SUICIDE IN VICTORIAN AND EDWARDIAN ENGLAND

Suicide in Victorian and Edwardian England

OLIVE ANDERSON

CLARENDON PRESS · OXFORD

1987

Oxford University Press, Walton Street, Oxford OX2 6DP
Oxford New York Toronto Melbourne Auckland
Delhi Bombay Calcutta Madras Karachi
Petaling Jaya Singapore Hong Kong Tokyo
Nairobi Dar es Salaam Cape Town
Associated companies in Beirut Berlin Ibadan Nicosia

Oxford is a trade mark of Oxford University Press

Published in the United States
by Oxford University Press, New York

British Library Cataloguing in Publication Data
Anderson, Olive
Suicide in Victorian and Edwardian England.
1. Suicide—Great Britain—History
I. Title
362.2   HV6548.G7
ISBN 0–19–820101–X

Library of Congress Cataloging-in-Publication Data
Anderson, Olive.
Suicide in Victorian and Edwardian England.
Bibliography: p.
Includes index.
1. Suicide—England—History—19th century.
I. Title.
HV6548.G7A53   1987   362.2   87–5613
ISBN 0–19–820101–X

Printed and bound by Butler and Tanner Ltd
Frome and London

ACKNOWLEDGEMENTS

IN writing this book I have incurred debts of many kinds, and I am glad to be able formally to acknowledge some of them here. I owe my thanks to the Dean and Chapter of Westminster Abbey for permission to study and quote from the inquest papers of the coroner for the City and Liberty of Westminster, and to the Keeper of the Muniments for his kindness in facilitating my use of these papers; to Miss N. Frith of Sheppard & Son, solicitors, Battle, for permission to study and quote from the inquest papers of N. P. Kell and Charles Sheppard deposited in the East Sussex Record Office; to Henry Cross & Sons, solicitors, Prescot, for permission to refer to the inquisitions of the Prescot manorial coroner deposited in the Lancashire Record Office; to HM Coroner, Bedfordshire, for permission to refer to certain coroners' records in the County Record Office; and to the Deputy Coroner for permission to study and quote from certain inquisition papers for the Hertford District, and the County Archivist of Hertfordshire for facilitating my use of these and other coroners' records. I am also grateful to the Corporation of London and the Deputy Keeper of the Records for permission to use the records of the coroners for the City of London and Borough of Southwark and other records at the Corporation of London Records Office; and to the Greater London Council for permission to use the papers of the coroner for Central Middlesex, 1862–74, and certain records of the Middlesex Sessions and Colney Hatch lunatic asylum in the custody of the Head Archivist of the Greater London Record Office. My thanks are also due to the County Archivists of Bedfordshire, Berkshire, East Sussex, and Lancashire, the Area Archivist for the West Devon Area, and the staff of the Archives Department, Marylebone Library, City of Westminster, and the Department of Manuscripts of the British Library.

Chapters 2 and 3 contain material (including Tables 1.1, 1.2, and 3.1) which first appeared in my article 'Did Suicide Increase with Industrialization in Victorian England?' published in *Past and Present*, 86 (Feb. 1980), pp. 149–73 (World Copyright: The Past and Present Society, Corpus Christi College, Oxford, England), and I am grateful for permission to make use of this material here. Chapter 4 contains material which first appeared in my article 'Suicide in Southwark, 1861' published in the *British Journal of Clinical and Social Psychiatry*, i (1982), pp. 92–4, and I am also grateful to the past and present editors of that journal for permission to use it here. Some of the material in Chapter 6 was first outlined in a paper presented to a Conference of the Society for the Social History of Medicine and summarized in the Society's *Bulletin*, 26 (June 1980), pp. 18–21, and I am likewise grateful for permission to draw upon it here. All quotations from Crown Copyright records appear by permission of the Controller of Her Majesty's Stationery Office.

Westfield College, London   O.A.

CONTENTS

LIST OF FIGURES

Figures 1, 2, 4, 8, 9, 10: photographs by Y. Sahota, Westfield College

LIST OF GRAPHS AND MAPS

Graph 2, Maps 3 and 6: photographs by Y. Sahota, Westfield College

GRAPHS

MAPS

LIST OF TABLES

ABBREVIATIONS

AR	*Annual Report*
BedsRO	Bedfordshire Record Office
BerksRO	Berkshire Record Office
BL	British Library
CI	Coroners' Inquests
CR	Coroners' Records
CLRO	Corporation of London Records Office
DNB	*Dictionary of National Biography*
ESRO	East Sussex Record Office
GLC	Greater London Council
GLRO	Greater London Record Office
Hansard	*Hansard's Parliamentary Debates*
HRO	Hertfordshire Record Office
IR	Inquest Records
LRO	Lancashire Record Office
LCC	London County Council
OPCS	Office of Population Censuses and Surveys
PP	Parliamentary Papers
WDRO	Devon Record Office (West Devon Area)

INTRODUCTION

For a very long time indeed psychiatrists and sociologists as well as moralists and social workers have made suicide one of their central concerns; and in the last generation suicidology has emerged as a speciality with its own journals, associations, and international congresses, and an annual output of books and articles running into hundreds of items. Historians, however, have contributed virtually nothing to this flow. Very little sustained research has been done on the history of suicide, apart from its role in literature and ethical debate. Suicidologists have sometimes regretted this neglect, and their interest in these pages can perhaps be hoped for with some confidence. But this is a historian's book. It was begun with the object of throwing more light on Victorian and Edwardian England, not on suicide, and it has been shaped by historical concerns, not suicidological debates. It is true that each of its four parts offers a historical dimension for one particular aspect of suicidology; yet each has its *raison d'être* in a distinctive set of historical issues, each is primarily based upon a particular sort of historical evidence, and each aims to practise a rather different kind of historical writing. As a whole this book will have failed if it does not persuade specialists in the history of the period that looking into suicide offers some rewards.

The suicide statistics of Victorian and Edwardian England are the concern of the first part. It may seem perverse to embark upon the first detailed study of Victorian and Edwardian suicide statistics at this juncture, since although generations of sociologists have made intensive studies of suicide based on official suicide rates, the defects of these statistics have at last been appreciated in the last fifteen years or so, and the validity of the statistical study of suicide has become controversial. As one sociologist has recently remarked,[1] however, what matters in using any set of official statistics is not whether it is accurate, but whether a correspondence has been established between its nature and the use to which it is put; and it is possible that the 'fit' of these particular official statistics is rather better with historical than with suicidological research.

[1] Taylor, *Durkheim and the Study of Suicide*, p. 122.

A very little investigation into the processes whereby Victorian and Edwardian suicide statistics came to be compiled makes it clear that concealment levels and official procedures for identifying and recording suicidal deaths varied greatly, both at different times and in different places. Accordingly these statistics, even more than most, need to be continually appraised in the light of as much contextual knowledge as possible and used with cautious discrimination. Plainly they can never establish what the suicidologist would most like to know: the real scale of suicide and its causes. But have they anything to tell the historian about the fifty years or so after they first began to be systematically compiled in the late 1850s? Fortunately it is possible to get behind the national averages which constitute the familiar official figures, and to construct various runs of suicide rates for different Victorian and Edwardian age and sex groups, occupations, and places. Can these specific suicide rates perhaps provide a rough index to the changing levels of stress experienced within these groups? Can they illuminate a little the changing significance for the subjective quality of life of such fundamental matters as work and habitat, age and gender, in the course of a half-century when some very substantial shifts in these respects probably took place? Given the dearth of other aggregate evidence on such questions, it seems worth following up the hints offered by the varying susceptibility to suicide shown by people of different age and sex, occupation and abode; and flickering though the light they throw on the social history of the emotions may be, these variations clearly illuminate the changing demographic, economic, and psychological significance of suicidal death in this period.

Taken by themselves, however, the upshot of such statistical investigations is necessarily very uncertain where subjective experiences of living are concerned. After all, what significance should be attached to suicidal actions? Today the meaning of suicide is a wide open question among specialists. It is no longer possible to assume that suicide rates provide an index of moral and social disintegration in any general sense, or to deny that, even for a single individual, suicidal behaviour may simultaneously have many meanings. What then were the commonest meanings of suicide in Victorian and Edwardian England? The ideas of a handful of well-known moralists, writers, and artists are familiar enough; but what were the thoughts and feelings of the many thousands of ordinary people who took their own lives? What were the commonest paths to suicide in certain places, among certain age groups, for men, and for women? How did the experience of suicide change between the mid-nineteenth and early twentieth centuries? Clearly it is only through again and again retrieving the ordinary person's experience of suicidal death that the bare bones provided by official statistics can be given flesh and made to function as the anatomy of an intelligible whole.

Retrieving in depth the personal experiences of suicide of completely ordinary people is the concern of the second part of this book. It is a concern which puts a premium on access to long, unselected and unbroken runs of detailed individual case histories. Very fortunately a few of these are available, in the form not of medical case histories (although some of these are to be found in professional treatises and journals, as well as in asylum records), but of the case papers kept by some coroners, and above all their verbatim notes of the evidence given at their inquests. In so far as the realities of suicide in ordinary life and the thoughts and feelings of the people involved can ever be laid bare, these coroners' case papers achieve this. Nevertheless the temptation has been resisted simply to report the mass of touching, surprising, and suggestive details, and to quote desperate scrawls and witnesses' words to convey 'as it really was' the texture of this unfamiliar part of Victorian and Edwardian life. Instead, the findings from these papers have been organized to express something of this texture and at the same time illuminate the ways in which place and time, gender, age, and occupation affected individual experiences of suicide.

Thus the second part of this book aims to be micro-history (specific-ally, 'people's history'), but micro-history which is throughout pressed into the service of macro-history. Fortunate accidents of archival sur-vival (and the kindness of present owners and custodians) have made it possible to compare experiences of dying by suicide in four very different parts of London in 1861–2, in rural Sussex at the same point in time, and in two of these same parts of London fifty years later; while other papers have supplied more scattered grounds for comparison. No doubt further intensive sampling would reveal a great deal more; but from these few hundreds of ordinary stories it is at least very clear that the meaning of suicidal actions in Victorian and Edwardian England (as of most other kinds of human behaviour) can be deci-phered aright only through reconstructing their context as completely as possible.

Part of the context of these actions, however, was the 'suicide culture' in which those who died by suicide had passed their lives.

What people thought and felt when they found themselves caught up in a situation of which suicide could be the outcome was partly settled by the ways of thinking and feeling about suicide which they had unconsciously absorbed from childhood onwards. There was no single universal Victorian or Edwardian outlook on suicide. The plain man's notions varied in different parts of the country, among different generations, and among different social groups; in other words, reactions to suicide varied within (it seems) certain overall patterns. Some of these patterns are more recoverable than others; none is easy to establish in the detail which alone carries conviction. Yet all are worth exploring, not only to complete the context of suicidal behaviour and so increase its intelligibility, but still more for reasons which have nothing to do with understanding suicide. For the way ordinary people responded to this particular human action—whether from afar in standard commonplaces, or at first hand when they found themselves involved as witnesses or jurymen—takes us deep into their ideas about sin and divine punishment, God and the moral law, death and the afterlife; and even deeper into practical everyday notions of morality, psychology, and pathology, and what one might call the etiquette of personal crises. These notions were very different from those of the handful of clergymen, intellectuals, and writers whose views have repeatedly been equated with nineteenth-century English ideas about suicide, and different too from the scraps of folklore reported to have 'lingered on' into the nineteenth century and beyond; but they are well worth trying to elucidate if the goal is a fuller comprehension of the hearts and minds of ordinary people in Victorian and Edwardian England.

Accordingly the third part of this book is intended as a contribution to the history of *mentalités*. The ideas and feelings of Londoners in the 1860s are constructed first, in order to supply a yardstick. Their stock emotional and moral responses to suicide can be plausibly deduced from the ballads and stories, plays, visual images, and jokes which they liked most, and from the varying tone and content of suicide reporting in the newspapers which in those years they were buying in very large numbers for the first time; while inquest proceedings reveal the kind of circumstances in which ordinary people who had been caught up in a case of suicide did or did not think suicidal actions unsurprising and forgivable. How ordinary people defined normal behaviour, what situations they saw as likely triggers of 'rash acts', what they reckoned the limits of endurance in such and such circumstances, and what they regarded as right and wrong in this or that relationship are all illuminated by depositions and jury verdicts. Such evidence is not easy to interpret, and outside London it is patchy and difficult to come by (at least for those who are not local historians on the spot); but it seems clear that everyday reactions to suicide were by no means either uniform or unchanging. Place was one significant element; time was another. For example, evidence available for 1893 and 1911 shows how ordinary Londoners' consciousness of suicide did and did not alter during the fifty years before the First World War; and the development of 'suburban' secretiveness about suicide as disgraceful and sordid, so often associated with 'Victorianism', seems on investigation not only to wear a rather different aspect, but to be the product of the late Victorian and Edwardian period and not of earlier years.

Still, the history of *mentalités* can never take the place of the history of action, however much it can illuminate it. To neglect what was done about suicide by those in positions of power and authority in society at large, or by those with the duty or desire to care personally for individuals who were sick in soul, mind, or body, would be to neglect the responses to suicide of the very people whose actions made most difference to the sort of life—and death—which befell ordinary people. The last part of this book, therefore, does not deal with the plain man's thoughts and feelings about suicide, nor with the vivid minutiae of individual experiences of suicidal death, nor yet with statistical aggregates. Its object is to describe and appraise the efforts to prevent suicide which were made with varying degrees of earnestness by those with power or authority, time or money, skill or influence. It leaves on one side the sermonizing and theorizing which constitute the familiar aspect of the educated response to suicide, and concentrates on deeds. Victorian and Edwardian England was particularly well supplied with men and women of energy, professional ambition, and social zeal, and the many sided work of suicide prevention which today attracts so much effort and debate has Victorian and Edwardian precedents in abundance.

This last part is thus a long one. In Victorian England, as today, some people sought to prevent suicide by social action and the creation of a deterrent environment, while others concentrated on helping individuals who were known to be at risk. To explore the efforts made by those who saw suicide as a problem of national well-being— spiritual, moral, mental, or physical—is to retrieve some little known aspects of the past working of this country's ecclesiastical, civil, and criminal law (aspects which were inevitably distorted during the crusade to secure the passing of the Suicide Act of 1961), and to fill a small gap in the history of concern with public health and safety (in the shape of attempts to create an environment where suicidal inclinations would be less likely and suicidal actions more troublesome and difficult). Equally, though, to study suicide prevention work among individuals at risk is to discover yet another chapter in the impressive history of Victorian and Edwardian philanthropic endeavour (particularly among those who became entangled with the law), as well as something about the contrasting practical roles of various categories of medical men—family physicians, police and prison surgeons, hospital staff, and asylum doctors—in the years when their work and their status were being transformed.

It will be plain that this is very much a generalist's book. Suicidologists may well be glad of this, and find it convenient to be offered within the same covers a historical dimension for four of their most discussed kinds of research: the study of rates and epidemiological and demographic distributions; of individual case histories; of cultural backgrounds; and of prevention techniques and crisis intervention. But I also hope that those who pick up this book because they are interested not in suicide, but in Victorian and Edwardian England, will find that one or other of its variegations suggests some link with their own concerns—whether those centre on age, gender, or death; on the past significance of place or work, or the social history of consciousness, law, or medicine; on mainstream ecclesiastical, administrative, or legal history; on history from below, or history from above. For this book is about a subject which has proved far more protean, as well as far more open to empirical research, than ever seemed possible at the outset, some ten years ago. Neglected angles still continually come into view, and second and third thoughts multiply; and many different sorts of specialists in both suicidology and history will surely find serious errors and omissions to point out. Still, it has already been too long in the making, and my hope must now be that it may whet the appetite of others to use in larger quantities the rich ingredients which I have only sampled.

PART I

STATISTICS

I

The Processes behind Victorian and Edwardian Official Suicide Statistics

WHEN Emile Durkheim decided in 1897 to use an exposition of suicide rates to demonstrate to the sceptical that social conditions and institutions were 'real, living, active forces' operating upon the individual in accordance with definite laws, he was embarking upon an enterprise which was by no means new. Even in 1857, when Henry Buckle published his *History of Civilization in England*, suicide statistics had already for a generation furnished a favourite proof for positivists throughout Europe that human actions are governed by mental and physical laws; and in his opening pages Buckle asserted again that the striking regularity in the annual numbers of suicides showed that even the most deliberately willed, solitary and eccentric action 'is merely the product of the general condition of society'.[1] Throughout most of the nineteenth century and beyond, suicide statistics were favourite weapons in the conflict between those who believed that individuals were willy-nilly ruled by the laws of 'social physics', and their opponents who insisted that human beings were not automatons. Accordingly from their pioneering days in the 1830s onwards, the moral statisticians produced an elaborate literature investigating statistically the links between suicide and level of education, marital status, occupation, and much else, and repeatedly deployed the official suicide statistics of Europe in an array of works intended to make clear the laws of human behaviour.

Yet one body of official statistics is conspicuously lacking from this expanding literature on suicide—those of England. Durkheim was entirely typical in listing as his principal sources for *Le suicide* the official statistical publications of Austria, Belgium, Bavaria, Prussia,

---

[1] Durkheim, *Suicide*, p. 39; Buckle, *History of Civilization in England*, i. 26–7. The nineteenth-century sociological literature is briefly surveyed in Giddens, 'The Suicide Problem in French Sociology', pp. 3–4. (Full bibliographical details of all works cited will be found in the Bibliography.)

Wurtemberg, Baden, the United States, Italy, Oldenburg, and France—
but not of England.[2] Only one continental scholar ever made direct use
of the English official suicide statistics in this period: Enrico Morselli,
Professor of Psychological Medicine in the Royal University of Turin,
in his *Il Suicidio*, published in 1879 and translated into English in
1881; and the very thoroughness and success of his comprehensive
international survey made such English figures as he provided seem all
that were needed. Nor was this continental neglect remedied in England
itself. In the first half-century after the regular publication of English
official suicide statistics began, only one private citizen, the epidemiologist J. N. Radcliffe, put them to serious use,[3] although two
government statisticians, W. Millar of the Army Medical Department and William Ogle of the General Register Office, made a special
study of the suicide returns to which they had official access.[4] Their
excellent learned papers, however, reached only a restricted audience.
As another able government statistician, Robert Giffen of the Board
of Trade, recognized in 1886, 'knowledge of the statistics of suicide
was not very widely distributed' in England.[5]

Among English and continental writers alike there was thus a neglect
of English official suicide statistics which was strange indeed at a time
when statistical studies of suicide proliferated throughout Europe.
How did this situation come about? To begin with, English government
publications were remarkably late in including such figures. Not until
the later 1850s did suicide statistics at last begin to appear regularly
each year, first in the remodelled judicial statistics published by the
Home Office from 1856, and then within the revised mortality statistics
published in the annual reports of the Registrar-General of Births,
Deaths and Marriages from 1858. Even so the availability of these
figures was often not realized, partly perhaps because Buckle's very
well-known and much translated book, which had been written just
before they began to appear, specifically stated that none were

---

[2] Durkheim, *Suicide*, p. 52. Another indication of Durkheim's unfamiliarity with the
English suicide statistics is his notion that the collection of 'supposed causes' was
currently being abandoned: ibid., p. 151. A brief description of the nature of the English
official suicide statistics in this period will be found in the Appendix.

[3] For the use made of these statistics by Radcliffe (1826–84: *DNB*), see ch. 3, pp. 74–
77. All this work was done before Radcliffe became one of the Privy Council's first
public health inspectors in 1869.

[4] Both presented the results of their researches to the Statistical Society (later the
Royal Statistical Society): see Millar, 'Statistics of Deaths by Suicide among H.M.'s
British Troops', and Ogle (1827–1912: *Munk's Roll*), 'Suicides in England and Wales'.

[5] Discussion following Ogle, 'Suicide in England and Wales', p. 130.

published. Moreover, neither the judicial statistics nor, at first, the Registrar-General's reports presented the suicide figures in a convenient form for purposes of serious research. The coroners' returns in the judicial statistics related to populations which were usually unknown, since their jurisdictions rarely corresponded with any other administrative area; while the General Register Office only began to publish separate annual tables of deaths from suicide in 1867, and soon ceased to break these down regionally, although details were always given of sex, age, and method.[6] The English official suicide statistics, then, got off to a slow start, and long remained comparatively undigested and difficult to use.

Much more inhibiting, however, was the bad reputation these statistics had on the continent for exceptional unreliability. Indeed, the first continental scholar to insist that they deserved as much credit as those of any other country, as well as the first to use them since Morselli, was Durkheim's outstanding pupil Maurice Halbwachs; and this was as late as 1930.[7] In Durkheim's own day it had long been axiomatic that concealment was especially rife in England, especially of suicide committed by drowning. Two facts continually reinforced this perennial continental distrust: English retention of an archaic system of coronatorial investigation of suspected unnatural deaths which was utterly unlike anything known abroad,[8] and continental failure to appreciate the improvements achieved in death certification and forensic medicine in England from 1836 onwards.[9] Even the patient Morselli never mastered the system, and in a confused passage diffused the belief that the English authorities were exceptionally careless and the English statistics therefore exceptionally 'inexact'.[10]

If ignorance and misunderstanding led to continental neglect, why then did English writers not remedy the situation? Their failure to do so was surely in the main a by-product of the failure of sociology to take root in England. The belated inclusion of suicide data in official publications came at a time when the first wave of statistical social

[6] For a critical general analysis of these statistics, see Brend, *An Inquiry into the Statistics of Deaths from Violence and Unnatural Causes in the United Kingdom.*

[7] Halbwachs, *Les causes du suicide*, p. 28 n. 2, pp. 53–7.

[8] The implications of the differences between the continental and English systems are speculated upon by J. B. Speer, Jr., in his essay review of T. R. Forbes, *Crowner's Quest*, pp. 353–6.

[9] On these improvements see Havard, *The Detection of Secret Homicide*, especially ch. 4.

[10] Morselli, *Suicide*, p. 25.

research was in decline and 'maudlin philanthropy', case work, and then field surveys were very much in the ascendant.[11] As any bibliography of publications on suicide in this period will show,[12] English contributions were few indeed by international standards, and apart from the work of medical men based upon clinical observations, consisted chiefly of continuations of the moralizing or anecdotal traditions of the seventeenth and eighteenth centuries. The statistical articles by Radcliffe, Millar, and Ogle already singled out were in a class of their own, and were the products of a generation which was dying out by the 1880s. They can be supplemented only by a few paragraphs occasionally included in their annual official reports by Ogle himself, by one of his successors, T. H. C. Stevenson, and above all by the dynamic first statistical head of the General Register Office, William Farr.[13] Throughout the whole of the nineteenth and early twentieth centuries only three book-length English studies of suicide were published, all of them by medical men: Forbes Winslow's *The Anatomy of Suicide* (1840), W. Wynn Westcott's *Suicide: Its History, Literature, Jurisprudence, Causation and Prevention* (1885) and S. A. K. Strahan's *Suicide and Insanity: A Physiological and Sociological Study* (1893).[14] Undeniably, French, German, and Italian writers dominated the study of suicide. Their researches certainly fell 'into a statistical groove', as Westcott complained in 1885,[15] but this was a groove to which English statistics contributed little, and that little usually at second hand. These prolific continental writers relied for their material on England upon Morselli's exhaustive international survey of 1879 and the handful of English books and articles just mentioned.[16] A few hoary statistics

[11] Cf. Cullen, *The Statistical Movement in Early Victorian Britain*, pp. 148–9; Cole, 'Continuity and Institutionalization in Science', in Oberschall, ed., *The Establishment of Empirical Sociology*, pp. 73–129; Abrams, *The Origins of British Sociology*, p. 40.

[12] The standard example is Rost, *Bibliographie des Selbstmords*.

[13] These passages will be found in the *Registrar-General's 3rd AR*, pp. 78–82, *19th AR*, pp. 196–205, *26th AR*, p. 193, *43rd AR*, pp. xxvii–xxviii, and *75th AR*, *Supplement*, Part III, pp. xciii–xcvii. On William Farr (1807–83: *DNB*), see Eyler, *Victorian Social Medicine*.

[14] Winslow (1810–74: *DNB*) was the owner of a private lunatic asylum, Strahan was Assistant Medical Officer to two county lunatic asylums successively, and Westcott was a London coroner and Medical Officer of Health.

[15] Westcott, *Suicide*, p. 68.

[16] The only English sources cited by Durkheim were the articles by Millar and Ogle and the books by Westcott and Strahan already mentioned, although he frequently cited Morselli's English material. Similarly, the only English sources referred to in Legoyt, *Le suicide ancien et moderne*, are the articles of Millar and Radcliffe, and the book by Winslow, together with a paper by the actuary Samuel Brown (1810–75: *DNB*) in the *Assurance Magazine*, ii (1852), which is in fact mostly on marriage rates.

were thus constantly repeated, especially those for London between 1846 and 1850 which Buckle had published and the figures relating to the years 1872–6 given by Morselli. In short, nineteenth-century ideas about the incidence of suicide in England were usually illustrated by the official statistics rather than founded upon them; and the Edwardian statistical revival did little to change this state of affairs.[17]

The detailed study of these statistics is thus now being embarked upon for the first time. This might well seem a perverse undertaking, since the whole enterprise of the statistical study of suicide is currently under fundamental attack from some sociologists. Official statistics never record more than a sample of any form of deviant behaviour;[18] and official suicide statistics, it may be held, are not only incomplete and full of random inaccuracies, but also systematically distorted by the operation of death registration procedures. When the sociologist J. D. Douglas called for the abandonment of statistical research into suicide in the later 1960s, he argued that varying search processes, varying levels of official efficiency and medical training and above all varying definitions of suicide all systematically affect the working of death registration procedures and make the statistics they produce useless for research into the social meanings of suicide.[19] Today 'soft' statistics like those for suicide are very often said to throw more light on collection procedures than on the happenings they purport to enumerate. Even those who continue to defend their use concede that it is essential to find out more about how they come into existence, while the thoroughgoing sceptic concludes that even if there is a relationship between suicide and social factors, the suicide statistics are incapable of throwing any light upon it.[20]

To a historian, however, these doubts and criticisms do not seem particularly disconcerting. Victorian suicide statistics certainly present

[17] The suicide statistics were discussed by that very able jurist Sir John Macdonell (1845–1921: *DNB*) in his introduction to the Criminal Statistics for 1899 and much more briefly in the introduction to those for 1907 by W. J. Farrant (who became Superintendent of the Statistical Branch of the Home Office in 1895 after its long-overdue overhaul: Pellew, *The Home Office 1848–1914*, p. 105). A little passing use of contemporary English statistics was also made by the young Reginald Skelton in his 'Statistics of Suicide'.

[18] The implications of this familiar fact are well shown in Sellin, 'The Significance of Records of Crime', pp. 489–97.

[19] Douglas, *The Social Meanings of Suicide*, pp. 163–231.

[20] Counter-attacks on Douglas's work include Sainsbury, 'Suicide: Opinions and Facts', Besnard, 'Anti- ou anté-durkheimisme?' and more generally Hindess, *The Use of Official Statistics in Sociology*.

awkward problems and offer limited rewards; but in this they are not essentially different from other Victorian official statistics. Historical evidence is often valuable indirectly for the light it throws on the situation which brought it into existence, as well as directly for the information it contains; and its usefulness always depends as much upon how accurately the historian can interpret and evaluate it as upon its own intrinsic quality. Accordingly it is a basic historical routine to investigate at the outset who produced the evidence being used, and when, why and how, so that it can be appraised for both accuracy and bias. In the case of official returns this means their evaluation in the light of as full an understanding as possible both of how they were collected and transmitted to higher authorities and of the interests and abilities of the people concerned in these tasks, as well as their appraisal in the light of popular, specialist, and political attitudes towards their subject and the process of collection, together with the severity of punishment for default.

Each of the three underlying weaknesses to which sociologists have recently paid so much attention—that definitions are variable, official processes uneven in efficiency, and concealment widespread—are all weaknesses which a historian is accustomed to find in any body of returns, *mutatis mutandis*. So far as a historian of suicide is concerned, their existence dictates not that the statistical evidence should be ignored, but that it should be used for appropriate purposes, and with care. This means not only that it is essential to find out as much as possible about how these statistics were produced and interpret them accordingly; but also that only very marked trends, differences in scale, or relationships should be taken seriously, and that their implications should be continually checked against other evidence, and heavily relied on only for those aspects of the subject which cannot be investigated otherwise. Inevitably it is in considering large aggregate questions about the incidence of suicide that the official statistics become altogether indispensable; and since a general framework can be established only by answering questions of this sort, it is such questions which will be tackled in the first part of this book.

At this point a major disclaimer must be made. The present investigation proposes to accept without more ado that the real scale of suicide is as uncertain in the past as it is in the present. Recently the true total of deaths by suicide in nineteenth-century England has been estimated by combining the number of suicide verdicts with a proportion of the verdicts of 'found drowned'.[21] No such surmises will be offered here, for what will be investigated is not the absolute but the relative incidence of suicide. Before embarking upon this enterprise, however, it is surely necessary in the light of what has just been said to consider how the official suicide statistics may have been affected by the processes which led in Victorian and Edwardian England to the registration of a particular death as a death by suicide.

In the Victorian period, professional expertise and orderly routines made some very substantial advances in the system for investigating sudden death, but always within an archaic feudal framework which was neither uniform nor centrally controlled. Nor is this surprising; for although English administration was remodelled between the 1830s and 1880s there was no revolution in government, and the traditional English reliance upon the initiative, responsibility, and money of local officers, corporate bodies, and even private individuals persisted everywhere. This amateurism and autonomy affected the system for investigating sudden death most tellingly through the 330 or so coroners who were its core.[22] Two-thirds of these were county coroners, and were elected at the hustings by the county freeholders (see Fig. 1), until the new county councils were given the duty of appointing them in 1888;[23] the rest were either coroners for a borough eligible to have its own coroner, and so appointed by a town council,[24] or were franchise

---

[21] Hair, 'Deaths from Violence in Britain', p. 15 n. 55.

[22] There is as yet no study of the ancient office of coroner in the age of reform. An excellent account of the coroner's legal position was given by J. Brooke Little to the committee appointed by the Home Office in 1908 to inquire into the law relating to coroners and coroners' inquests, and this will be found in PP 1909 [Cd. 4782] XV, pp. 1–32. The most useful practitioner's handbook is Jervis, *On the Office and Duties of Coroners*, and the best modern survey is probably that provided in Havard, *The Detection of Secret Homicide*, despite some anachronistic and over-simple historical judgements and occasional inaccuracies in historical details; see also, however, Wellington, *The King's Coroner*. The principal statute before the important Coroners (Amendment) Act of 1926 was the Coroners Act of 1887, 50 & 51 Vict., c. 71.

[23] 51 & 52 Vict., c. 41, s. 5. The last election was held on 11 June 1888, for the new District of North-East Middlesex. The photograph reproduced in Fig. 1 is thus misleadingly captioned 'the last "hustings" erected in England for an election of a coroner' in Jervis, *On the Office and Duties of Coroners* (7th edn.), p. 11.

[24] Under the Municipal Corporations Act of 1835, 5 & 6 Will. IV, c. 76, s. 62, every borough which had its own court of quarter sessions was required to appoint a fit person to be coroner of the borough. Under the Local Government Act of 1888, 51 & 52 Vict., c. 41, s. 38(5), however, quarter sessions boroughs with a population of less than 10,000 lost this power. The engagement diaries of R. B. Johns, coroner for Plymouth, 1892–7, vividly illustrate the borough coroner's position midway in the hierarchy of borough officers, and his integration into the local government network: WDRO, 95/160–4.

Fig. 1 The declaration of the poll at the hustings erected in Portland Place, London, for the election of a coroner for Central Middlesex, 11 May 1881

coroners appointed in the way prescribed by the charter which created the franchise (usually by the lord of the manor). Coroners' appointments were never made or even approved centrally, although they were direct officers of the Crown, and in no case were professional qualifications required. Most were solicitors already employed locally on public business (usually as Clerks of the Peace), who were often carrying on a family tradition; a fair number were medical men (as many as 14 per cent in the 1880s, as a result of the sanitarians' campaign for medical coroners), and a few were barristers or simply local figures. About 10 per cent held more than one coronership.[25] In practice all held office for life: there was no retiring age (and no pension), and they were removable for misbehaviour only by the Lord Chancellor or after conviction before a court of law. They settled their own procedure and could exclude the press and public from their courts if they wished; and neither the Home Secretary, the Lord

[25] In 1910 there were 360 coroners' jurisdictions and 330 coroners (200 county coroners, 76 borough coroners, and 54 franchise coroners): PP 1910 [Cd. 5004] XXI, p. 4.

Chancellor, nor any one else had more than the most limited control over them. Until 1860 all were paid for each inquest they held by a statutory fee plus mileage and expenses from the local rates, subject to the agreement of the county justices or borough recorder that the inquest had been 'duly taken'; after 1860, however, county coroners received an agreed annual salary, plus expenses—a victorious parliamentary conclusion to a decade of acute financial conflict between coroners and justices in many counties, and of wide-ranging debate on the office itself.[26] Even so, they long remained essentially office-holders, as opposed to public employees.[27]

Coroners—and above all, county coroners—were thus as much entitled to pride themselves on their independence as were their critics to deplore their arbitrary powers. Many of them, moreover, remained quite unaffected by the growth of professionalism within their own body, so that in 1893 more than half their number were still not members of the Coroners' Society formed in 1846 to promote (among other things) regularity and uniformity of practice.[28] Even as late as 1911 the diversity of practice between the eight London coroners was a constant annoyance to the tidy bureaucrats of the London County Council.[29] It was thus always probable that when a particular set of tendencies was strong in one coroner's jurisdiction, those operating within his neighbours' areas would be very different. This is a salient point; for it surely follows that however much administrative or socio-economic similarities in similar kinds of places or within a single region might promote similar patterns of under- or over-

[26] 23 & 24 Vict., c. 116. The debates of these years raised fundamental issues about the office, some of which are unsettled today, although others were decided in 1926. They have left many scattered written remains, both published and unpublished. Havard, *The Detection of Secret Homicide*, ch. 4 and especially p. 51, is too ready to credit coroners with a desire to advance forensic medicine and fails to appreciate the magistrates' side of this dispute. The latter is well conveyed in Middlesex Justices of the Peace, *Report of the Special Committee appointed at the Michaelmas Sessions, 1850*, while the coroners' case for proper professional remuneration is fairly stated in BL, Add. MSS 40,612, fols. 57–8. (I owe the thought of looking at Peel's papers for references to coroners' fees to a passage in the unpublished thesis by E. Sherrington, 'Thomas Wakley and Reform', ch. vii.)

[27] On the transition from officer to employee in general, see Chester, *The English Administrative System 1780–1870*, pp. 123–68. The assumptions involved are well illustrated so far as borough coroners are concerned by Clegg, ed., *Autobiography of a Lancashire Lawyer*, pp. 90–101, 113, 298–304. See also Eliot, *Middlemarch*, Book II, ch. 16.

[28] 154 coroners were members of the Society in 1893: PP 1893–4 (373, 402) XI, p. 130.

[29] PP [Cd. 5492], XIII, Appendix II, pp. 21–35 and especially paras. 9, 31, 32–7.

registration, these patterns were always likely to be disrupted by an individual coroner's personal interpretation of his office. Accordingly not only is biographical as well as local knowledge needed for the appraisal of the suicide statistics for particular areas, but it is probably safe to assume that across a large number of jurisdictions, coroners' individual idiosyncrasies tended to cancel each other out.

Was this so in every respect, however? Or were there some factors which did indeed regularly affect not simply the overall size of the sample represented by the official figures but its specific make-up, so that particular categories of suicides were always under- or over-represented? This is a crucial question. To answer it requires careful appraisal of each of the four stages by which a death came to be registered as one caused by suicide: the first or pre-coronatorial, at which it was settled whether or not a death should be drawn to the coroner's attention; the second or coronatorial, at which the coroner determined whether or not an inquest should be held on that death; the third or inquest stage, at which a jury decided whether or not a verdict of suicide should be returned; and finally the recording stage, at which the coroner and local Registrar of Deaths carried this verdict into the judicial statistics compiled by the Home Office and the death returns lodged at the General Register Office.

So far as the first stage is concerned, the key to its working is the persistent dearth of statutory provisions or administrative rules for calling the coroner's attention to sudden or suspicious deaths. Until 1853 statutory requirements of this sort were entirely lacking. From that year onwards all deaths which occurred in private lunatic asylums had to be reported to the local coroner, and from 1862 and 1865 so too had those in pauper lunatic asylums and prisons. By the turn of the century a report had also to be made of deaths which occurred in inebriates' retreats and reformatories, and among children being cared for for reward, and other special groups of this sort.[30] For all other deaths, however, a coroner had only four imperfect channels of

[30] The relevant legislation is 16 & 17 Vict., c. 96, s. xix, Act to amend the Regulation of the Care and Treatment of Lunatics, 1853; 25 & 26 Vict., c. 111, s. 44, Act to amend the Law relating to Lunatics, 1862; 28 & 29 Vict., c. 126, s. 20, Prisons Act, 1865; 42 & 43 Vict., c. 19, s. 27, Habitual Drunkards Act, 1879; 60 & 61 Vict., c. 57, s. 8, Infant Life Protection Act, 1897; 61 & 62 Vict., c. 60, s. 19(1), Inebriates Act, 1898; 8 Ed. 7, c. 67, s. 6(1), Children Act, 1908. The Local Government Board required all deaths of idiots and persons of unsound mind in poor law institutions to be reported, and the Factories and Mines Acts and Workmen's Compensation Acts *de facto* added similar obligations: Troutbeck, 'Inquest Juries', p. 50. All drownings in tidal or navigable waters also had to be reported: PP 1909 [Cd. 4782] XV, p. 18.

information: private individuals (who might sometimes want publicity in order to show up guilty parties but were usually anxious to avoid it); doctors (whose duty was no more than moral, and whose practices would suffer from too much zeal); policemen (whose constabulary regulations did not always formally instruct them to report sudden deaths to the coroner); and Registrars of Deaths (who were only ordered to report uncertified deaths to the coroner in particular areas and for particular reasons).[31] The flow of information through each of these channels might be regularly affected by a variety of factors.

Foremost among these was the varying popularity of different methods of suicide in different parts of the country and in different occupations and social classes, as well as in different age-groups and generations and between men and women. This mattered considerably, since some methods of suicide were much more easily concealed or mistaken for other modes of death than others, and in law a death had to be considered accidental until proved otherwise. The method least likely to permit concealment or mistake was hanging, and this was a method preferred by men rather than women, by the elderly rather than the young, and above all by the poor. In the 1860s it accounted for a much higher proportion of suicides registered in the north and north-west than in the south and south-east; but everywhere by the 1900s it was used less frequently than in the 1860s. On the other hand, the method most easily confused with accidental death, that of drowning, was everywhere used more by women than men, and used increasingly by young women; and was most popular, apparently, in the south-eastern counties.[32] Again, any method which rarely succeeded

---

[31] Noel Humphreys, who had spent a lifetime at the General Register Office, told the Medico-Legal Society in 1906 that instructions to Registrars to notify coroners of all uncertified deaths had only been issued exceptionally, for particular areas, and had aroused too much local protest to work well: Troutbeck, 'Modes of Ascertaining the Fact and Cause of Death', p. 112. The overall situation is described in PP 1893–4 (373, 402) XI, p. viii, and at more length in PP 1909 [Cd. 4782] XV, p. 14, Qs. 331–4, p. 45, Q. 1002, and PP 1910 [Cd. 5139] XXI, p. 10.

[32] For the methods of suicide employed in 1858–83 see Ogle, 'Suicides in England and Wales', pp. 118–21; for those used in 1901–10 see *Registrar-General's 75th AR, Supplement*, Part III, p. xcv; and for those used in 1912–60 see *Registrar-General's Statistical Review, 1961*, Part III, p. 263. Suicide rates by method can be calculated from the full mortality tables not only for England and Wales and for the registration division of London, but between 1858 and 1880 for all registration divisions, and between 1858 and 1910 for all registration counties. I have made these calculations for each registration county only for the decade 1861–70. Where these figures are concerned, however, it is important to note that a considerable (though variable) proportion of coroners' certificates did not specify the pathological cause of death: see p. 32.

swiftly was more likely to lead to medical attention and, in big towns, to hospital care, and both these developments (especially the latter) greatly reduced the chances of concealment. Poison, for example, often proved a very slow method and led to hospitalization; and poison was always commoner among women than men, and, in the 1860s, much commoner in London than elsewhere, although it became relatively more popular everywhere during the next fifty years. The use of razors and knives was another method which often led to hospitalization, and the incidence of this method was quite different, since it was far commoner among men than women, and in the 1860s commonest of all in the south midlands, although by the 1900s it was used decreasingly everywhere.[33] Variations in the incidence of particular methods of suicide, then, must have affected the flow of information to coroners about suspicious deaths among particular categories of people in particular places and at particular times.

A second important factor at this first stage was the activity of the police. So far as the new County Constabularies were concerned, the County Coroners Act of 1860 was something of a landmark in this respect. From 1836 onwards inquests became both more numerous and more expensive in many places for several reasons, notably the introduction of the new system of death registration and statutory fees for medical evidence and post-mortems. The old parish constables had a long tradition of acting as 'a sort of parish jackal' and lining their pockets by zealously reporting all bodies to the coroners, and eager constables, impecunious medical men, and officious or grasping coroners (who were nearly always 'of a lower social grade than county magistrates') all made heavy inroads into the county rates. Inevitably friction became acute in many counties, and culminated in magistrates not only disallowing coroners' fees, but also forbidding constables to report deaths to the coroner or to serve his summonses.[34] After a series of *causes*

---

[33] My generalizations about hospitalization are based upon the case histories studied, especially those discussed in Part II. Some discussion of the changing relative popularity of different methods of suicide will be found in ch. 10, pp. 362–75.

[34] The magistrates of the counties of Durham, Devon, Gloucester, Kent, Middlesex, Stafford, the West Riding, and Glamorgan disallowed fees on numerous inquests in the 1850s: PP 1860 (237, 237–I) LVII, pp. 3–6. Constabularies were instructed not to report every case of sudden death to the coroner in (among other counties) Durham, Gloucester, Northumberland, and the West Riding: PP 1860 (241) LVII, pp. 16–17, 30–1, 115, 131. These controversies were very much part of local politics for a time: see, for example, the public meeting at Gateshead reported in the *Daily Telegraph*, 19 Jan. 1860, p. 2. In fairness to the magistrates it should be noted that in Middlesex, for example, the cost of inquests increased sixfold in 1828–48: Middlesex Justices of the Peace, *Report of the Special Committee appointed at the Michaelmas Session, 1850*, p. 11.

célèbres and much debate among justices, coroners and their allies, a Royal Commission under the Peelite politician Edward Cardwell proposed in 1859 to reduce costs by ending the coroners' discretion and entrusting the responsibility for initiating inquest proceedings to the new County Constabularies. The next year, however, this proposal was scotched by a Select Committee under Robert Lowe, although the only one of this Committee's own recommendations to reach the statute book was the requirement already mentioned that magistrates should pay county coroners not by fees but by an annual salary, reviewable every five years in the light of the average number of inquests held in the previous quinquennium.[35] After this important victory for the coroners' lobby, reasonable informal rules were worked out in many counties for the guidance of constables in deciding which deaths to report to the coroner, and some county constabulary regulations came to include a formal instruction to call the coroner's attention to all sudden deaths.[36] More important than such variations in police instructions, however, were the great variations which always existed in the intensity of policing in relation to population and acreage, and hence in the proportion of suspicious deaths which became known to the police. Wherever there was a continuously patrolled police beat, a constable would almost certainly discover any case of suicide committed in a public place on that beat, and was also very likely to be called in for assistance when a suicide occurred in a working-class house (although inquest papers are naturally a poor guide to the frequency with which this did not happen); in the very largest towns, the police were often particularly shrewd in using their wide experience to decide which deaths to report to the coroner. In rural areas, however, the situation in all these respects was altogether different.[37]

---

[35] PP 1859 (sess. 2) [2575] XIII. 1, p. xix; PP 1860 (193) XXII, pp. iii–v; 23 & 24 Vict., c. 116, s. 4. This Act originated in a private member's bill inspired by the medical coroners' lobby and the populist radicals associated with them: cf. the draft legislation being circulated among sanitarians in 1856 in the volume of ephemera belonging to Henry Letheby, second Medical Officer of Health of the City of London, now in the British Library (shelf-mark 898 d. 17), and *The Lancet*, 1860, ii. 247, 8 Sept. The payment of coroners by salary was resisted in the House by the Home Secretary of the day, G. C. Lewis: *Hansard*, 3rd series, clviii, col. 1631, and clix, col. 2114.

[36] See, for example, Address of E. Eagles, Coroner for the County of Bedford, to the Peace Officers of the County of Bedford, 1 Jan. 1861, Beds RO, C.O.4, and PP 1909 [Cd. 4782] XV, p. 14, Q. 331

[37] Varying police practices are discussed further in ch. 8, pp. 287–90.

Another significant factor at this stage was the working of the new system of civil registration and medical certification of death. Both spread remarkably quickly in England and Wales after their introduction in 1836, despite the absence of any necessity for either before the burial of a body, and the fact that non-registration did not become a penal offence until 1874.[38] Local variations were nevertheless considerable, with uncertified deaths always fewest in the largest towns, and ranging, as late as 1882–92, from 8.8 per cent of all deaths in North Wales to a mere 0.9 per cent in extra-metropolitan Middlesex.[39] Admittedly certification did not necessarily ensure the detection of a case of suicide. Medical certificates of the cause of death were often criticized as being too readily given to private patients, and the police surgeon who said in evidence in 1893 that in private practice 'it does not seem to me to be any part of my duty to act as a private detective' was probably speaking for most of his colleagues. Doctors often seem to have shifted responsibility to the local Registrar by issuing a certificate in terms which they knew he would not accept, but which enabled them to avoid offending their patients.[40] Despite all this, however, no less an authority than William Ogle of the General Register Office was convinced that a low proportion of uncertified deaths and a high proportion of inquests often went together;[41] and it is certainly true that in the kind of large town where the proportion of uncertified deaths was low, poor law doctors, police surgeons, and

[38] Under the Civil Registration Act of 1836, to bury a body without the authorization of the local Registrar or coroner only became a penal offence if the Registrar was not notified within 7 days, and for this the penalty was £10: 6 & 7 Will. IV, c. 86, s. xxvii. When non-registration became a penal offence in 1874, the maximum penalty was only a fine of 40s.: 37 & 38 Vict., c. 88, s. 16. Legal proceedings were rare: PP 1893–4 (373, 402) XI, p. xix. For the progress of civil registration, see Glass, *Numbering the People*, appendix 4, 'Vital Registration in Britain during the Nineteenth Century', It was Farr's view that even before the Amending Act of 1874 'very few' deaths escaped registration: Farr, *Vital Statistics*, p. 527. In France, on the other hand, although medical verification became mandatory in 1866, fully a quarter of deaths were not indicated as being so verified as late as 1926: Douglas, *The Social Meanings of Suicide*, p. 223.

[39] In 1882–92 in London 1.1 per cent and in the largest towns 2.2 per cent of all deaths were not medically certified, while the proportion in England and Wales as a whole was 3.3 per cent: PP 1893–4 (373, 402) XI, Appendix no. 17, pp. 298–300. Ten years later the proportion of uncertified deaths in London had fallen to only 0.2 per cent, according to Noel Humphreys of the General Register Office: Troutbeck, 'Modes of Ascertaining the Fact and Cause of Death', p. 113.

[40] Walford, 'On the Number of Deaths from Accident, Negligence, Violence and Misadventure', p. 526; PP 1893–4 (373, 402) XI, p. 134, Q. 2556; PP 1909 [Cd. 4782] XV, p. 45, Qs. 1003–5.

[41] PP 1893–4 (373, 402), XI, pp. 224–5, Qs. 4053–6.

Registrars, as well as police constables, were inevitably all widely experienced in recognizing suspicious circumstances which called for investigation, and fully accustomed to working with the coroner and his officer.

Finally, it goes without saying that when private individuals were involved, everything depended on circumstances. A working-class man or woman who found someone *in extremis* or seriously ill but still alive was likely to summon the help of a neighbour, police constable or medical man, in that order; but if death had already occurred, what counted most was whether the finder was a relative, employer, or householder who was likely to be blamed for the attempt, or knew that some discreditable circumstances were likely to emerge at an inquest. Where the dead person was merely a lodger, or a customer at a public house or inn, or *a fortiori* some unknown stranger, a police constable would probably be fetched forthwith.[42] The poor rarely shared their betters' general distaste for publicity in cases of sudden or violent death, or their abhorrence of inquests.

Altogether, then, it is clear that there were indeed certain broad categories of suicide cases which were more likely to be reported to a coroner than others, although it is difficult to summarize them in a few words. For example, any case which occurred in a public institution was very unlikely to escape a coroner's attention; and the same is true of the suicide by hanging of a man living alone in lodgings in a large town, or the death by poison of a woman living with her family near a great hospital. At this first stage, however, the most consistently important factor was probably the presence of a police constable on the beat; and while this could increasingly be taken for granted in urban areas, it certainly could not be assumed in rural ones.

It is possible to be more precise about the biases built into the second stage of the process. Each coroner acted entirely at his own discretion in deciding whether to hold an inquest; but the pressures in favour of holding one were clearly strong. Directly or indirectly a coroner's income was always related to the number of inquests he held. There were no exceptions to this rule until 1883, when a local act fixed a coroner's salary for the first time; but the precedent thus set by Birmingham was followed by only a very few great cities, notably Liverpool and Manchester.[43] It is true that a coroner was sometimes restrained

---

[42] These generalizations are largely based upon the inquest papers studied.
[43] PP 1909 [Cd. 4782] XV, p. 6, Qs. 124–7. The salary of the coroner for Birmingham was fixed at £1,000. Borough coroners had a statutory fee of 20s. for every inquest

even after the act of 1860 by fears that some of his expenses might be disallowed,[44] or by a wish to avoid friction with the paying authority because he held other posts in local government (for example, as Clerk of the Peace, Medical Officer of Health, or Poor Law Medical Officer), or quite simply by other claims upon his time (the office was nearly always a part-time one). Nevertheless, coroners were perennially accused of burdening the rates with the cost of an unnecessarily large number of inquests, and all the more plausibly so since they often had to recoup heavy electoral expenses.

Quite apart from such personal financial incentives, some coroners chose to hold inquests very freely as a matter of political or professional principle. In the mid-nineteenth century the coroner's office simultaneously attracted the reforming enthusiasm of two entirely different kinds of radicals: populist vestry politicians, who believed the coroner's primary function was to check private crime and official negligence, whose watchwords were popular liberties, the ancient constitution, and no centralization, and whose prophet was Joshua Toulmin Smith; and public hygienists of the utilitarian sort, who believed the coroner's first object should be 'the promotion of sanitary measures', who agitated for the use of experts, efficiency and progress, held up continental practices as a model, and from 1857 enjoyed an annual field day at the congresses of the Social Science Association. The populists depicted the coroner as 'the magistrate of the poor' and maintained that inquests should be freely held because they were the historic—and only—safeguard of the humble against ill-treatment by magistrates, gaolers, and the new poor law authorities and police. (One of their great triumphs was the statutory obligation to hold an inquest on the body of every prisoner who died within a prison, while their failure to secure a similar obligation with regard to inmates of workhouses was one of their defeats). The sanitarians, for their part, insisted that an inquest should be held whenever the pathological cause of death was uncertain, and, moreover, that a post-mortem should be ordered, since only so could the country achieve accurate mortality statistics, the essential tool of enlightened social

which the recorder thought duly taken, with a further 6s. 8d. after the Coroners' Act of 1887, and 9d. for every mile over 2 miles travelled from their abode, plus expenses. Franchise coroners might be paid in the same way as either borough or county coroners, that is, either by fees or by a salary subject to quinquennial review.

[44] In particular, local authorities were perennially reluctant to pay for post-mortems, for which there was a statutory fee of 2 guineas: 6 & 7 Will. IV, c. 89, Sched. B(2).

policy.[45] Both groups of enthusiasts for the coroner's inquest had their heyday in the 1850s and 1860s; but both had their more moderate successors in the 1900s.[46] By that time the coroner's officer, rather than the coroner himself, decided in practice whether an inquest should be held, and there was some suspicion that cases concerning families who knew how to tip discreetly were dropped; but coroners' officers always denied that tips were so much as offered to them, let alone accepted, and were in any case only paid their full fees if an inquest actually took place.[47]

Clearly, then, the ratio of inquests held to cases reported was likely to be high everywhere throughout this period. Variations did occur; but by the early twentieth century at least, these followed a recognizable pattern and seem to have related predominantly to inquests which ended in verdicts of natural death. The proportion of inquests held by urban coroners was nearly twice as high as the proportion held by either country coroners or the handful of coroners paid by a fixed salary, since the latter tended to hold an inquiry only when there were some suspicious circumstances, whereas urban coroners often did so whenever the pathological cause of death was unknown.[48] This

[45] Thomas Wakley (1795–1862: *DNB*) was by far the best known of the populist coroners: see Sprigge, *The Life and Times of Thomas Wakley*, Finer, *The Life of Edwin Chadwick*, pp. 159, 199, 257, 388, 418, and also E. Sherrington, 'Thomas Wakley and Reform, 1823–62'. Other populist coroners were William Baker, also of Middlesex (see his *A Letter addressed to H.M.'s Justices of the Peace*) and J. H. Todd of Hampshire (see his *A Letter to the Revd. George Deane*). The fullest exposition of this aspect of vestry radicalism was given by J. Toulmin Smith (1816–69: *DNB*) in his *The Right Holding of the Coroner's Court*. Wakley's successor, Edwin Lankester (1814–74: *DNB* and see below, ch. 4) had a foot in both camps. The sanitarian campaign to upgrade coroners into an efficient part of the country's public health machinery was strongly supported by William Farr, notably by means of the comments and Tables of Violent Deaths which he inserted in the *Registrar-General's 19th AR*, pp. 196–205, which provided the coroners' lobby with welcome ammunition in their fight for coronatorial independence. (Edward Postle, one of the Norfolk magistrates, sent a circular letter on Farr's remarks to all chairmen of quarter sessions in Oct. 1858: Beds RO, C.O.4.) Both the populist and the sanitarian viewpoints on the coroner's office were expressed at the Congress of the National Association for the Promotion of Social Science in 1866: see its *Transactions*, pp. 228–92; it was an alliance between these two that secured the victory represented by the County Coroners Act of 1860. On these two viewpoints, see also below, ch. 10, pp. 347–8.

[46] Attitudes to inquest juries and to medical investigators formed the dividing line. The conflicting views of Edwardian coroners are clearly illustrated in the discussion on the paper read to the Medico-Legal Society by Troutbeck, 'Modes of Ascertaining the Fact and Cause of Death', pp. 106–17.

[47] PP 1910 [Cd. 5139] XXI, p. 133, Qs. 10, 150–2, p. 194, Qs. 11, 487–90; PP 1911 [Cd. 5492] XIII, p. 30, Q. 64.

[48] Brend, 'The Necessity for Amendment of the Law relating to Coroners' Inquests', p. 145.

divergence is not surprising. A busy urban coroner, unlike a country one, would be sitting in his court anyway, and such inquests could be completed very quickly; moreover, financial and practical considerations apart, such coroners were more likely than rural ones to be men with medical qualifications and keen sanitarians.[49] The varying 'character of the population' might also lead to such divergences, as the London coroners claimed. (In London in 1903–7 the proportion of inquests held ranged from 59 per cent of cases reported in the South-West District, to 90 per cent in the Eastern and Tower of London District.[50]) Everywhere, however, there were in-built pressures against allowing a case to be closed after merely informal inquiries; and in urban areas—apart from a small handful of cities—these pressures were rarely resisted even when there were no suspicious circumstances.

At the third stage, that of the inquest itself, the pressures were more complex. Three things could affect the likelihood of a suicide verdict being returned, apart from the plain facts of the case: the thoroughness of the preliminary investigations and hence the quality and nature of the evidence presented at the inquest; the calibre of the jury and coroner; and the relationship between them. All three were likely to be significantly different in the great towns from what they were in the less busy and less compact jurisdictions which covered most of the country.

In the major urban jurisdictions, and above all in London and the three provincial cities which were in a class of their own, namely, Liverpool, Birmingham, and Manchester, even the non-medical evidence was likely to be fuller and the witnesses better selected, since the coroner's officer in such places was usually a very experienced man who used effective search procedures, had some familiarity with the law of evidence,[51] and took very full statements from the witnesses (which might indeed merely be repeated at the inquest). The medical evidence itself was likely to be immensely superior, not only because of the higher proportion of hospitalized cases and the ready availability of laboratory facilities, forensic experts, and thoroughly experienced police surgeons, but also because the coroner involved was far more likely to be a self-confident man of some prominence, both locally and

---

[49] In 1884 over 20 per cent of borough coroners were medical men as against only 10 per cent of county coroners: see the *Law List* and *Medical Directory*.

[50] PP 1911 [Cd. 5492] XIII, Appendix II, p. 28, Table, and p. 34, para. 84.

[51] There were no strict rules of evidence at coroners' inquests.

in the Coroners' Society, who took a wide view of his office and was ready to do battle over the expense entailed by the lavish use of post-mortems and other expert evidence. Indeed, in some of these cities by the turn of the century, the paying authority was itself anxious to abolish the list of uncertified deaths, and therefore encouraged the coroner to do his work thoroughly.[52] Not surprisingly, it was London which produced that ratepayers' nightmare, a coroner who ordered expert post-mortems in 99.2 per cent of his cases but proved irre-movable.[53] (This was John Troutbeck, first treasurer of the Medico-Legal Society founded in 1901, and a zealous exponent in the 1900s of what had been since the 1870s the progressive answer to the mid-nineteenth century debate on whether coroners should have medical or legal qualifications: namely, that if they could not have both, they should be lawyers with regular assistance from specialists in forensic medicine.) Such extremism was rare—forensic experts were few, and in any case many coroners as well as the British Medical Association preferred to follow the strict letter of the law and employ the local practitioner or police surgeon concerned in the case.[54] Whoever per-formed them, however, post-mortems were certainly far more often ordered by town coroners than by country ones. Town coroners, moreover, received a high proportion of their cases from public hos-pitals, and upon these they had the benefit of free medical evidence, since until 1926 no doctor whose duty it had been to attend the deceased was entitled to be paid for giving evidence at an inquest upon his or her body.[55] (Near the great London teaching hospitals, such cases could, by the 1900s, account for as many as a third of all the inquests held, and elaborate medical reports were routinely furnished on each one.)

As for the quality of the jury, it varied widely; and this was an

[52] Westcott, 'The Coroner and his Medical Neighbours', p. 19.

[53] The British Medical Association had taken up the matter with the Lord Chancellor himself: PP 1911 [Cd. 5492] XIII, Appendix III, pp. 40–1 paras. 60–8.

[54] Westcott, 'The Coroner and his Medical Neighbours', pp. 18–19. A coroner was empowered to call to give medical evidence any qualified practitioner who had attended the deceased during his last illness or at his death, or failing this, any practitioner near where the death happened: Coroners Act 1887, 50 & 51 Vict., c. 71, s. 21(1). No official objections were made when experts were called instead, but much ill-feeling was caused among general practitioners.

[55] 50 & 51 Vict., c. 71, s. 22. Whether a workhouse infirmary was a public hospital for this purpose was a matter of legal debate. The London County Council chose to consider it was not, and paid fees to poor law medical officers who acted as witnesses: PP 1911 [Cd. 5492] XIII, Appendix II, p. 34, para. 78.

important matter, since the jury's verdict was final, however perverse it might be. Unlike other jurymen, coroners' juries needed no qualifications. In a rural area, it might be difficult to get together any jury at all, and 'poor and uneducated labouring men' were often summoned in such places, although coroners disagreed fundamentally on how far this made them any the worse jurymen. In a town, a few layabouts might make themselves perpetually available for the sake of a drink and the fee which some authorities paid to jurymen, or a hard-pressed coroner's officer might repeatedly summon the same easily accessible tradesmen (sometimes in the expectation of a tip to pass them over). To guard against these weaknesses it was common by the end of the century in efficient urban jurisdictions either to work through the voters' list, or to summon juries by streets; the coroner for Liverpool, for example, was by then giving his officer standing orders to 'avoid the day labourer' and 'get tradesmen, shopkeepers and merchants' and make sure of a jury equal to 'a delicate question' by choosing 'a better class of street'. City juries like this—and *a fortiori* the gentlemanly juries of the City and west end of London—were more likely to understand technical evidence and to be free from what Troutbeck called 'bias where people of a superior class are concerned'; and they were also more likely to have the courage of their opinions, since they would almost certainly not know personally the individuals concerned, and would themselves remain virtually anonymous.[56] Did this mean that the juries most likely to be independent of the coroner in reaching their verdicts were city ones? Hardly: for in a busy city district, which might yield an annual income of £2,000 or more,[57] the coroner himself

---

[56] Much of the evidence is conflicting, since the desirability of abolishing inquest juries was a deeply controversial issue. See, however, PP 1909 [Cd. 4782] XV, p. 77, Q. 2018, pp. 182–3, Qs. 5236–48, p. 186, Qs. 5354–66; PP 1910 [Cd. 5004] XXI, p. 13; PP 1910 [Cd. 5139] XXI, p. 96, Qs. 9027–33; PP 1913 [Cd. 6818] XXX, p. 58, Qs. 1682–4, p. 36, Q. 1127, p. 118, Qs. 3295–300, p. 140, Qs. 3953–7; Troutbeck, 'Inquest Juries', p. 51. The frequent recurrence of the same names in lists of jurors at inquests held in Paddington in the 1850s leaves no doubt that some urban jurors served very frequently, and indeed frequent summonses to serve were something of a tradesman's and shopkeeper's grievance: Marylebone Library, Registers of Coroner's Inquests, Paddington, vols. 3–4 and 'The Workhouse Test in St. Pancras', *Ratepayers' Journal and Local Management Gazette*, 26 July 1856, p. 76. Dickens discovered that the parish beadle counted on being bribed not to summon him: *The Uncommercial Traveller*, 'Some Recollections of Mortality', p. 195.

[57] In 1909 the two busiest London coroners had an income of £2,000–£2,500 a year: PP 1909 [Cd. 4782] XV, p. 70, Q. 1834. The annual income from the position of coroner for West Middlesex in the 1830s was never less than £1,500–£1,800: Sprigge, *Thomas Wakley*, p. 374, although many busy urban coroners employed a deputy, as did elderly

was often an exceptionally vigorous and forceful man. In the great mass of routine cases, it was everywhere the coroner who in practice decided the verdict. Nevertheless, wherever habits of deference were not overwhelmingly strong, a jury might reject his guidance if it conflicted with their own morality of suicide or their feelings towards the people concerned, or, above all, if the coroner appeared to be sheltering the local authorities. Juries chiefly showed their independence, however, not by returning a verdict indicating a totally different mode of death, but by delaying the proceedings, making a different choice among the possible kinds of suicide verdict from the one their coroner favoured, or adding a long rider to their verdict.[58] It was certainly not only in large towns that they could thus assert themselves. Hertfordshire agricultural labourers were indeed apparently acquiescent cyphers; but juries in rural Bedfordshire in the 1870s several times used their statutory right to insist on an adjournment in order to get a post-mortem and summon additional witnesses against their coroner's express wishes, and in the Rhondda in 1862 a jury saved a neighbour from a murder charge by returning a verdict of suicide on his victim in the teeth of the coroner's directions and of expert medical evidence.[59] In reality the distinctive feature of the minority of socially superior urban juries was perhaps not so much their independence as a reasoned respect for evidence, a capacity to refrain from irrelevant questions, and the avoidance of loose verdicts and futile riders. Altogether, it seems reasonable to surmise that in the big cities inquests were less likely than elsewhere to end in an open verdict or one of natural or accidental death when what was indicated was a verdict of suicide.

The fourth and final stage was that of report and registration. The findings of coroners' juries were reported to two different government departments, the Home Office and the General Register Office. Each process had its own history. Under the Municipal Corporations Act of 1835, borough coroners were required to send to the Home Secretary at the end of each legal year returns of the number of inquests they

invalids. (The use of deputies was not regulated by statute until the Coroners Act of 1887.)

[58] These long riders were often made much of in the press: see, for example, *Morning Advertiser*, 11 July 1856, reprinted in *Ratepayers' Journal*, 26 July 1856, p. 80. (There were three main categories of suicide verdicts: *felo de se*, 'temporary insanity' or 'mind unsound', and 'state of mind unknown', all of which are discussed in ch. 6, pp. 219–30.

[59] BedsRO, C.O.2/2, inquests held on 21 Sept. 1874, 12–13 July 1876, 26–7 Jan. 1877, 31 Dec. 1877; Thomas, 'Medical Men of Glamorgan', p. 127.

had held, together with the findings of the jury and costs incurred.
When the Home Office remodelled the annual judicial statistics in
1856, it decided to publish similar returns from all coroners as a branch
of the new Police Statistics. There was never any statutory obligation
upon franchise coroners to make such returns, nor was there any upon
county coroners until the Coroners Act of 1887. Nevertheless they all
'promptly complied', no doubt because they already kept registers of
the facts requested in order to establish the payments due to them. In
addition, however, in 1836, the first legislation on the civil registration
of deaths had required coroners to see that their juries inquired into
the particulars required by the new death certificates, and then to
report their findings to the Registrar of the district in which the inquest
was held (after 1874, this had to be done within five days).[60] By the
same legislation, the Registrar of Deaths was required in his turn to
enter these particulars in his register. These local Registrars were from
the beginning statutorily required to make a quarterly return to the
Registrar-General in London of all the deaths registered in their
districts, and the Registrar-General himself was required to make an
annual report to Parliament. At first the General Register Office only
occasionally published any of the information about mortality from
suicide it thus acquired. In 1858, however, a nosology was introduced
which listed suicide separately from violent death, so that from that
year onwards, deaths registered as caused by suicide appeared separately in the mortality tables in precisely the same way as a death
registered as resulting from any of the other causes of death listed in
the new classification.

Did either of these two channels, by which the findings of coroners'
juries entered the statistics of central government, divert or distort the
flow? Prima facie it might seem likely that the figures published by the
General Register Office would be more incomplete than those of the
Home Office, since they were based upon the coroners' returns only
at second hand. In the first year, there were indeed 10 per cent fewer
registered suicides than there were suicide verdicts—a shortfall vari-
ously blamed upon obscurity in the verdicts and duplicate coroners'
returns.[61] Thereafter, however, the discrepancy was never at all

---

[60] 6 & 7 Will. IV, c. 86, s. 25; 37 & 38 Vict., c. 88, s. 16.

[61] *Registrar-General's 19th AR*, p. 199; Radcliffe, 'On the Prevalence of Suicide in
England', p. 1. The number of suicide verdicts registered at the Home Office for 1861–
70 was about 0.4 per cent greater than the number of deaths by suicide registered at the
General Register Office, and for 1871–80 3 per cent smaller. By the early twentieth
century the discrepancy between the two totals was about 0.1 per cent.

sizeable, and was as likely to arise from a larger number of cases of suicide being returned by the Registrars than by the coroners as from the reverse. Of the two, it is intrinsically likely that the Registrars were more accurate and painstaking performers of clerical tasks than most coroners, and also that they maintained more uniform standards in such matters. They were drawn from the lower middle class, and were often relieving officers, tax collectors, postmasters, schoolmasters, drapers, and so on; they were all very closely supervised and disciplined by the General Register Office from the days of the martinet Major George Graham onwards; and they were not allowed to follow occupations considered incompatible with their duties.[62] The socially superior coroners, on the other hand, were not only holders of a uniquely independent office, but varied greatly in their calibre and ways of working, including the extent to which they employed clerical assistance (which had to be paid for out of their own pockets). Moreover, once these returns reached the two London offices, they were in far more punctilious and skilled hands at the General Register Office than they were at the Home Office, where the small statistical branch was the despised Cinderella of the department.[63] Probably, then, there is not a great deal to choose between the two sets of figures so far as simple reportorial accuracy is concerned, although those compiled by the General Register Office may possibly have the edge.

One fundamental difference between the two runs needs to be kept in mind, however. The statistics published by the Home Office related to suicide as a legal mode of death. So far as these statistics are concerned, ambiguity and error in the return itself (as opposed to the verdict which the return reported) can be discounted, apart from the occasional clerical slip and probably equally occasional duplication (in the interests of augmenting fee income). The Registrar-General's statistics, however, were concerned with suicide as a pathological cause of death, and for his purposes these returns were seriously affected by errors, omissions, and ambiguities in the certificates coroners gave. Not until 1926 were coroners statutorily obliged to make

[62] Farr, *Vital Statistics*, p. xix. A pawnbroker, undertaker, or licensee, for example, could not be a Registrar: PP 1893–4 (373, 402) XI, p. xxiv. Only very rarely was the same man both Registrar and coroner. In the first 29 years of civil registration only 4 out of a body of 2,200 Registrars were found guilty of making fictitious entries of death: Farr, *Vital Statistics*, p. 222; and the 'careful verification of local figures' by the General Register Office impressed the knowledgeable: Preston-Thomas, *The Work and Play of a Government Inspector*, p. 289 n. 1.

[63] Pellew, *The Home Office 1848–1914*, pp. 53–5, 108.

use of the printed forms supplied by the General Register Office for purposes of medical certification of death, and throughout the Victorian period the certificates they gave to the Registrars were often extremely vague. Even when a jury clearly defined the legal mode of death as suicide, it often gave no indication of the pathological cause of death—for example, whether death occurred from suffocation or by poison—and the coroner in his turn often failed to transmit to the Registrar such medical evidence on this point as had emerged at the inquest. Successive chiefs of the statistical department of the General Register Office repeatedly complained of this lack of precise information.[64] In this matter there were certainly significant geographical variations. Vagueness was particularly rife in country areas (above all in Wales),[65] where post-mortems were under-used, hospitalization rare, and medical witnesses prone to generalities and antiquated medical ideas. Time, however, wrought great changes. By 1911 the quality of the medical evidence given at inquests had everywhere improved so much that impressive results were achieved in response to a circular from the Registrar-General asking coroners to include in their certificates all the information available on the medical cause of death, even when it did not appear in the verdict. In that year, only 1.7 per cent of the deaths registered as caused by suicide were reported to the General Register Office without pathological details.[66] As pathological statistics, if not as legal ones, therefore, Edwardian suicide statistics are vastly superior to those produced in the mid-Victorian years.

Victorian and Edwardian suicide statistics were plainly shaped at every stage by the processes which produced them. Yet it would be a mistake to end here, for they were also shaped by another factor: the close integration of the system into local life. Three pressures arising from this deserve to be borne in mind.

The first is that of local topography. Until 1911, all deaths were registered in the district in which the body lay, and not in the deceased's usual place of residence. In any ecological study of suicide before 1911, therefore, it is always necessary to take into account local features

---

[64] *Registrar-General's 16th AR*, Appendix, p. 115; *25th AR*, p. 191; *50th AR*, p. xx.

[65] In 1861–70 (to take an extreme example) the nature of the returns for 47 per cent of the female cases of suicide registered in Monmouthshire was such that they could not be classified under any of the five main methods of suicide, and had to be listed under the heading 'Other or unspecified'.

[66] *Registrar-General's 74th AR*, p. xcv.

which were likely to increase artificially the number of suicide verdicts in a particular coroner's district—for example, an abundance of rivers, ponds or canals, or railway termini, or the presence of some renowned suicide spot. An exceptionally large concentration of certain residential institutions could also prove significant. It will be remembered that from 1853 onwards special statutory provisions were made for coroners to investigate the deaths of persons 'under the charge of a public body',[67] partly because Englishmen found it second nature to suspect authorities of abuse of power, and partly because officials themselves were increasingly desirous of avoiding the scandals and popular outcries so common in the early Victorian years. Other institutions soon began voluntarily to give instructions for all deaths not clearly from natural causes to be similarly reported. The presence of a large hospital, in particular, could substantially increase the suicide rate of a district.

A second distortion sprang from the fact that Victorian and even Edward communities almost always assumed that the gentlefolk among them were outside the rough and tumble of popular institutions, which undoubtedly included 'the people's court', alias an inquest. Until at least the end of the nineteenth century, and despite the efforts of Wakley and other coroners anxious to raise the status of their office, an inquest was irretrievably associated with undignified proceedings which went on in hired rooms in public houses, before very humble jurors (who might sometimes be allowed to solace themselves with beer and tobacco), amidst the coming and going of stray cats, dogs, infants, and members of the public;[68] and by law it included a view of the body, often unclothed and usually in some outhouse, by all the jury. To the poor a coroner's inquest (like a police court) might be a welcome source of drama and gossip; but to their betters it seemed chiefly a sordid source of low comedy (see Fig. 2). At the very end of the century permanent coroners' court rooms, mortuaries, and post-mortem rooms began to be provided by local authorities in large cities, and smaller towns began to hire rooms in the proliferating working men's clubs, institutes, and halls instead of in public houses.[69] Never-

---

[67] These are listed above in note 30.

[68] Wakley, as part of his efforts to raise the status of the coroner's office, insisted on comparatively high standards of propriety (cf. Fig. 2), and gave orders controlling the admission of strangers on 17 Oct. 1851: Marylebone Library Registers of Coroner's Inquests, vol. 2, flyleaf. Dickens (who is depicted on Wakley's left in Fig. 2) characteristically heightened reality in his description of the 'inkwich' at The Sol's Arms in *Bleak House*, ch. xi.

[69] At least as late as 1889 almost every inquest in Lancashire was held in a public

Fig. 2 Thomas Wakley (coroner for West Middlesex, 1839–62) holding an inquest, with Charles Dickens looking on at his left (n.d.: *c.*1840)

theless, journalists were still inclined to satirize 'crowner's quests', and a distinctly vulgar aura long clung around them. All this (and much else) conspired to keep inquests apart from the small separate world of 'the gentry'.[70] Police, doctors, juries, and coroners were all as a rule

house: PP 1910 [Cd. 5004] XXI, p. 151, Q. 10, 603. In London on the other hand as early as 1851 the gentlemanly coroner for the City and Liberty of Westminster reported that he had 'prevailed on several of the local authorities in my district, as well as governors of hospitals, to give me the use of board rooms, with a vast increase of comfort to myself': Middlesex Justices, *Report of the Special Committee appointed at the Michaelmas Session, 1850*, p. 48; and the coroner for the City of London often made similar arrangements. Gradually most London vestries provided suitable accommodation, and by the 1890s only 8 per cent of inquests were held in public houses. By 1897 the London County Council had fully met its obligation under the Public Health (London) Act of 1891 to provide proper accommodation for inquests, and the use of public houses ceased altogether. As for mortuaries, they began to be provided in London in the 1860s, although only 11 provincial boroughs had a mortuary of any sort in 1880: Burdett, *The Necessity and Importance of Mortuaries*, pp. 18–19. Contiguous mortuaries and coroners' courts were the ideal: Hardwicke, *On the Office and Duties of Coroners*, p. 5; and the London County Council set out to provide these after 1891: LCC, *AR for the year ended 31 March 1901*, pp. 193–6. Progress was checkered, however: see below, ch. 5 n. 82.

[70] On the rare occasions when an inquest had to be held on the body of one of the well-to-do and the body lay at home, Lankester's papers show that he held the inquest privately in the house, as requested by the relatives.

respecters of persons, at least until the very end of this period.[71] Accordingly, while it is difficult to see any evidence for selective registration of suicide by sex or age (apart from that indirectly brought about by different preferences for particular methods of suicide among men and women and among young and old), and while it remains no more than speculation that there was under-registration of suicide among those employed in such occupations as mining, quarrying, fishing, and railway work (which provided so many opportunities for taking fatal risks as to make suicide of the kind that would be recorded by a jury hardly necessary), there is nevertheless every likelihood that suicide among the upper and professional classes was always significantly under-registered in most neighbourhoods. William Ogle himself was convinced of this in 1886; and it is impossible to believe that he was wrong.[72]

The third and most important repercussion of the genuine localism of the system, however, arose from the very marked administrative as well as social dissimilarities in later nineteenth-century and early twentieth-century England between the great cities at the heart of nascent conurbations, and the rest of the country. This created in effect a two-tier coroner system. In most places the whole nature of English life and institutions reinforced the general rule that inquests were freely held, but slackly prepared and inexpertly conducted; but in a handful of exceptionally busy and compact jurisdictions which handled a high proportion of complex cases, things were far otherwise. In 1860 eight coroners accounted for 27 per cent of all the work done by the coroners of England and Wales; and in 1912 the eight coroners who each held over a thousand inquests a year accounted for nearly 21 per cent of all the inquests held.[73] Thus a very a small group of jurisdictions in London, Liverpool, and Manchester reached heights of coronorial professionalism which might indeed begin to be approached by the coroners for Leeds, Sheffield, and Birmingham, responsible as they were for over 500 inquests a year, but which for many reasons were hardly even aspired to by the bulk of their colleagues. Accordingly, it is overwhelmingly probable that the statistics emanating from these

---

[71] Arnold Bennett in *The Pretty Lady* (1918), described the 'icy radical' who presided over the 'small, close, sordid' coroner's court in Westminster as 'a disrespecter of persons above a certain social rank', who accordingly saw to it that the jury added a critical rider to their verdict on the Marquis of Lechford's daughter.

[72] Ogle, 'Suicides in England and Wales', p. 102.

[73] In 1958 the 13 full-time coroners dealt with about one-third of all cases: Thurston, *Coroner's Practice*, p. 5.

elite jurisdictions were more complete, more precise, and more intern-
ally consistent than those from the rest. They should therefore be
regarded with exceptional respect; while conversely the least respect
of all should be given to those emanating from backwaters where there
was too little work for expertise to develop or where the supporting
facilities provided by local authorities were rudimentary—in effect the
small borough coroners' districts which existed until 1888, thoroughly
rural districts, and most (although not all) franchise coronerships.

The mid-Victorian lobby for improved vital statistics and forensic
medicine never secured the adoption of the continental police system
of investigating sudden and suspicious deaths (although it came quite
close to success in 1859); and only a few local authorities (notably
Manchester)[74] ever employed special medical investigators, its other
favourite recommendation. Registrars continued to lack medical qualifications (and indeed much education of any sort); coroners continued
to be predominantly 'bustling attorneys'; and general practitioners
continued to resist encroachments upon their vested interest in providing post-mortems and medical evidence by forensic experts.[75] The
coroner system, however—like so many other English institutions—
had been made very sensitive to changing local circumstances by the
crucial legal and administrative developments of the 1830s, with their
provisions for a new kind of police, civil registration, remuneration
for medical witnesses, penalties for non-attendance at an inquest, and
much else.[76] The mid-nineteenth century brought some consequential
amendments and some important negative decisions, as well as a great
campaign to secure the appointment of medically qualified coroners,
although from the later 1870s radicalism in forensic medicine as in
civil registration was quiescent for a generation, and the proportion
of medically qualified coroners ceased to grow. (The Coroners' Act of
1887 was essentially no more than a great consolidating measure.)
What mattered most, however, was always the readiness of the local

[74] PP 1893–4 (373, 402) XI, p. x.

[75] For the attitude of general practitioners see PP 1911 [Cd. 5492] XIII, Appendix III,
p. 41, para. 62; Troutbeck, 'Modes of Ascertaining the Fact and Cause of Death', p. 95;
Westcott, 'Twelve Years' Experience of a London Coroner', pp. 17–18 and *idem*, 'The
Coroner and his Medical Neighbours', pp. 18–22.

[76] A comprehensive collection of the relevant statutes and statutory orders is provided
in Baker, *A Practical Compendium of the Recent Statutes, Cases and Decisions Affecting
the Office of Coroner*, Appendix, pp. 391–644. Absentee medical witnesses could be
fined £5: 6 & 7 Will. IV, c. 89, s. vi. In 1887 penalties were added of up to 40s. for
recalcitrant witnesses and £5 for defaulting jurymen: 50 & 51 Vict., c. 71, s. 19.

authority to pay for pathological investigations and the efficiency of the local police and medical facilities. Thus in the late Victorian and Edwardian golden age of large cities, city inquests were inevitably very different not only from those held in country areas, but also from those held in the same cities a generation or two earlier. These favoured places had come to possess *de facto* something very like the system so often advocated by utilitarian reformers, for they had salaried, full-time legal coroners, some of whom were also medically qualified, who sat in their own court houses (equipped with mortuary and post-mortem facilities) with all the authority of expert public functionaries (although they were the appointees of local and not central government). These coroners habitually used an experienced police officer to undertake investigations on their behalf, almost invariably called for medical evidence and post-mortems (although usually not from forensic experts), and followed a series of professional routines which made the expert private preliminaries to the inquest at least as important as the public enquiry itself.

This contrast is tangibly embodied in one of the few collections of coroners' papers spanning this whole period which is known to survive, that of the coroners for the ancient Borough of Southwark (which was under the jurisdiction of the Corporation of London).[77] Every coroner was obliged to deliver his account in the shape of a register of inquests held and expenses incurred to the paying authority every four months, and to draw up at the end of every inquest the formal legal document embodying the jury's finding known as an inquisition; but whether or not he kept any other records, and what form they took, was entirely for him to decide. In 1861 the coroner for Southwark (who was also coroner for the City of London) was one of the most professional of that generation, Serjeant W. J. Payne, the first president of the Coroners' Society of England and Wales; yet his system was simply to tuck inside his inquisitions—which were afterwards numbered and bundled up—three pieces of paper. The first was his printed letter to the beadles and constables of the parish where the body lay, ordering jurymen to be summoned to attend an inquest at a stated time and place (Payne was unusual in holding his inquests in a vestry hall or workhouse, rather than a public house); the second a list of those

---

[77] These papers are preserved in the Corporation of London Records Office. (Unfortunately the papers arising from coroners' inquests have often been destroyed when more than 15 years old, under the Public Record Office Schedule for the destruction of coroners' records issued in 1921.)

summoned (which Payne ticked to show those who actually served), together with a list of witnesses; and the third Payne's own hastily scribbled notes of the evidence given, which the witnesses signed. The papers produced by his Edwardian successor, F. J. Waldo, were markedly more formal, detailed, and precise. Waldo had been Medical Officer of Health for St George's, Southwark, and held a Diploma in Public Health and a Cambridge MD as well as being a barrister, magistrate, writer, and lecturer on medical jurisprudence and public health and (incidentally) a keen antiquarian. Immediately after his appointment in 1901 he arranged for his inquest papers to be bound into three separate series: first, the inquisitions themselves; then the depositions and other case papers; and finally a 'No-Inquest' series relating to the inquiries made into deaths in the workhouse and in the great lunatic asylum of Bethlem, all of which were automatically reported to him, although few required an inquest. Waldo's volumes of case papers offer a striking contrast to Payne's bundles. Four differently coloured printed documents were now routinely produced in the course of each inquest. First, and most important, since it determined the whole structure of the proceedings, was the General Report of the coroner's officer, Risby, a police sergeant based at the local police station; this consisted of a white form containing the answers to thirteen questions of fact, inside which was tucked Risby's handwritten report on his personal inquiries. Then there were the medical reports, which in Southwark frequently took the form of elaborate post-mortem reports from Guy's Hospital; and a blue printed letter from Waldo to the parish officers (in effect Risby), ordering the body to be removed to the mortuary and witnesses and jurymen to be summoned (which was done street by street). Lastly there were the notes made by Waldo's clerk of the witnesses' depositions at the inquest, which was always held in Waldo's own court room. This abundance of printed forms and clerical notes, the existence of a municipal mortuary with a post-mortem room and of a coroner's court room, and above all the central role played by the police sergeant who had been seconded to act as the coroner's officer, all clearly demonstrate how different the working routines and facilities of an Edwardian city coroner could be from those of fifty years before.

Outside the great cities, however, the system inevitably remained far weaker in expertise. Indeed, the gulf between inquests held in busy urban areas and those held in the rest of the country had probably never been so wide as at the turn of this century; for these new city ways of working were not the result of any formal changes, but rather a by-product of increased professionalism among city police, medical men, and coroners, and changing standards in urban local government. On the other hand, where the system remained most untouched by developing professionalism and the new civic gospel, it retained all the more surely and completely those twin sources of strength which would have been most in jeopardy had the coroner system been replaced by either of the two continental alternatives of the police or medical examiners: the support of ordinary citizens and ordinary doctors. In the detection of suicide, this broad acceptability at the level of everyday life meant that the English system enjoyed far more of one vital ingredient of success: individual co-operation from those with first-hand contacts with the case. In Victorian and Edwardian England no system, however superior in theory, could work well in practice unless it was flexible enough to be able to function both in some of the world's most highly developed cities and in the depths of the countryside, and was also free from any association with unfeeling investigations by alien and intimidating specialists who worked behind closed doors and were paid fat fees for their operations.[78] By 1911 around 36,000 inquests were being held each year, yet only three verdicts had been quashed by a higher court in the previous seven years; and at the end of an exhaustive Home Office inquiry, the committee acknowledged that they were 'astonished at the good work done by coroners: the discharge of their frequently very painful duties is effected with very little friction, and we attributed this to the good sense, tact and good feeling shown by the great majority of coroners in their dealings with the public.'[79] Until 1888 the bulk of English coroners were popularly elected by a mass franchise,[80] with only a minority appointed by local authorities or notables; they were, moreover, overwhelmingly part-timers, who were in no way isolated from everyday local life, and the verdicts at their inquests were given by any twelve or more 'good and lawful men' of the parish where the body lay, often sitting in the midst of many of their neighbours. In practice as well as theory such a system was essentially a democratic one, and

---

[78] See the points made in discussion by George Bernard Shaw, Luke White, MP and coroner for East Yorkshire, and S. F. Butcher, president of the Coroners' Society, at a meeting of the Medico-Legal Society: *Transactions*, iii (1905–6), pp. 108–10.

[79] PP 1910 [Cd. 5004] XXI, p. 4.

[80] Even the freehold of a burial plot sufficed to provide a qualification to vote in a poll for a county coroner. At Edwin Lankester's election as one of the coroners for Middlesex in 1862, there was a total poll of 10,894: see *DNB*.

remarkably independent of the higher reaches of political and social authority, and indeed of official control of any sort. It reflected at every turn not bureaucratic processes or laws and orders, but the prejudices, habits, and values of each particular locality in all the diversity of its public and private interests, conflicts, and routines.

In England, there were well over 300 largely autonomous local mechanisms for the registration of death by suicide. Despite its drawbacks, this system provided a powerful built-in safeguard not only against the emergence of any consistent pattern of selective under- or over-registration, but also against consistent habits of non-co-operation and silence which could have damaged its workings even more seriously. Nineteenth-century continental writers were clearly entirely correct to regard the English official suicide statistics as in a class of their own. What follows from this, however, is not that they should be despised or rejected as historical evidence, but that they should be evaluated with the aid of as much insight as can be mustered into the complex processes which produced and shaped them, and recognized as *par excellence* historical statistics which should be put to particular rather than general uses.

2

Gender, Age, Mortality, and Suicide

SHOULD the history of suicide be written separately for men and for women? In the nineteenth century it was usual to deal in suicide rates which related to persons, without distinction of sex. Not that it was supposed that the incidence of suicide was identical among both sexes: on the contrary, it was common expert knowledge that suicide was three or four times more frequent among men than among women, except during the late teens.[1] The difference was seen as essentially one of general level, however, so that there seemed no great objection to combining the figures for the two sexes. But was this view correct? The question is an important practical one, for clearly if the pattern as well as the scale of suicide was really very different for men and for women, any study based upon suicide rates for persons will depict a non-existent androgyn and thus be seriously misleading for both sexes.

All the major theories of suicide make it seem likely that the geographical, occupational, and age incidence of suicide was very different for the two sexes in Victorian and Edwardian England, given the wide differences at that time in what was expected of men and women, and in what they did. For example, if the main explanation of suicide is found in the disintegration of social ties and the increase of egoism and anomie under the impact of the division of labour, then it must have been highly significant that for very many years the industrial revolution hardly touched most working women. Equally, if neighbourhood ecology is stressed, it is important that the experience of living in a particular street can hardly have been the same for men and for women, so different were their roles; while if the causes of suicide are sought in the impact of various stages of the life cycle or in physical or mental disease, it is even more plain that wide differences are likely. Male and female suicide rates have certainly had separate dynamics during the twentieth century, for while suicide among men reached its highest level in 1931–4 and then began to fall, so that by 1976 it had

---

[1] See for example Morselli, *Suicide*, pp. 189–204.

Statistics

dropped to the level registered in 1867, among women it increased sharply after the Second World War until 1963, and then fell only slowly, so that by 1976 the level of suicide among women was still not below that recorded in the mid-1920s.[2] In short, it seems very probable that the history of suicide in Victorian and Edwardian England was very different among men and women. But is there any statistical evidence that this was so? There is; but a great deal of it deserves little weight. Registered cases of female suicide were comparatively few, especially before the 1890s, so that many taxonomies of female suicide statistics yield numbers which are very small. Female suicide rates are consequently apt to be very volatile; they have, moreover, a smaller range than male rates. Thus although there are often wide contrasts between male and female suicide rates, only those which rest upon a reasonably large numerical base can be taken to point to genuine divergencies.

Four broad differences between male and female patterns of suicide stand out in the statistics which meet this requirement.[3] First, differences of geographical incidence. Not surprisingly, in view of the smaller numbers involved, there were far fewer areas of consistently high or consistently low female suicide rates than of male. Such consistently high and low areas as did exist, however, by no means always coincided with the high and low areas of male suicide rates. It is notable, for example, that the trio of southern counties which consistently provided some of the highest male suicide rates in England before 1914—Sussex, Kent, and Surrey—never had more than average crude suicide rates for women; and in 1901–10 at least, these rates prove to have been in reality distinctly below the national average when allowances are made for the distorting effect of the age structure of the female population of these three counties. Second, differences in the socio-economic settings associated with high or low suicide rates. For example, mining areas usually had spectacularly low male suicide rates but quite high female ones; and similarly, although in the years immediately before 1914 standardized mortality rates from suicide for women were much the same in all three types of urban administrative areas but notably

---

[2] OPCS, Series DH1, no. 4, *Mortality Statistics 1976*, p. 68, Table 9. (The figures for 1976 were the most recent available at the time of writing this chapter; in the late 1970s suicide rates rose, but more for men than for women.) The figures for 1901–61 are surveyed in *Registrar-General's Statistical Review, 1961*, Part III, pp. 240–67; for continuations see Adelstein and Mardon, 'Suicides 1961–74', and McClure, 'Trends in Suicide Rate for England and Wales 1975–80'.

[3] Differences in method as opposed to incidence are discussed in ch. 10, pp. 364–7.

lower in rural districts, neither of these things was true of the rates for men. Third, different rhythms of change through time in the scale of suicide. For example, in national terms male suicide rates rose fairly steadily throughout this period, whereas female ones made one very sharp upward leap in the 1890s but in all other decades rose very little. And last and perhaps most suggestive of all, differences in the age incidence of suicide, both at the mid-century statistical outset, and during the long-term adjustments brought by the next fifty years. At the outset the typical pattern was a steadily rising incidence until old age for men, as against an earlier peak, and two sudden rises at puberty and the menopause, for women. From the 1880s onwards, however, the national figures exhibit markedly divergent trends in the suicidal behaviour of the two sexes in their late teens and even more in old age, with suicide increasing sharply in both age-groups among men, but growing very little or actually decreasing among women.[4]

All four of these differences revealed by separating male from female suicide statistics are more or less discordant with one or other traditional interpretation of suicide. Those listed under the first heading throw doubt on the long-held association of the highest suicide rates with the diffusion of unhealthy metropolitan influences; those under the second challenge the equally long established association of high suicide rates with social isolation and big cities; while those under the third hardly fit the familiar attribution of increased female suicide to increased female emancipation, nor do those under the fourth fit well with explanations of suicide in terms of the biological life cycle. The implication must be not only that some differences did exist between male and female patterns of suicide, but also that to investigate the incidence of suicide without making consistent distinctions of sex is to lessen the chance of understanding aright the suicidal behaviour either of men or of women.

Evidently the history of suicide among women and among men must be studied separately; and this conclusion is reinforced by two quite different considerations. The first is purely technical. It has always been believed that a higher proportion of female than of male cases of suicide escaped registration in the nineteenth century. This has usually been attributed to the much greater use women made of drowning as a method of suicide. ('Found drowned' was a recognized euphemism for female suicide long before G. F. Watts's well-known painting—see

---

[4] All these points are fully documented below, in this and the following chapter.

Fig. 6—was given that title in 1850.) Since there was often no clear
evidence of how the body came to be in the water, and in law sudden
death was presumed accidental until proved otherwise, a verdict of
suicide was easily avoided in drowning cases—at least until coroners
increasingly led their juries to accept circumstantial evidence on this
point. It has been argued, moreover, that families always have a greater
incentive to conceal female suicide;[5] and it is not improbable that in
cases of doubt there was often greater readiness to avoid verdicts of
suicide on women.[6] Altogether it is likely that there was indeed more
under-registration of female than of male suicide. Accordingly, it is
desirable to avoid weakening the male figures by amalgamating them
with the 'softer' female ones, in the interests of greater accuracy in the
description and interpretation of suicidal behaviour. Today, however,
there are other, quite different incentives to write the history of suicide
separately for the two sexes. It is now a truism that women have a
separate and (until recently) neglected history; yet surely it is not
women's history alone but the reconstruction of separate but parallel
histories for both men and women of specific aspects of human experience which will make it possible to appraise at all exactly the difference
between the sexes at given points in time, and thus to assess the
changing historical significance of sex and gender. At first glance,
indeed, separate but parallel histories of suicidal behaviour among
Victorian and Edwardian men and women seem particularly worth
while, as promising insights into the differences between male and
female experiences of urbanization and industrialization. Might not
sex specific suicide rates be used to quantify changing male and female
experience of social disorganization, and even to construct sex specific
indices of alienation, or at least of suffering and malaise? On reflection,
however, such great expectations must be laid aside. Lofty super-
structures like these could hardly be satisfactorily erected on the basis
of the statistics produced by Victorian and Edwardian ways of detecting and recording suicide; nor could they easily carry much weight
today, when the relationship between individual acts of suicide and
the social structure is a matter of fundamental dispute among suicidologists. Still, to reconstruct the separate histories of suicide among
men and women is certainly to be offered some hints on the changing

---

[5] Douglas, *The Social Meanings of Suicide*, p. 215 n. 61.
[6] Women who tried but failed to commit suicide were certainly treated more leniently
than men by the authorities throughout the later nineteenth and early twentieth centuries:
see ch. 8 n. 98.

significance in Victorian and Edwardian England of being male or female and above all to be given some clues to the links which may have existed between changes in the significance of gender, in the meaning of different stages of life, and in the incidence of mortality. It is this triangle of interconnections which the separate histories of suicide among men and among women will here be used to explore.

Nineteenth-century commentators on the relationship between sex and suicide repeatedly remarked that international statistics established two points: first, that men were more prone to suicide than women, and secondly, that female suicide rates although always comparatively low, increased markedly though briefly at both puberty and the menopause, whereas male rates rose steadily until old age, when they declined.[7] In England and Wales these generalizations have long ceased to represent reality. In the early 1960s, when the Registrar-General's office marked the passing of the Suicide Act in 1961 and the opening of a new era in the law of suicide by surveying the last sixty years of the old regime, the gap between male and female suicide rates was shown to have been closing since 1911–20. Suicide rates among the elderly had been higher than among the middle-aged since 1901–10 so far as men were concerned, and among women too since 1951; while suicide had been tending to decline in these sixty years among young women under twenty-five, even more than among young men.[8] But how far were these trends foreshadowed before 1900? How far were the generalizations pioneered in the mid-nineteenth century already ceasing to be accurate in England at the very time when they were establishing themselves among the well-informed?

So far as the greater overall frequency of suicide among men is concerned, the answer is plain: not at all. In each of the first five decades of English official statistics—the very decades when an ever-increasing advantage for women was also establishing itself in general mortality—the gap between male and female suicide rates widened. Thus, while the male suicide rate was greater than the female by a ratio of 2.9 to one in 1861–70, this ratio had risen to 3.3 to one by 1901–10.[9] Not until 1911–20 did the narrowing of the overall gap

[7] See for example Morselli, *Suicide*, pp. 213–20.
[8] *Registrar-General's Statistical Review, 1961*, Part III, p. 244, Table CXXIV, and p. 246, Table CXXV.
[9] These ratios are based upon the standardized figures given in *Registrar-General's 75th AR, Supplement*, Part III, p. ccxi, Table 10.

begin. Yet it would be a great mistake to rest content with this generalization; for its significance looks entirely different once it is set against the shift which was going on in the age patterns characteristic of male and female suicide rates. In 1879 Morselli summarized expert suicidological opinion neatly: 'the prevalence of men over women is *least* in youth, *greatest* in adults, whilst it becomes *small* in old age and decrepitude.'[10] Even in 1879, however, this formula hardly fitted the English statistics, and in the next thirty years three trends appeared which ran altogether counter to the accepted generalizations. First of all, from the 1870s recorded suicide increased especially steeply among men over the age of sixty-five, whereas among women it hardly increased at all among those aged between sixty-five and seventy-four, and actually declined among those over the age of seventy-five. Thus by 1901–10 suicide had become nearly eight times commoner among men over seventy-five than among women of that age, and nearly six times commoner among men between the ages of sixty-five and seventy-four than among women. From the 1880s onwards, then, it was among people over the age of sixty-five that the difference between the sexes was greatest so far as suicide was concerned; in this respect the behaviour of men and women in old age had become vastly more dissimilar in the later nineteenth century than it had been earlier. Secondly, although suicide increased among young people of both sexes, it increased far more slowly among girls aged between fifteen and nineteen than among boys, so that in 1901–10 the male suicide rate for the first time actually exceeded the female in this age-group, as well as in all others. Among men and women in the prime of life (that is, those aged between twenty-five and forty-four), however, although only among them, suicide grew at a very similar pace for both sexes between 1860 and 1910; and it was women of this age who were chiefly responsible for the massive increase in the female suicide rate which occurred in the 1890s.[11]

The upshot is clear: divergent trends for the two sexes among the young and old, and among them alone, were responsible for the increasing gap between male and female suicide rates between 1860 and 1910. This suggests immediately that the classic explanations of this gap—that women did not participate in collective life in the same way, and that they were more patient, resigned, and self-sacrificing—

[10] Morselli, *Suicide*, p. 213.
[11] For all these figures see *Registrar-General's 75th AR, Supplement*, Part III, p. ccxi, Table 10.

may have been very wide of the mark. Certainly the causes of suicide, whatever they may have been in that half-century, affected old men far more than old women; girls less than boys; and old women and girls less than women in their prime. Thus if the age and sex specific national suicide statistics are any guide at all, they point to an experience of old age which became more harsh for men but not for women from the 1870s, and an experience of puberty which became less difficult for girls than for boys from the 1890s; whereas in the prime of life the balance sheet between the sexes evened out so far as the trends of change were concerned.

Nation-wide generalizations, like these, however, are never very satisfying. Fortunately a more concrete picture of how the age incidence of suicide diverged among men and women in Victorian and Edwardian England can be constructed, with the aid of three comprehensive sets of local age and sex specific suicide figures published between 1858 and 1914: those for the 623 registration districts during the decade 1861–70; those for the county boroughs, urban districts, and rural districts for each year from 1911 onwards; and those for the division of London for each year from 1858. Each of these repays attention.

From the age and sex specific suicide figures for every registration district in the country during the 1860s—which make it possible to calculate and compare the suicide rates in provincial towns of different sizes and types in a way which will be described in detail in the next chapter—it transpires that it was in the two retirement resorts of Bath and Brighton and (much more remarkably) in industrial towns that the suicidal behaviour of the two sexes differed most sharply in old age. In Bath and Brighton male suicide rates were high at every age;[12] but in industrial towns suicide rates for men were never high until they jumped steeply upwards among those over the age of fifty-five. Among elderly women, however, suicide rates in industrial towns often fell even more than usual. Indeed, in the new industrial towns which were dependent not upon textiles but on the extraction or manufacture of mineral ores or chemicals, engineering, and so on, the gap between male and female suicide rates for those over the age of seventy-five

---

[12] The annual average suicide rate recorded for the registration district of Bath in 1861–70, namely 7.9 per million living, was very similar to that recorded in the period 1778–98 by the city coroner, which was 7.5 per million living. Five-sixths of those found to have committed suicide in 1778–98 were servants and labourers, and this, together with the high recorded levels of other sorts of violence, has been seen as evidence of 'a culture of deprivation and violence' and 'the absence of community among the labouring population': Neale, *Bath 1680–1850*, pp. 92–4.

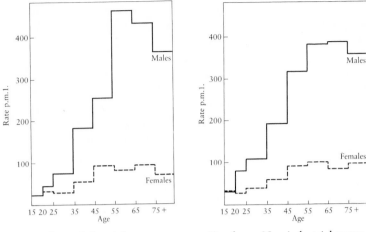

Graph 1.1 Industrial towns

Graph 1.2 Non-industrial towns

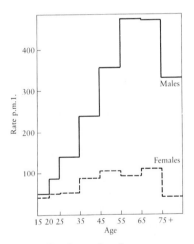

Graph 1.3 London

Graph 1. The age and sex incidence of registered suicide, 1861–70: 1.1 industrial towns; 1.2 non-industrial towns; 1.3 London

Source: Table 1.1.

Table 1.1. Average annual mortality from suicide per million living at eight different groups of ages in (i) industrial towns (types A and B), (ii) other provincial towns (types C, D, and E) with a population of more than 20,000, (iii) London and (iv) England and Wales, in the decade 1861–70

	15–19	20–4	25–34	35–44	45–54	55–64	65–74	Over 75
Male								
Industrial towns	22	44	74	183	255	465	433	364
Other provincial towns	32	80	109	191	318	382	386	358
London	49	86	140	238	356	473	471	328
England and Wales	28	59	93	163	263	377	359	251
Female								
Industrial towns	22	32	29	54	91	80	93	67
Other provincial towns	34	27	38	59	91	101	83	96
London	40	49	50	87	104	90	108	37
England and Wales	31	31	35	53	83	87	83	70

Source: Returns for the districts listed in Table 3.1, and for the division of London and England and Wales, in *Registrar-General's 35th AR, Supplement*, pp. 1–445.

was already wider in the 1860s than it had become in the country as a whole by 1901–10. Among young men under thirty-five, however, suicide was far rarer in industrial towns than in other sorts of town, and it was comparatively rare among young women too, except between the ages of twenty and twenty-four. (See Table 1.1 and Graphs 1.1 and 1.2.) Equally worth noticing is the fact that among girls between the ages of fifteen and nineteen suicide was much less frequent in big towns of every sort, except London, than it was elsewhere, since this implies that for girls though not for boys it was sheer urban size rather than urban economic structure which mattered. Indeed, in large towns with a population of more than 50,000, including London, girls of this age were already less prone to suicide than boys; so that the relationship between the sexes which became characteristic of this age-group in the national suicide statistics in the twentieth century had already come into existence in the 1860s in the country's most urban places (see Table 1.2).

The age and sex specific figures provided from 1911 onwards are

Statistics

Table 1.2. Average annual mortality from suicide per million living between the ages of fifteen and nineteen in provincial towns of three different sizes, London, and England and Wales, in the decade 1861–70

	Size I towns	Size II towns	Size III towns	London Division	England and Wales
Male	27	36	18	49	28
Female	22	21	35	40	31

Note: Size I towns, population over 100,000; Size II, population 50,000–100,000; Size III, population 20,000–49,000.

Source: As for Table 1.1.

much more elaborate geographically than these returns, but much less suggestive; and they are, moreover, too differently compiled for exact comparisons to be possible. Still, it is perhaps worth noting that by 1911–13 male suicide rates were highest over the age of sixty-five in all types of administrative area, so that it was only the tendency of suicide rates among women of this age to be lowest in smaller towns which made the divergence between the suicide patterns of the elderly become greatest in such places. It is certainly worth remarking that among women under twenty-five suicide was apparently much rarer in big cities than in smaller towns or even in rural districts. In the county boroughs of the southern region, in particular, suicide rates among young women were extremely low; while in the smaller towns of the north they were exceptionally high, indeed, nearly five times higher than in the county boroughs of the south and twice as high as in the county boroughs of the north.[13]

The third available set of place specific figures, those for London, calls for much more comment, for in London the age incidence of suicide altered quite dramatically for both sexes in the half-century before 1914, and London's suicide statistics always deserve exceptional respect—since they are not only the product of registration processes which were almost certainly exceptionally efficient throughout these years, but are uniquely consistent and abundant, and rest upon a

[13] 'Causes of Death at Different Periods of Life', *Registrar-General's 74th AR*, pp. 313–23, *75th AR*, pp. 329–39, *76th AR*, pp. 304–14. The estimated population of England and Wales and of the main divisions of England and Wales in the middle of the year 1911 is given in *Registrar-General's 74th AR*, pp. 4–5, Table 2. Summary Tables giving the annual mortality from suicide per million living in 1911, 1912, and 1913 in each type of administrative area and region in different age-groups and at all ages will be found in *Registrar-General's 74th AR*, pp. 63–70, Tables 24–7, *75th AR*, pp. 67–74, Tables 25–8, *76th AR*, pp. 67–74, Tables 25–8.

Table 1.3. Average annual mortality from suicide per million living in London and the provinces of England and Wales at all ages and at eight different groups of ages in the decennia 1861–70 and 1901–10

	All ages	15–19	20–4	25–34	35–44	45–54	55–64	65–74	over 75
Male									
London									
1861–70	135	49	86	140	238	356	473	471	328
1901–10	186	47	114	179	292	490	592	489	398
Provinces									
1861–70	93	25	54	84	150	247	362	314	236
1901–10	154	35	87	148	246	383	520	510	380
Female									
London									
1861–70	48	40	49	50	87	104	90	108	37
1901–10	55	26	47	62	92	134	124	97	33
Provinces									
1861–70	31	29	28	31	46	79	86	79	73
1901–10	48	36	45	54	78	105	106	86	52

Sources: Registrar-General's 35th AR, Supplement, pp. 2–5; *75th AR, Supplement*, Part III, pp. 2–5. (It should be noted that the General Register Office calculated the mean population for 1861–70 by taking the arithmetic mean of the population recorded in the *Censuses* of 1861 and 1871, but that for 1901–10 by assuming an increase by regular geometrical progression between the *Censuses* of 1901 and 1911.)

substantial numerical base. (London contained about 14 per cent of the country's population in the 1860s.)

Contrary to the impression so strongly conveyed by romantic writers and artists at the time, as well as social theorists, the sheer scale of suicide was not uniquely high in Victorian London, apart from one or two small areas (see Maps 4 and 5). There were many towns where suicide was more common than it was in the registration division or (after 1889) the administrative county of London (the counterpart of today's Inner London area)—and a good many counties too, for throughout this period London's rates ranked on average no higher than seventh among county suicide rates for men, and sixth among those for women (see Table 2). In the middle of the nineteenth century what was really distinctive about suicide in the metropolis was its exceptional frequency among young people, especially among young men. Thus although in 1861–70 London's overall standardized mortality ratio for suicide was 139 for men and 135 for women, its suicide rates for young men and women aged between fifteen and twenty-four were respectively as much as 71 and 58 per cent higher than those of the rest of the country.[14] Only the kind of ancient, multi-functional, medium-sized assize or county town which in any case had higher overall suicide rates than London (as will be explained in the next chapter), surpassed it in the frequency of suicide among young people; and the gulf was enormous between London and the industrial towns, with their exceptionally low suicide rates among those under the age of thirty-five (see Table 1.1). Moreover, since the young tended to use the most easily concealed methods of suicide, and in particular to avoid hanging,[15] even these very high suicide figures for young people in London were probably exceptionally incomplete. In mid-Victorian London, although not in England's other biggest towns and cities, the familiar nineteenth-century belief that it was in the great cities of Europe that suicide among the young was most rife, was abundantly true.

By the eve of the First World War, however, a transformation had taken place. When the metropolitan and provincial suicide rates are calculated separately, it emerges that the gap between the two was narrowing throughout the later nineteenth century (partly no doubt due to improved provincial efficiency in the registration of suicide), until by 1911–13 London's overall suicide rates were barely 11 per cent higher than those for the rest of the country—a very small excess for the world's biggest city (see Table 1.4).[16] Where men were concerned, the gap between metropolitan and provincial suicide rates was still widest among the young, although it was far narrower in 1901–10 than it had been in the 1860s, and there had actually been a small drop in the rates recorded for youths between the ages of fifteen and nineteen. Among women, however, the change had been massive. Suicide in London among girls between fifteen and nineteen was by

---

[14] The standardized mortality ratio expresses the number of deaths from suicide actually registered in London as a percentage of the number which would have been expected to be registered if each age-group in London had committed suicide with exactly the same frequency as the same age-group did in England and Wales. For the mean population in the decade 1861–70 and deaths from suicide at different ages in London, 1861–70, see *Registrar-General's 35th AR, Supplement*, p. 4; for annual rates of mortality in England and Wales from suicide per million living at nine different groups of ages, 1861–70, see *Registrar-General's 75th AR, Supplement*, Part III, p. ccxi, Table 10. Provincial suicide rates have throughout been calculated here by subtracting the suicide and population figures for London from those for England and Wales; both sets of figures were published each year in the Registrar-General's Annual Reports.

[15] Ogle, 'Suicide in England and Wales', p. 121, Table XI; *Registrar-General's 75th AR, Supplement*, Part III, p. xcv, Table XLV.

[16] For the crude male and female suicide rates in London and the provinces in 1911–13, see the sources cited in n. 13.

Table 1.4. *Male and female mortality from suicide in London as a percentage of mortality from suicide in the provinces at all ages and at four different groups of ages in the decade 1861–70 and the years 1911–13*

	All ages		15–24		25–44		45–64		Over 64	
	Males	Females	Males	Females	Males	Females	Males	Females	Males	Females
1861–70	145	155	171	158	162	177	136	121	150	115
1911–13	111	111	90	77	109	129	116	105	104	87

Sources: *Registrar-General's 35th AR, Supplement*, pp. 2–5; *74th AR*, pp. 4–5, pp. 313–27; *75th AR*, pp. 329–39; *76th AR*, pp. 304–14.

1901–10 nearly as much below the rate returned for girls in the rest of the country as in 1861–70 it had been above it, and even in absolute terms had dropped by 35 per cent; while among young women aged between twenty and twenty-four suicide rates had become virtually the same in London as in the provinces, although in the 1860s they had been 75 per cent higher (see Table 1.3). Evidently, then, although in the 1860s London had furnished a conspicuous exception to the rule already holding good in the provinces—that, for girls, the bigger the city the better—by the Edwardian period this rule applied to the metropolis as well. Among the elderly, too, the changes which occurred among female suicide rates are the more notable. Compared with the rest of the country, suicide in London increased little among men over sixty-five, and fell very little among women over seventy-five; but since high suicide rates among men over sixty-five and very low suicide rates among women over seventy-five were already being registered in London in the 1860s, the comparatively static incidence of suicide among people of these ages is hardly surprising. Among women between the ages of sixty-five and seventy-four, however, suicide in London actually fell by 10 per cent in these fifty years, although in the rest of the country it increased by nearly 9 per cent, so that among all women over the age of sixty-five, suicide diminished between 1861–70 and 1901–10 even more in London than in the provinces.

Thus suicide was rarer in Edwardian London than in the provinces among girls aged between fifteen and nineteen, as well as among men aged between sixty-five and seventy-four and among women over seventy-five. Among young men it still remained a place where suicide was notably more frequent than in the rest of the country; but this was probably not the result of high suicide rates among native-born young Londoners. London must always have been a place where an exceptionally high proportion of those who committed suicide within its boundaries were strangers; and the Censuses for 1901 and 1911 indicate that the largest influx of male immigrants into the capital was of men between the ages of twenty and twenty-four.[17] When in 1911 for the first time cases of suicide began to be allocated to the deceased's place of residence instead of to the registration district in which the body was found, it was the suicide rates for men aged between fifteen and twenty-four that fell most substantially. In the three years 1911–13 the suicide rate among London's own residents proved to be 10 per cent lower than the provincial one among men aged fifteen to twenty-four; 23 per cent lower among women aged fifteen to twenty-four; and 13 per cent lower among women over sixty-five.[18] (See Table 1.4.) In short, if mid-Victorian London never altogether deserved its long-standing reputation as the city of suicides, Edwardian London, unlike the mid-Victorian capital, was not even a city where suicide was rife among the young; indeed, the opposite was by then the truth.

Altogether it is plain that in the fifty years or so before 1914 some notable shifts had taken place in the relative proneness to suicide of members of different sexes of the same age, and also of members of the same sex at different stages of life. The main outlines of these changes are clear. The relationship between suicidal behaviour and gender had become markedly more pronounced among the elderly, as in old age men became much more prone to suicide but women much less so; and this state of affairs—so characteristic of England throughout the first half of the twentieth century—seems to have appeared first in London and the industrial towns. A second, milder shift in the relation between gender and suicide had occurred at the stage of late adolescence. Here the gap between the sexes had changed not so much its size as its nature. No longer did girls commit suicide more than boys at this age, but vice versa, as was to happen throughout the twentieth century; and it was in London and the biggest provincial towns and cities that this situation was first recorded. Another pair of

[17] It may also be worth noticing that in London in 1890–2 it was among men who committed suicide between the ages of 20 and 24 that the proportion was highest of those who had no occupation. (For the deaths from suicide of occupied males in London, 1890–2, see *Registrar-General's 55th AR, Supplement*, Part II, p. 4. The number of deaths from suicide of unoccupied males in London has been calculated by subtracting the number of deaths from suicide of occupied males from the total numbers of male deaths from suicide in London in 1890–2 given in the annual abstracts of deaths in London, classified according to sex, age, and cause, in *Registrar-General's 53rd–55th ARs*.)

[18] These calculations are based upon the sources cited in n. 13.

changes had occurred in the relative proneness to suicide of different age-groups within the same sex. The difference between the suicide rates of men at different stages of life had become much greater, since among young men suicide had been increasing comparatively slowly, while among old men it had been increasing comparatively quickly. This wide contrast had been slow to appear in London, but was already present in the 1860s in an acute form in the industrial towns. There, suicide among men aged between fifty-five and sixty-four was more than twenty times commoner than among youths aged between fifteen and nineteen, and ten times commoner than among young men aged between twenty and twenty-four—a contrast far greater than in other kinds of towns, and greater even than that which was to characterize the twentieth century. Among women of different ages, however, suicide rates continued to be far more similar than they were among men in different age-groups. True, the divergence between young and middle-aged women increased a little in this period, and particularly in London, where the fall in suicide among girls and its rise among middle-aged women were both very marked; but the suicide rates of young and old women grew closer together than they were ever to be again, especially in bigger towns and cities.

What happened, then, seems clear enough; but what lay behind these changes? Was an industrial environment good for young men, but bad for old? Was a big town environment good for young women, and also for old? Were the problems of old age becoming more taxing for men but less so for women, and those of youth becoming less intractable for both sexes, but especially for girls? In short, do these trends provide some indications of the subjective impact of industrialization and urbanization on people of different sexes and ages at different times? Perhaps they do. The indications they give hardly deserve serious attention, however, unless quite different kinds of evidence show them to be at least inherently plausible.

The sex and age incidence of suicide in industrial towns in the 1860s (see Graph 1.1) certainly seems entirely credible. It is now very clear that in Lancashire textile towns in the period 1841–61 life was exceptionally good for the young, but exceptionally bad for middle-aged and elderly men, although often not for middle-aged and elderly women. Life was better for the young partly because a wide range of jobs was open to them, but chiefly because the earning power of textile operatives reached its peak when they were in their late teens and twenties. Men in their late thirties and forties, however, had to move into lower-paid jobs as their dexterity, strength, and endurance declined, and were soon reduced to hawking, street-sweeping, and rag-gathering; and the cotton famine during the American Civil War can only have increased their vulnerability. Older women, on the other hand, were often valued as child-minders and housekeepers, since many young women worked in the factories. It seems likely, moreover, that wherever there were large-plant industries and non-craft occupations which required dexterity, endurance, or strength there was some penalization of older workers and emancipation of the young similar to that experienced in textile towns; in the iron and steel trades, for example, wages peaked between the ages of twenty-five and forty-five.[19] Thus in job opportunities, earning power, and status, the position of the young in industrial areas of this sort must have been much more favourable than in rural areas and non-industrial towns, where widespread parental ownership of the means of production, a restricted labour market, and the predominance in the urban male labour force of craftsmen, retailers, and professional men usually favoured the middle-aged and elderly.[20]

On the other hand, the finding that there was an association between urbanization and lower suicide rates among young girls runs altogether counter to nineteenth-century notions about the causes of female suicide and the significance of puberty. Then and long afterwards, it was platitudinous that what protected women from suicide was their passive, secluded lives; as Durkheim wrote in 1897, 'woman kills herself less ... because she does not participate in collective life in the same way'.[21] Only among young people in their late teens were virtually identical male and female suicide rates recorded,[22] and this was

---

[19] Anderson, *Family Structure in Nineteenth Century Lancashire*, especially pp. 25–7, 91, 102–3, 124, 143; Roebuck, 'When does Old Age Begin?', p. 420.

[20] In York, for example, a 'vast proportion' of the male labour force were craftsmen or dealers in 1851: Armstrong, *Stability and Change in an English County Town*, pp. 29, 189.

[21] Durkheim, *Suicide*, p. 341; cf. Morselli, *Suicide*, p. 197. It soon became commonplace to warn women that taking part in politics or 'matters best suited to men' would infallibly lead to higher female suicide rates; and to point out that women constituted a higher proportion of total suicides in England and the United States than they did in countries where women were less emancipated: see e.g., Mulhall, 'Insanity, Suicide and Civilization', p. 908.

[22] For example, in England and Wales in 1871–80 the mean annual suicide rate per million living aged between 15 and 19 was 24.74 for males and 24.20 for females: *Registrar-General's 43th AR*, p. xxviii, Table O.

ascribed without hesitation to 'sexual causes especially operative in the female at that time of life'. The assumption was always that if an unmarried girl committed suicide, it was because she had been seduced. Female 'precocity' and 'indulgence of lustful desires' at puberty seemed as certainly the explanation of these higher suicide rates among girls, as 'disturbed organic and psychical functions' were of the other brief rise in female suicide at 'the critical or menopausis epoch'; and since precocity was believed to be particularly stimulated by big city life, it seemed to nineteenth-century minds altogether unsurprising that the statistics of so many European states showed that it was in cities that suicide among young women was most common.[23]

Yet is the striking English trend towards lower suicide rates among adolescent girls in the biggest towns and cities throughout the later nineteenth century really implausible? In a big city, daughters away from home enjoyed far more autonomy, even if they were also more vulnerable.[24] Urban immorality and licentiousness were always exaggerated by reformers; and if a girl was pregnant and deserted, suicide might well be less likely to seem the only solution available in a big city than in the far more rigid, confined, and reputation-conscious environment of a small town.[25] It is true that the remarkably high suicide rates recorded for girls in London in the 1860s and 1870s seem to tell against this; but these high rates were not recorded everywhere, and suicide was very rare among girls living in St George's Hanover Square, for example, which was full of servant girls fresh from the country, and far commoner in a working-class residential area like St Margaret's and St John's, Westminster. In any event, London was surely a special case, with its magnetic pull for girls already in trouble, and its armies of prostitutes and domestic servants—the latter making up a third of its female population between fifteen and nineteen, and reckoned as prime consumers of the novelettes, ballads, and melodramas which presented suicide as the appropriate response for a girl in difficulties. (Not until the end of the century was the hold of

---

[23] Ogle, 'Suicides in England and Wales', pp. 127, 129; Morselli, *Suicide*, pp. 220–4. Precocious sexuality was commonly associated with female waywardness of every kind. It was indeed the case that the sexual lives of girls were 'seen as having greater significance than those of males': Gorham, 'The "Maiden Tribute of Modern Babylon" Re-examined', p. 379.

[24] Tilly and Scott, *Women, Work and Family*, pp. 116, 123.

[25] Even just before the First World War, to move from London to a 'feudal' country town like Hertford was to be overwhelmed by 'how drastic was the change': Swan, *My Life*, pp. 109–10.

these romantic stereotypes weakened with the advent of a new music hall popular culture of knowing larkiness.) Prostitutes, however, who seem in the early Victorian years to have been typically aged between fifteen and twenty-five, if York is any guide,[26] apparently became much less numerous in big towns from the 1860s.[27] There are indications, moreover, that in big cities sexual activity generally tended to become more limited and to begin later; that from the 1880s the new 'social purity' crusade was having an effect on lower-middle class and working-class morals and manners; and that by the turn of the century respectably brought up young town-dwellers were often sexually ignorant, as well as subject to far stricter care and control during their much-lengthened stay in the parental household.[28] Certainly illegitimacy rates in urbanized counties were consistently lower than in rural ones from at least 1870,[29] and sexual immorality was increasingly deplored as a characteristically rural vice. It may even be that the moralizing, romantic nineteenth-century association of suicide among young girls with seduction was as shakily grounded in fact as the most famous poetic expression of it, Thomas Hood's *The Bridge of Sighs*.[30] After all, however censorious the respectable became, Charles Booth found that the lower working class were characterized by 'loose views on sexual relations' even at the very end of the century.[31] Pre-marital sexual

[26] In 1842 74 cent of street-walkers known to the police in York were under the age of 26: Finnegan, *Poverty and Prostitution*, p. 81.

[27] This happened chiefly because of the changes in supply and demand associated with the demographic and economic changes in working-class life in these years and the professionalization of their trade: J. Walkowitz, 'Prostitutes and Working Women in Nineteenth-century Plymouth and Southampton' in Vicinus, ed., *A Widening Sphere*, p. 92; W. A. Armstrong, review of Finnegan, *Poverty and Prostitution*, in *Economic History Review*, 2nd series, xxxiii (1980), pp. 425–6; R. D. Storch, 'Police Control of Street Prostitution in Victorian London' in Bayley, ed., *Police and Society*, p. 67.

[28] Walkowitz, *Prostitution and Victorian Society*, p. 253; Bristow, *Vice and Vigilance*, pp. 127–30; Meacham, *A Life Apart*, pp. 66–7; Thompson, *The Edwardians*, pp. 64–6, 71. The mean age at marriage in the early twentieth century was the highest ever recorded in England.

[29] *Registrar-General's 72nd AR*, p. xxxv, Table xxviii, 'Annual Illegitimate Birth-Rates in each Registration County, 1870–1909'. For a table giving the rank order of counties by bastardy ratio in 1842, 1870–2, and 1900–2, see Laslett, Oosterveen, and Smith, eds., *Bastardy and its Comparative History*, p. 30. Declining national illegitimacy rates in the century after *c.* 1850 were an international phenomenon. An explanation is offered by Shorter, *The Making of the Modern Family*, pp. 80–98, but the whole question remains open to debate: see Laslett, Oosterveen and Smith, eds., ch. 1.

[30] See ch. 6 n. 32.

[31] This was in outer East London: Booth, *Life and Labour of the People in London*, Final Volume, p. 335. The domestic life and sexual behaviour of the poor is seen as unaffected by the new middle-class mores until the later nineteenth century by Stone: *The Family, Sex and Marriage in England*, pp. 679–80.

experience was always widespread and sexuality openly accepted, and it has been noticed by collectors that in well-worn songs girls left betrayed were not condemned and did not always show remorse; while recent work on the records of the Foundling Hospital has unearthed only one or two cases of attempted suicide among the hundreds of unmarried mothers who petitioned for the admission of their infants.[32] It is striking, too, that although the first thought of coroners and juries at an inquest on a girl was always to establish whether she had been pregnant, only once in the inquest papers studied here did this prove to have been so, and that was in rural Sussex.

Altogether, then, what the suicide statistics imply on the changing significance of age and gender in industrializing and urban environments seems not implausible. But what lies behind this altering relationship between suicide, age, and gender? To refer loosely to industrialization or urbanization seems unconvincing, particularly since the suicidal behaviour of young and old changed most substantially in London—a place which the industrial revolution almost passed by, and which had long been a great city. Fortunately, however, if London's statistics raise the most puzzling questions, their exceptional fullness also opens the way to a more exact and realistic understanding of what lay behind these shifts.

One additional factor suggested straight away is changes in health and morbidity. In London, it will be remembered, suicide rates among young people were extraordinarily high in the 1860s but thereafter fell continuously, except among young men aged between twenty and twenty-four. The drop among girls between fifteen and nineteen was exceptionally steep, and this may partly have come about not only because they benefited from the changes in sexual behaviour and attitudes already noticed, but also because they enjoyed a greater improvement in health than boys. Even in the 1860s the death rate among girls of this age had been lower in London than in the country as a whole, and it dropped from 5.04 per thousand living in 1861 to as little as 2.30 by 1904–8, chiefly as a result of improved resistance to tuberculosis.[33] In the later 1890s girls achieved lower death rates than

---

[32] Laslett, Oosterveen, and Smith, eds., *Bastardy and its Comparative History*, p. 54; Howkins, 'The Voice of the People', p. 70; J. R. Gillis, 'Servants, Sexual Relations and the Risks of Illegitimacy in London, 1801–1900' in Newton, Ryan, and Walkowitz, eds., *Sex and Class in Women's History*, p. 128.

[33] The death rate among girls aged between 15 and 19 has been calculated for the year 1861 from the figures in *Registrar-General's 24th AR*, p. 99, and *Census, 1861*, ii. xiv; that for 1904–8 is taken from *Registrar-General's 72nd AR*, p. 20, Table 19.

boys between the ages of fifteen and nineteen for the first time; and
this occurred sooner in London than in rural counties—not surprisingly, for female mortality from tuberculosis was persistently higher
in rural than in urban areas.[34] Since bad diet, confinement indoors,
and depression are all associated with tuberculosis, it seems reasonable
to conclude that the more copious food, outside stimulus, and fun
available by the end of the nineteenth century to working girls in big
towns and cities were improving their health and well-being. Matters
like these all seem potentially relevant to the steep fall in suicide rates
among young girls living in London—a fall which in the 1890s for the
first time made suicide less frequent among them than among girls
living in the provinces.

Why, though, did not only these adolescent girls, but also boys of
the same age and girls in their early twenties resort much less to suicide
by the turn of the century? Here it is surely essential to appreciate that
in Edwardian London young people between the ages of fifteen and
twenty-four or even older found themselves living through a definite
stage of the life cycle, as had certainly not been the case fifty years
earlier, and doing so on favourable terms, both economically and
psychologically. After 1870 the school-leaving age and the average age
at first marriage both rose, so that in London by the early 1900s school
attendance was compulsory until the age of fourteen, while the mean
age at first marriage was twenty-eight for men and twenty-six for
women.[35] During this long interval between school and marriage,
young Londoners of both sexes enjoyed economic advantages which
in the mid-nineteenth century had only been available in the new
industrial towns, and to girls, only in textile towns. Thanks above all
to the rapid growth of tertiary occupations, in London young people
were now in demand for an increasing range of jobs, at much higher
wages than in the provinces. These were jobs for which compulsory
education had given them the necessary basic skills: jobs in shops and
offices which took them outside domestic life altogether (a particularly
novel development for girls), placed them within a framework of

[34] The mortality of males as a percentage of that of females in each decennium from
1841–50 to 1901–10 at 12 groups of ages is given in *Registrar-General's 75th AR,
Supplement*, Part III, p. xxv, Table IX. Rural and urban contrasts in female mortality
rates are discussed in S. Johansson, 'Sex and Death in Victorian England, 1840–1910'
in Vicinus, ed., *A Widening Sphere*, pp. 163–81.
[35] *Registrar-General's 72nd AR*, p. xxi, Table XIV. The mean age at first marriage
was slightly lower in the provinces.

regular hours, impersonal routines, and defined responsibilities, and offered them good wages with a margin left over for pleasures (for they were jobs with poor prospects but high immediate pay).[36] The shoe-black brigades of the 1860s had entirely disappeared long before the 1900s, and only one boys' Home survived out of the nine which existed a generation before; while by 1911 only one in four of the girls aged between fifteen and nineteen who lived in London were domestic servants, and their pay and conditions had greatly improved.[37] (Victorian domestic servants were believed to have high rates of suicide, as well as of illegitimate pregnancy, drunkenness, and theft.) The steadier, higher incomes and increasing respectability of the London working-class family household, the greater care as well as discipline which young Londoners were apt to receive from their elders as well as from their betters (who had 'discovered' the problem of juvenile delinquency in the 1890s), and the wider range of leisure activities available to them—such things all went to create in London a framework for young adult living which was entirely different from the one which existed in the 1860s.[38] It may be too that changes of consciousness, and particularly a much diminished personal familiarity with violence and death, altered the subjective meaning of self-destruction for young people living in big towns and cities during this period. Certainly where it is possible to compare inquest papers for the 1900s with those for the 1860s, the depositions do indeed suggest that the work situations, emotional grievances, and punishments experienced by the young people who committed suicide in London altered greatly during these fifty years. In 1862, for example, when the eighteen year old Ellen Webb threw herself off Blackfriars Bridge after the dairyman who had employed her since she was nine as a living-in milk carrier discovered that she had not been handing over all the money she collected from his customers, this was a typical enough case; but it

[36] PP 1909 [Cd. 4632] XLIV, pp. 14, 16, 48; Booth, *Life and Labour of the People in London*, 2nd series, v. 319–21 and Final Volume, p. 43. Booth also noted that village youths who came to London (usually 'the cream') likewise found no difficulty in getting good jobs: ibid., 1st series, iii. 120. After the age of 21, however, boys in dead-end jobs found acute employment problems, and this may perhaps not be unconnected with the persistently high suicide rate in London among young men in their early 20s.

[37] *Census, 1861*, ii. 18, Table 10; *Census, 1911*, x(part 1). 90, Table 9. Much was made of the 'revolution in the conditions of female domestic service': see e.g. Pedder, *Where Men Decay*, pp. 51 et seq.

[38] In 1900–2, for example, London's illegitimacy rate was among the very lowest in the country, as indeed it always was between 1870 and the Second World War: Laslett, Oosterveen, and Smith, eds., *Bastardy and its Comparative History*, pp. 30, 64.

was a far cry from the equally typical case in 1911 of a sixteen year old office boy living with his street-seller parents and earning 10s. a week in a big firm in the City who poisoned himself because 'I felt upset no one had thought about my birthday.'[39]

What may explain, however, not the reversal but the reinforcement of the mid-nineteenth century pattern among those over the age of sixty-five, as male suicide rates crept a little higher still and female rates fell a little lower, so that the gap between the two grew ever wider? When this widening gap is seen in the new industrial towns, or even nationally, it is certainly tempting to see it as a reflection of the decasualization of male labour, devaluation of experience, and shortened working life so characteristic of an industrial economy, and to conclude that men over the age of fifty-five or sixty-five more and more frequently underwent an abrupt reduction of income and personal status which women escaped, since only in a few areas were women then fully part of the industrial economy. Such an explanation accords well with the fact that suicide among men over sixty-five was generally high in other industrial countries in the twentieth century, and that suicide among men of this age began to decline in England for the first time when the ten years' qualifying period for retirement pensions under the post-war social security legislation ended in the late 1950s.[40] Yet London's figures demonstrate that the new male labour patterns brought by industrial capitalism cannot be the only explanation. In London, where industrial capitalism came late, casual and craft labour were both widespread and persistent;[41] yet high suicide rates for older men were always recorded there. Moreover, as many as two-thirds of the men over sixty-five who committed suicide there between 1890 and 1892 were classified as 'occupied'.[42] This probably does not mean much; but it is notable that nationally, the highest suicide rates among men over sixty-five reported in 1878–83 were not among industrial workers, but in service occupations (which had high

---

[39] Both these examples are taken from the inquest papers of the coroner for the City of London, and both are referred to again below in chs. 4 and 5 respectively.

[40] These points were noted in the *Registrar-General's Statistical Review, 1961*, Part III, p. 248.

[41] Casual labourers and their families are estimated to have amounted to 10 per cent of London's population in a work whose central theme is London's casual labour problem: Stedman Jones, *Outcast London*, p. 56.

[42] This figure has been calculated from the tables cited in n. 17 to this chapter. It should be remembered that men who were temporarily out of work were still classified as 'occupied'.

suicide rates at other ages as well);[43] and that in 1911–13 suicide rates were highest in rural districts, not urban ones.[44]

Once again divergent health trends and divergent psychological and economic circumstances make what happened more intelligible. Suicide is closely associated with ill-health. It should therefore be noted that the gap between male and female mortality rates in old age widened in women's favour throughout this period, and particularly in London, where in 1904–8 the female death rate for the age-group sixty-four to seventy-four was only 76 per cent of the male, as against an average for England and Wales of 83 per cent.[45] It is true that longer life expectancy cannot necessarily be equated with better day-to-day health; but among these old people, this female advantage was the result, not of greater male proneness to fatal accidents or acute infections, but of women's superior toughness.[46] As for psychological and material deprivations, the significance of failing strength was always likely to be greater for men, quite apart from the earlier unemployability associated with many occupations in an industrial economy. Charles Booth concluded in 1894 that women were better off than men in old age, particularly in the towns, but that their position had probably always been better, whatever the environment, since they were better able to manage for themselves, could go charing, nursing, and so on, and were more willingly housed by their relatives.[47] Ties of affection were likely to be much stronger with mothers than with fathers.[48] Moreover, a sizeable proportion of these women over

[43] Ogle, 'Suicides in England and Wales', pp. 124–6, Table XIII.

[44] See the Registrar-General's tables cited in n. 13 to this chapter.

[45] *Registrar-General's 75th AR, Supplement*, Part III, p. xxv, Table IX, and *72nd AR*, p. 20, Table 19.

[46] In younger age-groups, longer female life expectancy was in principle not inconsistent with poorer female nutrition and a heavier incidence of minor ailments among women, as is remarked by Thane, 'Women and the Poor Law in Victorian and Edwardian England', p. 34. Old women in London in the decade 1901–10, however, had a longer life expectancy than old men, most strikingly because of a much higher male death rate from tuberculosis: *Registrar-General's 75th AR, Supplement*, Part III, p. 5, 'Deaths in Registration Counties, 1. London, 1901–10'.

[47] Booth, *The Aged Poor*, pp. 321–2, 331. In 1890–2 only 3.1 per cent of occupied males were over the age of 65 in London, compared with 3 per cent in the Registrar-General's Industrial Districts, 7.8 per cent in Agricultural Districts, and a national average of 4.6 per cent: *Registrar-General's 55th AR, Supplement*, p. clxvi, Table VI. Dock labourers, for example (an important occupational group in London), after the age of 50 found work hard to get unless trade was particularly good: Roebuck, 'When does Old Age Begin?', p. 420.

[48] Crowther, *The Workhouse System*, p. 234.

sixty-five must have been widows,[49] and the economic compensations of widowhood were probably greatest among the poorest families. Nor should the rise of grandmothering be forgotten: in the working-class culture of late nineteenth-century and Edwardian London, so home centred and matriarchal, there were surely many counterparts of the grandmothers who ruled over the manners and morals of Robert Roberts's corner of Salford in the 1900s.[50] Again, until the advent of old age pensions in 1908 the experience of old age was frequently determined by the policy of the local Union and individual adaptability to it. In London the ratio of indoor to outdoor relief was exceptionally high, even after 1894 (when some Boards of Guardians began to come under working-class control and give lavish out-relief); but women were always far more likely than men to be put on the outdoor list. (In London in 1892, 30 per cent of men over sixty-five were in workhouses and 7 per cent getting outdoor relief, but for women the proportions were very different: only 18 per cent were in the workhouse, while 15 per cent were getting outdoor relief.)[51] It is quite probable moreover that for men 'the House' was not only a more immediate threat, but also more unendurable when they came within its walls. Women, after all, were far more used to spending their lives confined within the same small community, and working-class wives had had a lifetime's experience of a 'master' as their intermediary with the outside world.[52] That highly experienced Superintendent Queen's Nurse, Miss Loane, noted that old men who had led an adventurous and wandering life felt 'enraged and desperate when confined to two bare rooms and a treeless yard'; whereas an old woman could be 'so clean and orderly in her ways that the workhouse rules would not press hardly on her'.[53] It is perhaps no accident that the inquest papers studied provide several instances of old men killing themselves rather than go into the workhouse, or when they had become inmates, but none of old women doing so. Altogether, there is much scattered evidence that in late Victorian and Edwardian towns and cities, includ-

---

[49] In 1901–10 among those over the age of 65 women outnumbered men by 3 to 2 in London: *Registrar-General's 75th AR, Supplement*, Part III, p. 5.

[50] Roberts, *The Classic Slum*, p. 43; Stedman Jones, 'Working-Class Culture and Working-Class Politics in London, 1870–1900', pp. 485–7.

[51] Booth, *The Aged Poor*, p. 14; PP 1892 (sess. 1) (265) LXVIII, pp. 14–15; PP 1895 [C. 7684] XIV, p. xvii.

[52] Cf. Davidoff, 'Mastered for Life: Servant and Wife in Victorian and Edwardian England', pp. 406–19.

[53] Loane, *Neighbours and Friends*, pp. 263, 318.

ing London, women were less vulnerable than men to old age.[54]

What, then, is the upshot? To nineteenth-century commentators, London's high suicide rates demonstrated 'the pernicious influence which the customs and habits of large cities exercise on the moral character of the individual'.[55] In reality, however, it is not their overall level but their variations which are significant; and these show not the pernicious moral effect of city life, but the influences which gender and stage of life, as well as physical, psychological, and material environment could all exercise upon individual consciousness, for good and for ill. To compare London's suicide patterns with those in other places during these years is again to see this network of influences at work, although not in identical forms. Essentially, what all these age and sex specific suicide statistics point to is two things, neither of which runs counter to other available evidence: first, the aggravation of the problems of old age where men but not women were concerned; and secondly, the advent in big towns and cities of a comparative paradise for young people, and especially teenage girls. From the point of view of the changing significance of gender at particular stages of the life cycle, the implication is that youth was acquiring a more similar meaning for each sex, but age becoming an increasingly different kind of experience. From the point of view of the changing significance of successive stages of life among those of the same sex, however, it is very striking that in 1911–13 a man over the age of sixty-five was nearly seven times more likely to commit suicide than a man between the ages of fifteen and twenty-four, whereas a woman over sixty-five was only one-and-a-half times more likely to do so than her junior. Women, it seems, were getting very much better than men at being old. It might be hazarded that the seven ages of man had always been more significant for him than the three ages of woman (delimited by the great reproductive milestones) were for her, and that in the later nineteenth century—unlike the later twentieth—this contrast grew even sharper and more ubiquitous. Such deductions carry some conviction, however, only because they do not conflict with what can be discovered from other sources; and it remains an open question whether suicide rates themselves can ever furnish an authoritative independent guide to the inner emotional history of any group.

---

[54] This may be a European phenomenon: Stearns, 'Old Women: Some Historical Observations', pp. 51–6.

[55] Morselli, *Suicide*, p. 203.

Yet if the incidence of suicide makes only an ambiguous contribution to the history of life in society, its place in the history of death in society is beyond dispute. True, suicide statistics are as enigmatic a guide to the feelings, responses, and perceptions surrounding death, as to experiences of stress and maladjustment to life; but they have a clear contribution to make to the understanding of the history of mortality, as indeed has the history of mortality to the understanding of suicide statistics. The context of self-destruction, after all, is created as much by experiences of death as by experiences of life; and any appraisal of the consequences of suicide (as opposed to its causes) must base itself upon the ratio of deaths from suicide to deaths from all causes, not the rates of mortality from suicide recorded among the living. So far, this investigation has placed suicide in the context of general mortality only in so far as it has been argued that age and sex differences in its incidence were partly the result of age and sex differences in morbidity, and that these can to a considerable extent be gauged from age and sex differences in mortality. But what was the changing overall incidence of suicide not among the living, but among the dead?

Between the late 1850s and 1913 the incidence of suicide increased nearly three times more among the dead than it did among the living. By 1911–13 it accounted for over ten in every thousand male deaths, instead of little more than four, as in 1861–70. There had thus been an increase of 142 per cent in the proportion of male deaths for which suicide was responsible, whereas the crude male suicide rate per million living had risen by only 52.5 per cent; and the difference between the two corresponding female rates of growth, which were 138 and 44 per cent respectively, was a little larger. Only among women aged over seventy-five did suicide account for a smaller proportion of deaths on the eve of the First World War than in the 1860s. Suicide was still not a major cause of death; but it had become a relatively more important one, and this had happened less because of the fact that a higher proportion of people were destroying themselves, than because mortality from parasitic and infectious diseases was diminishing, and accidents, negligence, and other forms of violence were proving less lethal.

What was the demographic and economic significance of these changes? Here sex and age specific figures are again the key; for age and gender affected the deaths of Victorians and Edwardians as powerfully as their lives. In this period, one change stands out: as a killer, suicide became most deadly among those in the prime of life, instead of among those aged between forty-five and fifty-four—a time when, in the 1860s, middle age was settling into old age. In the decade 1901–10, suicide was officially listed as one of the principal causes of mortality for men and women aged between twenty-five and thirty-five.[56] At every age between fifteen and forty-four, indeed, the proportion of deaths caused by suicide had more than doubled between 1861–70 and 1901–10; whereas among older people the increase in the proportion of deaths caused by suicide was comparatively slight, despite absolute rates of suicide among them which were nearly always far higher than those among their juniors.[57] The explanation of this contrast is simple: among men and women over forty-four, the general death rate had fallen very little, whereas among those under that age, above all among those under twenty-five, the great mid-nineteenth century causes of death had already become far less fatal.[58] Accordingly, in the case of women aged between twenty and twenty-four, for example, an increase in their suicide rate between 1861–70 and 1901–10 of only 45 per cent meant an increase of as much as 225 per cent in the proportion of deaths among these women for which suicide was responsible.

By 1901–10, not only did suicide account for more than twice the proportion of deaths for which it had been responsible in the 1860s, but its maximum toll was being levied where its demographic and economic significance was greatest: upon younger adults. In that decade, one out of every 36 deaths among men aged between twenty-five and forty-four—the age of maximum responsibilities and output— was from suicide, whereas in the 1860s the proportion had been only one out of every 96 or so. Even among men aged between twenty and twenty-four, who had comparatively low absolute suicide rates, one out of every 46 deaths had come to be officially ascribed to suicide, instead of one out of 143, as in the 1860s; although among men at the end of their working lives (aged sixty-five to seventy-four), among whom absolute suicide rates were much higher, suicide in 1901–10 still

---

[56] *Registrar-General's 75th AR, Supplement*, Part III, p. 1, Table XX.

[57] The ratio of deaths from suicide at different periods of life to deaths from all causes at the same periods of life is given for 1861–70 in *Registrar-General's 35th AR, Supplement*, p. lxxxix, Table 4, and for 1901–10 in *75th AR, Supplement*, Part III, p. clxxv, Table 6.

[58] There are some convenient tables in Logan, 'Mortality in England and Wales from 1848 to 1947', pp. 132–78, and OPCS, Series DH1, no. 3, *Trends in Mortality, 1951–1975*, p. 5, Tables 1.1 and 1.2.

accounted for only one out of every 128 deaths. Figures like these help to explain the renewed concern about the increase of suicide among younger people shown by authorities and social reformers alike in Edwardian England; and they were right to be concerned, for the standardized mean age of officially ascertained suicide was lower in 1901–10 than at any other time in the century after 1861,[59] while the real toll upon the young was even larger. From the point of view of national efficiency in the safeguarding of the country's productive and reproductive resources, suicide had thus acquired an altered significance by the Edwardian decade; and for ordinary people too, the fewer deaths then coming within their own experience were more likely to include a case of suicide, and moreover one which seemed an unmitigated waste of human life.

It would be a mistake to exaggerate either the psychological or the practical impact made by these changes in mortality from suicide, or to consider them in isolation from the impact of other changes in mortality and above all in modes of death. Feelings and ideas about suicide must always be affected by the nature of the total real-life experience of death. When death was common at every age, as it was in the mid-nineteenth century, suicide cannot have appeared in the same light as it did when old age alone had become the great killer. Between 1860 and 1913 the crude general death rate fell by 35 per cent; and by 1901–10 as many as 27 per cent of deaths were occurring over the age of sixty-five, instead of barely 19 per cent as in the 1860s.[60] Yet in this respect, the Edwardian experience of death remained closer to that of the 1860s than to that of today, when some three-quarters of deaths occur over the age of sixty-five. Probably what mattered more than the increased rarity of premature death in general, was the far greater rarity of violent and accidental death in particular. Between the 1880s and 1914 life was growing safer very fast. Not only were war casualties small, but mortality from industrial and road accidents was falling, and safety measures were beginning to be taken for granted, as they certainly had not been in the middle of the nineteenth century. The increase of 49 per cent in standardized male mortality

---

[59] For the standardized mean age of suicide in England and Wales, 1861–1948 see Swinscow, 'Some Suicide Statistics', p. 1420, Table 1.

[60] For the crude general death rate in England and Wales see Mitchell and Deane, *Abstract of British Historical Statistics*, pp. 36–7. For the numbers of deaths at different ages, see for the decade 1861–70 *Registrar-General's 35th AR, Supplement*, pp. 2–3; and for 1901–10, *75th AR, Supplement*, Part III, p. 3.

from suicide which took place between 1861–70 and 1901–10 thus has to be contrasted with a simultaneous decrease in male mortality from other forms of violence of 37 per cent, and from industrial and road accidents of around 50 per cent.[61] In short, if natural death was becoming less familiar, unnatural death was becoming even more so; and suicide accordingly stood out the more not only as an abnormal mode of death and a personal human drama (these it had always been), but also as a rare kind of happening altogether, and a socially significant one. It is a sign of the times that in 1896 *Pearson's Magazine*, that shrewd judge of what its lower middle-class readers wanted, sandwiched a popular version of current suicidology entitled 'Is Suicide a Sign of Civilization?' between Kipling's 'Captains Courageous' and an item on 'A Dog-fancying Duchess'.[62] Even to the ordinary slightly educated man, the social phenomenon of suicide had become mysterious and interesting, as the individual deed had always been.

If demographic facts are indeed among the determinants of popular moral ideas and consciousness,[63] it cannot seem surprising that by the turn of the century suicide so commonly appeared to ordinary town-dwellers in the light of a sad waste, above all when it occurred among younger people and children, whose lives were increasingly likely to be 'spared' in the normal course of events. Journalists saw explicit connections between improvements in health and well-being and suicide trends. The heavier periodicals were fond of blaming the increased safety of daily life for a decline in standards of 'courage and manliness' which allowed some people to resort more readily to suicide, and others to exonerate them for doing so.[64] Medical writers and 'advanced' thinkers were apt to go even further in associating suicide with 'loss of tone'. Thomas Hardy caught very accurately the talk of the time when in his ultra-modern novel evolved between 1887 and 1894, *Jude the Obscure*, he made the local doctor, 'an advanced man', comment on the suicide of Jude's children: 'It is the beginning of the coming universal wish not to live.'[65] Eugenically minded intellectuals abounded at this time, and some at least were prepared to draw the logical conclusion from this particular explanation of suicide: that self-

[61] Greenwood, Martin, and Russell, 'Deaths by Violence, 1837–1937', p. 147, Table 1, and p. 153, Table 5.
[62] Brand, 'Is Suicide a Sign of Civilization?', pp. 666–7.
[63] Ossowska, *Social Determinants of Moral Ideas*, p. 33; Hochstadt, 'Social History and Politics', p. 81.
[64] E.g. *The Spectator*, lxxii, p. 678 (19 May 1894).
[65] Hardy, *Jude the Obscure*, part vi, ch. 2.

destruction was not a waste of the nation's human resources, but a beneficial elimination of the least fit part of the race's breeding stock. 'True' suicide, by which they meant irrational suicide, they believed to be not the result of environment, but a manifestation of a degenerative disease transmitted by inheritance; and to them this seemed demonstrated by the finding that mortality from suicide, like that from other degenerative diseases, had increased in the last generation although the general death rate had fallen. Suicide was thus part of the mechanism which ensured 'the survival of the fittest'. It followed that it could be regarded as all to the good if these 'diseased unfortunates', by destroying themselves, removed the risk that they would perpetuate a diseased strain. Suicide could even be provocatively preached as in some circumstances a social duty.[66]

Was this unconventionally optimistic asssessment of the economic and demographic impact of suicide made by some *fin de siècle* intellectuals nearer to the truth than the popular view of suicide as a sad waste? It would certainly be a mistake to think that suicide cut a swathe through the most valuable sections of the country's human capital. Inevitably some of the most renowned suicides in this as in any other period were those of entrepreneurs, artists, politicians, and professional men in their prime; these, though, were the exceptions. The occupational suicide rates calculated in the General Register Office in the late nineteenth century show six occupations with rates more than double the average for occupied males between the ages of twenty-five and forty-four: soldiers, innkeepers, inn servants, and physicians, druggists, and lawyers, in descending order.[67] The soldiers' lead was a very long one. The high suicide rate in the Army certainly gave cause for concern, and in 1881 the annual Army Act for the first time made attempting to commit suicide a statutory military offence. Yet it was an acute problem only among troops serving in India and above all in

---

[66] Strahan, *Suicide and Insanity*, pp. 187–94; Perry-Coste, *The Ethics of Suicide*, pp. 4, 15–16. For Strahan, see ch. 1 n. 14. Perry-Coste (who had a London B.Sc. degree) argued from the position of a fervent opponent of 'professional Christianity'. The American statistician, Adna Weber, similarly insisted that 'suicide is one of the processes of natural selection': Weber, *The Growth of Cities in the Nineteenth Century*, pp. 402–3; but the most influential proponent of this view was no doubt Morselli, who concluded at the end of his internationally acclaimed work that 'suicide is an effect of the struggle for existence and of human selection': *Suicide*, p. 354.

[67] Ogle, 'Suicides in England and Wales', pp. 124–6, Table XIII. The 'all ages' occupational figures for 1890–2 and 1900–2 show similar rankings: *Registrar-General's 55th AR, Supplement*, Part II, p. clxv, Table V, and *65th AR, Supplement*, Part II, p. cxci, Table V.

cavalry regiments, at least in 1862–71, when it was very fully investigated; and although in that decade 663 non-commissioned officers and men were officially lost from suicide (an annual loss of 0.379 per thousand of the strength), this was proportionately lower than the losses from suicide suffered in many continental armies in this period.[68] As for the other occupations which had high suicide rates among those under the age of forty-five, they were occupations which (apart from the law) were also apt to have a very high general death rate, and a high insanity rate. As the statistical chief of the General Register Office put it in 1886, 'they are liable to suicide just as they are liable to other forms of disease.' In the case of the drink trades, for example, those who committed suicide were often also sufferers from alcoholism and diseases of the liver and urinary system—a statistical picture which the case histories encountered in inquest papers abundantly illustrate.[69] Moreover, since mortality from suicide was twice as high among unoccupied as among occupied men aged between twenty-five and sixty-four, a certain proportion of cases of suicide among men of this age (7.2 per cent in 1890–2), were of no economic significance.[70] Finally, it is notable that the lowest occupational suicide rates of all were always found among miners of every sort, railway workers and engine drivers, navvies and road labourers, fishermen and shipbuilders, and similar workers.[71] Evidently, whether or not suicide removed nature's weaklings as Social Darwinists liked to think, it certainly did not take its heaviest toll from the most productive sectors of the labour force.

No similar information is available about female occupational mortality—not surprisingly, since only 38 per cent of women at the end of the century were recorded as following a definite occupation.[72] It is consequently the demographic significance alone of changing female mortality from suicide in these years which can be appraised. Between the ages of twenty and forty-four, the increase in the ratio of deaths from suicide to deaths from all causes had been greater for women than for men, since at these ages general mortality decreased more

---

[68] Millar, 'Statistics of Deaths by Suicide among H.M.'s British Troops', pp. 187–92. Some continental figures are given in Morselli, *Suicide*, pp. 256–61.

[69] Ogle, 'Suicides in England and Wales', p. 116; cf. *Registrar-General's 65th AR, Supplement*, Part II, p. cix.

[70] *Registrar-General's 55th AR, Supplement*, Part II, p. 3, 'Mortality of Occupied Males (England and Wales), 1890–92'; p. 7, 'Mortality of Unoccupied Males, 1890–92'.

[71] See the tables cited in n. 67.

[72] *Registrar-General's 55th AR, Supplement*, Part II, p. vi.

among women.[73] Moreover, since the average age of suicide was always
lower for women than for men, the percentage of total deaths from
suicide which occurred under the age of forty-five was always higher
for women than for men, and between 1861–70 and 1901–10 had risen
from 51 to 56 per cent. (For men, the increase had been from 41 to 44
per cent.) Nevertheless, it is essential to remember that the scale of
suicide among women of all ages was still low, whether the number
of cases is judged relatively to the number of women living, or relatively
to the number of deaths due to other causes. Even its heaviest toll,
that taken upon women aged between twenty and twenty-four,
amounted in 1901–10 to only one out of every 77 deaths in that
age-group. Admittedly this was a very great increase compared with
1861–70, when suicide accounted for only one in every 250 deaths
among women of this age; but it was still far less than the one in
every 46 deaths for which suicide was responsible among men of the
same age in 1901–10. As for the childbearing population as a whole
(that is, women aged between fifteen and forty-four), suicide was
responsible for only one out of every 87 deaths which occurred among
them—a proportion which can hardly be regarded as of major demographic significance. Already in 1861–70 suicide had ranked no higher
than seventeenth for any female age-group, although it ranked thirteenth in the causes of death among men at every age between thirty-
five and sixty-four;[74] and in 1901–10 it still remained a much less
important cause of death for women than for men.

It would thus be a mistake to exaggerate either the demographic or
the economic consequences of suicide in Victorian or even Edwardian
England on the basis of the official mortality figures. True, these figures
show that by the early twentieth century the English experience of
death was already one in which suicide loomed much larger than it had
done in the middle of the previous century, while substantial increases
in the expectation of life for younger people had already begun to give
suicide its special modern significance as a cause of 'wasted' young
lives. Even so, many other causes of death continued to take a far
heavier toll, even among men and women under the age of forty-five.
The history of general mortality offers some clues to morbidity and
hence (arguably) to the incidence of suicide; and in the long term it

---

[73] See the tables cited in n. 57; and for the mortality of males as a percentage of that
of females in each decennium from 1841–50 to 1901–10, see *Registrar-General's 75th
AR, Supplement*, Part III, p. xxv, Table IX.

[74] *Registrar-General's 35th AR, Supplement*, p. lxxxix, Table 4.

probably affected moral ideas about death and suicide, as well as much else. Mortality from suicide itself, however, whatever its psychological repercussions, was never a major determinant of the quantity of human capital available in either Victorian or Edwardian England; and it is difficult to believe that it greatly affected its quality either, whether by removing the ablest or weeding out the weakliest of its components. In short, the demographic, economic, and psychological importance of the changing sex and age incidence of suicide among the dead, although real, was a limited one.

The causes, contexts, and consequences of suicide, however, are intimately linked not only with age, gender, and mortality but also with environment and place. In the nineteenth century, and even in the early twentieth, England was an immensely varied land; indeed, in Victoria's reign it was probably less homogeneous than ever before or since. How then did the quality of life vary in different parts of the country and in different socio-economic settings? The founding fathers of sociology would have been confident that this large question could be answered by constructing an index of regional suicide rates. Today it is a more limited question which seems both answerable and worth asking: what difference did where people lived in Victorian and Edwardian England make to their chances of dying by suicide? It is this question that will be tackled next.

3

The Geography of Victorian and Edwardian Suicide

Early Victorian progressives deeply believed in geography. Whether they emphasized physical laws or (like Henry Buckle) moral and intellectual ones, all positivists agreed that human actions were ruled by environment, not individual caprice. Before the triumph of criminal biology and then psychology at the end of the century, it was criminal sociology which flourished, and regional and local variations which were scrutinized for the key to deviant behaviour. Equally, before the victory of bacteriology around 1880, it was to environmental factors that medical men turned to explain the occurrence of disease. Thus for the early Victorians both moral and medical geography ranked high, and it was no accident that their time saw a golden age of geographic cartography, when the mapping of diseases and population densities, of criminal and moral offences, of literacy and industries, and much else, not only began, but often reached a very high technical level indeed.[1]

In this crusading heyday of ecological morality and medicine, social theorists and medical men who turned their attention to suicide inevitably tried to find a distinctive geographical pattern in its distribution. In England, however, there was too little serious interest in suicide for such efforts to be either early or profound, and the distribution of bastardy, drunkenness, cholera, and many other moral and legal offences and diseases had been mapped many times before the same treatment was at last given to suicide in 1859.[2] The young epidemiologist responsible for this pioneering work was John Netten Radcliffe. Radcliffe had become a specialist in cholera and other Levan-

---

[1]. Gilbert, 'Pioneer Maps of Health and Disease in England', pp. 172–83; Morris, *The Criminal Area*, pp. 37–64.

[2] When A. Guerry published his *Statistique morale comparée de la France et de l'Angleterre* in 1864, suicide was the only aspect of behaviour whose distribution was mapped in France, but not in England.

tine diseases during the Crimean War, when he had been attached to the headquarters of Omar Pasha, and on his return he was drawn into the circle of sanitarians and epidemiologists around John Simon of the Medical Department of the Privy Council. Within a few years he was to become honorary Secretary of the Epidemiological Society and to emabark on the epidemiological surveys for the Medical Department which culminated in his appointment as Public Health Inspector in 1869; but between 1858 and 1863 he was employed as sub-editor of the *Journal of Psychological Medicine*.[3] This periodical was founded, owned, and edited by Forbes Winslow, a busy successful alienist who had first made his name in 1839 with a paper on suicide to the Westminster Medical society which he quickly turned into a book which for forty-five years remained the only English treatise on the subject.[4] It was thus probably no coincidence that it was while he was Winslow's sub-editor that Radcliffe wrote upon suicide, beginning in October 1859 with a long, unsigned article in the *Journal* entitled 'On the Distribution of Suicides in England and Wales'.[5] This Article was accompanied by a full-page map (see Map 1), and in it Radcliffe used the topographical and statistical procedures and the terminology and concepts then in vogue among his fellow epidemiologists, all of which had recently been made more widely familiar by his friend John Snow's famous map of the cholera outbreak in the Broad Street area of London in 1854.[6] Using the inquest statistics which had just begun to be published by the Home Office, together with some special tables for 1852–6 recently produced by the General Register Office (and its earlier

[3] Radcliffe, whose work has already been mentioned (see ch. 1) was a 'soft-hearted', 'simple, honest' man, according to Sir John Simon's obituary of him: *Transactions of the London Epidemiological Society*, new ser., iv (1884), p. 121. His sub-editorship (which has escaped biographical notice) was recorded by Forbes Winslow when he resigned 'the editorial baton': *Medical Critic and Psychological Journal*, iii (1863), p. i. (This was the title given to the *Journal of Psychological Medicine* in 1861.) It seems likely that Winslow discerned a compatible assistant in Radcliffe not as an epidemiologist, but because in his first published work he had emphasized 'the great progress of physiology and psychology in enabling us to grapple with sensuous phenomena': *Fiends, Ghosts and Sprites*, p. 266.

[4] On Forbes Winslow, see ch. 1. n. 14. A full report of the star-studded discussion which followed Winslow's paper was printed in *The Lancet*, 1839–40, i. 291–3, 330–1, 371–2 (9, 16, 23 Nov.).

5 Radcliffe also published in the same issue a piece on 'The Aesthetics of Suicide', and it is very probable that he was the author of 'The Method and Statistics of Suicide', which had appeared earlier in the year.

[6] On epidemiological methods and concepts at this time, see Pelling, *Cholera, Fever and English Medicine, 1825–65*.

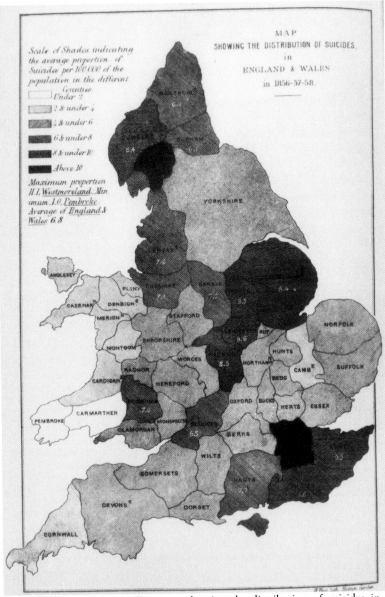

Map 1. J. Netten Radcliffe's map showing the distribution of suicides in England and Wales in 1856–8, published in the *Journal of Psychological Medicine*, xii (1859)

tables for 1838–40), Radcliffe mapped the county distribution of suicide between 1856 and 1858 as accurately as these statistics allowed. His scale of six shades revealed three 'suicidal fields' in England and Wales, that is, areas where suicide was exceptionally prevalent. He then tested the association of these 'suicide fields' with as many factors as possible, with the object of isolating 'the differential element in the aetiology of suicide, that is, that element which determines the act of destruction as an exceptional result of the widespread causes to which it is ordinarily attributed'. His conclusion was that this element was to be sought in 'a peculiar vicious or morbid tone of thought'—a phrase which offers a verbal echo of the finding that cholera propagates iself by 'morbid matter'[7]. In 1862 he 'attracted universal attention' when he read an updated (and subsequently thrice-published) version of his paper to the annual meeting of the National Association for the Promotion of Social Science,[8] a body with many links with the Epidemiological Society. This, however, was apparently the end of his epidemiological work on suicide.[9]

Radcliffe's work of 1859–62 remained unique. Fifteen years later, Morselli's exhaustive study of suicide in terms of international comparative moral statistics included a map of suicide in England which showed that in the years 1872–6 eastern and southern counties had higher suicide rates than northern and western ones; but in his text, Morselli merely remarked in passing that this distribution accorded with the general rule that suicide was lower in extreme climates and mountainous regions and higher in flat and fertile areas with great rivers.[10] Fifty years later still, in 1930, Durkheim's pupil Maurice Halbwachs produced a far more sophisticated version of Morselli's commonplaces, declaring that 'a relief map greatly helps to understand a suicide map', and arguing in the manner of Henri Berr that geographical factors are fundamental because they determine occupation,

[7] Radcliffe, 'On the Distribution of Suicides', p. 482. Radcliffe's mapping was inevitably inaccurate, since mortality from suicide was at this time not included in the annual mortality statistics, and he was therefore obliged to rely on the Judicial Statistics, despite the fact that (as he noted) 'the boundaries of a county do not always represent the actual limits of a coroner's district': ibid., p. 469.

[8] This paper made use of the statistics for 1858–60. It was printed not only in the *Transactions of the National Association for the Promotion of Social Science* for 1862 but also with little change in the *Social Science Review* as well as the *Medical Critic and Psychological Journal* for that year.

[9] The final number of Winslow's periodical, however, published in Oct. 1863, carried the last of Radcliffe's articles on the aesthetics of suicide (on which see ch. 7): 'Baits for Suicide: *Lady Audley's Secret* and *Aurora Floyd*'.

[10] Morselli, *Suicide*, Map 4 (at end) and p. 52.

occupation in turn determines way of living, and way of living determines susceptibility to suicide; yet his only suicide map of England simply plottted the coefficient of dispersion of county suicide rates in the years 1920–6.[11] In England itself there was no revival of the ecological approach to disease and deviance until after the Second World War. Not until 1955 was an ecological study published of suicide (connecting differences in the suicide rates of London boroughs with their social differences), and not until 1963 did maps showing mortality from suicide appear in a *National Atlas of Disease Mortality in the United Kingdom* prepared for a committee set up by the Royal Geograpical Society specifically to revive research in medical geography.[12]

Thus for nearly a century topographical comment on the distribution of suicide in England was rare; and this is hardly surprising, since in the later nineteenth and early twentieth centuries not only did epidemiology go into hibernation,[13] but such English work as there was upon the relationship between environment, and human behaviour and health, became permeated by an assumed dichotomy between industrial and agricultural environments, or later, between urban and rural ones. Occupational mortality, not hygienic topography, interested Farr's successors at the General Register Office;[14] and their strategy was to identify occupations or areas which were distinctively industrial or agricultural, in order to contrast a whole range of industrial and urban mortality rates with a range of agricultural and rural ones.[15] A lively mind might occasionally be struck by 'some extraordinary exceptions' which did not fit the assumption that suicide was

[11] Halbwachs, *Les causes du suicide*, p. 159, Planche V.

[12] Sainsbury, *Suicide in London;* Howe, *National Atlas of Disease Mortality in the United Kingdom*.

[13] Lilienfeld, '"The Greening of Epidemiology"', p. 527. The almost total neglect of vital statistics and environmental factors by Medical Officers of Health and other social workers after about 1880 was lamented by Sir Arthur Newsholme (1857–1943: *DNB*): *Fifty Years in Public Health*, pp. 113, 275.

[14] Old-stagers who still hoped to produce 'Sanitary Maps' deplored with feeling the changes which Farr's successors made in the presentation of the country's vital statistics: for example Haviland, *The Geographical Distribution of Disease in Great Britain*, pp. 290–1, 341–2.

[15] This was the strategy which Farr's successor, William Ogle, and even more Ogle's successor, John Tatham, pursued in the three Decennial Supplements for which they were responsible, namely, those for 1871–80, 1881–90, and 1891–1900. Not until 1919 did the General Register Office (whose Chief Statistician was by then T. H. C. Stevenson) publish, with some comments, a table of county suicide rates, and this was still designed to assist comparison between urban and rural rates: *Registrar-General's 75th AR, Supplement*, Part III, pp. xcvi–xcvii, Table XLVI.

higher in industrial and urban areas than in agricultural and rural ones,[16] but it was within the terms of this assumption that the spatial distribution of suicide continued to be analysed. The geography of Victorian and Edwardian suicide thus remains *terra incognita*, except for the few years studied by Radcliffe and Morselli and the county rates plotted on the two maps they published.

But was there any true geography of suicide in Victorian and Edwardian England and Wales? Were there, that is to say, any persistent and substantial variations in the incidence of suicide in different parts of the country? And if so, were these variations associated with particular regional or local cultures and thus strictly topographical; or were they associated with particular socio-economic habitats wherever they might be situated, and thus ecological? Such questions, unfortunately, must always be tackled in terms of administrative areas—unlikely though it is that regional or local differences in disease or behaviour will ever be co-extensive with official boundaries. So far as suicide is concerned, it is only for the registration counties in the years between 1858 and 1910 that it is possible to calculate a long unbroken series of sex specific local official suicide rates which cover the whole country and are capable of being standardized to allow for variations in the age structure of the population. Were there, then, any registration counties for which markedly high or markedly low suicide rates either for men or for women were persistently recorded between 1858 and 1910? This must be the initial question.

At first glance, the most striking characteristic of Victorian and Edwardian county suicide rates (see Table 2) is their homogeneity.[17]

---

[16] For example, Skelton, 'Statistics of Suicide', pp. 475–6.

[17] This is equally true of the crude county suicide rates for 1858–60 and 1911–13, which have been omitted from Table 2 for reasons of space. The method of calculating these rates was as follows. Except for the decades 1861–70 and 1901–10, the number of deaths by suicide registered in each registration county was found from the 'Abstract of Deaths in the Registration Counties of England and Wales' published annually in the *Registrar-General's AR*. For 1861–70, the number of deaths registered in each registration county was calculated from the Returns for the Registration Districts of England and Wales published in the *Registrar-General's 35th AR, Supplement*, pp. 1–445; while for 1901–10 the suicide rates for each county were taken from the *Registrar-General's 75th AR, Supplement*, Part III, p. xcvi, Table XLVI, with the exception of those for North and South Wales, which were separately calculated from the *Registrar-General's 64th–73rd ARs*. The mean population for each decade was taken as the figure given by the General Register Office. (It should be noted that for the first two of these five decades the General Register Office calculated the mean population by taking the arithmetic mean of the population rcorded in the two relevant Censuses, but that for later decades it assumed an increase by regular geometrical progression between the two Censuses.)

Table 2. *Average annual suicide rates per million living in the registration counties of England and Wales in five successive decennia, 1861–1910*

	MALES					FEMALES				
	1861–70	1871–80	1881–90	1891–1900	1901–10	1861–70	1871–80	1881–90	1891–1900	1901–10
London (metropolitan Middlesex Surrey, Kent)	135	130	144	161	186	47	44	45	51	55
Surrey	139	129	147	177	179	41	32	39	44	50
Kent	140	135	162	182	191	38	32	38	42	49
Sussex	139	159	156	158	175	22	46	45	40	45
Hants	99	111	118	145	160	27	29	30	33	46
Berks	101	100	128	136	179	36	44	37	43	49
Middlesex	127	134	119	122	142	46	42	37	31	46
Hertfordshire	97	68	116	111	123	26	32	37	30	32
Buckinghamshire	66	108	118	121	151	21	30	21	31	36
Oxfordshire	92	113	93	124	140	23	22	37	51	40
Northants	109	112	140	162	188	37	32	53	53	68
Hunts	94	84	91	126	185	44	28	34	61	50
Bedfordshire	64	96	101	108	166	19	17	24	34	34
Cambridgeshire	81	92	109	128	185	26	28	34	41	47
Essex	82	94	109	118	144	24	29	33	38	40
Suffolk	93	121	146	189	205	39	39	44	42	54
Norfolk	99	115	126	155	170	28	26	32	46	59
Wiltshire	86	73	80	102	114	25	29	22	22	37
Dorset	71	73	81	130	143	36	28	25	34	38
Devon	104	113	120	158	182	33	29	33	34	39
Cornwall	49	57	72	99	121	23	24	25	29	28
Somerset	97	102	104	136	159	34	32	29	45	56

Gloucestershire	82	95	101	135	149	25	32	32	42	48
Herefordshire	100	94	88	141	123	34	38	49	41	45
Shropshire	83	83	107	127	159	30	35	29	46	45
Staffordshire	68	74	96	119	149	22	32	35	42	48
Worcestershire	74	92	109	136	153	16	31	35	37	53
Warwickshire	117	144	144	151	170	39	46	51	54	48
Leicestershire	115	122	142	170	176	47	40	43	52	47
Rutland	180	207	213	187	124	43	86	71	28	58
Lincolnshire	106	120	114	139	154	56	35	39	46	46
Nottinghamshire	116	124	138	161	176	41	39	38	50	60
Derbyshire	106	127	99	128	157	41	30	36	43	43
Cheshire	85	114	106	121	148	27	32	36	43	52
Lancashire	105	105	120	138	154	31	34	40	47	53
W. Riding	93	107	126	129	165	34	35	41	49	54
E. Riding	83	111	105	132	175	43	37	38	44	57
N. Riding	68	127	85	98	126	39	35	26	39	50
Durham	64	71	73	105	130	26	28	25	34	33
Northumberland	77	102	108	128	145	32	31	46	57	44
Cumberland	131	141	146	133	136	46	41	42	38	35
Westmorland	119	142	181	184	191	29	28	51	33	71
Monmouth	46	58	63	86	100	16	30	15	42	41
South Wales	47	56	61	77	88	25	29	27	26	36
North Wales	41	51	60	91	103	9	24	22	25	31
England & Wales	99	107	118	137	158	34	35	37	44	49

Sources: See ch. 3 n. 17.

The differences between them prove to have been far smaller throughout this period than the differences between the county rates for other criminal offences (such as drunkenness), or other individual choices (such as modes of marriage), or for pauperism, or even most diseases.[18] Welsh county suicide rates had their own uniquely low range of values; but no English county suicide rate was more than 54 per cent above or below the national average in the 1860s, and by the 1900s, when registration processes were operating more uniformly throughout the country, the range of variation was down to 33 per cent either way. Thus in the 1860s the highest male county suicide rate in England (that for Sussex) was only about three times greater than the lowest; and by the 1900s it was less than twice as great.[19] Female county suicide rates, moreover, had a still narrower range, and one which altered very little throughout this half-century—although for many individual counties, female rates were based upon such small numbers that they were inevitably erratic from one decade to another.

The frequency of suicide was thus noticeably similar throughout the country, always excepting Wales. Why then did this go unremarked, at least until the appearance in Paris in 1930 of M. Halbwachs's comparative study?[20] No doubt this chiefly happened because the publication and study of suicide statistics began so tardily in England, and because in the later nineteenth century hygienic topography was dismissed as old-fashioned and superficial, and the demonstration of urban/rural contrasts was assumed to be what mattered. Another more technical reason, however, may have been the failure of the General Register Office to standardize areal suicide rates until 1919. It was well realized that any suicide rate which took no account of the age structure of the population concerned could be seriously misleading. Any figures which did not show the expected contrast between urban and rural

---

[18] The wide range of county rates in 1902 for pauperism, tuberculosis, criminal offences, and so on is shown by the demographic maps at the end of Bartholomew, *The Survey Gazetteer of the British Isles*, Plates 35–8. For a histogram showing the wide range of county civil marriage rates at this time, see Anderson, 'The Incidence of Civil Marriage in Victorian England and Wales', p. 53.

[19] In 1959–63 the deviations from the national average of the standardized mortality ratios for suicide for the counties and county boroughs of England and Wales were far greater, and ranged from 160 and over, to less than 55: Howe, *National Atlas of Diseases Mortality*, pp. 100–5. To some extent, however, this must have been the result of separate calculation of the standardized mortality ratios for counties and county boroughs, and hence the tabulation of figures for administrative counties which relate only to the urban and rural districts within each county.

[20] See Halbwachs, *Les causes du suicide*, chs. 6–7 and especially pp. 157–9 and p. 184, Table XXIII. Halbwachs's work, however, attracted little attention in England.

suicide rates, therefore, were confidently dismissed as simply the result of local variations in age structure. In reality, standardization has proved to entail only quite small corrections wherever it has been undertaken for this study;[21] and in 1919, when the General Register Office itself came to standardize a wide range of urban and rural death rates for the years 1911–14, its figures showed that the difference between urban and rural mortality from suicide was actually smaller than that between urban and rural mortality from any of the other eleven causes of death compared in this way.[22] The range of variations in English county suicide rates was genuinely remarkably narrow; and as between counties, at any rate, there seem no contrasts dramatic enough to point clearly and irresistibly to an environmental aetiology or to a persistent local suicide culture.

Within this limited range of variations, however, there were indeed a handful of male county suicide rates which were consistently substantially above or below the national average; and these undeniably act as signposts to the whereabouts of the country's 'black' and 'white' suicide areas, in the limited sense in which such strong terms can be applied to Victorian and Edwardian England. Strikingly enough, the 'suicide fields' around London and in the midlands and the north which had been identified by Radcliffe in 1859 are still recognizable fifty years later. In each of the five decades between 1861 and 1910,

[21] For 1901–10 standardization involves corrections for over a third of county suicide rates, but of no more than between 5 and 10 per cent. When the General Register Office standardized mortality from suicide for the years 1911–14, it found with surprise that the effect was not very great: *Registrar-General's 80th AR*, p. xc. (Standardized mortality ratios, that is, the ratio of the number of suicide verdicts actually registered to the number which would be expected if each age-group in the area in question had committed suicide with exactly the same frequency as did that age-group in England and Wales as a whole during the period in question, have been found by calculating the arithmetic mean number in each age-group above the age of 10 in each registration county from the Censuses taken at the beginning and just after the end of each decade, and then calculating the expected number of cases for each of those age-groups in that county from the age specific national suicide rates given for each decade between 1861 and 1910 in the *Registrar-General's 75th AR, Supplement*, Part III, p. cciii. For the decade 1901–10 this operation has been performed for each registration county, with the exception of Rutland and Huntingdon, whose populations were too small for this to be worth while, with the results shown in Map 2; otherwise, standardization has been carried out only in selected cases. All the deviations of the crude rates from the national mean discussed in the immediately following passages, however, are too large for it to be at all likely that standardization would remove them.)

[22] Where suicide was concerned, the urban excess was less than 9 per cent. At the opposite extreme, urban mortality from measles was 146 per cent higher than that in rural counties: *Registrar-General's 75th AR, Supplement*, Part III, p. xcvi, Table XLVI, and pp. ccxii–ccxvii, Table 11.

London and the contiguous counties of Kent, Surrey, and Sussex were in the top quartile of male county suicide rates, and so was Westmorland; and for four of these decades Nottinghamshire, Leicestershire, and Northamptonshire in the east midlands were in the same position. Among female county suicide rates, only London was always in the top quartile; but Nottinghamshire always had a rate above the national average—a consistency achieved by no other county. Where were the 'white' areas, however? Clearly in the far west and north-east. North and South Wales, Monmouthshire, Cornwall, Durham, and the North Riding of Yorkshire were all in the bottom quartile of male county suicide rates in all five decades; and North and South Wales and Cornwall were also there for female county suicide rates, as too was County Durham for forty out of these fifty years. Two other south-western counties, Wiltshire and Dorset, likewise kept a place in the bottom quartile of male county suicide rates for forty years, and Wiltshire did so for female rates also (see Table 2).

The geography of suicide in Victorian and Edwardian England and Wales is thus clear enough in county terms. If Westmorland's figures are disregaded as too small to have real weight, two 'black' and two 'white' areas stand out: the black in the south-east and the east midlands, the white in the far west and north-east. This distribution is an unexpected one, and has iconoclastic implications. To begin with, it is surprising that London, 'the City of Dreadful Night', proves to have been simply one of a group of counties with consistently high suicide rates, and to have ranked (as was remarked in the previous chapter) on average no higher than seventh among them for male suicide, and sixth for female. Neither here nor in the rest of this picture is there much support for the long-established association of the highest suicide rates with urban, industrial areas and the lowest with rural, agricultural ones. Evidently in Victorian and Edwardian England rural counties could have consistently high suicide rates, and non-rural counties consistently low ones. Sussex and Durham provide perhaps the most striking demonstrations of this. Sussex was to a large extent a rural county; yet of all the counties where suicide was regularly very high, Sussex was the one where it was so most consistently. Durham, on the other hand, had a negligible agricultural population; yet its suicide rates were only about half those of Sussex. Equally notable, moreover, is the persistent absence from the top quartile of the three most completely industrialized counties of all: Lancashire, the West Riding, and Staffordshire. In every decade, in short, urban and industrial counties, rural and agricultural counties, and altogether hybrid ones, all appeared in very similar proportions in each quartile of county suicide rates.

Where does a county map of the dynamics of suicide growth show that suicide increased most steeply, however? National suicide rates were rising throughout this period, and especially from the 1890s; and to contemporaries there was nothing puzzling about this. They deplored it; but they were keenly conscious that they were becoming a nation of dwellers in great cities, and suicide was closely associated with great cities by a network of familiar literary and visual images as well as by traditional moral, medical, and sociological discourse. Yet what the county suicide rates reveal is that it was as often in rural as in urban areas that male suicide was increasing most rapidly in these years. For women the situation was different: in several rural counties, notably Lincolnshire, female suicide actually declined. So far as male suicide was concerned, however, of the seven counties where crude suicide rates increased between 1860 and 1910 by more than twice the national average amount—Bedfordshire, North Wales, Cornwall, Buckinghamshire, Cambridgeshire, and Staffordshire—only one, Staffordshire, was not a rural county.[23] Moreover, this increase was certainly not simply the result of an ageing male population in the countryside. In North Wales, for example, even the standardized male mortality ratio for suicide rose from 39 to 59 between 1861–70 and 1901–10; while in Cornwall it rose from 52 to 72. Equally, by 1901–10 a third of the eighteen counties which had a standardized mortality ratio for suicide of over 100 were very rural ones (Suffolk, Westmorland, Somerset, Cambridgeshire, Berkshire, Bedfordshire: see Map 2);[24] although in many other rural counties suicide remained genuinely very low. What happened in Suffolk is especially notable, for from the 1880s its male suicide rate rose so steeply that by 1901–10 it was surpassed only by that for Sussex, and had reached an annual average of 205 per million living—a level 22 per cent higher than would have been expected given the age structure of Suffolk's population.

The county geography of both the statics and dynamics of suicide thus accords ill with established theories and expectations; and its

[23] A rural county is defined here as one in which over 34 per cent of the population was still rural in 1911 according to the calculations of Bowley, 'Rural Population in England and Wales', pp. 605–6, Table III.

[24] In all these counties rural inhabitants accounted for over 38 per cent of the population in 1911.

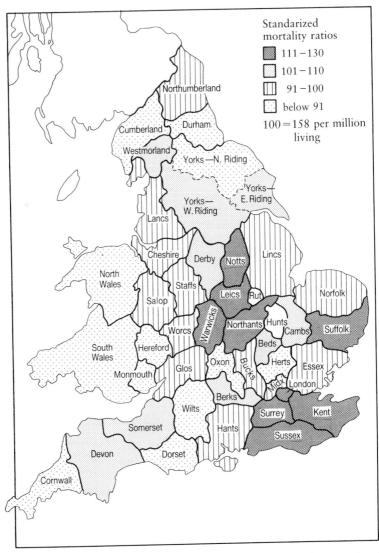

Map 2. Registered male mortality from suicide in the registration counties of England and Wales (excluding Rutland and Huntingdon), 1901–10: standardized mortality ratios

Sources: see note 21.

surprising features cannot be explained away by bureaucratic variations any more than by local demographic abnormalities. When the exceptionally elderly populations of most rural counties and the exceptionally youthful ones of some industrial counties are taken into account, the trends and relationships apparent in the crude suicide rates may indeed be modified, but they do not disappear; and although patchily increased rural efficiency in the registration of suicide no doubt counted for something, it cannot be a sufficient explanation of rising male suicide rates in certain rural counties, since in the same counties female suicide rates remained comparatively stable or even declined.[25]

Plainly close investigation is needed; but can it be achieved? Registration counties have serious limitations as units of study, for they often contained places of very dissimilar types. A few of them were indeed entirely non-rural and non-agricultural throughout this period; but even the most rural county included some sort of town and had many inhabitants not occupied in farming, market gardening, fishing, or forestry. It follows that although the absence of high suicide rates for Lancashire, Durham, Glamorgan, and Middlesex may well be enough to establish that high suicide rates did not necessarily accompany intense industrialization and urbanization, their presence for Sussex and Suffolk is certainly not sufficient to demonstrate that high suicide rates could exist in rural and agricultural areas, since Sussex and Suffolk each contained a very large town, namely Brighton and Ipswich. Clearly the geography of suicide in Victorian and Edwardian England can only become more intelligible if it is possible to press into use a series of suicide statistics relating to areas more socially and economically meaningful than the registration counties.

Fortunately this can be done for one decade, although only for one. It will be remembered that for the decade 1861–70 the General Register Office published separate mortality figures for each registration district in the country. These have already been used to throw light on the age and sex incidence of suicide; and it is also possible to use them to arrive at a truly urban and a truly rural suicide rate, by grouping together on the one hand the figures for the twenty-eight most com-

[25] With trends like these in the registration county figures, it is not surprising that the elaborate figures by administrative area provided after 1910 show that except in the northern region, it was in rural districts and not urban areas that the highest male suicide rates were returned in 1911–13, and that only in the southern region was this accounted for by a high suicide rate among men over the age of 45: *Registrar-General's 74th–76th ARs,* tables cited in ch. 2 n. 13.

pletely rural districts in England, and on the other, those for the eighteen districts contained within those provincial towns which had a population of over 100,000.[26] When this is done, the resulting purely urban suicide rate proves to have been only a little over a fifth higher than the purely rural one where men were concerned (101 per million living, as against 82.3); although the difference was wider in the case of women (33 per million living, as against 22.4).[27] It will be remembered that figures for less heterogeneous units than the counties were not again provided until after 1910. These new figures show, however, that in 1911–14 the differences were notably small between the overall suicide rates in the three major types of administrative areas which then existed (county boroughs, urban districts, and rural districts), and that the standardized male suicide rate in county boroughs was only 7.8 per cent higher than that in rural districts.[28] It seems fair to say, then, that there does seem to have been some tendency for male suicide rates to be higher in entirely urban areas than in rural ones, but that even in the middle of the nineteenth century the difference was not great, and by the early twentieth century it was small indeed.

The belief that high suicide rates are characteristic of a modern industrial and urban way of life has played too central a role in theories of both suicide and society to be quickly dismissed as inapplicable to Victorian and Edwardian England and Wales. Clearly the question of the relationship between suicide and particular environments needs to be attacked more closely, and above all in much less general terms. After all, few specialists today would be inclined to think that any simple contrasts could be established between urban and rural or industrial and agricultural areas in Victorian England; and this is so, because these now seem not only overlapping rather than mutually exclusive categories, but also very variegated ones. The differences between industrial complexes, resorts, and administrative, professional, or business and commercial centres now seem fun-

---

[26] These 28 rural districts are those identified as the most purely rural by Bowley, and listed in his 'Rural Populations in England and Wales', p. 620, Table IX. The 18 urban districts are the districts situated within those provincial towns which had a population larger than 100,000 in 1861–70, as listed in the first column of Table 3.1 in this chapter.

[27] The figures for the rural districts concerned will be found in *Registrar-General's 35th AR, Supplement*, pp. 1–445; those for the urban districts concerned are given in Table 3.1 in this chapter.

[28] The official standardized male suicide rates for county boroughs, other urban districts, and rural districts in 1911–14 were respectively 151, 144, and 140 per million males living: *Registrar-General's 80th AR*, p. xc, Table LXIX.

damental, as do those between (for example) animal-rearing and arable areas, or between closed and open villages; while cultural cohesion no longer seems something to be automatically associated with rural rather than urban communities. On the face of it, then, it now seems unlikely that suicide in Victorian and Edwardian England would have been especially a concomitant of every kind of town life and no kind of country life. Is it feasible, however, to test these suspicions? Fortunately, the uniquely detailed figures available for 1861–70 can once more be pressed into service.[29] By grouping together the 623 registration districts in different ways, it is possible to isolate the suicide rates of many different kinds of communities, while still keeping a reasonably large numerical base for each of them and taking into account their different age structures. In the present instance priority has been given to the analysis of suicide rates in urban settings—partly because it is less practicable to isolate homogeneous yet numerous rural populations, but chiefly because of the leading role in both expert and popular thinking which has always been played by ideas about urban suicide.

The starting-point of this analysis is therefore a taxonomy of urban suicide rates. London's suicide statistics, as has already been said, are unique, like London itself, and best treated separately. Seventy-six provincial urban districts have therefore been used. They have been grouped with a matrix of fifteen cells according to population size and type (see Table 3.1). Between them these districts contained in this decade some 31 per cent of the country's population, and accounted for 3,254 male and 1,151 female registered cases of suicide; and in this matrix, they provide thirteen pairs of male and female suicide rates (see Table 3.2).

What emerges from this taxonomy of urban suicide? First, some confirmation that a town's size usually mattered less than the kind of town it was: suicide was slightly more frequent in towns of 50–100,000 inhabitants than in those with a population of more than 100,000, but very much more frequent indeed in ancient multi-functional or entirely non-industrial towns with a population of 20–49,000. Secondly, reinforcement for the conclusion, already suggested by the county

---

[29] A more detailed and in some ways more wide-ranging exploration of the ground covered in this section will be found in Anderson, 'Did Suicide Increase with Industrialization in Victorian England?', in which Table 3.1 first appeared. I am now less convinced, however, that the detection and registration of suicide was likely to have been less efficient in non-industrial than in industrial towns, as was suggested there (p. 164).

figures, that really high suicide rates rarely accompanied industrialization, but that very low ones often did. Apart from the central districts of Manchester, Liverpool, and Birmingham, it was only in

Table 3.1   Registered cases of suicide in the decade 1861–70 in seventy-six urban registration districts of England and Wales, classified by size and economic type

	Size I	Size II	Size III
Type A	Bradford	Blackburn	Ashton-under-Lyne
	Chorlton	Bolton	Burnley
	Hunslet	Halifax	Bury
	Leeds	Huddersfield	Dewsbury
	Manchester	Oldham	Macclesfield
	Salford	Preston	Rochdale
		Stockport	Wakefield
			Wigan
	492,035 M.P.	422,909 M.P.	366,608 M.P.
	485 M.S.	493 M.S.	371 M.S.
	537,090 F.P.	458,366 F.P.	388,915 F.P.
	151 F.S.	161 F.S.	138 F.S.
Type B	Aston	Merthyr Tydfil	Darlington
	Birmingham	Stoke-on-Trent	Dudley
	Newcastle	Sunderland	Gateshead
	Sheffield	Wolverhampton	Guisborough
			(Middlesbrough)
			Prescot (St Helens)
			South Shields
			Tynemouth
			Walsall
			Warrington
			West Bromwich
			Wolstanton (Burslem)
	303,473 M.P.	208,320 M.P.	391,593 M.P.
	314 M.S.	119 M.S.	224 M.S.
	308,719 F.P.	203,729 F.P.	379,693 F.P.
	112 F.S.	50 F.S.	92 F.S.
Type C	Bristol	Southampton	Birkenhead
	East Stonehouse		Cardiff
	Hull		Gravesend
	Liverpool		Medway (Rochester
	Plymouth		and Gillingham)
	Portsmouth		Newport
	Stoke Damerel		Swansea
	West Derby		
	435,891 M.P.	21,435 M.P.	166,002 M.P.
	459 M.S.	26 M.S.	131 M.S.
	463,853 F.P.	24,300 F.P.	163,074 F.P.
	169 F.S.	8 F.S.	44 F.S.

Table 3.1 (continued)

	Size I	Size II	Size III
Type D		Leicester Norwich Nottingham	Carlisle Coventry Derby Northampton Worcester
		110,318 M.P. 164 M.S. 130,230 F.P. 61 F.S.	105,943 M.P. 140 M.S. 114,997 F.P. 45 F.S.
Type E		Bath Brighton	Cambridge Canterbury Chester Colchester Croydon Exeter Ipswich Oxford Reading Yarmouth York
		64,950 M.P. 96 M.S. 87,866 F.P. 38 F.S.	201,983 M.P. 232 M.S. 220,298 F.P. 82 F.S.

Note: Size I, over 100,000, Size II, 50–100,000, Size III, 20–49,000 inhabitants. M.P./F.P. denotes mean male/female population; M.S./F.S. denotes male/female suicides.

Source: Registrar-General's 35th AR, Supplement, pp. 1–445.

ancient multi-functional or entirely non-industrial towns and cities that suicide rates approached or surpassed those of London. In the seaports and textile towns they were decidedly lower; in the new towns of the second stage of industrialization they were usually very low indeed; and strikingly low suicide rates were always returned for mining areas. Only slightly less notable, however, are the low rates returned in booming seaports and in smaller industrial towns based on the extraction or manufacture of minerals and chemicals, as against those returned not only in the largest cities of these two types, but also in towns of different type but the same size. (See Table 3.2). Lastly, dissimilarities emerge in the sex and age incidence of suicide in different kinds of towns (as will be remembered from the previous chapter), with suicide rates in industrial towns proving to have been abnormally low among young men and abnormally high among men over the age

Table 3.2. A taxonomy of urban suicide in provincial England and Wales, in the decade 1861–70: average annual mortality from suicide registered per million living

	Size I Males/Females		Size II Males/Females		Size III Males/Females	
Type A Towns (textile manufacturing)	98.5	28.1	116.5	35.1	101.2	35.5
Type B Towns (iron and coal, cutlery, engineering, china, glass)	103.4	36.3	57.1	24.5	57.2	24.2
Type C Towns (seaports)	105.3	36.4	121.2	32.9	78.9	27.0
Type D Towns (ancient towns and cities with some new industry)			148.6	46.8	132.1	39.1
Type E Towns (non-industrial county or assize towns, resorts, residential centres)			147.8	43.3	114.9	37.2

Note: England and Wales, males 98.8, females 33.7; Division of London, males 134.8, females 47.9.

Source: Table 3.1.

of fifty-five, and the lowest suicide rates for girls being returned in the largest size of town, whatever its economic type (see Tables 1.1 and 1.2).

In 1861–70 male suicide rates were substantially lower in medium-sized and small new industrial towns and small seaports than they were in completely rural registration districts (where, it will be remembered, the male suicide rate was 82.3 per million living). On the other hand, the female suicide rate was never quite so low in any of these sorts of town as it was in the most purely rural districts (where it fell to 22.4 per million living). In ancient multi-functional or entirely non-industrial towns, however, both male and female suicide rates could be almost twice as high as rural ones. Clearly, then, the narrow excess of aggregate urban suicide rates over rural ones conceals a situation in which certain types of towns in reality had far lower suicide rates than even the most rural areas, whereas other entirely different kinds of towns had far higher ones. In themselves these wide urban variations are hardly surprising; but it accords ill with traditional suicidology that suicide should have been rife not in the industrial centres created by either the first or the second wave of the industrial revolution, but in ancient multi-functional and residential towns. For men over the age of fifty-five industrial towns and cities did indeed often deserve their reputation as black areas where suicide was concerned; but only for them.

The micro-geography of urban suicide thus proves to have been very diverse indeed in the one decade before 1911 for which it can be reconstructed; and urban size alone does little to make its variations comprehensible. There seem to be three possible keys, however, to what lies behind this complex picture: stage of urban development; local attitudes towards self-destruction; and local occupational structure. Of the first, the seventy-six districts just analysed provide many examples, for in towns which were then growing at their fastest and whose economic structure was at its most open (as in Middlesbrough, for example), the suicide rate was even lower than would have been expected in view of the very high proportion of young male immigrants such towns always attracted, and in view of the under-registration perhaps particularly likely in such a place. By definition, however, stage of development cannot explain a particular level of suicide for any length of time. It can do nothing, for example, to explain such permanent phenomena as the extremely low levels of suicide always common in Glamorgan, North Wales, and Cornwall. Here, the second key seems the appropriate one; for so dissimilar were the economies of these areas by the beginning of the twentieth century as to suggest that what was at work may have been shared psychological deterrents, stemming perhaps from a common chapel culture or other collective traditions. Possibilities like those, however, although they may be suggested by statistical evidence, cannot be given substance by it. At this point, therefore, what will be investigated is the third possibility, namely, relationships between suicide and occupational structure.

Occupational mortality was a leading concern of Farr's two immediate successors at the General Register Office, William Ogle and John Tatham. In their day hygienic topography ceased to preoccupy the public health world, and Farr's elaborate district mortality tables were first compressed into half the space by no longer being published separately for males and females,[30] and then jettisoned altogether.

---

[30] This was justified as 'not merely to economise space, but to give a broader and therefore more secure basis for the calculation of rates, and also in order to meet the practical requirements of the Medical Department of the Local Government Board': *Registrar-General's 45th AR, Supplement*, p. iii.

Instead, Ogle began to move towards investigating occupational mortality, and Tatham completed the change in the two decennial supplements published under his aegis, in 1897 and 1907, which provided elaborate occupational mortality statistics for 1890–2 and 1900–2.[31] Soon after he came to the General Register Office, however, Ogle had personally used the mortality returns for 1878–83 to investigate the links between occupation and suicide, and he announced his results in a paper given to the Statistical Society in 1886 whose findings have already been repeatedly drawn upon.[32]

What then was the occupational incidence of suicide in the late nineteenth century? Although soldiers, those in the drink trade, and professional men always had by far the highest suicide rates, suicide rates half as high again as the average for all occupied males were consistently recorded among all sorts of artisanal and service occupations. On the other hand, although the lowest suicide rates of all were always found among miners of all kinds, rates half as low again as the average were regularly recorded among workers engaged in the manufacture of most metals and chemicals, china, glass and paper, ropemakers, and all sorts of outdoor workers, including agricultural labourers (but not farmers). (See Table 4.) Admittedly, Ogle's and Tatham's statistics relate only to a period of eleven discontinuous years, and their categories often do not clearly distinguish between craftsmen and operatives. The numbers recorded for most occupations (apart from the professions) were cumulatively fairly substantial, however; and both Ogle and Tatham standardized their rates to allow for the very different age structures of different occupations. On balance, therefore, the association of the lowest and highest occupational suicide rates with particular occupations seems sufficiently well established to deserve serious attention.

To nineteenth-century sanitarians, these variations in the occupational incidence of suicide made obvious sense.[33] By their reckoning, the suicide-prone occupations were 'unhealthy' ones (by which they meant that they were apt to involve mental strain, or habits of intemperance, or lack of fresh air and exercise). Moreover, they gave easy access to some familiar means of self-destruction while a man was 'in the mood'; and such commentators often noticed how commonly a

---

[31] *Registrar-General's 45th AR, Supplement*, p. lxi, Table P; *55th AR, Supplement*, Part II, p. clxv, Table V; *65th AR, Supplement*, Part II, p. cxci, Table V.

[32] Ogle, 'Suicides in England and Wales'.

[33] The sanitarians' views on suicide are discussed at length in ch. 10

Table 4. *William Ogle's table of average annual suicide rates per million living among males in different occupations aged between twenty-five and sixty-five, in the years 1878–83*

All males 222			
Soldier	1,149	Tanner, currier, furrier, saddler, leather goods maker	249
Inn, hotel servant	650	Miller	239
Innkeeper, publican, spirit, wine, beer dealer	474	Textile factory worker	229
Medical practitioner	472	Painter, plumber, glazier locksmith, gasfitter	224
Chemist, druggist	444	Blacksmith	222
Barrister, solicitor	408	Bookseller, grocer, draper, tobacconist, general shopkeeper	218
Butcher, fishmonger, poulterer, greengrocer	407	Carter, carrier, haulier	214
Domestic servant	377	Carpenter, joiner	213
Hairdresser, hatter, glover, umbrella, stick maker	364	Sawyer	201
Cheesemonger, butterman, milkman	353	Metal worker	201
Commercial traveller, broker, agent	346	Policeman	201
Cabinet maker, upholsterer, French polisher, undertaker	341	China, earthenware, glass worker	193
Commercial and law clerk	329	Wheelwright, coach, carriage maker	183
Baker, confectioner	328	Agricultural, general, road, railway, clay, gravel, sand labourer	177
Watchmaker, philosophical instrument maker, jeweller	315	Mason, bricklayer, builder, tiler, slater, plasterer, whitewasher	175
Porter, messenger, watchman	314	Gardener	160
Coachman, cabman, flyman, stableman, groom	303	Fisherman	150
Schoolmaster, teacher	290	Quarryman	141
Farmer, grazier	270	Clergyman, priest, minister	139
Printer, bookbinder	262	Shipwright, shipbuilder	96
Tailor	256	Miner	74
Shoemaker	252		

Source: *Journal of the [Royal] Statistical Society*, xlix (1886), p. 108, Table 4.

man took his own life with the special instruments of his trade, so that soldiers used guns, butchers used knives, photographers used cyanide of potassium, and so on.[34] True, they entirely ignored the degree of group solidarity characteristic of an occupation—something which today might well be regarded as the most likely dividing line between occupations which were and were not especially suicide prone—and they paid little attention to the possibility that a depression of trade might temporarily increase suicide in a particular occupation. (Only

[34] See e.g. Ogle, 'Suicides in England and Wales', pp. 121–2, and Farr's comment on the paper by Millar, 'Death by Suicide among H.M.'s British Troops', p. 191.

for farmers did Ogle consider the possibility of a link between their high rate of suicide in 1878–83 and the depression in cereal farming.)[35] Fluctuations like these, however, cannot account for the persistent occupational patterns which recur throughout the years investigated at the General Register Office. Plainly these patterns do deserve some credence—and none the less so because those uncovered in the mid-twentieth century were very broadly the same.[36]

Once this occupational incidence of suicide is taken into account, much becomes unsurprising in both the geographical distributions observed in the county suicide rates and the socio-economic distribution of urban suicide discovered in 1861–70. Industrial occupations, after all, are strikingly absent from the lists of occupations with consistently high suicide rates, whereas those lists include an abundance of the professional, artisanal, and service occupations which were characteristic of all commercial, business, administrative, and residential centres, whatever their size or location. Both these facts accord well not only with the fundamental point that suicide was always comparatively evenly distributed throughout the country, but also with the observation that in 1861–70 it was much less high in industrial centres and seaports than it was in ancient towns and cities with mixed functions, or in wholly non-industrial ones. The census enumerators' books for Lewes in 1871, for example, show an ancient county town with very many inhabitants who followed occupations which were listed as suicide prone,[37] and this makes it unsurprising that the male suicide rate in the district of Lewes was more than twice the national average in the 1860s. Conversely, the lowest occupational suicide rates recorded were those for mining; and the match between the counties where suicide was rarest and the geographical distribution of iron, copper, lead, tin, and coal mining is very close indeed, for all the 'white' suicide counties—north and south Wales, Cornwall, Durham, and the North Riding—were important mining areas in the mid-Victorian period.[38] Similarly, the few industrial workers for whom Ogle and Tatham recorded suicide rates substantially above the average—namely,

[35] Ogle, 'Suicides in England and Wales', pp. 113–14.

[36] See Greenwood, Martin, and Russell, 'Deaths by Violence, 1837–1937', p. 158, Table 9A, and *Registrar-General's Decennial Supplement, England and Wales, 1951*, Occupational Mortality, Part II, vol. 1, Commentary, p. 69, Table DL.

[37] Brent, ed., *Lewes in 1871: a Household and Political Directory*.

[38] The map showing the distribution of the occupations of the people published in the Census of 1851 is useful in connection with all these points. (A reproduction of this map will be found in the back pocket of J. H. Clapham, *An Economic History of Modern Britain: Free Trade and Steel, 1850–1886* (Cambridge, 1932).)

hosiery workers in 1871–80; file, tool, cutlery, and scissors makers in 1890–2; and pottery, earthenware, silk, satin, and crape workers in 1900–2—all followed occupations which were highly localized;[39] occupational geography thus makes unsurprising both the high suicide rates characteristic of the east midlands, and the rising suicide rate already remarked upon in Staffordshire at the end of the century. Rates well below average, however, were listed for the kinds of occupation to be found in seaports and the new industrial towns based upon the manufacture or extraction of minerals and chemicals, and this too is in harmony with the pattern of urban suicide found in the 1860s.

Is the correct conclusion, then, that 'the geographical distribution of suicide was due not to purely geographical conditions, but to the nature of the chief occupations in which the inhabitants were engaged', as Ogle assured the Statistical Society in 1886?[40] After all, how a man made his living was indeed the great shaper of an individual's life, just as local occupational structure was the great shaper of socio-economic environments. Ought we then to agree that what mattered was not where a place was, but the kind of economy it had? Was there no true topography of suicide at all in Victorian and Edwardian England, but only an ecology of suicide? In reality, sweeping conclusions of this sort would be mistaken; and that not merely because the distribution of suicide prone occupations does not invariably neatly coincide with that of area suicide rates, for some such discrepancies are hardly surprising. What stands in the way of their acceptance is the fact that they altogether fail to account for two important segments of the situation: female suicide, and suicide in Wales.

Any close correspondence between the kind of work women did and their proneness to suicide is hardly to be expected in this period, and certainly could not be proved. The General Register Office excluded women from its studies of occupational mortality because, it will be remembered, only 38 per cent of them were recorded as having a definite occupation, as against 98 per cent of men.[41] Even in the three counties where paid employment for women was most widespread— Lancashire, Nottinghamshire, and Derbyshire—no common pattern of female suicide is discernible, adjacent though these counties are.

---

[39] *Registrar-General's 45th AR, Supplement*, p. lxi, Table P; *55th AR, Supplement*, Part II, p. clxv, Table V; *65th AR, Supplement*, Part II, p. cxci, Table V.

[40] Ogle, 'Suicides in England and Wales', p. 134.

[41] See ch. 2 n. 72.

Probably some indirect relationship did indeed exist between the male occupational structure of a place and female suicide patterns there, since occupational structure strongly affected local ways of living; and this may lie behind the fairly similar rank order of male and female suicide rates in different types of town shown in the taxonomy of urban suicide constructed for the 1860s.[42] On the other hand it is difficult to see any clear relationship between local levels of nuptiality and fertility—which were both affected by local male occupational structure—and female suicide rates. In mining areas, for example, which always had high nuptiality and fertility rates, the incidence of female suicide varied greatly from one locality to another, although the incidence of male suicide was strikingly similar. Yet if well-marked socio-economic and demographic patterns are difficult to discern in the distribution of female suicide, so too are strictly topographical ones. Indeed, only three features are sufficiently marked to be singled out. First, overall female suicide was always above average in London, although between 1858 and 1910 London dropped from first to eighth place in the rank order of county suicide rates for women; secondly, female suicide did not increase in rural areas in the late nineteenth century in the same way as male suicide; and finally, the relative level of female suicide was higher in smaller towns compared with other sorts of environments than was the relative level of male suicide there.[43] Arguably, however, it is precisely this lack of clear spatial patterns in the incidence of female suicide which may be significant (in so far as it is not simply the result of the much smaller numbers involved); for it both lends support to the now sometimes challenged stress upon the comparative unimportance for women of any environment but their personal, family, and neighbourhood one, and by its very dissimilarity from the sharp, well-defined patterns of male suicide strengthens the case for acknowledging the paramount influence of occupation on the incidence of suicide among men.

To turn to the peculiarities of Welsh suicide rates, however, is to realize that even where men are concerned occupational structure cannot altogether explain why suicide was more frequent in some places than others. By English standards, recorded suicide in Wales

[42] As will be seen from Table 3.2 in this chapter, the only substantial difference in rank order was with regard to medium-sized seaports and to a lesser extent textile towns, which ranked respectively ninth and eighth for females in this set of 13 suicide rates, but fourth and fifth for males. These differences, however, are not unintelligible.

[43] See Tables 2 and 3.2 in this chapter, and the figures by administrative area for 1911–13 cited in ch. 2 n. 13.

was very rare among all ages and both sexes, everywhere, and at all times. Admittedly, these low levels of suicide can to some extent be explained by the dearth in Wales of the kind of towns and occupations where suicide was most frequent. Professional men, clerks, artisans, and almost all those workers (apart from farmers) who had high occupational suicide rates were comparatively rare in the Principality, whereas most of the occupations with low suicide rates were very heavily represented indeed—notably mining of various sorts, quarrying, and agricultural work. It is impossible to accept these remarkably low Welsh suicide rates as simply a by-product of the Welsh economy, however. To begin with, during the second half of the nineteenth century different parts of Wales grew increasingly dissimilar from an economic point of view; yet during the same period standardized mortality ratios for male suicide grew increasingly similar throughout the Principality. By 1901–10—a decade when the contrast between the industrial south-east and the rest of Wales was very sharp indeed—the standardized male mortality ratios for suicide were virtually the same in Glamorgan, the rest of the south, and north Wales (see Table 5). It was not male, but female suicide rates, which differed widely

Table 5. Standardized mortality ratios for deaths from suicide in Wales in the decades 1861–70 and 1901–10

	1861–70		1901–10	
	Males	Females	Males	Females
North Wales	39	22	59	62
South Wales	49	74	59	81
Glamorgan	53	86	55	69
England & Wales	100	100	100	100

Sources: Registrar-General's 35th AR, Supplement, pp. 410–45; *64th–73rd ARs*, Abstracts 'England and Wales: Causes of Death at Different Periods of Life' and 'Causes of Death in Registration Counties'; *75th AR, Supplement*, Part III, p. xcvi, Table XLVI.

in Wales, and these were very low in the north, and very high (by Welsh standards) in the south. It would be a mistake to make too much of these female suicide rates, for the numbers involved were not large. Still, it does seem that although the varying propensities to suicide in Wales may well have had some connection with broader economic trends (it was in the most rural Welsh counties that male suicide grew fastest in the late nineteenth century), they did not simply reflect variations in occupational structure; and this conclusion is reinforced by the persistence a century later of the pattern observable in the later nineteenth century.[44]

Even more compelling reasons for resisting simple occupational explanations of the peculiarities of Welsh suicide rates are implied by the fact that all crime rates were low in Wales in the later nineteenth and early twentieth centuries, and not only suicide rates. From the 1860s the idea gained ground that Wales was an especially peaceable and law-abiding place, where temperance and a strict moral code reigned; and this was not simply the fruit of nonconformist propaganda, but was borne out each year by the Judicial Statistics. Yet did these statistics merely reflect the weakness of local government machinery and the forces of law and order in Wales, aggravated by the reluctance of neighbours to inform on each other and the unwillingness of juries, magistrates, and coroners to convict? It is certainly possible that hostility was even more widespread than in England to the new police, as well as to Anglican landowning holders of local offices; and it must be remembered that most Welsh coroners were county coroners, and therefore until 1888 elected by the county freeholders (usually very small landowners) and after 1888 appointed by the strongly anti-establishment Welsh county councils. Perhaps concealment and perverse verdicts were indeed more frequent than in England; but this is speculation, since the behaviour of Welsh coroners and their juries remains largely unknown.[45] In any case, it is difficult to see how excessive under-registration could have been responsible to any great extent for low suicide rates in Wales, in view of the peculiarities of the sex, age, and geographical distribution of the cases which were actually registered there. For example, how could the responses of neighbours, police, juries, and coroners in districts like Merthyr Tydfil in the 1860s have led to nearly all the cases among women being officially registered as suicide, but very few of the cases among young men—especially since it was among young men that the proportion of friendless immigrants was highest? Again, forensic

[44] *Registrar-General's Statistical Review, 1971*, Part I, Tables, Medical, p. 263, Table 19. It was in the most rural counties that the real frequency of suicide increased most between the 1860s and 1901–10: cf. Table 5 in this chapter.

[45] Perhaps G. Overton, coroner for North Glamorgan and an ironmaster's son, was a populist of the Wakley stamp—he was mooted by the Merthyr Chartist, Gould, as a parliamentary candidate for the borough: Jones, 'Dr Thomas Price and the Election of 1868 in Merthyr Tydfil', p. 257 n. 115. However this may have been, Overton failed to dominate his jury in 1862 in the case of Jane Lewis: Thomas, 'Medical Men of Glamorgan', p. 127.

medicine was very undeveloped and the new police very thin on the ground in rural Wales;[46] yet in 1911–13 it was not the rural areas or small towns which registered the lowest suicide rates (except among young people under the age of twenty-five), but the handful of county boroughs and, most striking of all, Cardiff and Swansea, places where standards of policing, death certification, and medical and coronatorial expertise were all comparatively high.[47]

Altogether, it seems most probable that these low Welsh suicide rates reflect a level of suicide which was genuinely low (although no doubt not so low as the official statistics suggest), just as low Welsh crime rates in this period have recently been argued to be real so far as the native Welsh were concerned.[48] If this is so, then surely the distinctive incidence of suicide in Wales must be ascribed essentially to the distinctiveness of Welsh culture, with its ancient stress upon the solidarity of kin and neighbours, its lasting disinclination to crimes of personal violence, and its strictly Bible-based moral code, which from the 1850s onwards achieved a central position, thanks above all to the chapels. Strong deterrents to criminal—and suicidal—behaviour were widespread, in the shape of taught prohibitions, unconscious inhibitions, and the supportive solidarity and moral sanctions of family, neighbours, and chapel.[49] Given all this, it seems overwhelmingly likely that cultural restraints were the decisive influence in inhibiting Welsh suicide, although admittedly they were powerfully reinforced by the peculiar occupational structure of the later nineteenth-century Welsh economy, just as they were undermined in rural Wales as the century wore on by the collapse of traditional rural communities.[50]

[46] Among the county coroners, only the coroners for North and East Glamorgan ever handled enough cases to become really professional; and the proportion of suicide verdicts which gave no pathological details was always exceptionally high in Wales.

[47] In 1882–92 Cardiff had one of the lowest proportions of uncertified deaths in the country and one of the highest proportions of inquests: PP 1893–4 (373, 402) XI, p. 299. In 1898 Swansea had the lowest suicide rate recorded for any large town in England and Wales, and Cardiff the sixth lowest: *Judicial Statistics, 1899*, part I, p. 41. For the figures in 1911–13 see the tables cited in ch. 2 n. 13.

[48] Jones, 'Crime, Protest and Community in Nineteenth-Century Wales', p. 14; Howell, *Land and People in Nineteenth Century Wales*, p. 156.

[49] Cf. e.g. E. Jones, 'Tregaron' in Davies and Rees, eds., *Welsh Rural Communities*, p. 98, and Williams, 'Customs and Traditions Connected with Sickness, Death and Burial in Montgomeryshire in the late Nineteenth Century', pp. 56, 61.

[50] Between 1861–70 and 1901–10 the male suicide rate for the 3 most rural counties of Wales (namely, Cardigan, Montgomery, and Flint in 1861–70 and Cardigan, Montgomery, and Merioneth in 1901–10) rose from 45.4 per million males living to 82.5; whereas the male suicide rate for the 3 least rural counties (Glamorgan, Monmouth, and Denbigh) rose far less, from 49.7 to 55.3 per million males living.

Both local occupational structure and cultural traditions, then, might make suicide rather more or less likely in particular parts of Wales or provincial England. But what of London, it may be asked? After all, London was a registration division made up of three registration counties and 29 registration districts, and containing some 14 per cent of the country's population within an area of only 78,000 acres: surely its suicide statistics offer a unique opportunity for micro-studies of the links between socio-economic environment and propensities to suicide? Unfortunately they do nothing of the sort, for the simple reason that (as was observed in the first chapter) until 1911 deaths were registered not in the deceased's district of residence, but in the district in which the body was found; and in London far more than anywhere else there was a considerable likelihood that these two would not be the same. There, any outer district was within quite easy reach of any inner one; increasing numbers of people worked in one registration district and slept in another; great hospitals like Guy's and St Bartholomew's acted as magnets for casualties over a wide area; and newspaper items, local lore, popular novelettes, ballads, visual imagery, and melodramas all conspired with these facts to inflate the number of suicide verdicts registered in a small handful of districts.[51] In the 1860s, for example, one registration district within the square mile of the City had the lowest female suicide rate in London while its close neighbour had the highest female (and male) suicide rate not only in London, but in the whole of England and Wales.[52] This is a striking juxtaposition; but it would be a great mistake to assume that it has any light to throw on the ecology of suicide. Maps of suicide rates in Victorian and Edwardian London are by no means useless. Even more than other suicide maps, however, they need to be recognized for what they are: portrayals of the spatial distribution not of acts but of verdicts of suicide. In a statistical study of the ecology of suicide they are best left on one side, unreliable indicators as they are of the whereabouts of those parts of the metropolis whose inhabitants were especially apt to take their own lives.

In the end, the most striking fact about the distribution of suicide rates in Victorian and Edwardian England remains its uniformity. Only

[51] The reputation of certain places in central London as suicide spots is very neatly conveyed in a satirical plea for safety measures published anonymously, during Dickens's editorship, in *Bentley's Miscellany*, vi (1839), pp. 540–2.

[52] The two City registration districts concerned were East and West London respectively: *Registrar-General's 35th AR, Supplement*, p. 35.

when a much more microscopic scale is used than for other statistics of mortality, crime, or individual behaviour does a pattern begin to emerge which hints at some links between environment and tendencies to suicide. Whether those links were forged chiefly by occupation and economic environment or chiefly by cultural traditions seems to have varied not only between men and women, but in different parts of the country. There is more than a peculiar economic history behind the distinctiveness of Welsh suicide rates, and other regions too may have had something of a suicide culture of their own. Certainly the statistics offer no support for associating suicide at this time with large cities and industrialization. On the contrary: rising male suicide in many rural areas from the 1880s suggests that in times of hardship and frustration agricultural workers turned not only to politics and trade unionism but also to violence upon themselves as substitutes for arson and violence.[53] Equally, the far greater frequency of suicide in the 1860s in ancient county towns and purely residential places than in mining areas and new industrial towns, as well as the steadily narrowing gap between metropolitan and provincial suicide rates, provide further evidence that urban and industrial centres and even London itself were places which increasingly offered not only far greater hopes of betterment, but also more support to the unfortunate, than did the Barchesters and Middlemarches of the time.[54] In short, there is indeed a geography of suicide in Victorian and Edwardian England and Wales, although not a deeply defined one; but it is a geography which must be understood in terms of local traditions as well as occupational settings, and which certainly should not be equated with any simple contrasts between urban and industrial as opposed to rural and agricultural ways of life.

[53] Cf. D. Jones, 'Rural Crime and Protest' in Mingay, ed., *The Victorian Countryside*, ii, 576.

[54] In the Edwardian period—sometimes called the golden age of British cities—this is not surprising; but even for the earlier part of the century, much recent writing makes this very plausible. For example, it has recently been concluded that urban disamenities had only the most trivial influence on trends in the quality of life for labourers in nineteenth-century Britain: Williamson, 'Urban Disamenities, Dark Satanic Mills, and the British Standard of Living Debate', p. 76.

PART II

EXPERIENCES

4

Dying by Suicide: London, 1861–1862

How has the experience of dying by suicide changed through time? Were the thoughts and feelings of someone who embarked upon suicidal actions different when the law of suicide was different, and when the plain man made different assumptions about heaven and hell and the circumstances in which suicide was natural or forgivable? Has the sort of person most likely to experience this kind of death altered, whether in terms of sex or age, family circumstances and health, or occupation and social class? Have some paths to self-destruction become far more well trodden, at least for certain age or sex groups; or have the precipitating causes of suicide remained essentially the same? Over the last century or so the methods most commonly used by those taking their own lives have certainly altered a great deal; but has this greatly changed the last stages of the experience of dying by suicide, or merely altered the impact of intervention?

Questions like these can hardly be answered by statistics. At best, official statistics can reveal only three things about the experience of suicide: how common it was formally adjudged to be in a particular place; how often it there befell men as compared with women and one age group as compared with another; and what method was used most frequently by different sex and age-groups. In short, statistics can establish the bare bones of this aspect of past experience, but no more. Even less to the point are the oft-told stories of the suicides of the celebrated—for example, of Benjamin Haydon the painter or John Sadleir the swindler and Member of Parliament—since by definition these are altogether unrepresentative. Clearly only long unbroken runs of ordinary case histories can provide insights into the experiences of the many completely obscure men and women who committed suicide in Victorian and Edwardian England. But do such case histories exist? Fortunately they do, thanks to the verbatim notes of witnesses' depositions made by a few coroners at their inquests.[1] Notes like these are

[1] County, borough, and franchise coroners all needed to keep registers of the inquests they held, whether for the purpose of submitting their accounts to the authority which

more vivid than clinical case records can ever be (although medically interesting cases can be found in medical journals and treatises, and asylum registers sometimes record details of their suicidal patients), and their purport can often be made clearer still with the aid of local press reports. Such private papers are rare; but some survive, and have generously been made available for study.

These are potentially very valuable records, and in this and the following chapter they have been used as the core of three studies designed to bring into focus the impact upon ordinary experiences of suicide not only of change through time, but of different settings and environments as well.[2] The first draws upon the exceptionally copious papers relating to inquests held in London in the early 1860s in order to delineate the experience of suicide in mid-Victorian London, and thus establish a bench-mark against which other experiences can be appraised. This study is based upon a close consideration of every case of suicide registered by two London coroners between January and December 1861 and by a third between mid-July 1862 and mid-January 1863, amounting altogether to a total of 101 cases. These three coroners were regularly responsible for around half the suicide verdicts registered in Victorian London, and their jurisdictions included examples of nearly every type of district which was contained within that city of staring contrasts. London had long been unique, however, and Londoners were always reckoned a special breed of people; moreover, as has already been pointed out, suicidal behaviour in big cities and in the countryside have always been held to be quite different. A second, similar study has therefore been made of the thirty-four cases of suicide which were registered in the same period in an intensely rural area: the part of east Sussex known since the eleventh century as the Rape of Hastings. Provincial inquest papers for this period are rare, and these papers for the Rape of Hastings between 1859 and 1866 seem to be the only substantial run for the middle years of the century at present available. It is therefore fortunate that they relate to an area which was not only very rural, but also lay within a county whose suicide statistics (as was noticed in the previous chapter) are excep-

---

paid them or making returns to the Home Office, and these registers, and to a lesser extent the inquisitions themselves (that is, the formal legal document embodying the jury's verdict) are not uncommonly preserved. Other inquest papers for this period are rare, however, and particularly verbatim notes of depositions of the sort so heavily used here (which were the private property of the coroner concerned).

[2] For a brief description of these records, see Appendix II.

tionally interesting. Finally, in order to explore the significance for this aspect of human experience not only of place but of the passage of time, a similarly intensive study has been made of the twenty-three cases of suicide recorded in 1911 in two of the same London jurisdictions studied earlier, those of the City of London and Borough of Southwark—apparently the only coronatorial jurisdictions for which voluminous inquest papers survive in a long enough run to make it possible to compare mid-Victorian and Edwardian experiences of suicide in exactly the same place.

What can we recapture, then, of the experience of dying by suicide in mid-Victorian London? The three coroners whose papers provide an opportunity to see into this hidden world were very different men indeed, with widely different styles of working. Two of them, Serjeant William Payne, coroner for both the City of London and the Borough of Southwark, and Charles St Clare Bedford, coroner for the City and Liberty of Westminster, were lawyers and old hands, accustomed to be consulted on the controversial issues which had for a generation surrounded their office. Payne belonged to a dynasty of old-style City office-holders. He had been elected to his two franchise coronerships (which were customarily held by the same person) by the City's Common Council in 1829, and for a decade after 1833 he also held the post of Chief Clerk at the Guildhall, until in 1843, at the age of forty-four, he was called to the bar and moved higher up the hierarchy of legal offices. When an association to protect coroners' interests was formed during the prolonged struggles before the legislation of 1860, he became its first president; and until his death in 1872 he remained a proponent of the assimilation of the pay and status of coroners to those of 'other judges', and (apparently) of the use of a medical subordinate to undertake preliminary inquiries and post-mortems where necessary.[3] St Clare Bedford, the appointee of the Dean and

[3] So claimed Henry Letheby, Medical Officer of Health for the City of London: *Report to the Commissioners of Sewers . . . on Certain Imperfect Mortality Returns*, p. 8. William Payne (1799–1872: Boase) was succeeded by his eldest son, William John Payne (1822–84: Boase), who had been his deputy since 1843 and coroner for the Duchy of Lancaster Liberty since 1857. In the early 1850s his emoluments amounted to about £500 a year, and were causing no friction: PP 1854 [1772] XXVI, p. 604. His 'energy and initiative' in founding the Coroners' Society in 1846 have been singled out for praise: Havard, *Detection of Secret Homicide*, p. 66. This body, however, surely grew from the Committee of Coroners established in 1843 to try to secure acceptable legislation on coroners' duties and remuneration (which had repeatedly slipped through their fingers since 1816), and of this Committee Payne was not a member: BL, Add. MSS 40,530, fols. 31–5 and 40,612, fols. 57–8.

Chapter of Westminster Abbey (whose Chapter Clerk he was), held his franchise coronership even longer, from 1843 to 1888. A licensed attorney since 1833 and as convinced as Payne that the first purpose of his office was not 'the promotion of sanitary measures' but 'the prevention, detection and punishment of crime', St Clare Bedford was a much less thrusting man. Exceptionally conscientious, gentlemanly, and fair minded, he was turned to for advice by the Middlesex Justices at the height of their conflict with their two renowned coroners, Thomas Wakley and William Baker.[4] Both Payne and St Clare Bedford confined themselves at their inquests to asking the routine questions recommended in practitioners' handbooks (the latter doing so more thoroughly than the former); and both noted the medical evidence only briefly, and did not make a habit of ordering a post-mortem. The third member of this trio, Dr Edwin Lankester, was a coroner of an entirely different breed, however, for he believed passionately that the first purpose of a coroner must indeed be 'the promotion of sanitary measures'. In July 1862, when his papers begin, he was as yet wholly inexperienced, for he was fresh from his election as county coroner for the newly created Central District of Middlesex. His strenuous and expensive election campaign had been backed by the leading sanitarians of the day. For them, Lankester was an ideal candidate, for he was not only Medical Officer of Health for St James's Westminster and a leading figure in the Association of Metropolitan Medical Officers of Health, but also a well-known and effective scientific writer and lecturer. Lankester was determined to demonstrate to the full that the coroner's office, provided it was placed in medical hands, could indeed powerfully advance the cause of public health in a locality.[5] He ordered post-mortems as a matter of routine, made full and expert notes of all the medical evidence given, and in his early days occasion-

[4] Middlesex Justices of the Peace, *Report of the Special Committee appointed at the Michaelmas Session, 1850*, pp. 42, 48, St Clare Bedford to Thomas Turner, 30 Dec. 1850 and 13 Jan. 1851. (These controversies are briefly referred to in ch. 1 n. 34.) On Charles St Clare Bedford, see the *Clergy List* and *The Times*, 23 June 1888, p. 14, col. 1.

[5] Dr Edwin Lankester (1814–74: *DNB*) was an exceptionally good-looking, energetic, genial 'man of science', who deserves a biography. His popular bestseller, *Half Hours with the Microscope*, went through several editions between 1859 and 1905. A friend of Dickens and Jerrold in the early 1840s, as well as of the epidemiologists Snow and Radcliffe, he was a regular writer for the *Daily News*. His 8 children included Sir Ray Lankester (1847–1929: *DNB*). His election was a milestone in the campaign for medical coroners, and was very fully covered by *The Lancet*: see for example 1862, ii. 45 (12 July). He often expounded his conception of the coroner's office: for example, ibid., 1863, i. 608 (30 May).

ally sketched the scene described by witnesses and took almost verbatim notes of everything said at his inquests.

These three coroners differed greatly; but their four Districts differed even more. Industrial Southwark was as unlike the commercial and financial purlieus of the City, as it was unlike the conspicuous wealth and back-alley poverty of Westminster, or the rookeries of Holborn and St Giles, respectable Islington, rowdy St Pancras, or genteel Marylebone, Paddington, and St John's Wood—all of which fell within Lankester's sprawling District of Central Middlesex (see Map 3). Thirteen registration districts lay wholly or in part within the boundaries of these four jurisdictions (see Maps 3, 4, and 5). Their mortality figures for the decade 1861–70 suggest that only in Bedford's jurisdiction of Westminster were suicide rates everywhere high by London standards, and then only for men. In the City, high rates in the western and central parts were counterbalanced by low ones in the east, and in Southwark suicide rates were round about the metropolitan average; while throughout Lankester's spreading domain, they tended to fall below it (see Maps 4 and 5). These same figures also suggest that the high suicide rates among young men which have already been noticed as characteristic of mid-Victorian London occurred only in the non-industrial central districts: they were not recorded in either the inner industrial zone or the suburbs.[6] To study the individual stories behind these statistics, however, is to realize that different neighbourhoods differed widely not merely in the scale of suicide, nor even in its sex and age incidence, but in the texture of the experience of dying by suicide itself. This may well seem unsurprising. The different parts of London interacted with each other far less in the 1860s than they do today,[7] and their 'aborigines' (to use a catchphrase of that time) were often portrayed as utterly distinct 'tribes'.[8] Age and sex structure,

---

[6] For the location of these 3 sorts of area, see Stedman Jones, *Outcast London*, p. 141, 'Map of Inner Industrial Perimeter'.

[7] The lack of interaction between physically close but utterly different classes, occupations, and ways of living in inner London is probably linked with its haphazard, complex street plan, which persisted until well into the era of street improvements, building developments, and slum clearances of the Metropolitan Board of Works (1855–89), as is suggested by that topographically very correct writer, Sadleir: *Forlorn Sunset*, p. 500, postscript.

[8] This separateness was in no way lessened by the fact that many of the dwellers in these slummy enclaves picked up a living from the needs and habits of the well-to-do households adjoining, in the way described (but not perhaps altogether correctly interpreted) by Malcolmson; 'Getting a Living in the Slums of Victorian Kensington', pp. 28, 34, 45.

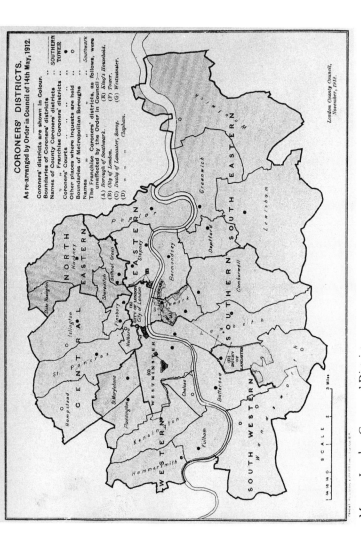

Map 3. London Coroners' Districts, 1912

Note: The boundaries of the three Franchise Coroners' Districts studied here, labelled 'A', 'B', and 'G' above, remained the same throughout. The Central Middlesex District of 1862, however, was much more extensive than the Central London District of 1912, for it included rural Middlesex as well as parts of the Western and North-Eastern Districts shown here.

Source: LCC, *London Statistics*, xxii. 1911–12.

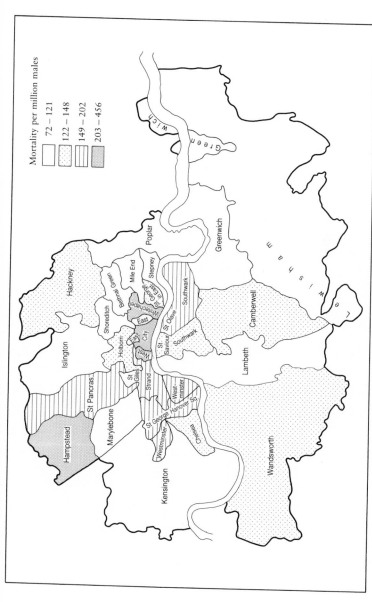

Map 4. Average annual male mortality from suicide in London registration districts, 1861–70.
Source: Registrar-General's 35th AR, Supplement, pp. 26–45.

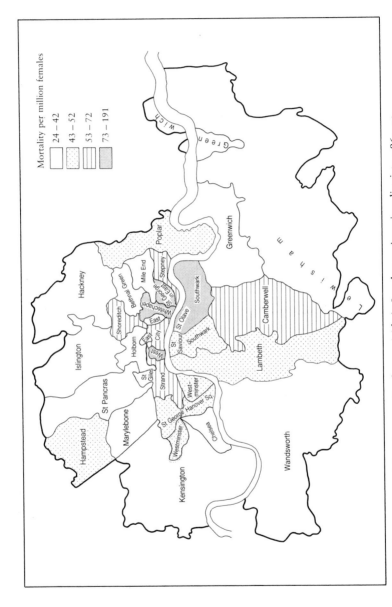

Map 5. Average annual female mortality from suicide in London registration districts, 1861–70

Source: As for Map 4.

morbidity and housing conditions, occupations and level of income, living habits—all these always affect local patterns of suicide, and all these varied greatly between each of these four Districts, even more than they did within them.

It would be a great mistake to assume that these differences in suicide patterns simply reflect demographic, economic, and social contrasts between different parts of London, however, if only for the technical reason already touched on more than once.[9] Every dead body lying within the boundaries of a coroner's jurisdiction fell within his purview, wherever the dead person might have lived; and in inner London, coroners often found themselves holding inquests upon the bodies of people who had lived outside their jurisdiction but died within it. Three topographical accidents in particular always affected not only the size of a coroner's load of suicide cases, but also its nature—since different sorts of people tended to have characteristic methods of committing suicide, and hence to be more likely to die in certain sorts of places. One of these was the location of those perennial magnets, canals, ponds, and rivers, and of such suicide spots as were currently notorious; another was the distribution of railway termini with their surrounding networks of hotels, carriers' quarters, and coffee houses;[10] and a third was the location of workhouses used as public mortuaries and even more of a handful of well-known large hospitals, to which police and public took accident cases from far afield. Each had its own effect. For example, young women (who always particularly favoured drowning) had learnt from innumerable novelettes and ballads as well as many well-publicized real-life examples to make for the Regent's Canal, the swing bridges over the Docks, the stretch of the Thames between London and Westminster Bridges, or Hampstead and Highgate ponds; while skilled workers and better-off people, who unlike unskilled labourers did not favour hanging but poisoning, cutting or stabbing themselves, were more likely to survive long enough to be hurried off to one of the great central hospitals before they died.

Urban geography and the varying efficiency of local police and medical men, as well as the demographic, economic, and social characteristics of different neighbourhoods thus made the experience of dying by suicide different in different parts of mid-Victorian London. These differences cannot be reduced to a single series of contrasts, whether

---

[9] See above pp. 32–3, and p. 102.
[10] See Kellett, *The Impact of Railways on Victorian Cities*, p. 319.

ecological or any other. Yet so real were they that it is necessary
to draw four separate profiles of suicide: in Southwark, the City,
Westminster, and central north London.

Southwark in 1861 was a place of busy wharves and warehouses, with
a famous brewery (Barclay & Perkins), a large engineering works
(Maudslay, Son & Field), and a multitude of smaller industrial
concerns.[11] Not surprisingly, since it was part of London's old industrial zone, it had few domestic servants and few immigrants;[12] women
did not greatly outnumber men, and the age structure of its population
was close to the London mean, with 16 per cent of its men and 19 per
cent of its women above the age of forty-five. At 25.3 per thousand
persons living, its average annual death rate was not the highest in
London, although it was slightly above the metropolitan average of
24.3.[13] Its inhabitants were not quite the most closely packed together
of any in the capital,[14] but there were some notorious 'nests of dirt,
vice and overcrowding' in the district around St Peter's church near
Southwark Bridge; in Mint Street and Kent Street (now Tabard Street)
around St George's; in the streets and alleys between Gravel Lane and
Blackfriars Road on either side of the Brighton & South Coast Railway;
and in the New Cut between Blackfriars and Waterloo Roads, a great
haunt of low prostitutes.[15] (Southwark's prostitutes were the poorest
in London, according to the metropolitan police.)[16] Three aspects of
its topography tended to increase its coroner's load of suicide cases:
its riverside position, abutting upon two of the busiest free bridges
across the Thames, London Bridge and Blackfriars Bridge (Southwark
Bridge was a toll bridge until 1864, and little used);[17] the presence of
two busy railway termini at London Bridge and a surrounding network

[11] For Southwark's occupational structure, see *Census, 1861*, pp. 21–34, Tables 11
and 12. As well as the *Censuses*, local Directories and newspapers were constantly
referred to in working on the inquest papers discussed here; and *Bacon's New Ordnance
Atlas of London and the Suburbs* was used for the topography and street names of
London at this time.

[12] Jones, *Outcast London*, p. 139, Table.

[13] *Registrar-General's 35th AR, Supplement*, pp. 4–5, 40–1.

[14] See ibid., p. clxv, Table 56.

[15] Hollingshead, *Ragged London*, pp. 165–83; Weight, 'Statistics of the Parish of St
George the Martyr, Southwark', pp. 50–71. As in many other parts of central London,
overcrowding in north Southwark increased as a by-product of street improvements
and railway extensions: Dyos, 'The Slums of Victorian London', pp. 37–8; Jones, *Outcast
London*, p. 162.

[16] Mayhew, *London Labour and the London Poor*, iv. 266, Table.

[17] Reddaway, 'London in the Nineteenth Century: IV', pp. 167, 171.

of cheap hotels and coffee houses;[18] and finally the presence of two great hospitals, St Thomas's (which did not leave its original site until the autumn of 1862) and Guy's, to which in 1861 (as for generations) south Londoners were accustomed to bring accident cases of all sorts.[19] Yet suicide verdicts were apparently not exceptionally common here. In the decade 1861–70 only 161 suicide verdicts were recorded in the registration district of St Saviour's and St George's Southwark and Newington, which contained the greater part of Payne's jurisdiction,[20] so that the official annual average suicide rate there was 143 per million males living (as against 135 for the whole division of London), and 44 per million females living (as against 48 for the whole division of London). (See Maps 4 and 5.) It was the comparative frequency of suicide among those aged between thirty-five and sixty-four which led to this small excess among men; whereas it was its comparative rarity among women under forty-five which brought down Southwark's female suicide rate.[21] There is little more to be learnt about suicide hereabouts from the official statistics. Payne's notes on the eighteen cases on which he recorded a verdict of suicide during 1861, however, establish the outlines of an experience of suicide in this mid-Victorian community which is so distinctive that it is not misleading to offer one man's story—a Dickensian Christmas story without a happy ending— as representative.

In the early hours of New Year's Day 1861, fifty-three year old Charlie Sudds shouted yet again, 'A merry Christmas and a happy new year to all', and blew his brains out with a large horse pistol. He fell heavily on the bedstead in his downstairs parlour in Webber Street behind Waterloo Road, and died immediately. That Christmas Eve he

---

[18] Hobhouse, *Lost London*, p. 150. As the natural terminus for coaches running south, Southwark had long had large and important inns.

[19] Steele, 'Numerical Analysis of the Patients Treated in Guy's Hospital', pp. 387–8, 398, Table xi. In 1861 the presence of Bethlem Hospital did not increase the number of suicide verdicts registered in Southwark, although it certainly did do so in some years. For other public institutions there, see *Census, 1861*, i. 218.

[20] Payne's jurisdiction extended over about half of the registration district of St Saviour's, St George's, and Newington, and a small part of the registration district of St Olave's and Bermondsey: see Maps 3, 4 and 5. Its boundaries were those of the old Borough of Southwark, consisting of the 3 manors over which jurisdiction was granted to the City in the sixteenth century (or the 5 parishes of St George's, St John's, St Olave's, St Thomas's, and St Saviour's), as opposed to those of the parliamentary borough created in 1832 or the metropolitan borough created in 1899. There is an excellent map showing these ancient boundaries in Johnson, *Southwark and the City*, at end.

[21] *Registrar-General's 35th AR, Supplement*, pp. 4–5, 40–1.

had suddenly been sacked from the engineering shop where he had worked as a millwright for twenty-five years (perhaps Powis & James at the top of his street); his old master had died, and 'the new man wanted to get someone cheaper.' On New Year's Eve there had been a family gathering at his married daughter's house near by. He had been restless, his son-in-law remembered, but after all he had many things to vex him. 'A dreadful pain at the back of his head' had plagued him for some time, and moreover the loss of his job was a serious matter, for London was in the middle of its worst winter for years, frost had closed the Thames, and business was very slack—that indeed was why his employer needed to cut his wages bill.[22] An hour or so after midnight struck, Charlie Sudds had walked home alone. He exchanged some seasonal back-chat with the Rittmans, who had been his fellow lodgers for the last ten years. When his wife came in, he said he would hide so that she should think he was still out, and when she had gone upstairs, he lit a fire in their parlour and called to her to come down. But instead she chose to go out to first-foot yet more relations, whereupon Charlie Sudds went into the kitchen for a gun (why it was there was never explained: he had not joined one of the new Volunteer Rifle Corps), and 'hollered out that he would fetch his wife and shoot himself'. At this his wife's sister (who had walked back with her) ran out to fetch a policeman; but when she and the policeman arrived, Charlie Sudds had already shouted his final season's greetings and was dead. That night he had certainly 'had a little drop', as his son-in-law put it, and he was in the habit of 'drinking a little some-times'; but he was usually 'pretty steady' and was highly respected in the neighbourhood, as the *South London Chronicle* duly reported that Saturday.[23]

Charlie Sudds was typical of those who committed suicide in mid-Victorian Southwark in a number of ways. Demographically—since he was a man, aged between forty-five and fifty-four; and in social status—since he was a highly skilled but not self-employed worker (he might equally typically have been an entirely unskilled casual labourer: it was the middling class, the master craftsmen, and the semi-skilled who were conspicuously lacking among Southwark's suicides). The situation which precipitated his action—unemployment, with no more

---

[22] Hollingshead, *Ragged London*, pp. 3–5; Scott, 'Intemperance and Pauperism', p. 486.
[23] CLRO, CR, Southwark, 3 Jan. 1861, inquest no. 5, Charles Sudds; *South London Chronicle*, 5 Jan., p. 5 (where Sudds's name is wrongly given), and 12 Jan. 1861, p. 4.

than a little drinking—was equally typical of Southwark, although comparatively rare in the three other metropolitan areas for which similar evidence is available. He was also representative enough in his lack of any substantial history of bodily or mental disease. Only about a quarter of those who ended their own lives in Southwark were suffering from some organic disease (all of them men aged about fifty). None had previously been in a mental asylum, although two were considered to be deranged by the house surgeons who saw them after their admission to hospital, and a quarter had made previous suicide attempts (which may suggest some psychiatric disorder).

In one final respect Sudds was typical of those who committed suicide not only in Southwark but in all the other metropolitan areas which can be studied in this way: he was not living alone, but amidst a network of relations and fellow lodgers. Some three-quarters of those upon whom verdicts of suicide were recorded in Southwark in 1861 were married; and of the four who were not, all lived outside the Borough, and only one (a young waiter who had just lost his job at the Great Western Railway Hotel and been jilted by his girl)[24] did not live with or among relations, or with an old master. In the 1860s there was an acute working-class housing shortage in inner London, so that relatives often lived together, while even the most respectable working men lived, like Charlie Sudds, as lodgers in houses with multiple tenancies. On the face of it, in mid-Victorian London family quarrels might be expected to have precipitated suicide far more often than loneliness or isolation. Yet apparently family strains were relatively unimportant, as they seem to have been for Sudds. Only one Southwark case belies this, and this is also the only case involving someone under the age of twenty-five—that of a young Bermondsey outworker, Will Pragnell, who swallowed some of the corrosive sublimate he used in his work as a brass finisher, because his mother called him lazy and refused him opium, although he was depressed and tired; and even the Pragnells were not on really bad terms. 'Mother, don't fret,' he said as she took him to Guy's. 'I've done it and it will soon be over!' (She claimed he had not been 'right in his head' since an accident when he was fifteeen, and that they 'had to watch him'.)[25]

The way Will Pragnell had 'done it' is worth noticing, since Sudds's use of a gun was altogether odd. In Southwark the chosen door to death was usually the one which a man's occupation made it easiest

[24] CLRO, CR, Southwark, 11 Sept. 1861, inquest no. 173, William James Brunsdon.
[25] Ibid., 22 Oct. 1861, inquest no. 202, William Pragnell.

for him to open. In this industrial quarter, work quite often brought familiarity with chemicals, and for men poison was the commonest single method of suicide—more than twice as common as in London as a whole, and nearly five times more common than in England and Wales.[26] It was certainly not the Thames which was this riverside borough's usual gateway to suicidal death, as the Seine seems to have been for nearby Parisians;[27] in 1861 the only man living in Southwark who was recorded as having drowned himself was a wharf labourer,[28] and he was taking a way out which his daily routine had made obvious, not succumbing to the pull of 'the river of suicides'.

What of the final process of dying, so often painfully prolonged? Southwark's two great hospitals brought many more dead bodies into Serjeant Payne's jurisdiction than did the proximity of the Thames. Half of the men upon whom he registered verdicts of suicide in 1861 died at St Thomas's or Guy's; and the care these two hospitals gave must have significantly altered the experience of dying after a suicidal attempt in this part of south London. Between 1854 and 1861, seven out of eight of all the women and three out of four of all the men who were admitted to Guy's after attempting suicide recovered.[29] Inevitably these cases included many whose attempts had not been very serious, but the detailed medical evidence given by the house surgeons on the treatment of those who did die, makes it easy to understand why this hospital received high official praise in 1863.[30]

So far nothing has been said about the feminine experience of suicide. In mid-Victorian London, the process of daily living was widely different for women and for men, and so too was the experience of suicide revealed in these papers. For men, three things especially affected how easily they found themselves on the paths which led to suicidal behaviour, and which gateway to suicidal death they took at the end: personal physique and temperament, abode, and, above all, occupation. For women, the impact of physique, temperament, and abode was not at all the same, while the great formative pressures of defined, paid occupation were either comparatively weak or altogether lacking, although their work imposed pressures of its own. Verdicts of death by suicide were everywhere much more rarely recorded on

---

[26] For the incidence of suicide by poison in the Division of London and in England and Wales in 1861, see *Registrar-General's 24th AR*, p. 140.

[27] Cobb, *Death in Paris*, p. 4.

[28] CLRO, CR, Southwark, 18 Feb. 1861, inquest no. 50, Henry Edwards.

[29] Steele, 'Numerical Analysis of the Patients Treated in Guy's Hospital', pp. 387, 398.

[30] PP 1864 [3416] XXVIII, p. 580.

women than on men (as has already been noted), and this gap had been widening for some years. In the decade 1861–70 the gap was particularly wide in Southwark, since three male deaths by suicide were officially recorded there for every one female death by suicide, and the suicide rate for women was only 31 per cent of that for men. (In the Division of London as a whole it was 36 per cent.) It is thus not surprising that in 1861 Payne recorded a verdict of death by suicide on only four women, as against fourteen men.

As it happens, however, these four women exemplify very well the characteristics of the feminine experience of suicide, at least as it is revealed in mid-Victorian inquest papers. This seems everywhere to have been far more inward looking and homogeneous, and much less patterned by a diversity of external factors than that of men. For women there were, apparently, two main paths to suicide. The first and most well-trodden was drink, and this they travelled with men on equal terms. (That drink played a lesser role than unemployment in precipitating male suicide in Southwark was unusual, to judge from other inquest papers.) The second, however, was especially their own: the path of brooding self-reproach and desponding worry about emotional loss and separation from loved ones. For them, work-related problems and organic illness less often played a decisive role; while they tended to differ in the ages at which they were most likely to commit suicide (in the way analysed in Chapter 2), and to come from humbler social groups than men. Altogether it is thoroughly typical that three of these four Southwark women were in their early fifties, with stable marriages to unskilled workers, and that two of them persisted in 'fretting' about family cares which their husbands were taking in their stride, while the third 'used to drink for four or five days, off and on'. Is it not unexpected, either, to find that the fourth, Louisa Townshend, was a thirty-one year old prostitute living apart from her 'surgeon' husband, and keeping a shop in the notorious area off Tabard Street; and that although neither friendless not without resources, she was 'in the habit of sending out for two or three quarters of gin a day'.[31] The methods of suicide these four women chose were equally unsurprising. Two—both working women in their fifties— hanged themselves; and although a mere one in five of the women who committed suicide in London at this time used this method, it was always the way preferred by older working people. A third walked from Camberwell to drown herself in the Thames—and everywhere

[31] CLRO, CR, Southwark, 22 Aug. 1861, inquest no. 161, Louisa Townshend.

drowning was chosen by twice as many women as men; while Louisa Townshend sent out her housekeeper's little girl for essence of almonds—much used as a flavouring for sweetmeats and liqueurs as well as a perfume for pomade, and hence a favourite source of hydrocyanic acid for women who 'entertained' men in their rooms.

In mid-Victorian Southwark five main currents thus flowed and intermingled to carry men and women towards suicide: drink; bodily and mental illness; unemployment and business troubles; public disgrace and private self-reproaches; and family strains, emotional disappointment, and bereavement.[32] The combination is an accustomed one. Here, however, where working people were crowded together in an old industrial quarter which was very sensitive to seasonal fluctuations, the last final push to suicide in 1861 again and again came from a man's work situation. Only among women did suicide not run in a distinctive local channel chiefly carved out by occupational geography. Here, where even more than elsewhere suicide was the resort of later middle age and not of youth, self-inflicted death seems rarely to have been chiefly a means of revenge, and comparatively seldom the sequel of an earlier escape through drink; most often it was itself the primary escape route from self-blame or self-pity, foreboding or hopelessness, pain or fatigue.

It was a very different experience of suicide that Payne encountered on the days when he held inquests across the river in his other jurisdiction, with a jury of 'superior intelligence' made up of 'tradesmen and the higher classes beside him',[33] and a punctilious reporter from the *City Press* in attendance.[34] The 1860s was the decade when the City took its largest step away from being a residential and industrial

---

[32] E.g. the prospect of an operation at Guy's for 'a stoppage in his water' was the immediate cause of a 55 year old man's throwing himself from an upstairs window (ibid., 11 Mar. 1861, inquest no. 65, William Drew); a long-serving chemist's porter reacted to a new employee's complaint of him to his employer with, 'It's all over with me. I'm ruined now', and a draught of prussic acid (14 Nov. 1861, inquest no. 219, James Jeffries); a 56 year old 'sober, hardworking, industrious' wife and mother became increasingly depressed when she could not work as much as usual, and hanged herself (21 May 1861, inquest no. 118, Maria Cox); and after 37 years of marriage the prospect of going to the workhouse and being separated from her husband, a casual labourer who could find no work, seemed unbearable to Mary Hines after she had had a pint of beer (9 May 1861, inquest no. 112).

[33] PP 1860 (193) XXII, p. 16, Q. 478, evidence of Mr Serjeant William Payne.

[34] Every inquest in the City was unfailingly reported soberly and unsensationally in the *City Press*.

area, and lost a third of its population. True, this was a process which affected its intensely crowded eastern fringes comparatively little. These were increasingly being assimilated into the neighbouring clothing manufacturing districts of Whitechapel, Bethnal Green, and Stepney, and demographically they were not altogether unlike industrial Southwark. In the rest of the City, however, drastic redevelopment was going on.[35] The poor were being squeezed into and across the western borders, as the central area became a complex of substantial banks, offices, and warehouses linked by wide new thoroughfares. Clerks, warehousemen, messengers, porters, and inn servants predominated among the City's workers, although in the west around Paternoster Row the largest single male occupation was printing; but increasingly these workers were coming in daily from homes outside the City boundaries.[36]

This sharpening economic and demographic contrast between the eastern quarter and the rest of the City was paralleled in contrasting suicide rates, for in 1861–70 the male suicide rate in the western district of the City was four times as high as in the east, and the female suicide rate more than eight times as high (see Maps 4 and 5). Nevertheless it would be a mistake to assume that the first contrast was the chief cause of the second. To some extent, it is true, the people living in the eastern fringes were probably genuinely less prone to suicide, for it will be remembered that industrial workers and unskilled labourers did tend to have low suicide rates;[37] but the difference was probably also partly the accidental creation of the smallness of the resident populations concerned, particularly in the west, and above all, of urban topography. For example, after it had been rebuilt in the 1820s London Bridge seems to have been less used by 'jumpers' (as opposed to those who climbed down the landing steps underneath) than Blackfriars Bridge in the west of the City, which was an unrivalled magnet for early Victorian London servant girls bent on suicide. Again, the railway termini were concentrated in the central and western quarters of the City, where Liverpool Street, Blackfriars, Cannon Street, and Ludgate Hill stations were all located, leaving only Fenchurch Street station in the east; and the many large hotels and ex-coaching inns in the west and centre were heavily used by sojourners from the provinces

[35] Some of the ostentatiously handsome office buildings which had just gone up are illustrated in Summerson, 'The Victorian Rebuilding of the City of London'.

[36] *Census, 1861*, i. 204, ii. 21–9, Table 11; Jones, *Outcast London*, pp. 161, 231–2.

[37] See Table 4 in ch. 3.

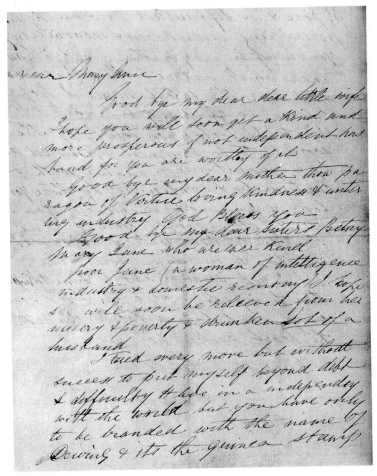

Fig. 3 A suicide note written near Paternoster Row on 13 June 1861: George Dewing's farewell to his 'dear dear little wife'

and abroad (who were always apt to include more than their fair share of suicides).[38] In the eastern fringes, moreover, accident cases were probably removed over the City boundary to the nearby London Hospital in Whitechapel Road, whereas Bart's Hospital in the north-

[38] Staying at a hotel in the City was a normal holiday or business practice until 1914, as is well brought out in Howgego, *The Victorian and Edwardian City of London* (not paginated).

west corner of the City certainly attracted accident cases from far afield, as it had done for centuries. Indeed, the presence of this great hospital is probably the chief key to the western part of the City's spectacular suicide rates, just as it is to its general mortality rate of double the metropolitan average. All things considered, it is no surprise that in 1861 only two of Payne's City verdicts of suicide were recorded in the east, nor that in the whole decade 1861–70 only twenty-two suicide verdicts were recorded in the east out of a total for the City of

154.[39] Accordingly, to investigate the experience of suicide in the mid-Victorian City through its coroner's eyes is to concentrate upon its central and western districts.

A bankrupt thirty-nine year old printer of Bath Street, near Paternoster Row, George Dewing, may aptly stand as the representative of those who committed suicide in the City in 1861, and unlike Charlie Sudds of Southwark, he can speak for himself, for he left a long letter addressed to his wife (see Fig. 3). 'Good bye my dear dear little wife', he wrote to Mary Anne in their bedroom on Monday morning, 13 June 1861, 'I hope you will soon get a kind and more prosperous if not independent husband for you are worthy of it.' He went on:

Good bye my dear mother thou paragon of virtue loving kindness and untiring industry God bless you. Good bye my dear sisters Betsey Mary Jane who are ever kind. Poor Jane (a woman of intelligence industry and domestic economy) I hope she will soon be relieved from her misery and poverty and drunken sot of a husband. I tried every move but without success to put myself beyond debt and difficulty and live in an independcy [sic] with the world but you have only to be branded with the name of Dewing and its the guinea stamp to be poor and in difficulties however Vigilant, persevering industrious & economising you may be. My father grandfathers uncle aunts sisters brothers [sic] cousins &c that bear the fated name I hope I leave no offspring behind to inherit it, to be look [sic] upon coldly by the world to be shunned and frowned at by acquaintance and treated with a contumely and contempt by those you love and respect all because you are poor and fates against you.

He continued to cover his double sheet of writing paper in his spidery hand: 'I leave these continued losses and Crosses it may hap to encounter some other but I had some years of them and kept them to myself in hope the times woud [sic] change but hope differd [sic] makes the heart sick no more.' And he ended: 'farewell farewell George.' Later that morning his wife found him unconscious in his armchair with this letter beside him (it is now tear-stained); and five days later she told the jury that although he was in good health, apart from bronchitis, he had taken cyanide of potassium because 'the embarrassment in his affairs' had caused him to be 'very despondent'.[40]

The first way in which George Dewing was representative of those who died from suicide in the City was in being still comparatively young. In 1861 almost 54 per cent of these particular unfortunates were under the age of forty-five, as against only 44 per cent of their

---

[39] *Registrar-General's 35th AR, Supplement*, pp. 120–1.
[40] CLRO, CR, City, 18 June 1861, inquest no. 106, George Dewing.

counterparts in the Borough of Southwark and 39 per cent of suicides in the whole of England and Wales.[41] He was typical too in the matter of socio-economic class. In the City, those who took their own lives tended to be lower middle-class people (at least a fifth of them had servants), or, less often, semi-skilled workers: characteristically they were master tradesmen, wholesalers, or retailers, or perhaps clerks or commercial travellers. This dissimilarity from Southwark's suicides was not simply the corollary of the City's very dissimilar social and economic structure, for it is not only skilled industrial employees who are (naturally enough) missing from the City's suicides, but also unskilled manual labourers, whom the City possessed in similar abundance to Southwark, in the shape of messengers, porters, and the like. Again, Dewing was typical in having had good health, apart from the bronchitic 'fits' which even at the inquest could not be made into much. In the City ill-health played a smaller role as a preliminary to suicide than in any of the other areas for which evidence is to hand; and when it was significant, it less often took bodily than mental shape—an unusual state of affairs. Finally Dewing was typical not only of the City, but of all the other areas which have been studied, in that he was living amidst a network of relations—his farewell letter apostrophizes a whole tribe of Dewings. It is true—and not surprising—that in the central district of the City a few of the people who destroyed themselves (three out of the total number of twenty-four) were merely travellers passing through; but of the rest, all but two or three were living in the midst of relatives, and all but one were apparently doing so with no great strain. (The one exception was a thirty-one year old greengrocer, who hung himself in his loft near Printing House Square when he could endure no longer his wife's unending accusations that he was 'carrying on with the servant girl'.)[42] Here, family tensions were as little important as the setbacks of young love; and among men, family bereavements did not prompt suicidal disorientation until extreme old age.

So far as the demographic, socio-economic, and domestic profile of suicide in the City is concerned, George Dewing is thus altogether representative. He is not so, however, in the thoughts and feelings which led him to end his life. This may seem surprising, since few literary stereotypes of Victorian suicide are more familiar than that of the business man driven to suicide by financial embarrassments; yet

---

[41] *Registrar-General's 24th AR*, pp. 120–1.
[42] CLRO, CR, City, 20 Feb. 1861, inquest no. 42, William Pares Lee.

the truth is that for no one else in the City in 1861 were business difficulties or unemployment the trigger of self-destruction. For two people, it is true, work had provided opportunities for pilfering which ended in a day of reckoning; but what they could not face apparently was disgrace, not—or not yet—material hardship.[43] Certainly the seasonal fluctuations in trade and employment which so often precipitated suicide in industrial Southwark did not loom large among those who destroyed themselves during the same months on the other side of the river. The main high road to suicide in the City was neither the road George Dewing travelled, nor the one Charlie Sudds found himself upon: it was alcoholism. In the City, although heavy drinking was often associated with difficulties at work or separation from a spouse, again and again the latter seem to have been the consequence of the former, and not the reverse. Perhaps this is not difficult to understand. Some of these cases suggest that in an economic structure like that of the City, where contacts and organized good fellowship were particularly important,[44] drinking habits were more likely to become ingrained; others, that part of the explanation is that so many of the City's inhabitants worked in inns and eating houses,[45] work which was later repeatedly shown to be especially associated with both alcoholism and suicide; while yet others suggest a link with living in the most grossly overcrowded areas, especially where the women were concerned.[46] The range of individual circumstances is too wide for dogmatic generalization, however. All that can be said categorically, is that in 1861 nearly half of the City's suicides were notoriously heavy drinkers (as against just over a quarter in Southwark); and that it is in the City that the link between suicide and alcoholism seems strongest in mid-Victorian London.

What of the final experience of suicidal death? The Thames was certainly not the City's road to suicide, any more than it was Southwark's. In so far as the City had its own peculiar method, it was to jump from a height—not surprisingly, given its tall buildings, and that

[43] Ibid., 12 Feb. 1861, inquest no. 37, Thomas Frakes; 24 Jan. 1861, inquest no. 18, Ellen Webb.

[44] Cf. the Fellowship form of organization among City porters and the nineteenth-century role of dinners and public houses in this: Stern, *The Porters of London*, pp. 198, 211–12, 251, 287.

[45] For example, CLRO, CR, City, 15 Jan. 1861, inquest no. 13, Francis Richard Holden; and 28 Aug. 1861, inquest no. 139, Thomas Henry Rennick.

[46] Ibid., 20 Dec. 1861, inquest no. 196, Ann Ridgway of 18 Shoe Lane, Farringdon Without; and 24 Dec. 1861, inquest no. 197, Priscilla Munro of 17 Thavies Inn, Holborn Hill.

its two most far-famed suicide spots were the Monument and the iron gallery at St Paul's. (Dewing was unusual in using poison; but then, his was one of the few City occupations which involved familiarity with chemicals.) Hanging, however, was the method which just over half these men used, most often from a bedpost, sometimes from banisters, or from the pipes of a water-closet; and since hanging was usually swift and sure, this may help to explain why only comparatively few of them died slowly, and in hospital.

As for the feminine experience of suicide in the City, it offers few surprises. Here, women suicides were outnumbered by men rather less heavily than in Southwark (the ratio was 2.4 to one instead of three), but here as elsewhere their social class was rather lower than that of their male counterparts: only one of them was married to a man in that class of small employers and non-manual workers which produced so many of the City's male suicides. All were wives or widows, except the eighteen year old Ellen Webb, whose story has already been told;[47] and it was Ellen Webb, predictably enough in view of her age and sex, who provided the only case of suicide by drowning recorded in the City in this year. There were no prostitutes in this group; the City was not an area for either brothels or street-walking. All these women lived in the midst of relatives, and their dealings with their families were rarely represented as unhappy. Only one, Ann Ridgway, had had constant fights with her jobbing lighterman husband, before she finally hung herself in the kitchen of the overcrowded house in Shoe Lane where they lived with their seven children; and she was a heavy drinker.

In the City as elsewhere, heavy drinking and 'nerves' were thus the two clear paths to suicide for women, and here, as elsewhere, the latter was the special lot of women in their fifties. A wife whose lethargic brooding over the death of a daughter ten years before ended in her taking oxalic acid; a widow whose perpetual worry lest she should be a burden to her postman son ended in her cutting her throat:[48] women like these had their counterparts in Southwark, as had the drunkard Ann Ridgway. One woman's story, however, shows how these two well-trodden feminine paths to suicide could sometimes intersect. At the end of 1860 a fifty year old domestic servant in Edinburgh married a widower who had two teenage children. They came to London, and lodged in one of the most overcrowded and dubious quarters of

---

[47] See ch. 2.
[48] CLRO, CR, City, 20 Ap. 1861, inquest no. 73, Mary Whitney; 20 Aug. 1861, inquest no. 134, Harriet Knights.

Holborn, Hatton Wall. The husband, David Scrymgeour, worked as a currier, the boy went to school, and the girl out to service. Agnes Scrymgeour was not in need—'he used to give her sixteen shillings a week and paid the rent besides'—but she grew very miserable, and begged him to send her home to Scotland. This dour man would not quarrel with her; but he would not speak to her either. After six months of constant drinking, which she paid for by pawning her husband's things, she told a fellow lodger that 'she felt as if she could kill herself'. When her husband in due course found her with a laudanum bottle beside her, he still said nothing, but gave her an emetic and took her to Bart's. There she died, still wishing to go back to her mother two miles outside Edinburgh, and leaving her husband to offer the jury an interpretation of her action which was as coldly moralistic as it was shallow: 'I think she was ashamed of herself.'[49]

To turn to Westminster is to encounter yet another distinctive mid-Victorian experience of dying by suicide. Charles St Clare Bedford's District, with very roughly a quarter of a million inhabitants, was rather bigger than both of Payne's put together.[50] It covered the whole gamut of poverty and wealth, running as it did from the crowded alleys of Soho and the Strand (where there was a density of 249 persons to an acre in 1861), through the much more mixed parishes of St Martin's in the Fields and St James's Piccadilly to the fashionable purlieus of Mayfair, as well as the new residential estates in Pimlico and Belgravia, and the office developments which had just begun to push out working families and small shopkeepers from Westminster.[51] At one extreme was the registration district of St George's Hanover Square, where the average annual death rate in the 1860s was only 88 per cent of the metropolitan average, where there were no more than seventy-five men to every hundred women, and 23 per cent of these were girls aged between fifteen and twenty-four; where 60 per cent of all the occupied women and 14 per cent of all the occupied men over twenty were domestic servants and where (not surprisingly, in view of these large numbers of domestic servants) over half the inhabitants had been born outside London. At the other extreme was the district of St Margaret's and St John's Westminster, where many of London's

---

[49] Ibid., 28 Feb. 1861, inquest no. 46, Agnes Scrymgeour.
[50] This estimate of population is necessarily a rough surmise, since only the boundaries of the jurisdiction of the coroner of the City of London coincided with a census area.
[51] Hollingshead, *Ragged London*, pp. 102–5.

working poor still huddled in the Lanes and 'Rents' behind the newly constructed thoroughfare of Victoria Street. There, the average annual death rate was over 108 per cent above the metropolitan average; men were only narrowly outnumbered by women, and the female population certainly did not include armies of young girls up from the country to work in domestic service, for only 29.6 per cent of occupied women and only 3.2 per cent of occupied men over twenty were domestic servants, and most of the inhabitants had been born in London.[52] (The slums of central London, it should be remembered, were always 'settlement tanks for submerged Londoners', not for immigrants.)[53]

Demographic and socio-ecological differences like these might be expected to be reflected in different scales of suicide. Yet this was not so. The suicide rates of all three of the registration districts which lay substantially within St Clare Bedford's jurisdiction fell within the upper quartile of metropolitan suicide rates, with St George's Hanover Square recording the highest male, and the amalgamated district of St James, St Martin's, and the Strand, the highest female rate of the three. (See Maps 4 and 5.) On the other hand, there were differences in the age incidence of registered suicide which seem notable. In the seventy-six cases registered in 1861–70 in the district of St George's Hanover Square, it was among men under forty-five that suicide rates were most heavily in excess of the metropolitan average, whereas in the fifty-seven cases registered in the still partly industrial areas of St Margaret's and St John's, this excess was concentrated among men aged between fifty-five and seventy-four.[54] Are there traces here of the contrast already noted in the provinces between the pattern of suicide in non-industrial urban areas, where abnormally high rates were often recorded among young people, and the pattern characteristic of industrial areas, where suicide rates often rose sharply among men over the age of fifty-five?[55] The female figures are too small to deserve much analysis; it is worth noticing, however, that in St George's Hanover Square, only two cases of suicide were recorded between 1861 and 1870 among its 11,678 girls aged between fifteen and twenty-four, many of whom were servant girls up from the country, whereas in St Margaret's and St John's, a quarter still full of working-class families,[56] five cases of

---

[52] *Registrar-General's 35th AR, Supplement*, pp. clxv, 26–9; *Census, 1861*, ii. 21–34, Tables 11 and 12; Jones, *Outcast London*, p. 139, Table.

[53] Dyos, 'The Slums of Victorian London', pp. 29–30.

[54] *Registrar-General's 35th AR, Supplement*, pp. 26–9.

[55] See above ch. 2 and Table 1.1

[56] This was one of the areas investigated in 1840 by a working committee of the

suicide were recorded among half this number of girls. Perhaps this is another hint that the state of affairs already noted in the provinces existed within London itself, and that there too a less confined, more anonymous big-city environment had advantages for girls.[57]

But how far did local topography affect these statistics? There were still no railway stations in this district (Victoria was still being built and Charing Cross was not opened until 1864), and St George's Knightsbridge was the only hospital of any size (Westminster, Charing Cross, and King's College Hospitals were then all quite small). On the other hand, St Clare Bedford's jurisdiction included the largest barracks in the capital (and soldiers were always notoriously prone to suicide),[58] and many acres of those accustomed resorts of the desperate, the royal parks. (The Serpentine in Hyde Park was so notorious a suicide spot that the Royal Humane Society had employed boatmen to keep watch and maintained a 'receiving station' there since the late eighteenth century.) As for Waterloo and Westminster Bridges and the Adelphi Arches, they were so regularly depicted in mid-Victorian literary and artistic stereotypes as the final bourne of women in distress that it is surprising not that the Strand was the section of this jurisdiction with the highest female suicide rate, but rather that there were not far more female deaths by suicide registered there.[59]

To pass from the City of London to the City of Westminster had been for many centuries to cross a frontier which was not a purely conventional one; and to study St Clare Bedford's inquest papers is to realize that this was as true of suicide as of more public matters. 'The Season' made the weather in Westminster, and not only for such workers as tailors, dressmakers, and high-class furniture makers, but for all the many men and women who lived by providing personal services for the nobility and gentry.[60] Four-fifths of those who committed suicide in Westminster in 1861 worked in the tertiary sector of the economy, providing services of one kind or another, as compared with just over half in the City and less than a quarter in Southwark.

London Statistical Society: 'Report on the state of the working classes in the parishes of St Margaret and St John, Westminster', *Jnl.* [*Roy.*] *Stat. Soc.*, iii (1840), pp. 14–24.

[57] See ch. 2 and Table 1.2.

[58] *Census, 1861*, i. 216, ii. 21.

[59] As will be seen from Map 3, the immediate area of the Adelphi Arches fell within the jurisdiction of the coroner for the Duchy of Lancaster Liberty (Savoy), not the coroner for Westminster. On the Serpentine, see ch. 10 n. 36.

[60] *Census, 1861*, ii. 21–34, Tables 11 and 12; Hall, *The Industries of London since 1861*, p. 28.

A 'gentleman's gentleman' thus aptly represents the experience of suicide there.

Just before midnight on Friday, 26 July 1861, towards the end of the Season, James Mason, the valet of Lord Ashburton, the Peelite politician,[61] was standing in his master's town house in Piccadilly (Bath House, pulled down in 1960), when his employer's Groom of the Chamber handed him a note. He read it by the gaslight in the hall and 'rushed upstairs very fast indeed, without a candle'. In the morning the housemaid who went to make his bed found his door locked. When she found it still locked at four o'clock in the afternoon, a carpenter, a locksmith, and a policeman from St James's Park were all called in. They forced the door open, and saw the forty-five year old valet hanging from his bedpost by his own scarf, dressed only in his day shirt. In the room were a few jottings about horse-racing, coins to the value of £1. 6s. 6d., and a letter to his brother in Newbury in Berkshire telling him that he was probably about to be dismissed; but the disturbing note he had been given the previous night was missing, and so was his gold watch. Here was a tale of mystery and drama in an aristocratic household, and the local newspaper's racy crime reporter did it full justice.[62] At the inquest, however, the evidence needed careful summing up, for three possible explanations emerged. The first and obvious one, that Mason had placed some disastrous bets, became less convincing when the publican in Shepherd's Market who had handled his betting flatly denied that Mason had been betting at all heavily. Perhaps then his dismissal was the crucial factor? Here the key witness was Lord Ashburton's surgeon, James Rice.[63] He revealed that although Lord Ashburton had been regretfully obliged to give Mason notice to leave on 5 August, owing to his growing habit of drinking, he had already settled an annuity of £20 a year on him in 1857, when he completed twenty-one years in his service. Mason would therefore have had something 'to tide him over'. The surgeon implied a third explanation: he described Mason as 'a peculiar silent man'. Lord Ashburton's Groom of the Chamber and Mason's betting agent agreed that he had often been 'very excited', 'very nervous', 'very reserved', and was altogether just the sort of peculiar person who might be

---

[61] William Bingham Baring, 2nd Baron Ashburton (1799–1864: *DNB*), Secretary to the Board of Control, 1841–5, Paymaster-General of the Forces, 1845–6.

[62] 'Suicide of Lord Ashburton's Valet', *West Middlesex Advertiser*, 3 Aug. 1861, p. 3.

[63] The *Medical Directory*, shows that Rice (who was MB (Lond.), MRCS, and LSA) had trained at King's College Hospital and was at this time Surgeon to the Westminster Dispensary in Broadway and living off Langham Place.

expected to commit suicide. After a brief consultation, the jury agreed to return the usual verdict of temporary insanity.[64]

The case was novelettish; yet it brings out accurately enough some of the characteristic flavour of suicide in Westminster at this time. Like many others who ended their lives there, Mason was not London born; he was no longer young (although at forty-five he was rather below the average age of male suicide in Westminster, which was close to fifty); and he was not a family man (the proportion of Westminster suicides living with relations was not so high as in the other districts studied, although still in the region of two-thirds). He was a service worker, and a skilled one at that, as were about half of Westminster's suicides (who included such lower middle-class figures as a commercial traveller and a printer's clerk and, higher in the social scale, a former Army captain).[65] Only in the matter of health was Mason rather unrepresentative; for to judge from St Clare Bedford's rather scanty medical notes, bodily and mental illness loomed larger in Westminster than elsewhere (although this was perhaps simply because in 1861 those who destroyed themselves tended to be older there than in the other districts studied). Six men had some illness or disability, although of a chronic rather than acute kind; two had recently been discharged from a lunatic asylum; and three more had made previous attempts or threats to kill themselves. (One of these last, however, was not so much disturbed as outrageously spoilt—Samuel Walton, the only child of doting elderly parents, who had never been denied anything by his comfortably off hairdresser father, a vestryman of St George's, until at the age of twenty he demanded to be set up with £100 a year so that he could take a Lambeth prostitute to wife.)[66]

Does this suggest that in Westminster bodily illness and psychiatric disturbance were most likely to carry someone to suicide? It is true that in a broad sense ill-health dominated these people's lives just before they ended them quite as frequently as did heavy drinking; and equally true that drinking was far less prominent in Westminster than

[64] Westminster Abbey Muniments, CI, 31 July 1861, inquest no. 69, James Mason.

[65] Ibid., 11 Mar. 1861, inquest no. 83, John Cox, and 5 June 1861, inquest no. 22, George Ball Stokes. An inquest 'held by Mr St Clare Bedford on Mr Charles Benjamin Blade, formerly an officer in the Army, at his residence in Cumberland Street, St George's Hanover Square on 26 October 1861' was reported in the *South London Chronicle*, 2 Nov. 1861, p. 7. I have found no notes of this inquest, however, among St Clare Bedford's papers.

[66] Westminster Abbey Muniments, CI, 13 Nov. 1861, inquest no. 19, Samuel George Walton; 'Melancholy Case of Love and Suicide at Pimlico', *West Middlesex Advertiser*, 16 Nov. 1861, p. 3.

in the City, while unemployment and economic worries were much less salient than in Southwark. What really characterizes this group of suicides in Westminster, though, is the role played by emotional loss, among men as well as women. It seems fair to say that the triple linkage which appears and reappears in different proportions in every district studied—between heavy drinking, difficulties connected with work, and ill-health—became in Westminster a fourfold one, in which emotional loss played a greater part than difficulties connected with work, although a smaller one than ill-health. Mason was thus quite typical in the combination of factors which led him to suicide, since dismissal must have portended for him not only financial loss, but some loss of identity as well. The evidence given at the inquest suggests that he took his own life, not directly because he had been drinking heavily (although he had indeed increasingly been turning to drink), nor because of financial worries alone (although he certainly had these), but because of the disturbing effect upon his introverted and moody personality of the imminent loss of his important position within the nobleman's 'family' which had been his world throughout his adult life.

As for the actual experience of dying by suicide, in Westminster as nearly everywhere else, this meant more often than not the experience of hanging. Sometimes, as for Mason, there was no very convenient bracket to hand: he must have clasped his hands over his knees to prevent them reaching the bed, for the height of his bedrail from the mattress was only just over 3 feet. Drowning was not common here, despite the nearness of the Thames, and in this non-industrial area poison was rarely employed, although young Samuel Walton drank cyanide of potassium from the photographic equipment his indulgent father had given him. Cut-throat razors were used much more often than in the City or Southwark; and death seems to have come quickly more often than in either of those two districts. Here, as elsewhere, those who found an ominous locked door or an apparently dead or dying relative, sent for the usual trio of a neighbour, a policeman, and a local surgeon; but only on three occasions was the casualty then moved to hospital. In 1861 Westminster's hospitals did not serve as collecting points for suicide cases for miles around, as did the three really big London hospitals, Bart's, Guy's, and St Thomas's. On the other hand Westminster, equally with the City, provides an early example of the trend towards the use of local government buildings for coroners' inquests.[67] St Clare Bedford had long considered 'the

[67] See ch. 1 n. 69.

holding of inquests in obscure public houses most objectionable',[68] and in 1861 less than a third of the Westminster inquests which ended in suicide verdicts were held in taverns. It was in the board room at the Mount Street workhouse (alias the vestry room of St George's Hanover Square) that the socially very mixed juries of this district very often gathered, with gentlemen sitting side by side with clothes-dealers and their like. (This was where Mason's body was taken and the inquest upon it held.)

What of the women who took their own lives in Westminster? In 1861 the ratio of male to female suicide was higher there than in either Southwark or the City, and only four deaths by suicide among women were recorded by St Clare Bedford in that year. Once again, however, these four fall into the two familiar categories, for three of them were deeply distressed older women, while the fourth was a drunken young harridan. Not one was a seduced young girl up from the country, despite the large numbers of girls in service thereabouts. The three older women concerned had all had some fairly recent bereavement, but all were living with relatives. One was clearly suffering from more than the natural depression of mourning; for to a married woman of fifty-seven, the deaths of her parents should hardly have seemed 'losses she could not bear up against'.[69] The fourth woman of the group, Eleanor Horner, was a prostitute from the notorious area of Cornwall Road in Lambeth, near 'Whoreterloo'. She had probably expected to be rescued when she rolled herself over the parapet of Waterloo Bridge after a policeman broke up her Saturday night fight with her landlady; but she was not, and her body was carried up river to Westminster. Eleanor Horner was precisely the sort of woman whose attempts at

[68] Middlesex Justices of the Peace, *Report of the Special Committee appointed at the Michaelmas Session, 1850*, p. 48, letter of Charles St Clare Bedford to Thomas Turner.

[69] Westminster Abbey Muniments, CI, 15 Mar. 1861, inquest on Ann Elizabeth Goudge. After she had been rescued from the Serpentine by a policeman who had been fetched, Mrs Goudge was taken to the Royal Humane Society's 'Receiving House' and put into a warm bath for three-quarters of an hour, and then taken to St George's Hospital, Knightsbridge, where she died. Charles Hunter, a young ex-House Surgeon at St George's, tried to use the inquest to support his publicization of the medical case against the hot-bath treatment of the drowned and in favour of the new 'Ready Method', that is, the system of artificial respiration recently devised by Marshall Hall (1790–1857: *DNB*), the discoverer of reflex action. He briefed St Clare Bedford with a list of questions to ask J. S Christian, the Medical Officer of the Royal Humane Society (who still clung to the old method), and the Medical Officer of St George's Hospital; and the medical evidence is indeed extremely full on this important and then controversial issue. (St Thomas's Hospital, unlike St George's, was then still using the bath: CLRO, CR, Southwark, 18 Feb. 1861, inquest no. 49, Henry Edwards.) See also ch. 10 n. 37.

suicide the *Daily Telegraph* was at this time urging its readers not to waste their charity upon: women who threw themselves into the river in a tipsy brawl when they saw someone was at hand to fish them out quickly.[70] She certainly provides a much more realistic illustration of the women who threw themselves off 'the Bridge of Sighs' than does the romantic visual and literary image of the day, for these women were indeed often prostitutes from the red-light area of the south bank, and when prostitutes attempted suicide, it was not remorse but drunkenness which was usually the precipitant. 'I shall soon get D.T.', Lushing Loo had told Henry Mayhew not long before, 'and then I'll kill myself in a fit of madness.'[71]

As it happened, it was in Westminster that the third of the mid-Victorian London coroners whose inquest papers have survived, Edwin Lankester, lived and carried out his modestly paid duties as Medical Officer of St James's.[72] After his election in July 1862 as coroner for Central Middlesex, Lankester found himself regularly driving north-wards from his house in Savile Row to hold around twenty inquests a week in that sprawling, wedge-shaped jurisdiction—a jurisdiction which was far larger than that of Westminster, containing as it did close to a million people, and stretching from Westminster's northern boundary of Oxford Street as far as rural South Mimms (although the parishes falling outside the metropolitan registration division will be disregarded here). A bird's eye view of Central Middlesex would have shown an artisan and middle-class area, which had comparatively few semi-skilled or wholly unskilled male labourers and few female sweated workers, but often many domestic servants, and thus resembled the western much more than the eastern or southern districts of London.[73] Seen at close quarters, however, Lankester's jurisdiction falls into four distinct parts, each with its own demographic, socio-economic, and

[70] Westminster Abbey Muniments, CI, 17 July 1861, inquest no. 48, Eleanor Horner; *Daily Telegraph*, 31 Aug. 1860, p. 4.
[71] Mayhew, *London Labour and the London Poor*, iv. 224. 'Lushy' was the Cockney underworld's word for drunk: Hindley, *The True History of Tom and Jerry*, p. 186. The petty criminality and alcoholism common among ordinary prostitutes at this time is well described where those in York are concerned in Finnegan, *Poverty and Prostitution*, chs. 3 and 5.
[72] In 1866 Lankester's salary as Medical Officer of Health was £150: Stewart and Jenkins, *The Medical and Legal Aspects of Sanitary Reform*, Table 1, opposite p. 80. Lankester was always in financial difficulties after his expensive election campaign of 1862: see *DNB*.
[73] Jones, *Outcast London*, p. 389, Table 15.

occupational flavour,[74] but each making it easy to understand why in the 1870s Central Middlesex was the metropolitan district in which juries most often returned a verdict of death accelerated by privation or from starvation.[75]

The most well-to-do part was the western one, stretching from Marylebone to Paddington and Hampstead. John Hollingshead caught Lankester's Marylebone exactly when he wrote of it in 1861 that 'terraces and squares of private mansions, as much as large factories and centres of industry, attract a crowded dependent population', and went on: 'Near the stable there is generally a maze of close streets, containing a small greengrocer's, a small dairy, a quiet coachman's public house, and a number of houses let out in tenements. These shelter a large number of bricklayers, carpenters and similar labourers, with their families, and many laundresses and charwomen.'[76] Those who could not quite afford Mayfair or Belgravia settled in these terraces and villas (as did the Gazebees in Trollope's *The Small House at Allington*);[77] so that it was upper middle-class families who lived here in symbiotic relationship with the poor and attracted a tribe of young servant girls to the district. Marylebone's eastern side was very different. This was north London's superior equivalent of the squalid, dangerous red-light area in Lambeth and Southwark. Elegant, decorous brothels studded the area between Great Portland Street and Cleveland Street, and well-dressed street-walkers operated in Regent's Park and Primrose Hill.[78] Adjoining Marylebone, however, was St Pancras, and St Pancras had far fewer social pretensions. St Pancras was dominated not by service workers, but by highly skilled craftsmen—musical instrument makers, cabinet makers, and the like; and its male population was younger and much less heavily outnumbered by women. It provided a kind of skilled working-class buffer between upper middle-class Marylebone and the eastern segment of Lankester's domain, lower middle-class Islington. Islington was still essentially a dormitory suburb for 'clerks with large families and small salaries', as

---

[74] See *Registrar-General's 35th AR, Supplement*, pp. clxv, 28–33; *Census, 1861*, ii. 21–34, Tables 11 and 12.

[75] See e.g. PP 1878–9 (245) LXI, pp. 2–3. Such Returns were annual from 1871.

[76] Hollingshead, *Ragged London*, p. 143.

[77] Trollope's *The Small House at Allington* conjures up well the social nuances in the early 1860s of addresses in Mayfair, Pimlico, Bayswater, and St John's Wood. See especially ch. 40, 'Preparations for the Wedding'.

[78] Mackenzie, *Marylebone*, pp. 93–4; Mayhew, *London Labour and the London Poor*, iv. 267.

it had been in 1836 when 'Boz' sketched the morning exodus in its streets towards the City.[79] On its southern borders, however, lay the only section of the ancient industrial perimeter of the cities of London and Westminster which fell within Lankester's jurisdiction: the poor and desperately crowded districts of St Giles and Holborn, Clerkenwell, and Fagin's territory of Saffron Hill.[80] Here domestic servants were fewer than anywhere else in Lankester's area, and women preponderated far less. Here too the death rate was extremely high and the housing shortage acute. The old industries of printing, book-binding, and precision work were still followed; and attic workrooms were crammed with the people dishoused by the creation of New Oxford Street and the complex of railway lines behind Farringdon Street and King's Cross stations. It was above all in its notorious housing conditions, even more than in its demographic, occupational, or social and economic texture that this last part of Lankester's District was most unlike the rest.[81]

Once again these contrasts were not reflected in the local official suicide rates. Leaving aside the thinly populated semi-rural district of Hampstead, all five of the registration districts which fell wholly or mainly within Lankester's jurisdiction—Marylebone, Pancras, Islington, Holborn, and St Giles—had suicide rates below the metropolitan average,[82] with the exception of Holborn and St Pancras so far as male suicide rates were concerned (see Maps 4 and 5). Indeed, in Islington male suicide rates were low enough to fall into the bottom quartile of male suicide rates in the twenty-nine metropolitan registration districts. Thus Lankester, unlike Payne and St Clare Bedford, was working in a part of London where the overall scale of suicide tended to be rather low by metropolitan standards, although not by provincial ones. Even by metropolitan standards, however, the experience of suicide was exceptionally common here among young people, although often comparatively rare among men over the age of fifty-five; in other words, in these north London areas the age incidence of suicide

[79] Dickens, *Sketches by 'Boz'*, e.g. 'Scenes: I. The Streets—Morning' and 'Tales: XI. The Bloomsbury Christening'.

[80] Jones, *Outcast London*, pp. 140–2; Hollingshead, *Ragged London*, pp. 14–34; Greenwood, *Unsentimental Journeys*, pp. 127–8; Hall, *The Industries of London*, pp. 28, 72, 97; Bédarida, 'Londres au mileu du xixe siècle', p. 280.

[81] *Census, 1861*, ii. 21–34, Tables 11 and 12; *Registrar-General's 35th AR, Supplement*, pp. clxv, 32–3; Jones, *Outcast London*, pp. 167, 175–6, 189.

[82] Only a small part of the registration district of Paddington fell within the Central Middlesex jurisdiction. Still, its nature, and especially the presence of St Mary's Hospital there, tended to increase the load of suicide cases.

followed the pattern which seems characteristic of non-industrial urban neighbourhoods, and not that typical of either rural or industrial ones.

Yet, it would be a mistake (as always) to attach too much significance to these local suicide figures without considering the topographical factors which may have helped to shape them. Lankester's domain contained a string of railway termini, running from Farringdon Street in the east to Paddington in the west, but no really large hospitals to distort the mortality pattern: even the largest north London hospital, the Middlesex, had only 259 patients in 1861. The institutions which potentially most affected the suicide side of his work were quite different: barracks and workhouses. Marylebone and St Pancras housed a concentration of soldiers (always prone to suicide) second only to that in Westminster,[83] and contained London's two largest workhouses,[84] whose 2,686 inmates were often ailing and feeble-minded and thus above-average suicide risks; and St Pancras work-house was particularly heavily used in 1861 as a mortuary by the police. Much more important, however, was the exceptional abundance of parks and open spaces. Hampstead Heath (a traditional resort for those intent on violent death by shooting, whose deep ponds on its Highgate side were easily accessible from the newly built-up areas of north London), Regent's Park, Primrose Hill, the northern fringe of Hyde Park, and Kensington Gardens—all these brought work to Lankester, the more so since all these places, except the Heath, were favourite resorts for prostitutes. Lastly, and most important of all, the Regent's Canal wound across Lankester's domain, from Paddington, through Marylebone and Camden Town, to Islington.[85] The gateways to the towing path were never locked, and the canal inevitably acted as a magnet for those bent on suicide—particularly women, to whom drowning in this canal's deep waters occurred as an obvious resort especially readily. St Mark's bridge, indeed, was an unromanticized north London 'Bridge of Sighs' in miniature, much used as it was by pedestrians, particularly prostitutes cutting through Regent's Park from Primrose Hill to Great Portland Street. With its low parapet only

---

[83] *Census, 1861*, i. 216.

[84] St Marylebone workhouse was for long the largest in the country, and in 1862 came to the end of the worst period of its history: Neate, *The St Marylebone Workhouse and Institution*, pp. 1, 18, 26.

[85] For the course of this canal, see the sketch map in Denney, *London's Waterways*, p. 57.

3 feet high, it provided a notorious temptation to impulsive suicide attempts by the young and the dissolute.[86]

Facts such as these perhaps help to explain one of the most striking points to emerge from Lankester's exceptionally full early case notes: the very high proportion of women among his suicide cases. In his first six months as coroner, the suicide verdicts Lankester's juries recorded on men outnumbered those recorded on women by only 1.6 to one—whereas in Westminster, it will be remembered, suicide verdicts on men outnumbered those on women by as many as four to one. Nor was this a mere accident; for over the whole decade 1862–71 the suicide verdicts recorded by Lankester included a higher proportion of female cases than did those recorded by Payne and St Clare Bedford.[87] To some extent, no doubt, this higher ratio simply reflected the fact that in Lankester's jurisdiction women outnumbered men slightly more than they did in St Clare Bedford's and much more than they did in Payne's; yet this hardly seems enough completely to explain the narrower gap in these north London districts between male and female familiarity with suicide. At all events, Lankester's notes, unlike the others, provide a run of suicide cases which is sufficiently evenly balanced between the sexes (with fifteen female cases and twenty-four male) to permit sustained comparison of the experience of suicide among women and among men, and to allow the feminine instead of the masculine experience of suicide to serve as the basis of analysis. A woman may thus very fittingly stand as the representative of those who took their own lives in north London in 1862.

On Monday, 1 September 1862, a porter by the name of William Lindley took precautions against subsequent charges against himself by fetching two policemen to 4 Hall Place, near Maida Vale, to act as witnesses while he opened his lodger's locked door. Inside, the three men saw the lodger, Emma Austin, and a laudanum bottle, and thereupon sent to Paddington Green for a local medical man, Dr J. S. Beale. He pronounced her dead, and her body was taken to the Paddington dead-house, where it remained until Thursday, when Lankester held an inquest upon it at the Dudley Arms public house, close by in Harrow Road. Emma Austin was not a young woman, although the

---

[86] St Mark's bridge was (and is) the boundary between St Marylebone and St Pancras; hence mere accident determined whether a case of suicide by drowning from this bridge was registered in the former or latter district. This bridge is further discussed in ch. 10.

[87] In Central Middlesex the proportion was 41 per cent, as against 33 per cent in Westminster and 35 per cent in the City and Southwark: *Judicial Statistics, 1862–1871*, Part I, Table 11.

Bayswater Chronicle's reporter so described her,[88] no doubt in an attempt to make her story as romantic as possible. She was forty-two, and was living in lodgings apart from her husband, working all day as a laundress with her landlord's wife. On Saturday afternoon she had gone out at 4.30 to get money to pay her rent from her husband, a plasterer living in Lisson Grove, but he had refused to give her any, and she had returned to her lodgings in an excited mood. Clearly there was some feeling at the inquest that Henry Austin had behaved badly, for he defended his refusal by asserting that she was a chronic drunkard and had been drunk on Saturday, and that he had been 'obliged to part with her, to save himself from being imprisoned for debt'. Mrs Lindley on the other hand insisted that Emma Austin had not been 'tipsy' either before or after she met her husband that last Saturday, and that she had only seen her 'occasionally the worse for liquor'. William Lindley kept out of this conflict of evidence, and told the jury he knew nothing of the dead woman's habits. It was agreed, however, that she had tried to make away with herself once before; and the jury's sympathy was aroused by 'a quantity of poetry' dedicated to her husband which she had left on the mantelpiece.

> The treasure I have had and lost,
>   Oh, could I but regain,
> Not for all the wealth the world might cost,
>   I would not act the same.

> My Harry to my arms once more,
>   Oh, could I have you again,
> Then to my God I would implore,
>   For happiness to remain.

> Oh Harry! is your heart so hard
>   That it can no more relent
> To the prayer of your penitent,
>   When she says she does repent?

To the jury as well as to the *Bayswater Chronicle*'s reporter these efforts at versification established that Emma Austin had been 'of a romantic tendency', and by extension, in an unsound state of mind; but it was the medical evidence which clinched the matter, for Lank-

---

[88] 'A Romantic Suicide', *Bayswater Chronicle*, 6 Sept. 1862, p. 5.

ester had ordered a post-mortem, as he routinely did, and Dr Beale reported 'that the state of the brain indicated unsoundness of mind.'[89]

Emma Austin's history illustrates the difference between the feminine and masculine experience of suicide in north London in 1862 in several ways. To begin with, she was middle-aged, not elderly. (Over half of the men in question were over the age of fifty-five, but only an eighth of the women.) Then too, she was living alone in lodgings with people who were not her relatives. (Half of the women in this sample were living alone, but only a quarter of the men.) Moreover, she was poor, and spent her days doing humble work with another unskilled worker in a backyard; and this too is typical, for these women suicides were ending lives which had been lived at a lower social and economic level than those of their male counterparts. (When those who committed suicide in north London in these six months are grouped into five socio-economic categories,[90] women greatly outnumber men in the lowest category, but in every other class the opposite is the case. Clearly it is necessary to remember that as female Chartists had been saying twenty years earlier, women always suffered more in bad times than men.)[91] Again, she was typical in that she had made a previous attempt to end her life. (Over half of the women in this sample had previously attempted or threatened suicide, but less than a third of the men—a contrast which is altogether unsurprising, since women everywhere were regarded as readier both to threaten and to attempt suicide than men, although they far more often failed in their attempts.)

Yet Emma Austin's story equally illustrates how much men and women who died by suicide shared a common experience. The current which mainly carried her to suicide was one which swept along both sexes alike: alcoholism. For both the men and the women in this sample, heavy drinking was apparently the most frequent path to suicide: 'apparently', for perhaps this factor was apt to be exaggerated at inquests, since it would exonerate the survivors from blame. At the inquest on Emma Austin the jury heard a friend minimizing her drinking habits and her alienated spouse emphasizing them, and this situation was not unusual. Even so, it seems fair to say that drink dominated the last part of the lives of over a third of these men and women; in this quarter of London, drink was the most common prelude

---

[89] GLC, Central Middlesex IR, Box 1, 4 Sept. 1862, inquest no. 142, Emma Austin.
[90] The occupations placed in each of these 5 socio-economic groups were those listed in Jones, *Outcast London*, pp. 355–6.
[91] Jones, 'Women and Chartism', p. 6.

to suicide for both sexes, and in every social class. Bodily and mental ill-health came far behind, as the second most potent precipitant of self-destruction; but with regard to this, feminine and masculine experience did differ, since organic illness was much more likely to set men on the path to suicide (after all, they were usually older), and mental illness or depression was more likely to catch up women in its net. Altogether, three-quarters both of the men and the women in this sample were either alcoholics, or sufferers from a serious organic illness, or from depression or some other mental disorder serious enough to have warranted medical attention. By comparison, economic and emotional triggers were insignificant. Yet when they did operate, they too did so in a rather different way for the two sexes. When the trigger was an economic one, for women it was not disappointed expectations or 'reduced circumstances' which proved unbearable, but sheer primary poverty—not surprisingly, since they were more often alone, shifting for themselves, and at the very bottom of the social pyramid. As for emotional shock and strain, although they were even less often the chief precipitant, women were their victims far more often than men. In north London, of the two varieties of female suicide already identified as typical, the drunken harridan predominated; but there were also some middle-aged women who brooded and fretted their way to suicide—women like Margaret O'Brien, whose son had left home seven years before and who murmured continually, 'My poor boy, what has become of him?', and Mary Cooper of Camden Town, whose long grieving for her youngest daughter's death ended in her slipping out to the canal close by.[92] Such women had few male counterparts.

Did the very last hours of these men and women tend to differ? In this respect Emma Austin illustrates what was shared rather than what was different in male and female experience, for poison was a way of dying chosen equally readily by both sexes in these districts of north London.[93] On the other hand, here as elsewhere, suicide meant drown-

---

[92] GLC, Central Middlesex IR, Box 1, 23 Aug. 1862, inquest no. 98, Margaret O'Brien, and 9 Aug. 1862, inquest no. 58, Mary Frances Cooper; *St Pancras News and Middlesex Advertiser*, 16 and 30 Aug. 1862.

[93] Although nationally the reverse was always the case, in Central Middlesex poison was still more often used than hanging in 1883–4: Westcott, *Suicide*, p. 149. The poison most often used was oxalic acid, a cheap everyday substance which became widely used for suicide from the 1820s, after some fatal accidents had led to warnings being given against confusing it with Epsom salts, so that its properties became 'familiarly known': Christison, *Treatise on Poisons*, p. 194. On suicide by poisoning, see ch. 10.

ing for very many women, whereas this was rarely the death men chose: they found it much easier to use knives and razors. (Seven of these fifteen women drowned themselves but only two of the twenty-four men concerned, although nine of the men used knives or razors.) Again, none of these women died in hospital, for most of them were already dead when they were found; whereas the more adventurous methods which tended to be used by men meant that three of this particular sample were taken there, one to University College Hospital, one to St Mary's, and one to the Royal Free.[94]

The masculine and feminine experiences of suicide were thus not identical. Quite apart from these differences at the moment of death itself, the demographic, socio-economic, and medical profile of those who died in this way was not the same for each sex. Clearly a different sort of person was a high suicide risk among women and among men. Yet it would be wrong to ignore how similar were the actual triggers of suicidal behaviour for both sexes. Drink and what went with it— money troubles, family tensions, and physical decay—was the great common denominator; and although the two other main pre-cipitants—illness, and troubles associated with work—did reflect differences in the bodily make-up of the two sexes and in their social and economic roles, these were differences of form rather than sub-stance.

Work, that great shaper of human lives, shaped the suicidal experi-ence of women as well as men, although its influence was less manifest when that work was domestic work done inside a family's own living quarters. Indeed, one reason why women who committed suicide tended to come from a lower social class than men may have been that only solitary women in the lowest social groups were fully exposed to the troubles associated with employment or the lack of it. Nearly half of these north London women had been supporting themselves, and to a greater or lesser extent their work patterned the way in which they died as well as the way in which they lived. For example, two female street-sellers from the slums of Clerkenwell and Holborn— tough, eccentric, independent old women, who were used to drinking hard and living rough—chose to make away with themselves when the cold weather began and they could not get a living, rather than

[94] GLC, Central Middlesex IR, Box 1, 26 Aug. 1862, inquest no. 105, William Henry Wilson; 24 Sept. 1862, inquest no. 176, Charles Pritchard; 7 and 10 Nov. 1862, inquest no. 10, Herman Nitche; *St. Pancras News*, 23 Aug. 1862 (the hospital to which Wilson was taken is erroneously reported as the Middlesex); 'Distressing Suicide in Kensington Gardens', *Bayswater Chronicle*, 27 Sept. 1862, p. 4.

put up with the four walls and sobriety of the workhouse.[95] A pair of prostitutes from the red-light area around Great Portland Street provide an instructive comparison. One, a brawling, drinking, machine-worker from Lincolnshire who had worked for seven or eight years as a prostitute, and whose head had already been badly cut, jumped tipsily over St Mark's bridge at midnight after two potential customers had robbed her of her earnings and she had failed to rob a third in her turn; the other, a refined Belgian courtesan whose employer had civilly given her to understand that he no longer needed her services as the French-speaking 'housekeeper' of his discreet Newman Street brothel when the International Exhibition closed in December 1862 and her foreign 'visitors' departed, quietly poisoned herself with the essence of almonds she was using to perfume a pomade.[96] Both the moment and the manner of the deaths of women like these, as well as their latent susceptibility to suicide, were more strongly patterned by their occupations than were the deaths of any of the men in this sample, not excepting the masterful John Ballard, a teetotal lecturer who had taught himself Greek and Hebrew and 'other sciences', but lost his job as one of Cubitt's élite corps of foremen through his 'unyielding temper'. (He contracted with the War Office to repair bedsteads used in the Crimea, but hung himself in his own loft off the Caledonian Road when some of his repairs were rejected as below standard: 'he never could bear failure.')[97]

One final point deserves to be briefly made. For men and women alike the reality of dying by suicide was very different from the familiar literary and artistic stereotypes. No more often than their male counterparts did women destroy themselves on the mere impulse of the moment. Jealousy, passion, unrequited love, and distress over false charges and misunderstandings were motives which emerged at these inquests as rarely for them as for men, and illegitimate pregnancy and detected adultery figure in these cases not at all. Taken as a whole, the differences between the two sexes' experience of suicidal death were

[95] GLC, Central Middlesex IR, Box 1, 16 Oct. 1862, inquest no. 37, Ann Bush; 6 Nov. 1862, inquest no. 100, Mary Brown. During the fine months, such women commonly tramped the country or went off to work in market gardens: Mayhew, *London Labour and the London Poor*, i. 516–17.

[96] GLC, Central Middlesex IR, Box 2, 13 Dec. 1862, inquest no. 114, Naomi Bailey, and 8 Dec. 1862, inquest no. 98, Constance Van den Alleele; *St Pancras News*, 20 Dec. 1862; *Marylebone Mercury*, 13 Dec. 1862, p. 2.

[97] GLC, Central Middlesex IR, Box 1, 1 Nov. 1862, inquest no. 87, John Ballard; *St. Pancras News*, 8 Nov. 1862. Ballard had earned the large sum of £200 a year as a Cubitt foreman. On this élite corps, see Hobhouse, *Thomas Cubitt*, pp. 263, 292–3.

by no means all-embracing, and related less to final circumstances and precipitating motives (as romantic folk-lore and suicidology held), than to the early beginnings of their journey on the road to suicide and the ultimate manner of their self-destruction.

Each of these mid-Victorian London coroners encountered a distinctive experience of suicide, as he held his inquests in his own enclave. Charlie Sudds's ending was part and parcel of life as it was lived in industrial Southwark, just as James Mason's ending was part and parcel of life in Mayfair, and George Dewing's of life in Newgate; and if in north London the relationship between environment in the widest sense and a particular experience of suicide is less clear-cut, this is simply because this relationship was necessarily a very variegated one in that sprawling jurisdiction. Yet it would be misleading to end upon this note, and emphasize only the local and the particular in the experience of suicide within mid-Victorian London. After all, however much the circumstances typical of their suicide cases were apt to differ, these three coroners saw and heard much that was broadly similar. Payne, St Clare Bedford, and Lankester would surely have united, for example, to disparage most of the current notions about the kind of person who committed suicide, and to emphasize how rarely these were seduced girls, frustrated young men, the poorest of the poor, or solitary wanderers alone in the great city. Equally, they would probably all have emphasized how confused were most of those who ended their own lives at the moment when they did what proved to be the fatal action, and how rarely they were both completely sober and in good health. It is likely that they would have presented drink as the great road to suicidal death for women as well as men, and that they would all three have dismissed as more or less insignificant ennui, romantic despair, and utter destitution, as well as those two other traditional leitmotifs, religious mania and fear of arrest at the hand of the law. They would have recognized that 'the river of death' with its 'Bridge of Sighs' accounted for very little of their work, and that it was the improvised cord, the bedroom razor, and the familiar poison bottle with which they and the big hospitals in their patch chiefly had to contend. Above all, they would surely have agreed that the experience of dying by suicide revealed month after month at their inquests was often a humdrum one, and as sordid as it was sad.

5

Another Place, Another Time:
The Rape of Hastings,
1859–66,
and London in 1911

How far was the experience of suicide encountered in mid-Victorian London a peculiar one, compared with that encountered in other places, or other times? To answer this question in terms of place needs substantial runs of provincial inquest papers, and these are apparently not forthcoming for any urban or industrial area.[1] For one rural district, however—the Rape of Hastings in east Sussex—a run of papers has recently become available which covers the years 1859–66 and yields as many as thirty-four suicide verdicts.[2] Thanks to these papers it is possible systematically to compare experiences of dying by suicide in London and in an altogether different kind of place during the same mid-Victorian years.

The coronatorial jurisdiction of the Rape of Hastings was a solidly rural one, with the little market town of Battle at its centre (see Map

---

[1] The inquest papers of the coroner for the manor of Prescot for 1851–9 have been deposited in the Lancashire Record Office, but contain only 3 suicide verdicts. Those for the Liberty of the borough and manor of Hungerford are in the Berkshire Record Office, but contain only 2 suicide verdicts for the whole period 1841–77. A substantial set of inquest papers for the Hertford District is in the Hertfordshire Record Office, but these relate to the years 1870–85. I have not succeeded in discovering any other case papers of this sort (as opposed to registers and inquisitions) for these years which relate to such places.

[2] These valuable papers, recently deposited in the East Sussex Record Office by the Battle firm of solicitors, Sheppard & Son, contain not only the inquest papers for 1859-66 of N. P. Kell and his deputy and successor Charles Sheppard (briefly described below in Appendix II), but also Kell's inquisitions for 1848–9, some bundles of newspaper cuttings, returns of fees submitted to quarter sessions in 1838–42 and 1860, counterfoil books of coroners' orders for burial, 1838–52, and papers relating to legislation for reforming the office of coroner, 1827–60. I am most grateful to Christopher Whittick of the East Sussex Record Office for informing me of this deposit soon after it had been received.

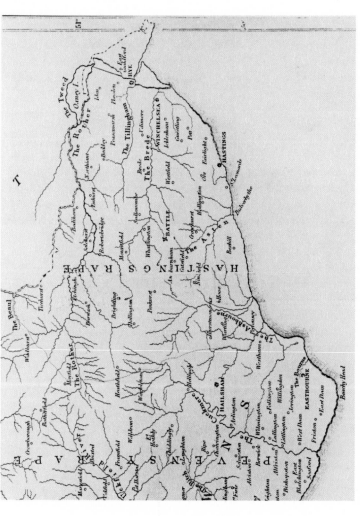

Map 6. The Rape of Hastings in 1864, as shown in M. A. Lower's map, reduced from the Ordnance Survey, published in *Sussex Archaeological Collections*, xvi. 1864

6).[3] It is true that part of the new watering place of St Leonard's-on-Sea fell within its boundaries, but the ancient towns of Hastings, Winchelsea, and Rye did not, for they had coroners of their own. For many years the coroner for the Hastings Rape was the clerk to the magistrates for the Battle Division of the Rape, Nathaniel Polhill Kell; and when he died in April 1865 another Battle attorney, his deputy Charles Sheppard, succeeded him in both offices.[4] Unlike their London counterparts, Kell and Sheppard had no special officer to assist them; but their relations with the local magistrates, notables, and police were harmonious, and they held some twenty-five inquests a year in inns, houses, and outbuildings, always with less delay than was usual in London, and often on the very day that death occurred.

Their large jurisdiction contained only around 50,000 people, but it stretched from the level land around Rye to the wooded hills of Battle Ridge and the more desolate slopes of the Weald. The population of these parts was still increasing, and more land was being cultivated than ever before or since, as arable, hop-gardens, pasture, or woodland. Almost half the men worked as agricultural labourers, although there were many small 'smock-frock' farmers in the Ticehurst and Hailsham districts, and a few squatters in the more barren parts of the Weald, as well as a number of large farmers and some fine gentlemen's estates. Each of its dozen or so large villages included among its thousand or two inhabitants its own tribe of craftsmen and tradesmen, from blacksmiths and wheelwrights to tailors and surgeons, for these were still very self-contained communities:[5] the two railway lines to Hastings had only just been finished.[6]

Demographically, as well as occupationally and topographically, the Rape was quite unlike London. Here, men outnumbered women

[3] The coroner for the Rape of Hastings was technically coroner by separate commissions for several other adjoining franchises, namely the hundreds of Foxearle, Gostrow, Robertsbridge, and Bexhill, and the manor of Battle: PP 1910 [Cd. 5139] XXI, p. 21. By 'the Rape of Hastings' is meant here the area of his authority.

[4] Kell (who came from a Lewes family of solicitors) was also Auditor of the Sussex and Kent Poor Law Union District and held various other minor offices. He had been in practice in Battle for over 40 years when he died at the age of 73: obituary, *Sussex Advertiser*, 25 Apr. 1865. His successor was coroner for some 50 years, and gave evidence to the Home Office committee on coroners in 1909 as a representative of the franchise coroners.

[5] *Census, 1861*, i. 246–7, ii. 106–36, Tables 17 and 18; *A Compendious History of Sussex*, i. i, xiv; Day, *Glimpses of Rural Life in Sussex*, pp. 1–2; Egerton, *Sussex Folk and Sussex Ways*, p. 131.

[6] For a sketch map of the railway lines and the canals in the area, see Armstrong, *A History of Sussex*, p. 61.

except among those aged between twenty and forty-four; and, more important still, the population was an older one, particularly where men were concerned. Longevity was common in these parts, and over 22 per cent of the men were over forty-five, as against only 16.8 per cent of men in London.[7] In the Rape, the annual average death rate in the 1860s was no more than some 17.3 per thousand living, as against 24.3 in London; and indeed these parts of Sussex were repeatedly singled out by the General Register Office as 'Healthy Districts'—not surprisingly, since it was among agricultural workers of every kind that the investigations into occupational mortality of the later years of the century found the lowest male mortality rates of all.[8]

Yet it would be a mistake to assume that mortality from suicide was any lower in the Hastings Rape than in London. It will be remembered that the county of Sussex consistently had very high suicide rates.[9] Only approximate figures can be given for the Coroner's District of the Rape of Hastings, for as usual the boundaries of coronatorial and registration districts did not coincide. In the three registration districts which fell chiefly within this jurisdiction, however, male suicide was nearly half as common again as in England and Wales as a whole and 8 per cent more common than in the registration division of London; only female suicide was below both the national and the metropolitan average.[10] Female suicide was also very substantially less common than in any of the four metropolitan Districts studied in Chapter 4; but male suicide rates here were very similar to those in Southwark and Central Middlesex, although lower than in the City of London and Westminster. It is in age incidence rather than in scale that the real statistical contrast is to be found, not only between the Rape and the division of London, but also between the Rape and both the country as a whole and such small non-industrial towns as neighbouring Hastings: for in the Rape suicide was far more frequently

[7] Virtually the whole of the registration districts of Battle and Ticehurst and most of that of Rye fell within the jurisdiction of the coroner for the Rape of Hastings, together with a corner of the registration district of Hailsham and a very little of that of Hastings. These and the following figures relate to the registration districts of Battle, Ticehurst, and Rye, and are based upon *Registrar-General's 35th AR, Supplement*, pp. 70–5.

[8] See e.g. *Registrar-General's 55th AR, Supplement*, Part II, p. clxxvi, Table 9, and p. clxxx.

[9] See Table 2.

[10] The registration districts of Rye, Battle, and Ticehurst had a male suicide rate of 148 per million living in 1861–70, as compared with a male suicide rate of 99 per million living in England and Wales and 135 in the Division of London. For women the corresponding figures were 30, 34, and 48: *Registrar-General's 35th AR, Supplement*, pp. 70–5.

something which was resorted to by the very elderly. In the three registration districts which covered most of this jurisdiction, the suicide rates registered in the 1860s for those over sixty-five were about three times higher than the national average, and twice as high as in the division of London. Among other age-groups suicide rates were nothing out of the ordinary, except among those aged between twenty and twenty-four years old. Indeed, among women living in the Rape in the 1860s suicide was virtually unknown except among those in their early twenties or late sixties or seventies.

Inevitably all these suicide rates registered in the Rape have a slender numerical base and must therefore be treated with circumspection;[11] but there is one pitfall inherent in the London statistics from which they are quite free. Mortality from suicide was far more purely native in these rural parts than it could ever be in the metropolis. Only St Leonard's attracted an influx of stangers, and as it happened, none of these committed suicide in these particular years. The railway navvies had departed at the end of the 1850s,[12] and there was no equivalent of the cliffs at Beachy head to act as a magnet for the desperate, and no hospital to serve as a collecting point for the dying.[13] Almost without exception, therefore, it was people whose families had lived in the neighbourhood for generations whose sudden deaths Kell and Sheppard were called upon to investigate; and they did so with the aid of juries who were equally local people, and who often themselves volunteered evidence from their own personal knowledge.

Such suicide as occurred here was thus genuinely indigenous, and this lends all the more significance to a final characteristic of these parts which calls out for emphasis; 'the distinctive Wealden formation of human nature', as one contemporary put it. East Sussex folk, and above all Wealden folk, were often regarded as a breed apart from other country-dwellers, much as Cockneys were from other city-dwellers. Today they readily seem archetypal 'open' villagers. Forthright and independent, matter of fact rather than superstitious, puritan and nonconformist in their religious views, given to horseplay and outspoken to the point of roughness, they were impatient of authority,

[11] The total number of suicide verdicts registered in the districts of Rye, Ticehurst, and Battle was 36; Hailsham added another 10.

[12] *Census, 1861*, i. 246–8, footnotes.

[13] The only local hospital was the East Sussex, Hastings, and St Leonard's Infirmary, with 22 beds: *Medical Directory, 1860*, p. 901. The county lunatic asylum was far distant, at Haywards Heath, although there was one very select licensed house for lunatics within the Rape, at Ticehurst: ibid., pp. 994, 996.

unsympathetic to hypocrisy, and altogether free from deference, sentimentality, or easy patter. Docility, apathy, and conformity had never been part of the style of this old smuggling area, which had at times seen virtual guerilla warfare with the Revenue authorities.[14] Significantly, the phase of 'the last labourers' revolt' which started in 1830 here in Battle and Brede, was the phase which attacked not threshing machines, but overseers and parsons' tithes; and it was pushed through not by labourers alone, but by labourers in full collusion with farmers.[15] Old radical centre that it was, it is no surprise to find that on Census Sunday 1851 there was a weak Anglican performance in the Wealden districts, and that a small band of 'Freethinking Christians' gathered in Battle, as well as a sizeable number of Unitarians and a large contingent of Baptists and Wesleyan Methodists.[16] Since in the early 1860s these villages were still largely untouched by any public opinion but their own, this deeply ingrained rebelliousness and toughness has a double significance for the historian of suicide; for it must have tended not only to weaken the social constraints and private fears which usually inhibited suicidal behaviour, but also to make juries less apt to fudge their verdicts.

For Kell and Sheppard suicide was certainly a familiar mode of sudden death: 17 per cent of their inquests in these years ended in a verdict of suicide, as against only 8 per cent of Lankester's first 500 inquests. To an extent which was seldom matched in London, however, suicide for them was something to be associated with men—and with old age, especially where such few women as did commit suicide were concerned. It is this last which is the most immediately striking difference. Urban coroners rarely had to investigate a case of suicide by a really old woman. Not once in the months studied here did Payne, St Clare Bedford, or Lankester deal with a case of suicide by a woman over the age of sixty-five; yet half of the handful of female suicide cases dealt with by Kell and Sheppard related to women in their

---

[14] Egerton, *Sussex Folk*, pp. 7–11, 28–30, 103, 108; *Glimpses of Rural life in Sussex*, pp. 48–52; and cf. Rule, 'Social Crime in the Rural South in the Eighteenth and Early Nineteenth Centuries', pp. 144, 146. For a summary of 'open' township characteristics and some remarks relating them to the Heathfield–Burwash–Battle area, see Mills, *Lord and Peasant in Nineteenth-Century Britain*, pp. 102, 117, Table 6.1, 119–20.

[15] Hobsbawm and Rudé, *Captain Swing*, pp. 78–84, 174, 176, 185, and Appendix III, Table of Incidents. It has recently been argued, however, that the degree of social conflict in open parishes and specifically in Burwash has been underestimated: Wells, 'Social, Conflict and Protest in the English Countryside', especially pp. 121–2.

[16] PP 1852–3 [1690] LXXXIX, pp. 16–17. Cf. Coleman, 'Southern England in the Census of Religious Worship, 1851', p. 162.

seventies.[17] From the point of view of occupation and social class, however, what sort of people were committing suicide in these long-lived, self-contained, independent-minded communities? The answer is clear enough: rarely agricultural labourers or the very poor; often craftsmen and tradesmen, farmers and innkeepers, persons of some local standing.[18] Still less often than in London was suicide an experience which befell the poor and humble; and even those few women who committed suicide were not drawn from lower social groups than their male counterparts, as they tended to be in London.[19] Suicide was something to be associated with those same village leaders who in 'the bad times' had been ringleaders of the riots against overseers and parsons, men 'in a somewhat superior condition of life', whose wages (as the trial judge had said in 1831) were 'such as to place them far above the reach of want';[20] and this is the less surprising since investigations of occupational mortality later repeatedly showed suicide to be much commoner nationally among farmers and craftsmen than among agricultural labourers.[21]

If suicide was not usually the resort of the poor, neither was it chiefly the resort of the lonely and isolated. Here, as in London, two-thirds of the men who ended their own lives were living with relatives, and the others usually had relations close at hand; while virtually all the women in question were living with relatives. Family relationships which showed proper consideration and loyalty seem to have been valued less sentimentally than in London, but even more highly; and although no family quarrels came into the open at these inquests, in a few cases hints appear that the treatment rightly due from a husband, son, or brother had not been forthcoming. Such behaviour seems to have been disapproved of by the jurymen (to judge from their

[17] The proportion of suicide verdicts in these inquest papers which related to men over 65 was also higher than in those of the three London coroners studied, but not by very much: 15 per cent as against 11 per cent.

[18] Only a fifth of the men on whom suicide verdicts were returned were labourers or paupers. The remaining four-fifths included, for example, a miller, blacksmith, tailor, shoemaker, painter and glazier, farmer, and auctioneer and house agent. Large numbers of artisans and craftsmen, farmers and shopkeepers are seen as characteristic of 'open' villages, and such people were generally more prone to suicide than labourers: see Table 4.

[19] Only one of these women, a former servant, fell into the lowest of the five socio-economic categories used (see ch. 4 n. 90); the others were the wives or widows of farmers, innkeepers, a carpenter, and the like.

[20] Hobsbawm and Rudé, *Captain Swing*, p. 207.

[21] See Table 4; *Registrar-General's 55th AR, Supplement*, Part II, p. clxxvi, Table 9; *65th AR, Supplement*, Part II, p. xliv.

questions, and their 'medium' verdicts), just as it had apparently distressed those whose deaths they were investigating.[22] As a rule, however, these Sussex inquest papers portray those who committed suicide as having been living among companionable relatives and friends remarkably like those conjured up by a local memoirist of that generation of Wealden people: intensely neighbourly and helpful, affectionate, 'unready with their tongues to promise, but with true, warm hearts'.[23] Lack of human contact or support was the background to suicide here even less than in London.

How far was that background ill-health? The answer is plain: very far indeed. Nowhere in London (apart perhaps from Southwark, that solidly working-class area) did ill-health play anything remotely approaching the truly major role it played in the Rape. Over three-quarters of those who took their lives in this rural area had not been in good health, as against about a quarter in London. Insanity, certified or medically suspected, was rare; but various fevers and organic diseases, 'pains in the head', failing powers, the depression of old age, and a range of nervous ailments were all attested to have been present again and again. In none of these cases did Kell or Sheppard order a post-mortem; but almost invariably they heard medical evidence, and in very many cases this was not confined to the condition in which the deceased had been found, but also rehearsed some previous medical history. In short, although this district as a whole was an outstandingly healthy one, the opposite was true of those of its people who committed suicide.

The difference between the profile of suicide in rural east Sussex and in London was thus not simply a reflection of the demographic and socio-economic contrasts between the two areas. Its incidence among the elderly was far heavier, the contrast between male and female suicidal behaviour far wider, and the role of ill-health much greater than might have been predicted from a straightforward demographic and socio-economic comparison. Its distinctiveness in such ways strengthens the suspicion that the pattern of suicide in the Rape may also have differed significantly in more elusive matters as well—

---

[22] ESRO, A 1684, inquests of 17 Apr. 1859 on Mary Martin, 19 June 1861 on James Campbell, 22 June 1863 on Jesse Simpson; *Sussex Advertiser,* 26 Apr. 1859 (Mary Martin), 30 June 1863 (Jesse Simpson). 'Medium' verdicts (that is, verdicts that there was not sufficient evidence to say whether the deceased had been of unsound mind) were returned on Mary Martin and James Campbell.

[23] Day, *Glimpses of Rural Life in Sussex*, p. 28. Alice Day belonged to an old Wealden family, and was remembering her girlhood in the 1870s and 1880s.

in reasons, motives, and what people thought they were doing when they killed themselves. Certainly the paths along which these east Sussex men and women travelled to suicidal death were not the same as those which were most often trodden in London. To begin with, they were far less varied: bereavement, jealousy, and emotional loss figured almost never, and domestic troubles, material want, and loss of work scarcely more often. Only three of these Sussex unfortunates were medically considered insane, although several were rather simple-minded; and a smaller proportion in the Rape than in London had previously threatened or actually attempted to destroy themselves. The most important single precipitating cause of suicide in London, heavy drinking, operated in barely 10 per cent of these deaths, and not at all among the women: the drunken harridan so common among London suicides makes no appearance here. Perhaps this ought not to be surprising. Male mortality from alcoholism was shown to be lower in both 1880–2 and 1890–2 among agricultural labourers than in any other occupation,[24] and female alcoholism was always regarded as very much a city vice. Beer, not gin, was the Sussex drink, and although the farm labourer had his pint on Saturday evening, drinking it 'in faith', believing it built up his strength and cured a variety of ills, as one old inhabitant of this part of Sussex put it, 'there are few drunkards among our fixed field cottagers.'[25] On the other hand, real or imagined humiliation and loss of neighbourly or family esteem, feelings of 'not being taken so much notice of' as formerly, or of having been treated high-handedly, or of being 'looked cold upon' by people, all pre-cipitated suicide far more often in Sussex than in London, and were at work in well over a third of these cases. But what carried men and especially women to suicide in the Rape was above all pain, sickness, failing powers, and the depression associated with these things. Here, those who killed themselves rarely acted in a momentary fit of temper, any more than as a result of a bout of drinking. Quite often they did what they did because they could not bear to lose face; but usually they had behind them days, weeks, or months of pain or 'lowness', nervous tension or sleeplessness, senile confusion or feelings of loss of health and strength.

Did any of this affect their final experience of death? Theirs were

[24] *Registrar-General's 55th AR, Supplement*, Part II, p. clxxvi, Table 9.
[25] Geering, *Our Sussex Parish*, pp. 33–4, 187–93. Geering's parish was Hailsham, on the western side of the Rape; and he went on, 'It is among the odds and ends of our working men we must look for the careless professional drinker' (p. 187).

the timeless methods of suicide. They hung themselves: two from a familiar and convenient tree, other indoors from a beam, or a nail in a wall or door—the bedposts and water-closet pipes which were so much used in London were rarities in these villages and hamlets. The men drowned themselves, much more often than did men in London— usually in ponds and wells, but one man in the sea, and one, with dogged determination, in a shallow little stream. Two shot themselves; but none jumped from a height or under a train, and not one used poison. Country work did not then involve the constant use of poisons; and moreover they lacked both the London street culture which made the properties of poisons used for murder and suicide common knowledge, and the many London chemists' shops where laudanum, oxalic acid, and the rest could easily be bought. Throat-cutting was used by the women, however, with a frequency so exceptional as to prompt separate consideration. This apart, there is nothing surprising here: the routines and resources of the countryside shaped the way these people died, as they had shaped the way they lived.

As for the moment of death itself, it was more often a solitary one for these country men and women than it was for London's suicides. Here, medical intervention played a tiny part, not only because there were no casualty departments in east Sussex (although it is true that only Hastings had a hospital), and certainly not because of any dearth of medical men (these abounded in the Rape), but for the simple reason that most were already dead when found. Only 11 per cent of the men, although a majority of the women, were still alive when they were discovered. Of these survivors, all except one had cut their throats. Thus when suicide brought prolonged torments, for these country men and women they were those not of poison, as in London, but of a severed wind-pipe. Their wounds were stitched up by the nearest surgeon, their families and neighbours gathered round, as well as the village constable and sometimes a minister, and few lingered long. Far more often, however, suicidal death in the Rape was a lonely business completed with no human witnesses, sometimes quickly, but sometimes only after stubborn and grotesque efforts.

And after death? Country news travelled fast, and coroner and jurymen met very quickly. (Thirteen jurymen was the number Kell expected the constable to summon). More often than in London they deliberated not in a public house but in some private dwelling or outbuilding; and this not at all from respect for the privacy proper to gentlefolk, as in London, but simply as a matter of practical

convenience. At these inquests medical evidence was virtually always
given, but police evidence naturally played a much smaller part than
in the metropolis.[26] These two conscientious country coroners directed
their questions first towards establishing that the fatal act had been
suicide, and not homicide or accident; and after this, towards clarifying
the deceased's state of mind at the time. The press cuttings Kell
collected on suicide in 1843–45 suggest that he had been struck by
Wakley's colourful assertion (following the M'Naghten trial) that
unless the evidence fully justified a verdict of insanity, the jury ought
to return a 'medium verdict' as between 'temporary insanity' and *felo
de se*, and simply declare that there was not sufficient evidence to show
the deceased's state of mind.[27] Apparently the forthright, unsentimental
Sussex juries who assisted Kell and his deputy and successor agreed
with this view, which was perhaps often expounded to them in sum-
mings-up; for almost one in five of their suicide verdicts was 'state of
mind unknown', instead of the usual 'mind unsound' or 'temporary
insanity'.

These verdicts were never hastily reached; and thanks to the care-
fulness with which the facts were explored and recorded, these inquest
papers give some hints of the ways in which the differences between
rural and metropolitan suicidal behaviour may have reflected not only
differences in occupations, morbidity, and population structure, but
also differences in habits and attitudes, feelings and beliefs. The first
such hint concerns the medical habits and ideas of ordinary people.
Then, as now, the intention to die was often not a clear-cut one; and
this was so not only because suicide was sometimes an appeal for help,
but also because even more often than today it was sometimes a flight
from physical pain. When physical pain becomes intolerable, the means
of flight will be dictated by whatever therapies and pain controllers
are familiar and immediately available. Between self-destruction and
self-medication there is thus always a grey area; but it is a grey area
whose nature and riskiness are always variable. To mid-Victorian
Londoners and industrial workers, the most familiar and readily
accessible escapes from pain were opiates and alcohol; in the country,

---

[26] The East Division of the County of Sussex Police Force totalled only 125 persons
in the year ending 29 Sept. 1868: PP 1868–9 (22) XXXI, p. 154. Wilfrid Scawen Blunt
vividly describes an inquest held on his estate in the Sussex Weald in 1908 which sounds
very like those of the 1860s: *My Diaries*, pp. 622–3.

[27] The bundle of press cuttings labelled 'Suicide' contains cuttings of this summing-
up of Wakley's, and of several inquests held by Wakley in which the verdict returned
was that of 'Suicide, but no evidence to show state of mind': ESRO, A 1684.

neither of these was so widely used. In the Rape of Hastings village surgeons and village people alike still regarded vigorous blood-letting as a primary means of relief. The Rape was one of those country districts where there were so many small farmers and such good chances of getting poor law and 'club' appointments in the bigger villages, that the ratio of medical men to population was high.[28] Those who ended their own lives in this country district seem to have received more medical attention during their lifetime than their London counterparts, whether as poor law or club patients, or simply as customers dealing with the village surgeon as they did with the village tailor or shoemaker; and in this very varied host of medical men it was the tradesman-surgeon and unqualified practitioner or assistant who predominated.[29] Of the twenty–four medical men who gave evidence at these rural suicide inquests, a quarter had no recognized medical qualifications at all, two-thirds had qualified before 1850, half had had no hospital training or experience, and only two had a physician's qualifications. None of this deterred any of them from general practice, however;[30] and herabouts medical men evidently still treated their patients by means of violent bleeding, blistering, and purging, and talked of soothing, conserving, or stimulating 'organic nervous power' or relieving congestion. This was the kind of approach which their patients wanted and understood. After all, even the up-to-date Mrs Beeton included instructions on leeches, blisters, purges, and 'How to Bleed' in the first aid section of her *Household Management* in 1861; and these village people certainly saw sickness as something which ramified through the whole of body and mind and required not specific localized treatment, but the vigorous general remedies long familiar among them, and given a new lease of life by the enthusiasm for therapeutic blood-letting among advanced medical men between the 1820s and 1840s.[31]

[28] Rivington, *The Medical Profession*, p. 4.
[29] Details about all the medical men in the Rape, as well as those who gave evidence at the inquests studied, have been compiled from *Kelly's Post Office Directory of Sussex, 1867* and the *Medical Directory*. A good many were entered in the former as carrying on a trade, and were not given the suffix 'Esq.' This was a period of very rapid change in medical education and status, and this host of medical men ranged from the unqualified William Press of Hurst Green who had been practising since before 1815, to his neighbour John Taylor, who had been on the Army medical staff in the Crimea, contributed to *The Lancet* and *Medical Gazette*, and came to Ticehurst fresh from King's College Hospital and two London infirmary appointments.
[30] 'The ancient boundaries of practice had been entirely broken down' in the previous generation: Holloway, 'Medical Education in England, 1830–1858', p. 309.
[31] Beeton, *Book of Household Management*, pp. 1061–95. The medical and lay evi-

All of this is an important key to some of these east Sussex suicides. Mary Martin of Wartling, for example, had been treated by leeches for a complaint affecting her head in 1853, and when her headaches returned in 1859, the surgeon who attended her (and who had qualified at Bart's in 1849), prescribed 'an issue in her arm to relieve her system'. After a few weeks, however, this 'dried up and ceased to operate', according to the woman who helped her with her washing, and her headaches grew worse. In these circumstances, and so well accustomed as she was to the therapy of blood-letting, it seems very understandable that when Mary Martin was found dead one morning she had not hanged, nor poisoned, nor drowned herself, but had cut her throat.[32] Most suggestive of all, however, is the evidence given at the inquest on Sarah Goble, a pious old Wesleyan widow lady who lived on the outskirts of Battle. She had been complaining of palpitations and pains in her head, and of not being able to sleep; and one morning after breakfast she cut her throat with the penknife she used in her sewing work. When her servant found her she was still conscious, and the police sergeant who hurried round asked her, ' "How came you to do this?" She said, "My head." I said, "Why did you do it?" She said, "To ease myself." I said, "Did you intend to cut it so much as you have?" She said, "No." '[33]

Again, local habits and mentalities may have shaped local suicidal behaviour not only through the medical mores characteristic of any lavishly doctored country area at that time, but also through the moral attitudes and patterns of behaviour peculiarly characteristic of east Sussex and the Weald. Deliberately to end one's own life involved a clear flouting of authority and convention. The French founding fathers of suicidology regarded high suicide rates as a consequence of insubordination to the established order, and hence as a specifically 'modern' development which was especially rife in towns and among

dence given at these inquests fully bears out the presumption that around 1860 run-of-the-mill country medical men and *a fortiori* most of their patients still spoke and thought in terms of humoral or tension pathologies (on which see Shyrock, 'Nineteenth-Century Medicine: Scientific Aspects', p. 882) and still placed great faith in bleeding. On the brief new vogue for vigorous blood-letting *c.* 1820–50, see Niebyl, 'The English Blood-Letting Revolution', *passim*, and especially pp. 479–80. In early Victorian novels 'the inevitable remedy for almost every kind of ailment was always bleeding': Brightfield, 'The Medical Profession in Early Victorian England', p. 241.

[32] Esro, A 1684, inquest of 19 Apr. 1859 on Mary Martin.
[33] Ibid., inquest of 11 Sept. 1862 on Sarah Goble.

emancipated political and intellectual elites.[34] Englishmen, however, had always been 'an ungovernable people', and the nineteenth-century English countryside was not everywhere phlegmatic and deferential, even when the last labourers' revolt was over and better times had come. As was remarked earlier, the area of Battle and the Weald had been a centre of political radicalism and economic protest in the bad times after Waterloo, and even more significantly, had long been an area where people were stubbornly impatient of authority and 'found back' if they were treated high-handedly or punished.[35] Thus it may not be pure coincidence that so many of the men who took their own lives hereabouts (and contributed to making this an area of high official suicide rates) belonged to the group reckoned to be the most 'stiff-necked' and unshackled by convention of all, the tradesmen; or that the corner where suicide inquests were held most frequently was around Burwash, a Wealden area notorious in the previous century for smuggling, sheep-stealing and burglary, violence and lawlessness.[36] Certainly there are hints that some of the men who killed themselves had been in a mood to spite authority at the time. Thus Thomas Moon of Whatlington, just outside Battle, who would have been in his thirties at the time of the Battle riots over parish allowances, hanged himself in 1864 partly because he resented not 'having his parish pay when he thought he ought to'. His outdoor allowances had only been stopped for one week, and he was not in actual want, but he had visited the Union medical officer to complain of his treatment, and been indignant about it to his neighbours. Again, there is Henry Weston, a hard-drinking, highly literate sixty-two year old painter and glazier, who had vowed that he would never go to the Lewes house of correction, and kept his vow by hanging himself with his handkerchief and necktie from a water pipe when he found himself in the Burwash lock-up on the way to serve four months' hard labour at Lewes for wife-beating.[37]

Finally, it is notable that there is no echo here of that cocky cynicism which can sometimes be heard in the London evidence, for example, from the dustyard worker James Harris of Paddington, who 'used to

---

[34] E.g. Durkheim, *Suicide*, pp. 241–76; Bayet, *Le suicide et la morale*, part IV, ch. 5 (the last half of this volume is not paginated in the only copy to which I have had access).

[35] Egerton, *Sussex Folk and Sussex Ways*, p. 11.

[36] Geering, *Our Sussex Parish*, p. 54; Lower, *A Compendious History of Sussex*, i. 90.

[37] ESRO, A 1684, inquests of 18 May 1864 on Thomas Moon and 2 July 1865 on Henry Weston; *Sussex Advertiser*, 7 June 1864, p. 6, and 8 July 1865, p. 4.

say he did not believe there was a God, but he believed there was a Devil'.[38] Quite the reverse: among some of these old Sussex men and women there survived that link between despair of personal salvation and thoughts of suicide which had been commonplace among ardent Puritans in Bunyan's day and continued easily to be suspected in religious 'enthusiasts', but which is never encountered in the mid-Victorian London cases which have been studied.[39] In this connection it is worth noting that according to its Rector the suicide prone area of Burwash was 'essentially Puritan in its Church views', that the adjoining Hailsham district in particular was a centre of old Nonconformity, and that Wesleyanism had early taken root in the eastern parts around Battle.[40] Certainly it is striking that in accounting for her old father having shot himself in bed, Elizabeth Thomas laid less stress on the fact that his faculties were seriously impaired (as was emphasized by the young surgeon attending him, Roger Duke, fresh from Guy's), than on her recollection that 'I have heard him when in this desponding state [from bodily weakness] say that he was such a great sinner he must go to hell and he feared he should be tempted to make off with himself. He had a great feeling he was such a sinner he could not be forgiven.' Similarly, an elderly Wadhurst farmer, James Harmer, seems readily to have assumed that suicidal melancholy was the consequence of despair of personal salvation, for when one of his labourers ('forty years in my employ', and soon to drown himself) fell into 'a low desponding state' in 1863 as he had done twenty years earlier, 'I asked him if it was his future state, and he said partly so.'[41] Suicidal despondency, and indeed any and every kind of suicidal behaviour, had once universally been spoken of as the work of the Devil. When old Elizabeth Sutton of Dallington excused herself to her daughter-in-law for having got into their farm pond by saying 'the Devil pulled her in', she was echoing a very ancient idea. To the

---

[38] GLC, Central Middlesex IR, inquest of 18 Aug. 1862 on James Harris—a dustman whose habits and outlook matched very closely the description of dustmen given in Mayhew, *London Labour and the London Poor*, ii, 176–7.

[39] This link is touched upon briefly by Thomas, *Religion and the Decline of Magic*, p. 474, and more fully by MacDonald, 'The Inner Side of Wisdom: Suicide in Early Modern England', pp. 574–8.

[40] Egerton, *Sussex Folk and Sussex Ways*, p. 103; PP 1852–3 [1690] LXXXIX, pp. 16–17.

[41] ESRO, A 1684, inquests of 4 May 1863 on Stephen Thomas and 24 Nov. 1863 on Thomas Pomfrey. Cf. Mr Wiseman's cautionary tale of Mr Badman's brother, whom for his sins God gave up to be his own executioner: Bunyan, *The Life and Death of Mr Badman*, pp. 256–7.

younger woman, however, her mother-in-law had simply long been 'very wandering', and indeed Elizabeth Sutton probably meant little by her old-fashioned turn of phrase—a turn of phrase partly kept familiar, no doubt, by the archaic formula still sometimes used when juries returned verdicts of *felo de se*, murder, or manslaughter.[42] Certainly when she did finally kill herself a fortnight later, she was filled with an even older instinct: that sense of the very aged that the time for dying has come so often noted by anthropologists and folklorists, and exemplified again a few miles away thirty years later when Wilfrid Scawen Blunt's eighty-four year old wood-reeve after due deliberation hanged himself in his cart-shed.[43] 'All be done, all be done', Elizabeth Sutton muttered repeatedly when she got up one May morning in 1863. Two daughters and a young grandson had just died; she was seventy-one and unable to do anything; and she quietly cut her throat.[44]

In rural east Sussex the experience of suicide was thus both subjectively and objectively different from what it was in London. Here it was more often horrifyingly violent and sombrely deliberate; and it was sad rather than sordid. The currents carrying people to self-destruction seem to have been deeper and stronger; fleeting squabbles and resentments were as comparatively rare as drunken boldness or gloom. These deaths were more often a response to deeply felt rebuffs and long-standing bodily suffering, and thus more often wear an innocent and sadly logical air. They were the handiwork of people who were serious and unsentimental in their conception of their rights and responsibilities. Members of diffuse communities of neighbours and relations as they were, their vulnerability was perhaps all the greater to the loss of any central element of their self-respect and way of life. Health and strength, family loyalty and support, neighbourly esteem and a proper pride all seem to have had a weightier significance here; and it is such things, as well as the obvious differences in their daily habits and ways of getting a living, which explain why, in rural east Sussex and in London, the sorts of people who killed themselves were not the same, any more than were the pressures which pushed them towards self-destruction, or the ways in which they finally ended

---

[42] These inquisitions might still begin with the words 'not having the fear of God before his eyes, but being moved and seduced by the instigation of the Devil': see the specimens in that much-used practitioner's handbook, Jervis, *On the Office and Duties of Coroners* (3rd edn., 1866), pp. 358–62.

[43] Blunt, *My Diaries*, p. 213. Blunt's estate of Crabbet was towards the west of the Weald.

[44] ESRO, A 1684, inquest of 18 May 1864 on Elizabeth Sutton.

their lives. In the early 1860s, the significance of place in south-east England was evidently still great enough for tangible and intangible factors to work together to produce local experiences of suicide which differed in coherent and strongly patterned ways although they existed only fifty miles away from each other.[45] How far was this true of the rest of England? This is something we may never be able to settle.[46] If distinctive local patterns did indeed exist up and down the country, however, it follows that to generalize about the meaning of suicide even for a single generation or in a single decade with no regard to place, must be to remain at a superficial level of understanding.

Was place more or less important than the passage of time? How significantly did one generation's experience of suicide differ from another's? Was there an Edwardian experience of suicide, as opposed to a mid-Victorian one? A close comparison of Edwardian and mid-Victorian experiences of suicide in exactly the same spot is clearly needed to answer such questions. Unfortunately this is not easy to achieve, for unbroken runs of coroners' case papers which span the nineteenth and twentieth centuries are very rare indeed. One such series does exist, however, in the shape of the meticulously kept papers of the franchise coroners for the City of London and the Borough of Southwark; and with their aid it becomes possible to tackle the question of how the experience of suicide changed with the passage of this particular half-century.

How different was the experience of suicide in the City in 1911 from what it had been in 1861? Few parts of the old inner London area had changed so fundamentally during these fifty years. By 1911 the City had very largely lost its residential character. Its inhabitants (who had become overwhelmingly adults) had dwindled to little more than a fifth of their number in 1861, and in 1901–10 accounted for only 0.5 per cent of the population of the registration division of London, as against 3 per cent in 1861–770.[47] The number of suicide verdicts registered in the City had also dwindled, and in 1912 numbered only

---

[45] Cf. C. Phythian-Adams on the 'invisible barriers between one locality and another' in the early-Victorian English countryside: Mingay, ed., *The Victorian Countryside*, ii. 619.

[46] Local newspaper reports alone are unfortunately not enough, for they remain on the surface of events. They can usefully supplement inquest papers, but they can never take their place.

[47] *Registrar-General's 35th AR, Supplement*, pp. 4, 34–5, and *75th AR, Supplement*, Part III, pp. 4, 128.

twelve, as against twenty-four in 1861. Moreover, only one of these twelve verdicts related to a woman, whereas in 1861 the City had been responsible for 11 per cent of all London suicide verdicts on women.[48] Admittedly men had come to outnumber women among the City's inhabitants in the intervening years, instead of vice versa;[49] still, this demographic shift alone was far too small to account for the drastic change in the sex ratio of City suicide verdicts. Had suicide become, then, an enormously more common experience among the men living in the City, but a far rarer one among the women? Not at all: for only one of the suicide verdicts returned in the City in 1911 related to a person who had actually lived within the City's boundaries. Here is the really salient fact in the Edwardian situation, and the really significant change.

For a long time the City had been a place where suicide verdicts were comparatively numerous in proportion to its residential population. In 1911, as in 1861, this was partly the result of demographic abnormalities and two topographical accidents: the presence of a great river and a great hospital. The Thames and St Bartholomew's were still drawing within the City's boundaries the bodies of those who had lived in its hinterland or, sometimes, far beyond its borders. In the summer of 1911 the bodies of a servant girl from Clapham and a dairyman's assistant from Stepney were picked up near Temple pier, and a steamer plying from Margate brought in the body of a passenger who had lived in Southend and had jumped overboard; while in the same months an Islington warehouse porter and a Shoreditch totter who had taken poison were both rushed to Bart's.[50] All these had close counterparts in 1861. In 1861, however, over two-thirds of those on whom City juries brought in verdicts of suicide were men and women

---

[48] In 1861, 63 women were registered as having died by suicide in the registration division of London: *Registrar-General's 24th AR*, p. 143. Payne's inquest papers for 1861 contain 7 verdicts of suicide on women.

[49] For every 100 women, 105 men lived in the City in 1911, as against only 92.7 in 1861: *Census, 1911*, x, Part 2, p. 380, *Census, 1861*, i. 196.

[50] (Since access to inquest papers less than 100 years old is subject to certain restrictions, these cases are referred to by number and date of inquest only.) CLRO, CR, City, inquest no. 120, 9 Aug. 1911, and 'Tragedy of Unrequited Love', *City Press*, 12 Aug. 1911, p. 7; inquest no. 101, 8 July 1911 and 'Embankment Tragedies', *City Press*, 15 July 1911, p. 7 (this case was also reported in the *Daily Chronicle, Daily Express, Daily Mail, Daily News*, and *The Times* of 12 July 1911); inquest no. 82, 12 June 1911, and 'Suicide from a Steamer', *City Press*, 17 June 1911, p. 7; inquest no. 83, 16 June 1911; inquest no. 102, 14 July 1911, and 'Suicide by Laudanum', *Morning Advertiser*, 15 July 1911, p. 6.

who had had their homes in the City. For them suicide was still predominantly a domestic affair, taking place within their own living quarters (which were often one and the same with their workplace), so that suicide was then no more unlikely to befall a woman in the City than anywhere else. By 1911 this had ceased to be the case. Only one resident inhabitant of the City took his own life there in that year; and he was an unmarried warehouseman lodging in one of the many eating houses in Bartholomew's Close, and working just outside the City boundaries, in Clerkenwell.[51]

What kind of suicidal experience, then, had taken the place of the domestic experience so common in 1861 and so rare in 1911? Certainly not that of the visitor passing through. In 1861 sojourners and those who had come up from the provinces in search of anonymity and relief did indeed swell the City's quota of suicides; but in 1911 such people were far more likely to be drawn to the much talked-of 'West End' and the new imperial capital which had arisen inside the circle of railway termini, where clustered such magnets as Hyde Park and Piccadilly Circus, Trafalgar Square and the Embankment. It was something altogether new which had become characteristic of the Edwardian City: commuter suicide. Half these City suicides of 1911 were men who travelled to work in the Square Mile every day, but lived outside it. In 1861 a distinction of this sort between domestic suicide and workplace suicide would have had little meaning, since most of those who then died by their own hands in the City lived in the building where they worked, or very near it. By 1911, however, the City had acquired its twentieth-century character, and had become a place for day commuters, not local workers;[52] while its streets were memorable for the absence of women,[53] as they were not either fifty years earlier, or fifty years later.

The question to be asked is thus clear enough: what led these male commuters to poison or shoot themselves at work instead of in the suburb where they lived? True, that timeless reason for workplace suicide—that there, the tasks and tools of a man's trade provided both convenient and familiar means of self-destruction—had not entirely disappeared in the Edwardian City (for example, a young electrician poisoned himself at the General Post Office in St Martin-le-Grand with

[51] Inquest no. 11, 13 Jan. 1911, and 'Tragic Suicide in Bartholomew Close', *City Press*, 21 Jan. 1911, p. 7.
[52] Caretaking was a major occupation of the City's tiny resident population in 1911: *Census, 1911*, x, Part 2, pp. 380–2.
[53] Willis, *101 Jubilee Road*, p. 41.

a corrosive solution used in his work there as a circuit attendant).[54] It was far rarer, however, than it had been in 1861; and in any case workplace suicide must surely be distinguished from commuter suicide, which is to be equated not with the lethal possibilities offered by a particular occupation, but with working and sleeping in two places distant from each other. In what ways could this divorce of work and home lead a man to commit suicide in his workplace in 1911? Two factors emerge very clearly in these City cases: the greater likelihood at work of seclusion and freedom from disturbance, particularly for a principal or anyone who had access to these large buildings after office hours; and the certainty of sparing wives or children the additional distress of finding a dead or dying husband or father in some familiar room. A third factor is hinted at, however, which is truly peculiar to commuter suicide, as these are not: the special tension which could be produced by this new way of living, which prescribed two very dissimilar kinds of conduct and achievement, in two sharply contrasted environments. For example, to an office boy constant paternal discipline in a crowded, impoverished home could suddenly seem intolerable in the cheerful, cocky atmosphere of a large firm in a new office block; while to a professional man the exacting but largely subjective standards of competence developed in the previous generation could make a City office a harrowing daily test of personal adequacy which financial success alone could not prove had been satisfactorily passed.[55] Each day, moreover, the commuter was presented with a locale for suicide which was free from the associations and inhibitions of home and neighbours, yet which needed to be neither deliberately sought out nor accidentally encountered. The growth of commuting thus established in the twentieth century a new variety of suicide, distinct not only from domestic suicide but also from occupational suicide and from suicide in public places outdoors, and with its own special facilities and opportunities as well as its own precipitating moods and tensions. In 1911 there can have been few other places where this new phenomenon was as frequent as in the City; and fifty years earlier it had not existed, even in the City.

This apart, how much had the profile of the typical City suicide

---

[54] CLRO, CR, City, inquest no. 72, 29 May 1911, and 'Suicide', *City Press*, 3 June 1911.
[55] CLRO, CR, City, inquest no. 34, 1 Mar. 1911, and 'Going Where Daisies Grow', *City Press*, 4 Mar. 1911, p. 7; inquest no. 143, 9 Oct. 1911, and 'City Solicitor's Suicide', *City Press*, 14 Oct. 1911, p. 7.

changed? Even more than in 1861, the typical City suicide was exceptionally likely to be young, as well as male. In the City, the mean age
of male suicides had fallen to 37.7 years in 1911 as against forty-four
in 1861, and as many as three-quarters were under the age of forty-
five, as against a London average of only 47 per cent.[56] Again, an even
higher proportion of City suicides were living with relations in 1911—
92 per cent, as against 70 per cent in 1861—and nearly half of these
were apparently happily married. The only one who lived alone was
also the only one who lived within the City's own boundaries: the City
had ceased to be a place for family households. As for the occupation
and social standing of these City suicides, white-collar and professional
workers continued to be well represented, as they had been in 1861;
but the skilled and semi-skilled craftsmen and tradesmen who had
preponderated earlier had now been replaced by unskilled workers of
much lower status—warehousemen, porters, and the like. Indeed, this
was the chief alteration which had taken place in the profile of the
typical City suicide, and it is not a surprising one, since the decline or
removal of the City artisan had been rapid in the second half of the
nineteenth century.

   Were the most likely paths to suicide still the same? Financial and
romantic worries continued to be of little importance, and bereavement
was even more insignificant than before. One very striking change had
taken place, however: in 1911 not a single suicide in the City could be
ascribed to excessive drinking, that major factor in some 42 per cent
of cases in 1861. Instead, the commonest road to suicidal death had
become ill-health, mental as well as bodily: this seems to have been a
serious factor in at least half these cases in 1911, as against only a
quarter in 1861. It is true that the City coroner in 1911, Dr F. J. Waldo,
unlike Serjeant Payne, was a highly qualified and experienced medical
man as well as a barrister,[57] and that the questions which he routinely

[56] Where no references are given for the City figures appearing in this section, they
have been calculated from the cases in the inquest papers. For the average age of male
suicides in the registration division of London in 1911, see *Registrar-General's 74th AR*,
p. 314.

[57] Frederick Joseph Waldo, MA, MD (Cantab.), MRCS, DPH, JP, and Barrister at
Law of the Middle Temple, was appointed coroner for the City of London and Borough
of Southwark in 1901, at a salary of £1,250 for the City and fees of £126 19s. 4d. for
Southwark, from which he paid for a deputy, clerk, travelling, stationery and printing,
and other out-of-pocket expenses. Unlike his predecessors, Waldo was required by the
Common Council to devote his whole time to his duties as coroner. He ordered post-
mortems 'in nearly all cases', and 'took his time' over inquests, as he told the Home
Office Committee on Coroners in a detailed and valuable description of his working
methods: PP 1909 [Cd. 4782] XV, pp. 70–7, Qs. 1819–2105.

asked, *au fait* as he was with the latest aetiologies of suicide, must
have tended to elicit links between a particular suicidal death and the
deceased's bodily or mental health which could hardly have emerged
in 1861. It would never have occurred to Payne to inquire, as Waldo
always did, whether the deceased had ever had sunstroke or fits,
been abroad (especially to the tropics), taken drugs, or had influenza,
although Payne too might well have asked whether the deceased had
ever had any injury to the head, financial worries, love troubles, or
delusions, as well as whether he or she drank or had any mental trouble
in the family. This altered routine questioning must at least partly
account for the frequent appearance in these cases of two factors which
were not thought of in 1861 but were widely associated with suicide
in 1911: the effects of heat, and the aftermath of influenza. The summer
of 1911 was quite exceptionally hot (in London temperatures were
registered of 96 degrees in July, 100 degrees in August, and 94 degrees
in September),[58] and the effects of sunstroke and dehydration were
much discussed; while it was by then regarded as well established that
influenza 'leads to melancholia and depression and produces insanity'.
'They get all forms of insanity from influenza', a police surgeon told
the jury at one of these suicide inquests. Another recently accepted
'cause' of suicide was 'neurasthenia', a term newly current to indicate
a condition 'on the borders of insanity', as the doctors of both the
City solicitors who shot themselves in October 1911 explained to the
jurymen.[59]

   To some extent the greater emphasis upon specific bodily and mental
disorders in these inquest proceedings must simply have reflected
increased lay and professional knowledge of such matters. There had
certainly been no diminution in awareness of alcoholism in these years,
however, to explain the virtual disappearance of heavy drinking from
these depositions; and this considerable change must surely be regarded
as a genuine one, and a consequence not only of the altered socio-
economic background of the people concerned, but even more of the
known increased sobriety of Londoners in the early twentieth century,
compared with fifty years before.[60] Finally, aggressive suicide was still

[58] LCC, *London Statistics*, xxii (1911–12) 68.

[59] CLRO, CR, City, inquest no. 11, 13 Jan. 1911; inquest no. 141, 4 Oct. 1911; inquest
no. 143, 9 Oct. 1911.

[60] How the role of good fellowship, drink, and drinking places had changed within
the Square Mile itself remains to be expounded; but even in the poorer parts of
Edwardian London on Sundays 'drunkenness was seen only in the lowest quarters':
Willis, *101 Jubilee Road*, p. 69. Drink consumption per head peaked in the United

rare in 1911 as it had been in 1861, despite the high proportion of younger people (always most prone to this kind of suicide) among those involved. Only twice does suicide seem to have been used as a weapon in a tense emotional battle: by Harry, the sixteen year old office boy from Walworth mentioned earlier, who felt his mother had turned against him, and by a twenty year old 'daily' living with her parents in Clapham who was desperate for revenge on the boy next door, who had tried to shake her off after she had had an abortion.[61] The typical picture is rather one of flight: flight from loss of self-esteem (in the case of the two solicitors), flight from the unnerving prospect of emigration to Australia (in 1911 emigration from London to Australia swelled into an unprecedented flood),[62] or flight from nagging bodily ailments (neuralgia combined with a broken engagement pushed one office supervisor to an overdose of the patent medicine he had borrowed from a typist, in the atmosphere of *bonhomie* prevailing as the City emptied on Christmas Eve).[63]

The thoughts and feelings of this Edwardian generation can be more intimately known than those of their predecessors, since six of them left a note, and three others murmured explanations before they died. One of the most explicit is the letter sent by Harry the office boy, 'from one in misery to the only one who thinks of me', his 'little sweetheart' who alone had sent him a birthday card. 'Me and mother had a row last night and I am shure I did not deserve it,' he wrote in a farewell letter which he put in the office box for posting. 'I never thought she would turn on me in the way she did but it won't take long to end it all. . . . I am going to the land where the daisies grow and the sun shines always and where there is no sorrows to share you all share the same that is joy for ever.'[64] How did it come about that this family row ended the way it did? Some knowledgeable comments on the quick, jolly, independent-mannered office boys who were the cream of the Board Schools' products were offered at exactly this time by Alexander Paterson, than at the beginning of his work in boys' clubs and fresh from teaching in a Board School in Harry's part of London. Their

Kingdom in 1875–6 and was declining throughout the decade 1900–9: Dingle, 'Drink and Working-Class Living Standards in Britain, 1870–1914', p. 609.

    [61] CLRO, CR, City, inquest no. 120, 9 Aug. 1911, and inquest no. 34, 4 Mar. 1911.
    [62] LCC, *London Statistics*, xxii (1911–12), 118.
    [63] CLRO, CR, City, inquest no. 141, 4 Oct.; inquest no. 143, 9 Oct.; inquest no. 135, 27 Sept.; inquest no. 187, 27 Dec. 1911.
    [64] Ibid., inquest no. 34, 1 Mar. 1911. The birthday card is preserved with the rest of the papers.

high wage of 10s., he noted, always made their adolescence a chancy business, for the father usually earned little (Harry's father was a street-seller with sixteen children, all but one younger than Harry, and Harry's wage was 10s.), and the centre of authority as well as love in the family was the mother. Everything therefore depended on how a boy's relationship with his mother stood the strains of the surrender to her of most of his wages and his staying out late with his 'crowd' or a girl. (Harry had been given a clout for coming home at a quarter to eleven the night before he poisoned himself.) 'These boys', Paterson found, 'cling to the visible and concrete' (Harry's grievances were that his mother had pawned his clothes and that none of his family had remembered his birthday); and they knew only two responses to life: the farcically comic or the morbidly sentimental. Usually Harry's style was the former (he was 'always jolly'); but in the face of what he felt as a rebuff, he, like many of the other youngsters Paterson had observed, 'put on his coat with the sudden and unreasonable dignity of the Cockney and walked away rather loftily into a very uncertain future'—although Harry's chosen exit 'to Glory' was a corrosive poison kept in a clerk's drawer. 'I felt upset because no one had thought about my birthday', he told his father as he lay dying in Bart's, and said he was sorry.[65]

In being so positive about his reasons, Harry was quite typical. Only a humble, and much older, warehouse porter confessed, 'I don't know what made me do it' (and on the form from Bart's reporting this man's death is pencilled, 'Father and a child of his *queer*').[66] The rest either offered apologetic explanations along the lines perenially familiar ('Rather than be a burden to my dear ones I must die', 'My dear wife I am worn out and going to have a rest'), or used the clichés current in popular journalism to justify their action: 'this instinct keeps saying why do you live why not end it all', 'life is not worth living', 'from the agony I have been through for no reason whatever I can only come to the logical conclusion that if there is a god that he is not so good as is made out.'[67] These last were the words of a figure who might have been the hero of an early novel by H. G. Wells: a young man who had risen into a white-collar occupation (he was a publisher's clerk, whereas his father was a carman in Manor Park), but was deeply

---

[65] Paterson (1884–1947: *DNB*), *Across the Bridges*, pp. 21–2, 29, 32, 47, 121, 125–6, 135. Paterson made much of these boys' impulsiveness: p. 185.

[66] CLRO, CR, City, inquest no. 83, 16 June 1911.

[67] Ibid., inquest no. 135, 27 Sept. 1911.

retiring and lacking in self-confidence (he was a quiet, intensely religious Protestant Truth Society supporter), 'had not a young lady and never went out at night'—and none of the phrases he used would ever, surely, have been written at this social level in 1861.

Indeed, the details of these escapist suicides which preponderated so markedly in 1911 make it all the easier to understand how the increased frequency of suicide provided further proof of the younger generation's loss of moral fibre to the many then disposed to see signs of race degeneration everywhere.[68] It was after all not severe pain, or hardship, or dishonour which unnerved these people, but rather some threat, real or imaginary, to their comfort or self-esteem. Fanciful introspection, disproportionate anxiety, deluded judgement do indeed all seem to have played a much larger role than in 1861; and this, together with the disappearance of drunken suicide, means that subjective factors seem to have come to matter more than objective ones, and ingrained personality patterns to have counted for more than external circumstances among these Edwardian City suicides.

What of the actual experience of dying? In 1911 poison was the modal method of suicide in the City, whereas in 1861 hanging had been the commonest single method there, as elsewhere. This was a change which was in harmony with national trends.[69] The kind of poison most often used had altered too, from opiates to corrosive poisons. These last, though very painful, did not necessarily kill quickly, and four of those who poisoned themselves were taken to St Bartholomew's still alive. The great majority of all these suicides, however, were already dead when found, although this did not necessarily mean that they had died alone and without witnesses. (A dairyman's assistant from Bethnal Green who took a header from the Embankment may have counted on being rescued, for there were a number of people around.)[70] In whatever manner they died, however, in 1911 the bodies of these people were taken to the exceptionally well-

---

[68] On this turn-of-the-century association of degeneracy and neuroses with suicide, see below, pp. 336, 390–1. To link the two was an international commonplace: cf, the opening of Chekhov's *On Official Business* (1899), 'In the old days your gentleman, so-called, would shoot himself because he'd embezzled public money, but your present-day suicide does it because he's fed up with life and depressed' (*The Oxford Chekhov*, ed. Hingley, ix. 112). (I owe this reference to Dr Roy Foster.)

[69] In 1911 the proportion of male suicides in England and Wales who used poison was 14 per cent, as against 7 per cent in 1861, and the proportion who hanged themselves was 29 per cent, as against 48 per cent in 1861: *Registrar-General's 24th AR*, p. 124, and *74th AR*, p. 550. On changes in methods of suicide generally, see ch. 10.

[70] CLRO, CR, City, inquest no. 101, 8 July 1911.

equipped City mortuary beside the Coroner's Court in Golden Lane where all inquests now took place; and it was here that the post-mortems which had become so normal were conducted, and here that the jury formally viewed the body before Waldo signed an order for burial—or in one case, for cremation, when such had been the dead man's unusual wish.[71]

In the City, then, the experience of suicide was substantially different in 1911 from what it had been in 1861. It had become a commuter's, not a resident's experience; an experience of men not women, and of professional and business men and unskilled workers, not craftsmen and skilled tradesmen. Equally, it had come to be precipitated by introspective brooding and by physical and psychological disorders rather than by heavy drinking or loss of livelihood; and to be an experience culminating not in hanging, but in corrosive poisoning, a shot in the head, or a jump into the Thames.

The City was undeniably a singular place, however, and likely to be a-typical in all things, suicide included. How far, it must therefore be asked, can similar changes be observed in Waldo's other jurisdiction? The Borough of Southwark had certainly changed less than the City. It now straddled two of the new metropolitan boroughs, Southwark and Bermondsey (see Map 3); but poverty and overcrowding were still rife, death rates high, and open spaces few. Local authorities here had been very slow to take up the civic gospel and provide baths and libraries, even though in western Southwark rateable values were high.[72] (As it happened, the unhealthiest parish of all, St George's, was especially well known to Waldo, since he had been its very active Medical Officer of Health until his appointment as coroner in 1901.)[73] In this part of inner London, population did not begin to fall until the turn of the century, and in 1911 it was still some 12 per cent greater than it had been in 1861.[74] Here the preponderance of women over

---

[71] Waldo gave a full description of the whole procedure to the Home Office Committee on Coroners: PP 1909 [Cd. 4782] XV, pp. 70–7.

[72] *Census, 1911*, viii. 558; *London Manual, 1899–1900*, pp. 70–1; Booth, *Life and Labour*, 3rd series, iv. 8–15, 52–4.

[73] *Southwark and Bermondsey Recorder and South London Gazette*, 19 May 1911, p. 4, editorial. Waldo's 'plain speaking' while Medical Officer of Health of St George the Martyr, Southwark, has recently been credited with renewed vestry activity there in public health matters: Owen, *The Government of Victorian London, 1855–1889*, pp. 321–2.

[74] LCC, London Statistics, xxii (1911–12), 30–1.

men, already far less than the London average in 1861–70, had virtually disappeared; but although a higher proportion of its men were now over the age of forty-five, overall the age structure of its population remained very close to the London mean.[75] Such socio-economic and demographic changes as had happened were thus small compared with those which had taken place in the City; and similarly, although changes had occurred in the suicide verdicts registered here, they were less drastic than those on the other side of the Thames. In 1911 the number of suicide verdicts recorded in the Borough was two-thirds of the number recorded fifty years before; and verdicts on men out-numbered those on women by only 2.6 to one, instead of 3.5 to one as in 1861. Nor was the statistical context very different, as far as can be judged. The greater part of the Borough fell within an area where in 1911 the suicide rate among male residents was very close to the London average, although that among female residents was high (instead of rather low, as in the 1860s, when non-residents were included in local mortality statistics).[76]

Yet for the Borough, as for the City, it would be a great mistake to approach the question of the changes which had occurred in the experience of suicide in terms of changes in local suicide rates and the local resident population, and for the same reason: none of the men and women upon whom verdicts of death by suicide were recorded in the Borough in 1911 had actually been resident within its boundaries, except one. Already in 1861 nearly 40 per cent of the Borough's suicides had lived outside its perimeter (as compared with some 30 per cent of the City's suicides), and by 1911 residential suicide had shrunk to as small a trickle in the Borough as it had in the City. In the Borough, however, social and economic shifts bore little responsibility for this state of affairs. Rather, the same topographical characteristics which had created a uniquely high proportion of non-resident suicides in 1861 were bringing in an even higher proportion fifty years later: its great hospitals, its railway stations, and its waterfront. As always, Guy's Hospital received cases of attempted suicide from miles around; and others were brought from even further afield to that

[75] These generalizations are based upon the figures for the registration district of St Saviour and the registration division of London in 1861–70 and 1901–10: *Registrar-General's 35th AR, Supplement*, pp. 4–5, 40–1, and *75th AR, Supplement*, Part III, pp. 4–5, 136.
[76] The male suicide rate in the metropolitan borough of Southwark in 1911 was 167 and the female suicide rate 73 per million living, while the corresponding figures for the Administrative County of London were 165 and 53: *Registrar-General's 74th AR*, pp. 314, 336, *Census, 1911*, Part 2, pp. 292, 362.

equally esteemed institution, Bethlem Hospital for the insane. The 'feeble ward' of the Mint Street workhouse added its small share, as did that perennial collecting point, the railway terminus at London Bridge; while the wharfs along the south bank were still providing jumping-off spots for those familiar with the working river front. Thus, although the experience of suicide in the Borough reflected less than ever the experience of living within its boundaries, this had not happened because of great shifts in its occupational structure.

Perhaps then the profile of the typical suicide was unchanged in Southwark? So far as age was concerned, this was so. The typical suicide continued to be markedly older in the Borough than in the City, just as in 1861. Most suicides there were still people between the ages of forty-five and fifty-four, and some 55 per cent of suicide verdicts still related to those over the age of forty-five. In Southwark, as in the City, the proportion of suicides who had been living with relatives had grown yet higher (indeed, the only person without a domestic background was a man who had been an inmate of the 'feeble ward' in the Mint Street workhouse).[77] Where changes had most strikingly occurred was again in occupation and status; for although the proportion who had been unskilled workers had changed very little and remained around 40 per cent, the artisans and semi-skilled workers of 1861 were entirely absent in 1911 (as in the City), and had been replaced by middle or lower middle-class people—shopkeepers, licensed victuallers, and the like.

How far had the precipitating causes of suicide changed? Self-reproaches, bereavements, family worries, and disappointments in love, unimportant in 1861, made no appearance at all in 1911. On the other hand, bodily and mental illness continued to be a factor in almost two-thirds of the cases investigated in 1911, as it had been in 1861, although in 1911 pain and disability were sometimes feared rather than actual. (For example, a prosperous master printer commuting from Camberwell to the City cut his throat in his first-class railway compartment because he was convinced that his dyspepsia was cancer, and that the time had come for him to die: 'as thy days, so shall thy strength be', stayed in his mind.)[78] Two notable changes, however, can be observed. First, although alcoholism had not entirely disappeared

---

[77] The circumstances of one of those upon whom a suicide verdict was returned in the Borough in 1911 remain unknown, since he was never identified.

[78] CLRO, CR, Southwark, inquest no. 74, 6 Apr. 1911, and 'East Dulwich Printer's Suicide: Unfounded Fear of Cancer', *South London Press*, 7 Apr. 1911, p. 7.

in Southwark as it had in the City, the two men whose suicide was attributable to heavy drinking had both followed occupations in which alcoholism was a chronic hazard: one was a retired publican, the other a former ship's steward and waiter.[79] Otherwise, drinking figured barely at all, and the hard-drinking women who so often appeared among the suicide cases of 1861 had disappeared in 1911 from Southwark, as much as from the City. More striking still, and more unexpected: loss of work and money troubles, which in 1861 had played a more important role in the Borough than in any of the other districts investigated, were of central importance in 1911 in only one case—that of a greengrocer with a mortgage, who borrowed money in order to put up a stand of seats in his shop on the route of George V's Coronation progress in June, lost business during the upheaval, and then was unnerved by the slack trade during the intense heat of that August.[80] It would be foolish to make too much of a sample as small as this one (which totals only eleven cases). Still, it is no doubt true that for working people at any rate loss of earnings had become less of a catastrophe hereabouts: out-relief was humanely administered and generous in these parts well before old age pensions began in 1908, and the Board of Guardians of St Olave's (which covered the eastern corner of the Borough) had been one of the first to be captured by working men after the electoral changes of 1894.[81]

What of the experience of suicidal death itself? Just as in the City, that experience had ceased to be the experience of strangulation by hanging; and in Southwark, death from taking poison was no longer exceptionally frequent as it had been in 1861. Instead, three kinds of suicidal death were all equally common: death from cutting the throat with a knife or razor; death from jumping into the river from one of the wharfs; and death from swallowing a corrosive poison. To half these men and women (and that was an even higher proportion than in 1861), death came in hospital, sometimes after many days, once after as long as two weeks. For none of them—apart from the two men suffering from delirium tremens—was suicide preceded by rowdy scenes or threats of self-destruction. These men and women of the

[79] CLRO, CR, Southwark, inquest no. 125, 31 May and 2 June 1911; inquest no. 155, 20 July 1911, and 'Suicide of a Bermondsey Publican—Amazing Hallucinations', *Southwark and Bermondsey Recorder and South London Gazette*, 21 July 1911, p. 5.

[80] CLRO, CR, Southwark, inquest no. 172, 25 Aug. 1911, and 'Empty Coronation Stands Worry Causes Suicide', *Southwark and Bermondsey Recorder and South London Gazette*, 1 Sept. 1911, p. 7.

[81] For the situation in 1899–1900, see Booth, *Life and Labour*, 3rd series, iv. 55–6, 138–9.

south bank—older than their Edwardian counterparts in the City, and in every sense more sober than their own predecessors fifty years before—most often quietly said 'Goodbye', or simply went out for a walk to the river after tea and soused mackerel with the family.

And afterwards? Every detail of what followed had changed, even more than in the City. After 1908 all inquests were held in the commodious former police court in Montague Street. Jurymen could now apply for 2s. for every sitting at which they served (an offer which most of them took up), and their only complaint was that they had to march through the streets under the eye of Waldo's officer in his police sergeant's uniform to perform the obligatory viewing of the body, since the dilapidated mortuary was a quarter of a mile or more from the court.[82]

In Southwark as in the City the experience of suicide was indeed different from what it had been fifty years before. It was different, moreover, in a broadly similar way; and this makes one readier to attach some significance to this small handful of cases. In these two corners of inner London, those who died from suicide in 1911 were even less often local inhabitants than they had been in 1861. That great mid-Victorian high road to suicide, heavy drinking, was now rarely trodden, except by those whose occupation placed them especially close to it. Another familiar path to suicidal death was also less frequented: that of loss of work and financial trouble. On the other hand, other worries had come to loom larger: dread of disease, of insanity, or of professional inadequacy. More often than before, suicide presented itself as a tempting escape—and an escape not from tragic sorrow or suffering, but rather from worry, depression, and self-dissatisfaction. The drunken, violent suicide so common in London in 1861 is not encountered here in 1911; but neither is that matter-of-fact, resolute suicide of extreme old age or physical disability found in mid-Victorian rural Sussex. The details of these Edwardian cases seem to reflect and echo the changes which (as will shortly be argued) had taken place in the plain man's attitudes to suicidal behaviour; and perhaps this is no coincidence. After all, in 1911 the favourite headlines

---

[82] Waldo used his juries' grumbles to support his pressure for a satisfactory mortuary in Southwark: *South London Press*, 14 Apr. 1911, p. 4, and 'Southwark Mortuary', *Southwark and Bermondsey Recorder and South London Gazette*, 4 Aug. 1911, p. 7. (Although accommodation for the holding of inquests had been made a statutory responsibility of the London County Council, mortuaries remained the responsibility of the metropolitan boroughs: see ch. 1 n. 69.)

of suicide reports in the popular press—'Tired of Life', 'Life is Too Hard', 'Is Life Worth Living?'—were clichés which had been circulating for a generation; and their reappearance in the last scribbles and murmurs of some of these unfortunates makes it tempting to surmise that not only had the circumstances to which suicide seemed an appropriate response changed over the years, but that they had partly done so under the almost subliminal influence of the changing catchphrases and images surrounding suicide in the popular mind.

However this may be, to study these inquest papers of 1911 is certainly not to encounter either the sordid, melodramatic experience of suicide often revealed in the corresponding papers for 1861, or the direct and often physically brutal experience of suicide encapsulated in the papers for rural Sussex in the 1860s. Instead, it is to be shown experiences often physically less harrowing, but more closely linked with private disturbances and subjective inner strains. The Edwardian aura of suicide as it was unfolded at these London inquests was neither squalid and violent, as in the mid-Victorian metropolis, nor sombre and sturdy, as in mid-Victorian rural Sussex; but rather a hysterical and convoluted escape from private feelings and fears.

What then is the upshot? Surely that the experience of dying by suicide, like any other experience, was very much part and parcel of a particular historical context. Two of the most direct ways in which this was so will be left for later discussion. The changing moral, emotional, and aesthetic aura surrounding suicide in ordinary life inevitably helps to establish the sort of situation to which suicide seems an appropriate response, and hence affects who embarks upon suicidal behaviour, and in what frame of mind and spirit; and these intangibles will be the theme of the immediately following chapters. Equally inevitably, changes in the accessibility, familiarity, and convenience of different means of self-destruction help to determine which people make use of them, as well as the experience of death (or survival) which follows; and this topic will be explored in some detail later,[83] although it will already have been deduced that the shift to those less violent, more passive methods of suicide so characteristic of the period since the First World War was beginning in the half-century before 1914. Reports of individual cases leave the impression that in the 1860s extremely brutal suicides, with massive bleeding and dismembering, were less common in London than in country areas; while in the same decade the first

---

[83] See ch. 10.

official statistics show a far higher proportion of suicides being carried out by poison in London and the industrialized parts of the midlands and the north than in rural counties.[84] During the next fifty years the proportion of men who killed themselves by some handy everyday poison doubled, and the proportion of women who did so increased by 75 per cent.[85] Admittedly, apart from the opiates, most of these substances—vermin killers, weed killers, cleaning fluids, above all carbolic acid—brought an agonizing death, unlike those later favourites, coal gas and (later still) analgesics and soporifics.[86] Still, to swallow a bottle of patent medicine or even carbolic acid required less determination and immediate physical courage than to use a knife, a razor, or even a rope, and the consequences of this could already be seen in the Edwardian period, even though the most dramatic increases in the availability of suicide to the timid, the tired, or the undecided were yet to come.

Quite apart from these two direct connections, however, there were also a multiplicity of indirect links between suicidal experiences and historical context, and to study inquest papers closely is to become convinced that these, although much less obvious, were probably at least as significant. Three such connections seem particularly worth notice.

The first is the link with the history of the family. Today those who are divorced, single or widowed, recently bereaved or living alone, are always understood to be especially at risk where suicide is concerned.[87] Evidently then the incidence of suicide is likely to be affected by shifts in household size and in age and sex specific death rates on the one hand, and alterations in family feelings and relationships on the other. Such matters have begun to preoccupy historians only in the last ten or fifteen years. Already, however, it seems plain that in the rapidly

[84] I have calculated the percentage of registered suicides attributed to poison in each county in the decade 1861–70 from *Registrar-General's 24th–33rd ARs*, Annual Abstracts, 'Deaths from Different Causes Registered in each of the Registration Counties', Class V, Order 4. In the registration division of London, 15 per cent of male and 24 per cent of female registered suicides in this decade were by poison, as against 7 and 16 per cent respectively in England and Wales as a whole. The proportions using poison were markedly below the national average in the southern counties, the North Riding, and Westmorland.

[85] See ch. 10 n. 68.

[86] For the poisons favoured before 1914, see ch. 10 n. 83, and for later trends see *Registrar-General's Statistical Review, 1961*, Part III, p. 263, Table CXXXII.

[87] Cf., for example, the social and medical profile of the suicidal person given by Sir Martin Roth and K. Schapira in Richardson, ed., *The British Encyclopaedia of Medical Practice: Medical Progress 1972–73*, p. 267.

expanding towns of mid-nineteenth century England working-class households were often very large, complex, and familistic;[88] and this realization, together with much work on urban housing shortages,[89] makes it the less surprising that the inquest papers discussed here so rarely show social isolation as a possible predisposing factor to suicide. On the contrary, life at close quarters with a variety of relations and step-relations, landlords and lodgers, had been the usual experience of these people. Again, it is currently often argued that the evolution of the working-class family from an economic to an emotional unit cannot have proceeded very far until the arrival of growing working-class prosperity in the later nineteenth century, since poverty tends to restrain emotions which run counter to economic needs. To early Victorian working-class husbands and fathers, 'wives and children stood as both the major obstacles to financial security and the chief means of warding off destitution'; and working-class autobiographies of the first two-thirds of the nineteenth century have been found to be far from dominated by bereavements, frequently though these happened.[90] Findings like these make it both less surprising and more significant that bereavement played so small a part in precipitating the mid-Victorian cases of suicide studied here, despite the high death rates of the 1860s.

Where suicidal behaviour among children and young people is concerned, important clues are furnished by two quite different aspects of the history of the family: the persistence of the home workshop and of outwork, so that many family households still had to co-operate as productive units; and sharpening disagreement about the proper scope of parental control and punishment. The general impression left by delving into reports of individual suicide cases in the period 1840–80 is that children and young adults who took their own lives often did so as a retort to harsh treatment, in order to make authoritarian parents repent of their conduct and to inflict punishment upon them in their turn. Where domestic outwork persisted, family exploitation was implicit in the process of production, as was shown in the case of the young Bermondsey brass finisher mentioned in the previous chapter, whose mother called him lazy because he could not finish the

---

[88] See Anderson, *Approaches to the History of the Western Family 1500–1914*, p. 26, and *Family Structure in Nineteenth-Century Lancashire*, p. 43

[89] E.g. Wohl, *The Eternal Slum*; Jones, *Outcast London*; Dyos, 'The Slums of Victorian London'.

[90] Vincent, *Bread, Knowledge and Freedom*, pp. 52, 56, 60.

work he had in hand and refused to let him have any opium, although he had had no rest all night. For him, some corrosive poison used for bronzing provided a more permanent escape than the opium his mother had refused.[91] In very much the same spot, fifty years later, when the sharpest boys from unskilled working-class big-city families were able for a few years in their late teens to earn high wages in dead-end office jobs and yet were expected to hand over nearly all their earnings to their mother and let her pawn their clothes and control their comings and goings as before, bitter feelings of not being properly appreciated at home could easily flare up, as they did for Harry, the office boy from Walworth, whose story was told earlier in this chapter.[92] In the later nineteenth century opportunities for such family tension multiplied, as the age of marriage rose and the transition to adulthood became more drawn out at a time when most working-class children in urban industrial areas lived at home until they married, and the concept of adolescence had not yet replaced the traditional semi-dependent status of youth.[93] So long as their children lived at home, most working-class parents seem to have expected to retain some control over their children's activities and to chastise them for wrong doing and disobedience. Punishment for not 'helping out' or for keeping late hours or bad company, the advent of a new step-mother, being forbidden to go on outings with friends or to invite a sweetheart to visit the home (a significant step)—such things were a familiar cause of suicidal behaviour.[94] In 1875 a Hertfordshire doctor suggested without hesitation that a son found hanging from one of the rafters in a small shed in the family's backyard, after being told that he must earn something or leave, 'might have been trying to frighten his father and mother, and that he carried it too far'.[95] A beating, or indeed harsh words, given or expected, had always been capable of the same consequences, as when in 1856 the twelve year old son of a Sheffield

---

[91] See ch. 4, p. 119.

[92] See pp. 170-1.

[93] Anderson, *Approaches to the History of the Western Family*, pp. 26-7; Gillis, *Youth and History*, p. 61.

[94] All these causes of friction are exemplified in the much-reported case of Ellen Norton, a 17 year old who worked in a trimming warehouse in Finsbury: *Jnl. of Psychological Medicine*, xiii (1860), pp. lix-lx; *Morning Advertiser*, 19 Jan. 1860, p. 6; *Reynold's Newspaper*, 22 Jan. 1860, p. 13. Another much-reported case was that of Annie Green, the 17 year old daughter of a music-hall proprietor, whose parents had tried to stop her affair with a married man: *Daily Telegraph*, 7 June, p. 6, 9 June, p. 6, 11 June, p. 2, 1860.

[95] HRO, CR, Hertford District, Bundle T, inquest of 9 June 1873, David Trigg.

table-blade forger jumped into the canal, leaving a note to say: 'It is for you hitting me.' (He had been sent on an errand three times, and had been hit for not doing it properly.)[96] Much of this is no doubt perennial in juvenile suicide. Still, at a time when working-class circumstances rarely allowed children to be exempted from the burdens of making a living, when parents and children were increasingly living under the same roof for longer than ever before, and when there was little or no idea of adolescence as distinct from childhood and adulthood (despite the fact that some teenagers began to earn good wages), suicide had a special role to play in the family strategies of young people which was at least partly a product of that particular phase of family history.

The second link between suicide and its historical context which calls for comment here is that with the history of work and business. Quite apart from the new tensions and opportunities produced by the rise of commuting—which were quite distinct both from the tensions perennially associated with every workplace and from the opportunities offered by the growing use of poisons, cutting instruments, and machinery—there were two features of Victorian working life which had special relevance. Today unemployment is often seen as a potential precipitant of suicide. In mid-nineteenth century England, however, livings were rarely made through regular employment along twentieth-century lines, and the emotional as well as the financial significance of being out of work was very different. One thing greatly increased the risk of emotional damage when someone lost a 'situation': the much more personal nature of working relations. The size of most undertakings was so small that personal relations inevitably counted for much, and dismissal, or a master's preference for a newcomer, could very easily be felt as a deep personal affront, particularly after long years of service. (Such feelings, it will be remembered, were among those influencing Charlie Sudds the engineer and James Jefferies the chemist's porter in Southwark in 1861.)[97] Most vulnerable of all to such feelings were domestic servants; and these in the second half

---

[96] This note was reported to begin with the couplet (in Roman capitals) 'Art thou gone? Shall thy step on the green hills no more/Give the echoes of music that charmed us before?': *Jnl. of Psychological Medicine*, ix (1856), p. lxix. Rather similar was the case of the 13 year old John Cousens, who was believed to have stolen some money and 'was afraid', the jury concluded, 'to go home for fear of correction': ibid., xi (1858), p. xxxvii. For the case of Anne Luke of Plymouth, who jumped out of her bedroom window after being thrashed by her father (ibid., pp. lx–lxii), see ch. 7 n. 14.

[97] See ch. 4 nn. 23, 32.

of the nineteenth century made up an exceptionally large proportion of the labour force, amounting to between 14 and 15 per cent.[98] Domestics often became so much part of the family that to lose a situation might almost be to lose all sense of identity. Such a loss was one of several factors behind James Mason's suicide in Bath House in 1861, described in the previous chapter, and it seems to have been the major element in the suicide in Ware in 1884 of a devoted employee who had been found a good new situation and had no money difficulties, yet was 'troubled in his mind through leaving his place', so fond had he been of his old master.[99] For a living-in servant (who was indeed part of the family in the older sense of that word), the death of an employer could be more upsetting than that of a close blood relation, since it removed at one stroke food, shelter, wages, and the most familiar human contacts and surroundings. There was nothing unique about the case of Rebecca Collins, who in 1862 resorted to opium three months after the death of the elderly lady with whom she had lived as companion for forty-three years; although she had been given a home by her dead employer's nephew, 'she imagined she was doing everything wrong.'[100]

A very different feature of mid-nineteenth century work and business which contributed special pressures making for suicide was the tempting responsibility given to even quite humble employees to collect and handle cash, the large number of informal credit transactions and the very personal nature of many money dealings, together with the readiness of employers, customers, and indeed all and sundry to suspect wrongdoing.[101] In 1862, it will be remembered, an eighteen year old Clerkenwell milk carrier, Ellen Webb, was given the responsibility of collecting the money her employer's customers owed for their milk, kept back some £12 or so, and drowned herself when found out.[102] So common was embezzlement, however, that it was not only those who

[98] McBride, *The Domestic Revolution*, p. 36.

[99] HRO, CR, Hertford District, Bundle T, inquest of 28 Mar. 1884, Charles Woodley. For James Mason, see ch. 4.

[100] GLC, Central Middlesex IR, Box 2, inquest no. 63, 29 Nov. 1862, Rebecca Collins. In the City in the previous year a much older man became 'very desponding on account of the death of the gentleman with whom he was', although he had an annuity of £50 a year and 'two £5 notes by him', and cut his throat: CLRO, CR, City, 6 Aug. 1861, inquest no. 127, Frederick Walbancke.

[101] On this widespread presumption of fraud, see Marriner, 'English Bankruptcy Records and Statistics before 1850', p. 358.

[102] See above, ch. 2 and ch. 4 n. 43. (Ellen Webb's story encourages doubt about 'the virtual disappearance of the milkmaid from the streets of London' by the 1850s, postulated on slight grounds in Atkins, 'The Retail Milk Trade in London', p. 523.)

had indeed been guilty of diverting other people's money to their own use who panicked, but also sensitive worriers and the out of sorts, who easily convinced themselves that suspicion was about to fall upon them.[103] Others believed that they would never succeed in collecting the monies due to them and so would be 'ruined'—a foreboding which seems to have been almost as frequent in real life as in fiction. At these humble levels, financial morality was even less clearly defined than at the levels dealt with in the Bankruptcy Acts; and petty entrepreneurship and money-lending could often lead to disaster less from deliberate fraud than from sheer bad luck and the informal, personal nature of everyday financial transactions at that time. The evidence given at mid-Victorian inquests in the semi-rural areas just outside London, far more often than that given in London itself, shows some real or imaginary trouble connected with handling other people's cash as a precipitating factor—not only among commercial travellers and debt collectors (who were notoriously prone to fraud), but also, for example, for the secretary of a local branch of a friendly society, a newly appointed parish overseer, and the foreman of a large farm. (This last had collected money from the men for beer at harvest time in August 1878 and lent it to one William Richardson; the next August he was pressed to pay the £16. 16s. owing for the previous year's beer, but Richardson had died, the foreman thought he would never get the money back—and shot himself.)[104]

A third notable link, however, and perhaps the closest of all, is the link with people's health and medical ideas. Today it is taken for granted that suicide is associated not only with chronic organic illness, but also with alcoholism and hypochondria, to say nothing of feelings of anxiety, guilt, and worthlessness.[105] The incidence and nature of such things, however, as well as notions of pain control and therapy, have clearly altered greatly through time. Little of the social history of sickness and hypochondria, or of medication, has yet been written; still, three changes stand out as closely linked with mid-Victorian and Edwardian experiences of suicide. The first is the changing nature of the grey area between self-medication and suicide. It has already been remarked that the chosen means of flight from intolerable physical

---

[103] For an example of this, see HRO, CR, Hertford District, Bundle T, inquest of 24 June 1884, William Bacon.

[104] GLC, Central Middlesex IR, Box 1, inquest no. 146, 15 Sept. 1862 at Whetstone on William Ede; HRO, CR, Hertford District, Bundle T, inquests of 2 July 1883 on John Coleman; 13 Aug. 1872 on Daniel Harvey; 8 Aug. 1879 on William Reed.

[105] Richardson, ed., *The British Encyclopaedia of Medical Practice*, p. 267.

pain is always dictated by whatever pain controllers are familiar and immediately available, and that in the 1860s laudanum, alcohol, and blood-letting were still the pain relievers which ordinary people were most familiar with and relied upon. It was argued earlier that the habit of looking to blood-letting for relief may account for certain suicides from self-administered cuts (as it certainly partly accounts for that of the artist Haydon);[106] and in the absence of evidence that suicidal intentions were likely, it was notoriously difficult to be confident that death from an overdose of laudanum was deliberate, since the quantity which could be safely taken varied enormously, and laudanum was a routine cheap stand-by in both professional and lay medication, and one moreover which was often taken on sugar and hence had no disagreeable taste to act as a safeguard.[107] At the end of the century blood-letting was obsolete and laudanum was acquiring a different aura;[108] but new links between suicide and self-medication were forged by the boom in proprietary medicines, particularly those based on chlorodyne—a boom which the medical profession's hostility quite failed to check, and which created new possibilities of overdose.[109]

Another matter of some importance (also noticed earlier), is the changing scale of drunkenness and alcoholism. Both were widespread in the mid-nineteenth century, as arrest statistics and medical writings bear out. The habits of 'the higher classes' had improved, that leading early Victorian physician and ethnologist, J. C. Prichard, remarked, but 'intoxication, as is well known, is still lamentably prevalent among the lower orders, and dram-drinking is a very frequent habit, especially

[106] Haydon's diary shows that he believed that when their blood began to flow, the suicides Castlereagh and Romilly must have achieved relief from the congestion on the brain from which he believed they (and he) suffered. In the hot summer of 1846 this idea of congestion on the brain which had to be relieved grew on him, and on 23 June he shot himself in the head and then cut his throat: Hayter, *A Sultry Month*, pp. 81, 114–15.

[107] Christison, *A Treatise on Poison*, pp. 631, 657–9; Lomax, 'Uses and Abuses of Opiates in Nineteenth-Century England', pp. 167–8. An example of the ambiguity of such cases occurs in Westminster Abbey Muniments, CI, 29 Nov. 1861, inquest on John Sullivan, where the verdict was 'death from the effects of an overdose of laudanum' (in this case, apparently, only a pennyworth of four drops).

[108] See Berridge and Edwards, *Opium and the People*, p. 225.

[109] Fraser, *The Coming of the Mass Market, 1850–1914*, pp. 139–41; Berridge and Edwards, *Opium and the People*, pp. 125–31; Lomax, 'Uses and Abuses of Opiates in Nineteenth-Century England', p. 174; Peterson, *The Medical Profession in Mid-Victorian London*, pp. 256–9. For an example of suicide by patent medicine in the City, see p. 170. The nauseating taste of the patent medicine taken, Anti-Kamnia, led the Divisional police Surgeon to argue against all the other witnesses that the overdose could not have been accidental.

in large cities, even among females and persons not of the very lowest grade in society.'[110] Suicide was well known as a possible result of drunkenness (which commonly induced a fatal daring and blindness to cause and effect), as well as of chronic alcoholism, with its emotional disturbances and delusions. From the 1860s, however, temperance pressure mounted,[111] and cheap mass-produced consumer durables as well as smoking were very rapidly substituted for heavy drinking in the 1880s and 1890s.[112] At the same time there was a swing to lighter beers,[113] while the damage done by drink must have been further reduced by the increased protein in working-class diets.[114] This is the context of that steep reduction in the links with drunkenness and alcoholism which emerged so strikingly when experiences of suicide in the City and Southwark in 1911 were compared with those of 1861. This particular difference, moreover, was one which must have changed the characteristic texture of dying by suicide quite markedly, for alcoholic suicidal behaviour was impulsive, sudden and indeed sometimes downright accidental, marked as it was by 'utter care-lessness' (as that very experienced late-Victorian specialist, G. H. Savage, put it).[115] The young tailor who killed himself in Bloomsbury in 1862 was entirely typical. After a fortnight's drinking spree, he went up to his third-storey room and, so his companion told the jury, 'said twice, "I am coming down". I said, "All right", and heard him fall into the street ... Whenever he was the worse for drink he acted like a madman.'[116] It is above all the frequency of drunken and alcoholic suicide in mid-Victorian London which gives the experience of dying by suicide there its distinctively casual, often sordid texture, so unlike not only the more deliberate suicidal behaviour characteristic of rural Sussex at that time, but also the more neurotic and introspective suicide found in Edwardian London.

[110] He went on, 'in public lunatic asylums in England, in a great proportion of the cases, dram-drinking is the exciting cause': Prichard, *A Treatise on Insanity*, pp. 204-5. For arrest statistics, see Harrison, *Drink and the Victorians,* p. 315.

[111] Harrison, *Drink and the Victorians*, ch. 11.

[112] Dingle, 'Drink and Working-Class Living Standards in Britain', pp. 618–21; Cart-wright, *A Social History of Medicine*, p. 116. Interestingly, some recent statistical medical research has indicated that the consumption of spirits had a diminishing link with male suicide after the late nineteenth century: Low, Farmer, Jones, and Rohde, 'Suicide in England and Wales', p. 361.

[113] Harrison, *Drink and the Victorians*, p. 314.

[114] Cartwright, *A Social History of Medicine,* p. 116.

[115] Savage, 'Suicide as a Symptom of Mental Disorder', pp. 15–16.

[116] GLC, Central Middlesex IR, inquest no. 105, 26 Aug. 1862, William Henry Wilson.

Almost equally worth comment, however, is the link with the waxing and waning of particular phobias, obsessions, and hypo-chondrias. Perhaps the men and women of the latter part of the nineteenth century were especially vulnerable to such fears, surrounded as they were by an environment in which folk remedies had largely disappeared but orthodox medicine had little to offer, and in which bogey diseases multiplied and quackery flourished as never before nor since, thanks to the popular press and the penny post.[117] In the second half of the century fear reigned particularly in one area: that of sexual disorders. Increasing medical evasiveness and public reserve, together with the quacks' calculated alarmism, worked together to multiply feelings of guilt, foreboding, and despair. Hypochondriasis associated with the sexual act is particularly relevant to the history of male suicide. Men were often prone not only to dread venereal disease, but also to believe that some quite minor condition had made them impotent. Honeymoon suicides were familiar enough to specialists,[118] although few cases were so well publicized as that of the unfortunate coroner for Staffordshire who killed himself on his wedding night in 1860 because he thought himself impotent. (He had a hernia, and this was then taken unnecessarily seriously by many people.)[119] Most damaging of all, however, were the terrifying fears whipped up in the 1860s and 1870s of the consequences of masturbation.[120] Never-ending and very expensive postal doctoring was prescribed by the quacks for its purportedly alarming results, which they identified as ranging from indigestion and headaches to general loss of health and vigour.[121] The postal operations of one sharp practitioner, Dr Henry Smith of Burton Crescent, Tavistock Square, led in the early 1860s to enough suicides among young men to bolster up loud denunciations of him in the

[117] Cf. Smith, *The People's Health*, pp. 418–20.

[118] Savage, 'Suicide as a Symptom of Mental Disorder', pp. 29–33.

[119] Inquest on G. H. Hinchcliffe, *Jnl. of Psychological Medicine*, xiii (1860), pp. lxv–lxvii.

[120] Much attention has recently been paid to this: see Hare, 'Masturbatory Insanity'; MacDonald, 'The Frightful Consequences of Onanism'; Engelhardt, 'The Disease of Masturbation'. An apt critical aside on such work, however, is offered in Smith, *The People's Health*, p. 296. In Britain G. H. Savage was by no means the only leading medical man who taught that 'the real danger arises from making too much fuss about this vice': Savage, 'Suicide as a Symptom of Mental Disorder', p. 30.

[121] See e.g. the advertisements for 'Consultations by Correspondence' and such pamphlets as 'Health Lost and Regained: Advice to Young Men on Subjects of Vital Importance' contained in Henry Smith, *An Alphabetical List of Diseases and their Remedies* (1877).

British Medical Journal;[122] and it so chances that one of his victims in 1861 was a young under-gardener at Ashburnham Place in the Rape of Hastings, who after twelve months of 'doctoring', 'feared he would come to poverty', felt no better, but could not reveal his secret to Battle's leading practitioner, Dr James Watts. 'Non-development of the organs of generation', was what Watts reported at the inquest held after this unhappy man had drowned himself; and that altogether orthodox local worthy went on to assure the jury that 'irregular habits invariably reduce the powers of the mind and enfeeble the body.'[123] By the end of the century such ideas were becoming old-fashioned among medical men, but they had been given a new lease of life in educated lay circles as alleged cause and effect of the current bogey of race degeneration, while even in their crudest form they were slow to disappear among the simple. As long as they lasted they remained all too potent a source of a certain kind of suicidal behaviour, utterly unlike that of the drunk or alcoholic—hesitant and painful, and reached as the climax of long depression, sleeplessness, and worry.

Connections like these could be multiplied. What has been said already, however, is surely enough to confirm that only at a level of generalization so broad as to be almost meaningless is it right to portray as unchanging and universal either the experience of suicide, or the circumstances which precipitated it. The sort of people who took their own lives, the paths which led them to that ending and the experience of dying in this way were plainly all deeply affected by specific historical contexts. Admittedly the impact of social position remains elusive; but whether the mainspring of suicide is sought in the inner life of individuals, in the ecology of an immediate environment or in pressures of a much more general social sort, it is clear that time and place were always forces to be reckoned with.

---

[122] *British Medical Jnl.*, 1865, i. 106, 303, 28 Jan., 25 Mar. It has been suggested that the medical profession's antipathy to sex quacks was the deeper because they shared so many beliefs and practices: Smith, *The People's Health*, p. 302.

[123] Esro, A 1684, inquest of 17 Apr. 1861, John Milichamp. 'Doctors in those days did not give in to nerves', recollected a Sussex parson in reminiscing about Watts and other local medical men: Ellman, *Recollections of a Sussex Parson*, p. 249.

PART III

ATTITUDES

6

Standard Commonplaces and Personal Reactions: Mid-Victorian London

If suicidal behaviour can be understood only in the light of the time and place where it occurred, it is clearly necessary to reconstruct commonplace ideas and feelings about suicide in specific milieux. Equally, to understand official responses to suicidal behaviour calls for some insight into the prejudices and unspoken assumptions of jurymen and ordinary citizens as well as authorities and experts. Commonplace ideas and feelings about suicide are also worth reconstructing, however, for reasons which have nothing to do with suicide. After all, attitudes to suicide are closely connected not only with ideas and feelings about death and what comes after and the great question of man's 'right to die', but also with beliefs about the probable consequences of sickness and stress of body and mind, the normal limits of human endurance, and the permissible ways of expressing shame, jealousy, and anger, or cowardice, remorse, and despair. They thus open a window into the plain man's moral and religious sentiments and sensibilities, as well as into his medical and psychological notions. Where Victorian and Edwardian England is concerned, insight into such matters seems particularly worth seeking, since variations in attitudes to suicide may suggest something about the impact of widely different and rapidly changing ways of living upon elusive feelings and ideas which are central to the inner relationships linking communities, families, and individuals.

Three groups of broad generalizations have hitherto been pressed into service to describe the thoughts and feelings about suicide of ordinary people in nineteenth-century England. The broadest of all are the generalizations based upon folklore and anthropology. 'The primitive suicide horror', it is often claimed, exercised a permanent influence on attitudes to suicide.[1] All over pre-industrial Europe,

---

[1] For example, Thurston, *Coroner's Practice*, p. 101; Alvarez, *The Savage God*, p. 45; Fedden, *Suicide*, pp. 13, 27–48.

including the British Isles, a suicide's corpse was regarded with special fear, and had to be buried apart or pinned down, for a suicide's ghost was restless and hostile and would seek to wander, at least until the hour of its natural death.[2] Specialists, however, have never allowed that such ideas necessarily indicate horror, scorn, or abhorrence.[3] After all, suicide was often expected and sometimes admired in the aged or the suffering; and if the corpses of suicides were treated with special caution because they had succumbed to the temptings of the Devil, or because they had been desperate or angry in their last moments and were likely to haunt the living in order to complete their 'unfinished business', in this they were treated no differently from the corpses of all those who met with a violent end.[4]

In striking contrast to such folkloric accounts of popular attitudes are the deductions repeatedly drawn by lawyers, moralists, and satirists since the early 1700s from the readiness of English coroners' juries to declare that at the moment of the fatal deed those who killed themselves had been insane. Here too, however, there has been no unanimity. Did the habit of shunning a verdict of *felo de se* demonstrate that juries felt a humane tolerance or romantic sensibility towards those who died by their own hand? Or were they—or their coroner—simply responding to bribery and other pressures from those anxious to ensure honourable Christian burial of the deceased and even more to prevent the forfeiture of goods to the Crown or, later, the voiding of a life insurance policy?[5] 'Great folk' had always had 'countenance in this world to drown or hang themselves, more than their even Christian',

---

[2] A much-used authority for such statements is Westermarck, *The Origin and Development of the Moral Ideas*, ii. 255. It will be remembered that Ophelia 'should in ground unsanctified have lodg'd/Till the last trumpet': *Hamlet*, Act V, scene 1. The burial of suicides in Victorian and Edwardian England is discussed in ch. 8.

[3] This was a late misapprehension, according to the Victorian folklorist J. C. Atkinson: *Forty Years in a Moorland Parish*, p. 217. Westermarck noted that it was comparatively rare for savages to attach any stigma to suicide: *The Origin and Development of the Moral Ideas*, ii. 240; and in an influential article Zilboorg argued that primitive societies idealized suicide even more than they feared it: 'Suicide among Civilized and Primitive Races', pp. 1361–2.

[4] Atkinson, *Forty Years in a Moorland Parish*, p. 217; Westermarck, *The Origin and Development of the Moral Ideas*, ii. 239; Blauner, 'Death and Social Structure', p. 382.

[5] Sprott, *The English Debate on Suicide from Donne to Hume*, p. 157; Moore, *A Full Inquiry into the Subject of Suicide*, i. 323, 332; Williams, *The Sanctity of Life and the Criminal Law*, p. 236. Defoe's *A Review of the Affairs of France* provides early evidence of complaints that bribes to coroners were behind these verdicts: no. 60, 30 Sept. 1704, p. 255. The same charge was introduced into the third and all subsequent editions of Wheatley (1686–1742: *DNB*), *A Rational Illustration of the Book of Common Prayer*: see pp. 568–9. (The third edition of this work first published in 1710, appeared in 1720.)

as the clown in *Hamlet* had complained.[6] Were eighteenth- and nine-teenth-century juries simply extending down the social scale that freedom from the legal penalties for self-murder which had long been enjoyed by those of family and substance?[7] Did moral condemnation of suicide remain widespread, even though legal penalties fell into disuse long before their statutory abolition?[8]

Most familiar of all, perhaps, are certain semi-sociological gener-alizations specifically related to social change during the nineteenth century. The masses, we are told, always had an attitude to suicide which was entirely different from that of the cultured and worldly élite, and in nineteenth-century England popular intolerance of suicide was given a fresh lease of life by three developments. First, 'the rise of the suburban spirit' made suicide seem less a sin or a crime than a social disgrace, a low affair 'tainted with the musty odour of the backstairs'; then, growing familiarity with the medical men's associ-ation of suicide with insanity fastened upon it 'all the superstitious fear of the queer and the mad' and hardened family intolerance of suicide, since it came to imply a hereditary taint of mental disease; and finally, the prevalence of poverty created an economic prejudice against suicide, since it deprived the family unit of a member's earnings.[9] Among the cultured few, counter-currents flowing from the Enlight-

---

[6] *Hamlet*, Act V, scene 1.

[7] Some of the harshest eighteenth-century criticisms of coroners' juries were directed at their favouritism, not their leniency: Bartel, 'Suicide in Eighteenth-Century England', p. 151. Blackstone simply condemned the irrationality of the habit of juries of assuming that the very act of suicide was evidence of insanity: *Commentaries*, iv. 189. Bentham, however, asserted roundly that 'it is only the poorest of the poor that . . . are ever found to be in their senses, and their wives and children to be proper victims for the rigour of the law': *Principles of Penal Law*, Part II, Book IV, section 4, *Works*, i. 480; and this was a common theme of late-eighteenth and early-nineteenth century satirists, including Byron (see *Don Juan*, Preface to Cantos VI–VIII).

[8] Williams, *The Sanctity of Life and the Criminal Law*, p. 239. Moore argued in 1790 that it was their 'very horror of the crime' which induced juries to conclude that a suicide must have been insane, especially when they followed the first impressions of their sensibility rather than principles of sound reason; and went on to offer an early contribution to the long debate on whether every act of suicide was itself a proof of 'moral' madness, a 'madness of the heart': *A Full Inquiry into the Subject of Suicide*, i. 324–35.

[9] Fedden, *Suicide*, pp. 14, 43, 230–1, 248–50, 260. Fedden acknowledged his especial debt to Bayet, *Le suicide et la morale*, and many writers in their turn have acknowledged a special debt to Fedden: for example, Alvarez, *The Savage God*, p. 239 n. 4, and Porterfield, 'The Problem of Suicide' in Gibbs, ed., *Suicide*, pp. 289–90. Thus directly or indirectly, Bayet's strongly anti-clerical contribution to the French sociological debate on suicide has been the source of widely circulated notions about English attitudes to suicide in the nineteenth and earlier twentieth centuries.

enment and Romanticism were making suicides 'for love' and those 'with a philosophic flavour' acceptable all over Europe, and for them, the morality of suicide became merely a matter of circumstances. For the many, however, a suicide in the family was increasingly something to be hushed up or conveniently glossed over as the result of mental aberration;[10] so that 'oddly enough', writers in this vein have concluded, 'it would seem at first sight that the law in nineteenth-century England was better disposed to suicide than the people.'[11]

There is thus a medley of generalizations in circulation, none of them free from ambiguity. Is it possible to discover more exactly how ordinary people in specific times and places thought and felt about suicidal behaviour, what moral judgements they passed upon it, and how they accounted for it? Is it possible, that is, to define and illustrate the suicide cultures of Victorian and Edwardian England? Here, as in any enquiry into past *mentalités*, it is important to distinguish stock commonplaces from first-hand reactions. For the former there is no shortage of evidence. Current euphemisms and colloquialisms, catch-words and slang all offer some hints; popular ballads and verses, stories and plays, and the verbal and visual images and emblems of suicide offer many more important clues; while the coverage given by reporters in commercially successful journals indicates by its omissions as well as its tone and scale the expected attitudes of specific kinds of readers. Admittedly, indirect evidence like this is tricky to interpret, and reveals more about those who had at least a few pence to spare than about the rough poor, more about Londoners than those living in the country-side or in provincial towns, and more about the years after 1855 than before, when the cheap press was not so abundant. Even at its most puzzling it has a validity, however, which the confident assertions of those professionally concerned with other people's minds and souls can never match. Personal reactions must be sought elsewhere: in the records of inquest proceedings. Even the baldest registers which indicate only the kind of suicide verdict chosen by the jury in a given case have something to offer; although naturally far more can be learnt from those rare newspaper reports which cover the inquest as fully as the story of the suicide itself, and recount not only the cross-exam-ination of witnesses by coroner and jury, but also the speed and unanimity with which the verdict was reached and the bystanders'

---

[10] Rosen, 'History in the Study of Suicide', p. 280.
[11] Fedden, *Suicide*, p. 261.

reactions. Most valuable of all, however, are those coroners' papers which include verbatim notes of the witnesses' depositions. Admittedly the evidence witnesses gave must often have been disingenuous, and was always shaped by the coroner's questions, just as verdicts were always influenced by him; still, witnesses (like juries) could be obstinately independent,[12] and these depositions reveal the first-hand reactions of ordinary people involved in a case of suicide in a uniquely direct way. Unfortunately (as has already been said), such depositions apparently survive in large numbers for only one area of mid-Victorian England: London. Inevitably, therefore, the starting-point for this enquiry must again be London.

Among mid-nineteenth century Londoners, suicide was very far from being a taboo subject. On the contrary, among both middle and working-class people it was as favourite a topic as any other kind of death, and did not necessarily arouse feelings of horror or condemnation, still less of supernatural dread. A good suicide was almost as gripping as a good murder, and far more interesting than most fatal accidents. If a case involved goings-on likely to incur public disapproval, the individuals concerned naturally tried to conceal them; but their efforts were always likely to be frustrated by the eagerness of reporters to retail precisely such details to their readers. Four different genres of suicide were very familiar: the sad, the wicked, the strange, and the comic. Each was associated with certain stock character types. (To think in terms of character types came easily to mid-Victorians, since their teachers, preachers, and entertainers all favoured this ancient way of interpreting human behaviour.) For each type there was an appropriate vocabulary and iconography, conveying, as required, sentimental or charitable pathos, didactic moralizing, prurient or gruesome sensationalism, bizarre interest, ironic humour, or vulgar farce. To some extent the nature of the occasion settled which vocabulary was used. Very often, however, the tone of the discussion reflected a decision to regard a particular death as belonging to a particular genre of suicide; and this decision necessarily rested chiefly upon how the circumstances surrounding the deed were interpreted, and hence reflected not only run-of-the-mill moral and religious notions, but also

---

[12] Examples of such independence on the part of juries can be found in Birmingham (see ch. 7 n. 16), North Glamorgan (see ch. 3 n. 45), Bedfordshire (BedsRO, CO 2/2, 26 and 27 Jan. 1877, inquest on M. Harris, and 31 Dec. 1878, inquest on E. Goodman), and London (*The Lancet*, 1902, ii. 1478, 29 Nov.).

popular psychological and medical ideas, and current emotional and aesthetic sensibilities. It goes without saying, therefore, that the commonplaces about suicide current among mid-nineteenth century Londoners were neither static nor uniform.

Perhaps the most useful initial guides to these commonplaces are the best-liked ballads, plays, stories, prints, paintings, and illustrations of the day. In the 1840s two ways of seeing suicide had gripped so many imaginations so strongly that they continued to shape ordinary outlooks not only in the 1860s, but long after. Of these two new elements in Victorian urban consciousness, by far the more deep rooted was the one which applied to suicide the commonplaces of the sexes' 'separate spheres'—commonplaces which were then becoming part and parcel of respectable attitudes at every level. The age-old contrast between male and female suicide depicted suicide as an escape from sexual dishonour for women, but from worldly dishonour for men; now it was emphasized and elaborated and given a distinctive emotional, moral, and symbolic twist. Among women, suicide by drowning was shown as the reluctant last resort of the seduced and abandoned (and therefore starving and despairing); whereas among men, suicide by shooting, throat-cutting, or hanging was presented as the quickly chosen escape of the proud, the weak, or the wicked from financial ruin, disgrace, or retribution. Very rarely indeed was sexual remorse shown as prompting a man to kill himself.[13] Dickens's earlier novels perfectly expressed (and no doubt reinforced) this application of the sexes' separate spheres to suicidal behaviour. Thus the villains Ralph Nickleby and Jonas Chuzzlewit are both made to take their own lives when they find themselves 'grovelling in the dust';[14] and in *The Chimes* there is baffled amazement when the wealthy banker Deedles shoots himself with no such provocation: 'No motive. Princely circumstances!'[15] Thirty years later, when Charles Reade made a ruined speculative builder cut his throat and Anthony Trollope (with greater topicality) made a ruined financier throw himself under an express train, both were doing precisely what their readers still expected.[16]

[13] Colonel Bracebridge succumbed to this in Charles Kingsley's *Yeast* (1851), ch. 16; but for Adolphus Crosbie 'there was too much manliness in him for such an escape': A. Trollope, *The Small House at Allington* (1864), ch. 28.

[14] See *Nicholas Nickleby* (1838), ch. 62, and *Martin Chuzzlewit* (1844), ch. 51. The suicide of Mr Merdle, 'the greatest Forger and the greatest Thief that ever cheated the gallows', is of the same kind: see *Little Dorrit* (1857), Book II, ch. xxv.

[15] *The Chimes* (1844), p. 114.

[16] Reade, *Put Yourself In His Place*, ch. i; Trollope, *The Prime Minister*, ch. lx.

Male suicide was thus most often shown simply as the fitting end of
a villain or a weakling. Significantly, it rarely attracted the illustrators
and artists of the day.

This was certainly not the case with the way of seeing female suicide
perfected in London in the 1840s. So deeply did its verbal and visual
stock-in-trade enter into popular consciousness, that to this day
notions of suicide in Victorian England centre around images of a
distraught girl flinging herself from a high bridge, or a beautiful
woman's damply draped body 'Found Drowned' and lying by moonlight near Waterloo Bridge, the bridge which from 1844 became for
all the world 'the Bridge of Sighs':

> One more Unfortunate,
> Weary of breath,
> Rashly importunate,
> Gone to her death!
>
> Take her up tenderly,
> Lift her with care;
> Fashion'd so slenderly,
> Young, and so fair![17]

It was this romantic stereotype of female suicide which was completely
familiar in kitchens and music halls, as well as in parlours and drawing-
rooms; so much so, indeed, that in real life a girl standing at a riverside
in the early morning might attract casual joking calls of 'What, are
you going to drown yourself so early?'[18] In the iconography of the
day any young woman depicted as lingering near deep water was
immediately understood to be deserted or 'fallen', and contemplating
suicide. The many who saw the plate of 'The River' drawn by 'Phiz'
to accompany Chapter xlvii of *David Copperfield* in 1849 (see Fig. 4),
for example, did not need to read the text to know that the distraught
girl shown there was a prostitute who knew that she 'belonged to the

---

[17] This poem, first published in May 1844 and still one of the best-known of all
Victorian poems, was an immediate and immense success on both sides of the Atlantic:
Clubbe, ed., *Selected Poems of Thomas Hood*, pp. 317–20. In 1846 an American musical
troupe touring England set it to music with great success: Tillotson, ed., *Letters of
Charles Dickens*, iv. 510–11 and n. 4; it was often translated into visual terms, as for
example by G. F. Watts in 'Found Drowned' (see Fig. 6): Phythian, *George Frederick
Watts*, p. 42; and it was soon familiar enough to be parodied and used in advertising:
see n. 46.

[18] This happened beside the river Derwent in Old Malton, Yorkshire: 'Romantic
Suicide', *Lloyd's Weekly Newspaper*, 17 Mar. 1861 (1st edn.), p. 3.

Fig. 4 'The River': H. K. Browne ('Phiz'), plate to illustrate Dickens's *David Copperfield* (1849), ch. xlvii, 'Martha'

river'—although they might have been less articulate than Dickens made Martha in explaining the familiar symbolism:

It comes from country places, where there was once no harm in it—and it creeps through the dismal streets, defiled and miserable—and it goes away, like my life, to a great sea that is always troubled—and I feel that I must go with it![19]

In the same vein, in *Oliver Twist* (1837) the prostitute Nancy had pointed to the dark water under London Bridge and said, 'I shall come to that at last.'[20] For a woman, suicide by drowning was seen as the conventional aftermath of seduction and betrayal. 'He deceived me—left me—what had I then to do but die?', sobbed the heroine rescued from the Thames in *The Scamps of London* and *London By Night*, two melodramas which remained immensely popular for at least forty years after their respective first performances in 1843 and 1845.[21]

[19] *David Copperfield*, ch. xlvii.
[20] *Oliver Twist*, ch. xlvi.
[21] W. T. Moncrieff [pseud.], *The Scamps of London or The Cross-Roads of Life* (Dicks' Standard Plays, no. 472), Act II, scene 1, p. 11; Charles Selby, *London By Night*

Nevertheless it would be a mistake to suppose that this ubiquitous stereotype of female suicide was presented in exactly the same way in the novels, songs, and paintings enjoyed by the middle-class market as in the street ballads, melodramas, and prints which entertained humbler people. The difference is plain. For the middle class, the female suicide was essentially a sinner; for the working class, she was a victim. For the former, suicide was the inevitable final retribution for fornication or adultery. At first the sinner's lot was only loneliness and poverty: 'for suicide she was not yet ready, her cup was not full';[22] but in the end, for girls led astray:

> ... every lamp on every street
> Shall light their wet feet down to death.[23]

This was as favourite a theme of the moralistic sensationalism of the 1860s as it was of the pietistic sentimentalism current twenty or thirty years earlier.[24] By contrast, the unchanging message conveyed by the songs and melodramas which working-class people favoured was that 'the woman always pays' and 'the poor get all the kicks'. Their distracted heroine was usually allowed to be rescued at the last minute, and men and women alike evidently enjoyed hissing her heartless rich seducer, as their parents had done before them (although earlier, the Serpentine or an open window were perhaps more likely than the Thames to be the suicidal props).[25] Working-class people were thus offered a treatment of female suicide which was only superficially up-dated; whereas the middle-class public absorbed one which was increasingly pervaded by the fashionable new ideals of Woman and Home—ideals which in these same years were making it almost as common to sentimentalize 'fallen women' as to put on a pedestal 'the angel in the house'.[26] To an extent, each variant had its own iconography. It was a vigorous, realistic image of female desperation

---

(Dicks' Standard Plays, no. 721), Act I, scene 3, p. 6. The dates of first production given here are those noted on the copies of these plays in the Malcolm Morley Collection, London University Library.

[22] 'Zeta' [J. A. Froude], 'The Lieutenant's Daughter', in *Shadows of the Clouds* (1847), p. 250.

[23] William Bell Scott, 'Rosabell' (1837), first published in Leigh Hunt's *Repository*, and reprinted in Minto, ed., *Autobiographical Notes*, i. 152.

[24] 'In moral and religious tracts suicide is generally the orthodox termination to a career of female frailty': *Daily Telegraph*, 6 July 1860, p. 4.

[25] Pearl, *The Girl with the Swansdown Seat*, p. 63; Booth, *English Melodrama*, p. 126.

[26] The idealization of the prostitute in the 1850s and 1860s is discussed in Trudgill, *Madonnas and Magdalens*, pp. 289–91.

Fig. 5 'Suicide of the Drunkard's Daughter': George Cruikshank, 'The Drunkard's Children' (1848), Plate VIII

in the face of adversity to which Cruikshank gave classic expression in his dynamic drawing of the Drunkard's Daughter—'Homeless, Friendless, Deserted and Gin-Mad'—flinging herself from a high bridge (see Fig. 5).[27] Again, it was an upright female figure flying through the air which appeared on the cover of Dicks's penny acting edition of Selby's *London By Night*.[28] By contrast, the massive oil paintings, engravings, and etchings familiar to the well-to-do diffused a far more passive, sentimentalized, glamorous, almost salacious view of female

[27] The raw material of caricaturists is necessarily familiar themes and emblems, although the debt is a two-way one. 'The Drunkard's Daughter' was one of the series of 8 plates entitled 'The Drunkard's Children' which was issued as a sequel to Cruikshank's phenomenally successful series entitled 'The Bottle': Arts Council, *George Cruikshank*, p. 56. This phenomenal success, however, was not repeated: Evans, *The Man Who Drew The Drunkard's Daughter*, p. 134. It has been argued that Cruikshank possessed 'an extraordinary gift for striking a style that would alter public consciousness' and that his work 'contributed to various dimensions of the Victorian culture': James, 'Cruikshank and Early Victorian Caricature', pp. 115, 117. This claim could well be made with regard to suicide. Details of some dramatic realizations of 'The Drunkard's Children', culminating in the daughter's suicide leap, are given in Meisel, *Realizations* (which appeared after this chapter was written), pp. 138–40.

[28] See Dicks' Standard Plays, no. 721. This cover is reproduced (and dated 1886) in Meisel, *Realizations*, p. 140.

suicide, showing as they did a beautiful damply draped body lying under an arch by the river with a dramatic chiaroscuro provided by the stars, the dawn, or a bull's-eye lantern, and sometimes a supporting cast of policemen, watermen, or passers-by (see Figs. 6 and 7).[29] In such ways was the current idealization of 'Magdalens' reflected in the images of female suicide in London offered to the middle-class public at the Royal Academy's Summer Exhibition and in magazine and book illustrations.[30]

The second way of seeing suicide which entered urban consciousness in the 1840s was the by-product not of new ideals of womanhood, but of a new imaginative vision of the poor. In these years when 'the condition of England question' seemed urgent and pressing, the poor emerged as weak and helpless victims of the heartlessness and thought-

[29] With the addition of a guilt-stricken passing reveller, this was the scene in the large oil painting, 'Drowned! Drowned!', exhibited by Abraham Solomon at the Royal Academy in 1860: for descriptions and an engraving, see *The Art-Journal*, 1 June 1860, p. 171, and 1 Mar. 1862, pp. 73–5. Already in 1858 Lord G. Fitzgerald's very effective etching to illustrate Stanzas I and II of 'The Bridge of Sighs' used the policeman's lantern to flood the upper part of the drowned girl with light: see Fig. 7. Waterloo Bridge, 'The Arch of Suicide', had been renowned since its completion in 1819 for assignations and suicides. (Its penny toll was said to make it the most private place so near to the centre of London.) In 1840 around 30 suicides a year (or some 15 per cent of London's registered suicides) were committed from this bridge, according to the assistant sub-editor of the *Morning Chronicle*: Mackay, *The Thames and Its Tributaries*, i. 36. Sometimes, however, the arch in such paintings represents one of the notorious Adelphi Arches hard by, rather than an arch of Waterloo Bridge itself. These enormous subterranean vaults (illustrated in Hobhouse, *Lost London*, p. 96) were the last refuge of the fallen in the mid-nineteenth century, and a familiar icon of the Magdalen's suicide. (The Strand and Covent Garden close by were notoriously frequented by 'the ladies of the streets', and 'The Shades' under one of these arches had been in the 1840s one of the most disreputable pubs for prostitutes.) Not until the later 1860s was this stretch of the Thames embanked: Sheppard, *London 1808–1870*, p. 286; and it was easy to wade into the river from the shallow steps at the end of the vaults, as can be seen from the final scene in the well-known set of paintings in the Tate Gallery by Augustus Egg entitled 'Past and Present' (1858), where the adulterous wife huddles with her bastard baby beneath one of these arches, while her (and the viewer's) eye is drawn along a moonlit path to the water: see the reproduction in, for example, Wood, *Victorian Panorama*, p. 140.

[30] In a shilling handbook for visitors of *c.* 1872, a deserted but 'elegantly dressed young lady' who had been rescued from the river by a passer-by and handed over to rough but kindly policemen figured as one of the sights of a London police station: Diprose's *Book about London and London Life*, pp. 80–1, and see ch. 8, Fig. 11. The standard pathetic version was in the same year offered by an American travel book: see the frontispiece to Kirwan, *Palace and Hovel* (reproduced on the jacket of this book), and 'Secrets of a River': ibid., ch. xxx. In 1878 the 'special and extra' Christmas Number of *The World* (which provided light entertainment 'for men and women') included 'a double-page wood-engraving of a drawing specially made by Mr Luke Fildes to illustrate one of the stories, entitled: FOUND DEAD ON THE EMBANKMENT': *The World*, 25 Dec. 1878.

Fig. 6 'Found Drowned' (1848–50, 57 in. × 84 in.): G. F. Watts's massive translation into painting of Hood's poem, 'The Bridge of Sighs'

less incomprehension of the rich;[31] and no clearer demonstration could be offered of their plight than to show that many of them chose to end their own lives. Chartists, anti-poor law campaigners, and many vaguely radical reformers of the late 1830s and 1840s agreed in presenting suicides among the poor as the result of cruel wrongs,[32] and sought to use specific cases as moving appeals for the charity and goodwill which alone could bridge the gulf between 'the Two Nations'. Middle-class consciences were especially sensitive to the sufferings of factory children and seamstresses; and to show these two as driven to suicide was a favourite strategy for arousing and responding to public feeling.[33] The most effective practitioners combined verbal with visual images, since all agreed that effective illustrations were crucial to the success

[31] This altered consciousness has been explored at length in Smith, *The Other Nation*.

[32] Anti-poor law campaigners made much of cases of suicide which could be attributed to destitution, since they could be used to demonstrate that the poor preferred death to the workhouse. The tremendous publicity given to the case of Mary Furley, which inspired Hood's 'The Bridge of Sighs', should be seen in the context of the campaign to discredit the new poor law. (This 40 year old seamstress had tried to drown herself and her two children in the Regent's Canal after her purse was stolen, rather than return to Bethnal Green workhouse, in which, unlike the workhouse in Whitechapel, she had been badly treated.)

[33] Engels was altogether typical in choosing the case of a London needlewoman who had drowned herself to show the misery of the workers in 1844: *The Conditions of the Working Class in England in 1844*, ed. W. O. Henderson and W. H. Chaloner, pp. 239, 130.

Fig. 7 'The Bridge of Sighs': etching by Lord Gerald Fitzgerald in Junior Etching Club, *Passages from the Poems of Thomas Hood*, 1858

of monthly part novels, although they differed over whether their public, having been reared on prints and caricatures (like themselves), still liked to 'read' into illustrations a wealth of meaning about human

Fig. 8 'He drew nearer to the extremest verge': A. Hervieu, plate to illustrate F. Trollope, *The Life and Adventures of Michael Armstrong, the Factory Boy* (1840), ch. 27

character, motive, and action, or preferred realism.[34] Thus the cosmo-politan Mrs Frances Trollope's *The Life and Adventures of Michael Armstrong, The Factory Boy* (1839–40) carried a realistically direct full-page illustration by the French artist A. Hervieu showing the wretched Michael on the brink of a craggy precipice, with the cruel mills in the distance and the enticing river below (see Fig. 8);[35] while for the last part of *The Chimes* (1844)—Dickens's 'great blow for the poor'—Richard Doyle provided a frontispiece in the old detailed emblematic style depicting Trotty's vision of a desperate, homeless Meg clutching her baby on the brink of the river and tempted by a swarm of devils to plunge into 'that portal of Eternity'—a vision intended to demonstrate that 'there is no loving mother on earth who might not come to this, if such a life had gone before' (see Fig. 9).[36] In the same vein of social protest (although it was also loaded with sexual stereotypes) was Thomas Hood's phenomenally successful sequel to his 'Song of the Shirt', 'The Bridge of Sighs', published by Dickens's friend Douglas Jerrold in the newly founded and still radical *Punch* in May 1844.[37]

Thus in the early 1840s sentimental radicalism fully succeeded in making the suicide of the poor seem part of the wider social problem of poverty, to be remedied through charity and goodwill, and regarded

[34] Harvey, *Victorian Novelists and their Illustrators*, pp. 2–3, 179–80.

[35] On the contrast between the direct drawing of the French lithographers and the English caricaturist tradition, see Houfe, *Dictionary of British Book Illustrators and Caricaturists, 1800–1914*, p. 78.

[36] *The Chimes* (1845 edn.), pp. 164–6. *The Chimes* has been seen as 'the most con-centrated piece of socially committed fiction that Dickens ever wrote', and was intended to be of intensely topical reference. The Chartist *Northern Star* at once understood Trotty's vision of Meg hastening to the river's brink as 'a true picture of MARY FURLEY, and too many hapless ones who like her, have been driven to destruction': Slater, 'Dickens's Tract for the Times', in Slater, ed., *Dickens 1970*, pp. xii, 104, 122. In the figure of Alderman Cute Dickens was satirizing (and grossly distorting) the efforts of Sir Peter Laurie to stop an outbreak of suicide attempts from Blackfriars Bridge: see ch. 8 n. 94. He wanted to 'shame the cruel and canting': Tillotson, ed., *Letters of Charles Dickens*, iv. 201, 218, 232. It has been argued that the 3 pieces on suicide published in *Bentley's Miscellany* during Dickens's editorship 'attest to Dickens's considerable edi-torial interest in suicide' several years earlier: Gates, 'Suicide, *Bentley's Miscellany* and Dickens's *Chimes*'; but the argument is not persuasive, since all 3 pieces were in their different ways treatments of suicide of a kind long familiar in such journals.

[37] Although Hood's poem, like Dickens's *Chimes*, was inspired by the case of Mary Furley, he discarded his earlier lines which adhered to the facts in favour of a roman-ticized fictional version which 'makes the indictment of society more severe': Clubbe, *Victorian Forerunner*, p. 174. See also n. 32.

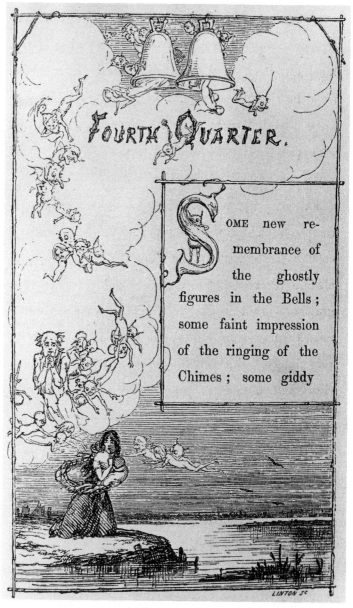

FOURTH QUARTER.

SOME new re-
membrance of
the ghostly
figures in the Bells;
some faint impression
of the ringing of the
Chimes; some giddy

Fig. 9 'She paused a moment on the brink': R. Doyle's frontispiece to the
Fourth Quarter of Dickens's *The Chimes* (1844)

with understanding and forgiveness.[38] By the early 1860s, it is true, disillusionment was setting in; and these years proved something of a subterranean watershed in the iconography of suicide, as in much else. The poor were beginning to appear not as feeble victims of society, but as degenerate, drunken tricksters and parasites who exploited the generosity of the well-to-do. Again, Dickens was a mouthpiece of the new mood. In 1844 he had thought it monstrous that suicide attempts should ever be treated lightly; but in 1860 in his family periodical *All the Year Round* he made a young Cockney sneer cynically of women 'jumpers': 'On'y mind you! There must be somebody comin'. They don't go aheaderin' down here wen there an't no Bobby nor gen'ral Cove, fur to hear the splash.'[39] In the 1860s what was developing was interest in the pathology of suicide attempts (as opposed to suicide itself), and a renewed perception of suicide as an individual, not a social problem.[40] The life-span of a widely diffused popular mood is always likely to be long, however; and among the lower middle-class shopwalkers and clerks who were then multiplying so rapidly in London, it was this attitude of vaguely radical compassion and forgiveness which entrenched itself as the normal response to suicide, precisely because it was then so hackneyed. Vulgarized philanthropy and vulgarized romanticism together ensured that the instinctive response of most Londoners in the 1860s to the usual kinds of suicidal death was to sigh over 'this melancholy event'.

Yet it would be a great mistake to forget that a third, utterly different treatment of suicide—the comic one—had flourished in the early Victorian years; for in the 1860s Londoners carried on laughing—in the right circumstances. Sometimes middle- and working-class people shared in the same jokes; but sometimes each laughed in their own way. There is nothing strange about this Victorian readiness to see suicide as funny. From at least the mid-seventeenth century,

[38] As a topical variant, it was made part of the problem of penal policy towards the poor by Charles Reade in 1856. Reade, inspired by the official reports on alleged abuses in Birmingham and Leicester gaols, shows a poor boy (Josephs) who had been thrown into prison for 'the smallest theft imaginable' (stealing food when starving) as driven to suicide to escape the tortures of the cruel governor: 'I shall tell Him what I went through first, and perhaps He will forgive me': *It Is Never Too Late To Mend*, Book I, ch. 20. Certainly the reader was expected to forgive Josephs.

[39] 'Wapping Workhouse', reprinted from *All The Year Round*, 18 Feb. 1860, in *The Uncommercial Traveller and Reprinted Pieces*, p. 20.

[40] Part of the background to this development was the reaction in the 1860s against the sentimentality of the immediately preceding decades and much alarmed concern about the 'demoralization' of the poor, on which see Jones, *Outcast London*, pp. 244–5, 251.

suicide had been treated as a slightly macabre jest, notably in burlesque almanacs.[41] Any abnormal experience is always likely to be reduced to manageability by laughter, and all the more so when it is one charged with emotion and entangled with such favourite butts as the Law and the Church; and nineteenth-century Cockney resilience and tough wit are proverbial. In the 1860s the best-liked comic treatments of suicide were those which made clever use of parody and word-play (then the favourite kinds of jokeyness)[42] to provide flippant versions of the moralizing, sentimental, and latterly the sensationalist 'straight' treatments of suicide which were currently so familiar. Two enormously successful suicide street ballads of the period, 'Villikins and his Dinah' and 'The Rat-Catcher's Daughter', both made lavish use of the favourite word-games of the 1860s to parody the usual romantic story of female suicide. At the end of 'Villikins' the performer shouted 'Moral', and bade 'all you young vimmen' and 'young fellers' to 'take a warning by her', and 'Never by any means, Disobey the guv'ner' and 'Mind who you clap eyes on'; but before this, his hearers had enjoyed a stream of Cockney dialect, pidgin Latin, pidgin French, and pidgin legal terminology, all in a neat pattern of alternating sung and spoken lines, solo and chorus verses.[43] 'The Rat-Catcher's Daughter' offered tongue-in-cheek sentimentality, not tongue-in-cheek moralizing; but it used the same verbal tricks.

> The Corrioner's Inquest on her sot,
> At the sign of the Jack i' the Vater,
> To find out what made life's sand run out,
> Of the putty liggle rat-catcher's daughter.
>
> The verdict was that too much vet
> This poor young woman died on;
> For she made an 'ole in the Riviere Thames,
> Vot the penny steamers ride on!
>
> 'Twas a haccident they all agreed,
> And nuffink like self slaughter;
> So not guilty o' fell in the sea
> They brought in the rat-catcher's daughter.[44]

[41] Capp, *Astrology and the Popular Press*, p. 129.
[42] On mid-nineteenth century humour, see Gray, 'The Uses of Victorian Laughter' and Bratton, *The Victorian Popular Ballad*, chs. 6 and 7.
[43] 'Villikins and his Dinah', which was 'during its run, as popular as any street song I remember', is printed in full in Ashton, *Modern Street Ballads*, pp. 98–100.
[44] 'The Rat-Catcher's Daughter' has often been reprinted: for example, in Cohen, *The Penguin Book of Comic and Curious Verse*, pp. 285–7.

Readiness to laugh at haunting by a suicide's ghost and the denial of Christian burial to someone guilty of *felo de se* is demonstrated by the almost as widely known ballad on 'Unfortunate Miss Bailey', who 'hanged herself one morning in her garters', then found that:

> The Crowner's Quest goes hard with me because I've acted fraily,
> And Parson Biggs won't bury me though I am dead Miss Bailey,

and thereupon haunted her seducer until he produced a guinea as a bribe for the sexton.[45] In 1868 those who read *The Owlet* were regaled with some verses headed 'The Age of Sighs' which began:

> One more unfortunate
> Laid on the shelf;
> Loveless—without a mate,
> All by her self;

and ended:

> Oh! 'tis most pitiful
> Near a whole city full
> Beau she had none ...[46]

In the same years another popular song, 'Isabella the Barber's Daughter', offered fun with sex-role reversal in the tale of a City clerk 'betrayed' by a 'faithless spinster' who rushes to the Thames's 'dirty water', although he is made to reflect in time that:

> There are fishes in the sea
> That have never been caught.[47]

Exaggerated burlesque patter was another current taste which could extend to include suicide. In the phenomenally successful *Ingoldsby Legends* (first published in 1840), Catherine of Cleves, when she found that her husband's minions had slaughtered her lover,

> ... Drank prussic acid without any water,
> And died like a Duke-and-a-Duchess's Daughter

In *Pickwick Papers* (1836) also, Sam Weller's flow of back-chat included 'There's nothin' so refreshin' as sleep, sir, as the servant girl

---

[45] Cohen, ibid., p. 284. This song was sufficiently widely known for the writer of an editorial in the *Daily Telegraph* of 6 July 1860 to take it for granted that readers would understand the implications of a reference to it.

[46] Hamilton, *Parodies of the Works of English and American Authors*, ii. 259.

[47] *The New Comic and Sentimental Song Book*, price 3d., p. 21. This is also in *Maclagan's Musical Age Songster*, price 6d.

said afore she drank the egg-cupful of laudanum.'[48] Nor were punning descriptions of suicide taboo. That professional punster, Thomas Hood, produced in 'Faithless Nellie Gray' a kind of feeble comic reverse of 'The Bridge of Sighs', full of weak puns about the 'soldier bold' who hanged himself, and thus a second time 'Enlisted in *the Line*'.[49] It seems all of a piece that the standard colloquialism for suicide from at least 1850 and well into the twentieth century remained 'making a hole in the water',[50] and that the formal Latin-derived term 'suicide' was not part of working-class speech—a fact which Dickens used to extract yet another smile in his piece on Wapping Workhouse in *All the Year Round*. 'A common place for suicide', he says of the swing bridge over some dark locks. 'Sue?' came the answer, 'Yes! and Poll. Likeways Emly. And Nancy. And Jane, and all the bileing.'[51]

The Law, the Church, and above all the moralizing and sentimental treatment of female suicide were thus laughed at light-heartedly in both streets and parlours. The poor-versus-rich theme of the melodramas also prompted some comic parodies. The classic in this vein is surely 'She was poor but she was honest':

> Standing on the bridge at midnight,
> She says, 'Farewell, blighted Love.'
> There's a scream, a splash—Good Heavens!
> What is she a-doing of?
>
> Then they drag her from the river,
> Water from her clothes they wrang,
> For they thought that she was drownded;
> When the corpse got up and sang:

[48] Barham, *The Ingoldsby Legends*, iii. 206–14; Dickens, *Pickwick Papers*, ch. xvi.

[49] Cohen, *The Penguin Book of Comic and Curious Verse*, pp. 194–6.

[50] E.g. 'Waterloo's the favourite bridge for making holes in the water from': Dickens, 'Down with the Tide', *The Uncommercial Traveller*, p. 528. For its continued use 60 years later, see Bennett, *Hilda Lessways* (1911), Book III, ch. iv, p. 257. Only in society and sporting circles, apparently, was the word 'suicide' itself given a slang use (to refer to four horses driven in a line) during the nineteenth century: Partridge, *A Dictionary of Slang*, i. 846, and cf. i. 398.

[51] Dickens, 'Wapping Workhouse', *All the Year Round*, 18 Feb. 1860, reprinted in *The Uncommercial Traveller*, p. 19. Ordinary people spoke of 'doing away with' themselves, 'making an end to things', and so on. The fullest discussion of the usage of the word 'suicide' (which is not in Dr Johnson's *Dictionary* of 1755) which I have come across is that of Pollock, C. B., in *Clift* v. *Schwabe*: *Law Times*, 18 July 1846, p. 345.

'It's the same the whole world over,
It's the poor that gets the blame,
It's the rich that gets the pleasure,
Isn't it a blooming shame?'[52]

This may be as late as the 1880s; but earlier, in the 1840s, there had been a different kind of dig at the toffs, when they appeared as a soft touch in the ballad of 'Veeping Bill', who 'gammoned' the 'flats' by conning them into believing he was a starving orphan just about to drown himself off Margate pier.[53] On the other hand there also existed a specifically middle-class suicide humour, which laughed at the attitudes to suicide which permeated early nineteenth-century German and French romanticism, and later at the constant trivializing use of suicide in the enormously popular new sensation novels of the 1860s. It will be remembered that Thackeray's version of 'Sorrows of Werther' ends:

> Charlotte, having seen his body
> Borne before her on a shutter,
> Like a well-conducted person
> Went on cutting bread and butter;[54]

and in the 1860s and 1870s the sophisticated were offered various pieces of frivolity which laughed at the current overworking of suicide as a standard prop in romances and plays (see Fig. 10).[55] Altogether, only one kind of suicide humour was rare in mid-Victorian London: the worldly, cultured, allusive irony which had been so often employed by satirists of English mores in the eighteenth century, in the days

[52] Cohen, *The Penguin Book of Comic and Curious Verse*, pp. 288–9. (The first use of 'blooming' in this sense noted in the *Oxford English Dictionary* dates from 1882.)

[53] Barham, *The Ingoldsby Legends*, 'Misadventure at Margate', ii. 223–8.

[54] Thackeray, *Miscellanies: Prose and Verse*, i. 64, and often reprinted.

[55] E.g. L. Oliphant, *Piccadilly: A Fragment of Contemporary Biography* (1870), pp. 99–102, and see Fig. 10. This spirited satire on the tone of fashionable London, which first appeared in *Blackwood's Edinburgh Magazine* in 1865 and went into its fifth edition in 1874, has also been seen as a parody of the conventional romance with its 3 phases of love, madness, and suicide: Read, *Victorian Conventions*, p. 25. Suicide is casually referred to at least a dozen times in those popular sensation novels by M. E. Braddon, *Lady Audley's Secret* (1862) and *Aurora Floyd* (1863). In W. S. Gilbert's satirical farce, *Engaged* (1877), the hero, his hopes blighted, announces that he is going to commit suicide, but desists as soon as he finds that he is rich: Rowell, ed., *Plays by W. S. Gilbert*, pp. 166–8. It will be remembered that the comic plot of Gilbert's *The Mikado* (1885) turns around the substitution of Nanki-Poo's execution for his suicide. R. L. Stevenson's stories, *The Suicide Club* (1878), however, apparently had their source in one of his cousin Robert Alan Stevenson's whimsicalities: Stevenson, *New Arabian Nights*, i. xxvii, Note by Mrs R. L. Stevenson.

Fig. 10 'The smile is very important—it shall play upon my lips to the end':
R. Doyle's skit to illustrate the disappointed lover's modish thoughts of suicide
in L. Oliphant's satire, *Piccadilly* (1870)

when England was believed to be uniquely 'the land of suicide'. A late
example of this kind of elaborate social satire upon London habits of
suicide appeared in *Bentley's Miscellany* in 1839 (when Dickens was
its editor), in the shape of a prospectus for a spoof joint-stock
company—'The London Suicide Company ... Chairman, the Lord

Viscount Gravesend, Secretary, John Mattocks, Esq.'—which amounted to a damning charge of self-interested neglect of proper measures of suicide prevention.[56] Such social satire, however, did not flourish in mid-Victorian London; and in the 1860s it was farce, word-play, and above all parody which ensured that Londoners laughed at suicide.

Londoners' sensibility to suicide thus had many sides. Yet what is absent is quite as significant as what is present. The suicide of lovers and sham suicide attempts were good for many laughs; but never suicide from want or pain. And if the scope of suicide humour was limited, the serious treatment of suicide was equally incomplete, at least by continental standards. Suicide was still not handled as though it were a morally neutral act. Under the influence of the romanticism indigenous to the English side of the Channel—humanitarian yet moralistic, woman-worshipping yet class conscious, sentimental yet chirpy—traditional attitudes had indeed been adjusted, but no more. Those satanic rebels, bohemian genuises, and blasé roués oppressed by ennui who were such routine characters in the fiction and plays of Orleanist France,[57] had not inspired a legion of early Victorian equivalents, any more than had the melancholic young Werther.[58] Instead, ordinary Londoners had been repeatedly shown suicidal death as the sad culmination either of the individual's sin or cowardice, or of the failings of modern England. True, by the 1860s the aura of want and destitution which had been made to surround suicide in the years of guilty concern about 'the Condition of England' was rapidly being replaced by one of maudlin sensationalism, and traditional expla-nations of suicidal behaviour in terms of worldly dishonour or dis-appointment in love were flourishing anew; yet the message also persisted that it was not always the individual who was to blame for 'the rash act'. In short, this generation of Londoners had never been

[56] *Bentley's Miscellany*, vi (1839), pp. 540–1. For various rather similar satires of the 1750s see Bartel, 'Suicide in Eighteenth-Century England', pp. 152–3.

[57] Their influence in making suicide fashionable in France is pursued at length in Maigron, *Le romantisme et les moeurs*, pp. 312–50. Perhaps the English failure to absorb the continental high romantic image of suicide as the fruit of egoism and anomie partly explains the divergence between continental and English studies of suicidal behaviour. This image, after all, has plausibly been seen as a major source of much continental theorizing, including that of Durkheim: Douglas, 'Suicide: Social Aspects', *International Encyclopaedia of the Social Sciences*, xv. 377.

[58] There were 7 English translations of Goethe's *Werther* between 1779 and 1809, but then none until 1854, when one appeared in Bohn's Standard Library: Long, 'English Translations of Goethe's *Werther*', p. 172.

shown suicide as glamorous or heroic; but neither had they been shown it as terrifying or disgusting. On the contrary, they had been continually invited to see those who took their own lives as fellow human beings, and to feel for them 'loving, not loathing'. Imaginatively, they were very familiar with suicide; but they were familiar with it primarily as yet another aspect of human behaviour which could stir laughter, tears, and perhaps a shake of the head, and which could and should be fitted into the context of ordinary human sympathy and experience.

How far did people transfer this imaginative sensibility to real life? In the mid-nineteenth century, ordinary Londoners were a good deal more likely than today to hear about cases of suicide, for although the official suicide rate was slightly lower in the 1860s than in the late 1970s,[59] the amount of space given to reports of suicide cases in every section of the press was then very much greater. Certain kinds of real-life murder and suicide remained as much a staple of popular entertainment as they had been in the heyday of street ballads and broadsides.[60] In journals catering for the lower middle classes, more-over, the reporting of inquests was further encouraged by the vestry radicals' enthusiasm for the coroner's court as the 'watchdog of the people' and by the radicals' slogan that it was the function of the press to expose that official inhumanity which they were eager to discover behind the deaths of those who had become involved with the new poor law and police. Except in so select a paper as the *Morning Post*, snippets on suicide inquests thus regularly filled the space between those two prime attractions, the columns of 'Sporting Intelligence' and 'Law and Police Intelligence' (in which last there also figured charges of attempted suicide). Indeed, so detailed and nation-wide was the reporting of a good suicide that the press was routinely blamed when-ever a rash of imitations occurred, and continually rebuked for titil-lating a public taste which in reality was very deep-rooted indeed. Good suicides, however, were rare. What was needed to satisfy all tastes was lavish quantities of high life and low life, romance and brutality, mystery and suspense, pathos and tragedy, business and domestic scandals, exotic foreigners and bizarre suicide methods, to-

---

[59] In 1861 the official suicide rate in the Registration Division of London was 88.8 per million living: *Registrar-General's 24th AR*, pp. 130–1 and *Census, 1861*, i. 196. In 1976 the official suicide rate in Greater London was 94.6 per million living: OPCS, *Mortality Statistics, Area, 1976*, Table 5, p. 83, and Table 1, p. 2.

[60] For the taste of the rough poor in London in the 1860s for ballads of crime and disaster, see [Johns], 'The Poetry of the Seven Dials', *Quarterly Review*, cxxii (1867), pp. 392–4, 398–400.

gether with implications of heartlessness and corruption on the part of the poor law authorities and the police. As it was, most suicides were too humdrum to be reported at all outside the local newspaper, and only a select few were featured prominently in the whole gamut of daily and weekly newspapers, from the *Morning Post* to *Reynolds's Newspaper*.

Even so, the routine press reporting of suicide in the 1860s undoubtedly repays close attention. In 1860 there were sixteen metropolitan dailies and an even greater number of weeklies;[61] and their suicide reporting furnishes a good guide to what the attitudes to suicide of each paper's readers were believed to be, precisely because—unlike that of local newspapers—it was highly selective. Yet for all its suggestive variety, this reporting also includes a significantly substantial common denominator.[62] In real life, as in fiction, the response most commonly expected to suicide was evidently pity. Not surprisingly, however, the circumstances which were regarded as deserving compassion were more varied and more humdrum, and the implied explanations of suicidal behaviour considerably more complex. In real life, suicide was not linked with romantic frustrations, impending bankruptcy or utter destitution so much as with worries over health, work or housing, with family misunderstandings or bereavement, in short, as J. Netten Radcliffe recognized, with 'disease, suffering and misery—circumstances, alas! of such a commonplace and familiar character, that they appeal most powerfully to the sympathies of many who know them from bitter experience'.[63] Equally, these newspaper readers and reporters evidently took it for granted that suicide might be simply the result of a sudden impulse getting the upper hand not only in a mood of depression, but during a fit of sulks or bad temper, jealousy or spite, or, most often of all, in a drinking bout. The stock journalese circumlocution, 'the rash act', conveys very well the hasty, impetuous, moody or obsessed state of mind which was evidently regarded as the

[61] Details of these newspapers and their target readerships will be found in C. Mitchell & Co., *The Newspaper Press Directory and Advertiser's Guide*, published annually after 1846.

[62] The section which follows is based upon a close comparative analysis of suicide reporting in Jan.–Mar. 1858, Jan.–Feb. 1860, Mar. 1861, and Feb. 1865 in the following London newspapers: *Daily News, Daily Telegraph, Morning Advertiser, Morning Post, Morning Star, The Standard, The Times*, and (among the weeklies) *The Illustrated London News, Lloyd's Weekly Newspaper, News of the World*, and *Reynolds's Newspaper*; and also upon less systematic use of *The Times* and *Daily Telegraph* over much longer periods.

[63] Radcliffe, 'English Suicide-Fields', p. 707.

normal accompaniment of suicidal behaviour; and to such a suicide, the normal response was one of tolerant pity. Thus in real life, as in fiction, the sad suicide was by far the most familiar genre.

Yet it would be a great mistake to suppose that in real life any more than in fiction suicide was invariably seen as sad. It is true that in the press only attempted suicide was treated quizzically,[64] and that suicide itself was never laughed at (although it would be wrong to infer from this that in private talk it was never treated with sardonic humour or irony). Nevertheless it was certainly occasionally presented as despicable, shocking, and wicked, just as it was in fiction; and moreover it was acknowledged to be sometimes puzzling, as it rarely was in art. Thus when suicide was achieved by meticulous planning and with sober deliberation and yet none of the expected circumstances or motives could be found, the response was at best suspended judgement. Suicide from *taedium vitae* and utilitarian or philosophic suicide were entirely alien notions in real-life reporting, as in fiction; and 'cheating the gallows' got no more sympathy from these Londoners than it had from generations of their ancestors.[65] Outright condemnation was always likely to be the reaction when a man who was reckoned a villain—a swindler, say, or a heartless murderer—killed himself deliberately and from self-interested motives;[66] although when suicide was the corollary of a compassionate murder committed by a distraught parent or lover in circumstances of acute want or suffering, condonation was *de rigueur*. In short, the reportorial and the purely imaginative treatments of suicide shared a broad similarity.

Since every newspaper tried to slant its reporting to suit the tastes of its target readership, the amount of space given to suicide cases varies considerably, as does the sort of case selected for mention, and the tone in which it was written up. What can be learnt from these variations? First, women at least as much as men were evidently

[64] For example, when the crinoline of a smart lady's maid prevented her from drowning when she jumped into the Serpentine this was reported widely: see for example *The Times*, 12 Jan. 1858, p. 4, col. e, and *Illustrated London News*, 16 Jan. 1858, p. 58.

[65] Bracton for a time in the thirteenth century gave the name of *felo de se* only to a criminal who killed himself in order to escape a worse fate: Pollock and Maitland, *The History of English Law*, ii. 488; and 7 of the 16 verdicts of *felo de se* returned in the City of London and Borough of Southwark in 1788–1829 related to prisoners in Newgate or in Poultry Compter: Forbes, 'Crowner's Quest', p. 38.

[66] There was an outcry, for example, when the jury failed to return a verdict of *felo de se* on the reprieved murderer G. V. Townley when he committed suicide: see n. 107. Trollope made the shrewd barrister Mr Wharton employ counsel at the inquest on his swindler son-in-law in order 'to avoid a verdict of *felo de se*': *The Prime Minister*, ch. lxi.

expected to find the subject interesting. It was in family papers that coverage was most extensive and odd corners were routinely filled with snippets on suicides.[67] Thus the *Daily Telegraph*, a very successful penny daily which aimed to be a family as well as a political and commercial paper for the new lower middle classes, not only reported interesting inquests more fully than any other paper but also frequently printed short items on suicide, most of which were captioned 'sad', 'melancholy', or 'painful', and written up accordingly. By contrast, newspapers which did not aim at family entertainment covered suicide cases in a more limited and selective way. The *causes célèbres* were always mentioned, even by a paper like the *Daily News* which was very sparing in its reporting of crime; but otherwise, it was chiefly male suicides in the world of the paper's readers which were noted.[68] Secondly, those who were expected to have the largest appetite of all for such matters were the new lower middle classes—the shopwalkers, clerks, and their families; and the angle they were thought to prefer was domestic pathos. The copious coverage of the *Daily Telegraph* was unrivalled in its sentimentality, whereas the uniquely varied readership of the mid-nineteenth century *Times* was offered a worldly wise handling which emphasized the odd and the curious, and that journal of the social élite, the *Morning Post*, as a rule ignored such matters altogether. Similarly with the cheap Sunday weeklies: all those read by artisans, domestic servants, and small traders dealt in 'appalling' and 'extraordinary' suicides as well as 'melancholy' ones, but the one with the largest proportion of lower middle-class readers, *The News of the World*, gave the subject the most lavish but also the tamest treatment.[69]

The nature of the commonplaces about suicide which circulated in London around 1860 thus begins to take shape. The man—and the woman—in the London streets encountered none of the 'primitive suicide horror' regarded as a continuing phenomenon by some writers, and was even less burdened with the petty embarrassment about

[67] This was not true, however, of *The Illustrated London News*—perhaps because it was expected to be especially read by 'the younger generation' in the family.

[68] Thus *The Times* chiefly reported suicides among those in the public service and in society, whereas the *Morning Advertiser* (the licensed victuallers' widely read newspaper) chiefly reported suicides among shopkeepers and business men.

[69] *Reynolds's Newspaper* was comparatively sparing in its coverage of suicide, as of all violence and crime, but the cases it did cover were treated in its usual thrilling style. On the differences between these Sunday newspapers, which had a large working-class readership, see V. Berridge, 'Popular Sunday Papers and Mid-Victorian Society', in Boyce, Curran, and Wingate, *Newspaper History*, pp. 247–64.

suicide so often attributed to respectable Victorians. On the contrary, suicide was then a topic which ordinary Londoners found thoroughly interesting. In that great city—where the new, less politically minded, fully literate but uncultured lower middle class was already growing rapidly—the old crude thrill offered by all violent deaths was beginning to be outclassed by a new chatty sentimental interest in the lives and endings of other people. Attitudes to suicide, as to any central aspect of human behaviour, were not simple. Class and environment, sex and age, all helped to determine which feelings, which moral judgements, and which rational explanations came most readily to which people; and even to the same person there was little likelihood that all cases of suicide would be seen in an identical light. What was very widely taken for granted was on the one hand that suicide was usually a sad ending which deserved pity and condonation; but on the other that it was occasionally thoroughly wicked, and moreover that not every suicide attempt need be taken seriously.

Nevertheless, it would obviously be quite wrong to assume that people who were personally caught up in a case of suicide responded along these standard lines, familiar though they might be. In mid-Victorian London, each case of suicide directly involved at least twenty to twenty-five people, whether as officers of the coroner's court, jurymen, or witnesses, and these men and women were not responding to a death which had already been categorized as this or that sort of suicide, or even as suicide at all: they were themselves involved in making sense of what had happened. The purpose of every inquest was to establish how the body upon which it was held came to meet its death, whether from natural causes, accident, homicide, or suicide; and then, if it was decided that death was self-inflicted, to consider the state of mind of the deceased at the moment of the fatal deed, in order to determine whether the crime of self-murder (*felonia de se*) had been committed. Juries were thus not only drawing upon their notions of the aetiology of suicide, but also expressing their interpretation of the law and of their own responsibilities. It was therefore medical, psychological, jurisprudential, and penal notions which were called into play, rather than habitual emotional and moral responses to suicide (although these must certainly have counted for something); and the proceedings of coroners' juries reveal as nothing else can do both the plain man's understanding of the likely distinguishing features of suicidal death, and his opinions upon how such a death ought to be treated by the law of the land.[70]

Accordingly, these proceedings deserve close attention. This claim may seem surprising, in view of the long-established habit of remarking that English juries, whenever they could not avoid a suicide verdict altogether, routinely brought in a verdict of suicide 'while of unsound mind' merely as a formula to save the deceased's family from the worst consequences of such a death. To study inquest proceedings in detail, however, is to become convinced that this familiar view not only overstates the uniformity of suicide verdicts and understates the attentiveness to the evidence shown by at least some juries, but also offers an explanation of their proceedings which is somewhat wide of the mark.[71] Certainly at the inquests held by Payne, St Clare Bedford, and Lankester verdicts were not a foregone conclusion, proceedings were serious and business-like, and juries (made up of 'tradesmen and the higher classes' and often of 'superior intelligence')[72] heard substantial medical as well as lay evidence. Naturally they could be swayed by a forceful coroner; but they could also stubbornly follow their own insights and prejudices.[73]

To interpret the proceedings of inquest juries aright, they must first be put into context. It is important to remember that the ideas of ordinary people about what behaviour was criminal and what the penalty ought to be for a given offence were often very different from the precepts of lawyers and judges; and that it was the ideas of ordinary people which often shaped the practical working of the law, thanks to trial by jury, together with reliance (until the later nineteenth

---

[70] The evidence given by the deceased's friends and relatives, it must be remembered, was always patterned by the purpose of the inquest, and no doubt often disingenuous.

[71] The jury system functioned very differently in different places: see ch. 1, especially pp. 28–9; and since it was efficient coroners who kept full inquest papers, and since no doubt efficient coroners tended to improve the working of the inquest system in their district, any study like the present which is largely based upon inquest papers will probably tend to reach more favourable conclusions than would often have been deserved.

[72] Evidence of Serjeant Payne on London juries: see ch. 4 n. 33. The lists of jurors summoned to serve in Westminster show them to have been of similar social standing. Lankester 'never tolerated tobacco, or beer, or anything that detracted from the dignity of the inquiry': *Transactions of the National Association for the Promotion of Social Science*, 1866, p. 293.

[73] E.g. the verdict of *felo de se* on Robert Goring mentioned in n. 79 was returned against the wish of G. S. Brent, deputy coroner for the Western Division of Middlesex: *Daily Telegraph*, 14 May 1861, p. 6; whereas in the notorious case of George Victor Townley the formidable Lankester got his way: see p. 229.

century) upon private prosecution. Thus when conviction for a given offence would have brought a penalty which was considered much too severe, there was commonly great reluctance to prosecute, unwillingness on the part of the grand jury to find a true bill at assizes or, if the case came to trial, a habit of down-grading the offence to a lesser one or of outright acquittal.[74] Offences which did not seem to injure anyone else and offences against the person were particularly apt to be regarded tolerantly. It is accordingly not surprising that inquest juries often baulked at returning a verdict of *felo de se*—a verdict which would entail legal penalties which were reckoned not only futile as a deterrent but also usually over-severe for such a deed as suicide was popularly held to be, especially since they fell not upon the offender but on family and friends. These penalties certainly had not lapsed in the 1860s. Until 1870, all those convicted of any felony suffered civil death, and their property was therefore forfeited to the Crown.[75] It is true that long before this the whole mechanism of forfeiture had fallen into disrepute, and it had become common for forfeited chattels to be returned by the Crown.[76] Nevertheless, the operations of mercy were erratic;[77] and although by the early nineteenth century coroners rarely drew up an inventory of the goods of someone adjudged *felo de se*,[78] forfeiture proceedings were not completely a dead letter.[79] By this time,

[74] In the Black Country in 1835–60 only 15 of 39 women tried for infanticide were found guilty, and these were given only prison sentences; and of 56 people indicted for murder, only 8 were convicted, and of these only 4 were executed: Philips, *Crime and Authority in Victorian England*, pp. 254–61.

[75] In 1870 forfeitures for treason and felony were abolished by the statute 33 & 34 Vict., c. 23.

[76] In 1668 Pepys secured the King's assurance that his late brother-in-law's estate would be returned to his family if his death was found to be self-murder. To his dismay, however, his brother-in-law's house proved to stand within the Liberty of the Dean of St Paul's, and certain members of the jury proved hostile. Finally, however, the safe verdict of 'died of a fever' was given: Latham and Matthews, eds., *The Diary of Samuel Pepys*, ix. 32–4, 43, 49, 78. Perhaps the rarity of verdicts of *felo de se* from the late seventeenth century onwards ought to be seen as initially more a side-effect of the defeat of the Crown by localism and private property than a consequence of altered religious or ethical attitudes towards the act of suicide (as is often suggested, for example by MacDonald, 'The Inner Side of Wisdom', p. 578). Contemporaries certainly regarded a verdict of *non compos mentis* as intended to safeguard property rights from the depredations of officials: see n. 7; and the man most likely to be adjudged *felo de se* was thus naturally the man who was propertyless or a stranger.

[77] For the fluctuating proportions restored by the Crown from year to year in the 1860s, see *Hansard*, 3rd series, cci, col. 1689, 31 May 1870.

[78] In 1850 this had not been done for 30 years in Bristol, for 'the feelings of the public are opposed to it': Grindon, *Compendium of the Law of Coroners*, p. 61.

[79] As late as 1861, when a gentleman who had shot himself on Primrose Hill was adjudged *felo de se* by a Camden Town jury, the coroner concerned (Wakley's deputy,

however, the real threat to the property rights of the heirs or creditors of suicides was coming from the directors of life insurance companies. In mid-nineteenth century London, life insurance was becoming increasingly common. After the leading case of *Clift* v. *Schwabe* (1846) a series of cases in the courts,[80] together with a number of statements and decisions by life insurance companies, convinced the public that a verdict of *felo de se* would certainly void a policy, but that with any other kind of suicide verdict the insurers would probably pay up.[81] Thus the spread of life insurance confirmed juries in their traditional equation of neighbourly solidarity with a *non compos mentis* verdict— much to the disgust of the life insurance industry.[82] The other practical penalty still enforced against those adjudged *felo de se* in the 1860s was dishonourable burial: and this was no light matter to that extremely funeral-minded generation.[83] The body of a *felo de se* was buried privately by the police on the coroner's order between the hours of nine and twelve at night, as the law continued to require until 1882. After 1823 burial had to take place in a burial ground and not in the public highway; but no religious rites in a consecrated burial ground could be obtained for a *felo de se* until the Burial Act of 1880.

Thus even in the 1860s a jury which avoided the verdict of *felo de se* was not merely sparing a family social disgrace, but defending their rights against the Church, the Crown, and insurance companies; and London juries had always defended with gusto the rights of ordinary citizens against the rich and powerful. Admittedly Victorian inquest juries went to extreme lengths: perhaps as few as 3 per cent of all their suicide verdicts were verdicts of *felo de se*.[84] Essentially, however, the

G. S. Brent) said in court that he would submit an inventory of the deceased's property to the Queen's Remembrancer: 'The Suicide on Primrose Hill', *Daily Telegraph*, 14 May 1861, p. 6.

[80] See *Halsbury's Laws of England*, 3rd edn., xx. 274–5, sects. 543–4.

[81] Cf. Westcott, *Suicide*, pp. 51–6, and Appendix, 'The Attitude of Assurance Companies to Suicide', p. 180. This subject is elaborated upon in ch. 8.

[82] Expressed, for example, by Cornelius Walford (1827–85: *DNB*), in 'On the Number of Deaths from Accident, Negligence, Violence and Misadventure', p. 526.

[83] On the burial of suicides, see ch. 8. Their bodies were never sent for dissection in the Anatomy Schools, however, although this was sometimes urged as a deterrent: see e.g. Copland, *A Dictionary of Practical Medicine*, p. 650, section 380.

[84] *Felo de se* verdicts were not separately enumerated in the inquest statistics until after 1893, when great variations between different jurisdictions were revealed—no doubt a perennial state of affairs. In the City of London and Borough of Southwark in 1788–1829 2.3 per cent of male and 0.3 per cent of female suicide verdicts were verdicts of *felo de se*: Forbes, 'Crowner's Quest', p. 13, Table 2. Metropolitan juries, however, were probably particularly sparing with these verdicts: see below, ch. 7, pp. 237–9.

infrequency of these verdicts is simply yet another instance of the long-acknowledged contrast between the severity of the letter of the unreformed law, and the mildness of its practical operation: once more, public opinion had 'snatched the Sword from the hand of the Law'.[85] This does not mean that jury proceedings simply indicate popular disapproval of the existing law of suicide. On the contrary: in so far as they were not mere unthinking routine, they furnish an unrivalled guide to the jurisprudence of self-inflicted death which was acceptable to ordinary people, as well as to popular notions about the causes of suicidal behaviour; and hence it is particularly valuable to consider the circumstances in which juries did very occasionally reject a verdict of suicide 'while of unsound mind', or 'temporary insanity', and return instead a verdict of either *felo de se* or 'state of mind unknown'.

Verdicts of *felo de se* were not mere random aberrations, but expressions of popular repugnance for a particular case of suicide which was seen as truly constituting a criminal offence and meriting the loss of civil rights. In law, it should be remembered, *felonia de se* had two essential ingredients: the fatal deed had to be a *willed* action, and it had to be *part of an evil design*.[86] The first requirement raised questions of the circumstances in which a man was not fully responsible for his actions, and hence of popular notions of mental illness; the second involved conceptions of evil, and hence of popular ethics. In London in the early 1860s a suicidal death aroused no pity when there was strong evidence that it had been deliberate and very carefully organized or ingeniously contrived; or when someone caught up in a network of deeds popularly regarded as evil had apparently consciously calculated that to kill himself would bring material benefits. Examples of such cases in London between 1861 and 1866—all of them adjudged *felo de se*—are the suicides of Thomas Richardson (a soldier absent without leave who had an incestuous relationship with his married sister: both poisoned themselves in their bed of shame in a City inn); Robert Goring (a well-to-do convert to Roman Catholicism, whose

---

[85] Bulwer, *England and the English*, i. 74. Why then, it may be asked, were these verdicts of temporary insanity particularly notorious? No doubt as time went on this owed much not only to their extreme frequency, but also to the fact that they persisted long after such practices had become rare (for *felonia de se* remained a criminal offence until 1961, despite calls for its abolition in the mid-nineteenth century floodtide of criminal law reform); although it must also be acknowledged that the issues raised by the law of suicide cut uniquely deep, and that for 2 centuries both liberal doctrinaires and their conservative opposite numbers had good reason to hold this piece of pragmatism up to ridicule.

[86] Cf. Jervis, *On the Office and Duties of Coroners*, 3rd edn., 1866, pp. 142–3.

suicide note to the well-known Jesuit activist Father William Eyre enclosed £70 'as a token of my love for the Catholic Church and interests' and aroused all the prejudices of popular Protestanism); William Hunt (perpetrator of a spectacular triple murder of his wife and two little girls in a cab, who poisoned himself when the new detective police hammered on his door); and William Vellens (a bitterly unsociable jobbing carpenter, who locked himself into his room for a month to make a guillotine which allowed him to kill himself instantaneously with a single movement).[87] Thus the ordinary Londoner still condemned outright suicidal behaviour which offended his deepest prejudices, and the kind of cool, deliberate self-destruction which had long been reserved for villains in English tales and melodramas (however much it had been glamourized and admired across the Channel).

'State of mind unknown' was a rather more frequently recorded verdict than *felo de se*. 'This 'medium verdict' had been particularly recommended by Thomas Wakley in the 1840s after the M'Naghten case, where he was one of those who denounced what some saw as the abuse of the plea of insanity in the courts; and the suicide verdicts recorded in his last registers, when not 'mind unsound', are all 'state of mind unknown'.[88] This was the natural verdict to return when the deceased was unidentified or a stranger, but it could also represent a kind of suspended moral judgement when a jury was not prepared either to condone the deed or to condemn it outright—as happened when there was clear evidence of some material motive or of that secretive or calculated planning which juries found so distasteful, yet no sign of that emotional stress which would have indicated a verdict of 'mind unsound', nor of those links with serious crime or grossly anti-social behaviour which might have led to a verdict of *felo de*

[87] All these cases were widely reported in the press: see e.g. *Morning Post*, 6–8 Mar. 1861 (Richardson); *Daily Telegraph*, 6–7 May 1861 (Goring); *Daily Telegraph*, 9–14 and 17 Nov. 1863 (Hunt); *The Times*, 28 and 30 Mar. 1866 (Vellens). On Father Eyre, see Boase, *Modern English Biography*. The jury were divided over Hunt and Vellens. Two further examples may be given: a unanimous verdict of *felo de se* was returned on John Sadleir, the Member of Parliament, speculator, and swindler who shot himself in 1856, and won general approval; and a Paddington girl who had insisted on carrying on an affair with a married man only escaped a verdict of *felo de se* after two adjournments had allowed the production of evidence of her virginity and of her addiction to romantic novels: *Daily Telegraph*, 7, 9, and 11 June 1860, inquest on Annie Green.

[88] See ch. 5 n. 27; and Marylebone Library, Registers of Coroner's Inquests, Paddington, vol. iv, and GLC, Coroners' Registers, Western Middlesex, 1856–62, vol. ii. (I have studied closely only the verdicts registered in Wakley's district in 1861.)

se. Thus, for example, a carefully arranged suicide which had been accomplished with a secretiveness and reserve which amounted to deceit of friends and neighbours was left in this moral limbo, even though it transpired that there had been desperate financial need; so too was the suicide of someone who although informally accused of serious crime, had nevertheless been much provoked and misunderstood.[89] Verdicts like these were not numerous;[90] but they show that even in mid-Victorian London, condonation of suicide was neither invariable nor automatic.

Suicide verdicts, however, reflect not only the plain man's moral sentiments, but also his medical and psychological ideas. It is clear that the ordinary layman's aetiology of suicide made a verdict that suicide had been committed 'feloniously, wilfully and of malice aforethought' seem as a rule genuinely wide of the mark, and one that it had been committed 'while of unsound mind' seen entirely plausible and proper—given the meaning he attached to the phrase 'unsound mind'. 'Normal' suicidal behaviour was always associated with a state of diminished responsibility and never with any general evil design, and thus met neither of the strict legal requirements for the criminal offence of *felonia de se*. London juries always investigated the biography of the deceased as well as the location and circumstances of death. The questions they asked show that the typical suicide was expected to have been 'dull' or 'desponding', to have had worries about money, work, health, or housing, quarrels with parents, lover or spouse, or to have been prone to drink. In the case of a woman, lactation and recent childbirth, as well as pregnancy, 'delayed menstruation', and the menopause, were all regarded as likely to precipitate suicide. (Lay and medical opinion agreed that these natural functions lessened responsibility and rationality.) A history of mental illness, shock or depression,

---

[89] Inquest on Mary Allways, *Annual Register, 1844*, Part II, p. 134; inquest on William Jackson, ibid., *1878*, Part II, pp. 3–4. The same non-committal verdict was returned by one of Wakley's juries in 1858 on a surgeon who surreptitiously poisoned himself at the end of a visit to an old friend in Hampstead in which he had not revealed that at that very moment the sheriff's officer was taking possession of his house in Cheapside under an execution for £31: 'Suicide of a City Surgeon by Prussic Acid', *Daily Telegraph*, 19 Aug. 1858, p. 7.

[90] In the only years for which national figures are available, namely 1894–9, some 7 per cent of all suicide verdicts recorded that there was no evidence to determine the state of mind of the deceased: *Judicial Statistics, 1894–1899*, Table XXX, 'Coroners: Verdicts of Juries', footnotes to totals of 'While Insane' verdicts. As 'A Young Lawyer' writing from London pointed out in 1866, a verdict of 'state of mind unknown' was strictly speaking tantamount to a verdict of *felo de se*, since in law a man was sane until he was proved insane: *Jnl. of Social Science*, i (1866), pp. 250–1.

and of repeated suicidal threats or attempts, were also part of the expected picture.[91] The underlying assumption throughout was that people who behaved suicidally were 'in a state', 'very nervous', 'bad in their head', 'strange at times', or simply drunk (and in law, drunkenness could rebut intention).[92]

Plausible evidence of such things seemed proper ground for a verdict of suicide 'while of unsound mind'—a verdict which to the ordinary man in the street carried no implications of true insanity. Only polemicists exploited these verdicts in contemporary controversies on the deterrent value of a severe penal code and the incidence and definition of insanity proper; and only such people equated the custom of returning a verdict of 'mind unsound' or 'temporary insanity' in the typical case of suicide with the controversial attempts then being made to extend the plea of insanity in murder trials.[93] The commonsense view of self-murder was that it was quite different from true murder, just as the commonsense view of the abnormal state of mind associated with suicidal behaviour was that it was quite different from certifiable

---

[91] This is a summary of the impression left by far too many cases to list. For good examples of the questions asked by jurymen, however, the full printed reports of the inquest on George Victor Townley may be cited: see e.g. *Daily Telegraph*, 17 Feb. 1865, p. 5. For medico-legal views on women, see Smith, *Trial by Medicine*, ch. 7.

[92] 'Drunkenness is not of itself an excuse for the crime, but it is a material fact in order to arrive at the conclusion whether or no the prisoner really intended to destroy his life': Wightman, J., in *R. v. Doody*, 1854, Cox, ed., *Reports of Cases in Criminal Law*, vi. 463; cf. Walker, *Crime and Insanity*, i. 178–9.

[93] In psychiatry 'mind unsound' was a term which had a wider meaning than 'temporary insanity'. In 1904 R. H. Wellington, deputy coroner for Westminster and South-West London, launched a somewhat pedantic attack on verdicts of 'suicide whilst temporarily insane': see his paper, 'The Verdict of "Suicide whilst Temporarily Insane": A Legal Contradiction'; and in June 1922 the Council of the Coroners' Society agreed that a verdict of temporary insanity should not be recorded: Jervis, *On the Office and Duties of Coroners* 7th edn., 1927, p. 188; see also ch. 8, pp. 264–5. So far as Victorian inquest verdicts are concerned, however, 'temporary insanity' seems to have been widely used by reporters and laymen (although not by the authors of practitioners' handbooks) simply as a convenient generic term or a handy piece of informal shorthand. Victorian inquisitions themselves are sometimes docketed 'temporary insanity' but carry within the regular formula, 'not being of sound mind, memory and understanding, but lunatic and distracted'. Victorian coroners varied in their personal practice. Wakley claimed that not one verdict of temporary insanity had ever been recorded in the Western Division of Middlesex during his time as coroner: *The Lancet*, 1860, ii. 193, 25 Aug. Lankester in his notes used the phrase 'unsound state of mind', as did those admirers of Wakley, Kell and Sheppard, in the Rape of Hastings, while St Clare Bedford employed 'while insane' and Payne 'temporary insanity'. 'Unsound mind', 'temporary insanity', and 'being lunatic' were all used by the coroners for Bedfordshire, Hertfordshire, and Hungerford whose papers have been studied, and 'temporary derangement' appears in the Prescot papers. The significance of such variations remains to be investigated.

lunacy:[94] in nine cases out of ten, self-murder was the deed of people who were desponding and distracted and not fully responsible for their actions, and who would not have got into such a state if their circumstances or health had been different.

These commonsense explanations of suicide were apparently reinforced by vague notions of current medical views. Some rudimentary acquaintance with the main drift of long established medical opinion on disorders of the nerves and brain is suggested by the evidence given by witnesses and their turns of phrase, even after allowances have been made for the prompting supplied by the questions of coroners and their officers. Nor is this surprising. Family medical reference books were circulating more and more widely in that era of cheap encyclopaedias, and were teaching that mind and body were inseparable, that the nervous system was susceptible to fear, grief, or anxiety, that brain fever might be expected from such stresses, as well as from 'night-watching, hard drinking, anger, stoppage of the usual evacuations, and external injuries to the head',[95] and that 'most forms of insanity are preceded by a period during which the patient is not quite himself ... Suicide is greatly to be apprehended in a good many cases, perhaps the majority.'[96] Similar notions were diffused by mid-nineteenth century fiction, in which 'brain fever' figured spectacularly;[97] and perhaps most effectively of all, by the medical evidence invariably called at these London inquests, and sometimes reported in Londoners' local newspapers. 'Her mind was very much upset and she did not sleep', deposed one surgeon in a suicide case; and another, 'her nervous system might have been in an irritable state from suckling her child', and again, 'under the influence of suppressed menstruation women frequently go mad', or, 'the wound at the back of the head might have set up a state of cerebral excitement.'[98] Any past blow on the head or bout of 'brain fever' was

---

[94] In 1862 the Court of Criminal Appeal itself ruled that attempted suicide was not attempted murder within the meaning of the new Offences against the Person Act: *R. v. Burgess*, 1862, fully reported in Leigh and Cave, *Crown Cases Reserved*, pp. 258–62. Any bizarre or gross breach of the moral order was commonly called 'mad' or 'insane' in ordinary speech: Smith, *Trial by Medicine*, p. 121.

[95] Buchan, *Domestic Medicine*, p. 166. This handbook first appeared in 1769 and went through many editions. It may be remembered that Mrs Tickit, the housekeeper in Dickens's *Little Dorrit*, 'always had *Dr Buchan's Domestic Medicine* on her knee': Book I, ch. 16.

[96] Lankester, ed., *Haydn's Dictionary of Popular Medicine and Hygiene*, pp. 315–16.

[97] See Petersen, 'Brain Fever in Nineteenth-Century Literature: Fact and Fiction'.

[98] CLRO, CR, City, 20 Aug. 1861, inquest no. 134, Harriet Knights; GLC, Central

made much of as predisposing someone to the kind of incipient mild insanity associated with suicidal behaviour, as was any past trauma, or a family tendency to suicide or insanity.[99] Talk of having 'a bad head' or 'the nerves' was a familiar part of ordinary mid-Victorian parlance, and medical men prescribed for a whole range of disorders of the temper, nerves, and judgement as a matter of routine. In daily life, as in medical handbooks and at inquests, conditions like these were commonly connected with many emotional as well as physical causes, and were read into everyday symptoms like sleeplessness, headaches, erratic behaviour, forgetfulness, and irritability.

At inquests such symptoms were naturally sought assiduously and frequently found; every scrap of suitable evidence was exploited to the full whenever the usual wish to give the deceased the benefit of any doubt was present. Witnesses evidently shared the jury's expectation that suicide would be found to be connected with a predisposing history of 'brain fever', 'nerves', irritability, and pains in the head, and with precipitating circumstances such as worry, excitement, quarrels, ill-health, and unemployment, as well as the most likely cause of all, drinking. They sometimes seem to have been puzzled when they could remember nothing of the sort and yet death did indeed seem to have been self-inflicted. Some of them used language harking back to the older monistic pathology and spoke in terms of nervous tension; but many more spoke in terms which faintly echoed the newer localized pathology and implied that they saw the eccentricities and upsets they described as akin to a kind of incipient brain illness.[100] What was conjured up was a psychological state when for the time being the deceased was 'not himself'.

Thus a verdict of 'while of unsound mind' can rarely have done violence to the consciences even of jurors who prided themselves on 'knowing their duty'.[101] Each of them had sworn to give a true verdict,

---

Middlesex IR, Box 1, 11 Dec. 1862, inquest no. 104, Charlotte Howard and 13 Dec. 1862, inquest no. 114, Naomi Bailey; ibid., Box 47, 18 June and 2 July 1874, Jessie Fraser.

[99] Two examples, chosen out of very many, will be found in CLRO, CR, Southwark, 25 Mar. 1861, inquest no. 79, Florence McCarthy; GLC, Central Middlesex IR, Box 1, 3 Nov. 1862, inquest no. 87, John Ballard.

[100] For example, CLRO, CR, Southwark, 23 Feb. 1861, inquest no. 55, Henry Ambridge, and ibid., City, 26 Feb. 1861, inquest no. 42, William Lee; Westminster Abbey Muniments, CI, 17 Sept. 1861, James Purdy.

[101] Bentham was surely showing his notorious inability to appreciate how the ordinary man's mind worked when he assumed that jurymen perjured themselves in giving *non compos mentis* verdicts: *Works*, i. 479.

not only according to the evidence, but also according to 'the best of my skill and knowledge'.[102] So far as the aetiology of normal suicide was concerned, the layman's 'skill and knowledge' envisaged a wide variety of predisposing and exciting circumstances which were all linked with a comprehensive range of symptoms and conditions associated with a person's being more or less 'not himself'; and the dominant medical opinions of the day contributed to and confirmed these commonsense ideas. In the mid-nineteenth century only the lawyers were moving in the direction of a narrower definition of insanity. In 1843 the formulation of the M'Naghten rules 'symbolised and exacerbated' the endemic and much publicized medico-legal conflict over the defence of insanity,[103] and limited insanity in law to the intellectual incapacity to distinguish between right and wrong. Coroners' juries, however, were never prepared to use this exacting definition. To them, the typical suicide might well know that what he was doing was wrong, and yet at that moment not be altogether sane; and current medical and psychiatric orthodoxy supported them in this view.

Londoners north of the Thames who came within the sphere of those two altogether exceptional medical coroners, Edwin Lankester and his predecessor Thomas Wakley, were encouraged to go much further than this in relating suicide to organic disease, and inducted into the novel teachings on forensic psychiatry pioneered in mid-nineteenth century London. Both men were outstanding medical publicists, and both made a point of seeing that their juries were provided with medical evidence which was easily intelligible, as well as full and exact. In the 1860s, no coroner was more in the public eye than Lankester. He held a coronership which was not only the second busiest in the country, but which had been regarded ever since Wakley's election in 1839 as the showpiece of the crusading movement for transforming the coronership into an office for medical men, and hence into an instrument of improved public health, scientific death registration, and better forensic medicine. Lankester deliberately sought to use his inquests to educate the public, and since he was already a household name as a popular writer and lecturer on science, as well as a zealous sanitarian, he had some success. Unlike most

[102] The oath to be taken by the jury is printed in Jervis, *On the Office and Duty of Coroners*, 3rd edn., p. 404.

[103] Smith, *Trial by Medicine*, p. 3. On this conflict between lawyers and medical men, see also Quen, 'An Historical View of the M'Naghten trial', p. 51, and West and Walk, eds., *Daniel McNaughton*. (There are several alternative spellings of M'Naghten's name.)

coroners at that time, he insisted on post-mortems on a very lavish scale;[104] and his habit of particularly drawing attention to the state of the deceased's brain as revealed by the autopsy must have helped to familiarize newspaper readers as well as those in the inquest room with the current progressive medical view that suicidal tendencies were usually a manifestation of brain disease, and that this might well be demonstrated in lesions, diseased membranes, or other organic abnormalities. He insisted that juries could understand even difficult cases, 'if they were addressed in Saxon and not in Latin'.[105] At his most sensational suicide inquest, that held in 1865 on George Victor Townley (a murderer whose sentence had been commuted to penal servitude for life after conflicting expert opinions on his sanity, and who had killed himself in Pentonville prison), Lankester used his cross-examination of the prison surgeon to instruct the jury in the possibility of a latent condition of homicidal and suicidal insanity, and to bring out the abnormal weight of the deceased's brain. He firmly overruled their scepticism about the chaplain's strong assertion of Townley's 'moral insanity' (a concept which had been given much public notoriety by its use in Townley's reprieve the previous year), and insisted that 'moral insanity was recognised by writers on this form of disease.' He wound up with a reminder that in cases of this kind the deceased was always entitled to the benefit of any doubt, and at the end of this *tour de force* secured a verdict of 'unsound mind' instead of *felo de se*.[106] To many ordinary citizens, however, as well as to younger psychiatrists like Henry Maudsley, this seemed plain nonsense.[107] From this time onwards it became increasingly common for leading psychiatrists and medical men to make a point of disowning the extreme view of the ultra-humane reformers of Lankester's generation, so flamboyantly

[104] Lankester told the National Association for the Promotion of Social Science that 'in cases of persons found hanged, and of persons seen to drown, I have not usually ordered *post mortem* examinations, but even in these cases, where suicide has taken place, some light might have been thrown upon them by the examination of the brain, which, if diseased, might account for the tendency to commit suicide': Lankester, *The Sixth Annual Report of the Coroner for the Central District of Middlesex*, p. 16. (Lankester published his annual reports to the National Association as shilling pamphlets, as part of his publicity effort.)

[105] 'The Extension of Coroners' Jurisdiction: Discussion', *Transactions of the National Association for the Promotion of Social Science*, 1866, p. 293.

[106] There is an especially full account of this much-reported inquest in *Reynolds's Newspaper*, 26 Feb. 1865, p. 5. For Townley's trial for murder, see Smith, *Trial by Medicine*, pp. 131–4.

[107] See e.g. 'Letter to the Editor', *Bell's Weekly Messenger*, 18 Feb. 1865, p. 5; and [C. Robertson and H. Maudsley], 'The Suicide of George Victor Townley'.

publicized by Forbes Winslow in the 1840s and 1850s and still doggedly preached by J. G. Davey in the 1870s:[108] namely, that suicide was invariably a manifestation of mental disease, and hence that the verdict of *felo de se* was never justifiable.

So far as the general public was concerned, however, this was a view which was known, but never generally accepted. Jurymen and witnesses alike had fairly clear ideas of the circumstances which normally led to suicide 'while of unsound mind'; and only when the evidence fitted in with these expectations was the normal verdict returned. (Juries sometimes insisted that unless a post-mortem was ordered and gave clear evidence of brain disease, they would return a verdict of *felo de se*.) Equally, it was only when a death fitted in with these ideas that it was categorized as a suicide at all. Then as now what was important was whether or not a typical suicidal biography and typical precipitating circumstances emerged from the evidence heard.[109] When jurymen did not find the pointers they were looking for, they returned an open verdict—as indeed was their duty, since suicide was a criminal offence, and the presumption of innocence therefore applied. Thus, for example, when an unknown man standing on the bottom landing of the stairs at London Bridge jumped into the water, the jury established two significant facts: that this happened at high water, and that the man jumped with all his clothes on, including his cap; after which they would only say that 'they had no evidence for what purpose' he jumped into the river. Again, when it emerged that a labourer who had been found dead from an overdose had been in the habit of taking laudanum and had sent 'the girl' out for a pennyworth when he could not sleep, but all other questions drew a blank, they would only say that he 'died from the effects of an overdose of laudanum'.[110]

The ideas of ordinary people about suicidal behaviour were thus closer to those of the medical men than to those of the lawyers; but they were not identical with either.[111] They never swallowed the extreme dogmas expounded by some alienists of that day, and did not

[108] Davey, 'On Suicide, in its Social Relations', pp. 230–55.

[109] The processes in the 1860s in the metropolitan districts studied here were in many ways strikingly like those revealed by an investigation undertaken in the 1970s into current processes: Atkinson, *Discovering Suicide*, chs. 6 and 7.

[110] CLRO, CR, City, 11 Oct. 1861, inquest no. 157, Man Unknown; Westminster Abbey Muniments, CI, 19 Nov. 1861, John Sullivan (cf. ch. 5 n. 107).

[111] The inherent conflict between medical and legal notions of crime, insanity, and responsibility is the theme of Smith, *Trial by Medicine* (which was unfortunately not

exonerate every suicidal action without exception as the result of mental ill-health. On the other hand, they certainly did not agree with the lawyers that every man capable of distinguishing right from wrong must be held fully responsible for his actions, and were prepared, like so many medical men of the time, to recognize that conduct was governed by the emotions quite as much as by the intellect, and to see both as linked with bodily health. More important among the humble, however, may have been their ingrained aversion from notions of free will. Unlike many more prosperous and articulate mid-Victorians, the kind of people usually summoned to give evidence at these inquests did not feel that they were the masters of their fate or the captains of their soul. They readily attributed what happened to them either to fate, or to the villainy of their fellow men. For humble people, extenuating circumstances always loomed large: after all, in daily life they were very familiar with the irresistible pressure of circumstances, just as their imaginations had been fed upon tales of suicides as victims rather than as sinners. 'We're none of us our own keepers', those on remand in Clerkenwell prison for attempted suicide often told the disapproving chaplain;[112] and this may have been as important a source of their tolerant realism as their comparative insensitivity to the gross physical mutilation which then accompanied many suicides. Very occasionally suicide seemed part and parcel of a villain's villainy and was condemned as such; but usually it seemed no more than act of sickness, weakness, folly, or sheer inadequacy, done under the pressure of debilities, provocations or hard luck which might have beaten any one.

Although they nearly always saw it as excusable, these people did not admire or defend suicide. In first-hand confrontations with it, although not in conventional stereotypes, the role of drink or spite was recognized and even in the sensational press or ballads and melodramas of the day, those who killed themselves were not given adulation or even respect. Outright condemnation was meted out to the rare case which forfeited sympathy by embarking on self-destruction in cold blood, or from self-interest, or as part of a chain of misdeeds; while upon the unintelligible and eccentric, judgement was apt to be suspended. It would thus be wrong to say that suicide was never

published when this chapter was written). Although verdicts of *non compos mentis* returned by inquest juries are not considered in this book, its discussion of insanity and responsibility in Victorian trials is indirectly very relevant to this topic.

[112] Horsley, *Jottings from Jail*, pp. 96–7.

condemned as an evil deed and a cowardly escape from the claims of the community. Yet this was a rare response. Mid-Victorian Londoners readily conceded diminished responsibility when told of familiar stresses, for their entertainments, traditions, moral instincts, and medical notions all usually enabled them honestly to condone a suicidal death as the act of an 'unsound mind'. In mid-nineteenth-century London, suicide was accepted as a fact of life and a familiar incident in comedy as well as in tragedy and melodrama; it was written about freely in the press, talked about and laughed over; but in real life it was always most likely to be responded to (as it was by the prisoners in Pentonville in 1865) with exclamations of 'poor fellow, poor fellow'.[113]

[113] This was the response of his fellow prisoners when Townley killed himself before their eyes as they came out of morning chapel: *Lloyd's Weekly Newspaper*, 19 Feb. 1865 (2nd edn.), p. 12, and [Robertson and Maudsley], 'The Suicide of George Victor Townley', p. 67. It provides a good example of the way in which first- and second-hand responses to suicide might differ, for the response of the outside world to this news was unsympathetic. (A brief outline of some of the points made in this chapter will be found in Anderson, 'Suicide in Victorian London'.)

7

Other Places, Other Times

How typical were mid-Victorian Londoners' attitudes to suicide? How different were the ideas and feelings of their contemporaries in provincial towns or the countryside? And how did the ideas and feelings of ordinary Edwardian Londoners differ from those of their fathers or grandfathers? Only the efforts of many local historians can make it possible to offer substantial answers to these questions. Some pointers do exist, however, to mid-Victorian provincial and rural outlooks, and many more to Edwardian ones in the metropolis. It is thus not altogether premature to raise with regard to attitudes to suicide those same fundamental questions of geographical diversity and change through time which have just been confronted with regard to the experience itself of this kind of death.

How much did attitudes to suicide vary in different parts of mid-Victorian England? Were Londoners' attitudes sufficiently representative for it to be clear that generalizations about the persistent popular horror of suicide need to be discarded? Or were these attitudes confined to a new urban popular culture whose relationship with traditional *mores* has yet to be properly evaluated? Three preliminary points can be made in response to such questions.

First, there is indeed evidence that in rural areas folk attitudes to suicide had not disappeared in the mid-Victorian period; but these survivals can only be understood aright if they are placed in the context of folk attitudes to other kinds of death, other sins, other crimes, and rural mentalities as a whole. For example, the belief (so often noted by folklorists) that the ghost of a suicide was restless and apt to wander, was also held about the ghost of anyone who died unprepared and with his sins upon him, or (sometimes) who had not had his feet tied together in his coffin.[1] 'No one cared to go after dark to the cross roads where Dickie Bracknell, the suicide, was buried with a stake through

---

[1] Thomas, *Religion and the Decline of Magic*, p. 595; Obelkevich, *Religion and Rural Society*, p. 297. For folkloric accounts of attitudes to suicide, see ch. 6 nn. 3 and 4.

his entrails', Flora Thompson recollected of her north Oxfordshire village in the late 1880s, 'or to approach the barn out in the fields where he had hung himself some time at the beginning of the century. Bobbing lights were said to have been seen and gurgling sounds heard there.' There were plenty of other haunted spots around this village, though, and in any case, 'it was all entertainment; nobody really believed in ghosts.'[2] Then too although suicides were indeed often buried in the 'backside' of the churchyard and without any service, in this they were treated no differently from the unbaptized.[3] It is true that in the countryside, much more than in the towns, burial practices must have supported the belief that suicide was a sin which jeopardized salvation, since in rural areas the churchyard remained the only burying place (whereas in towns there were from the 1850s extra-mural cemeteries which included ground outside the jurisdiction of the established Church, in which all and sundry could be buried with any decent rites which were desired). Nevertheless, even in a remote country parish a broad-minded parson might seem to absolve a suicide's sin by conducting the funeral in the normal way—as happened at Clyro in Radnorshire in the 1860s, when to everyone's surprise a girl who had drowned herself was buried opposite the church door with the usual ceremony.[4]

Again, although suicide was certainly talked of as the work of the Devil, so too were other sins. The literal reality of the Devil was taken for granted in daily speech by many people, especially older people, humble working people, and those who lived in areas with a legacy of puritanism or of evangelical revival. The Devil, however, represented not only external supernatural evil, but also ordinary human weakness. The common conscience or moral code, it has been aptly said, was personified in the Devil, as it also was in ghosts.[5] Talk of the Devil driving a man to destroy himself, as of a suicide's ghost haunting the spot where he had killed himself, reflects the fact that suicide was seen as a sinful deed rather than any unique or supernatural horror. There is thus no need to linger too long over the confidence of an old gardener in Radnorshire in 1874 to the young parson Kilvert that 'some years

[2] Thompson, *Lark Rise to Candleford*, pp. 293, 60.

[3] And not only the unbaptized, for 'from the seventeenth to the nineteenth century at least, it remained a vulgar belief that the northern part of the garth was more suited for the burial of strangers, paupers, unbaptized infants, those who had died a violent death, and, in particular, suicides': Burgess, *English Churchyard Memorials*, p. 25.

[4] Plomer, ed., *Kilvert's Diary*, ii. 48, i. 156.

[5] Obelkevich, *Religion and Rural Society*, pp. 276, 283.

ago ... the Devil tempted him to destroy himself because he was so wicked[6]', any more than over the language used by seventy-year old Elizabeth Sutton of Dallington in in 1864, when she apologized for the trouble she had caused by saying that 'the Devil had pulled her in' to the pond.[7] Finally, it should be remarked that although folklorists often say that a suicide's corpse was believed to be unlucky, Victorian country inquest papers do not show any special aversion to the corpses of suicides (which occasionally had to be left in the family's living quarters until the inquest), nor any reluctance to touch the bodies of those who had taken their own lives.[8] On the contrary, although in London the first step was usually to send for a policeman and a surgeon, in the country it was usually to cut down, bind up, pull in, or otherwise tend the dying or the dead, and to follow this with a series of practical actions (such as changing wet clothes), which suggest a matter-of-fact handling of the situation.[9] In short, folk attitudes to suicide have too often been studied in isolation, or in the context of myth and magic; and studied moreover through the evidence of words, not deeds. As a result they have tended to be presented in too melodramatic and lurid a light. In the mid-Victorian countryside, traditional ways of talking and behaving did survive, and suicide was certainly seen as a sin; but there seems little evidence of taboo, unique dread, or primitive horror.

Secondly, there is a variety of evidence which indicates that this wrong act was not everywhere regarded in the same way as it was in London. That rural attitudes to those who were guilty of the sin of self-destruction were harsher than metropolitan ones is suggested by looking into both the conventional clichés which circulated among country people and also their first-hand responses to specific cases. The new sentimental attitudes to the suicide of the poor which were so widely diffused in London during the years of concern over 'the condition of England question' apparently made little headway among farm servants and farmers. In the kind of reading matter intended for country readers in the 1860s it was plain, simple, traditional treatments which were preferred for suicide—as for other subjects. *Bell's Weekly*

---

[6] Plomer, ed., *Kilvert's Diary*, iii. 47.

[7] See ch. 5, p. 163.

[8] I have found no sign of that reluctance to touch those who were unmistakably dying (from whatever cause) which an observant Queen's Nurse found among the poor 50 years later: Loane, *An Englishman's Castle*, p. 137.

[9] This generalization is based upon the cases in the Rape of Hastings discussed in ch. 5, and a number of isolated other cases.

Messenger (a sixpenny newspaper with a rural, agricultural, Conservative readership) reported suicide cases sparingly,[10] and as a straightforward aspect of violent crime and in a conventionally moralistic tone, so that J. G. Davey, that dedicated campaigner for humane social attitudes to suicide, was provoked to attack its columns for preaching the orthodox doctrine that judges and juries, clergymen, and all those in authority had a duty to combat suicide by meting out to it the punishment and condemnation it deserved.[11] The *Annual Register*, which was read in a higher level of rural society, sedately reported suicides together with other criminal cases in its *Chronicle* until the mid-1870s. Older tastes prevailed too in fiction and in comic patter: it was Scott, not Dickens, whom Flora Thompson found to read in her hamlet in the 1880s, and her neighbours in Juniper Rise responded with fits of laughter to a travelling cheap-jack's variant of the nonsense suicide ballad which had been a favourite for at least two centuries:

> There was a man in his garden walked
> And cut his throat with a lump of chalk,
> His wife, she knew not what she did,
> She strangled herself with the saucepan lid.
> There was a man and a fine young fellow
> Who poisoned himself with an umbrella.
> Every Joey in his cradle
> Shot himself dead with a silver ladle.[12]

In first-hand encounters with suicide in provincial towns and villages, neighbours and bystanders seem to have been readier than Londoners to express moral judgements both on those who took their own lives and on those whom they blamed for driving an aged parent, spouse or child to do this desperate deed. No English counterpart has been encountered of the events in Ballygriffin, Tipperary, in 1864, when the country people prevented the burial service being held in the churchyard over the body of their unpopular landlord, Sir Thomas Judkin Fitzgerald, whose suicide they considered should have been

---

[10] The one suicide inquest to which it gave much space in 1861 was that on Robert Goring (see ch. 6 n. 87), no doubt because of its links with traditional anti-Popish feeling: *Bell's Weekly Messenger*, 11 May 1861, p. 67.

[11] Davey, 'The Prevalence of Suicide', p. 512. I have not been able to trace the 'recent long article by John Temple Chipchase in *Bell's Weekly Newspaper*' [sic] which provoked Davey's indignation.

[12] Thompson, *Lark Rise to Candleford*, pp. 370, 135.

adjudged *felonia de se*.[13] There are a number of cases, however, of deaths by suicide attracting enough indignant sympathy for crowds to administer 'rough music' to those they held responsible for the deed. In 1859 one of the leading shopkeepers in Plymouth was booed and jostled when he arrived for the inquest on his eighteen year old daughter, whom the crowd considered had killed herself because her father had treated her too severely (inside the inquest room, there was 'a roar of execration' at the sight of the clothes-line with which he had beaten her).[14] Similarly in Leicester in 1858, when the mother of four small children drowned herself in the river Soar after she had seen her husband in the street with his arm around a girl 'with whom he was known to have established an improper intimacy', the people of the neighbourhood were 'so exasperated against the guilty pair' that the police had to interfere for their protection, the windows of the house where the girl lived were broken, and she had to be removed from the inquest room in a cab.[15] Crowd action like this shows very clearly that suicide was not only regarded as a personal sin, but sometimes as a sin which ought to be visited upon the heads of others.

Country juries, coroners, and magistrates all seem to have been prepared to follow a more severe line than their metropolitan counter-parts. At rural inquests medical coroners were rare, post-mortems infrequent, jurymen often very humble people indeed, and local attorneys usually the leading figures. The non-committal 'medium' verdict, 'state of mind unknown', seems to have been little used,[16] unless it happened that the local coroner, like N. P. Kell of the Rape

---

[13] *Annual Register*, 1864, Part ii, pp. 67–9.

[14] Inquest on Anne Luke: *The Times*, 2 June 1860, p. 12, col. c, and *Jnl. of Psychological Medicine*, xiii (1860), pp. lx–lxii.

[15] Inquest on Mary Stringer: *The Times*, 25 Jan. 1858, p. 6, col. f.

[16] In 1865 in South Lancashire this verdict seemed a novelty worth commenting upon to the Liverpool correspondent of the *British Medical Journal*: 'Coroners' Inquests', 1866, i. 29, 6 Jan.; although 'A Young Lawyer' in London pointed out that 'the above finding is not so uncommon as the writer of the above paragraph seems to think, as it occasionally appears in the reports of coroners' inquests in the newspapers': *Jnl. of Social Science*, i (1866), p. 251, and see also ch. 6 n. 90. It is notable that when a stranger from Northampton committed suicide in a Birmingham hotel in 1858 after first trying to murder the woman who was passing as his wife (for 'if he could not have her, nobody else should'), the coroner did not suggest that there was insufficient evidence to show the deceased's state of mind, but told the jury that 'in the absence of evidence of irritability they must say the deceased was *felo de se*'. The jury, however, insisted on an adjournment, which allowed evidence to be produced of insanity in the family, excitability, addiction to liquor, and 'dulness', all of which, the coroner allowed, 'dispelled the idea of *felo de se*': *Saturday Evening Post*, 13 Feb. 1858, p. 3.

of Hastings,[17] had read in his newspaper about Wakley's support for this verdict as often the most appropriate, and had introduced his juries to this way of avoiding the choice between a verdict of felony or of insanity by leaving open the questions of state of mind and responsibility. When non-committal verdicts of this sort were recorded, it looks as though this was a response less to the absence of evidence as to state of mind, than to the presence of indications of wrong behaviour either by the deceased, or by close friends or relations. After all, a verdict of 'mind unsound', it must be remembered, exonerated from blame not only the deceased, but also his near ones. In rural Sussex that exoneration was withheld not only from a pregnant girl and a crippled visitor who perhaps seemed to have abused the hospitable kindness shown to him, but also where a wife had deliberately deceived the surgeon as to the nature of her dying husband's injuries, where a son had had words with an aged father about the work his father was doing for him, and where a husband might have been guilty of some improper or hurtful behaviour towards his gentle wife.[18] Similarly, in rural Hertfordshire in 1873 a 'medium' verdict was returned on a young man who might have been trying to frighten his parents because they had told him he must earn something or leave home.[19] As for the verdict of *felo de se* itself, this seems to have been given more readily outside London. In rural Hertfordshire, 5 per cent of the suicide verdicts registered between 1827 and 1840 were *felo de se*, whereas the corresponding proportion in the Eastern District of Middlesex in much the same period (1819–38) was only 0.6 per cent;[20] and a sample search of the returns of deaths reported to the Bedfordshire county police in

---

[17] See ch. 5 n. 27 for the press cuttings which N. P. Kell collected of verdicts of 'state of mind unknown' returned in London.

[18] ESRO, A 1614, inquests of 18 Sept. 1862 on Mary Ann Balcomb; 18 Jan. 1866 on John Weeks; 28 Feb. 1859 on John Cockett; 19 June 1861 on James Campbell; 19 Apr. 1859 on Mary Martin. A sixth 'medium verdict' was given on 28 Feb. 1865 on William Parks, a deformed hawker from the Union workhouse, whose suicide (by holding his face down in a shallow stream) had been a remarkably deliberate act, in cold blood.

[19] HRO, CR, Hertford District, Bundle T, inquest of 9 June 1873, David Trigg. His mother 'knew of no love affair', but a neighbour had 'heard him complain that he had been harshly spoken to'.

[20] Three verdicts of *felo de se* and 56 of insane suicide were registered in Hertfordshire: HRO, CR, Register of Inquests, 13 Sept.–18 Nov. 1840. In the Eastern District of Middlesex 4 verdicts of *felo de se* and 679 lunatic suicide verdicts were recorded: Forbes, 'Coroners' Inquests in the County of Middlesex, England 1819–42', pp. 377, 389. In Wiltshire between 1752 and 1796 as many as 11 per cent of all suicide verdicts were verdicts of *felo de se*: Hunnisett, 'The Importance of Eighteenth-Century Coroners' Bills', p. 129.

1861 revealed that the five cases of suicide reported in that year included one adjudged *felo de se*.[21] In Wolverhampton in 1860 a jury unanimously and immediately returned a verdict of *felo de se* on a young woman who threw herself down a pit shaft, apparently because a miner gave evidence that she placed her hands on the rail and twisted herself right over, and they assumed she did this 'in a sudden fit of jealousy'—that favourite explanation of a young girl's suicide,[22] and one which had also accompanied a verdict of *felo de se* on a girl in Barton-on-Humber in 1837.[23] Where murder was followed by suicide (as was not uncommon), provincial juries seem to have been readier to judge the suicide *felo de se*.[24] Finally, the *Judicial Statistics* for the early 1860s allow it to be categorically asserted that in the rural shires south of the Mersey and the Humber, the offence of attempted suicide was handled far more severely than elsewhere; there, a much higher proportion of those charged with this offence were sent for trial, and when tried, were actually convicted and sentenced. In the rural counties of Cornwall, Dorset, Northamptonshire, Hertfordshire, and Surrey, justices and assize juries were hardest of all on this offence; whereas those in London (and the two densely populated industrial counties of Lancashire and Warwickshire) were outstandingly lenient.[25] Altogether, it seems clear that Londoners' attitudes were far from universal.

A third and last point deserves to be made. Generalizations about 'the provinces' are valuable in demonstrating the contrasts between London and the rest of the country; but not otherwise. That there were differences between the suicide cultures of various parts of mid-Victorian England and Wales seems clear enough; and the question to

---

[21] Beds RO, C.O. 3, Returns of Deaths Reported to the Police, sheet for 1861.

[22] 'Determined Suicide of Young Woman' [Phoebe Davis], *Daily Telegraph*, 7 Jan. 1860, p. 2. The evidence is substantially different (and more melodramatic) in the reports in *Morning Advertiser*, 6 Jan. 1860, and *Reynolds's Newspaper*, 8 Jan. 1860, p. 12.

[23] Inquest on Catherine Foster, *Essex, Herts and Kent Mercury*, 22 Aug. 1837.

[24] See e.g. the inquest on Henry Fawson at Coventry (although the jury took 2 hours to reach this verdict): *Daily Telegraph*, 8 Feb. 1860, p. 7; and, more strikingly, that on Dr Alfred Warder reported in *Annual Register*, 1866, Part ii, pp. 93–7; whereas in Camberwell in the rather comparable sensational case of Samuel William Hunt, this London jury could reach only a majority verdict of *felo de se* even after a lengthy consideration: *Daily Telegraph*, 14 Nov. 1863, p. 2.

[25] In 1861–6 10 counties (containing 15 per cent of the population) reported no trials at all for attempted suicide; 6 (containing 33 per cent of the population) committed for trial less than 10 per cent of those taken into custody for this offence; and 3 (containing 4 per cent of the population) committed for trial over a third of those taken into custody for this offence: *Judicial Statistics, 1861–66*, Part I, Police, Table 4 and Criminal Proceedings [Table 2]; and cf. ch. 8, Tables 7.1 and 7.2.

address is therefore where these cultural boundaries ran, and how they should be explained. Were socio-economic similarities or ancient geographical unities more important as sources of dividing lines? Were there significant differences between big cities, small towns, and rural villages; between different occupations; or between one region of the country and another? Were attitudes to suicide more matter-of-fact in areas of mining and heavy industry or persistent acute poverty than they were in small textile or market towns? Did small towns more readily than big cities see suicide not as a personal act, but as an act with social implications, upon which they were prepared to express a judgement? Was there more tolerance of suicide in areas of isolated, independent hill farms than in closed villages where farm servants worked constantly together under the close surveillance of squire and parson? Did those living in the northern Border counties—so often influenced by Scottish law, which never regarded suicide as a crime— take less trouble to conceal suicide or to punish those who attempted it than did those living in an area like East Anglia, where clerical magistrates were most common and the Puritan inheritance was strongest, and which had a reputation for hard revengefulness? Does the proposition that regional subcultures were much less salient in England than in France need qualification where suicide is concerned?[26] There are hints of all these things; and the actual implementation of the law suggests that both local conditions and regional traditions left their mark. After all, 'soft' attitudes to attempted suicide were regularly associated (as has just been said) with the busy magistrates of the most urbanized and industrialized areas— but also with those of the Border counties of Cumberland and Westmorland, which were neither. Reluctance to treat attempted suicide as an offence deserving trial at assizes might have many origins, including purely practical ones; but it seems it might also spring from a regional habit of regarding suicide itself as no crime.

All that can be said with confidence at present is that magistrates, juries, and bystanders in the metropolitan area were more lenient to both suicide and attempted suicide in the mid-Victorian years than were their counterparts in the provinces, but that this greater overall provincial severity concealed wide variations. It remains to be investigated whether these variations were in some way associated with particular regions (with the south-east and south-west particularly

[26] Obelkevich, *Religion and Rural Society*, Appendix, p. 333.

inclined to harshness and traditionalism); with particular kinds of settlements (with the independent and scattered more tolerant than the closed and tightly knit); or with the dominance of particular types of occupation (with those involving daily familiarity with bodily violence or sudden death least inclined to sentiment or subterfuge); or even with local dynasties of coroners.[27] In the same way it remains to be seen whether tolerance of suicide was anywhere connected with 'the triumph of liberty' and acceptance of a man's right to order his own affairs, including his dying (as Bayet maintained), or with a low estimation of individual importance (the thesis which Bayet associated with Durkheim).[28] Certainly there is little evidence that among ordinary folk in mid-Victorian England it was anywhere connected with ideas of this sort.

The contrast between metropolitan and provincial attitudes around the 1860s must not be over-emphasized. Everywhere suicide was reckoned a sin. Even in London, ordinary people about to end their own lives often trembled at their sinfulness (to judge from the few notes they left behind them), although they hoped, falteringly, for God's forgiveness. 'In hopes the Almighty will pardon me; was I sure of that, I should leave the world without the least regret', wrote one sixty-four year old seamstress in 1844. 'My God, O my God, pray forgive me and take care of my dear wife', scrawled an old house-painter in his last throes in Kentish Town in 1874.[29] Yet although suicide was everywhere reckoned a sin, the gravity and the bearing of its sinfulness was seemingly not everywhere the same. In London around 1860, suicide was a sin which the moral, emotional, patho-logical, and even religious platitudes circulating at various social levels combined to make seem often a hard stroke of luck or a symptom of illness, but above all a private, personal matter, which called for human understanding and forgiveness and rarely for judgement. In the countryside older, simpler, harsher responses were still forthcoming, and judgement fell more readily upon the living as well as the dead for a deed which could still affront the collective moral feelings of a community. What emerges in one vital respect, however, is not differ-

---

[27] Personal links of various sorts between a coroner and his successor were very naturally common, the most usual being that of paternity, as in Bolton in 1876: see Clegg, ed., *Autobiography of a Lancashire Lawyer*, pp. 298–304.

[28] Bayet, *Le suicide et la morale*, pp. 792–5.

[29] *Annual Register*, 1844, Part ii, p. 134: GLC, Central Middlesex IR, Box 47, 14 Apr. 1874, inquest no. 21, John Goodcliffe, paper found on body.

ence, but similarity: nowhere in mid-Victorian England, apparently, did the attitude prevail that suicide was glamorous, courageous, or right.

How long did these attitudes persist? As early as 1859 J. N. Radcliffe detected disturbing portents of change in 'the aesthetics of suicide', and by 1863 he saw signs that sympathy and even approval might soon be solicited not only for the criminal, but for the crime of suicide itself. His concern was not for the 'most ignorant classes' but for the literate, whose minds were fed mainly on the most trashy romantic literature of the day or the most exciting events in the current news and were thereby familiarized with a treatment of suicide which he deplored. Above all, Radcliffe was concerned for the young people of the highly educated classes. To him, 'Wertherism' was one of the characteristics of the new sensation novel, and those two spectacular bestsellers, M. E. Braddon's *Lady Audley's Secret* and *Aurora Floyd*, were both 'baits for suicide'. He admitted that the actual deed of suicide figured in neither story; but he argued that the ready way in which their most sympathetic characters toyed with the idea of suicide was the thin end of the wedge.[30] In 1863 such fears were surely much overdone. Mrs Braddon's references to suicide seem entirely within the conventions of melodrama (as do many other features of the sensation novel); and even Radcliffe admitted that no open apologists for suicide had yet arisen in England, as they had in France.

Thirty years later, however, the aesthetics of suicide had indeed changed altogether, and apologias for suicide abounded in advanced circles. In the early and mid-1890s, to enthuse about suicide as 'this beautiful act' and romanticize those with 'the courage to break away from the banquet of life' was standard form among aesthetes and would-be bohemians,[31] just as proponents of 'the new morality' liked

[30] Radcliffe, 'Baits for Suicide: *Lady Audley's Secret* and *Aurora Floyd*', *passim*, and 'English Suicide-Fields, and the Restraint of Suicide', pp. 706–7. See also his articles of 1859 and 1861, 'The Aesthetics of Suicide'.

[31] After the first London performance of Ibsen's *Hedda Gabler* on 20 Apr. 1891, 'this beautiful act' became something of a catchphrase, as is well brought out in the skit on *Hedda Gabler* in F. Anstey, *Mr. Punch's Pocket Ibsen*, pp. 108, 124. J. M. Barrie's first play, *Ibsen's Ghost*, also burlesques Hedda Gabler's suicide; and Compton Mackenzie recollected a Sunday gathering in a Kensington Bohemian household in the mid-1890s when 'a young women in a floppy brown and orange dress read us a short story about some man who had committed suicide so beautifully that we felt at the end of it we all ought to commit suicide ourselves just as beautifully': *Our Street*, p. 278. For the original pasages, see *Hedda Gabler*, Acts III and IV in McFarlane, ed., *The Oxford Ibsen*, vii. 249–50, 260, 262.

to depict suicide as sometimes the final proof of unselfish love or the way to keep a dream secure.[32] To some extent this was simply yet another demonstration of the *fin de siècle* determination to admire anything unconventional and perverse, although at a deeper level suicide might indeed seem the gateway to Arcadia, or to that self-realization which was a central goal of 'decadence':[33]

> Who kills
> Himself subdues the conqueror of kings;
> Exempt from death is he who takes his life.[34]

From the 1870s, moreover, voluntary euthanasia had articulate advocates,[35] and utilitarian and individualist, and then eugenic and collectivist arguments in defence of at least a limited right of suicide were all voiced.[36] By the 1890s it was commonplace for those who claimed to be 'thinkers' as well as for aesthetes to speak in their different ways freely and favourably of suicide.[37] Increasing publicity was given to the 'suicide mania' discerned among young people and children, which began to be seen as the outcome not simply of 'civilization' or educational 'over-pressure', but of 'new views of life, the beginning of the coming universal wish not to live' (as with Jude the Obscure's children).[38] The much-publicized upward jump in official suicide and attempted suicide rates which took place in the early 1890s

---

[32] For example, Grant Allen, *The Woman Who Did,* ch. 24, and 'The Missing Link' in *Ivan Greet's Masterpiece Etc.,* p. 189; Le Gallienne, *The Romance of Zion Chapel,* p. 296; Dowson, 'The Statute of Limitations' in *Dilemmas,* pp. 138–9; This treatment of suicide, however, is one of the aspects of 'decadence' whose beginnings can be found in the 1860s: see e.g. the altruistic suicide which forms the climax of *Meg,* the novel published in 1868 by Mrs Elizabeth Eiloart, an active feminist: Mitchell, 'Sentiment and Suffering', pp. 42–3. Galsworthy's treatment of suicide in 1906 as 'that final renunciation of property' is very much that to be expected from such a writer at that time: *The Man of Property,* ch. 8.

[33] Jackson, *The Eighteen-Nineties,* pp. 21, 152, 160; Fletcher, 'The 1890s', p. 348.

[34] *The Testament of John Davidson* (1908), quoted in Jackson, *The Eighteen-Nineties,* p. 219.

[35] For a survey, see Van der Sluis, 'The Movement for Euthanasia, 1875–1975'.

[36] See e.g. Mallock, 'Is Life Worth Living?' (which achieved immense publicity); Bonser, '*The Right to Die*'; Wells, *Anticipations,* p. 300; and the references given in ch. 2 n. 66.

[37] For examples see the volume of Dorothy Richardson's long quasi-autobiography which covers the later 1890s—'If you knew you were not wanted you ought to get out of the way. Chloroform. Carbolic Acid': Richardson, *Pilgrimage: Backwater,* p. 244; and 'Nessa and I have been arguing the ethics of suicide all the morning, as we are alone': Virginia Woolf to Violet Dickinson, 30 Apr. 1905, Nicolson, ed., *The Flight of the Mind,* p. 189.

[38] See ch. 2 n. 65, and on educational 'over-pressure' see ch. 10 n. 32.

DIAGRAM № 3.– SUICIDES AND ATTEMPTED SUICIDES.

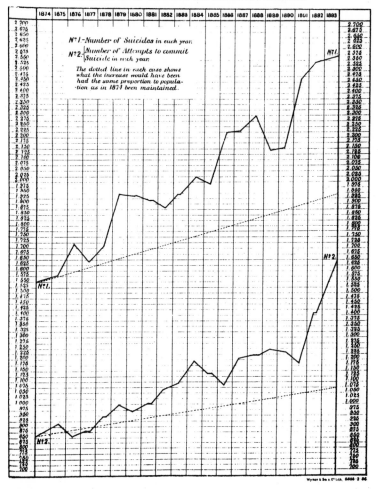

Graph 2. The growth of suicide and attempted suicide, 1873–93, as shown in the *Judicial Statistics* for 1893, published in 1895

(see Graph 2) was inevitably interpreted as yet another alarming sign that the rising generation was weak-kneed and degenerate.[39] In short, shifts in attitudes to suicide (and much else) which had been fore-shadowed for a generation reached a kind of exhibitionist climax in

[39] This upward jump was depicted in a large-scale diagram (reproduced here as Graph 2) given prominence in the first volume of the remodelled *Judicial Statistics*,

the early 1890s.[40] In 1893 especially—a year which saw the production of six of Ibsen's plays in London (as well as Pinero's *The Second Mrs Tanqueray*) and a long hot summer with much press reporting of suicides, particularly of two ostentatiously 'Ibsene' cases—attitudes to suicide provided a touchstone of alignment to 'the modern movement'.[41] The late Victorian and Edwardian revolt in matters moral and aesthetic thus very definitely included suicide within its scope; and although the aesthetic cult of suicide proved as short lived as other aspects of aestheticism,[42] the ethics of suicide long continued to be enthusiastically debated by the avant-garde.[43]

Yet it would plainly be a great mistake to take it for granted that any similar revolution occurred in the attitudes to suicide of ordinary people. Two questions call out for investigation (and here they will once more be tackled with primary reference ot Londoners): first, how far were ordinary people affected by 'decadence' and 'the new morality', even at the height of their vogue in the early 1890s? And secondly, can any lasting, substantial changes be discerned in everyday attitudes to suicide by the eve of the First World War, as compared with the 1860s?

Fortunately, so far as the first of these questions is concerned some very useful evidence has been left behind as a by-product of one characteristic of the 1890s: its deliberate showmanship. In these years, minor 'advanced' figures and newspaper editors co-operated to whip up heated public debates in the correspondence columns of popular newspapers, in order to advertise themselves and their views, and

published in 1895. On the late-nineteenth century European preoccupation with degeneracy, see Chamberlin, 'An Anatomy of Cultural Melancholy'; some repercussions of this on English efforts to prevent suicide are discussed in ch. 9, p. 336 and see also ch. 2, pp. 69–70. It has recently been remarked that degeneration theory provided some of the premisses of Durkheim's *Suicide* (1897): Nye, *Crime, Madness and Politics in Modern France*, p. 144.

[40] Cf. H. E. Gerber, 'The 90s: Beginning, End or Transition?' in Ellmann, ed., *Edwardians and Late Victorians*, pp. 50–79

[41] The 6 plays are listed in Jackson, *The Eighteen-Nineties*, p. 253. The two 'Ibsene' suicide cases were the Canterbury suicides (reported in *The Times*, 12 June 1893 and throughout the press), and that of Ernest Clark, discussed later in this chapter.

[42] 'In 1900 everybody got down off his stilts; and henceforth nobody drank absinthe with his black coffee ... nobody committed suicide ... or if they did I have forgotten': Yeats, introduction to *The Oxford Book of Modern Verse, 1892–1935*, p. xi.

[43] This very topical subject was chosen for the opening article of the first issue of the *Sociological Review* in 1908: Westermarck, 'Suicide: a Chapter in Comparative Ethics'; and could still provoke an exceptionally prolonged discussion among the members of the Medico-Legal Society 14 years later: Earl Russell, 'The Ethics of Suicide'.

to boost circulations.[44] Shoals of letters from the general public on disputable topics thus came into print; and in August 1893 such a correspondence took place on 'the suicide mania', with sackfuls of letters reaching the editor, of which well over fifty were published. The newspaper concerned was the *Daily Chronicle,* a radical-liberal daily which at that time had the largest circulation of any London daily, and which used a skilful blend of liveliness, variety, seriousness, and thoroughness to make itself a very acceptable mouthpiece of advanced opinion, much read by trade unionists and the upper working classes as well as by middle-class people.[45] It is thus not surprising that when on 14 August 1893 a young carpet designer with frustrated poetic aspirations by the name of Ernest Clark decided to shoot himself at Liverpool Street station after a fortnight's holiday in Cambridgeshire with his young lady and the works of Meredith and Gautier, and to win publicity for his last thoughts on Life, Love, and Beauty, he chose to post his long suicide note and last poem to the editor of the *Daily Chronicle.*[46] In the January Parliamentary recess that journal had run a much-discussed correspondence on 'Is Christianity Played Out?'; and now in the silly season of the summer recess, between 16 August and 24 August, it ran another under the headline 'Tired of Life'.[47] For days London had been sweltering in a heat wave, and at that period very hot weather was expected to precipitate a wave of suicides. The subject was thus a good choice for a summer stunt. Moreover, a great fillip was given on the second day by a provocative letter from the notorious Ibsenist and dramatic critic, William Archer, suggesting that suicide should be officially facilitated through the provision of 'lethal chambers'. This was quickly and virulently ridiculed by the young writer Richard Le Gallienne, who was then using every device that occurred to him to build up a reputation. Other minor figures joined in: the American writer Harold Frederic, the cartoonist G. R. Halkett, the radical journalist J. Morrison Davidson and the then secretary of the London Ethical Society, Findlay Muirhead.[48] Most of the letters

[44] Ellen Moers, *The Dandy: From Brummell to Beerbohm,* quoted in Fletcher, 'The 1890s', pp. 348–9.

[45] Havighurst, *Radical Journalist,* pp. 54, 60.

[46] Clark had (mis)copied into his memo book the well-known lines beginning, 'La vie est brève.' His father gave evidence that he was 'a great reader': 'The Suicide at Liverpool Street Station', *Standard,* 18 Aug. 1893, p. 3.

[47] Whittington-Egan and Smerdon, *The Quest of the Golden Boy,* pp. 209, 232–3.

[48] On Le Gallienne's participation see Whittington-Egan and Smerdon, ibid., pp. 232–4. For biographical details of Le Gallienne (1866–1947) and William Archer (1856–1924) see *DNB*; on Harold Frederic (1856–1898) see *Dictionary of American Biography*; on

printed, however, were from ordinary men and women (if those who write letters to newspapers can ever be so regarded); and since the editorial staff of the *Daily Chronicle* certainly knew how to please their readers, these fifty or so letters may be taken to provide a cross-section of the opinions then held on 'the suicide mania' by middle-class and seriously minded working-class people in London. (Only a few letters from provincial correspondents were printed.)

What then were the attitudes of these ordinary Londoners? To an extent which is striking (unless it is simply the result of editorial selection) they were prepared to accept the *Daily Chronicle*'s lead, and to equate arguments about the current cult of suicide with arguments about suicide in general. Interest in normal suicide, and knowledge of it, are conspicuously lacking throughout this debate. Only one correspondent—a veteran inquest reporter—pointed out that Clark's case was altogether a-typical, and that *taedium vitae* was really a very rare cause of suicide indeed;[49] almost everyone else discussed suicidal behaviour in terms of the *fin de siècle* romanticism of Clark's last words: 'I object to life. I hate and despise it.'[50] Most of them attempted to refute the 'new philosophy of suicide'. They usually did so, however, not on a priori grounds but on utilitarian or hedonistic ones, and sought to deter other Ernest Clarks from suicide not by asserting that the deed was intrinsically wrong, but rather by urging that life was, or could be, tolerable and worth while. Two things are notable about these lay sermons. First, that they *were* sermons. Only four correspondents offered a brisk practical prescription like that of 'C.W.': 'castor oil, and rest, and a little healthy romance reading would soon stop morbid self-inspection'; and only one letter was humorously ironical (evidently suicide humour was either dying out, or was not regarded as acceptable in this particular context).[51] Secondly, it is notable that between the three different kinds of sermon which were proffered—based upon humanism, Christianity, or patriotism—equal space was allowed to humanism and Christianity by the liberal-radical

G. R. Halkett, caricaturist and writer (1855–1918) see Waters, *Dictionary of British Artists Working 1900–1950*; on J. Morrison Davidson see Smith, *The London Heretics*, p. 132; and for the identification of Findlay Muirhead see Spiller, *The Ethical Movement in Great Britain*, p. 68 n. Another contributor was James Ashcroft Noble, a Liverpool businessman who contributed to *The Yellow Book*: Whittington-Egan and Smerdon, *The Quest of the Golden Boy*, p. 49.

[49] D. Oliver, 'Tired of Life', *Daily Chronicle*, 22 Aug. 1893, p. 3.
[50] 'Tired of Life', ibid., 16 Aug. 1893, p. 3.
[51] 'C.W.', ibid., 19 Aug. 1893, p. 8; George Samuel, ibid., 21 Aug. 1893, p. 3.

Chronicle, but patriotism ('the Englishman's motto is, "Never say die"') was lightly represented. Thus a wide spectrum of Christian opinion got into print, ranging from the ostentatiously up-to-date ('the new spirit that is abroad will one day be the world's regeneration ... we must work out the education and development of the race') and the bright 'mission' approach ('what we want is a Correspondence Church, run by Dean Farrar ... W. T. Stead, and Hugh Price Hughes'), through the orthodoxies of 'Thou shalt not tempt the Lord thy God' and 'the Catholic faith will prevent suicide' (which inevitably provoked a Protestant counter-claim), to humble personal testimonies to 'the power of the voice of Jesus' (which went down better with other correspondents than long-winded clerical trendiness).[52] Hell went unmentioned; but clearly it would be a mistake to suppose that Christianity was 'played out' among the *Chronicle's* readers in 1893. Equally, the editor allowed a wide spectrum of heretical opinion to get into print; although here, if the Theosophists are left out of the reckoning, there was rather less variety than among the Christians. Members of the Ethical Movement and the Social Democratic Federation agreed in urging that brotherhood and hopes of social progress were what made life worth living. Only one old radical campaigner, J. Morrison Davidson, stated categorically that 'deliberate suicide is simply the ultimate expression of moribund individualism and the competitive system of production and distribution; the root of the suicide mania, therefore, will be extirpated in time', with the triumph of co-operation; meanwhile, cowards ought to pull themselves together and sing 'Jerusalem'.[53] 'In the abode of the common people are consolations', encouraged 'a friend of Krapotkin' [*sic*], G. H. Perris of Chiswick.[54] 'We must work for the race, not ourselves', and, 'the one anodyne is sympathy with others', wrote one correspondent after another—even those so apparently unaware of organized progressive movements as to be capable of suggesting the setting up of an association 'working for the evolution of a more perfect humanity' at a time when London was fuller of precisely such groups than ever before or since.[55] The same gospel was preached in the single leader published

[52] See the letters in the *Daily Chronicle* from respectively John Page Hopps, 19 Aug., p. 8, the Revd. Holden Sampson, 22 Aug., p. 3, 'H.A.B.', 19 Aug., p. 8, 'Osyth', 22 Aug., p. 3, 'One Who Smells Jesuits Around', 24 Aug., p. 3, 'Ex-Soldier', 17 Aug., p. 5, Edward Beedoe, 18 Aug., p. 5, R. Padgham, 19 Aug. 1893, p. 8.

[53] Ibid., 23 Aug. 1893, p. 3.

[54] Ibid., 22 Aug. 1893, p. 3.

[55] E.g. T. F. Simmons, 17 Aug., p. 5, Walter C. Tracher, 18 Aug., p. 5, 'J.E.S.' and

on the subject: the current 'giving up' mood was condemned and blamed upon egoism, and the depressed were exhorted to have faith in 'the immense possibilities of human improvement'.[56]

For very few of the *Daily Chronicle*'s correspondents was suicide not an ethical question in 1893, and this was as true of atheists and socialists as of Christians and patriots. Indeed, it was frequently the heretics who offered the clearest moral condemnation of suicide, while the Christians often simply implied that for them the question would not arise, since for a Christian, life was necessarily worth living. In other words, as so often happened in these years, it was the hedonistic rewards of Christianity which were emphasized, rather than its super-natural authority; while altruistic moralism flourished vigorously on the heretical side of the fence. Certainly the aesthetes and egoists and ruthless eugenicists were left high and dry in a small minority. Apparently the new Bohemian taste for suicide was altogether wrong to progressive middle-class and upper working-class Londoners, although only a few of them went so far as to regard the subject in the manner of *The Independent and Nonconformist* as 'disgusting, dangerous and demoralising', and better not discussed at all.[57] The *fin de siècle* cult of romantic, egoistic, doctrinaire suicide won much attention but little admiration or even tolerance—just as earlier varieties of 'Wertherism' had made little impact in England, compared with the Continent.

What of everyday attitudes to 'normal', ordinary suicide? Con-servative opinion leaders were certainly fond of claiming that they had altered greatly. Preoccupied as they were with the regression, decadence, and loss of belief in divine providence which they espied all round them, they castigated 'growing tolerance' for suicide, lamented that 'suicide is now regarded with sympathy rather than with abhorrence', and in 1910, when the revision of the Prayer Book was under way, complained that in the last fifty years the Church as well as public sentiment had become injuriously tolerant of suicide.[58] It

'C.E.', 19 Aug., p. 8, John B. Shipley, 22 Aug., p. 3, 1893. Some of these many organizations are discussed in Smith, *The London Heretics*.

[56] *Daily Chronicle*, 19 Aug. 1893, p. 4. Probably the writer was the Revd W. D. Morrison, the penal reformer (1852–1953), who was the *Chronicle*'s leader writer on prisons and penal reform at this time and wrote on suicide on other occasions: Havighurst, *Radical Journalist*, p. 56.

[57] 'A Gruesome Controversy', *The Independent and Nonconformist*, 24 Aug. 1893, p, 150.

[58] See *The Spectator*, lxii. 364–5 (16 Mar. 1889); Henson (1863–1947: *DNB*), 'Suicide', p. 67; *The Spectator*, civ. 920 (4 June 1910).

would be a mistake, however, to regard rhetoric like this as necessarily any better founded than most assertions about the good (or the bad) old days. In essentials the moral, aesthetic, and even aetiological responses of ordinary people to suicide were probably much the same at the beginning of the twentieth century as they had been fifty years earlier. Public utterances by public persons, the practice of parsons, and the prescriptions of specialists had indeed altered in ways which will shortly be described, and all these encouraged the notion that tolerance of suicide was a recent mushroom growth. Yet it seems that so far as the plain man's ways of understanding, judging, and above all feeling about suicide were concerned, continuity was greater than change. True, in 1893 the *Daily Chronicle* discerned a great change during the last twenty to thirty years, and claimed that 'nineteen out of twenty people now believe in the propriety of suicide under certain conditions ... The idea of suicide as a sin hardly exists in popular consciousness. Pity, or the conviction that the act was a rash one, represents the nearest approach to moral reprobation.'[59] It is difficult to see, however, either that this analysis was strictly correct with regard to the 1890s or that it could not have been equally well applied to the 1860s. At the end, as in the middle of the century, suicide was condoned 'under certain conditions'. When it was committed in sickness, want, sorrow, or other unnerving stress, it always seemed understandable enough, and a deed which could be expected to be forgiven by a man's Maker as well as by his fellows. In the 1890s, as in the 1860s, most suicides did in fact seem to take place in some such circumstances, and most suicides accordingly aroused sentimental pity—to the disapproval of the hard-liners of both generations.

On the other hand, at the end as in the middle of the century, suicide which seemed the result of cool egoism or cowardice was strongly condemned. The *Chronicle*'s own correspondence columns demonstrate that its leader writer was wrong in supposing that in 1893 'the idea of suicide as a sin hardly exists in popular consciousness.' Most correspondents did regard Ernest Clark's deliberate act of suicide as morally reprehensible, although not many of them used the historic language of religion to condemn it. To sample suicide notes written in London in 1911, moreover, is still to come across such perennial phrases as 'hoping for forgiveness from all', or 'I despise myself for

[59] *Daily Chronicle*, 19 Aug. 1893, p. 4.

what I am doing ... Everybody will say I am bad and wicked.'[60] On the eve of the First World War, the normal suicide verdict of London inquest juries continued to be some variant of 'while of unsound mind';[61] but they still gave this verdict not because they did not regard suicide as a sin, but because they did not regard it as normally either a crime or a deed deserving the penalties still prescribed by the civil and canon law. As the barrister Richard O'Sullivan emphasized to the Medico-Legal Society in 1922, juries regarded suicide as 'something which the ordinary man does not do, and which the ordinary man ought not to do', and the verdict of 'temporary insanity' seemed to them the way 'to put it somehow right';[62] and in Edwardian even more than in mid-Victorian London, lay medical and psychiatric ideas may well have made such a verdict seem accurate enough, as familiarity spread with the idea of neurasthenia and a 'borderland' between normality and insanity, and with the notion that normality could be equated with an equilibrium which was easily disturbed. It is true that some legal pedants joined the traditionalists in campaigning at the turn of the century for a return to verdicts of *felo de se*; but Richard Le Gallienne was surely showing again his flair for playing the right notes to the gallery when he declared that those who found 'temporary insanity' verdicts absurd were interpreting insanity far too narrowly, and certainly far more narrowly than did ordinary jurymen: 'It should be defined as when the balance of the man's nature is not even.'[63]

What of the frequent claim by moralizing contemporaries that the Edwardian press was guilty of sensational, emotional handling of suicide and of giving it prominence, and that this demonstrated the change in popular attitudes to suicide from abhorrence to sympathy? In so far as the line taken by a commercially successful newspaper does indeed offer some indication of the likely attitudes of its readers this claim, if well founded, would certainly weaken the case for continuity just put forward. But was it well founded? A close comparative analysis of suicide reporting in London newspapers in March 1861 and July 1911 suggests that even in the 'yellow press' suicide was in fact playing a lesser role in 1911 than it had done in the mass circulation

[60] 'Sisters Found Drowned' (a case reported in virtually every newspaper), *The Times*, 15 July 1911, p. 7, col. d; 'Leeds Woman in Thames', *The Standard*, 20 July 1911.

[61] The *Judicial Statistics* for 1913 show that in the County of London 98.9 per cent of all suicide verdicts were verdicts of insanity, or of 'no evidence to determine the state of mind of the deceased': Table XXXI, p. 119.

[62] Discussion on paper by Earl Russell, 'The Ethics of Suicide', p. 44.

[63] *Daily Chronicle*, 21 Aug. 1893, p. 3.

newspapers of fifty years before, and that what had changed was typographical and journalistic techniques rather than the line taken on suicide.[64] In 1911 as in 1861, suicides (like homicides, daring robberies, conflagrations, and other disasters) were used to provide mass entertainment; but by 1911 so much else had been trivialized that these traditional topics were necessarily reported more selectively in order to make room for a whole range of foreign and home 'stories'—about the royal family, events of 'the Season', politicians and international crises, the unemployed, animals and family life, as well as sport, crime, and 'romance'. The spacious lay-out of the new halfpennies, too, meant that there was no longer any need for the routine small-print 'fillers', which suicide cases often conveniently provided for old-fashioned closely covered pages. It is true that when the halfpenny tabloids did report a suicide, they did so stridently, offering a strong 'angle' by means of double or triple-banked cross-headlines and sub-headings, and exaggerating, distorting, and padding out the story; but this was necessary in order to make it as likely as all the rest of their copy.[65] Such spectacular slickness was indeed new; but the sentimentality and sensationalism which contemporaries emphasized certainly was not.

Overall, fewer suicide cases got reported in 1911 than in 1861; and in some papers, those few cases which were thought worth featuring were handled much more dramatically than before, like everything else. These two changes, however, hardly warrant the conclusion that readers' attitudes to suicide either had altered very much, or were being drastically reshaped, especially since not all newspapers, even among the popular press, had taken to the new style of reporting. The *Morning Leader* and the *Star*, among the halfpennies, paid little heed to suicide; the *Daily Telegraph* had long lost its zeal for suicide

[64] See Lee, *The Origins of the Popular Press in England*, pp. 117–30. A comparison might well be made with the withering away of press reporting of executions: ibid., p. 102.

[65] A good example is the handling of the suicide of two servant girls at Brent in July 1911. The *Star* (an evening halfpenny paper) scooped the story and gave it a large display on 12 July. On Thursday 13 July (or Sunday, 16 July, in the case of the Sunday papers) it was reported throughout the press, in instructively different ways. The *Daily Mail* splashed it over p. 3: 'SISTERS DROWNED TOGETHER/DEATH EMBRACE OF TWO GIRLS/BUNDLE OF LOVE LETTERS'; while at the opposite end of the spectrum the *Morning Post* (the top people's penny daily) devoted a scanty 2 column-inches to the story in a baldly factual style, although it included the information that both girls were 'to leave service'. The old-fashioned *Morning Advertiser* was the only paper which on the same day also offered snippets about a 'suicide through unemployment' and another through incapacitating illness.

reporting; and although the *Standard* provided a steady coverage of coroners' inquests, it did so staidly—while the *Morning Advertiser* still handled suicide, like everything else, exactly as it had done in the 1860s. Moreover, debatable though the relationship between the values implied in the media and those actually held by their publics must always be, it is difficult to see that this relationship was likely to have been any more potent where the 'new journalism' was concerned than it was in the case of popular melodramas or novelettes. In all three everything was larger than life, and probably recognized to be so by everyone—except (apparently) susceptible adolescents. 'Maudlin sentimentality' about suicide was being deplored in 1860, and indeed much earlier still; and the more florid forms this sentimentality took at the turn of the century were surely simply an expression of the self-indulgent emotionalism characteristic of every aspect of middle-class and respectable working-class taste at that time, and not an indication of any great changes in the substance of popular feelings or moral attitudes.

At the end as in the middle of the century,[66] many things made it natural for ordinary people to condone most cases of suicide and subscribe to a verdict of 'temporary insanity': miscellaneous lore about the physical, mental, and emotional causes and consequences of someone 'not being himself'; easy feelings of pity; a vague ethic of 'do as you would be done by' and lower down the social scale the fatalistic acceptance that 'it could happen to any of us'; and among the poor the rarity of any sense of a duty to struggle against pain and weakness combined with almost universal moral and religious tolerance and a habit of explaining even the worst sin in their book with, 'They can't be right in their head. No one in their senses would go for to do such a thing.'[67] Nevertheless there were always some cases in which absolution was withheld, and to make away with oneself was in the abstract held to be wrong, however rarely ordinary people ever formulated their ethical position.[68] The reaction of the poor to wrong-doing, according to a sensitive Edwardian observer, the Queen's Nurse

---

[66] It is worth noting that the comparative continuity during the same time-span of working-class religious values and assumptions has been remarked upon: McLeod, *Class and Religion in the Late Victorian City*, p. xi.

[67] Loane, *The Next Street But One*, pp. 78–9, and *An Englishman's Castle*, p. 137.

[68] For a small shopkeeper to make elaborate and long drawn out suicide plans, justifying them to himself with, 'I don't see it does any harm to anyone' and 'there was nothing more to hope for but unhappiness', as did H. G. Wells's Mr Polly, was a sign of that character's eccentricity: *The History of Mr Polly*, pp. 244, 248.

Miss M. Loane, was 'I wonder he durst';[69] and suicide, it may be remembered, was always 'the rash act' in popular newspapers. The continuing compassionate condonation of 'normal' suicide was surely all of a piece with the uncomplicated ethical and religious attitudes of the respectable poor and those immediately above them, with their casual deism, their easy acceptance of death and immortality, and the familiar tangibility to them of Heaven, but not of Hell.[70]

Yet it would be wrong to conclude that no significant changes at all occurred in the attitudes to suicide of ordinary people during these fifty years or so. One important part of the context which shapes everyday attitudes to suicide is current attitudes to other kinds of death; and much has recently been made of the transformation of death in the early twentieth century for the first time in western history into an embarrassing and forbidden subject, and of dying into a process to be controlled by doctors and hidden away in hospitals.[71] Certainly from the 1870s there was a dwindling taste for deathbed scenes, elaborate burial ceremonials, and the accoutrements of public mourning, although outside the metropolis and at the bottom of the social scale old ways lasted longer. Is there any evidence that suicide, like natural death, was being extruded from the realm of the familiar in the late nineteenth and early twentieth centuries, and pushed into that of the remote and embarrassing? To those who believe that 'some time after Waterloo' suicide became 'a social disgrace' and was 'forced underground' by bourgeois 'Victorianism',[72] this question will seem perverse. Yet if, as has been argued here, suicide was in reality not 'kept out of sight' in the mid-nineteenth century among ordinary people, it clearly needs to be asked what other, later pressures concealed it from view, in so far as it 'went underground' at all.

[69] Loane, *The Next Street But One*, p. 88. Miss Loane unfortunately knew men far less intimately than women and children. George Sturt (1863–1927: *DNB*), however, commented on the absence of speculative thought and the fatalistic, stoical temper of his Surrey villagers: 'G. Bourne' [pseud.], *Change in the Village*, p. 130.

[70] Loane, *The Queen's Poor*, pp. 33, 46, 108, and *An Englishman's Castle*, p. 59. The tangible reality of Heaven is borne out by some suicide notes: cf the suicide note left by Harry of Walworth on p. 170.

[71] Ariès, *Western Attitudes Towards Death*, pp. 85–107; Illich, *Medical Nemesis*, pp. 122–50, and the references given there.

[72] Fedden, *Suicide*, pp. 247–9. Recently it has been suggested that suicide has changed from being a mortal sin to being another 'dirty little secret' as a result of having become since 1897 a subject for intensive scientific research: Alvarez, *The Savage God*, p. 69. Suicide has been a favourite subject for intensive scientific investigation, however, since the early nineteenth century: see ch. 1 n. 1.

In addressing such a question it is again essential to distinguish between shifts in the responses of members of a family to a case of suicide in their midst, and shifts in routine attitudes to suicide among the uninvolved. So long as official classification of a death as suicide brought with it practical penalities (as it might still do under civil and canon law, even in the early twentieth century), a family must have been anxious that a death from suicide should be called by another name, particularly when they were people of standing and substance. Whether or not they also sought to conceal a suicide in order to avoid purely social penalties, however, must surely have depended very much on such things as a family's social position, on how it made its living, and on how far the circumstances associated with that particular suicide were likely to seem discreditable in the eyes of neighbours. Among working people, who readily blamed suicide upon fate or human victimization and not on the individual concerned, suicide can rarely have seemed to threaten family disgrace unless the family itself seemed to blame for the deed—as not infrequently happened. Shopkeepers, lodging-house keepers, and publicans, however, seem to have been particularly anxious to conceal a suicide on their premises, no doubt because they had custom to lose; while, for example, a lower middle-class man whose father had spent some time in a workhouse, or a lower middle-class mother who knew her unmarried daughter had given herself an abortion and been jilted repeatedly, understandably tried hard to prevent the enquiries being set on foot which would lead to these facts getting out at an inquest.[73] It has too often been forgotten that the English system of investigating sudden death was a peculiarly open one, and involved washing everyone's dirty linen not only in a public inquest room, but probably in the local newspaper as well. An inquiry was thus not usually welcome.

By the early twentieth century, certain developments may have made an inquest even less welcome to a family than it had been fifty years earlier. For one thing, inquest post-mortems had become more common everywhere, and in certain districts of London, they were an invariable rule;[74] and dissection of any kind (like cremation) remained

[73] GLC, Central Middlesex IR, Box 47, 22 Dec. 1874, inquest no. 194, Henry Dixon; CLRO, CR, City, inquest no. 120, 9 Aug. 1911. When a policeman took a City clerk who had poisoned himself to a chemist's for chalk and water, he was ordered out of the shop: ibid., inquest no. 135, 27 Sept. 1911, and 'A Chemist's Legality', *City Press*, 30 Sept. 1911, p. 6.

[74] The proportion of inquest cases (not including hospital cases) on which post-mortems were ordered by the 8 coroners in the London County Council's area in 1903–

extremely repugnant to all but a progressive highly educated few. Among lower middle-class people personal success and happiness were increasingly admired and increasingly attributed to competitive achievement, so that suicide may more easily have seemed a humiliating confession of defeat, and one which brushed off upon the deceased's relations—given the percolation downwards of the mid-nineteenth century middle-class ideal of the close-knit mutually supporting family. Again, in a London made up of 'villages', whose population had become residentially more stable, and which contained a larger proportion of people susceptible to the claims of propriety and respectability, and anxious and able to 'keep themselves to themselves', the publicity of an inquest must have become more distasteful to still more families. Drunkenness and insanity, in particular—each of which was often presented as behind suicidal behaviour—were far more of a slur by the early twentieth century than they had been fifty years earlier, and each had come to be quite widely associated with transmissible physical degeneracy.

For uninvolved outsiders, on the other hand, it may have become even easier to exonerate from all blame someone who committed suicide (and his family also), if only because the level of suffering and unhappiness which people were expected to tolerate had fallen, and because suicide was increasingly seen as a matter not calling for moral judgement. Probably neither the diminishing social importance of death nor the decline of dogmatic religion and of belief in divine punishment for sin was as important here as increasing familiarity with a continually widening range of quasi-medical explanations for suicidal behaviour which removed it altogether from the sphere of human responsibility. Three such explanations—hot weather, influenza, and 'over pressure'—had certainly become commonplace even among quite humble people; while among the many who were concerned with current 'social problems', the transformation of attitudes to unemployment ensured sympathy for any suicide attributable to that great Edwardian talking-point. Yet the more and more explicit stress on the pursuit of individual health and happiness which marked the end of the nineteenth and the beginning of the twentieth century must have made so clear a demonstration of personal unhappiness as suicide an increasingly sensitive topic, even if the changing conventions in discourse about death were not enough to make it altogether taboo;

7 ranged from 23.2 to 99.2 per cent, with an average of around 70 per cent: PP 1911 [Cd. 5492] XIII, p. 28.

while the removal of suicide from the familiar atmosphere of everyday life may well have been encouraged by the new style of selective, high-powered, exaggerated newspaper coverage of suicide, and even more by the availability in all big cities of very many better sources of interest and entertainment than a run-of-the-mill suicide.

All this is necessarily speculative. There is clear and abundant evidence, however, on one matter certainly likely to affect popular sensibilities: that is, the shutting away of the official processes for investigating sudden death from Londoners' casual, everyday experience. In the late nineteenth and very early twentieth centuries, it will be remembered, a series of practical changes occurred in these processes. From the late 1850s public mortuaries began slowly to be provided, so that a corpse no longer had to remain among relatives and neighbours until the inquest could be held.[75] With this development went another important change: the replacement of the local public house as the usual place for an inquest, first by a room in some public institution, and then, in the busiest jurisdictions, by a specially built coroner's court-house, situated as a rule next to the local authority's mortuary and post-mortem room. By 1910 only one metropolitan borough (Woolwich) did not have a purpose-built coroner's court-house;[76] and some of these substantial buildings still stand as solid evidence that for Edwardian Londoners inquests were no longer the accessible, informal, unmysterious neighbourhood events they had usually been in the 1860s.

Suicide was being removed from the workaday experiences of ordinary Londoners in these years not only by the building zeal of urban authorities, but also by the increasing use made by busy coroners of bureaucratic routines and professional expertise. The emergence of the coroner's officer as a full-time investigator meant that far fewer lay witnesses were summoned to attend an inquest, and that inquest proceedings became much more streamlined, with prepared statements being read out and signed in the inquest room. Similarly, the increasing use of post-mortems and pathological analyses and of expert witnesses meant not only that juries had their minds made up for them more often than before, but that the technical language in which cases were

---

[75] The first London parish to acquire a mortuary was St Anne's, Soho, in 1856: Cardwell *et al.*, *Two Centuries of Soho*, p. 88. The credit for this step was claimed by Joseph Rogers, who was then on the Burial Board appointed by St Anne's vestry: Rogers, *Reminiscences of a Workhouse Medical Officer*, p. 239. On the provision of mortuaries and coroners' court-houses, see ch. 1, n. 69.

[76] LCC, *London Statistics*, xx (1909–10), p. 260.

often discussed might create an aura of arcane mystery in the court room, and in the newspaper reports as well. Most important of all, probably, the position of coroners everywhere became much more professional and clearly defined during the fifty years after the epoch-making County Coroners' Act of 1860, while for London coroners (with the exception of the franchise coroners among them) the twenty years after they came under the aegis of the new London County Council in 1889 were even more formative. Although there was still no formal requirement of any professional qualifications, by 1909 the great majority of the country's coroners were solicitors, with a few barristers and a number of medical men; only a few franchise coroners were 'persons of no attainments' either medical or legal.[77] The eight London coroners were all either lawyers or medical men or both, and several of them were leading luminaries of the Medico-Legal Society or the Coroners' Society. In 1888 the ancient ties between county coroners and 'the people' had been broken at last by the abolition of their election by all the freeholders, and the substitution of appoint-ment by the new county councils. The result of the last election of a county coroner was declared to a large cheering crowd at Hackney town hall on 11 June 1888.[78] Thereafter the excitements and fam-iliarities of the hustings—with all their canvassing, bribery, and speech-making—were lost, and coroners joined the ranks of expert salaried officials appointed by local government authorities, uniquely hybrid creatures though they still remained. By the early twentieth century the way was open for a second long-mooted break with the populism of the office—the statutory empowering of coroners to hold an inquest alone, without a jury, which finally came in 1926.[79]

Well before then, however, the role of neighbours and bystanders, witnesses and jurymen had already shrunk and dwindled, and the whole process of investigating a case of suspected suicide had become shrouded in an atmosphere of officialdom, expertise, and formality. In London (and other big cities) the process of officially establishing a

[77] PP 1909 [Cd. 4782] XV, p. 3, Qs. 58–9.

[78] *The Times*, 14 June 1888, p. 11, col. e. To the Lords, then considering the County Councils Bill, this seemed to show yet again the impossibility of allowing election by the freeholders to continue. The appointment of coroners by the county authority, instead of the Lord Chancellor, was the result of an opposition amendment: *Hansard*, 3rd series, cccxxvii, cols. 956–8, 22 June 1888.

[79] 16 & 17 Geo. V, c. 59, s. 13, Coroners (Amendment) Act, 1926. On the increasing professionalization of the coroner system, above all in London and a few other great cities, see ch. 1, pp. 37–8.

death as suicide had become essentially a matter for a team of experts and professionals, and not for the common man. The contrast between Dickens's description in 1853 of the lively 'inkwich' held amidst the bagatelle board, spittoons, and pipes of the Sol's Arms in Holborn in an atmosphere of beer, tobacco-smoke, spirits, and sawdust and Arnold Bennett's picture of the impersonal proceedings in the coroner's court-house in Westminster sixty years later, surely demonstrates how accurately each author could convey the texture of collective experience in the London of his day. In both the Sol's Arms and the court-house the room was crowded and malodorous; but there similarity ends. 'The coroner', wrote Bennett,

had arrived on the stroke of the hour, in a silk hat and frock coat, with a black bag, and had sat down at his desk and begun to rule the proceedings with an absolutism that no High Court Judge would have attempted ... There was no appeal from the ukase of the coroner ... With the doctor alone the coroner had become human.[80]

There is little trace here of 'the people's court'. The investigation of suicide had been taken over by professionals; and hand in hand with this and other less tangible changes, perhaps, had come the shrinking of this way of death into an awkward topic best avoided instead of yet another familiar part of the human condition. This was a shift in the attitudes of ordinary people which happened not in mid-Victorian but rather in Edwardian times, however, and one which was stimulated not by rampant 'Victorianism' but by a complex of changes which are characteristic of the close of the Victorian era, not its heyday.

---

[80] Dickens, *Bleak House*, ch. 11; Bennett, *The Pretty Lady*, ch. 35, p. 249. In 1913 another prolific writer drew a sharp contrast between a friendly inquest held in a country inn, with cake and wine for the witnesses, and the 'far, far more grim and awe-inspiring' proceedings at the big Coroner's Court near King's Cross some 20 years later, with its high dais for the coroner and box-like witness stand: Mrs Belloc Lowndes, *The Lodger*, chs. xviii–xix.

PART IV

RESTRAINTS

8

The Sermons and Sanctions of the Law

In the middle of the nineteenth century a new era opened in the long endeavour to prevent suicide through the sermons and sanctions of the law, for in these years a new offence was developed: the offence of attempted suicide. So long as the law concerned itself only with accomplished suicide, its preventive role could not extend beyond attempting to diffuse throughout society the consciousness that suicide was a criminal act which entailed grave penalties. Once mere suicidal behaviour became an offence, however, the machinery of the law could be used to deter from further attempts those particular individuals who had shown themselves to be at risk, and the law could become an instrument not only of social discipline, but of individual case work as well. In short, it could—and did—become a contrivance for rehabilitation as well as for punishment and intimidation.

This did not mean that the old deterrent role of the law was ever completely abandoned. True, the twin difficulties which perennially undermined the attempt to control suicide in this way were particularly acute in the middle years of the nineteenth century. Never were there larger numbers of sympathetic jurymen eager to mitigate the vicarious punishment of family and friends which was the only sort of penalty which this particular offence could ever entail; and never were there more medical men and ordinary people who were honestly convinced that most of those who took their own lives were 'out of their mind' and therefore not responsible for their action.[1] Accordingly, never were verdicts that the deceased had taken his own life 'while of unsound mind' more common. Yet was it right that coroners' juries should shield nine-tenths (or more) of suicides from the arm of the law in this way? This was always the central question; and in the second half of the nineteenth century it was given new point by its entanglement with a number of topical controversies. First, in the 1850s and 1860s the validity of the insanity defence in murder trials

---

[1] See ch. 6.

became one of the most hotly debated medico-legal issues of the day, and inevitably some of its proponents feared that the lavish use of 'temporary insanity' verdicts in cases of suicide would discredit the whole notion of the insanity defence. Equally, those public health enthusiasts who wished to make the coroner the centre of a system of medical police feared that the plethora of such verdicts would discredit both the coroner's office and his inquests; zealous clergymen lamented the way in which they undermined the teaching and discipline of the Church; life insurance companies considered them almost tantamount to fraud; and at the turn of the century the new breed of moral authoritarians who deplored the current permissiveness of the law and the softness of sentencing condemned them as proof of the absurd lengths to which harmful sentimentality could go.[2] Altogether, neither at the beginning nor the end of Victoria's reign was interested support lacking for the policy of controlling suicide through meting out severe penalties for the deed.

Yet how vigorously were the sanctions and sermons of the law ever applied in practice? The answer to this question is not the foregone conclusion it may seem to be, for not one but three branches of the law were involved. It is true that the criminal law of suicide (upon which attention has always concentrated) was almost a dead letter, since inquest juries ensured that the crime of self-murder was a rare one.[3] Still, as has already been emphasized, it was not entirely unknown; and from 1882, when (as the incidental result of reform in other areas of the law) all the penalties imposed by common and statute law for the crime of *felonia de se* had been removed,[4] legal pendants and moral vigilantes could argue that verdicts of 'temporary insanity' had now lost their practical point and served only to discredit inquests and support a harmful sentimentality towards suicide, and that coroners could and should now persuade their juries not to be afraid to return a verdict of *felo de se*. So said the editor of one standard

---

[2] For examples of such views, see *The Lancet*, 1860, ii. 193, 25 Aug.; Gurnhill, *Morals of Suicide*, i. 206–7; Butler, *Suicide or Murder*, p. 7; Bishop of St Alban's (E. Jacob), *Chronicle of Convocation, 1909*, 18 Feb., p. 37; 'H.', 'Correspondence', *Spectator*, civ. 920 (4 June 1910).

[3] Moreover, inquisitions were traversable, although applications for a writ of *certiorari* were rare. For an example of a husband who took this step when his wife was adjudged *felo de se*, see 'On Suicide—Verdicts of Felo-de-Se', *Jnl. of Psychological Medicine*, iii (1850), pp. 25–7.

[4] The relevant statutes are 33 & 34 Vict., c. 23, Felony Act, 1870; 43 & 44 Vict., c. 41, Burial Laws Amendment Act, 1880; 45 & 46 Vict., c. 19, Interments (*Felo de Se*) Act, 1882.

legal handbook from 1889 onwards;[5] so argued very forcefully Richard
Henslowe Wellington, founder-secretary of the Medico-Legal Society
and a busy London deputy coroner;[6] and so too suggested a committee
of bishops to the Home Secretary in 1910.[7] In the decade before 1914,
a handful of coroners put these views into practice.[8] Most ordinary
people, however, probably agreed that to impose on a family the
social stigma entailed by such a verdict was indefensible pendantry.[9]
Nationally, although the proportion of suicides who were adjudged
felo de se doubled and numbers peaked in 1909 with 137 such verdicts,
they still amounted to less than one in twenty of the total,[10] and in

[5] 'In the absence of evidence of unsoundness of mind, the verdict of *felo de se* must
still be directed and returned': Wharton, *The Law Lexicon*, 8th edn. (1889), p. 297. This
passage does not appear in previous editions, but was retained in subsequent ones. (On
the other hand, successive editions of Jervis, *On the Office and Duties of Coroners*,
show no change in the procedures recommended in cases of suicide.)

[6] Wellington, 'The Verdict of "Suicide Whilst Temporarily Insane": A Legal Contradiction'. This paper was subsequently published as a pamphlet. It was given a mixed
reception in *The Lancet*, whose editor would go no further than the opinion that 'in
existing circumstances, coroners should guide juries to abstain from "temporary insanity" where the act was apparently that of a sane man performed deliberately': 1904, ii.
771, 10 Sept. See also ch. 6 n. 93.

[7] The response of Winston Churchill (then Home Secretary) was that 'it would be
very inadvisable to go back to the old verdict of *felo de se*': *Chronicle of Convocation,
1911*, 14 Feb., p. 19.

[8] In 1910 there were 5 coroners whose juries returned more verdicts of *felo de se* than
of 'temporary insanity', namely, E. A. Gibson and Alfred Appleby of the County
Boroughs of Manchester and Newcastle upon Tyne respectively, J. Hyslop Bell and
John Graham of the Districts of Stockton Ward and Chester Ward in Co. Durham, and
Dr L. Drage of St Alban's, Herts: *Judicial Statistics, 1910*, Part I, Table XXXI, p. 127.
A third of the male and half the female verdicts of *felo de se* returned in England and
Wales in 1910 were returned at inquests held by the first 3 of these coroners. See also
Brend, 'The Necessity for Amendment of the Law relating to Coroners and Inquests',
Table V, p. 159, and *An Inquiry into the Statistics of Deaths from Violence and
Unnatural Causes in the United Kingdom*, Appendix III, pp. 76–7.

[9] Brend, 'The Necessity for Amendment of the Law relating to Coroners and Inquests',
p. 160. On one occasion when Gibson led his jury to return a verdict of 'insufficient
evidence to show state of mind' the solicitor for the family pointed out that it was a
serious matter for the relatives not to have the verdict of 'suicide while insane' and
offered further evidence on the deceased's state of mind, in vain: *The Lancet*, 1906, i.
1501, 26 May. In 1912, however, an inquest was quashed because the relatives had not
been given the opportunity to be present to testify to the deceased's state of mind: Jervis,
On the Office and Duties of Coroners (1927 edn.), p. 187.

[10] See *Judicial Statistics, 1909*, Part I, Table XXX, p. 117. *Felo de se* verdicts (excluding
those returned on murderers who committed suicide) rose from an annual average of
1.4 per cent of male and 1.1 per cent of female suicide verdicts in 1893–8 to an annual
average of 3.5 per cent of male and 2.1 per cent of female suicide verdicts in 1909–13;
indeed, the proportion of *felo de se* verdicts in the City and Southwark was higher in
1909–13 (at 7 per cent of male and 10 per cent of female suicide verdicts) than it had
been in 1788–1829 (when the corresponding figures were 2.3 and 0.3 per cent): see

1910 the Home Office committee on coroners recommended that the verdict of *felo de se* should be abolished altogether.[11] The fact was that after 1882 it was from the civil and ecclesiastical law, and only rarely and indirectly from the criminal law, that practical penalties for the deed of suicide were to be hoped or feared; for in neither civil nor ecclesiastical law was the weight to be attached to inquest verdicts of 'temporary insanity' ever a settled question, and in neither were the penalties attached to a verdict of *felo de se* whittled away by the impact of legislation, as they were in criminal law.

How substantial was the practical impact of the sermons and sanctions of the civil law? As was briefly remarked earlier, from the 1850s onwards more and more people were brought potentially within their scope by the juxtaposition of two facts: the very great expansion of life insurance business, and the common law rule that any felonious act resulting in death invalidated a policy on the life concerned. Around 1850 probably less than 0.4 per cent of the population had insured their lives, and virtually all of these were the landed, professional, and commercial sections of society.[12] From 1853, however, life assurance premiums were allowed against income tax, and more and more middle-class people took out policies; while from the 1870s industrial life assurance companies were successfully selling policies to very large numbers of ordinary working people, in competition with local friendly and burial societies.[13] By the end of the century a coroner could expect to find that very many of those who committed suicide had insured their lives, although often only for some such sum as £15.[14]

Yet while the number of policy-holders expanded enormously, the likelihood that death by suicide would entail loss of benefits became very small. In the earlier nineteenth century Assurance Offices usually inserted, and enforced, a clause whereby suicide voided the policy, although at the insurer's discretion the 'office' or surrender value (that is, a proportion of the premiums paid) was returned to the

---

Judicial Statistics, 1909–13, Part I, Annual Tables, 'Coroners: Verdicts of Juries', and Forbes, 'Crowner's Quest', p. 13, Table 2.

[11] PP 1910 [Cd. 5004] XXI, p. 20. It was in order to prove that the verdict of *felo de se* had become so rare as to be ripe for abolition that a leading coroner of the previous generation, A. Braxton Hicks, suggested to the Home Office that *felo de se* verdicts should be recorded in a separate column in the *Judicial Statistics*, as was done from 1893: *Judicial Statistics, 1893*, Part I, p. 34.

[12] Cockerell and Green, *The British Insurance Business*, p. 37.

[13] Ibid., pp. 38–41.

[14] This was the experience of F. J. Waldo as coroner for the Borough of Southwark in 1901 and 1911: CLRO, CR, Southwark.

representatives or family of a suicide.[15] Not surprisingly, the mid-century years of expansion threw up several leading cases on the effect of suicide on life insurance policies. For policies with no special conditions about suicide, the most important landmark was the ruling in *Horn* v. *the Anglo-Australian and Universal Family Life Assurance Company* in 1861 that such contracts were voided only when death was caused by the felonious act of the assured, and not when the assured was insane. Whether the verdict of a coroner's jury was conclusive in establishing insanity for this purpose, as juries themselves certainly believed,[16] was never decided in the courts;[17] companies preferred to pay up (although no doubt many insurance men agreed with Cornelius Walford that they were continually defrauded by coroners' juries).[18] Such unconditional policies, however, were comparatively rare, and usually everything turned upon the precise wording of a clause in the contract explicitly excepting death by suicide. Rulings very much in the companies' favour were given in two leading cases of the 1840s, *Borrodaile* v. *Hunter* (1843) and the even more renowned *Clift* v. *Schwabe* (1846), in which on appeal to the Exchequer Chamber the majority decided that a suicide exclusion clause applied even when the assured committed suicide while of unsound mind, provided he knew what he was doing and was capable of appreciating the consequences of his act.[19] This judgement was so widely regarded as unfair, however, that it was a pyrrhic victory. (The Assurance Office concerned felt it wise to compromise, and returned all the premiums paid, together with interest at 4 per cent, to the assured's widow.) Not only alienists, but the authors of the standard treatises on the law of life assurance and medical jurisprudence published their approval of the argument of the dissentient Lord Chief Baron, J. F. Pollock, and his conclusion that 'the act the result of any *delusion*—physical, intellectual or moral—is not the act of *the man*.'[20] Lay opinion was equally

---

[15] Bunyon, *A Treatise upon the Law of Life Assurance* (1854 edn.), p. 72. Actuaries watched all special risks carefully in the 1840s; indeed, it was an actuary, R. Thompson Jopling, who in 1851 published the first full-length statistical study of English suicide: see his 'Statistics of Suicide'.

[16] Cf. Cook, *Insanity and Mental Deficiency in Relation to Legal Responsibility*, p. 97.

[17] *Halsbury's Laws of England*, xxii. 275.

[18] Walford, 'On the Number of Deaths from Accident, Negligence, Violence and Misadventure', p. 526.

[19] Bunyon, *A Treatise upon the Law of Life Assurance* (1854 edn.), pp. 75–7; *Law Times*, 18 July 1846, p. 342.

[20] Bunyon, *A Treatise upon the Law of Life Assurance* (1854 edn.), p. 72; Taylor,

clearly not on the companies' side. For the first time, many people began to argue that since the risk of suicide was taken into account in calculating premiums, it was unjust for companies to refuse to pay when suicide was the cause of death.[21] More irresistible still was the general climate of opinion created by the reasoned belief of so many mid-Victorian medical men that those who took their own lives were almost invariably suffering from mental disease and therefore no more responsible for their action than 'if they had burst a blood-vessel'. Throughout the 1860s and 1870s that tireless publicist for 'the social rights of the insane', the alienist J. G. Davey, denounced the refusal to pay in full when death was caused by suicide as 'in all respects incompatible with an advanced psychology, and at variance with a due sense of right and common justice'; and by 1878 he correctly discerned that this practice was doomed.[22]

Their reputation among their customers had come to matter more to insurance companies than the rulings of the courts. They could not afford to disregard the strongly argued views of the educated, or the sentimental sympathies of the man in the street, still less to challenge explicitly the verdicts of coroners' juries. 'An insurance office is the creature of public opinion, and the reputation of illiberality is esteemed fatal to its progress', acknowledged the first treatise on the law of life assurance as early as 1854.[23] Throughout the next twenty years new companies vied with each other in cut-throat competition for new business, advertising more widely, promising more largely—and relaxing their conditions.[24] Within a generation the condition against suicide was becoming a rarity, except with respect to a limited initial period after the grant of the policy.[25] In 1885, when W. W. Westcott asked thirty-two companies for their regulations in order to give the subject extended treatment in his book on suicide, he found that nine of them made no mention of suicide, seventeen excluded it for limited periods ranging from one month to five years, and only six had a clause excluding this risk altogether. Much more important, he found that in

---

The Principles and Practice of Medical Jurisprudence, p. 1041; cf. 'A Jurist', letter to the editor, *Jnl. of Psychological Medicine*, i (1848), p. 328.

[21] Jopling, 'Statistics of Suicide', Part 1, p. 308.

[22] Davey, 'Life Insurance Offices and Suicide', p. 108; 'On Suicide, in its Social Relations', p. 252. See also his 'Life Insurance and Suicide', p. 281.

[23] Bunyon, *A Treatise upon the Law of Life Assurance* (1854 edn.), p. 72.

[24] Cockerell and Green, *The British Insurance Business*, pp. 39, 44–5.

[25] The change is recorded in the third edition of Bunyon's treatise, *The Law of Life Assurance* (1891), p. 95.

practice, unless they suspected fraud, all the companies paid in full, or nearly so, in cases of suicide.[26]

In the 1890s—that decade of polarization, when self-consciously 'new' ethical attitudes favouring suicide were met by pressure for greater severity and firmer teaching against it—opinions inevitably differed over whether it was desirable that (as one barrister emphasized) 'in England at the present time the suicide suffers no civil disability whatever.'[27] In 1904 the *Saturday Review* attacked outright the insurance companies' habit of waiving even clauses excluding suicide committed within a specified time limit, as not only an incentive to crime but unfair to other policy-holders, who had to bear the loss.[28] To well-informed Edwardians the old view that life insurance policies deterred suicide by providing both 'a restraint on the mind and conduct of the assured' and a 'pecuniary interest' for watchfulness on the part of his family must have become altogether implausible.[29] Life insurance policies had long been taken out by little people, however, and among humble men and women there were probably many who still thought vaguely, like H. G. Wells's Mr Polly in 1910, that a death which looked like suicide might make 'difficulties about the life insurance'.[30] Precisely what deterrent effect such vague ideas exercised must remain an open question; the most that can be urged is that among ordinary working people they were probably quite widespread.

Were the terrors of the ecclesiastical law also blunted in these years? In England the treatment of the bodies of suicides was never a battleground between Church and State, as it was in France,[31] for in England Church and State were in entire agreement that there was no 'right to die'. Yet it would be a great mistake to dismiss this question as an insignificant one in Victorian and Edwardian England. How the bodies of suicides ought to be buried was one of the many controversies through which the newly vigorous later-nineteenth century Church of England expressed its intensely conflicting views of true churchmanship; while how suicides were actually buried was something which necessarily concerned a growing number of people at first hand, as the number of suicide verdicts recorded each year climbed from

---

[26] Westcott, *Suicide*, pp. 54, 180–1. In 1904 R. Henslowe Wellington also made this point: 'The Verdict of "Suicide whilst Temporarily Insane"', p. 89.

[27] Strahan, *Suicide and Insanity*, p. 198.

[28] 'Suicide and Insurance', *Saturday Review*, 18 May 1904, xcvii. 685–6.

[29] Bunyon, *A Treatise on the Law of Life Assurance* (1854 edn.), p. 72.

[30] Wells, *The History of Mr Polly*, ch. 7.

[31] Bayet, *Le suicide et la morale*, pp. 786–92.

one thousand in the 1850s to over three thousand in the early 1900s.

What actually happened at the graveside was settled directly and immediately by the interpretation given to the law of the Church by the individual priest concerned; but indirectly and in the long term it was affected by the transformation in urban burial facilities which took place in the third quarter of the nineteenth century. In England, every parishioner had a right to burial in his parish churchyard. Suicides were no exception (although custom often led to their burial on 'the backside of the church', as was noticed in Chapter 7);[32] and even those found guilty of *felo de se* were statutorily required to be buried in the churchyard from 1823 (when their burial at a crossroads and with a stake in the heart was prohibited).[33] Not every parishioner, however, had a right to 'Christian burial'—that is, to the Burial Office of the Church, with its consoling assurances of salvation and resurrection. A rubric introduced in 1661 prohibited (as it still does) the use of the Burial Office 'for any that die unbaptized, or excommunicate, or have laid violent hands upon themselves'. Such silent interment was a heavy punishment, and no less so to the Victorians than to their forebears, since theirs was a society which attached deep importance to mortuary ceremonies of all kinds, and at every level regarded funerals as public occasions.

It was thus a matter of some significance how the clergy interpreted this rubric. Was Christian burial to be denied to all those who had 'laid violent hands upon themselves' without exception? From 1767 Richard Burn, and a series of later authorities upon ecclesiastical law, including A. J. Stephens, H. W. Cripps, and that distinguished pair Sir Robert Phillimore and his son W. G. F. Phillimore, all held that 'idiots, lunatics and persons of insane mind, not being deemed responsible for their acts, are not to be understood thereby'; and furthermore, that the coroner's jury was the proper judge of whether a particular person who took his own life had been insane when he did so.[34] On the other

---

[32] See ch. 6 n. 3. This northern part of the churchyard was consecrated ground, like the rest of the churchyard, and it is an error to suppose (as for example does Puckle, *Funeral Customs*, p. 152) that suicides, even those adjudged *felo de se*, had to be buried in unconsecrated ground.

[33] 4 Geo. IV, c. 52, s. 1.

[34] Richard Burn (1709–85: *DNB*) made the first point in the first edition of his *Ecclesiastical Law* (1763), i. 192 and the second in the second edition (1767), i. 243–4; and no alterations were made in subsequent editions. The views of Robert Phillimore (1810–5: *DNB*) were first published in the last edition of Burn's work, which he edited in 1842, making substantial additions. They reappear in the first edition of his own *The Ecclesiastical Law of the Church of England* (1875), i. 858–60; and were left unchanged

hand, such a standard commentary on the Prayer Book as Charles Wheatly's (which was steadily reprinted from 1710 to 1863) asserted roundly from 1720 that 'there is no reason, because a Coroner prostitutes his oath, that the Clergy should be so complaisant as to prostitute their office' and agree to read the Burial Service over suicides judged *non compos mentis* at a coroner's inquest; and this stance was shared by Wheatly's mid-Victorian successor, J. H. Blunt, who held that though 'the verdict of the coroner's jury should have respectful attention, it is not to be considered as an invariable law for the clergyman.'[35]

So what was Victorian clerical practice? In the early nineteenth century it seems to have been usual to regard a verdict of 'temporary insanity' as authorizing Christian burial. In 1845 H. W. Cripps remarked (in the first edition of his *Practical Treatise on the Laws relating to the Church and the Clergy*) that so far as he had been able to ascertain, this custom of 'acknowledged propriety' was always followed.[36] Within a few years, however, such a bland assertion of clerical consensus had become less plausible. Between about 1850 and 1880 argument about the clergyman's right to refuse Christian burial to the unbaptized and to evil-livers was endemic and clerical practice variable; and two things ensured that the burial of suicides too became a matter of contention. The first was the aftermath of the Tractarian revival. In the great mid-Victorian controversies over doctrine and liturgy, over the revision of the canons and the Prayer Book, over Church discipline and the responsibilities of the individual priest with the cure of souls, the burial of suicides was no more than a minor and marginal matter; nevertheless, it was part and parcel of these great

by his son, W. G. F. Phillimore (1845–1929: *DNB*), when he revised his father's treatise in 1895: *The Ecclesiastical Law of the Church of England*, 2nd edn., i. 670–1. Burn is also followed by Stephens, *A Practical Treatise of the Laws relating to the Clergy*, i. 197, and by Cripps, *A Practical Treatise on the Laws relating to the Church and the Clergy* (1st edn. 1845), pp. 687–8. (This passage still appeared, in abbreviated form, in the seventh and last edition of this work, by A. T. Lawrence and R. Stafford Cripps (1889–1952: *DNB*), at pp. 634–45.)

[35] Wheatly, *A Rational Illustration of the Book of Common Prayer* (1858 edn.), p. 569; Blunt (1823–84: *DNB*), *The Book of Church Law* (2nd edn.), p. 180. In 1790 the Revd Charles Moore deplored the non-enforcement of the penalties for suicide, including deprivation of Christian burial, and thought that the corpse might with advantage be exposed naked to public view and then given for dissection: *A Full Inquiry into the Subject of Suicide*, i. 339; while John Wesley in 1784 urged Pitt to check suicide by hanging the bodies of those who were guilty of it in chains: Lecky, *England in the Eighteenth Century*, iii. 140.

[36] Cripps, *The Laws relating to the Church and the Clergy*, p. 688.

debates.³⁷ For a clergyman called upon to decide whether to grant or withhold Christian burial to a suicide, charity to the departed and pastoral care for mourners easily came into conflict with 'stewardship of the mysteries of God' and conscientious care for the teaching and discipline of the Church.³⁸ On this as on so many other matters, high and low churchmen were divided not only from each other, but among themselves. A second set of factors further increased clerical disagreements. Between 1840 and 1880 (as has already been remarked) the asylum movement and a series of celebrated trials ensured publicity for the currently favoured medical position that insanity must be regarded as a physical disease which might affect the feelings and the will even when the intellect was unimpaired; that consequently even someone whose reasoning faculties were sound could nevertheless be insane and therefore not responsible for his actions;³⁹ and that the act of suicide was almost always an indication of insanity. Churchmen who accepted these well-known views could not fail to believe that most suicides should no more be held responsible for their action by the Church than by the secular law. The denial of Christian burial was quite useless as a deterrent, that devout Evangelical Lord Shaftesbury assured the Lords in 1882: the best prevention of suicide was early treatment and care in an asylum.⁴⁰ In 1865 a well-known high church-man, G. E. Biber, preached (and published) a sermon distinguishing at length 'the act of suicide' from 'the crime of self-murder', and explained that the Burial Office was meant to be denied only to

the high-handed wickedness of those who, either in frantic unbelief, having lived 'without GOD in the world', or in wild despair under the terror of the just punishment of their crimes, or in defiant rebellion against GOD, flinging back to HIM the gift of life which HE bestowed on them, have 'laid violent hands upon themselves'.⁴¹

---

³⁷ On these debates generally, see Jasper, *Prayer Book Revision in England* and Peaston, *The Prayer Book Revisions of the Victorian Evangelicals*.

³⁸ In 1856 Charles Reade made the good prison chaplain, Mr Eden, agonize long over whether Josephs had used 'angry or bitter words' before he took his own life: 'I am trying to learn the fate of this immortal soul.' It was not enough for him, as it was for Evans the turnkey, that the boy 'was driven to death' by the cruelty of the prison governor: *It Is Never Too Late To Mend*, ch. 22.

³⁹ On the 'novel visibility' of the insanity defence in the mid-nineteenth century, see Smith, *Trial by Medicine*, p. 3.

⁴⁰ *Hansard*, 3rd series, cclxxi, cols. 13–15, 22 June 1882.

⁴¹ Biber (1801–74: *DNB*) was a member of the Council of the English Church Union in 1863–4. His sermon was inspired by the suicide of a well-known parishioner, the banker W. G. Prescott, who was said to have been ill for some time. He argued that 'it is impossible to conceive that God would judge such an act on the same footing as acts

Clergymen unable to accept such ideas, however, could find themselves, as one such complained to his brethren in Convocation, 'in the painful dilemma of wearing at the grave the mask of hypocrisy and dissimulation, or of being branded as bigots and transgressors of the law'.[42] Three quite different remedies for this state of affairs were put forward in clerical circles in the 1860s and 1870s. The first, was for each priest to take Church discipline back into his own hands by refusing, even after a verdict of 'temporary insanity', to read the Burial Service in those cases where 'circumstances have come to his knowledge which make it plain that there was no such insanity as to deprive the suicide of ordinary moral responsibility': only so could 'the scandal and encouragement to suicide which result from a too easy compliance with the jury's verdict' be prevented. This was the solution urged by that prolific author of successful ecclesiastical handbooks, the old-fashioned high churchman J. H. Blunt; and Blunt believed that few suicides were really insane.[43] Such advice was not only impracticable, however, but unacceptable to the ecclesiastical lawyers (who deplored its cavalier attitude to evidence),[44] and to those who were convinced (like Shaftesbury) that the insanity verdicts of coroners' juries were

done in the indulgence of the instincts of our nature, and in deliberate and conscious opposition to the sense of moral responsibility', and reminded his hearers that none 'is exempt from the danger of ... a few drops of blood surcharging the weary brain, or a fever fit exciting the unstrung nerves ... leaving his actions subject to the control of morbid, all but unconscious, and it may be fatal impulses': *The Act of Suicide as Distinct from the Crime of Self-Murder*, pp. 7, 9, 12. The essential theological question is whether mental disease which does not impair the intellect can nevertheless diminish the freedom of the will and consequently absolve from moral guilt. J. A. Ryan argued in 1910 that it could: *Catholic Encyclopaedia*, viii. 42.

[42] C. R. Knight, *Chronicle of Convocation, 1879*, 24 June, p. 121.

[43] Blunt, *The Annotated Book of Common Prayer*, p. 294 (this handbook went through 7 editions between 1866 and 1903); see also n. 35. Blunt drew no distinction between suicide and self-murder. His view was that 'it is not always, or often, that madness leads persons to self-murder, but passion, fear of shame, and unbelief in a future life': *A Key to Christian Doctrine and Practice*, p. 136. There was much legal debate over whether the word 'suicide' covered all cases of self-destruction. In *Clift* v. *Schwabe* (1846), Rolfe (1790–1868: *DNB*) held that in common language every act of self-destruction was suicide, provided the probable results were known, and Parke (1782–1868: *DNB*) that the word 'suicide' was used to avoid the limitations of 'self-murder': *Law Times*, 18 July 1846, p. 342.

[44] When in 1872 W. G. F. Phillimore provided revisions and additions for a second edition of Blunt's *The Book of Church Law*, the words in *The Annotated Book of Common Prayer* just quoted were included but given quite a different emphasis by the addition of a long sentence warning the priest of the danger of coming to an opinion on the strength of hearsay evidence given without the sanction or solemnity of an oath, and with perhaps a very indifferent and careless sense of responsibility in the speaker, and no sifting or cross-examination: *The Book of Church Law*, 2nd edn., p. 180.

medically correct. A quite different solution was supported by the low
churchmen of the Prayer Book Revision Society, whose chief objection
to the existing situation was not that it encouraged suicide, but that
it profaned the Burial Service and obliged the officiating clergyman to
say over the body of a suicide words which he could not conscientiously
use, most notably, 'Forasmuch as it hath pleased Almighty God of His
great mercy to take unto Himself the soul of our dear brother here
departed'. These Evangelicals proposed that the Burial Service itself
should be amended so that it became humble and deprecatory, and
suitable for use not only over suicides, but over the notorious evil-
livers whom the clergy were obliged to bury not merely by a customary
charitable interpretation of the rubric, as in the case of suicides, but
by law.[45] Any proposal which involved altering the Burial Service itself,
however, had too many implications to have any chance of success in
Convocation, and it was a complex third scheme which was finally
put forward by both Houses of Convocation in 1879, as part of a set
of comprehensive proposals for changes in the canons of the Church
and the rubrics of the Book of Common Prayer. First, the rubric should
be altered to exclude from the Burial Service not 'any that have laid
violent hands upon themselves', but 'any who having laid violent hands
upon himself, hath not been found to have been of unsound mind'.
Secondly, over such persons it should not be unlawful for a priest, at
the request of the kindred or friends of the deceased and after silent
interment had taken place, to read portions of the Prayer Book and of
scripture which had been approved by the bishop and were not part
of either the Burial Service or Holy Communion. Lastly, at the burial
of those who had been found to have been of unsound mind, it should
be lawful for the priest, at the request or with the consent of the
kindred and friends, to use a shortened form of the Burial Service
which omitted the controversial passages of confident hope.[46] Here
was a compromise carefully adapted to meet many different objections
to the existing state of Church law; and in 1880 it was brought before
Parliament. Its function there, however, was simply to help the new

---

[45] C. R. Knight, *Chronicle of Convocation, 1879*, 24 June, pp. 119–23; Bligh, *Lord
Ebury as a Church Reformer*, p. 160. Ebury (1801–93: *DNB*) made annual attempts to
get Parliament to take up the amendment of the Prayer Book.
[46] Convocation of Canterbury, *Report on the Rubrics of the Book of Common Prayer*,
p. 47; [Proposed] *Constitution and Canons Ecclesiastical of the Church of England*,
Canon XXVI, p. 15, bound as appendix to *Chronicle of Convocation, 1879*. The final
discussions can be followed in *Chronicle of Convocation, 1879*, 24 June, pp. 119–26, 1
July, pp. 268–9, and 3 July, pp. 364–70.

Liberal Government to get a Burial Bill through both Houses and thus settle the last of those great Nonconformist issues which were the stuff of politics between about 1850 and 1880; and when it proved a Parliamentary liability, not an asset, it was dropped.[47]

For twenty years the question of the burial of suicides had been drawn into the great ecclesiastical battles over Prayer Book revision. Now in 1880 it was caught up in the last great political battle over Nonconformist citizenship, and it was this political entanglement which brought practical results. The matter was never so much as mentioned in Parliament's debates; yet when the Burial Laws Amendment Act of 1880 finally reached the statute book, as a by-product the legal position with regard to the burial of suicides was changed substantially. First, this Act made it lawful at any burial whatsoever for any form of orderly religious service to be performed in the churchyard by someone other than a clergyman of the Church of England. Secondly, it made it lawful for the clergy of the Church of England, in any case where the Burial Office was prohibited by the rubric and in any other case at the request of the relatives or friends, to use at the burial a consolatory service of portions of the Prayer Book and scripture prescribed or approved by the bishop of the diocese.[48] Thus not even those adjudged *felo de se* need now be buried silently, nor need they (thanks to a short separate act of 1882)[49] be buried privately at night: it was now permissible, although not obligatory, for a clergyman to read a consolatory service at such funerals; alternatively, the relatives could now arrange for some person

---

[47] The best brief account is probably that in Marsh, *The Victorian Church in Decline*, pp. 257–63. Between 1881 and 1887 distinctions in burial on the grounds of the beliefs of the deceased or the circumstances of his death were forbidden by French law in the interests of Protestants and Jews, so that in France too suicides benefited in these years by a side wind: Bayet, *Le suicide et la morale*, p. 792.

[48] 43 & 44 Vict., c. 41, ss. 1, 6, 13.

[49] 45 & 46 Vict., c. 19, Interments (*Felo de Se*) Act, 1882. This bill passed the Commons without discussion, but in the Lords the Muslim Stanley of Alderley (1823–1903: DNB) argued that private burial at night of a *felo de se* should still be required, since 'it had a deterrent effect on public opinion'. His view was countered, however, by those two Evangelical allies in good works, the third Earl Fortescue (1818–1905: DNB) and the seventh Earl of Shaftesbury (1801–85: DNB), together with the Lord Chancellor of the day, the high churchman Selborne (1812–1895: DNB): *Hansard*, 3rd series, cclxxi, cols. 13–14, 22 June 1882. It is worth remarking that Forbes Winslow, that great enthusiast for the abolition of the verdict of *felo de se* on the grounds that all acts of suicide were acts of insanity (and exponent of the insanity defence in murder trials) was also a fervent Evangelical and doer of good works, who moved in the same circles as Shaftesbury.

not a clergyman of the Church of England to perform a religious service at the burial.[50] (Methodist ministers, for example, had been freed from the burial rubric as early as 1786.)[51] The settlement of 1880 exorcized 'the Burial Question' from politico-ecclesiastical debate at last. For the clergy, however, since in the end the rubric had been left unchanged and unclarified,[52] the central practical problem with regard to suicide remained: did a verdict of 'temporary insanity' conclusively entitle a suicide to burial according to the usual rites of the Church of England, or not?

What had clerical practice been during the thirty years or so when 'the Burial Question' in all its ramifications was keenly debated? It seems likely that most clergymen accepted a 'temporary insanity' verdict as authorizing them to give Christian burial;[53] but certainly not

[50] A proposal emanating from the Evangelical and extreme Liberal Mackarness of Oxford (1820–89: *DNB*) to make it lawful 'on sufficient cause' to read a shortened form of the Burial Office over those excluded by the rubric was made by the Royal Commission on the Rubrics in its fourth Report: PP 1870 [C. 218] XIX, Schedule, pp. 30–1. Two Evangelical members, the Peelite Harrowby (1798–1882: *DNB*) and the Liberal Charles Buxton (1823–71: *DNB*), wished to exclude those who had laid violent hands on themselves from this concession, while two Tory ritualists, Earl Beauchamp (1830–91: *DNB*) and Canon Robert Gregory (1819–1911: *DNB*) wished to include them. The proposal was agreed *nem. con.* when that old-fashioned moderate, the amiable Ellicott of Gloucester and Bristol (1819–1905: *DNB*) proposed that this shortened Office should not be used without the bishop's permission. By 1879, however, Convocation had agreed that the Shortened Office should not be used for the excluded categories, and controversy had shifted to whether a simple consolatory service should be held not at the graveside, but in the church, after the interment, as was the high church view, so that the popular mind should not think that it was a Burial Service which was being given; and whether the bishop's sanction should *not* be required, in order to avoid giving the imprimatur of the superior authority of the diocese to this concession. For suicides not found to have been of unsound mind, it was felt impossible to provide a service; yet some consolation was felt to be due to the mourners. Even this, however, provoked objections, for example from Pusey's friend, Archdeacon Harrison (1808–87: *DNB*), who 'could not think of affording such consolation as would nullify the work of the Church': *Chronicle of Convocation, 1879*, p. 365.

[51] Rowell, *The Liturgy of Christian Burial*, p. 94.

[52] As a result section 13 of the Burial Laws Amendment Act created a very flexible situation indeed, which left open such controversial issues as whether the service should be at the graveside or in the church, during or after interment, and should or should not include passages from the Burial Service—as well as making the provision of any such service entirely discretionary. The Act was very much what its running title described it to be, and no more: 'Relief of clergy of Church of England from penalties in certain cases'. Nor is this surprising: throughout, the salient controversy was that about the burial of the unbaptized, not about the burial of suicides.

[53] It will be remembered that the villagers of Clyro were surprised in the 1860s when their vicar (R. Lister Venables, brother of the writer G. S. Venables) buried 'with the usual ceremony' a girl who had drowned herself; but Kilvert did not note what the jury's verdict on this girl's death had been: see ch. 7 n. 4.

all did so. High churchmen might object to an action which nullified the teaching of the Church and threw discipline into lay hands (in the shape of coroners' juries); but equally a low churchman might have conscientious objections to implying the salvation of an individual sinner, whereas a high churchman might take the view that only those who out of 'perverse will' had rejected God would be damned, and might stress charity and the corporate life of the Church.[54] One much-publicized rejection of a jury's verdict by a low churchman came in December 1848, when a Cambridge clergyman refused to bury a parishioner on whose body the jury had returned a verdict of 'found drowned' because he considered the dead man a notorious evil-liver and in reality a *felo de se*, since he had fallen into the river while drunk. For this, though, he was cited to the Court of Arches; and to the great indignation of Evangelicals, that Court held that the mere opinion of the clergyman did not justify refusal of the Burial Service.[55] In 1859 similar indignation was aroused among conservative high churchmen, when the refusal of a Leicestershire clergyman to bury a parishioner upon whom a coroner's jury had returned a 'temporary insanity' verdict, on the grounds that the rubric excluded *any* that laid violent hands upon themselves, led to an indignant petition to Parliament (backed by militant Dissent) and an exclamation from the woolsack by the then Lord Chancellor (Campbell, a Scotch Presbyterian) that 'the vicar had no right to form and act upon his own opinion, contrary to that which had been expressed by the jury'—a view immediately and wholeheartedly rejected by *The English Churchman*.[56]

In these very same mid-Victorian years, however, burial was in

---

[54] Keble had defended the expressions of hope in the Burial Service in 1836, and many years later Pusey defended the Athanasian creed, saying, 'the Judge of all will condemn only those who have, out of perverse will, rejected Him': Jasper, *Prayer Book Revision in England*, pp. 42, 112. 'Perverse will', so G. E. Biber argued in 1865, was the vital ingredient of self-murder as opposed to suicide: see n. 41. High churchmen very often recommended the adoption of the Roman rubric, which permitted the Christian burial of suicides of unsound mind: see e.g. 'Liturgical Revision', *Church Quarterly Review* iii (1876–7), p. 62. In the mid-Victorian years only a few high-and-dry churchmen like Blunt seem to have been troubled by the fact that in England a coroner's jury was the judge of the deceased's insanity, and that this was a much-criticized tribunal.

[55] On this case (*Cooper v. Dodd*), see Little, *The Law of Burial*, p. 8. Ebury made much of it, and of the remonstrance to the archbishops and bishops signed (he said) by 4,000 clergy: Bligh, *Lord Ebury as a Church Reformer*, pp. 161–3, 187–8.

[56] *Hansard*, 3rd series, clv, cols. 2–3, 19 July 1859 (none of the bishops was present); *The English Churchman*, 21 and 28 July 1859, pp. 684, 717. The case was a complicated one: see *Leicestershire Mercury*, 2 July, p. 5, and 30 July, p. 8, 1859.

reality slipping out of the hands of the Church altogether, and whether or not a suicide was given some kind of Christian burial was coming to depend less and less on the decision of an Anglican clergyman. By 1876 it was estimated that two-thirds of the population had access to burying places outside the jurisdiction of the Church of England, and could make arrangements for burial with whatever religious service they chose.[57] From the 1830s commercial cemeteries had been opening in big cities, and from 1852 onwards an important series of Burial Acts ensured that in towns of any size churchyards were replaced as burial grounds by municipal cemeteries. In these new cemeteries, the law required one section to be provided which was outside the jurisdiction of the Church and in which anyone could be buried in any 'decent and solemn manner'.[58] Thus a quite unintended consequence of sanitary necessity and financial economy, combined with the political need to satisfy the Nonconformist lobby, was that silent burial of suicides could easily be avoided in towns some twenty or thirty years before the Burial Act of 1880 finally made it unnecessary anywhere—even in villages where churchyards were still the only burying place.

What many people wanted, however, was 'a proper Church funeral', despite the extra fees it cost. In very large towns and cities this could be secured easily enough. In very large cemeteries a rota of clergymen were on duty between 10 and 3 o'clock each weekday, and when the coroner's order to bury was presented to the cleric on duty, he rarely knew, and had no right to enquire, what had been the cause of death of the body awaiting burial at the gates of the cemetery.[59] But what happened on occasions when the clergyman knew all the circumstances? Usually the full Burial Service was used; but not always. From the 1890s, especially, there were growing clerical doubts about the burial of suicides with the full rites of the Church, as steeply rising suicide rates became a matter of increasing public concern, verdicts of 'temporary insanity' were more often criticized while remaining almost as common as ever, and more and more clergymen became convinced

[57] This estimate was given in 'Modern Dissent', *Church Quarterly Review*, iii (1876–7), p. 504.

[58] That is, one section was to remain unconsecrated. In 1855, however, it was provided that the whole new ground might be consecrated if the vestry unanimously so resolved, and this occasionally happened, for example in Durham. For the private enterprise cemeteries of the 1830s and 1840s see Curl, *The Victorian Celebration of Death*, pp. 79–110; and for the Burial Acts from 1852 onwards, see Little, *The Law of Burial*, pp. 83–219, and PP 1897 (312) XI, Select Committee on Burial Grounds, Minutes of Evidence.

[59] Wellington, 'The Verdict of "Suicide whilst Temporarily Insane"', p. 90.

that the Church must concern itself with current social and moral problems.[60] There was continuing uneasiness that harm was done in a parish when the priest seemed to be using the words of the Prayer Book insincerely. In 1908 feelings like these prompted the rural deans of the diocese of Truro to ask Convocation for guidance.[61] The burial of suicides had last been debated by Convocation in the 1870s, and since then the Church's method of dealing with questions relating to the rubrics and Prayer Book had become pastoral rather than legal. Authoritative discretion to settle such issues was now claimed for the bishop of each diocese; and by 1908 the bishops almost to a man were eager to promote the Church's 'social witness'.[62] The episcopal committee of five (most of them veterans of the social gospel) which worked between 1909 and 1911 to draw up general guiding principles on the burial of suicides, though anxious not to push the clergy into developing 'a professional conscience', was more anxious still to bring 'the moral witness of the Church' to bear on the formation of a sounder public opinion, especially with regard to the verdicts of coroners' juries. It would have liked an 'authoritative pronouncement' from the bishops or the state that in future verdicts of *felo de se* must be expected to return into common use. The Home Office, however, vetoed this latest example of episcopal over-enthusiasm in tackling the problems of the day, and the committee's final report confined itself to spelling out what ecclesiastical practice should be in the current situation.[63] A *felo de se* must be interred silently, or with some special penitential service. The vast majority of other suicides, however, should be buried

---

[60] An early example of this mood is the 'Service of Reconciliation' held in St Paul's on 13 Oct. 1890, 4 weeks after a man had shot himself while a prebendary was preaching and thus 'polluted and profaned' the cathedral. The service was held on the petition of the high church dean, R. W. Church (1815–90: *DNB*), or in effect (since Church's health had failed) of his right-hand man, Canon Gregory, and the chapter of the cathedral to the Bishop of London, then the social gospeller Frederick Temple (1821–1902: *DNB*), who took the advice of his chancellor, T. H. Tristram, QC. *The Times* considered this ceremony ('impregnated with pre-Reformation principles') uncalled for, and the psychiatrists deplored as typical of a lawyer Tristram's refusal to attach proper weight to the jury's verdict that this man was partially insane: [D. H. Tuke and G. H. Savage], 'Suicide in St Paul's Cathedral', *Jnl. of Mental Science*, xxxvii (1891), pp. 113–15. On the movement at the turn of the century in favour of a return to verdicts of *felo de se*, see p. 264.

[61] *Chronicle of Convocation, 1908*, 5 May, pp. 89, 94; ibid., *1909*, 18 Feb., pp. 34–35.

[62] On the increase in the authority of the bishops and the promotion of diocesan consciousness, see Chadwick, *The Victorian Church*, ii. 347–50, 359–65; and on the victory of the 'social gospel' among Church leaders, see Norman, *Church and Society in England, 1770–1970*, ch. 6, and Jones, *The Christian-Socialist Revival*.

[*see page 280 for footnote 63*]

with the full rites of the Church, and this not only because the verdict of a coroner's jury deserved the utmost deference (for the reasons which had been urged by ecclesiastical lawyers from Burn onwards), but also because it was very often altogether 'true and just' to ascribe the act of suicide to 'the mysteries of mental disease'. If, nevertheless, an incumbent felt 'a real and serious difficulty', he must immediately consult his bishop, and abide by his decision; and very occasionally that decision would have to be that the full rites must be refused. The bishops felt confident, however, that suitable alternative forms of service for such cases could readily be devised, and could be made acceptable to the relatives if a full explanation was given to them beforehand 'considerately and gently'; and they hoped that in due course an agreed alternative service would be given reassuring familiarity and authority by being included in a revised Prayer Book.[64]

Thus by 1911, in the matter of the burial of suicides as of much else, the Church was asserting its autonomy (in this case from the verdicts of coroners' juries), but was doing so with the utmost discretion and with much emphasis upon the authority of the bishop within his diocese. Browne of Bristol might declare that 'a little wholesome severity [in the burial of suicides] would strike the parishioners in a way which would do untold service';[65] but in practice Convocation's insistence in 1911 that the decision to refuse the full rites should lie

[63] As president of the upper house Randall Davidson, the Archbishop of Canterbury (1848–1930: *DNB*) nominated to this committee not only that veteran of the Guild of St Matthew, Stubbs of Truro, who had presented the petition and became convener, but also Talbot of Winchester (1844–1934: *DNB*) and Paget of Oxford (1851–1911: *DNB*), both members of the Christian Social Union, and Ridgeway of Chichester and Jacob of St Albans (1844–1920: *DNB*)—who was no doubt added because of his leading role over the Burials Act, 1901: *Chronicle of Convocation, 1909*, 18 Feb., p. 39.

[64] Their fellow bishops found their Resolutions acceptable, with slight alterations: *Chronicle of Convocation, 1911*, 4 and 6 July, pp. 327–32, 410. Their report was printed and sold by the SPCK for 2*d*., and presumably had a wide clerical circulation. The proposed Prayer Book of 1928 included additions and permissive deviations of the kind desired by this committee, although not a separate Order for the Burial of Suicides. The alternative form of service which had earlier been authorized for use in the Diocese of Oxford in cases of suicide where the Prayer Book service could not be used is printed in Church Information Office, *Ought Suicide to Be a Crime?*, appendix E, pp. 52–6.

[65] Browne (1833–1930: *DNB*) was supporting a proposal to refuse to allow the body of a suicide to be brought into the church: *Chronicle of Convocation, 1911*, 4 July, p. 331. The keenest advocate of a strong line was Charles Gore (1853–1932: *DNB*), the Christian Social Union leader, who said he had always acted upon the principle that the bishop could vary the Burial Service in the case of a man who had laid violent hands upon himself (by implication, regardless of whether or not a verdict of 'temporary insanity' had been given): ibid., pp. 330, 332.

with the bishop probably made severity not more frequent, but simply less erratic. The 'central churchmanship' which was then in the ascendant was one of charity and hope; and the lower clergy (with whom the initial moves rested) were most of them far closer to ordinary lay opinion than their bishops. Altogether it is no surprise to find that the *Prayer Book Dictionary*, for example, both in its first edition in 1912 and its second in 1925, stated flatly that the verdict 'while of unsound mind' entitled the relatives to claim Christian burial for a suicide.[66]

Thus between 1852 and 1880, as an unintended consequence of its concern with the quite unrelated issues of public health and Nonconformist citizenship, Parliament ensured that no suicide, even one adjudged *felo de se*, need be buried without religious rites of some kind. The Prayer Book, however, continued to prohibit the use of the Burial Service for 'all who laid violent hands upon themselves'; and no *felo de se* seems knowingly to have been buried with the full rites of the Church, although most clergymen were prepared to accept a 'temporary insanity' verdict as exonerating suicides from responsibility for their sinful deed, and to read the Burial Service over their remains. Some clergymen, however, were not so complaisant; and during the controversies over degeneracy and moral decline at the turn of the century, such refusals attracted enough notice for 'advanced' writers to lament 'how often the poor consolation of a religious service is refused by the clergy'.[67] In reality such refusals were rare, and in any case likely simply to lead to burial by a Wesleyan minister instead. Yet such occasional stringency, when combined with the personal teachings of the clergy and above all the continued presence in the Prayer Book of the rubric of 1662, must have kept alive vague fears and uncertainties about how a suicide would be buried, especially in country parishes. Even in Edwardian England the sanctions of ecclesiastical law cannot entirely have lost their force.

It would be a mistake to discount altogether the residual terrors of the law in preventing suicide. Popular morality was not identical with the law of the land, but neither was it wholly unaffected by it;[68] and

[66] In both editions, however, it was clearly implied that the current practice was open to criticism: Harford and Stevenson, eds., *The Prayer Book Dictionary*, 1st edn., pp. 115, 765, 2nd edn., pp. 114, 773.

[67] Strahan, *Suicide and Insanity*, p. 198. For the opposite view that the clergy were too lax, see Gurnhill, *The Morals of Suicide*, i. 208–9 and 'H.', Correspondence, *Spectator*, civ. 920 (4 June 1910).

[68] In 1874 William Cory (1823–92: *DNB*) found in north Devon that 'it turns out true, as I expected, that the main education of farmers, tradesmen and labourers is given

the continued existence of legal penalties for self-murder, even though they were only occasionally and erratically enforced, must have helped to sustain traditional feelings that suicide was 'a bad deed', best concealed (like other such deeds), and if known, needing convincing explanation. Criminal, civil, and ecclesiastical law alike, however, were all ineluctably reduced to little more than residual deterrents of suicide by the same double difficulty—that self-destruction was an offence for which only innocent survivors could be punished, and one which was honestly believed to be usually committed when someone was not in his or her right mind. As a result, whether from considerations of equity, of commercial advantage, or of pastoral care, the very persons who might have been expected vigorously to enforce the various branches of the law against accomplished suicide usually allowed public opinion to fend off its penalties through the mechanism of inquest verdicts of 'temporary insanity'.

Nevertheless it would be quite wrong to suppose that attempted suicide began to be treated as an offence simply because the laws penalizing accomplished suicide were seen to be incapable of achieving that combination of retribution, deterrence, and reformation which was widely expected from every branch of the penal system in the nineteenth century. On the contrary: each aspect of the development of this new offence had its own independent dynamics, and this is as true of police practices with regard to taking into custody, and magistrates' methods of disposing of those brought before them, as of the sentencing practices followed at quarter sessions and assizes. Increasingly it was through these channels that the efforts of the authorities to curb and prevent suicide were made; and since the doings of police officers, magistrates, and judges were always very much more systematically recorded than those of the coroners, clergymen, and insurance company directors who were responsible for implementing the law against accomplished suicide, the changing handling of attempted suicide can be reconstructed considerably more exactly.

Only the advent of the new police made it practicable routinely to treat attempted suicide as an offence; and this fact in itself was enough to ensure that although this offence began to be developed as early as the 1830s in the metropolitan area, this did not happen everywhere in

by the law, of course through inherited and accumulated perceptions . . . law gives them a constant (?low) standard of right and obligation': Cornish, *Letters and Journals of William Cory*, p. 365.

the provinces until some fifty years later. Certainly the sharply rising rate of arrest for attempted suicide at the end of the century (see Graph 2) does not necessarily furnish conclusive proof of that *fin de siècle* suicide mania which so concerned contemporaries. The marked dissimilarity in the curves of the arrest rates recorded over the decades by the metropolitan and provincial police forces is alone enough to suggest that variations in these rates of arrest are as much a part of the history of the police as of the history of attempted suicide. Indeed, this was surely inevitable; for since the English legal system was an accusatorial and not an inquisitorial one, attempted suicide could never become more than an occasional and incidental concern of the law until a large number of people both had knowledge of a significant proportion of suicide attempts and also systematically brought charges against the attempters. Before the advent of a policed society a parent might occasionally charge a child with attempted suicide, or a master an apprentice, and magistrates often found themselves dealing with those who had tried to commit suicide either just before or just after their arrest for some serious crime; but charges of attempted suicide were not part of the justices' routine work-load.[69]

In London, before the establishment of the new Metropolitan Police in 1829 and the City Police ten years later, watchmen had often been instructed to be on the alert to prevent fatal accidents near favourite suicide spots, just as the Royal Humane Society's boatmen had long patrolled the Serpentine.[70] After 1829, however, a new era quickly began. It did so, because the new police concentrated their efforts not upon preventing or detecting serious crime, but upon establishing public order in the streets.[71] To this end, they zealously took into custody the drunk and disorderly, prostitutes, vagrants and beggars,

[69] The offence of attempted suicide does not appear in magistrates' books of ready reference until after 1850. Of the many such handbooks published by George C. Oke (1821–74: *DNB*), the first to include it was the second edition of *The Magisterial Formulist* (1856), at p. 351, closely followed by the fifth edition of *The Magisterial Synopsis* (1857), at p. 614. Thereafter it was always included in handbooks of this sort.

[70] In 1827, for example, 'Davis the watchman had been cautioned that unhappy females are continually attempting to drown themselves' from Blackfriars Bridge: *The Times*, 12 Apr. 1827, p. 3, col. d. On the Royal Humane Society's patrols, see ch. 10.

[71] Initially 85 per cent of arrests by the Metropolitan Police were for vagrancy, prostitution, drunkenness, and disorderly behaviour, and most of the remaining 15 per cent were for petty larceny and pick-pocketing: Ignatieff, *A Just Measure of Pain*, p. 185. This growing intolerance of rowdiness and violence in public places must be associated with the 'revolution in manners' connected with (among other things) the evangelical revival.

rogues and impostors—and those who tried to commit suicide.[72] There is nothing surprising about this. Suicide attempts were often a by-product of the drunkenness and violence which loomed so large in the street life of early-nineteenth century London; sometimes too they expressed that dogged resistance to the workhouse system and refusal to apply to the relieving officer which created many urban police problems in the 1830s and beyond, including behaviour intended to ensure a night spent in the lock-up instead of the casual ward; and sometimes they were begging dodges, like the feigned war wounds, dependent families, and other ploys used by astute beggars. Thus the petty offenders who were the chief target of the new police overlapped with many of the sorts of people who were prone to make public suicide attempts. After 1829, policemen on the beat in the metropolitan district took those whom they found trying to commit suicide to the station-house; and, equally important, the superintendents and inspectors at the station did not discharge these people when they had sobered down or cheered up (as the City Police often did, even in the late 1840s),[73] nor did they regard these cases simply as averted accidents (as the Liverpool police long did).[74] On the contrary, they almost invariably proceeded to charge them before a magistrate, and to charge them moreover not with being drunk and disorderly or some such familiar blanket offence, but specifically with attempting to commit suicide. As a result, even in the 1830s an average of fifty-eight persons each year were charged with attempted suicide in the metropolitan police district; and in the 1840s the number was three times as high. Altogether, between 1841 and 1850, 623 men and 1,184 women were so charged. Indeed, where women were concerned, in that decade attempted suicide accounted for 2.5 per cent of all offences known to the Metropolitan Police, although for men the proportion was a mere 0.7 per cent. According to the returns, the overwhelming majority of these people, and especially the women, were partly or wholly illiterate; and most of them (and again, especially the women) were servants,

---

[72] Cases of arrest for attempted suicide were reported in increasing numbers in *The Times* from 1830 onwards. In 1861, 61 such cases were reported, as against 5 in 1827: Palmer's Index to *The Times*. For a typical early case, involving street-walking, drunkenness, and brawling, see *The Times*, 15 Oct. 1834, p. 4, col. b, case of Mary Bowling.

[73] As late as 1847–9, no more than 40 per cent of those taken into custody by the new City police were being taken before the magistrates: Rumbelow, *I Spy Blue*, pp. 229–30, Appendix 6.

[74] Until 1863 cases of attempted suicide were classified as accidents in the Liverpool Police Returns: see e.g., *Porter's Tables*, 1842, p. 165.

labourers, or had no occupation at all.[75] It was indeed the street poor who were being brought in for this offence in these early years.[76]

It would be a great mistake to suppose, however, that any special explanation is required of either the new practice of systematically arresting those who attempted to commit suicide in public places, or the new routine of following arrest with a charge before a magistrate. Both were plainly part of the new standard of public order and style of metropolitan policing which appeared at this time; or, as some historians would prefer to say, both were part of a new conception of social discipline and the new set of techniques deployed for its enforcement, in which street discipline shared the same origins as the discipline of the factories and schools, prisons and reformatories, workhouses and asylums.[77] Certainly the new severity towards suicidal behaviour was part of the effort to enforce seemliness, law, and order in a teeming city. All suicide attempts in public places created scenes likely to attract crowds, provoke excitement, and obstruct and distress passers-by; while many were the accompaniment of the public drunkenness, violence, non-co-operation with authority, fraud, and imposture which were prime targets of the new police. As for police strictness, obedience to rules and avoidance of discretionary release of those taken to the police station were always insisted upon by the first Metropolitan Police Commissioners.[78] To some extent, however, the new severity was also a development of the older paternal insistence that a watch should be kept to prevent dangerous accidents among the citizens.[79] For example, it had long been recognized that an outbreak of

---

[75] The tables which G. R. Porter of the Statistical Department of the Board of Trade submitted to Parliament for the years 1831–50 include police returns which give some statistics for the offence of attempted suicide from 1831 onwards. From 1837 the 'degree of instruction' of those taken into custody for this offence by the Metropolitan Police is shown, and from 1838 their age, as well as their sex, although occupations are given only for those arrested in 1840. Of those arrested for attempted suicide in the metropolis in 1841–50, 15 per cent of the men and 7 per cent of the women could 'read and write well' or had 'superior instruction' (although the corresponding figures for all those arrested in the metropolis in this decade were lower still, at 7 and 2 per cent).

[76] It was this sudden increase in arrests, as well as the colourful utterances of Sir Peter Laurie and the *cause célèbre* of Mary Furley, which made the authorities' treatment of suicide attempts such a topical question for Dickens to handle in 1844: see ch. 6 nn. 32 and 36.

[77] Ignatieff, *A Just Measure of Pain*, pp. 214–15.

[78] The first Metropolitan Police Commissioners objected to station-house discharge, and until 1869 required inspectors to report all discharges and the reasons for them: Miller, *Cops and Bobbies*, p. 63.

[79] At first the Metropolitan Police Commissioners thought of this police action in terms of preventing accidents, and included those who had been saved from committing

suicide attempts by a particular method at a particular spot required to be checked promptly, since suicide spread by imitation; equally, since it was well established that the authorities should play many different paternalistic roles towards the poor and suicide attempts were known to be sometimes appeals for sympathy or exhibitions of 'maudlin self-abandonment', it easily seemed (given the moral theories of the day) that such people should be taught a salutary lesson.

Public welfare, public decency, and public order, all seemed to require a crackdown on suicide attempts; and since these were exactly the goals of the new Metropolitan Police, the sharp rise in the metropolitan arrest rate for suicide attempts in the 1840s is entirely understandable. In that decade about one person in every 13,000 who lived in the metropolitan police district was arrested for attempted suicide. In the 1860s the proportion rose to about one in every 11,000, and it remained at this level until the 1890s—those years of apparent suicide mania—when it rose to one in every 10,000 (cf. Table 6.1).[80] At first

Table 6.1. Attempted suicide: average annual arrest rate per million living in the metropolitan police district in selected decennia and quinquennia, 1841–1913

1841–50	1861–70	1871–80	1893–7	1909–13
76.9	93.9	90.1	99.8	78.4

Sources: Porter's Tables, 1841–50, Metropolitan Police Returns; *Miscellaneous Statistics of the U.K., 1861–79*, Crime &c: Metropolitan Police, no. 2; *Metropolitan Police Commissioner's ARs, 1880, 1893–97, 1909–13*, appendix: Offences for which Apprehensions were Effected; *Censuses* (see ch. 8 n. 80).

glance this steadily high arrest rate in the later nineteenth century may seem surprising, until it is remembered that although far higher standards of public sobriety, well-being, and discipline were then well established, so too was an increasing readiness in domestic emergencies

suicide in an account of the number of lives saved by the police: PP 1834 (600) XVI, p. 8, Q. 111. A policeman on duty near the river might run after those whom he suspected might try to jump in, 'reason' with them, and then allow them to go home, as did Sergeant Taylor: *The Times*, 5 Nov. 1841, p. 8, col. a.

[80] For the estimated population of the metropolitan police district in 1841 and 1851, see PP 1867–8 (89–I), LVII, and for its population in each census year from 1861 to 1911, see *Census, 1911*, i. 646, Table 24.

to fetch the nearest policeman, as the service role of the bobby on his beat came to be emphasized and quite widely accepted. As a result, suicide attempts inside as well as outside working-class homes increasingly ended in an arrest, sometimes to the surprise of those involved. (Middle-class households were much less likely to run for help from a passing policeman.) Not until the early twentieth century did the metropolitan arrest rate fall quite substantially (see Table 6.1), and then probably in response to new attitudes towards petty crime and the use of some police discretion with regard to this particular offence, rather than to any real drop in the number of suicide attempts.[81]

London was unique, however, for a long time. In the 1840s, the only other place where a substantial number of arrests for attempted suicide were reported was Manchester; and even the new Manchester City Police made only 92 such arrests in 1841–50, compared with the 1,807 arrests made by the Metropolitan Police—although the sort of people arrested were very similar, that is, chiefly youngish, illiterate, and out-of-work women (though women outnumbered men less heavily in Manchester than in London).[82] As late as 1872 a shilling handbook to London singled out as one of the distinctive sights of a London police station a 'young lady' who had been rescued from the river and brought in by rough but kindly bobbies (see Fig. 11). In 1872–3, 54 per cent of the cases of attempted suicide reported in the whole of England and Wales did indeed come from the Metropolitan Police;[83] and although thereafter provincial arrests increased very rapidly, especially in the 1890s (see Table 6.2), the provincial arrest rate never equalled the metropolitan one, even in densely populated, highly urbanized industrial areas, although arrests in such places were always much com-

---

[81] In 1928 the then Inspector of Constabulary remarked that although instructions were given to the Liverpool police not to prosecute routinely for this offence as early as 1903, similar instructions were not given to the Metropolitan Police until 1916: Dunning, 'Discretion in Prosecution', p. 46. Nevertheless at a high level discretion in prosecuting for this offence was certainly exercised earlier in the metropolis (see, for example, the case described in Strahan, *Suicide and Insanity*, p. 202), and this may have encouraged some discretion both in reporting and in taking into custody.

[82] The Manchester Police Returns for 1845–50 record the age, occupations, and other personal details of those arrested for attempted suicide, while in Hull and Birmingham a mere handful of arrests were made for this offence, and in Liverpool such episodes were still classified as accidents: see *Porter's Tables*.

[83] For no other offence was the proportion of cases reported by the Metropolitan and City Police higher than 33.3 per cent: *Judicial Statistics, 1873*, Part I, p. xiv. On the 'young lady' at the police station, see ch. 6 n. 30.

Fig. 11 The Metropolitan Police dealing with a case of attempted suicide, as shown in Diprose's *Book about London and London Life, c.1872*

Table 6.2. Attempted suicide: average annual number of apprehensions in the metropolitan police district and the rest of England and Wales in selected decennia and quinquennia, 1861–1913

	1861–70	1871–80	1893–7	1909–13
Metropolitan police district	334	390	610	569
Provincial England and Wales	300	467	1250	1830

Sources: Row 1, as for Table 6.1; Row 2, *Judicial Statistics*, Part I, Police Returns: Indictable Offences—Total Crimes, Apprehensions, &c.

moner than they were in rural districts (see Table 6.3).[84] To some extent this disparity may genuinely have reflected a higher incidence of suicide attempts in urban industrial areas, as contemporaries usually

[84] The 5 industrialized counties in Table 6.3 are Lancashire, Yorkshire (West Riding only in 1909–13), Durham, Staffordshire, and Glamorgan; and the 6 rural counties are Hereford, Shropshire, Norfolk, Suffolk, Cambridgeshire, and Huntingdonshire. (These are the counties shown to have respectively the smallest and largest percentages of rural inhabitants in Bowley, 'Rural Population in England and Wales', p. 605, Table 3.) It should be pointed out that the figures in rows 2 and 3 of Table 6.3 relate to cases known to the police, not apprehensions. For this particular offence, however, these 2 figures were almost identical: see *Judicial Statistics*, 1862–66, Part I, Police, Table 5, and ibid., 1909–13, Tables XIX and XXII.

assumed;[85] but to some extent it must also simply have reflected the far greater likelihood of detection in heavily built-up neighbourhoods, where policemen covered a much smaller beat and outdoor suicide attempts were often heavily concentrated in a few well-known and much patrolled spots—although it may be worth remembering that in many northern industrial boroughs the police seem to have become

Table 6.3. *Attempted suicide: average annual arrest rate per million living in the metropolitan police district, the five most highly industrialized and the six most completely rural counties of England and Wales, 1861–6 and 1909–13*

	1861–6	1909–13
Metropolitan police district	103.4	78.3
Industrialized counties	18.7	69.4
Rural counties	10.9	15.2

Sources: Row 1, as for Table 6.1; Rows 2 and 3, *Judicial Statistics*, Part I, Police Returns: Indictable Offences—Nature of Crimes in each District; and see ch. 8 n. 84.

vigorous instruments of the local authorities' zeal for moral discipline and good behaviour,[86] in a way which few rural County Constabularies would have been likely to parallel.[87] At all events, when provincial police forces routinely took into custody those individuals whose attempts at suicide came to their attention, they probably did so essentially for the same reasons as the Metropolitan Police: that is, less in order to punish or prevent attempts at suicide for their own

[85] Notably W. C. Sullivan (see ch. 11 nn. 69 and 82), who offered an elaborate explanation of this disparity based upon the assumption that it was real: 'The Relation of Alcoholism to Suicide in England', *passim*. That very sensible jurist John Macdonnell (1845–1921: *DNB*), however, doubted 'whether the figures as to attempts to commit suicide are so complete or trustworthy as to warrant any very precise conclusions': *Judicial Statistics, 1899*, Part I, p. 39.

[86] This is the argument of Storch, 'The Policeman as Domestic Missionary' and 'The Plague of the Blue Locusts'.

[87] The style of county and borough forces was very different. Chief Constables were usually drawn from broadly the same class of country gentry as the county magistrates (who were the county police authorities until the establishment of Joint Standing Police Committees under the County Councils Act of 1888), and were often ex-Army officers and independent, self-confident men, who ran their forces more or less without interference. The Head Constables of borough forces, by contrast, were nearly always men risen from the ranks, and were closely supervised by their watch committees of petty bourgeois aldermen and councillors: Critchley, *A History of Police*, pp. 140–4, Martin and Wilson, *The Police*, pp. 9, 10, 30, Steedman, *Policing the Victorian Community*, pp. 42–3.

sake, than as part of a general effort to enforce higher standards of public order, decency, and safety in the towns and cities of an expanding society.[88]

Whatever the explanation of this new police practice, however, it had one inevitable result: from the 1830s metropolitan magistrates regularly had to deal with men, women, and children brought before them on a charge of attempted suicide, and from the 1860s provincial magistrates, particularly in urban areas, were also confronted with such people. Sometimes these cases were a significant addition to magistrates' work-load; sometimes they were very few and far between. (At the Guildhall, such offenders accounted for some 5 per cent or more of all those brought before the Justices in 1861; whereas in Highgate and Edmonton nearly fifty years later they accounted for less than 0.3 per cent of the cases dealt with in petty sessions.)[89] These offenders could not be tried summarily, with the exception, after 1879, of children whose parents or guardians raised no objection, and, after 1899, of consenting juveniles.[90] How then did magistrates dispose of them?

What proportion were committed for trial at quarter sessions or assizes? Any general answer to this question would be misleading, for the practice of magistrates in different kinds of area varied widely. It has already been remarked that there was always a group of 'soft' counties where less than 5 per cent of those taken into custody for attempted suicide were sent for trial, and another group of 'hard' counties where over a third were dealt with in this way. The 'soft' counties, however, always contained nearly half the total population of England and Wales, since they were usually urbanized, industrialized ones; they tended, therefore, also to be areas where the arrest rate for attempted suicide was high. Thus as a rule there was an inverse relationship between the arrest rate and the committal rate for

---

[88] In Edwardian reports of Metropolitan and City Police action, 'suicides attempted, prevented by police' were still listed immediately above such items as 'fires attended', 'dogs restored to owners', and 'runaway horses stopped': LCC, *London Statistics*, xvii (1905–6), 208.

[89] CLRO, Guildhall Justice Room, Magistrates' Charge Book, 1861; GLRO, Petty Sessional Records, Highgate petty sessions, PS H/1/7–9, 1905–7 and Edmonton Division, PS E/E/2/57–60, 1910. (The Guildhall Justice Room dealt with all those apprehended in the western part of the City, and this included that favourite spot for suicide attempts, Blackfriars Bridge.)

[90] 42 & 43 Vict., c. 49, s. 10 (1), Summary Jurisdiction Act, 1879; 62 & 63 Vict., c. 22, s. 2, Summary Jurisdiction Act, 1899.

attempted suicide in a given area: where the local police force brought in large numbers of attempters, local magistrates were very selective in sending them for trial, and vice versa.[91] In London, where the police were very zealous, only about 2 per cent of the many thousands of people who were charged with attempted suicide were sent for trial before the 1880s (see Table 7.1). At first, indeed, such people were

Table 7.1. *Attempted suicide: committals for trial as a percentage of apprehensions in the metropolitan police district and the rest of England and Wales in selected decennia and quinquennia, 1861–1913*

	1861–70	1871–80	1893–7	1909–13
Metropolitan police district	2.2	1.9	4.5	10.4
Provincial England and Wales	9.6	13.8	12.9	11.4

Sources: as for Table 6.2.

always summarily dealt with as rogues and vagabonds, or drunk and disorderly persons, or on some similar alternative charge.[92] Not until 1841 were two persons, both women, sent to stand trial specifically for attempting to commit the felony of suicide; and these two trials were altogether exceptional, and intended to be so. They caused a great stir,[93] and were still remembered twenty years later—chiefly no doubt because one of the two committing magistrates was the most colourful City alderman of the day, Sir Peter Laurie, and because that universally read writer, Dickens, had relentlessly caricatured in *The Chimes* Laurie's bluff belief that suicide attempts could be 'put down' by a few exemplary sentences.[94] It is true that metropolitan magistrates began sending for trial more freely from the 1880s, and by 1909–13 were doing so in 10 per cent of the attempted suicide cases which came

[91] See ch. 7 n. 25

[92] None of the 587 men and women taken into custody by the Metropolitan Police for attempted suicide in 1831–40 was committed for trial for that offence: *Porter's Tables, 1831–40*, Metropolitan Police Returns. For examples of their being dealt with summarily under other charges, see *The Times*, 15 Oct. 1834, p. 4, col. b (Thames Police Office) and 3 Nov. 1841, p. 7, col. 1 (Guildhall).

[93] The new departure was widely reported: e.g., *The Times*, 5 Nov. 1841, p. 8, col. a, and as late as 31 Aug. 1860 was referred to in an editorial in the *Daily Telegraph*.

[94] Laurie had a reputation for exceptional shrewdness on the bench: [Grant], *Portraits of Public Characters*, i. 130, and 'City Magistrates, no. 1: Sir Peter Laurie', *Illustrated London News*, 21 Jan. 1843, p. 40. For Dickens's caricature of him as Alderman Cute in *The Chimes*, see ch. 6 n. 36. For Laurie's own appraisal of the results of his action, see *The Times*, 13 Nov. 1844, p. 7, col. f; and for a much later defence of his policy by an experienced prison chaplain, see Horsley, 'Suicide', p. 512.

before them (see Table 7.1); but this was probably not because they were taking a harder line, but because the significance of committal was changing radically in these years, as 'progressive' alternatives to prison sentences were more and more freely used by the courts.[95] As for the provinces, trial was always rare in highly urbanized, industrialized counties, where suicide cases came before the magistrates almost as often as in London. Trial was equally infrequent in the Border counties of Cumberland, Westmorland, and Northumberland, although almost certainly for quite a different reason: in Scotland suicide was not a criminal offence, and in this as in other matters the functioning of English law in the Borders was probably much affected by Scottish habits and practices. The only magistrates who were always quite likely to send for trial someone charged with attempted suicide, were those in the rural shires south of a line between the Mersey and the Humber (see Table 7.2); and they were rarely confronted with such people.[96]

Table 7.2. *Attempted suicide: committals for trial as a percentage of appre-hensions in the metropolitan police district, the five most highly industrialized and the six most completely rural counties of England and Wales, 1861–6 and 1909–13*

	1861–6	1909–13
Metropolitan police district	1.9	10.4
Industrialized counties	1.9	4.9
Rural counties	7.7	32.7

Sources: Row 1: as for Table 6.1; Rows 2 and 3: as for Table 6.3 and *Judicial Statistics, 1861–66*, Part I, Criminal Proceedings, [Table 2] and ibid., *1909–13*, Table VI.

For most urban magistrates, committal for trial was thus an unusual way of dealing with a charge of attempted suicide. What sort of offenders were singled out for this exceptional treatment? The Judicial Statistics indicate only that (as usual)[97] men were more likely to be

---

[95] See pp. 305–7.
[96] Perhaps significantly, some of these rural 'hard' counties were also counties where clerical magistrates clustered most thickly: see PP 1873 (388) LIV and cf. ch. 7, p. 240. It should be noted that these variations, and their nature, make it more intelligible both that contemporary descriptions of magistrates' behaviour were so contradictory, and that complaints of excessive leniency outnumbered complaints of harshness.
[97] On the more lenient treatment of female offenders in general, see Cox, *The Principles of Punishment*, p. 145.

committed than women.[98] The calendars of prisoners sent for trial at Middlesex quarter sessions and assizes, however, together with some surviving depositions, magistrates' reports, and petty sessional records for the London area,[99] show clearly that as a rule those sent for trial either had already made several attempts to commit suicide, or were bad characters with previous convictions for other offences. Occasionally a first offender was made to undergo the ordeal of trial, presumably as a salutary shock—for some lay magistrates (especially, apparently, suburban and rural ones),[100] as well as many clergymen and moralists,[101] never lost faith in the power of 'the sermons of the Sessions' to deter people from suicide attempts. Usually, however, trial was reserved for hardened offenders. It is easy to understand why this was so. The great majority of these cases, after all, were dealt with by stipendiaries and above all by the twenty-three metropolitan police magistrates; and these men were well abreast of current penal ideas. From the later 1860s penal thinking distinguished sharply between the wilful and persistent criminal and those who became offenders simply from misfortune, incapacity, drunkenness, or lack of proper care and training. The 'criminal class', it was held, should be made to serve severe prison sentences in conditions as harsh as possible; but 'hopefuls'

[98] In 1870–9 only 5.3 per cent of the women as against 8 per cent of the men apprehended for attempted suicide were sent for trial: *Judicial Statistics*, Part I, Police, Table 5; while in 1893–1913 41 per cent of those apprehended for attempted suicide were female, but only 27 per cent of those sent for trial: ibid., Tables V and XIX. This disparity between the sexes, however, may partly have been the result of the methods preferred by women (drowning and poisoning), which were more ambiguous than the methods preferred by men. It is worth noting that 76 per cent of the women but only 68 per cent of the men who were discharged for this offence were discharged for want of evidence in 1870–9: ibid., Table 5.

[99] The calendars and depositions in the Middlesex Sessions Records (GLRO, MJ/CP/B and MJ/SPE) have been worked through for 1861–5 and 1905–7 and sampled for 1869, 1871–2 and 1881. Of the petty sessional records preserved at the GLRO, the records for Highgate in 1905–7 and the Edmonton Division in 1910 have been worked through, and a number of others sampled. At the CLRO, the Guildhall Justice Room Magistrates' Charge Books for 1861 and 1863 were worked through, and the Registers and Notes of Evidence for 1900 and 1910.

[100] Of the 15 prisoners tried for attempted suicide at Middlesex quarter sessions in 1905–7, 5 had been sent for trial by the magistrates of well-to-do, suburban Highgate, and only one by those of densely populated, working-class Tottenham: GLRO, MJ/CP/B 42 and 43; again, in 1907–9 the Highgate magistrates sent 3 of their 17 cases of attempted suicide for trial, whereas in 1910 the Tottenham magistrates discharged all 15 of their cases: GLRO, PS E/E2/57–60; PS/H/1/7–9.

[101] The one-time prison chaplain J. W. Horsley continually expressed this faith in his widely read writings, and was much quoted by others: Horsley, *Jottings from Jail*, p. 258, *Prisons and Prisoners*, pp. 171–2, 177; Gurnhill, *The Morals of Suicide*, i. 208, Henson, 'Suicide', p. 75.

who might be deterred from further lapses by proper treatment should either be given no more than a token prison sentence, or be fined, bound over, held to bail, or sent to an appropriate institution (a workhouse or lunatic asylum, a reformatory or industrial school, or, after 1898, an inebriates' home).[102] A few years' experience in a busy police court abundantly demonstrated both that some of those who made suicide attempts fully deserved to be reckoned hardened offenders, and that such people were in a small minority. In reality what was remarkable about this offence was not (as the public supposed) the lenient attitude of magistrates towards it, but the tiny proportion of those taken into custody for it who could be reckoned true criminals and—almost equally important—the exceptional difficulty of assembling evidence of their intention which would be likely to convince a jury.[103] (If the defendant could establish that he was too drunk to know what he was doing, for example, he would be acquitted.)[104] Most of these offenders, accordingly, were discharged: this was what became of 92 per cent of those taken into custody by the Metropolitan Police in the 1830s, and it was still what became of 74 per cent of them in 1909–13, when the proportion discharged was smaller than it had ever been before.[105]

Yet it would be quite as mistaken to suppose that magistrates simply dismissed these people with a lecture, as to suppose that they sent most of them for trial. It is true that contemporaries often blamed 'philanthropic magistrates' for doing precisely this. Those with first-hand experience of the police courts, however, did not allow such statements to pass;[106] and the historian has only to go behind the misleading baldness of the statistics to see for himself how varied were

---

[102] See McConville, *A History of English Prison Administration*, i. 327–64.

[103] Very many more of these offenders were always discharged for want of evidence, than were discharged for want of prosecution: for 1870–9, see n. 98. Statistically, this offence was also exceptional in that nearly all the cases recorded as known to the police were taken into custody in this period. (In the metropolitan police district in 1909–13, the figure was 99.1 per cent, as against only 79.8 per cent for the whole range of principal offences: *Metropolitan Police Commissioner's ARs, 1909–13*, Appendix, no. 25).

[104] See ch. 6 n. 92.

[105] The figure for the 1830s is calculated from *Porter's Tables*, Metropolitan Police Returns; and that for 1909–13 from *Metropolitan Police Commissioner's ARs, 1909–13*, Appendix, no. 23.

[106] E.g. when W. W. Westcott said in the course of a paper to the Medico-Legal Society in 1905 that it was usual to dismiss those who had attempted suicide with a mere caution, two knowledgeable members, J. Wells Thatcher (1856–1946: *Who was Who*) and Dr James Scott (on whom see ch. 11, pp. 392–3) immediately corrected him: Westcott, 'On Suicide', p. 97.

routine procedures among metropolitan magistrates for dealing with alleged suicide attempts. All of them, however, had one essential practice: remand for a week, for daily visits from the prison chaplain and if necessary the surgeon.[107] Given the increasingly professionalized prison service of the later nineteenth century, a week's remand—occasionally renewed for a second week, though rarely for longer—could plausibly be expected to serve two useful purposes. First, it ensured that someone who had apparently tried to take his own life received medical treatment and moral counsel, and had sobered up or calmed down before he was left to his own devices; that is, it was a safety precaution, to be compared with the locking up overnight of those who were drunk and incapable. (In Victorian England there was a great gulf between a 'House of Detention' and a 'House of Correction', and real punishment could be equated only with the penitentiary discipline of the latter.) Secondly, however, remand made possible a serious attempt to deal with each case individually in an informed and therefore more effective way. To do this, the examining magistrate needed to know not only what the police could tell him about the circumstances of the alleged attempt (such as whether the person in question had seemed drunk at the time and whether there was evidence that he knew rescue was likely, or had previously attempted or threatened suicide), but also something about the personal circumstances of the alleged attempter; and these could best be discovered by the chaplain and surgeon, the two key officers in the prison, who would try to find out whether there was acute poverty, ill-health, or evidence of insanity, whether there were 'friends' who would provide a home (especially in the case of a girl), and whether there was any prospect of work for those who had none.

As it happens, the mid-Victorian workings of this system of remand in London can be unusually fully reconstructed. More than half of all the cases of attempted suicide recorded in the metropolis were sent to the special remand prison maintained by the Middlesex magistrates at Clerkenwell, and a variety of evidence survives on what happened to them there,[108] where they sometimes made up around 3 per cent of the

---

[107] In the early 1860s the Justices sitting at the Guildhall were already remanding about three-quarters of their attempted suicide cases in this way: CLRO, Guildhall Justice Room, Magistrates' Charge Books, 1861 and 1863.

[108] Unfortunately (although not surprisingly) all this evidence comes from the prison staff. The annual reports to the Middlesex Justices for 1847–78 (apart from 1876) from the chaplain, and some from the surgeon, are preserved at the GLRO: MA/RS/1 for the printed series, and MJ/OC, for the manuscript reports; see also MJ/SP/1873/Oct./16,

inmates. During their week on remand, it was the duty of the chaplain and surgeon to give them what advice and treatment they could; but more importantly, a report had to be submitted to the committing magistrate on each individual case at the end of the remand, setting out what seemed to be the most appropriate action for him to take. In the years between 1848 and 1878, it was still the chaplain's and not the surgeon's advice which was decisive (except in cases of suspected lunacy).[109] Changing penal ideas were already beginning to deprive prison chaplains of the absolutely central role given them by early Victorian penal theory; but their daily ministrations to each prisoner were still reckoned important, and the growing weight attached to the medical officers' functions never destroyed their official prestige (although to the prison inmates the chaplain was 'Lady Green', unless he proved otherwise, and 'gammoning' him was a favourite ploy).[110] Four very different clergymen followed each other at Clerkenwell before it was closed in 1886. Each left his mark on the way magistrates dealt with those whom they remanded there on a charge of attempted suicide. Their efforts will be fully considered in the next chapter. All that need be said here is that two of them, George Hough and Joseph Wheeler (both enthusiastic young missioners) suggested to the magistrates an increasing variety of ways in which the 1,385 men and women charged with attempted suicide who were remanded to Clerkenwell between 1868 and 1875 might be helped to overcome the weaknesses, hardships, and difficulties which had led them to attempt suicide. Only 22 per cent of these cases were simply discharged. Six per cent were released on their own recognizances and 2 per cent were sent for trial. All the rest, however, were given what seemed appropriate assistance. Many were returned to friends or relatives or 'sent back to their friends in the country'; some were started in a trade or found work, or helped to emigrate to Canada or the United States; others were sent to hospital

18, 37A (the remaining Sessions Papers for this period were uncatalogued and therefore unavailable at the time when this work was done). In addition, the last chaplain of Clerkenwell, J. W. Horsley, was an enterprising publicist, and when the appearance of Morselli's *Suicide* in translation in 1881 made the subject a talking-point, he utilized his prison experiences in a timely article, 'Suicide'. When Clerkenwell closed in 1886, he again utilized his case-notes in *Jottings from Jail*, and for the next 20 years continued to rework this material on attempted suicide.

[109] Naturally the major role given to the chaplain in cases of attempted suicide was regarded as a serious mistake by those who were convinced that suicidal behaviour was always a sign of insanity and therefore called for medical attention: see e.g. Davey, 'The Prevalence of Suicide', p. 519. The surgeon's role is discussed in ch. 11.

[110] Greenwood, *The Seven Curses of London*, p. 178.

or to a lunatic asylum, industrial school or refuge, or put in touch with the Discharged Prisoners' Aid Society; and many were sent to the workhouse.[111]

These particular decades of the 1860s and 1870s probably saw the heyday of enthusiasm for chaplaincy counselling on remand as an instrument of suicide prevention.[112] It is true that in the early twentieth century a very fully developed routine of remand for reports from both chaplain and medical officer was evidently still being used by City magistrates;[113] but it seems that some lay magistrates in outer north London were then using remand only in selected cases and chiefly to secure a medical report, and that this was perhaps the practice of some police magistrates also.[114] For juveniles, moreover, remand had never been considered desirable: the risk of contamination from old lags was too great. Instead, metropolitan police magistrates were early users of the practice of binding over or taking bail from a parent, or (after 1857) of a spell in an industrial school—until progressive opinion turned against institutionalization, when they began to employ various workers to keep an eye on such offenders after they left the court. In the metropolitan area it thus probably made little difference when children became triable summarily for attempted suicide in 1879, and juveniles in 1899, and equally little when the system of probation orders was introduced in 1907, or when, after 1908, children and juveniles had to be tried separately at special sittings.[115] Of the first twenty-five cases of attempted suicide which came before the metropolitan Juvenile Courts, six were placed on probation, two discharged

---

[111] See the reports of Hough and Wheeler to the Middlesex Justices, GLRO, MA/RS/1/501, 508, 514, 516, 521, 526, 531, 536; MJ/OC/65; MJ/SP, 1873 Oct/18.

[112] Perhaps it is significant of a changing climate that Clerkenwell's last chaplain, Horsley, was sceptical about the results of his predecessors' labours, and always maintained that the best preventive of suicide attempts would be sentences of hard labour: 'Suicide', p. 512.

[113] CLRO, Guildhall Justice Room, Registers and Notes of Evidence, 1900 and 1910.

[114] This impression with regard to lay magistrates is gained from the petty sessions registers of the Highgate and Edmonton Division (GLRO, PS/H/1 and PSE/E2) together with the calendars of prisoners tried at Middlesex quarter sessions (GLRO, MJ/CP/B) and above all the depositions relating to these prisoners, 1905–7 (MJ/SPE). With regard to the police magistrates' courts, the Edwardian routine was still remand at Tower Bridge, but it is not clear that this was equally true of Bow Street: PP 1908 [Cd. 4439] XII, p. 31, Q. 339, and p. 41, Q. 579.

[115] H. Curtis Bennett of Bow Street told the Home Office that the metropolitan police courts were in effect using a probation system several years before the Probation of Offenders Act of 1907: Bochel, *Probation and After-Care*, p. 20.

on recognizances, one sent to reformatory school, one committed for trial, and all the other charges were dismissed or withdrawn;[116] and there was nothing novel about any of this.

To assume, however, that these metropolitan practices were typical of the whole country would obviously be as wrong as to assume that they were successful. Very few other parts of the country had prisons which were used exclusively for remand; and both the staff of Clerkenwell (and of its successors, Holloway and Brixton prisons), and the hard-working metropolitan police magistrates whom they served, must have been exceptionally experienced and professional in their approach, as well as exceptionally well placed to make experiments in rehabilitation. Lay magistrates were usually conservative, and particularly in rural and suburban areas probably handed cases of attempted suicide less flexibly than stipendiaries, and much less flexibly than the metropolitan police magistrates.[117] Yet when a new magistrates' handbook was published in the 1880s, it was the flexible metropolitan approach which was held up as the norm;[118] while in Liverpool at the turn of the century, procedures were certainly very similar to those in London—perhaps not surprisingly, since it was always the Liverpool police who came nearest to rivalling the number of arrests for attempted suicide made by the metropolitan force,[119] and Liverpool's stipendiary magistrate was as busy (and as well paid) as the chief metropolitan magistrate himself.[120] Provincial practice, however, awaits investigation in local sources. What has been given

[116] *Metropolitan Police Commissioner's AR, Appendix, 1910 and 1911,* no. 24, and *1912 and 1913,* no. 25. For the arrangements for implementing s. 111 of the Children Act, 1908 in the metropolitan police court district, see LCC, *London Statistics,* xxii (1911–12), p. 289.

[117] County Benches in general had a reputation for ferocity: cf. 'a man would rather be had up three times before the Borough [Maidenhead] than once before the County [Berkshire]', Russell, *My Life and Adventures,* p. 175.

[118] Wigram, *The Justices' Note-Book* (1880), pp. 375–6. (Wigram sat on the Middlesex Bench.) New editions of older handbooks, however, continued simply to tabulate the legal position: for example, Stone, *The Justices' Manual,* 21st edn. (1882), p. 760, and Oke, *The Magisterial Synopsis,* 14th edn. (1893), ii. 908.

[119] For the practice in the 1890s at Walton prison, to which the Liverpool police courts sent those charged with attempted suicide on remand for medical observation, see the article by the Deputy Medical Officer there, Sullivan, 'Alcoholism and Suicidal Impulses', pp. 259, 270. In Salford in 1915, the stipendiary's approach was the practical 'philanthropic' one of the London police courts, at least in the case of Mrs Mary Munro: Roberts, *The Classic Slum,* p. 195.

[120] Both had a salary of £1,500 in 1873: PP 1873 (192) LIV. In the Edwardian East End underworld, Liverpool was said 'to have the hottest police force in the world': Samuel, *East End Underworld,* ii. 78.

priority here is the disposal policy of the City and metropolitan police magistrates, who undoubtedly handled far larger numbers of attempted suicide cases than any other magistrates.[121]

It remains to be considered how this disposal policy can be explained. How did it come about that although the police regarded themselves as prosecuting agents for this offence, these busy professional magistrates did not?[122] In Victorian and Edwardian England, 'philanthropic' magistrates were repeatedly blamed for treating suicide 'lightly' by the many who believed that their kindness simply encouraged such attempts; and today the wisdom of their low-key approach could again be questioned, since parasuicide is found to be less frequent in a hostile society, and vice versa.[123] It would be a great mistake, however, to assume that the attitude of these magistrates was the result of sentimentality. To them, attempted suicide was probably neither a deed of portentous moral significance to be equated with murder, nor an act of tragic despair calling for the world's pity, but simply one of many offences, mostly very petty, which had to be dealt with week after week, and whose origins and significance were even more varied than most. True, not until 1925 did Parliament downgrade the legal status of attempted suicide into that of a minor offence, triable in petty sessions and police courts; yet in practice police magistrates always dealt with such cases summarily, and disposed of the overwhelming majority of them themselves.[124] Quite often an attempter could formally be dealt with summarily on some other charge, since suicide attempts were frequently associated with some petty offence, and indeed were often enough made in a police cell by someone

---

[121] Even in 1909–13 the Liverpool and Manchester police forces reported only 779 and 469 cases of attempted suicide respectively, while the Metropolitan Police reported 2,843 cases and was thus still responsible for a quarter of the cases of attempted suicide reported in England and Wales: *Judicial Statistics, 1909–13*, Part I, Table, Indictable Offences: Nature of Crimes in each District.

[122] This contrast was singled out for notice in 1928 by the then Inspector of Constabulary, who consequently attached considerable significance to the instructions given to the Liverpool police in 1903 to prosecute for attempted suicide only 'when there was some definite circumstance calling for punishment or the order of a Court presented the only chance of refuge and asylum for one too weak to stand alone': Dunning, 'Discretion in Prosecution', p. 46.

[123] Baechler, *Suicides*, pp. 403, 442.

[124] 15 & 16 Geo. V, c. 86, s. 24, Criminal Justice Act, Schedule Two. When in 1908 the lobby for inebriates' reformatories urged that it was vital to increase magistrates' powers to deal with attempted suicide by bringing it within the scope of summary jurisdiction, the Bow Street magistrate, H. C. Bennett, retorted that he invariably dealt summarily with attempted suicides: see ch. 11 n. 84.

already taken in on another charge (commonly that of being drunk and disorderly). In short, successive generations of busy urban magistrates handled cases of attempted suicide very much like the rest of their work-load, using their own experience and initiative within the framework of whatever was the outlook of their particular generation upon the causes of petty crime and the best way of dealing with it.

Year after year their experience showed them that a suicide attempt sometimes sprang from want and misfortune, sickness or despair; but also that it sometimes sprang from loss of self-control through drink, brawling or sheer moodiness, silliness or incompetence; and that not infrequently it was a way of blackmailing family, friends, or lovers, manipulating the authorities,[125] or softening up the charitable and gullible public.[126] (Metropolitan police magistrates always had particularly good reason to know this last, since after a touching case had been reported in the police columns of the newspapers, the magistrate concerned was often inundated with ear-marked donations sent to him through the post by the soft-hearted.)[127] In the 1830s and 1840s—when the majority of those brought before them for attempted suicide were out-of-work young women and when resistance to the new poor law was at its height—magistrates were particularly conscious of the links between these attempts and poverty, prostitution, and reluctance to apply to the parish relieving officer, as well as of the element of hysterical imitation which could cause a particular type of attempt to multiply. In the 1860s, by contrast, they more readily associated them with ingrained rowdiness and fraudulent mendicancy (both then much denounced); while in the 1900s they particularly linked them with female alcoholism and male unemployment—two great preoccupations of those years.[128] Yet this was *par excellence* deviant

[125] It was almost axiomatic among experienced prison administrators that suicide attempts among those serving a penal sentence (as opposed to those charged, remanded, or awaiting trial) were usually feigned: see, e.g. Griffiths (1838–1908: DNB), *Secrets of the Prison House*, ii. 183–4, 194; Hopkins, 'Suicides and Malingerers', pp. 110–11.

[126] Warnings against faked and exhibitionist 'cries for help' were quite common: cf. ch. 4 n. 70 and ch. 6 nn. 39, 53.

[127] In 1841 the magistrate who heard the charge against Harriet Camp (a respectable married woman with 5 children and an unemployed husband, who had tried to drown herself from Blackfriars Bridge because she could not bear to see her family without food and her husband would not apply for relief), gave her a small sum in the usual way and then, after the case had received publicity, was sent a number of donations, ranging from £5 downwards: *The Times*, 28 Oct., p. 7, col. b, 5 Nov., p. 8, col. 1, 9 Nov., p. 7, col. c, 1841. In 1861, the police magistrates were still the preferred charitable agencies of the general public: PP 1861 (180) IX, p. 80, Q. 2184, p. 84, Qs. 2243–6.

[128] The generalizations in this paragraph are based upon impressions given by news-

behaviour to which the appropriate judicial response was unsure, so varied were the circumstances surrounding it (as any metropolitan charge book makes clear). To a kind, conscientious, or hard-pressed magistrate, remand for investigation must therefore have seemed obviously useful, and this no doubt is why it so quickly became recommended practice.

It is equally easy to understand why magistrates increasingly decided upon binding over in these cases, or holding the attempter or a relation to bail. After all, those arrested for a suicide attempt were quite often female, and very often young and impressionable, with no settled intention to end their lives.[129] Magistrates had always been prone to extract a promise not to do such a thing again, and had liked personally to entrust the offender to a relation; and these practices were formalized when progressive penal thought and practice moved away from prison sentences for first offenders towards various forms of court order.[130] By the middle of the 1890s as many as 18 per cent of those arrested for attempted suicide in the metropolitan police district were being bound over or held to bail;[131] and reasonably so, if the experience of one police magistrate appointed in 1899 was typical—for he found that as a rule they did not come before him again, 'if wisely dealt with by friends or relations'.[132] To these busy urban magistrates remand very commonly seemed judicious, aid or after-care quite often appeared

paper police reports and autobiographical recollections, as well as charge books and magistrates' registers.

[129] Attempted suicide was typically an offence of those under the age of 35, and unplanned. For some profiles of the typical attempted suicide, see Horsley, 'Suicide', pp. 506–7 and *Jottings from Jail*, p. 243; Sullivan, 'The Relation of Alcoholism to Suicide', pp. 266–9; East, 'On Attempted Suicide', pp. 442, 455. The conclusion of a recent study of the treatment of criminal violence in this period is apposite here: 'The "hot-bloodedness" of the violent man was permitted to excuse a great deal, especially since his turpitude could be blamed on drink, was usually impulsive, and brought him little profit': Gatrell, 'The Decline of Theft and Violence', p. 300.

[130] For mid-Victorian examples of the homily followed by the exaction of a promise not to make another attempt, see CLRO, Guildhall Justice Room, Magistrates' Charge Books, 1861, 1863; and for examples of later practices such as the formal binding over of a father in the sum of £10 for 6 months, and discharge on the prisoner's own recognizance of £5 for 6 months, see ibid., Registers, 1900 and 1910.

[131] *Metropolitan Police Commissioner's AR, 1893–97*, Return of Offences for which Apprehensions were effected: Indictable Offences. In 1909 Bennett of Bow Street (who claimed 23 years' experience) said: 'The usual thing is to put them back if they have not anybody with them, and send for their friends and get their friends' bail for them and let them go': PP 1908 [Cd. 4439] XII, p. 41, Q. 579.

[132] Chapman, *The Poor Man's Court of Justice*, p. 203. Chapman's court of Tower Bridge (formerly Southwark) had many attempted drowning cases.

appropriate, and one form or other of binding over increasingly seemed worthwhile; but only rarely did a case of attempted suicide seem to call for such strong measures as trial at quarter sessions or assizes.

Yet it would be wrong to conclude that the sentencing practice of these courts can be ignored so far as attempted suicide is concerned— if only because the examining magistrate's decision must always have been influenced by what he expected to be the likely outcome of a trial. What then was the usual fate of the few sent to stand trial for this particular offence? Undeniably it had its full share of diversity and unpredictability. Unless cases were very carefully selected and prepared, the grand jury might well find 'no true bill' or the trial jury return a verdict of 'not guilty', since in the eyes of ordinary people an attempt at suicide easily seemed not to merit condign punishment. This happened frequently in early trials for this offence: only fourteen of the thirty-six people committed for trial for attempted suicide in the metropolitan area between 1841–50 were convicted and sentenced;[133] and the first national figures show that in 1861–5 'no true bill' was found against 11 per cent of those committed for trial, while another 11 per cent were acquitted.[134] By 1909–13 these proportions had been halved, and conviction was as likely for attempted suicide as for most other offences,[135] presumably because better preparation and more experience had led to a closer fit between the reactions of juries and examining magistrates to a given body of evidence. On the other hand, by this time there may well have been even more geographical variation than before in the sentencing of those found guilty, for after 1889 all cases of attempted suicide were tried at quarter sessions unless the High Court specifically directed trial at assizes (which happened in only about 17 per cent of cases);[136] and sentencing at quarter sessions was always particularly erratic, since legally qualified chairmen were rare outside urban areas.[137]

---

[133] *Porter's Tables, 1841–50*, Metropolitan Police Returns.

[134] *Judicial Statistics, 1861–65*, Part I, Criminal Proceedings [Table 1].

[135] Ibid., 1909–13, Table V.

[136] This was in incidental result of 52 & 53 Vict., c. 12 (Assizes Relief Act, 1889). The proportion of cases sent to assizes has been calculated here from the *Judicial Statistics*, Part I, Tables I, III, and V.

[137] See Jackson, *The Machinery of Justice*, pp. 107–8. In cases of attempted suicide, Surrey quarter sessions had a reputation for severity, whereas Middlesex quarter sessions before the great reorganization of 1889 was known for leniency over this as other offences: Horsley, *Prisons and Prisoners*, p. 179; Chesterton, *Revelations of Prison Life*, p. 312. My sampling of the Gaol Calendars for 1868 confirmed that there were indeed wide differences in sentencing, with quarter sessions at Louth (Lincolnshire), Wol-

What is notable in national terms, however, is less the increase in the proportion of those tried for attempted suicide who were found guilty, than the growth of the practice of dealing with those against whom this charge was proved with a court order and not a custodial sentence, whether in prison or, after 1898 and for alcoholics, in an inebriates' reformatory.[138] In the 1860s, 13 per cent of those tried for attempted suicide were dealt with by court order (usually for discharge on bail), and 19 per cent in the 1870s; but by 1893–7 this proportion had risen to 40 per cent, and by 1909–13 it had reached 58 per cent (see Table 8.1). Thus the swing away from custodial sentences so

Table 8.1. *Attempted suicide: percentage of those tried in England and Wales who were (a) given a prison sentence (b) dealt with by court order, in selected decennia and quinquennia, 1861–1913*

	1861–70	1871–80	1893–7	1909–13
Prison sentence	60	53	40	28
Court order	13	19	40	58

Sources: Judicial Statistics, 1861–80, Part I, Criminal Proceedings [Table 1]; ibid., *1893–7, 1909–13*, Table V.

notable generally after the Probation Act of 1907 was well established by the mid-1890s so far as attempted suicide was concerned, and already included twice as many of those tried as was ever the case before 1914 for other offences.[139] In attempted suicide cases, however, the preference for bail probably reflected not so much the new penal thinking which affected criminal administration generally at the turn of the century as the perennial legal ambivalence towards suicide and

verhampton (Staffordshire), and Newington (Surrey) giving hard labour for suicide attempts: PRO, HO 140/2–4.

[138] In 1899–1907 29 men and women convicted of both attempted suicide and habitual drunkenness were committed to these reformatories: PP 1908 [Cd. 4342] XII, p. 5. In 1908–13, however, only 12 of those tried for attempted suicide received such a sentence: *Judicial Statistics*, Part I, Table V—a diminution which no doubt reflects the disenchantment with the policy of committal to inebriates' reformatories indicated in MacLeod, ' "The Edge of Hope" ', p. 240. The temperance lobby at this time estimated that two-thirds to four-fifths of those who attempted suicide were alcoholics: cf. ch. 11, p. 397.

[139] Comparisons with a number of broad categories of offences can conveniently be made by consulting Gatrell, 'The Decline of Theft and Violence', pp. 342–70, Tables A1–A5, col. 11, and Tables B1–B3. On the changes in the administration of criminal justice around the turn of the century designed to reduce the number of people needlessly or erroneously sent to prison, see Manchester, *A Modern Legal History of England and Wales*, pp. 258–9.

attempted suicide, both of which were heinous offences according to the letter of the law, but usually venal ones in public opinion and judicial practice. Certainly this particular trend away from custodial sentences was not accompanied by what according to progressive penal theory should have been its corollary, namely, prison sentences which, when given, were always sufficiently long for remedial influences to take effect. On the contrary: the proportion of those imprisoned for attempted suicide whose sentences were for merely one month or less was even higher in the mid-1890s than it had been in the 1860s and 1870s, when short sentences were most used in sentencing generally.

Table 8.2. *Attempted suicide: percentage of those tried in England and Wales who were given a prison sentence (a) at assizes (b) at quarter sessions in 1893–7 and 1909–13*

	1893–7	1909–13
Assizes	49	42
Quarter sessions	38	26

Sources: *Judicial Statistics, 1893–97, 1909–13*, Part I, Tables I and III.

Not until 1909–13 did sentences of over a month predominate for this offence in the very small proportion of trials which by then ended in a custodial sentence (see Table 9.1), and by this time almost a third of these sentences were going to offenders with previous convictions.[140]

Table 8.3. *Attempted suicide: percentage of those tried who were given a prison sentence (a) in the metropolitan police district (b) in the rest of England and Wales in 1893–7 and 1909–13*

	1893–7	1909–13
Metropolitan police district	30	18
Provincial England and Wales	42	30

Sources: Row 1, *Metropolitan Police Commissioner's ARs, 1893–97, 1909–13*, appendix: Committals for Trial, with Results; Row 2, as in Table 8.1.

Two large exceptions to these national trends, however, must be pointed out. In the first place, the few prisoners tried at assizes after 1889 were little affected by the trend away from custodial sentences (see Table 8.2), and were also more likely to be given sentences of over a month (see Table 9.2). There is nothing surprising about this, since it was hardened offenders, and above all those charged with additional

---

[140] Of those convicted for the offence of attempted suicide in England and Wales, 31 per cent had previous convictions in 1909–13, as against 21 per cent in 1893–7: *Judicial Statistics*, Part I, Table IX.

Table 9.1. *Attempted suicide: percentage of those sentenced to prison in England and Wales who were given a sentence of one month or less in selected decennia and quinquennia, 1861–1913*

	1861–70	1871–80	1893–7	1909–13
	60	50	70	44

Sources: Judicial Statistics, 1861–80, Part I, Criminal Proceedings [Table 1]; ibid., *1893–97, 1909–13*, Tables II and IV.

Table 9.2. *Attempted suicide: percentage of those sentenced to prison in England and Wales who were given a sentence of one month or less (a) at assizes (b) at quarter sessions, 1893–7 and 1909–13*

	1893–7	1909–13
Assizes	59	46
Quarter sessions	72	44

Sources: See Table 9.1.

indictable offences, who were sent for trial at assizes. (Indeed, the charge of attempted suicide may sometimes have been used to 'get' offenders when a conviction could not be secured for another offence.)[141] Secondly, in the metropolitan police district sentencing was even more out of step with national trends—but in exactly the opposite direction. There, not only did the swing away from custodial sentences for attempted suicide move much further and much faster than in the provinces (see Table 8.3), but the few prison sentences given were overwhelmingly for longer periods (see Table 9.3), exactly as progressive penal thinking prescribed. Between 1893 and 1897, only 30 per cent of those tried for attempted suicide in the metropolitan police district were given a prison sentence, as against 42 per cent in the provinces; and only 17 per cent of these sentences were for one month or less, as against a massive 76 per cent of provincial sentences. In the metropolitan area, for the great majority of those tried (and by 1909–13 this meant for 82 per cent), the outcome was a solemn undertaking not to repeat their attempt, probably reinforced by the giving of

---

[141] In 1909–13 there were 108 additional indictments against the 226 persons tried at assizes for attempted suicide, but only 37 additional convictions against them. By contrast only 1.6 per cent of those tried at quarter sessions for attempted suicide were charged with other offences: *Judicial Statistics*, Part I, Tables I and III, cols. 27 and 28.

Table 9.3. Attempted suicide: percentage of those sentenced to prison whose sentence was for one month or less in (a) the metropolitan police district (b) the rest of England and Wales, 1893–7 and 1909–13

	1893–7	1909–13
Metropolitan police district	17	17
Provincial England and Wales	76	49

Sources: Row 1, as for Table 8.3; Row 2, as for Table 9.1.

sureties and perhaps supervision by an officer of the court for six months.

These developments in metropolitan sentencing practice are only adumbrated in the Judicial Statistics. They can be given substance by the calendars of prisoners for trial at Middlesex quarter sessions and the depositions relating to these prisoners, which show what happened in a busy court with a professional chairman whose cases came entirely from the metropolitan police district.[142] Between 1861 and 1865, under the chairmanship of Judge William Bodkin and his deputy Joseph Payne (when penal thinking favoured severity), a charge of attempted suicide was proved against two men and six women at Middlesex quarter sessions, each of whom was given a prison sentence, although only one was for as long as twelve months. (This woman had four previous convictions, and had tried to strangle herself when taken to the police station for attempted burglary.)[143] In contrast, in the three years between 1905 and 1907, under Sir Ralph Littler, KC (when both the court's catchment area and penal fashion had greatly altered),[144] a

---

[142] The metropolitan police district extended over several counties, and cases were sent to several different quarter sessions, as well as to the Central Criminal Court.

[143] Payne (1797–1870: Boase), the brother of the coroner, Serjeant William Payne, whose papers were used intensively in Part II, tended to give more severe sentences for this offence than Bodkin (1791–1874: *DNB*): GLRO, MJ/CP/B/8–12, and MJ/SPE, Bundles for Dec. 1862, Sept. 1863, May, July, and Sept. 1864, Aug., Sept., and Dec. 1865. (The sentence mentioned was given on 27 Sept. 1864 to Frances Galloway, whose previous sentences included one sentence to 4 years' penal servitude.)

[144] In 1889 the inner metropolitan part of Middlesex, which fell within the new Administrative County of London, ceased to send cases to Middlesex quarter sessions, whose work-load was thus sharply reduced, and whose chairman and deputy chairman ceased to be paid. Sir Ralph Littler, KC (1835–1908: *DNB*) was chairman both of Middlesex Sessions and of Middlesex County Council from 1889 until his death, when he was succeeded in the former post by his deputy, Montagu Sharpe. Arthur Harding remembered Littler as 'the hottest judge in England' and took care never to go thieving within the boundaries of Middlesex: Samuel, *East End Underworld*, ii. 76.

charge of attempted suicide was proved against eight men and seven women, but only four were given a prison sentence. Three of these were for twelve months, and went to solitary women in need of much surveillance and assistance; the fourth was for one day, and was given to a forty year old tailor with a wife and friends, work and a house, but a drinking problem. As for the remaining eleven people concerned, two were found insane, three discharged, and the other six dismissed on their own recognizances to appear for judgement if called upon— recognizances which ranged from £2 for a Brentford servant girl to £20 for a sixty year old case-maker.[145] Such sentences were clearly not out of accord with the Edwardian progressives' belief that sentencing should look 'more to the character of the criminal than to the crime'.[146]

In the metropolitan area there had evidently been a rejection of the idea (so common in most late-Victorian courts) that when a charge of attempted suicide was proved a token prison sentence should always be given, not in order to reform the individual concerned, but simply to support the idea that attempted suicide was a criminal offence.[147] It would accordingly be wrong to assume that it was conversion to faith in severity as the best way to check suicide attempts which led metropolitan magistrates to become increasingly ready in the 1890s and 1900s to commit those charged with attempted suicide for trial, just when provincial magistrates were becoming more reluctant to do so (see Table 7.1). What caused them to send for trial 10 per cent instead of 2 per cent of those who came before them on this charge was surely their growing confidence in the higher courts as sources of appropriate help and assistance for the weak and vulnerable.

In the fifty years after about 1830, one of the many ways in which England became a policed society was thus in the matter of suicide attempts. The ordinary machinery of law and order became a major agency for the prevention of suicide, and one which aimed to function not so much through teaching cautionary lessons to the public at large, as through deterring and rehabilitating those individuals who had shown themselves to be likely to make such attempts. Not surprisingly,

---

[145] GLRO, MJ/CP/B/42–3, and corresponding bundles of MJ/SPE.

[146] Enunciated, for example, by the young Hugh Gamon, *The London Police Court*, p. 233. Cf. the police magistrate Cecil Chapman on the slow change from retaliatory to reformative punishment: *The Poor Man's Court of Justice*, p. 17.

[147] For a criticism of this practice voiced in 1893, see Strahan, *Suicide and Insanity*, p. 201.

this branch of the law operated quite differently from the rest of the criminal law. The recorded incidence of this offence, unlike crimes of theft and violence, rose steeply from the end of the nineteenth century (see Graph 2); and an arrest was made in virtually every case which the police reported as known to them. Yet those arrested were rarely sent for trial, although their offence purported to be a serious one and was never included among the many made triable summarily. Again, the few who were indicted almost always pleaded guilty by the latter part of the nineteenth century, and were very rarely acquitted; yet a sizeable proportion of those against whom this charge was proved, never received a prison sentence. In short, the operation of the newly developed law of attempted suicide, like that of the much older law of suicide itself, was distinctly *sui generis*.[148] As a corollary, the persons who determined the impact of the law on this particular kind of deviant behaviour were not the usual ones. The staff of the penal prisons were altogether unimportant: in 1909–13, for example, only some 2 or 3 per cent of those charged with attempted suicide received a prison sentence, and of these, only a fraction were in prison for more than a few days. Nor was the role of circuit judges and magistrates in quarter sessions much more significant: for in 1909–13 only about 11 per cent of those charged with this offence ever came before them. It was not through the process of trial, conviction, and sentencing that the machinery of the law usually worked to prevent suicide, but through the night at the police station, through the examining magistrate's reproof, caution, and practical assistance, and through the individual attention given by the chaplain and medical officer of the local prison used for remand. Moreover, since three or four great cities accounted for the bulk of those taken into custody for this offence,[149] the work of the law was overwhelmingly the responsibility of a very few individuals: the metropolitan police magistrates, their counterparts in Liverpool, Manchester, and Birmingham, and the chaplains and medical officers of their remand prisons.

Did this mean that the operation of this part of the law responded

---

[148] For the operation of other branches of the law in this period, see Gatrell, 'The Decline of Theft and Violence', pp. 342–70, Tables A1–A5 and B1–B3.

[149] In 1866–7 the metropolitan police magistrates and 10 stipendiary magistrates dealt with about two-thirds of the cases of attempted suicide known to the police in England: see *Judicial Statistics, 1866–67*, Part I, Police, Table 4, and PP 1873 (192) LIV. In 1909–13 about half the cases of attempted suicide reported by the police occurred in districts with stipendiaries: *Judicial Statistics, 1909–13*, Part I, Table, Indictable Offences: Nature of Crimes in each District.

more to changes in attitudes to suicide than to the pressures which affected the administration of the rest of the criminal law? So far as the magistrates were concerned, it clearly did not. When an attempt seemed part of a pattern of established criminal behaviour, or was deliberately fraudulent or compulsively repeated, they treated it like the serious offence it always was in law; but otherwise it was given the same mixture of prompt restraint, reproof, and practical help as the general run of family troubles, drunkenness and destitution, malingering and personal violence among the poor. (The suicide attempts of the well-to-do rarely came before them.) Men of strong personality as they often were, and well known locally, most metropolitan police magistrates seem to have worked rapidly and shrewdly but with underlying kindness and a judicious use of their court's poor box. (They were distributing some £10,000 a year in the late 1860s.)[150] The best of them 'kept their law in the background and dealt with men and women face to face as men themselves'.[151] They by no means always sided with the police.[152] In effect they were key figures at the centre of a growing volume of social work, both public and private, and in many ways the urban successors of the paternal country justices of the old regime. Certainly in their dealings with those brought before them on a charge of attempted suicide it was not the penal side of the law which was uppermost, nor its majesty, solemnity, and impartiality, but the elements of impromptu justice exercised through the understanding of individual circumstances, and of mercy demonstrated through the use of judicial discretion. Lay justices in country districts (who encountered suicide attempts only rarely) may well have had different attitudes; but for busy professional magistrates, 'putting down suicide' seems to have been part and parcel of their many-sided daily round, and no more.

For the prison chaplains and medical officers whose reports these

---

[150] Hawkesley, *The Charities of London*, p. 7. The police magistrates did not relieve the absolutely destitute from their poor boxes, for in a day or two they would be destitute again; 'that is a proper case for the poor law': H. Selfe of the Thames Police Office, PP 1861 (180) IX, p. 172, Q. 4114.

[151] Lieck, *Bow Street World*, p. 130. For other first-hand impressions of police magistrates at work in the late nineteenth and early twentieth centuries see Holmes, *Pictures and Problems from London Police Courts*; Gamon, *The London Police Court*; Chapman, *The Poor Man's Court of Justice*. In the City, where the Aldermen sat as Justices, the chief clerk's role was far more important; but in 1909–13, for example, only 6 per cent of the cases of attempted suicide dealt with in the metropolitan area came before the City Justices.

[152] For specific examples of Edwardian police magistrates' criticism of the police, see Samuel, *East End Underworld*, ii. 194, 199, 202, 331.

hard-pressed men often relied upon heavily, however, the case was different. They were the acknowledged experts upon both suicide and social problems—the clergy by right of inheritance, as it were, the medical men by right of recent conquest. By the late nineteenth century, full-time medical appointments in the country's few large prisons tended to be held by men who used their position to conduct clinical research, published their results in professional journals, were active in professional societies, and participated in the round of professional conferences; while the chaplains of the major prisons often continued their predecessors' habit of publishing their reflections upon their special experiences of work among the poor and sinful, took part in the activities their particular variety of Churchmanship supported, and participated in the network of organizations and meetings which increasingly brought together social workers of every shade of religious opinion and of none. In short, everything conspired to make medical officers and chaplains medical men and clergymen first, and members of the prison service second;[153] and hence to ensure their awareness of current discussion of the significance and proper treatment of suicidal behaviour.

Altogether, it would be a great mistake to suppose that where attempted suicide was concerned, the primary role of the law in Victorian or Edwardian England was to punish. The machinery of the courts was indeed an indispensable part of efforts to prevent suicide. It was so, however, not because of Victorian or Edwardian faith in penal custody or the deterrent effect of severity, but because it served to identify those at risk in the big cities where known suicide attempts were most frequent, and channel towards them expert medical and psychiatric attention and the help of the social workers of the day. What mattered as much as the new police practice of bringing before a magistrate those who tried to commit suicide, was the magistrates' practice of seeking advice and assistance through the remand system and from the charitable organizations which increasingly clustered around the prisons and the courts. In reality suicide prevention was carried out through a network of links—formal and institutional, but also personal and individual—of the kind so characteristic of state and society in Victorian and Edwardian England, where the distinctions were often blurred between official and voluntary organizations and

---

[153] For the professionalization of clergymen and medical men in the mid-Victorian period which is the background to this state of affairs, see Heeney, *A Different Kind of Gentleman*, and Peterson, *The Medical Profession in Mid-Victorian London*.

between public and private action. Accordingly, although the sermons and sanctions of the law are indeed the appropriate starting-place for a study of Victorian and Edwardian suicide prevention, they are no more than that; and it is the other strands in the network which must now be examined.

9

Good Samaritans

The mighty river flowing dark and deep,
    With ebb and flood from the remote sea-tides
Vague-sounding through the City's sleepless sleep,
    Is named the River of the Suicides;
For night by night some lorn wretch overweary,
And shuddering from the future yet more dreary,
    Within its cold secure oblivion hides.

One plunges from a bridge's parapet,
    As by some blind and sudden frenzy hurled;
Another wades in slow with purpose set
    Until the waters are above him furled;

So far, what James Thomson wrote in 'The City of Dreadful Night'
in 1874 had literal as well as poetic truth. Not so, however, his next
lines, for he went on:

They perish from their suffering surely thus,
For none beholding them attempts to save.

The reality was far different. Only a tiny handful of rationalists and
bohemians were ever prepared to allow a fellow human being to drift
unchecked into

That one best sleep which never wakes again.[1]

Quite the contrary: every successive phase of Victorian and Edwardian
philanthropic endeavour produced its own characteristic attempts
to save would-be suicides from a self-inflicted death. In Thomson's
day, the great mass of charitably inclined and more or less comfortably-
off people whose ideas on suicides came from newspapers and maga-
zines, supplemented by popular poems and plays, pictures, ballads,

---

[1] 'The City of Dreadful Night', Stanza xix, *Poems and Some Letters of James
Thomson*, ed. Ridley, p. 201.

and stories, easily thought of suicide attempts as a by-product of poverty and sin. After all, the suicide attempts of the virtuous well-to-do seldom became public knowledge, since they usually escaped the attention of the police;[2] and when they did, they were easily seen as symptoms of brain fever, over-pressure, neurasthenia, and the like. Where those who were very far from having 'everything to live for' were concerned, however, common sense ruled out such explanations. To the plain man, the suicide attempts of the poor and outcast nearly always seemed a cry for help, and help not from medical men or psychiatrists, but from fellow human beings like himself.

Help to their fellow men was precisely what an impressive proportion of Victorians and Edwardians dedicated a great deal of their time and money to providing; and their strenuous efforts to seek and to save the sad, the suffering, and the sinful inevitably led them into encounters with some who were ready to take their own lives. Not until the turn of the century, however, did they make any attempt to mount a special effort aimed directly and exclusively at preventing suicide. To philanthropic Victorians, the suicide attempts of the poor were the by-product of their way of life, and not of mental disease or neuroses, still less ennui or romantic introspection. Their efforts to prevent suicide were therefore subsumed within their efforts to eradicate whatever they saw as the root of individual sin and suffering. It follows that the suicide prevention work of the Victorians can only be understood, and indeed espied, by looking at the changing scene of Victorian charitable effort in general. Since saints and samaritans far outnumbered sanitarians and sociologists in that scene, evangelistic endeavours to rescue the perishing will here be given pride of place over the social and environmental measures urged by public health enthusiasts and social scientists; and once more London will be the focus of attention, not only because it accounted for so many of the country's recorded suicide attempts, but also because it was increasingly the centre of organized charity.

Initially, pure evangelism dominated the activities of those alarmed by the state of the urban poor. True, throughout the nineteenth century there was no lack of people who believed that saving faith alone would bring betterment of life and that sound religious teaching was the only sure road to social order; but only in the early Victorian years did urban philanthropy as a whole concentrate upon the effort to bring to

[2] East, 'On Attempted Suicide', p. 449.

the poor definite religious instruction.[3] As part of this effort, unde-nominational City Missions were started in London, Manchester, and Liverpool in the 1830s, and these Missions were responsible for the adoption of a major innovation in evangelistic technique: the system of regular street-by-street home visiting of a whole district by paid lay workers who were themselves working-class people. It was the London City Mission, founded in 1835, which pioneered this system, although its methods were quickly copied and developed by other bodies;[4] and it continued to lead in this field, as Charles Booth found in the early 1900s. By that time it employed over 400 Agents, each of whom was expected to pay a monthly visit to about 650 families, and 'to pioneer a pathway among the most wretched and debased of our fellow creatures'.[5] These Agents stayed in the same district for many years, covering every street, bringing those with alms in touch with the needy (although not giving alms themselves), and 'putting in a word for Christ'. They were neither condescending nor disciplinarians (often they were themselves former artisans); and more than all their imitators, they seem to have been in tune with the outlook of the people they visited and comparatively acceptable to them.[6] Universal home visiting was also at the heart of the mid-nineteenth century pastoral revival in the Church of England; and in this, the clergy in crowded urban parishes were assisted by a multitude of different sorts of workers.[7]

As a matter of simple chance, any district visitor whose work was truly unselective would be likely sooner or later to rescue some would-be suicide by timely assistance or interruption; while a regular, friendly visitor might build up enough knowledge of an individual at risk to feel 'called' to pay a visit at an unusual time, and thus save a life. Inevitably, too, such visitors would sometimes find themselves listening to outpourings at moments of crisis, and providing sympathy, advice, and help. The experiences of a London City Missionary who worked for twenty-one years in the King's Cross district may stand as representative. His recollections in 1861 have the same straightforward,

---

[3] See the oustanding study by Simey, *Charitable Effort in Liverpool in the Nineteenth Century*, pp. 33–45.

[4] Bosanquet, *London*, pp. 70–4.

[5] Its Agents then included 117 Special Missionaries, some of whom covered places where would-be suicides were especially likely to be encountered, such as hospitals: *London City Mission Magazine.* lxxii (Oct. 1907), p. 248.

[6] Booth, *Life and Labour*, 3rd series, vii, 289–90.

[7] Heeney, *A Different Kind of Gentleman*, pp. 59–63.

practical tone which impressed Charles Booth forty years later.

Once [a] man had the rope round his neck when I knocked at his door; my visit was made the means of defeating his purpose, and he lived to become a reformed character. On another occasion I had to assist in restoring life to a woman who had attempted to drown herself. Once a woman walked about the room for some minutes with a razor in her hand, protesting she would cut her throat, while no one being in the house but myself, I had to remain with her a long time till aid arrived, to prevent the rash act.[8]

So far as the London City Mission was concerned, its secretary was probably speaking for many generations of Missionaries when he assured a reporter in 1907 that they had found their work was used by God to prevent suicide, and knew from their own experience that through their words 'better feelings can often be implanted in those out of whom life seems crushed by despair, drunkenness, losses or financial troubles'.[9] Admittedly, district visitors with a less comprehensive coverage or a more stridently pious tone, or those who were well-to-do amateurs, can hardly have had the same opportunities or chances of success. Still, by trawling as intensively and systematically as they did from the 1830s onwards, all these fishers of men were likely to find themselves occasionally saving lives in the course of trying to save souls.

Organized large-scale help for would-be suicides, however, was the product of certain quite different developments which came about in the middle of the century. In the 1850s and 1860s very many zealous Christians became convinced that the gospel which they preached to the poor and outcast would fall on stony ground unless they first provided for their pressing bodily needs; and to finance this 'souperism', they increased their subscriptions to charity.[10] The sheer number of charitable organizations rose even more, however, since this new belief in practical philanthropy coincided with a vogue for specialization, both in evangelism and in good works. These were the years of Moonlight Missions and Thieves' Suppers and innumerable other melodramatic enterprises, all of them deliberately concerned with 'the Sunken Sixth', and reflecting the romantic sensationalism then coming into fashion generally, and the sensationalist methods of the revival of 1859 in particular; and such enterprises had their counterpart in bricks and mortar in the shape of a mushroom growth of refuges and reforma-

[8] 'A Farewell Report of a Missionary after Twenty-One Years' Labour in the King's Cross District', *London City Mission Magazine*, xxvi (Oct. 1861), p. 222.
[9] *Daily Express*, 11 Jan. 1907, p. 5.
[10] Bowen, *The Idea of the Victorian Church*, p. 266.

tories, institutes and industrial schools, and 'Homes' of every description.[11] It was thus altogether predictable that Christian philanthropists who encountered would-be suicides in the 1850s and 1860s would feel moved not only to preach and pray, but to find out why these people had behaved so desperately, and then to use the multiplying resources of organized charity to provide suitable cases with shelter, work, medical care, or whatever seemed needed. What was not predictable, however, was the crucial development: the emergence of a few experts who were responsible each year for trying to start on a new life hundreds of people who had come close to suicide, and in so doing made growing use of these voluntary organizations. In the metropolis this came about simply because this last flowering of Evangelical philanthropic vigour coincided with the first appearance of a flow of people charged with attempted suicide, and sent to Clerkenwell, the Middlesex remand prison, for its chaplain's attention. At this time several key posts in Middlesex Sessions happened to be held by redoubtable Evangelicals and keen supporters of these new philanthropic organizations,[12] who saw to it that clergymen of Evangelical mould, 'conversant with the habits of the poor', were appointed as chaplains of Middlesex prisons.[13] It is therefore altogether understandable that from the 1850s onwards men and women charged with attempted suicide came to constitute an important 'sphere of duty' for successive chaplains of Clerkenwell, who saw them as 'poor, wretched, and often outcast, destitute creatures';[14] and understandable too that they were given exactly the same kind of help as their counterparts outside prison were receiving from other Evangelical workers.

[11] These efforts are described in Heasman, *Evangelicals in Action, passim.* Their concrete results can best be appreciated, however, by a glance at Sampson Low, *The Charities of London in 1861.*

[12] Henry S. Pownall, Chairman of Middlesex Sessions 1843–76 and *ex officio* a Visiting Justice of all 3 Middlesex prisons, was, like the great majority of Middlesex magistrates, a stout 'Protestant': see PP 1870 (259) VIII, esp. p. 68, Qs. 1735, 1750, p. 69, Q. 1769, p. 73, Q. 1814. Pownall was on the General Committee of the Reformatory and Refuge Union, while Joseph Payne, Deputy Assistant Judge of Middlesex quarter sessions (see Ch. 8, n. 143) was a prominent figure in this Union: cf. *The Reformatory and Refuge Journal*, i (Jan. 1861), p. 55, and xi (May 1863), p. 67.

[13] A vacant chaplaincy was advertised, and might draw a dozen applications: PP 1870 (259) VIII, p. 63, Qs. 1674, 1678. Visits of chaplains to prisons had to be provided under 4 Geo. IV, c. 64, s. 70, and Justices were obliged to appoint to every prison a Church of England chaplain (who had to be full-time in a prison with more than 100 inhabitants) under 28 & 29 Vict., c. 126, ss. 10, 11. Only after the centralization of local prison administration in 1878 were prison chaplains appointed by the Home Secretary (and in effect by the chairman of the Prison Commissioners).

[14] Chaplain's report for 1871, GLRO, MA/RS/1/521.

The decade of the 1850s thus saw the beginning of a distinct phase of philanthropic suicide prevention, with the creation of a network of agencies offering help to the sort of people then being arrested for attempted suicide, and, much more important, the identification of the prison chaplain as the person whose task it was not only to give moral advice, but to find out what practical help was most needed in a given case, and then persuade the examining magistrate that the arrangements he recommended were appropriate. In so far as mid-Victorian London ever had a suicide prevention agency, it was surely located in the chaplain's office in Clerkenwell prison.[15] The effectiveness of this phase of suicide prevention work thus depended on two things: how shrewd and skilful the chaplain was in his dealings with those in custody in the cells, and how well he knew his way about the philanthropic world; and what he did both as a personal counsellor and as a *de facto* welfare officer was inevitably shaped by his conception of his role as a clergyman, as well as his personality and experience of life. What happened in this phase of suicide prevention work was determined, therefore, by the interaction of trends in churchmanship and social work with the changing personal style of the four men who were chaplains at Clerkenwell between its reopening in 1847 and its final closure in 1886.

The first of these four, George Jepson, established that providing practical help to those remanded on a charge of attempted suicide was part of the chaplain's regular work, and saw the number of such cases sent to him climb from about 100 a year in the 1850s to over 150 a year in the early 1860s—'a remarkable instance of progressive usefulness', as he put it.[16] As early as 1851, his conversations in the cells convinced him that many attempts at suicide could be prevented by the setting up of a 'Public Reformatory Institution' where 'wretched outcasts of society' could find a refuge from temptation and crime.[17] In these optimistic expectations Jepson was altogether typical.

> Success to Refuges, success
> To plans Reformatory,
> For they're the things the world to bless.
> And add to England's glory,

---

[15] Two cells knocked into one made this office: Horsley, '*I Remember*' p. 77.

[16] What follows is based chiefly upon the annual reports of the chaplains of Clerkenwell House of Detention to the Middlesex Justices: see Ch. 8 n. 108. This particular passage occurs in the report for 1860; GLRO, MA/RS/1/473.

[17] Chaplain's report for 1851, GLRO, MA/RS/1/430.

declaimed that inveterate rhymester, Judge Payne, fresh from sentencing at Middlesex quarter sessions, to a meeting of the Reformatory and Refuge Union in 1863;[18] and between 1846 and 1859 alone, the number of such shelters in London grew from three to fifty.[19] (The shortage of housing for the London poor was then acute.) To these establishments Jepson sent some 9 per cent of the women remanded to Clerkenwell for attempted suicide, beginning in 1848 with one placement in the Guardian Society's asylum and another in the Refuge for the Destitute. Both these institutions accepted women aged between fifteen and twenty-five, on condition that they agreed to stay for at least a year, be taught by a schoolmistress, and do laundry work, domestic work, and needlework inside the Home 'until their character is improved and a situation procured for them'.[20] What of the many not eligible for such places? Admission to a workhouse or a hospital was arranged for about 7 per cent of those sent to him, men as well as women; and a handful were started off with a small sum of money, or sent back to their usual employers. For almost two-thirds of his cases, however, Jepson's solution was to put them in the care of their parents, relatives, or friends, and to this end he arranged reconciliations, reunions, and the payment of travelling expenses.

Jepson's work had fallen into something of a groove by the time he died in 1867, after twenty-four years at Clerkenwell. The three much younger men who succeeded him relied markedly less on promises of care from relatives or friends, and very rarely gave sums of money (giving alms was by then regarded as not sound philanthropic practice), although they provided some help in kind, gave introductions to potential employers, and generally acted as mediators. Their policy was to make use of an increasing variety of voluntary and semi-official charitable organizations; so much so, indeed, that in the year before it closed Clerkenwell enlisted the help of twenty-three different charities—far more than any other prison.[21] Increasingly, men and women were handled differently. Not surprisingly, men and boys were more rarely dealt with by getting a relative or friend to undertake to look

---

[18] *The Reformatory and Refuge Journal*, xi (May 1863), p. 69.

[19] See the list published by the Committee of the Reformatory and Refuge Union, *The Metropolitan Reformatories, Refuges and Industrial Schools*, 4th edn. (1859).

[20] Ibid, p. 5. 'A Vacancies list will be gladly forwarded to Magistrates and others', it was stated here.

[21] *Prison Commissioners' AR, 1885–86*, Part 1, Appendix no. 20, pp. 78–81. (Not all these charities necessarily gave aid to attempted suicide cases.)

after them than women and girls, and were more often started in a trade, sent to an industrial school, helped to emigrate, or placed in a workhouse;[22] and they were also far more often simply discharged or put on bail.[23] An increasing proportion of the girls were sent to reformatory Homes,[24] despite the fact that these young chaplains shared the greater scepticism common in philanthropic circles in the 1860s and 1870s, knew very well that only a few would stay more than two or three months in any Home, and lamented that 'drink often makes the reclamation of these poor creatures an apparently hopeless task'. The new orthodoxy was that drink, even more than lack of sound instruction, was the root of all evil, and that many of the poor were far from deserving; and to this they subscribed. Serious attempts at suicide they held were rare. A suicidal gesture was the favourite ploy of drunken women and silly girls, and in any case the police had often made an arrest merely because of drunken suicide threats or suspicious behaviour.[25]

This kind of brisk approach reached its apogee under John Horsley, the born administrator, fund-raiser, and public relations man who was chaplain between 1876 and 1886.[26] By then between three and four hundred cases of attempted suicide were coming to Clerkenwell each year; and Horsley believed his experience showed that both

---

[22] As an illustration of the close links between prison chaplains and philanthropists and slum missioners, it may be noted that emigration was first arranged for cases of attempted suicide (one going to Canada and one to the United States) in 1872–3, the very time when a 'flurry of activity' among the philanthropic emigration societies (which included the Clerkenwell Emigration Club) was producing a record number of assisted emigrants: Malchow, *Population Pressures*, pp. 18, 43, and the time when the chaplain of Clerkenwell prison, Joseph Wheeler, was a clergyman who had spent 3 years working on emigrant ships for the Thames Church Mission.

[23] The chaplains' annual reports show that in 1867–75 48 per cent of men were discharged, 6 per cent put on bail and 31 per cent returned to their relatives; whereas the corrresponding figures for women were 24 per cent, 4 per cent, and 44 per cent respectively.

[24] In 1867–75 14 per cent of females remanded for attempted suicide were sent to Homes.

[25] Report for 1875, GLRO, MA/RS/1/536 and for 1872, MJ/OC/65, fol. 688. Wheeler seems to have grown more disillusioned as time went on: cf. his report for 1875 (MA/RS/1/536) with his reports for 1870 (MA/RS/1/516) and 1871 (MA/RS/1/521).

[26] After Clerkenwell closed, Horsley ran the Waifs and Strays Society for 2 years; later, as a slum vicar and social gospeller, he ran Southwark's Public Health Committee and Board of Guardians (becoming mayor of Southwark in 1910), as well as serving on the council of the Church of England Temperance Society and the Anti-Gambling League and founding the Guild of SS Paul and Silas: see *DNB* and his own copious and clearly self-satisfied writings, especially '*I Remember*'.

romantic and sociological ideas about the cases of suicide were mistaken. Suicide, like every other kind of sin, crime, and misery, was caused by intemperance, impurity, laziness, and bad temper, and nothing else. Horsley, though, had not been up at T. H. Green's Oxford for nothing, and he insisted that society shared in the responsibility for these failings.[27] Suicide attempts could be drastically reduced if magistrates gave a few exemplary sentences, if the press stopped reporting cases sympathetically and in detail, if inebriates were sent to reformatories, if workhouses ceased to bring up girls to be backboneless, sulky, and silly, and if all children without exception were taught some sound eschatology and the duty of self-control.[28] Meanwhile he was prepared to work hard for the drunken, feeble, violent, blackmailing wretches sent to him, and to give them the firm treatment he often considered they needed. He particularly believed in firm treatment for alcoholics, and shared the avant-garde faith of the 1870s that they could be cured by a period of compulsory detention (and drying out).[29] He instanced with satisfaction the case of an alcoholic woman who had come under his care several times for attempting to drown herself:

At last I persuaded a magistrate to give her three months in default of bail (cruel only to be kind), that there might be some chance of getting the drink out of her ... and obtaining her some shelter at the end of the time. I was soon enabled to get her a chance of regaining a character and self-respect, and her livelihood in service. A strict hand on her has been necessary, but in good situations she has been ever since.[30]

But Horsley was not only firm and self-assured; he could be generous, and he was always resourceful. He preached, lectured, wrote, and begged to get money for a private 'Chaplain's Fund' which he could spend entirely at his own discretion, and he claimed that he 'took no notice of creed in affording help'.[31] He used some of this money, for example, to send to a Home for Inebriates a hotel-keeper's widow

---

[27] The duty of 'hindering hindrances' to a good life was one he never failed to preach. (Horsley went up to Pembroke College in 1863.)

[28] Horsley first propounded his views on the causes of suicide as a counter blast to Morselli in his article, 'Suicide', and developed them subsequently in *Jottings from Jail*; see especially pp. 46, 68, 244–52, 256–9. His *Prisons and Prisoners*, ch. 8, adds little.

[29] Cf. MacLeod, "The Edge of Hope", pp. 225–31.

[30] Horsley, *Jottings from Jail*, p. 121. Horsley often insisted that 'much more than half the cases of attempted suicide ... would be attributable to intemperance': ibid., pp. 245–8; 'Suicide', p. 507; PP 1884–5 [C. 4402] XXX, p. 88, Q. 2245.

[31] Horsley, *Jottings from Jail*, pp. 109, 119.

'who had been under me for attempted suicide after d.t. Now she is in a good situation and one of the very few women I have known to be cured of intemperance.'[32] He exploited the possibilities open to a knowledgeable and efficient person who was able to bring several different charities to bear on a single case for different purposes at different junctures. For example, for a young mother driven to attempt suicide by her husband's brutality to her children he synchronized help from the London Society for the Prevention of Cruelty to Children, the Waifs and Strays Society, and the Sheriffs' Fund. With satisfaction he reported:

Not one of these societies could have efficiently dealt with the case in all its aspects and needs; but by co-operation all that was possible and desirable was done; and by experience bringing all their forces to bear on the case at the right time the good was done without delay.[33]

Continuity, combined with responsiveness to changes of emphasis in the wider philanthropic world, thus marks the work of these chaplains in channelling a variety of practical help towards those sent to Clerkenwell on a charge of attempted suicide; but what of their pastoral work in the cells—work which after 1863 was confined to those who registered as 'C. of E.', yet nevertheless included over 90 per cent of those remanded on this charge?[34] It goes without saying that the way in which this was performed depended above all on each chaplain's personal style, not only as a man, but as a Churchman, and on his conception of his calling. What then led successive generations of young clergymen to apply for the chaplaincy of Clerkenwell when it fell vacant? It would be wrong to emphasize too much that the salary of £200 and then £250 a year[35] was more than the average curate's stipend of £150, and that the supply of livings was far smaller than

[32] Ibid., p. 131. The same fund procured 'a few luxuries' for a woman dying in a workhouse infirmary: 'so often had she attempted suicide when drunk that one was thankful she was dying sober, and moreover penitent, as far as I could judge': ibid., p. 132.

[33] Ibid., p. 114.

[34] Among Roman Catholics the incidence of suicide attempts, as of suicide itself, was comparatively low. In 1868–77, 92.5 per cent of those remanded to Clerkenwell on a charge of attempted suicide registered as 'C. of E.' (that is, in effect, as neither Roman Catholics nor Jews): Horsley, 'Suicide', p. 504. Under the Prison Ministers Act of 1863 a prisoner not registered as 'C. of E.' was not to be visited by the chaplain unless his own denominational visitor had not visited him for 14 days, and was not to be compelled to attend any religious service of a persuasion to which he did not belong: 26 & 27 Vict., c. 79, ss. 4–5.

[35] PP 1852–3 (908) LXXXI, p. 9; PP 1878–9 (245) LXI, p. 5; PP 1880 (59) LIX, p. 9.

the supply of curates;[36] what should be stressed is rather the pull of successive ideals of the role of religion inside a prison.

When George Jepson became chaplain of Clerkenwell in 1848 it was widely believed that a chaplain could 'preach prisoners out of their evil courses'—a belief which was surely the penal counterpart of that faith in the power of religious instruction to solve the problem of poverty which marks the history of philanthropy in the same years. This was the era of 'the chaplain's reign',[37] when prison life revolved around his ministrations in chapel and in the prisoners' separate cells. Jepson came from the chief stronghold of old-fashioned Protestantism in Tractarian Oxford, St John's College,[38] and his annual reports suggest that he responded to his experiences much as might be expected from a man whose ideas were formed in the 1830s within an Evangelical milieu. He seems to have possessed the self-confidence characteristic of early Victorian Evangelical prison chaplains. Certainly he had an exceedingly optimistic estimate of the extent to which his efforts with those committed 'on the grave charge of attempted self-destruction' afforded them 'the hope of regaining, with God's blessing, the inestimable advantage of moral position and character'. On the other hand, he quickly stopped ascribing suicide attempts chiefly to the results of 'profligacy', and learnt to blame 'destitution and difficulty of employment, and occasional domestic quarrels' as well as 'prostitution and intemperance'; and his pioneering welfare work suggests that he was kind and prepared to take pains for his charges. The language of his reports also suggests, however, a rather conventional, narrowly pious and moralistic man, and it seems all too likely that in the cells he was regarded as a 'Lady Green' and gulled in the usual way—a suspicion strengthened by his report in 1864 that some of his female cases had tried to commit suicide through 'a desire to escape, at any risk, from a life of vice and contamination'.[39]

---

[36] It has been calculated that in the 1860s there was reasonable maintenance available for only about one-third of the clergy: Heeney, *A Different Kind of Gentleman*, p. 111.

[37] Griffiths, *Memorials of Millbank*, i. 194–226. Although little attention has been paid to later phases of the prison chaplains' work, much has recently been written on this earlier era: see e.g. Henriques, 'The Rise and Decline of the Separate System of Prison Discipline'.

[38] Ward, *Victorian Oxford*, p. 84. Jepson took his BA and Deacon's and Priest's Orders in 1837. (The basic facts about all these clergymen's careers have been taken from *Crockford's Clerical Directory* and the *Clergy List*.)

[39] Chaplain's annual reports for 1851, 1856, and 1864, GLRO, MA/RS/1/430, 461, 489. In 1860 the Surgeon, Henry Wakefield (then an old man in his seventies) remarked in his report that 'the good advice [prisoners remanded for attempted suicide] have

Jepson's immediate successor, George Hough, appointed in 1867, spent only three years at Clerkenwell before being promoted to the far better paid chaplaincy at Westminster House of Correction. He was twenty years' Jepson's junior, and straight from curacies in two small villages in the west of England; and he remains a shadowy figure, apparently cast much in Jepson's mould.[40] But the next appointment brought a significant change, for it brought to Clerkenwell an early example of a new breed of prison chaplain: the home missionary. In the 1860s, discharged prisoners took their place among the many special groups of the poorest and most depraved which began to be separately catered for in a formal way at that time (St Giles's Mission was founded in 1860, the Metropolitan Discharged Prisoners' Aid Society in 1864, and Mrs Meredith's Prison Gate Mission was formalized in 1865); and such philanthropic enterprises had their evangelistic counterpart in the Home Missions mounted in the same years. Under Bishop Tait, the diocese of London was in the forefront of this effort to meet the spiritual wants of the poor and outcast, and a host of London Diocesan Missionary clergy, Scripture Readers, and Missionary Women began to work in the slums, in the docks, among the navvies building new railway lines,[41] and, in short, wherever the regular parochial organization of the Church seemed inadequate. The men and women incarcerated inside the prisons, however, could be reached only by those within the prison service. It was therefore entirely predictable that some of these missionary clergy would feel 'called' to work as prison chaplains: and so it turned out.

Joseph Wheeler, who came to Clerkenwell in 1870, was a product not of Oxford, but of the Church Missionary College in Islington. In 1863 he became a London Diocesan Home Missionary, and in 1867 he was appointed chaplain to the Thames Church Mission, where he worked on board the vessels and in the docks of the Port of London. His application for the vacant chaplaincy in this neighbouring prison was thus a natural step, for in Clerkenwell jail he would be working in the same poor quarter of London, helping, rebuking, and trying to

received from the chaplain, and the kindness shown to them during their imprisonment, have in many instances been attended with the happiest results': MA/RS/1/473.

[40] Hough's college was Pembroke, then a well-organized cheap college where liberal politics and Evangelical theology flourished: Ward, *Victorian Oxford*, pp. 134, 141. The salary of the chaplains of the Westminster House of Correction was £400: PP. 1852–3 (908) LXXXI, p. 10.

[41] See Diocese of London, *Bishop of London's Fund*, 1st annual report, June 1863–Dec. 1864, and successive reports and papers.

save much the same sort of people as before; and in fact he was to spend the rest of his life in prison work. Over twenty years later, he told a Home Office committee that his six years at Clerkenwell had given him a great deal of valuable experience, since about 5,000 men and women passed through that prison each year;[42] but from the outset he was certainly far better equipped for his work in the cells than either Jepson or Hough. He had plenty of first-hand knowledge of the behaviour and outlook both of the poor and outcast, and of the various religious and philanthropic organizations available to help them; and his inspiration was missionary hope, no more. His expectations from his own efforts were more modest than those of his predecessors, his view of attempted suicide less grave, his readiness to put the blame upon drink more emphatic, and his conviction that too much sympathy only encouraged such attempts very firm.[43] All things considered, it is a reasonable surmise that his pastoral style was less heavy-handed and more realistic and accessible than that of his predecessors.

Total transformation came only in 1876, however, when Wheeler moved on to the Female Convict Prison at Fulham, just when the long chairmanship of Middlesex Sessions by that stout Protestant H. S. Pownall came to an end. Out of thirty-six applicants for the post, the Justices chose a young high church curate working in the East End, John Horsley; and Horsley's appointment meant that prisoners in Clerkenwell felt very early the impact of certain trends in both church-manship and philanthropy which were soon to carry all before them. In the 1870s Evangelicalism was declining, and high churchmanship and the social gospel were in the ascendant. Many people were begin-ning to feel, as Horsley did, that 'personal service is the lesson of the Incarnation', and that 'personal regard and human sympathy can hardly be found in the operations of a Society.' The specialized organ-izations beloved by the Evangelicals, with their committees, agents, and subscription lists, were becoming old-fashioned. Young men bent on social service began to aim at empathy, nor charity, and to live in the slums themselves. Their aim was to turn the Catholic parochial ideal into a reality, and to identify their church with the local com-

---

[42] PP 1896 [C. 8154] XLIV, p. 89, Qs. 3733–4. On the Thames Church Mission, see *The Official Yearbook of the Church of England, 1889*, p. 127.

[43] See especially his reports for the years 1872, GLRO, MJ/OC/65, fol. 688 and 1875, MA/RS/1/536. By the 1870s it was generally accepted that it was misguided to expect to reform hardened criminals by preaching: cf. Griffiths, *Memorials of Millbank*, i. 205. Clerkenwell, however, received many first offenders.

munity; and to this end they cultivated the common touch, keeping open house, organizing clubs and activities of every sort, from boxing to seaside holidays, and often working in local government for the welfare of 'their' people.[44] Exactly such a one was John Horsley. While he was still at Oxford, he spent his vacations slumming in Shoreditch under H. D. Nihill, founder of the Sisters of the Poor, and in 1875 he went back there as Nihill's curate. Before this, however, in his first curacy under F. M. Cunningham, he had become known as a conductor of the short intensive parochial missions which were the high church counterpart in the 1870s of the revivalist campaigns of Moody and Sankey; and in 1878, soon after he went to Clerkenwell, he published a well-received handbook explaining how to run such campaigns.[45] His success as a revivalist is not surprising. Horsley was a handsome, extrovert man who led the singing himself, preached extempore sermons laced with humour and anecdotes, held relaxed, informal After-Meetings, and avoided 'an inquisitorial or detective spirit' in his private interviews with penitents, while helping them towards informal confession. For Horsley, the chaplaincy at Clerkenwell was a natural extension not only of his work as a slum curate in nearby Shoreditch, but also of his peripatetic revivalist campaigns. In 1875, the Governor and Visiting Justices of Leeds Gaol had taken the then unprecedented step of allowing a mission to be held inside the gaol, during a mission in Leeds;[46] but Horsley was well aware that as a rule only the prison chaplain could reach prisoners. His appointment made the men and women remanded to Clerkenwell among the first to experience the

[44] On the 'Parochial Idea' of the 1870s, 1880s, and 1890s, slum priests, and settlements see Pringle, *Social Work of the London Churches*, pp. 168–70; Bowen, *The Idea of the Victorian Church*, pp. 285–334; McLeod, *Class and Religion in the late Victorian City*, pp. 110–14, 127 n. 84; Inglis, *Churches and the Working Classes in Victorian England*, pp. 26–30; Jones, *The Christian-Socialist Revival*, pp. 79–82.

[45] Horsley and Dawes, *Practical Hints for Parochial Missions*. Dawes, later Bishop of Rockhampton, Queensland, was Horsley's brother-in-law. They secured a preface from the Revd George Body (1840–1911: *DNB*), on whose preaching, and on Anglo-Catholic revivalism generally, see Kent, *Holding the Fort*, pp. 236–94. H. D. Nihill was a leading member of the Society of the Holy Cross and a pall-bearer at the funeral of the most renowned of all Ritualist slum priests, Charles Lowder: Ellsworth, *Charles Lowder and the Ritualist Movement*, pp. 136–7, 140, 142, 168.

[46] Horsley and Dawes, *Practical Hints for Parochial Missions*, p. 81. The Gladstone Committee stimulated change here as in every department of prison administration, and after 1895 missions (attendance at which was strictly voluntary) were held in most prisons from time to time, on the grounds that they could do no harm and might do good: *Prison Commissioners' AR, 1897–98*, pp. 122–4 and *1898–99*, pp. 23–4, 31–2; Hobhouse and Brockway, eds., *English Prisons To-day*, p. 196 n. 29.

kind of chaplain familiar in the early twentieth century, when jovial, hearty 'Sky Pilots' had quite supplanted in the prison service the lugubrious 'Lady Greens' of earlier years.[47]

In prison, Horsley continued to behave like a high church missioner. He believed that prison work ought to be like a continuous After-Meeting, that is, a matter of informal prayer and teaching in the chapel, followed by private interviews in the cells when prisoners perhaps be led to make practical, limited resolutions of amendment. Inside and outside prison, he was a great believer in denouncing the sin, not the sinner; thought it important not to be sentimental with women; and complained of the 'chronic levity' of the girls.[48] (It vexed him that he could never get them to take a serious view of a suicide attempt.) He took hyprocisy and imposition for granted, and was pleasantly surprised by thanks for his after-care arrangements or the repayment of his loans.[49] His style was 'short straight talks', cheeriness and no nonsense, and this was very much the style of the future, however much his message itself was the familiar one of the need to repent and live a life of self-respect.

In method also, as well as in style, Horsley was very much the high church missioner, who always saw his task as being to hand on his converts to the permanent care of their regular parish priest. As each prisoner left Clerkenwell, he wrote (so he claimed) to their parish priest, 'commending them to their notice, sympathy and aid', and in the busy summer months, when suicide attempts always peaked, this meant about a dozen letters a week on behalf of those charged with attempted suicide. The recipients, he grumbled, 'usually shuffle off their responsiblity for them';[50] and at that time it was probably true that most parish clergy and lay workers cared little and knew less about what went on inside a prison—a state of affairs which Horsley energetically tried to remedy, making his own reputation in the process. He founded the Guild of SS Paul and Silas in 1881; and to the end of his days he liked to speak in the style of a prison chaplain, talked of

---

[47] This contrast was noted by the Recorder of London, Sir Ernest Wild, in his foreword to Jervis, *Twenty-Five Years in Six Prisons*, p. 7. Jervis was very much a chaplain in the same mould as Horsley, although a generation younger; and just after Jervis had left Wormwood Scrubs in 1902, Arthur Harding was amazed to find in the services there the same fervent evangelistic atmosphere as in the services he had been taken to when he was a Barnardo boy: Samuel, *East End Underworld*, ii. 72.

[48] Horsley and Dawes, *Practical Hints for Parochial Missions*, pp. 55–69, 80.

[49] Horsley, *Jottings from Jail*, pp. 96, 116, 119, 121.

[50] Ibid., pp. 94, 114–15.

'my friends in prison', and had ex-prisoners as his servants.[51] His success is clearly impossible to appraise. He evidently thrived on the comings and goings at Clerkenwell—'one has not the time to be depressed, nor the desire to moan over failures'—and his resilience can only have been an asset in his work in the cells.[52] He himself always insisted that, *pace* such writers on suicide as 'Dr Morselli', his own experience proved that 'the forces of free will and grace' were 'stronger than those of heredity and environment', and 'I suppose that no one in the world' (he impressed upon the readers of his article on suicide in *The Fortnightly* in 1881) 'has similar or as great opportunities of observing the phenomena of this particular crime.'[53]

From 1886 Holloway prison took over Clerkenwell's role, and the chaplain there, the former London Diocesan Missionary George Plaford (helped by Horsley's old assistant, H. G. Duffield) succeeded to Horsley's 'parish' stretching from Croydon to Edgware, and from Ilford to Staines.[54] Both these men died at almost the same time, and from 1893 their posts were filled by G. P. Merrick, already an experienced chaplain and *persona grata* at the Home Office, and A. K. Ramsay, formerly a curate in Hammersmith. After 1902 only women were sent to Holloway, and Brixton became the remand prison for men; and Merrick, by then first Chaplain-Inspector of H M's Prisons, promoted his assistant to the new post there, and then on Ramsay's death in 1906 replaced him with an experienced career chaplain of his

---

[51] He made his reputation during his 10 years at Clerkenwell with papers to the Church Congress and a Social Science Congress, and articles not only for *The Fortnightly*, but for *Macmillan's*, *The Pall Mall Gazette*, *The Echo*, and so on. His last publication was *How Criminals are Made and Prevented: A Retrospect of Forty Years* (1913).

[52] Horsley, *Jottings from Jail*, p. 127. He himself put in 6 hours a day, and he secured the help of a Scripture Reader in 1880 and an assistant chaplain in 1882: PP 1880 (59) LIX, p. 9; *Prison Commissioners' AR, 1879–80*, Part II, p. 21; *'I Remember'*, p. 110. Horsley always said he found prison work 'fascinating': ibid., p. 75. It may not be irrelevant that he married the Governor's daughter a few months after he went to Clerkenwell.

[53] 'Suicide', p. 504; *Jottings from Jail*, p. 239; *'I Remember'*, p. 95.

[54] So Horsley described his prison's catchment area: PP 1884–5 [C. 4402], XXX, p. 87, Q. 2234. Plaford was a graduate of King's College London, who first worked as a curate in Mile End and Whitechapel (where the outstanding Evangelical slum rector W. W. Champneys was at work), moved on to work among the railway navvies in north London, and then became a London Diocesan Home Missionary. After 7 years he was appointed vicar of St Paul's, Upper Holloway, and moved thence in 1873 to Holloway prison, where he spent the rest of his working life. Duffield came from St Gabriel's, Pimlico, and was much involved in the activities of St Giles's Mission. He also acted as secretary and treasurer of Horsley's Guild of SS Paul and Silas, and combined his duties at Clerkenwell with the chaplaincy of Newgate prison.

own sort, J. B. S. Watson.[55] Some of both Ramsay's and Watson's reports to magistrates on their Brixton attempted suicide cases survive, and show them in these Edwardian years still acting in the familiar way, advising prisoners and then the examining magistrates, administering the Pledge, promising help from the Sheriffs' Fund and arranging seaside holidays (sometimes now with active help from their wives).[56]

By this time, however, the prison chaplain's role in suicide prevention was long past its zenith. From the late 1880s prison welfare work in general was less and less the chaplain's preserve. The expansion of the prison education service, the introduction of lady visitors, special speakers, and lecturers, the new policy of inviting part-time assistance from the local parish clergy in order to secure freshness and variety in spiritual ministrations—internal developments such as these all made him less important within the prison service,[57] while wider trends lessened his prestige. Even more significant in the long term was the continuous redrawing of the boundary between the duties of chaplains and medical officers which was encouraged by the growing emphasis upon the physical basis of criminal behaviour and the beginning of psychiatric treatment in prisons.[58] Where attempted suicide

[55] Merrick's rise is an interesting one, although he did not win a place in *DNB*. He had held prison chaplaincies at Westminster, Millbank, and Wormwood Scrubs before his appointment to Holloway; was on the Gladstone Committee of 1894; and thereafter had an unstoppable career, serving as Visiting Chaplain to HM Prisons, 1896–1902, and becoming the first Chaplain-Inspector, 1902–21. He seems to have been a moderate social gospeller, and perhaps this was why he was chosen to sit on the Gladstone Committee. He was an ex-slum curate, and like others of his kind, an active supporter of the National Association for Promoting State Emigration and Colonisation: Malchow, *Population Pressures*, p. 136. Ramsay came straight from a curacy at St Stephen's, Hammersmith, to Holloway; whereas Watson had already held prison chaplaincies at Derby, Maidstone, and Hull when he was appointed to Brixton in 1906. For the 'great changes' at Holloway and Brixton, see *Prison Commissioners' AR, 1901–2*, p. 7, and 1902–3, p. 338.

[56] For example, the cases of Mary Arloff, 1 May 1900, and Thomas Bedford, 18 Feb. 1910: CLRO, Guildhall Justice Room, Registers and Notes of Evidence.

[57] On these internal developments in the Ruggles-Brise era of prison administration, see Rose, *The Struggle for Penal Reform*, p. 63; Thomas, *The English Prison Officer*, pp. 125–51; and more specifically PP 1898 [C. 8790] XLVII, pp. 12–13 and the annual reports of the Prison Commissioners. As Eustace Jervis (a Diocesan Missionary who began his career in the prison service in 1898) wrote in 1925, 'Nobody ever seems to have a good word to say for the chaplain of a prison': *Twenty-Five Years in Six Prisons*, p. 117. By 1938 the Convocation of York's concern over these changes in the chaplain's role prompted William Temple, then Archbishop of York, to raise the matter with the then head of the Prison Commission: Ruck, ed., *Paterson on Prisons*, pp. 125–6.

[58] 'The Medical Officer is the most powerful official in a prison', was the unequivocal opinion of the Prison System Enquiry Committee of the Fabian Research Department

cases were concerned, however, the most important immediate development was plainly the advent in the police courts of *de facto* probation officers.

Long before the Probation of Offenders Act of 1907 a number of busy courts were operating what was in effect a probation system. Here a watershed can be found in the later 1870s, when the Church of England Temperance Society began to maintain agents at some police courts to induce those who appeared there to take a pledge of abstinence from drink. By 1891 each of the thirteen metropolitan police courts was equipped with such an agent. These 'police court missionaries'—all appointed by the bishop of the diocese—seem to have been remarkably well chosen. Practical and alert, and apparently free from religiosity, they quickly convinced the magistrates that they could be trusted and were given almost a free hand. They were allowed to talk to the prisoners in the cells and waiting-rooms before they were charged, and then to stand beside the magistrate as the cases came up, putting forward points on the prisoners' behalf, and murmuring suggestions as to how they should be dealt with. They made it a rule only to offer to stand surety for cases they believed to be hopeful; but once they had taken on a case, they spared no pains.[59] As Charles Booth noted in 1903, they did not stint money when it was needed. These men had advantages which no chaplain could ever match. Equally in touch with all the philanthropic organizations, they could also use press publicity on behalf of their cases by enlisting the help of the reporters attached to their court;[60] they were entirely unassociated with prison discipline; and they came from much the same social class as those with whom they worked. (Thomas Holmes, the most renowned of them all, had been an iron-moulder in Walsall.) Unavoidably they were 'tarred with the denominational brush'; but they believed that deeds, not words, were the only way of 'giving Christ' to the needy. In the early 1900s their many progressive admirers agreed that to call them 'missionaries'—a name redolent of proselytes

in 1922: Hobhouse and Brockway, eds., *English Prisons To-day*, p. 256. See also Home Office: East and Hubert, *Report on the Psychological Treatment of Crime*, pp. 1–2; and ch. ii, pp. 389–401.

[59] Leeson, *The Probation System*, p. 5; Booth, *Life and Labour*, 3rd series, vii. 371; Williams, *Later Leaves*, pp. 390–1; Church of England Temperance Society, *Missionary Efforts*, pp. 4–6. (According to this lecture, written to accompany a set of lantern slides, the Society's police court work was 'very quiet and unobtrusive' until 1888.)

[60] Thomas Holmes acknowledged that he would have been unable to deal with many cases without the aid of press publicity: Holmes, *Pictures and Problems*, p. viii.

and sermons—was altogether misleading. They were more philanthropic than religious in their outlook, reported Charles Booth, and
'never spoke of spiritual influences' on their cases;[61] the police court
missionary aimed to be 'not a preacher, a censor, or a reformer, but
a kindly friend'.[62] Not even a new-style Sky Pilot could hope to be so
acceptable and practical a helper or so astute an investigator as these
genuine men of the people; and, most fundamental advantage of all,
no chaplain however zealous could undertake that continuing after-
care of a suicide case, stretching over months or even years and
extending to every mundane detail, which was routine for police court
missionaries.

Despite all this it would be a mistake to suppose that remand was
simply replaced by probation for cases of attempted suicide, or that
the chaplains' work was altogether superseded. Very often both chaplain and missionary were involved in the same case, and remand
often preceded *de facto* probation. Where it was necessary for family
circumstances to be investigated or practical arrangements made, the
magistrate's obvious choice was the police court missionary; where a
moral appraisal of someone who had tried to commit suicide was
needed, he might well appeal to the prison chaplain; but in either
event, the prisoner would probably be remanded. Thus, for example,
when Montague Williams had to deal at Worship Street police court
in 1891 with a friendless seventeen year old girl who had thrown
herself in front of a train, he remanded her and asked 'the clergyman
of the Jail' (no doubt George Plaford of Holloway) to report whether
she was worthy of his finding a home for her; but as soon as the
press publicity given to the case brought an offer of a home from a
shopkeeper and his wife in the North of England (wrote Williams), 'I
at once placed the facts of the case before the missionary attending
my court ... and he promptly opened up communications both with
the prisoner and with my correspondent.' The shopkeeper came to
Worship Street, and 'my court missionary saw the two off by train
... and the accounts he receives are eminently satisfactory.'[63] This
particular police court, however, had only had a missionary for a few
months. At the North London police court, where between 1889 and

---

[61] Booth, *Life and Labour*, 3rd series, vii. 376; see also Williams, *Later Leaves*,
pp. 390–1 and Lieck, *Bow Street World*, pp. 86–7.

[62] Thus the publisher's blurb for Holmes's *Pictures and Problems*. The work of this
'friend' is described in Gamon, *The London Police Court*, pp. 161–82.

[63] Williams, *Later Leaves*, pp. 395–7.

1905 a succession of new magistrates found the formidable Thomas Holmes in possession, remand seems very often to have been used simply to give him time to bring his resourcefulness to bear on a case. Thus a woman who had tried to commit suicide because of her husband's cruelty was remanded for a week while Holmes devised some arrangement. He found that he could negotiate a legal separation which gave the home and maintenance of 15s a week to the woman. 'This arrangement', wrote Holmes, 'met with the approval of the magistrate, who, on the remand, accepted sureties for the wife and let her go.'[64] Similarly, in 1907 Cecil Plowden at Marylebone police court remanded a servant girl who had tried to drown herself in the lake in Regent's Park, and whom he had persuaded to ask to go into a home, 'to enable the missionary, Mr Kirby, to find a suitable home for her'.[65] Increasingly, the police court missionaries were providing not so much a supplement to the remand system as it had operated in its mid-Victorian heyday, but rather an alternative to it. Indeed, so striking was the overall success of these agents of the Church of England Temperance Society that a host of imitators appeared, notably from the Church Army and the Salvation Army. By 1898 rival missionaries could sometimes be seen in a court, contending to be entrusted with a case by the magistrate,[66] although these newcomers were never given the privileges enjoyed by the CETS missionaries, and always remained at best free-lance workers.[67]

What then were the methods used by this important new group of workers among those taken into custody by the police for attempted suicide? The accepted spokesman of the police court missionaries has always been Thomas Holmes, an outstandingly successful publicist.[68] Like so many progressive social workers at the turn of the century, Holmes rejected the previous generation's emphasis on drink as the root of all evil;[69] and he insisted that his twenty years' experience as a

---

[64] Holmes, *Pictures and Problems*, p. 79. The *Law Lists* show that the North London police court had four different magistrates between 1891 and 1899. This rapid turnover was no doubt the result of the practice of offering police magistrates in order of seniority any vacancy which occurred. There was no demand for the North London court (a newly established one), and it was often a police magistrate's starting point.

[65] 'Tired of Life at Fifteen', *Daily Chronicle*, 10 Jan. 1907, p. 5.

[66] Maddison, *Hints on Rescue Work*, p. 7.

[67] Gamon, *The London Police Court*, pp. 167–8.

[68] For the early career of Holmes (1846–1918: *DNB*) see his own *Pictures and Problems*, pp. 21–2, and for his later years see Rose, *The Struggle for Penal Reform*, pp. 68–88.

[69] See e.g. *Pictures and Problems*, pp. 173, 276.

police court missionary had taught him that drink was not the most importance source of suicide attempts. Two other causes were far more to blame: social conditions, and 'the growth of insanity in the race'. 'Poor living', increasing age, crippling rents, and hopeless prospects—these, he said, he had found in hundreds of cases to be the cause of suicidal despair. He had invariably sent such people away on seaside holidays and provided them with suitable clothing, plenty of food, and some friends; but the truth was that 'when they come back, they have to face exactly the same conditions which brought them down before, except that the improvement in health and the sympathy are still there ... If we could supplement their incomes it might be some good, but we cannot.' As for his other great cause of suicidal behaviour, the growth of insanity, he believed that the only remedy was to shut up epileptics and 'those demented by strange feelings and delusions'. 'We want scientific men and Government to take up this great question', was his conclusion.[70] The gulf between such opinions and those of Horsley's generation was indeed a wide one. These, though, were Holmes's views in 1907, in the full flush of progressivism, and after he had risen to the post of secretary of the Howard Association. The likelihood is that his views in the 1890s as an obscure police court missionary were less dogmatic, as those of his fellow missionaries probably always were. In any case, whatever general conclusions these men did or did not draw from their conversations with the hundreds of people who appeared each year in the police courts charged with attempted suicide, the help they offered was always eminently practical. Unlike the prison chaplain, they did not work primarily through mobilizing the efforts of others, but themselves provided the care they felt was needed; and unlike him, they could be selective in those they tried to help. They undertook responsibility only for those whom they had given sureties for, or whom the magistrate had released on their own recognizance and a promise not to repeat the attempt, on the strength of the missionary's offer to take charge of them. If Holmes was at all typical, their strategy was then to change the circumstances of these people to an extent that enabled them to stand on their own feet. Holmes was against institutionalization.[71] He worked ingeniously

[70] Interview with Holmes reported in the *Daily Express*, 4 Jan. 1907, p, 8.

[71] The Howard Association (later League) campaigned from the 1880s against institutionalization, and supported boarding out and probation, so that Holmes's move to become its secretary in 1905 was for him a natural one: Bochel, *Probation and After-Care*, pp. 15–16; Rose, *The Struggle for Penal Reform*, pp. 50–1.

to keep homes and families together, arranged outings and amusements as well as good food and clothing, checked on hours of work, acted as an employment agency and careers adviser, and was generally prepared to provide supervision and support for years on end: 'The aim is to find a pathway for those to whom life offers only despair.'

One case may serve as an example of this style of suicide prevention work at its best. On the anniversary of her husband's death, a widow who had been living for four years in a single room, supporting her four small children by making matchboxes (seven gross a day, at twopence-three farthings the gross), tried to drown herself in the River Lea. Her dead husband had made her promise not to let the children go to a workhouse. She had made no appeal for help; no religious agency had visited her; none of the usual charitable organizations seemed to know anything of her. She was taken by the police to the North London police court.

She was not punished, God forbid! [wrote Holmes]; but the worthy magistrate kindly committed her to my charge. So I went with her to that little room ten feet by eight. I saw the wistful children almost famished, and sadly wanting clothing. I sent in food for them, and next day went again with clothing for all of them. I took them out, and bought new boots for them all, mother included ... I paid her little debts. I filled their cupboard with food. I stopped her from work. I compelled her to go out of doors. All this I could do as I continued to visit her, but no smile could I bring to her face, no hope into her heart. I got her nice clothing, but even that created no interest; there was nothing but dull, passive apathy and increasing weakness.

So Holmes sent the children into the country, and took the widow away to the seaside for a month with his own wife and two other women who had attempted suicide ('one was a fur-sewer, and had thrown herself in front of a train; the other a blouse-maker, who had taken laudanum'). He went on in this way for four years, until the eldest boy was old enough to be found a situation. Then, after several years of only sending a little help, Holmes found the youngest child ill and the mother refusing to call in the parish doctor, for fear the child should be separated from her in the infirmary. 'So I had again to begin my task, for I could not leave her in such misery'; and once more he produced better rooms, clothing, boots, situations, and a school for the girl. For the invalid mother, however, Holmes foresaw only a sombre ending. Her hope had long since become, not to die, but to live long enough to see her children self-supporting—'a hope that will

not be realised'.[72] Holmes often told this story, and no doubt it
lost nothing in the telling. Still, the patience, resourcefulness, and
imaginative goodwill behind these efforts to support someone who
had once attempted suicide seem undeniable, and make it easy to
understand both the (perhaps excessive) confidence magistrates placed
in such workers, and the admiration they inspired in Charles Booth,
that hardened surveyor of the London scene. Certainly it can be no
surprise that many of these missionaries were formally appointed as
probation officers after 1907, or that probation orders began quite
often to be made in the courts when a charge of attempted suicide had
been proved, immediately the law allowed it for an indictable offence.[73]
It had indeed been well established that given friendly, practical long-
term after-care, it was not inevitable that someone who had once tried
to commit suicide would repeat the attempt—although the cost of
such after-care in time and money might be very high.

Throughout the Victorian years, a closely linked network of agencies
of religious evangelism, private philanthropy, and official welfare and
reformatory work was responsible for the efforts made to look after
those known to the police to have attempted suicide, just as it was
responsible for most other Victorian social action in the big cities.
This network had its own internal dynamics of growth and change;
yet in essentials it showed a notable continuity. The people at risk of
suicide whom these agencies tried to help were solely those whom they
or the police chanced to encounter;[74] the help given them was always
similar to that given to other sinful and outcast, hungry and homeless,
foolish and fraudulent men and women; and it was always given
through the same agents and the same organizations as those used for
other social work. Victorian suicide prevention work did indeed reflect

---

[72] Holmes, *Pictures and Problems*, pp. 296–300. (This is surely the same case as that
described to Booth and reported in *Life and Labour*, 3rd series, vii. 374.) For other cases
of attempted suicide dealt with by Holmes, see his *Pictures and Problems*, pp. 77–81,
269–70, 325–7, *Known to the Police*, pp. 254–6, and *London's Underworld*, pp. 141–2.

[73] The enabling legislation was the Probation of Offenders Act, 1907 (7 Ed. 7, c. 17,
s. 1(2). In 1908–13 probation orders were made for 11 per cent of those convicted of the
offence of attempted suicide at assizes and quarter sessions: *Judicial Statistics*, Table V;
while in the metropolitan police district, probation orders were made in a quarter of
the cases of attempted suicide dealt with in 1910–13 in the Juvenile Courts set up under
the 1908 Children Act: see ch. 8 n. 116. For the appointment of missionaries as probation
officers, see Bochel, *Probation and After-Care*, p. 45.

[74] It is true that with the enormous growth of open air evangelism from the 1860s,
chance encounters between those bent on suicide and those bent on saving souls
increased; but the help offered was still the same as that offered to any other passer-by.

changing analyses of the problem of poverty, changing styles of philanthropic effort and penal policy, and changing kinds of churchmanship and evangelism; but it remained unaltered with regard to
the central matters of who was helped, how, and by whom, for
its mainspring lay in the persistence within the world of well-to-do
Christian philanthropy of both a way of seeing suicide attempts which
made them part of the general problem of the poor and outcast, and
certain fundamental assumptions about the range of possible responses
to poverty and wrong conduct.

In the early 1890s and early 1900s, however, received ideas about
the sources of human actions, the causes of social and economic
problems and the significance of suicide were all changing very fast. It
is accordingly not surprising that early in the new century a post-
Victorian phase of samaritan work among would-be suicides began;
all that is surprising is that it was started as late as 1907, and by a
popular newspaper in conjunction with the Salvation Army. On New
Year's Day, 1907, the *Daily Express* carried on its front page a banner
headline, 'General Booth Opens Anti-Suicide Bureau'. For the next
few days sensational stories, interviews, and letters about the new
Bureau at the Salvation Army's Headquarters in the City abounded
on the front page of the *Express*.[75] Running totals of 'Lives Saved'
were splashed across it; after a week, the figure had reached 194. 'The
War Against Suicide' was demoted to page 5 to make room for 'The
Romance of the Lady Bigamist' on January 11, and on January 15 it
was dropped completely; but by then the Anti-Suicide Bureau at 101
Queen Victoria Street had attracted so much interest and so many
correspondents and callers, that the Salvation Army was opening a
string of provincial Bureaux along the same lines.[76] Details of this
provincial work were apparently never published; but much was
written about the progress of the London Bureau—and understandably, since after five years it claimed to have had 4,754 callers.[77]

This Anti-Suicide Bureau marked a radically new departure in
suicide prevention work in two important respects. In the first place,
it reflected a widespread acceptance of suicide as a distinct social

[75] For a particularly colourful account of a visit to the Bureau (where 'death prowled
about me'), see W. Rolt White, 'At the Gates of Death', *Daily Express*, 7 Jan. 1907, p. 4.
[76] Leeds, Birmingham, Manchester, Bristol, Glasgow, and Newcastle were mentioned:
Daily Express, 5 and 10 Jan. 1907, p. 8; *The Standard*, 8 Jan. 1907, p. 4; *The War Cry*,
12 Jan. p. 9, and 19 Jan. 1907, p. 8.
[77] *Salvation Army Year Book for 1913*, p. 49. In 1907 the number of callers was 1,124:
White, *The Great Idea*, p. 106.

problem, and a major one at that. The Bureau's rules, its approach, its very title, all expressed a view of suicide which did not regard it as the corollary of poverty,[78] disease, prostitution, or even drink; while the fact that it owed its existence to a suggestion from the *Daily Express* (then fighting a circulation war with the *Daily Mail*), demonstrated that suicide had become the colourful sort of 'question' upon which the mass circulation national dailies fed. By then it was common knowledge that the statistics showed a steep increase in suicide and attempted suicide, and this increase had come to seem an expression of the problems of the post–Victorian world, since suicide was very widely associated with the stress of modern living and the supposed increase of insanity and onset of racial degeneration, as well as with the loss of religious faith. In the 1890s the 'suicide mania' had been the topic of the moment among the intelligentsia and their imitators; a decade later, it had percolated into the talk and reading of people at a much lower social level, largely through the new mass circulation weeklies and dailies. (It is surely no accident that about this time the word 'suicide' began to be widely used as a metaphor—for example, in talk of 'race suicide' as a dramatic euphemism for declining national birth-rates.)[79] There is thus nothing surprising in the decision of the *Daily Express* to boost its reputation for philanthropic concern, and at the same time ensure a flow of gripping copy, by starting the new year of 1907 with a suicide prevention campaign. To do this through William Booth, however, was a brilliant stroke. Ever since he embarked upon his sensational rescue plan for 'Darkest England' in 1890, Booth had been by far the most controversial figure in the country in the field of social work;[80] and yet another elaborate indictment of his ways (John

---

[78] One of the Bureau's Rules was, 'No financial assistance is promised': *Salvation Army Year Book for 1908*, p. 12. There was thus a sharp contrast between the Bureau and the only other organization dedicated especially to suicide prevention which I have found namely, the National Fund for the Prevention of Suicide through Poverty, started by the Food and Betterment Association of Liverpool (whose president was the city coroner) some time around the turn of the century. H. Lee Jones of this Association (later called the League of Well-Doers) employed methods very like Booth's, however, and appealed to the same vague longing to do good felt by lower middle-class people not hitherto active in charity work: Simey, *Charitable Effort in Liverpool in the Nineteenth Century*, pp. 119–20.

[79] Theodore Roosevelt's much-quoted phrase of 1902 is included in *Stevenson's Book of Proverbs, Maxims and Familiar Phrases*, p. 2240, sect. 4. English examples of the use of this popular metaphor include R. Rentoul, *Race Culture or Race Suicide: A Plea for the Unborn* (1906), and W. R. MacDermott, 'The Suicide of the Race', *Westminster Review*, clix (1903), pp. 695–703.

[80] Inglis, *Churches and the Working Classes in Victorian England*, pp. 204–9. A fairly

Manson's *The Salvation Army and the Public*), appeared just before the Bureau was opened. In the popular mind, though, Booth seemed a superman whose confident, sweeping remedies would set England to rights if he were only given the funds and support for which he endlessly appealed. Catchily named projects were his speciality, and on this occasion Booth's flair for publicity did not fail him. In reality a couple of officers were simply sitting at their roll-top desks at Headquarters much as usual (see Fig. 12);[81] but by christening them 'The Anti-Suicide Bureau' Booth skilfully conjured up not another charitable organization, still less another soul-saving mission, but a brand new, up-to-the-minute, expert advice centre. The word 'Bureau' was then just coming into use in the sense of an office with a specialized function;[82] and its choice perfectly epitomizes the advent of suicide in the popular consciousness as a problem of the day calling for specialized advice and expert attention.

In practical terms, however, a second feature of the Bureau was even more significant: it invited anyone at all with suicidal thoughts and feelings to contact it. As a result, help began for the first time to be offered before any actual attempt had been made, and to all who asked for it—instead of only those taken into custody by the police or encountered by mere chance. Not surprisingly, this self-selected clientèle proved to be widely different in social class, sex, and age, as well as in its problems. From the beginning, the Bureau was used not only by the poor, but by clerks, shop assistants, business men, in short, by precisely those lower middle-class people who had been conspicuously absent from the police courts, but were likely to read the *Express* and to find it convenient to call at Victoria Street or seek help by correspondence. As early as 4 January 1907, the *Express* was

---

typical attack is A. Osborne Jay, *Life in Darkest London: A Hint to General Booth* (1891); another is in H. Bosanquet, *Social Work in London*, pp. 341–8. *The Times* rightly remarked in commenting on the opening of the Anti-Suicide Bureau that 'opinions will always differ concerning the true value of the Salvation Army's social work': 24 Jan. 1907, p. 4, col. a.

[81] 'Lieutenant-Colonel' (later Commissioner) Unsworth explained that he mixed other business with his suicide work, so that no one should know which of his callers were potential suicides: *Daily Express*, 7 Jan. 1907, p. 4. Women callers were seen by 'Colonel' Mrs Barker, Chief Secretary of the Army's women's social work, and a widow with 24 years' service. On both these officers, see *Salvation Army Year Book for 1908*, pp. 62, 68. By 1955 the Bureau (which is briefly mentioned in the Army's official history) was 'associated with the Investigation Department at the Men's Social Work Headquarters': Sandall, *History of the Salvation Army*, iii. 300.

[82] See the *Oxford English Dictionary* and *Supplement*, s.n. 'Bureau'.

Fig. 12 The Anti-Suicide Bureau at work, as shown in 'News Pictures by Camera', *Daily Express*, 3 Jan. 1907

printing on its front page an appeal from the officer in charge of the men's section of the Bureau to employers who could give temporary work to solicitor's clerks, office handymen, business men, or mechanics to contact him, since the unemployed men coming to him were not suited for the kind of work offered by unemployment committees, and would not think of applying to any charitable organization; and in 1913 the Bureau was still reporting that 'there have been few applications from the working classes.'[83] Earlier, it had also been reported

[83] 'Applicants very largely represent the following classes: clergymen, missionaries, military officers, doctors, solicitors, chief constables, old sea captains, journalists, architects, schoolmasters, general tradesmen, bank clerks, hotel proprietors and publicans, mechanics, company promoters and others', was its claim: *Salvation Army Year Book for 1913*, p. 49.

that 'few women apply to the Bureau', and three-quarters of those seen in the first four days of 1907 were men.[84] This was surprising. The conventional wisdom was still that more women than men attempted suicide,[85] and in London the proportion of women among those arrested for this offence, although declining throughout the later nineteenth century, did in fact never fall below 45 per cent.[86] This mere trickle of women callers becomes not unintelligible, however, when it is remembered that the men who proved sufficiently articulate, resourceful, and attention-seeking to consult the Bureau were from the lower and middle bourgeoisie, and that their female counterparts were the very women most likely to be deterred from such a step by their restricted horizons and a multiplicity of limiting pressures, including less propinquity to Victoria Street and the City.[87] Finally, the Bureau's callers were often young, at least in its early days. Booth himself held that among young men living alone in London, 'employment is so precarious, they hesitate to marry', and that this made them particularly prone to 'loneliness and dissipation', the chief reasons for contemplating suicide which emerged from the first interviews;[88] but perhaps the explanation is simply that young clerks and shop assistants were more likely to respond to what was at the beginning something of a newspaper stunt.

Quite as important, however, as these differences of class, sex, and age between those who reached the police courts and those who consulted the Bureau, was the fact that the latter had usually got no further than thoughts of suicide. It is not surprising therefore that the

[84] *Daily Telegraph*, 5 Jan. 1907, p. 6. Unfortunately the figures published by the Salvation Army itself do not distinguish between men and women.

[85] Horsley, for example, always asserted that attempted suicide was a peculiarly female crime: *Jottings from Jail*, p. 242. Possibly he and other commentators were misled by the magistrates' habit of remanding a much higher proportion of women apprehended than men, and by the fact that those charged with attempted suicide accounted for a considerable proportion of all women taken into custody, but only a very small proportion of men. (In the metropolitan police district the respective proportions in 1909–13 were 10.2 and 0.86 per cent.)

[86] The *Judicial Statistics* show that 49.8 per cent of those apprehended in England and Wales for attempted suicide were females in 1867–9, 47.4 per cent were females in 1881–3, and only 41.4 per cent were females in 1893–7. The proportion in the metropolitan police district, however, was always higher. (For example, the Metropolitan Police Commissioner's Reports show that 52.6 per cent of those apprehended there for attempted suicide in 1893–7 were females; although by 1909–13 this figure had fallen to 45.5 per cent.)

[87] The explanation suggested by Rider Haggard, 'the great story teller', was 'the greater secretiveness of the sex': Haggard, *Regeneration*, p. 158.

[88] *Daily Telegraph*, 5 Jan. 1907, p. 6; *The War Cry*, 12 Jan. 1907, p. 9.

nature of the suicide problem seemed one thing to the Salvation Army
officers at the Bureau, and quite another to the medical officers in the
remand prisons who did so much to shape informed Edwardian
opinion. The latter knew nothing of those who had attempted, or
threatened, or merely contemplated suicide but had never been taken
into custody by the police; just as they knew nothing of those who
had been arrested but not remanded to prison. From their vantage
point alcoholism (above all), and then domestic troubles and feeble-
mindedness were the chief causes of suicide attempts, and certainly
not unemployment.[89] At the Bureau, however, things looked very
different. Between 1907 and 1912, 55 per cent of their callers gave
financial embarrassment or hopeless poverty as their reason for being
there, and another 5 per cent embezzlement or forgery; whereas drink,
drugs, and disease together were blamed by only 10 per cent.[90]

   Clearly the Bureau not only expressed a new way of seeing suicide
(and a way which has proved typical of the twentieth century), but
brought within reach of help quite new groups of people at risk. How
was this opportunity used? The truth is that in this, as in so many
other kinds of social work, the Salvation Army provided new bottles
for some very old wine. For fifty years and more, prison chaplains,
police court missionaries, and their philanthropic auxiliaries had
already been doing what the Bureau embarked upon with such fanfares
in 1907. Like them, the Bureau listened and gave advice—spiritual,
medical, legal, indeed advice of whatever sort seemed needed. Like
them, the Bureau tried to bring about reconciliations with relatives
and friends, and interceded with former employers. Like them, it gave
direct practical help on a limited scale—paying travelling expenses
home or to relations or a place of employment, making small grants
for the purchase of a stock of goods to sell, providing clothes or
recommendations to prospective employers, or occasionally making
arrangements for emigration. And like them, the Bureau used a system
of referrals, although only to the various departments of its own Social
Headquarters at Whitechapel (especially the Labour Bureau, Distress,
Investigation, and Prisoners' Aid Departments for men, and the
Affiliation, Women's Inquiry, and Slum Departments for women).[91]

---

[89] See Sullivan, 'Alcoholism and Suicidal Impulses', and East, 'On Attempted Suicide'.

[90] *Salvation Army Year Book for 1913*, p. 49. For earlier but closely similar percentages, see White, *The Great Idea*, p. 98.

[91] See the 'General Classification of Treatment' given in the *Salvation Army Year
Book for 1913*, pp. 49–50.

Only in two respects was its help novel in substance, and in each case the innovation seems a natural consequence of the fact that it was working outside the ambit of the law and with an altogether different clientèle. First, it promised complete confidentiality: 'nothing is committed to writing without express permission', 'no unnecessary inquiries are made into the antecedents or private circumstances of applicants', 'secrecy is inviolably preserved'.[92] Secondly, it undertook negotiations with creditors to gain an extension of time or secure agreement upon a composition—clearly a corollary of the special characteristics of its clientèle. Its style, on the other hand, does seem to have been very much its own, for it handled its visitors with a light touch and much cheerful raillery. In 1910 Rider Haggard thus described its methods:

A poor wretch staggers in ... He vapours about self-destruction ... He produces drugs or weapons ... But the Officers in charge laugh at him or give him a cup of tea ... They listen quite unmoved though not unconcerned ... When [the tale] is finished, they ask coolly enough why he considers it necessary to commit suicide for a trifling job like that ... Why, exclaims the Officer, there are a dozen ways out.[93]

This briskness may have seemed an appropriate way of defusing the situation, given that these callers were predominantly young men who had not got beyond thoughts of suicide; but it also reflected the Army's somewhat simplistic approach to suicide prevention. It is characteristic that the *War Cry* (the Salvation Army's own newspaper) thought that 'the suicide mania' could be checked in London if the Army was given funds to run a 'Lonely Man's Club': 'What we want is a great cheerful Institutional Home for those who are mentally depressed.'[94]

[92] Complete confidentiality was one of the Bureau's Rules: *Salvation Army Year Book for 1908*, p. 12. The General also undertook, however, to carry on some ambitious sociological research: 'Records will be kept of all cases that come to our notice, and they will be studied from a scientific point of view. We will try to find out to what this suicide mania is due, and we hope later to be able to deal with the cause in its incipient state. The sociology of the future will deal with causes, and not effects, and our study will help in this direction': *Daily Telegraph*, 5 Jan. 1907, p. 6. The classified lists of causes of suicidal inclinations published in subsequent *Year Books* show that these records were indeed kept.

[93] Haggard, *Regeneration*, p. 152. Haggard inspected the Salvation Army's controversial social work at General Booth's request (and despite strong dissuasion from the sceptical Conan Doyle), and presented the Army with the copyright of his enthusiastic (and catchily titled) report, *Regeneration*: Ellis, *H. Rider Haggard*, p. 189; Higgins, *Rider Haggard*, pp. 204–5.

[94] *The War Cry*, 12 Jan. 1907, p. 9.

Not surprisingly, responses to the Anti-Suicide Bureau were very mixed. Popular journalists, expressing the new consciousness of suicide as a social problem distinct from that of poverty, might declare that 'to make war on the dark shadows that encompass the human mind is as much a duty to our fellow-men as to give them food and a bed';[95] and some psychiatrists and men in public positions were found to support this line.[96] Many of those with extensive experience of suicidal behaviour, however, were distinctly guarded in their response. The Bureau's *raison d'être*, as its name implied, was the belief that what was required to stem the flood of suicide was an advice centre. But was this so? The *Daily Express* tried to elicit endorsements for the Bureau from such recognized authorities on social work as the secretaries of the London City Mission and the St Giles's Mission, as well as Thomas Holmes, by then a widely known personality; but none would go further than an acknowledgement that 'in many cases' advice was 'of great help', and all implied (quite rightly) that their own organizations had long been providing all that the new Bureau offered, and more. Thomas Holmes, indeed, declared outright that advice would help only a small minority of cases, and those the easy ones (notably young men alone in London who were not badly off, but easily became depressed after they had had a little to drink).[97] Medical men were even more lukewarm than social workers in their response. Some offered a reminder of the eugenicists' current teaching—that suicide should not invariably be prevented, since it was better for the community that those of diseased mind should cease to live and procreate; but that if indiscriminate suicide prevention was practised, then care should be taken to shut up permanently those suffering from more than temporary stress and depression.[98] Others pointed out that since suicidal impulses were usually very sudden, the Bureau could not possibly help more than a minority of cases;[99] and many clearly felt

---

[95] This newspaper comment is quoted in the *Salvation Army Year Book for 1913*, p. 50.

[96] One may cite Dr C. D. Sherrard of Lusted Hall, Tatsfield, Surrey, and Patrick Rose-Innes, Recorder of Sandwich and Eastgate: *Daily Express*, 5 Jan. 1907, p. 1.

[97] *Daily Express*, 4 Jan., p. 8, and 11 Jan., p. 5, 1907.

[98] Thus wrote H. R. Oswald, coroner for the South-East District of London, and one of the small band of coroners who were both medically and legally qualified: *Daily Express*, 7 Jan. 1907, p. 1.

[99] Thus wrote Dr E. F. Talbot MacCarthy, visiting physician to the British Hospital for Mental Diseases and formerly Visitor in Lunacy of the High Court of Justice, Ireland: *Daily Express*, 8 Jan. 1907, p. 1.

that what was needed was not 'good words' at all, but a doctor.[100] The coroner and medical man, W. Wynn Westcott, asserted categorically that of the cases of completed suicide in North London upon which he had held an inquest, at most 19 per cent might have been helped had they consulted the Bureau—to which the Bureau could have retorted that to them 'good words' had a far more practical meaning than he supposed, and that they had already successfully dealt with some of the very categories of people whom he declared they could not help.[101] Running through all these observations was the implication that the Anti-Suicide Bureau had an over-simple view of both the causes of the problem and how to tackle it; and this was essentially the criticism made of all the Army's social work at that time. Ever since the launch of the 'In Darkest England' campaign in 1890, the old hands who had long worked quietly and carefully among the poor and needy had agreed that the best that could be said of the Salvation Army was that, although their work was wasteful and in some ways positively mischievous through sheer naïvety, they were zealots who meant well.[102] What they might have added was that the Army alone not only set out to use strident publicity techniques to win popular support for its work, but did succeed in inspiring with enthusiasm for its simplistic utopian schemes and sensationalized 'Plans' to set the country to rights a new lower middle-class public which had never before been involved in organized charity.

The Anti-Suicide Bureau, 'the General's latest scheme of Hope and Help', certainly aroused sympathetic interest in organized suicide prevention work at lower social levels than in the past. The kinds of help offered were not in reality novel in themselves; but the Bureau made them available to a new clientèle, in a new way, and at a much earlier stage of the suicidal cycle than had ever been the case before. It thus marks something of a half-way house between the Victorian style of samaritan work, and the style characteristic of the twentieth

[100] E.g. 'A Well-Known Authority', *Daily Express*, 5 Jan. 1907, p. 8.

[101] Westcott, *Daily Express*, 9 Jan. 1907, p. 1. Westcott was here simplifying the analysis of his suicide cases in the years 1902–4 which he had presented in his paper to the Medico-Legal Society of 1905, 'On Suicide'. He considered that at most the Bureau might have helped where the cause of suicide was grief, domestic worries and debility, and 'unknown'—thus ruling out, for example, alcoholic excess and debauchery, his largest category, and one which the Bureau certainly claimed to help. In fact, only 4 or 5 of the Bureau's callers to its knowledge subsequently committed suicide: Sandall, *History of the Salvation Army*, iii. 301.

[102] This was the verdict of *The Times*, 24 Jan. 1907, p. 4, col. a.

century. Neither mid-nineteenth century Christian philanthropists nor Edwardian Salvation Army officers ever separated care for the body from care for the immortal soul; and both alike thought in terms of helping individuals in need and showing them the reality of a Gospel of Hope. With the advent of the Bureau, however, there began an organized attempt to make help freely available to those whose entanglement with suicide was entirely within their own thoughts and feelings, and to carry on this work quite independently of the machinery of the criminal law and make it accessible to any one in the whole country, or even the world.[103] These were departures which became thinkable only when social workers came to see suicidal behaviour as a problem distinct from other social problems, mysterious in its origins, and imbued with significance for the nation and indeed for the whole civilized world. In certain basic respects, then, those two developments characteristic of the later twentieth century—international samaritan agencies and widespread acceptance of parasuicide (as well as suicide itself) as one of the strategies used by the individual beset with problems—can both be traced back to Edwardian England.[104]

[103] 'In case of applicants being in the country two Salvation Army officers will be instructed by telegraph to call on them in plain clothes': *Daily Express*, 2 Jan. 1907, p. 1. By the end of the year the Army could claim that its war with suicide was a 'worldwide movement' and list 5 provincial offices and 20 'foreign agencies' in cities all over the world (in effect, wherever the Army was active): *Salvation Army Year Book for 1908*, p. 12.

[104] Cf. Baechler, *Suicides*, p. 442.

The Environmentalist Approach
to Suicide Prevention

Few Victorians or Edwardians would have been likely to equate efforts to prevent suicide with either the ambulance work of missionaries and philanthropists, or the sermons and sanctions of the law. What loomed largest in their consciousness was probably the contribution of the medical world, and above all the 'mad-doctors'. That contribution was a triple one, however, and came not only from psychiatrists, but from general practitioners and sanitarians as well; and it is the work of these last—the public health enthusiasts and their allies the social scientists—which forms a natural bridge between the endeavours of magistrates, clergymen, and philanthropists on the one hand, and the clinical work of general practitioners and psychiatrists on the other. To practising utilitarians like these sanitarians, suicide prevention was an aspect of social medicine, best tackled by the creation of an environment which would make suicide attempts both less likely to be contemplated, and more difficult to carry out.

There is nothing surprising about the belief of the medical and lay social reformers behind the early Victorian public health movement that suicide was another of the many causes of death which could be reduced by creating a healthier and safer environment. Preoccupied as they were with the health of towns and the 'Condition of England' question, the idea that suicide was linked with urban living and the conditions of modern society was to them quite as plausible and familiar as the idea that it was linked with insanity or individual constitution. Moreover, a number of the first generation of British sanitarians had absorbed the new continental statistical, epidemiological approach to social medicine,[1] and this approach from the beginning studied suicide as an epidemic disease and hence a problem

---

[1] On the antecedents of the sanitary movement see Rosen, *A History of Public Health*, ch. v, and his chapter 'The Evolution of Social Medicine' in Freeman, Levine, and Reeder, eds;. *Handbook of Medical Sociology*, pp. 30–60.

of public health. William Farr himself, that most influential of all Britain's mid-nineteenth century sanitarians, was studying in Paris in the year (1829) when one of the most renowned of these early epidemiological investigators of suicide, Esquirol, joined with others to found the *Annales d'hygiène publique*;[2] and it was an article published in that journal which stimulated him to undertake the pioneering epidemiological analysis of suicide in England which he included in the third official report of the Registrar-General of Births, Deaths and Marriages, published in 1841.[3] The sanitarians' strategy for the reduction of suicide was first expounded in these brief paragraphs of Farr's, and remained essentially unchanged for the rest of the century and beyond. It had two parts: first, the fostering of healthy minds in healthy bodies, through encouraging outdoor exercise, 'occupational hygiene', 'the regulation of the mind', and less publicity for 'detailed, dramatic tales of suicide, murder and bloodshed'; and secondly, the creation of an environment from which all tempting facilities for suicide had as far as possible been removed, so that suicide was both less easy to think of and to carry out. The relief of poverty, it should be noticed, was never on their agenda. As Farr said in this early study, 'it does not appear from the registers, that either poverty or riches have any great disturbing influence on the tendency to suicide': statistically, suicide was connected with drunkenness but not with destitution.[4]

What was the source of this two-pronged strategy? *Mens sana in corpore sano* was so much the characteristic Victorian conception of health that this psycho-physical prescription for the creation of a population which was less inclined to suicide may hardly seem to

---

[2] For a view of Farr as 'a product of the Parisian school of medicine' and student of the distinguished epidemiologist Louis, see Lilienfeld, ' "The Greening of Epidemiology" ', p. 514. Many Englishmen were then attracted to study in Paris by its brilliant medical school; and in addition, important French publications rapidly became known in Britain through reviews and translations. The new French approach to suicide was early drawn to British attention in this way: see e.g. the review published in the *Monthly Review*, x (new and improved series) (Feb. 1829), pp. 159–74 of J. P. Falret, *De l'hypochondrie et du suicide* together with Esquirol's article on suicide in his *Dictionnaire des sciences médicales*, and the translation published in Edinburgh in 1842 of A. Quetelet's seminal work, *Sur l'homme et le développement de ses facultés* (1835) (which discusses suicide in ch. II, sect. 2).

[3] Namely, M. Brouc, 'Considérations sur les suicides de notre époque', *Annales d'hygiène publique*, xvi (1836), pp. 223–62.

[4] *Registrar-General's 3rd AR*, Appendix, 'Violent Deaths', pp. 75–89, and especially pp. 81–2. 34 years later Farr again took up the subject of suicide in his annual official Letter to the Registrar-General: *Registrar-General's 26th AR*, Appendix, pp. 192–3.

require any particular explanation.[5] Still, it should be noted that although it was the French approach to social medicine which provided the sanitarians with their research procedures, their practical environmental recommendations stemmed from that programme of 'medical police' first expounded in Germany in the later eighteenth century. By the early nineteenth century this had become familiar to progressives throughout Britain through the wide-ranging influence of the Scottish universities at that time. From 1795 onwards Scottish medical lecturers regularly expounded 'the art or science of medical police', defined as providing for 'the various circumstances, inseparable from the aggregation of human beings within narrow limits, by which health may be affected',[6] through accident prevention, occupational hygiene, and 'the hygiene of procreation' as well as through personal and environmental sanitation and the control of communicable diseases.[7] The task of reducing suicide was an aspect of the task of improving 'the health of towns'; and Farr and his like proposed to undertake both by a combination of consensus and compulsion, education and legislation, and private and official action.[8] Indeed, while the legal-environmental approach to public health was in its heyday before the bacteriological theory of disease carried all before it in the 1880s very many reformers believed that the coroner himself—provided he was a medical man—could function not merely as a detector of felonious violence but as a great preventer of death, including suicidal death. Populists like Thomas Wakley, Toulmin Smith, and William Baker urged that holding inquests on deaths in institutions was the best protection for their inmates against the neglect and ill-treatment which they believed caused death not only by disease but by suicide;[9] while social scientists argued that inquests could provide essential information about those local environmental factors responsible for pre-

[5] The holistic Victorian conception of health is examined in Haley, *The Healthy Body and Victorian Culture*, chs. 1 and 2.

[6] This is the definition given by Robert Druitt (1814–83: *DNB*) in 'Short Notes on Some of the Details of Sanitary Police', p. 16.

[7] See Rosen, 'The Fate of the Concept of Medical Police, 1780–1890', pp. 107–8.

[8] All these were envisaged by Farr in 1841: *Registrar-General's 3rd AR*, Appendix, pp. 75–89.

[9] E.g. Baker, *A Letter ... on the Subject of the Increase of Inquests*, p. 6, and *A Practical Compendium*, pp. iv–v; Smith, *The Right Holding of the Coroner's Court*, p. 45. Deaths in workhouses were never made statutorily reportable to a coroner; but for the obligations laid on other institutions in this respect, see ch. 1 n. 30. For a wider argument on this theme, see the discussion of 'The Extension of Coroners' Jurisdiction' at a meeting of the sub-section on Repression of Crime of the National Association for the Promotion of Social Science: *Transactions*, 1866, pp. 228–36, 291–3.

ventable deaths,[10] and thus enable the coroner and medical officer of health to act in close alliance to educate local authorities and the public in desirable 'social arrangements for the preservation of life'.[11] This was the vision which inspired many sanitarians in the 1860s and 1870s to support the campaign for medical coroners—a campaign which reached its zenith of success in the 1880s,[12] when 46 coroners (or 14 per cent of the total) were medical men, most of whom held appointments in state medicine.[13]

The sanitarians' programme for the reduction of suicide is thus clear enough. The same cannot be said, however, either of the specific contribution made by this programme to the general movement for a healthier and safer urban environment, or of the impact on suicide rates of such environmental improvements as were achieved. Take, for example, the part of their programme which called for attention to occupational hygiene and outdoor exercise. When Farr found that the death registers showed that suicide was frequent among artisans, he at once drew the moral. 'The workshops of all artisans admit of immense improvements in ventilation', he pointed out in 1841. 'Cleanliness is greatly neglected. Neither the men nor all the masters

[10] Thomas Wakley, the fugleman of the movement for medical coroners, as well as a great populist, announced that he would regularly publish tabulated information gleaned from his suicide inquests, so that the community could discover 'what are the physical conditions which lead to this catastrophe': *The Lancet*, 1855, i. 47–8, 13 Jan.

[11] Edwin Lankester, 'On Some Points of Relation between the Office of Coroner and that of Medical Officer of Health', paper given on 16 May 1863 to the Association of Medical Officers of Health, reported in *The Lancet*, 1863, i. 608, 30 May. Lankester himself tried to practice these ideas. (On these reforming conceptions of the coroner's role, see also ch. 1, pp. 24–5).

[12] William Hardwicke, Lankester's deputy and then successor as coroner for central Middlesex, recommended to the parliamentary committee of the British Medical Association in 1879 that the projected Coroners' Reform Bill should declare the new degree in state medicine offered by Dublin, Edinburgh, and Cambridge a proper qualification for appointment as coroner: *On the Office and Duties of Coroners*, p. 3. Hardwicke and his successor, G. P. D. Thomas, as well as Lankester, combined the posts of coroner and medical officer of health.

[13] They were medical officers of health, poor law medical officers, public vaccinators, certifying factory surgeons, and the like: see the *Law List* and *Medical Directory*. Mid-Victorian coroners' elections, and especially those held in Middlesex, were often used to publicize the case for medically qualified coroners. Not all sanitarians, however, took a rosy view of the potentialities of the office (one notable early dissenter was H. W. Rumsey: see his *Essays and Papers*, p. 167); and from the 1880s medical opinion was moving away from the doctrine that coroners ought to be medically qualified: see e.g. T. W. Grimshaw, 'The State in its Relation to the Medical Profession', *British Medical Jnl.*, 1887, i. 192, 29 Jan. By 1912 the number of medically qualified coroners had declined to 43, and by 1958 to 38: Thurston, *Coroner's Practice*, p. 10.

appear to be aware that the respiration of pure air is indispensable; that the body requires as much especial care as the tools, instruments and machines.'[14] Yet not until after the passing of the Workshops Regulation Act in 1867 was there any question of introducing controls in small workshops; and it is highly unlikely that awareness of the occupational incidence of suicide ever had much to do with the extention of industrial health and safety measures.[15] In any case, it will be remembered, it was such occupations as inn-keeping and hotel work, medicine, pharmacy, the Army, and the law which had the highest suicide rates of all,[16] and occupations like these were quite outside the scope of industrial legislation. Then again, in 1841 Farr had recommended as a means of reducing urban suicide the provision of 'facilities in towns for athletic exercises and simple games out of doors, which, while they bring the muscles into play, unbend, excite, and exhilarate the mind'.[17] For entirely general reasons, however, public health enthusiasts from the early 1830s supported exercise grounds;[18] and in any case these were rarely provided until the very end of the century. True, on Good Friday 1848 a 'Government Gymnasium' was opened on Primrose Hill, thanks to that leading official sanitarian, Lord Morpeth, then Chief Commissioner of Woods and Forests; and this was exactly what Farr had recommended, providing as it did simple gymnastic apparatus in an open space much frequented by north London's many artisans. This open air gymnasium, however, long remained exceptional.[19] Instead, mid-Victorian notables bestowed upon their fellow townsfolk neat parks where sports were often prohibited; and opportunities for organized outdoor exercise remained

---

[14] *Registrar-General's 3rd AR*, Appendix, p. 82.

[15] The standard late nineteenth century treatise, J. T. Arlidge, *The Hygiene, Diseases and Mortality of Occupations* (1892), is silent on the question of suicide.

[16] See ch. 3, Table 4.

[17] *Registrar-General's 3rd AR*, Appendix, p. 82.

[18] Notably R. A. Slaney, MP (1792–1862: *DNB*) who chaired the Select Committee on Public Walks. In supporting gymnastic exercises and outdoor activities for adults, the sanitarians were once more responding to continental developments. On British adaptations of German gymnastics, see McIntosh, *Physical Education in England since 1800*, pp. 81–2.

[19] It is shown in the *Illustrated London News*, 29 Apr. 1848, p. 283. (The spot is still used today in essentially the same way.) In 1867 Hardwicke, as medical officer of health for Paddington, reported that it was 'frequented by large numbers of young men': 'In What Form and to What Extent is it Desirable that the Public should Provide Means for the Recreation of the Working Classes?', *Transactions of the National Association for the Promotion of Social Science*, 1867, p. 473. In 1866 Liverpool acquired a public gymnasium, but this was a private benefaction: ibid., pp. 473, 556.

scarce enough to serve as the bait which attracted skilled workers, clerks, and shop assistants to the Volunteer corps, YMCA, and (from the later 1870s) working men's clubs, as well as to the many clubs run by Church missions and settlements. In Bristol, for example, the local authority did not provide sports grounds until 1905.[20] In short, it is difficult to believe that a desire to lessen suicide figured at all frequently among the many motives which lay behind Victorian efforts to encourage 'rational exercise' among the people, and quite impossible to surmise how many sedentary workers may have been saved from suicide by better health and spirits brought about by the improved facilities for outdoor exercise which did become increasingly available during the last thirty or forty years of the nineteenth century.

Even more uncertain is the impact of the sanitarians' emphasis upon mental and moral hygiene as an indispensable element in the total health which would reduce suicidal tendencies. Undoubtedly many early Victorians who worked for 'the improvement of mankind' shared Farr's belief that 'the educated classes' could best be preserved from suicide by being taught the importance of 'the regulation of the mind'. The power of the will was after all an article of faith in the 1840s, 1850s, and 1860s to many who had hardly heard of Conolly and the 'moral management' of mental derangement; and injunctions to be alert to control 'morbid sensations' (including thoughts of suicide) came from many quarters.[21] Thus for example the first medical officer of health for St George's Hanover Square, C. J. B. Aldis, followed his lecture to the Literary and Scientific Institute in Pimlico in 1860 on 'How to Ward Off Bodily Sufferings by Sanitary Improvement' with

---

[20] Meller, *Leisure and the Changing City, 1870–1914*, pp. 112, 116, 155, 171, 228; Bailey, *Leisure and Class in Victorian England*, pp. 82, 121, 129–32, 137–8; Cunningham, *The Volunteer Force*, p. 113. The Parks and Playgrounds movement of the late 1870s and 1880s is a sign that public provision for outdoor exercise for the urban masses was still comparatively rare, despite the calls for government gymnasia in the 1860s which came not only from the sanitarians but also from some of the newly vocal militarists and those alarmed by that other novelty of the time, the alleged degeneration of the human race.

[21] Some introduction to this strong mid-nineteenth century emphasis upon the part the will could play in controlling mental disorders is offered in Skultans, *Madness and Morals*, pp. 157–79, and its links with the teaching of eighteenth-century moralists are well indicated in Donnelly, *Managing the Mind*, pp. 127–8. A much-admired exposition of this theme was J. Barlow's lecture to the Royal Institution, *On Man's Power over Himself to Prevent or Control Insanity* (1843). Phrenologists (then at the peak of their influence) always maintained that mental health was the result of daily exercise of all the mental organs, and that slothfulness and over-indulgence were at the root of much insanity: Cooter, 'Phrenology and British Alienists, *c.* 1825–1845', p. 138.

another on 'The Power of Individuals to Prevent Melancholy in Themselves'. He advised that anybody who was afflicted with 'such moroseness as to suggest ideas of injury to themselves' should 'at once endeavour to make a strong effort of the will, in order to nip the premonitory symptoms in the bud'; while everyone should avoid habits likely to be injurious to the nervous system, particularly drinking, smoking, and 'ungoverned passions'.[22] A few months earlier Harriet Martineau had insisted in her column in *Once a Week* that suicide was perfectly preventable, if people would only have the common sense to avoid drink and other excesses and generally give a 'rational, honest, cheerful attention to the health of the head';[23] while blander medico-religious advice came from that successful family writer, the Baptist physician George Moore, to 'rest in God's love', 'associate with calm and loving minds', and turn to prayer.[24] Given indoctrination so pervasive, it would be wrong to dismiss out of hand the possibility that some were indeed inspired to struggle towards self-control and endurance.

On the other hand, the reformers' fond hope that the press might help by giving up suicide reporting remained no more than that. It was well known that one suicide at a particular spot or by a particular method, if widely reported, could trigger off many others; so much so that suicides from the Monument, the Duke of York's Column, and the new Clifton Suspension Bridge were cited by the eminent sanitarian Sir Benjamin Richardson in the 1860s as examples of death by 'emotional contagion'.[25] To such brisk persons as Harriet Martineau or C. J. B. Aldis, as to Alderman Peter Laurie a generation before, imitative outbreaks could easily be stopped by ridicule, punishment, or the erection of physical barriers;[26] but epidemiologists influenced by the French approach to suicide believed that appropriate education and voluntary self-censorship by the press would do more than any-

---

[22] Aldis (1808–72: *DNB*), *The Power of Individuals to Prevent Melancholy in Themselves*, pp. 13, 16–18.

[23] Martineau (1802–76: *DNB*), 'Self-Murder', *Once a Week*, 17 Dec. 1859, p. 510.

[24] Moore (1803–80: *DNB*), *The Power of the Soul over the Body*, pp. 350–2. According to Moore, this work was 'much plagiarised': ibid., p. viii; and another of his medico-religious works, *The Use of the Body in Relation to the Mind* (1846) was advertised by his publisher as 'a favourite with families'.

[25] Richardson (1828–96: *DNB*), *Diseases of Modern Life*, p. 473. (This book, although published in 1876, reprinted essays published 11 years earlier. Clifton Suspension Bridge over the Avon gorge was used for suicide even before it was opened in 1867).

[26] Martineau, 'Self-Murder', p. 512; Aldis, *The Power of Individuals to Prevent Melancholy in Themselves*, pp. 14–15. For Laurie's views, see ch. 8, p. 291.

thing else to check not only such outbreaks but also more deep-seated suicidal tendencies.[27] That expert epidemiologist, J. Netten Radcliffe, whose investigations of suicide were so outstanding for their thoroughness, concluded in 1859 that 'the differential element in the etiology of suicide' was always 'a peculiar vicious or morbid tone of thought'; and he never changed his opinion. For Radcliffe and those who thought like him, it was important not only to inculcate self-control through sound moral and religious instruction, but to influence poets, novelists, and painters to portray suicide with unprepossessing realism, and above all to persuade the press, 'the greatest teacher of them all', not only to restrict publication of details about suicide cases, but to 'declare a war to the knife … against all maudlin sentiment' on the subject.[28] Occasionally a newspaper did do this, although probably rather as a stunt;[29] and occasionally the details of some bizarre method of suicide might be suppressed at a coroner's request;[30] but by and large the treatment of suicide by all the media grew more sentimental and sensational rather than less. Restrictions like those imposed on the reporting of divorce cases, for example, were never introduced on the reporting of suicide; and by the end of the century the pseudo-scientific fatalism about the incidence of suicide which both Radcliffe and Farr had been so anxious to discredit in the 1860s was being given wide publicity in the popular press.[31] Altogether, if the increasingly slack 'tone' of the media disturbed Radcliffe in the early 1860s, fifty years later he would surely have lamented that it had ceased altogether to be a restraint upon suicide.

At the moment of Radcliffe's death in 1884, however, a quite different aspect of the contemporary mental environment was being singled out by those concerned with both public health and the reduction of suicide: 'over-pressure' in the new public elementary schools. That stress and suicide were connected was a very hoary

---

[27] Cf. Brouc, 'Considérations sur les suicides de notre époque', p. 261.

[28] Radcliffe, 'English Suicide-Fields, and the Restraint of Suicide', p. 710. On Radcliffe's warnings on the impact of reading matter, see also ch. 7 n. 30.

[29] In July and Aug. 1860 the *Daily Telegraph* gave highly coloured warnings to its readers against misplaced sympathy for fraudulent or trivial suicide attempts: 6 July, p. 4, 31 Aug., p. 4, 1860.

[30] This happened in Manchester in 1908 with regard to the then novel method of suicide by gas poisoning: *The Lancet*, 1908, ii. 1041, 3 Oct. (It may have been particularly novel in Manchester, where the penetration of gas to working-class homes was far slower than in most cities: Daunton, *House and Home in the Victorian City*, p. 240, Table 10-1.)

[31] See e.g. Brand, 'Is Suicide a Sign of Civilization?'

notion indeed,[32] and 'over-pressure' in general was a stock explanation of suicide among Victorian critics of 'modern living'. In the struggles over the Education Department's system of payment by examination results and the introduction of penny school dinners for under-nourished children, however, melodramatic links were discerned—and denied—between a (largely imaginary) increase in child suicide and 'brain-forcing' in public elementary schools, with much play being made with Dr J. Crichton-Browne's opinion that recent cases of child suicide demonstrated the current need to guard against the tendency of education 'to overthrow mental equilibrium'.[33] Yet it would be foolish to suppose that either the ending of payment by results or the beginning of penny school dinners owed much to alarm over suicide among school children; and certainly quite impossible to show that either of these contributed anything to the reduction of juvenile suicide rates. Here, as elsewhere, the practical effects of the sanitarians' efforts to create an environment which fostered healthy bodies in healthy minds and so nipped suicidal propensities in the bud, must remain an open question.

Fortunately some appraisal is possible of the other side of their policy—the creation of a deterrent environment, in which those in the mood for suicide would find it hard to accomplish and no one would have the idea suggested to them by the sight of a tempting means of self-destruction. Many people always found this goal unrealistic, for it was standard wisdom that if someone found they could not commit suicide in one way, they would do it in another. This, however, was precisely what the environmentalists denied. Many deaths by suicide, they claimed, were the result of the conjuncture of a mood and an opportunity; indeed, sometimes the mood was suggested by the sight

[32] See Rosen, *Madness in Society*, pp. 172–94. What was new in the early 1880s was the connection made between stress and the education given to working-class children in public elementary schools. The idea that prolonged study led to insanity, and hence to suicide, had been in circulation since at least the seventeenth century. 'Education and the nervous system' was a well-established topic of Victorian family handbooks, and dire warnings against 'forcing' were common: see for example Spencer's much-reprinted *Education: Intellectual, Moral and Physical*, pp. 174–88. Indeed, it was J. Crichton-Browne's chapter on precisely this subject for Cassell's *The Book of Health* (ed. M. Morris) in 1883 which was believed to have led to his being asked by the Education Department to report on the alleged over-pressure in public elementary schools: Leyland, ed., *Contemporary Medical Men*, ii. 32.

[33] *Hansard*, 3rd series, cclxxxii, col. 603 (26 July 1883); Sutherland, *Policy-Making in Elementary Education, 1870–1895*, pp. 245–56. For a rather different interpretation, see Robertson, 'Children, Teachers and Society: The Over-Pressure Controversy, 1880–1886'.

of an opportunity. As Farr wrote in 1861, 'In certain states the mind appears to be fascinated ... by the presence of a fatal instrument ...; and the withdrawal of the means of death suffices to save life.'[34] This was the rationale behind the environmental strategy for suicide prevention: that deaths by suicide were to some extent accidental, and could therefore be reduced by proper safety measures, like all accidents. Accident prevention had always been part of the science of 'medical police'; and in the early Victorian years, when domestic and industrial accidents were increasing sharply,[35] accident prevention won ready support from many kinds of people zealous for improvement. Thus many safety measures came to be adopted; and every type of safety measure might save the lives of some who had intended to die, as well as of very many more who had not.

The watchman on patrol at the place of danger is surely the oldest safety measure of all. From the late eighteenth century, boatmen were employed by the Royal Humane Society to prevent those who seemed to intend suicide from going into the Serpentine, and rescue those who attempted to drown themselves.[36] In the 1830s, however, the Society's Committee attracted some mockery for its apathy; and in the early 1860s, although it had set up 260 rescue stations with poles and rope drags for use in accidents or attempted suicide, it was clinging to out-of-date resuscitation techniques.[37] In 1860 the Society claimed to have rescued 27 people who had attempted suicide; but in 1880 the number had dropped to only 21.[38] Still, 'honorary and pecuniary' rewards continued to be offered for efforts at rescue (indeed, in Liverpool in 1852 one would-be suicide thought it prudent to wait until it grew

[34] *Registrar-General's 26th AR*, p. 193. Farr had made the same point in 1841: *Registrar-General's 3rd AR*, Appendix, p. 88, and repeated it in 1874 in the discussion following Millar's paper to the Statistical Society: 'Statistics of Deaths by Suicide among H. M.'s British Troops', p. 191. Farr's successor William Ogle also believed that it was the sight of an accessible instrument of destruction while in the mood which was fatal: 'Suicide in England and Wales', p. 110.

[35] Only in the nineteenth century did these account for the majority of violent deaths: Hair, 'Deaths from Violence in Britain', pp. 19, 21.

[36] The Society had erected a 'Model Receiving House' for the rescued in 1834 in Hyde Park (where it still stands): see the illustration and description in Royal Humane Society, *AR 1861*, p. 30. George III is said to have first had the idea of a receiving house here, and to have given the land for it: ibid., *AR 1974*, p. 12.

[37] 'Prospectus of a New Joint Stock Suicide Company', *Bentley's Miscellany*, vi (1839), p. 541. For its case against the new 'Ready Method' of artificial respiration (on which see ch. 4 n. 69), see Royal Humane Society, *AR 1861*, Appendix, pp. 31–8.

[38] Ibid., p. 19; Return of Rescues and Attempted Rescues by the Royal Humane Society, PP 1882 (34) LII, p. 61.

dark before going down to the docks, so as to evade the professional rescuers who hung around there);[39] and towards the end of the century amateur rescuers multiplied, thanks to the campaign to teach swimming and life saving and the founding in 1891 of the Life Saving Society, whose reports soon included items about would-be suicides whose lives had been saved by passers-by trained in the Society's techniques.[40]

Far more significant than any of this, however, was the regular patrolling undertaken by the new police. Their *raison d'être* was the prevention of public disorder, crimes, and accidents; and the prevention of suicide ranked as all three. Constables were early instructed to watch for suspicious behaviour on their beat; and in 1842, for example, the Liverpool police (who, it may be remembered, like the Metropolitan Police, at first reported suicides and attempted suicides as 'accidents'), claimed to have prevented eight suicides while patrolling the streets. (They had seen only five prevented by other people.)[41] Notorious suicide spots were regularly patrolled, so far as other duties allowed. Special vigilance was always expected around the many new bridges and deep and dangerous waterways constructed in the first half of the nineteenth century in many populous towns and cities, and above all in London.[42] Blackfriars Bridge in particular was watched by the new City Police, as it had been by their predecessors.[43] Toll-keepers on the Thames bridges were also expected to be on the alert. True, the satirical claimed that they were all deaf and paid no attention;[44] but in 1853 Charles Dickens's 'Waterloo' (*alias* the toll-keeper on Waterloo Bridge) ran after those whom he suspected of intending to jump and held them back, or if necessary raised the

[39] Read and Jebson, *A Voice in the City*, pp. 31–2. For the rewards offered under its Rules, see Royal Humane Society, *AR 1861*, p. 88. The sum of £179. 3s. 4d. was expended on honorary and pecuniary rewards in the year ending 31 Dec. 1860: ibid, p. 27.

[40] Such a rescue by two members of the Manchester City Police Life Saving Team was reported, for example, in Life Saving Society, *AR of the Central Executive Committee, 1896–97*, p. 25. The Education Department's Code of 1890 allowed swimming to count for attendance purposes, and thereafter swimming and life saving were taught in progressive Board schools: Smith, *Stretching their Bodies*, p. 99.

[41] *Porter's Tables, 1842*, p. 165; and see ch. 8, nn. 74, 79.

[42] For a diagram of London's new waterways, see Denney, *London's Waterways*, p. 13.

[43] See ch. 8, nn. 70 and 79. In 1844 'a police constable was constantly on duty to prevent the numerous attempts that were being made' from Blackfriars Bridge: *The Times*, 13 Nov. 1844, p. 7, col. f.

[44] 'Prospectus of a New Joint Stock Suicide Company', *Bentley's Miscellany*, vi (1839), p. 541.

alarm so that the watermen put off to rescue them.[45] All this was far surpassed, however, by the surveillance undertaken by the Metropolitan Police. Every year the Thames Division (which patrolled the river in galleys, and from 1885 in two steam-launches as well), reported that it had rescued some would-be suicides: six in 1874, eight in 1876 and as many as eighteen in 1885 (when nine more were reported to have been rescued by private persons).[46] By 1911 what was needed (according to Waldo, the leading sanitarian at that time among the metropolitan coroners) was not more rescuers but a chain of places along the Thames where the rescued could be given proper first aid.[47] Long before this, however, many suicides had been attracted away from the Thames and Serpentine to the new commercial docks and canals,[48] and these were often in the middle of poor and densely populated areas which were closely policed. From 1830, when the swivel bridge linking London Dock's New Eastern Basin with Shadwell New Basin was built, the police were constantly rescuing the local prostitutes from the deep water below—water soon dubbed 'Mr Baker's Trap', because of the many bodies, and therefore fees, it brought to the local coroner, William Baker.[49] From 1879 four constables were 'especially employed' in preventing suicides at the swing bridges of the London Docks, and in 1874, for example, prevented eleven persons, all drunk, from jumping into the water;[50] while in 1849 a 'Magdalene' told Mayhew how she had gone to the Regent's Canal to drown herself, but 'the policeman watched me and asked me what I was doing. He thought I looked suspicious, and drove me from the park. That saved my life.'[51]

---

[45] Dickens, 'Down with the Tide' (reprinted from *Household Words*, 5 Feb. 1853), *The Uncommercial Traveller*, pp. 529–30.

[46] *Metropolitan Police Commissioner's AR, 1874*, Appendix p. 96; *1876*, Appendix, p. 43; *1885*, Appendix, pp. 49–50.

[47] *Daily Express*, 12 July 1911, p. 1.

[48] In April 1837 the Medical Committee of the London Statistical Society correctly predicted that the canal building then going on would attract suicides away from Westminster to Regent's Park and Stepney: 'Suicides in Westminster from 1812 to 1836', *Jnl. [Roy.] Stat. Soc.*, i (1838), p. 110.

[49] Described by Dickens in 'Wapping Workhouse', *All the Year Round*, 18 Feb. 1860 (reprinted in *The Uncommercial Traveller*, p. 19), it long had a certain notoriety: see Horsley, *Jottings from Jail*, p. 256, and Williams, *Leaves of a Life*, i. 170. 15 women drowned themselves in 'Mr Baker's Trap' in Old Gravel Lane in the first 4 years after the bridge was built: *The Times*, 15 Oct. 1834, p. 4, col. b.

[50] *Metropolitan Police Commissioner's AR, 1874*, Appendix, p. 90.

[51] Mayhew, *The 'Morning Chronicle' Survey of Labour and the Poor*, i. 167, Letter VIII, 13 Nov. 1849.

Police surveillance regularly extended to the parks and the streets as well as the waterways. The constable who in 1907 saw a woman lying against a tree in Tottenham High Road, asked her what was the matter, heard she had taken poison, and hurried her off to the station close by for an emetic, was as typical as his predecessor over fifty years before who in 1862 heard the screams of a woman who had jumped into the Grand Junction Canal in Kensal Green, ran for assistance, and got her out.[52] Between 1859 and 1863 forty-one people, or one in five of all those known to the Metropolitan Police to have been 'saved' from suicide, indoors and out, were saved by the police themselves;[53] and sampling of the metropolitan magistrates' court records suggests that this was probably a fairly typical proportion. Nor is there anything surprising about this. The conception of 'preventive police' pioneered in the metropolis after 1829 had much in common with the conception of public health and orderly well-being which inspired the social reformers behind the early public health movement; and in practice the ethos, organization, and methods of the new police were all well adapted to the task of suicide prevention, encouraging as they did local knowledge, personal contact, and round-the-clock watchfulness, and the provision of (more or less friendly) advice, persuasion, and restraint by a local man on the beat who knew his own patch. Certainly the 'bobby' style of policing was far better suited to suicide prevention work than the 'cops' style could ever be.[54] Its converse, however, was that constables were on occasion interfering and impertinent busybodies, and were nearly always blatant respecters of persons in deciding whose behaviour was suspicious and whose was not. Certainly they were in no way exempt from the frailties which vitiate every kind of human patrol: slow-wittedness, negligence, and absence from the scene at the vital moment.

For these and other reasons, the preferred long-term safeguard where the most notorious suicide spots were concerned was never a

---

[52] Both these women were subsequently sent for trial at Middlesex quarter sessions (case of Mary Anne Tillman, committed for trial 2 Dec., GLRO, MJ/CP/B/9 and MJ/SPE/Dec. 1862; case of Nellie Gordon tried 13 Apr. 1907, MJ/CP/B/43 and MJ/SPE/Apr. 1907. By the 1900s, however, it was increasingly unlikely that a passing policeman would not be able to dive in himself to rescue someone at risk of drowning, for swimming and life-saving were then encouraged in many city forces: cf. Nott-Bower, *Fifty-Two Years a Policeman*, p. 188; also n. 40.

[53] *Miscellaneous Statistics of the UK*, Parts IV, V, and VI, Crime &c: Metropolitan Police, Table 6.

[54] For a comparison of these two styles of policing in the mid-nineteenth century, see Miller, *Cops and Bobbies, passim*.

patrol, but a fixed structure. Unfortunately, fixed structures—railings, fences, parapets, locked gates, safety nets—cost money; and public authorities, ratepayers, and property owners varied greatly in their readiness to foot such bills. This was certainly so in the metropolitan area. The most famous of all nineteenth-century English anti-suicide structures, the iron cage erected to enclose the viewing gallery at the top of the Monument in the City (see Fig. 13) was decided upon by the City Lands Committee only three days after the last fatal jump in 1842, and before public pressure in the press had gathered strength.[55] The City authorities, though, were always *sui generis*. More typical was the untidy situation which arose over Highgate Archway, a viaduct which runs across the Great North Road 60 feet below, and forms part of the boundary between two local authorities. In 1885 it began to acquire a 'sinister reputation' after 'four suicides in as many months', and the local coroner, G. P. D. Thomas, and his deputy, W. W. Westcott (both of whom were medical coroners who had specialized in the field of public health and safety) decided that the parapet must be made unclimbable. They saw to it that the jury added an appropriate rider, and made representations to both local authorities.[56] Hornsey Local Board promptly erected a palisade on the north side; but Islington Vestry dragged its feet and the south side for a time remained unprotected, except when a policeman could be spared to guard it.[57] Still, big progressive local authorities increasingly took it for granted that anti-suicide precautions should be incorporated in their constructions; and when the new London County Council (which had taken over responsibility for Highgate Archway) came to rebuild it in 1897, considerations of safety and aesthetics were combined in the specification of a high parapet topped by highly ornamental wrought-iron

[55] *The Times*, 23 Aug., p. 6, col. b, 24 Aug., p. 6, col. f, 1842. The cage was painted white to make it unobtrusive in the distance, ibid., 5 Nov. 1842, p. 2, col. f. The contraption attracted some mockery from continental visitors, as proof that the English themselves thought they were a suicide prone race. There were 6 well-publicized leaps from the viewing gallery in the period 1788–1842: Welch, *History of the Monument*, p. 54.

[56] Westcott, *Suicide*, p. 131. Thomas knew his way around local politics. He was medical officer of health for Willesden, had been for many years chairman of the Sanitary Committee of Paddington Vestry, and stood as the Conservative candidate for West Islington in the General Election of November 1885: Leyland, ed., *Contemporary Medical Men*, ii. 163–8.

[57] *Metropolitan Police Commissioner's AR, 1885*, Appendix, p. 49. For sketches of the tempting drop, old balustrade, and new railings, see *Pall Mall Gazette*, 10 Aug. 1885, p. 4, and *Graphic*, 10 Apr. 1886, p. 392.

Fig. 13 The anti-suicide cage over the viewing gallery of the Monument, as shown in *The Graphic*, 12 Dec. 1891

grilles and revolving *chevaux de frise* (still relied upon to prevent suicide there today).[58] The low bridge over the Regent's Canal near the Zoo, however, remained 'a temptation to suicide', despite the call for 'proper measures for public safety' made by Edwin Lankester and his jurymen in December 1862, immediately after a strong letter to *The Times* from Dr James Clark, who lived near by in St Mark's Square and was continually called out to attend those who had jumped into the canal. 'My own profession', he protested,

have been straining every nerve to remove the causes of disease and premature death by the adoption of proper sanitary and preventive measures. Surely it is equally the duty of our public authorities to make such a dangerous bridge and canal as secure as possible, and thus lessen the facilities for crime afforded to that increasing class of individuals whose morbid minds tempt them to seek relief for the real or imaginary ills of life by self-destruction?[59]

The high parapet which Clark wanted never materialized, however; drags, lifebuoys, and locked gateways to the towing path had to suffice.

Commercial companies were always apt to be even more difficult than local authorities to prod into action, whether by pressure from local coroners and their juries, local Members of Parliament, or the press; and it was especially unfortunate that the canals were so difficult to protect, since in the metropolitan area it was in the Regent's Canal, not the River Lea or Thames, that the proportion of suicidal drownings was highest.[60] Women in particular chose the canal: 'I went there because I thought I was more sure of death', explained one woman to Mayhew.[61] From 1878 Members secured parliamentary Returns which demonstrated how dangerous were the country's waters, and others which singled out the Thames, the Lea, and the Regent's Canal.[62] At

[58] London County Council, *An Account of the Bridges, Tunnels and Ferry belonging to the London County Council*, p. 13.

[59] *The Times*, 10 Dec. 1862, p. 10, col. b; inquest on Naomi Bailey, reported in *St Pancras News*, 20 Dec. 1862. Like Highgate Archway, this bridge marked the boundary between two local authorities (St Marylebone and St Pancras).

[60] The absolute number of suicides, however, was higher in the Thames, where 112 suicidal drownings were recorded in 1877–81; PP 1882 (257) LIV, pp. 2–3; PP 1882 (192) LII, pp. 2–3.

[61] Mayhew, *The 'Morning Chronicle' Survey of Labour and the Poor*, i. 167. In 1880 29 per cent of all registered female suicidal deaths by drowning in the UK were in canals, but only 18 per cent of male: PP 1882 (34) LII, pp. 56–7.

[62] These Returns showed that a verdict of suicide was returned on 49 of the 226 bodies taken from this canal in 1877–81 and an open verdict on another 115 bodies: PP 1882 (257) LIV, pp. 2–3. It is thus hardly surprising that in the Eastern Division of Middlesex, 52 per cent of all the suicidal drownings recorded by the coroner were in canals: PP 1882 (34) LII, pp. 14–15.

last, after a conference of vestries in 1896, the Members for the places most at risk—Poplar, Rotherhithe, Hoxton, Bethnal Green, and Bow—secured a private member's bill giving local authorities power to require fencing where a canal abutted the public highway; but this was not until 1898, and the Act applied only within the county of London.[63]

The one sphere where this kind of barrier to suicide was installed with such thoroughness as to be dramatically successful was in the country's prisons. As early as the 1850s, when hard labour and strict separation were attracting much denunciation as causes of insanity and suicide, some precautions began to be taken.[64] Waterpipes were boxed in, top galleries wired over, or netting hung across landings. In local prisons, however (although not in convict prisons or military prisons), suicide was sufficiently frequent in the 1870s for a major enquiry to be launched by the Home Office when it took them over in 1877.[65] As a result every possible physical obstacle to suicide was installed. 'We have taken all the precautions that suggest themselves', said the Medical Inspector of Prisons, R. M. Gover, in 1894;[66] and so effective were these, that even that dedicated critic of the prison regime of the day, W. D. Morrison, was obliged to admit that prison suicide had become virtually impossible to accomplish, and to claim that it had been perforce transmuted into insanity.[67] Physical barriers could certainly achieve an impressive degree of success in preventing suicide within the environment of a closed institution, or at a specific suicide spot. Yet to install such structures really extensively could never be practicable; and in any case the method of suicide which was growing most quickly in popularity in this period—poison—was one against which such barriers could offer no protection.[68]

---

[63] *Hansard*, 4th series, lix, cols. 18–20; 61 & 62 Vict., c. 16. In 1897, a similar Bill had been withdrawn: PP 1897 I, Bill no. 181.

[64] Charles Reade joined in this denunciation in 1856: see ch. 6 n. 38; and in the early 1860s Frederick Robinson alluded to the wiring over of the galleries of Brixton prison in one of his chatty tales: 'A Prison Matron' [pseud.], *Female Life in Prison*, ii. 151. For a photograph showing the safety-nets which came to be used in all English prisons, see Hobhouse and Brockway, *English Prisons To-day*, p. 321.

[65] *Prison Commissioners' AR, 1878–79*, Part I, pp. 17, 84–5; *1879-80*, Part I, pp. 18, 54–62.

[66] PP 1895 [C. 7702] LVI, p. 45, Q. 1372. Gover was a member of the Epidemiological Society, it may be noted.

[67] Ibid., p. 104, Qs. 2999 and 3009.

[68] Between 1858 and 1910 the proportion of suicides ascribed to poison almost doubled. In 1901–10 14.2 per cent of male and 27.7 per cent of female suicides were by means of poisons and poisonous vapours: *Registrar-General's 75th AR, Supplement*,

What was clearly needed in this situation was that third classic technique for promoting public safety: legal restrictions upon access to the sources of danger. As early as 1841 Farr had urged that suicidal deaths by poison could be reduced if poisons used for medicinal purposes were made obtainable only by medical prescription, and those used 'in the arts and manufactures' only against a certificate from the master.[69] The restrictions introduced before the First World War never approached such stringency.[70] Too many vested interests were involved for that; and moreover the primary object was always to prevent accidents or homicide, not suicide. 'You cannot legislate against suicide', was the perennial opinion, for 'if a person cannot have recourse to one mode of destroying his life, he will to another.'[71] Many medical men and sanitarians nevertheless remained convinced that to impose restrictions on the sale of certain poisons was the way to limit their misuse, even for purposes of suicide.[72] In this respect the pioneering Arsenic Act of 1851 was far less important than the Sale of Poisons and Pharmacy Act of 1868. This established a Schedule of poisons, which all had to be clearly and fully labelled and sold only by registered pharmacists. Those listed in Part I of the Schedule could be sold only to someone known by or introduced to the pharmacist, and only after the completion of an entry in his Poisons Register which recorded the date of the sale, the name and address of the purchaser and his sponsor, quantity sold, and purpose for which it was required.[73] These restrictions remained in force throughout the next forty years. Not until 1908 did an 'agitation for free trade in poisons ... got up by manufacturers, shopkeepers and dealers'[74] to satisfy the need of the farming community to buy poisons more easily, finally secure legislation which ended the pharmacists' monopoly over the sale of certain

Part III, p. xcv, Table XLV; whereas in the period 1858–83, the corresponding figures were only 7.9 and 14.5 per cent respectively: Ogle, 'Suicides in England and Wales', p. 118, Table IX.

[69] *Registrar-General's 3rd AR*, Appendix, p. 88.

[70] The restrictions imposed on narcotics are discussed in Berridge and Rawson, 'Opiate Use and Legislative Control', and in Berridge and Edwards, *Opium and the People*, Part III; see also Parssinen, *Secret Passions, Secret Remedies*, pp. 68–77.

[71] PP 1857 (sess. 2) (294) XII, p. 43, Q. 311, p. 68, Q. 568, p. 85, Q. 726; PP 1903 [Cd. 1443] XXXIII, p. 23, Q. 746, p. 38, Q. 1161, p. 41, Q. 1277, p. 67, Q. 2194, p. 82, Q. 2754.

[72] PP 1857 (sess. 2) (294) XII, p. 68, Q. 569, p. 89, Q. 751; Westcott (who held the qualifications of MB and DPH and was coroner for North-East London), *On Suicide*, p. 9.

[73] 31 & 32 Vict., c. 121, s. 17.

[74] T. H. W. Idris, MP, in cross-examination, PP 1908 (150) IX, p. 7, Qs. 92–4.

poisons in common use—two of them, as it happened, for suicide.[75] Neither before nor after 1908, however, were the statutory restrictions likely to be of major importance in preventing suicide, as opposed to accidental death or homicide. Indeed, to see a 'Poison' label on some bottle bought for a legitimate purpose long ago might actually suggest the idea of suicide to someone 'in the mood'—as Lankester said himself at one of his inquests, and as F. C. Calvert, the distinguished founder of Calvert & Co., always maintained.[76] In any case there were plenty of poisons to be had which were not scheduled. Even a Part I poison could easily be bought from a pharmacist by anyone with a plausible tongue and a calm manner,[77] and in the East End at any rate penny-worths of oxalic acid could readily (though illegally) be got in an ironmonger's.[78] On the other hand, scheduling a poison did apparently have a temporary deterrent effect, for the use of a popular poison for suicide dropped after it had first been scheduled: this happened with both laudanum and carbolic acid immediately after they had been placed in Part II of the Schedule, in 1868 and 1900 respectively, and again with laudanum after it had been placed in Part I in 1908.[79] Keen

[75] 8 Ed. 7, c. 55. The two favourite suicide poisons which could be sold by those who were not pharmacists under section 5 of the 1908 Act were hydrochloric acid and soluble salts of oxalic acid.

[76] Calvert (1819–73: *DNB*) was said to have been very reluctant to sanction putting 'Poison' labels on his firm's products: PP 1903 [Cd. 1443] XXXIII, p. 105, Q. 3342. He did believe, however, that increasing the difficulty of purchasing poison would reduce suicide by that means: PP 1857 (sess. 2) (294) XII, p. 68, Q. 569. Lankester suggested that seeing 'Poison' on a bottle of oil of almonds might have proved fatal to Constance van den Alleele (on whose case see ch. 4, p. 146): *Marylebone Mercury*, 13 Dec. 1862, p. 2.

[77] Inquest papers vividly illustrate the tales those bent on suicide told to pharmacists and their assistants, as well as the perfectly legitimate purchase of a poison subsequently used for suicide. For good examples see LRO, DDCs, Prescot Manorial Coroner, inquest on Michael Kenny, 1 Dec. 1853, deposition of Charles Webster, and Berks RO, H/JCi/3, inquest on John Bird, 10 July 1872, deposition of William Taylor.

[78] PP 1903 [Cd. 1443] XXXIII, p. 50, Q. 1501. Oxalic acid was always a working-class woman's favourite, for it was very cheap and in continual household use, for example for cleaning brass.

[79] Westcott repeatedly asserted that the great diminution in the number of deaths from carbolic acid which followed its addition to Part II of the Schedule in July 1900 demonstrated the great value of scheduling a poison: 'In my district the number of deaths [from carbolic acid] was at once halved': *On Suicide*, p. 10. Nationally, carbolic acid accounted for 12.7 per cent of female suicides in 1899, but for only 6 per cent in 1907: *Registrar-General's 62nd AR*, pp. 258–9 and *70th AR*, pp. 438–9. For the fluctuations in narcotic suicide rates, 1863–1910, see Berridge and Edwards, *Opium and the People*, Table 3 (not paginated) and for the numbers of narcotic and other suicidal poisonings, 1840–1926, see Parssinen, *Secret Passions, Secret Remedies*, Table 6, pp. 233–4. (There is an error in the heading of the third column of this Table, which should read, 'Opiate suicides as a percentage of total suicidal poisonings', not, 'of total suicides'.)

sanitarians always asserted that some people bent on suicide did indeed give up an intended purchase of poison when they found they had to go from shop to shop and answer questions and sign a Register in order to get a dose.[80] In 1900 the Coroners' Society was anxious for restrictions to be extended; and the addition of certain poisons to the Schedule in 1908 was some compensation for the relaxations introduced with regard to others, although far short of what the Society had recommended.[81]

All this, however, was much ado about little. What really patterned the choice of poisons for suicide was not the state of the law, but the role of particular poisons as tools of their trade for many people—industrial and agricultural workers, as well as (more notoriously) doctors, pharmacists, and photographers—and as an essential part of a household's routine domestic equipment.[82] As Farr and his like quite correctly emphasized, what was potentially fatal was for a man or woman in a suicidal mood to have at hand some instrument with which they were familiar in daily life, and which they knew could easily be used as a means of suicide. It is thus no surprise that in the thirty years or so before the First World War it was the handful of poisons which were then in everyday use which were also in common use for suicide, and these alone.[83] Ironically, the ready accessibility of one of the most popular suicide poisons of the 1890s and 1900s was the achievement of the sanitarians themselves. Poison had traditionally been a method preferred by women, by town dwellers, and by those

[80] This was Westcott's experience: PP 1903 [Cd. 1443] XXXIII, p. 50, Q. 1499. Coroners and magistrates, however, were apt to expect pharmacists to be more cautious (especially if their customers looked 'low and desponding') than was usually practicable: ibid., p. 50, Qs. 1506, 1525, 1527, and PP 1857 (sess. 2) (294) XII, P. 59, Q. 476. Too much was made of such episodes as that in Sheerness when an alert pharmacist gave an excited young woman who asked for arsenic some cream of tartar (labelled 'arsenic') instead: *Marylebone Mercury*, 1 Nov. 1862, p. 3.

[81] See the proposals put forward by Westcott with the authority of the Coroners' Society: PP 1903 [Cd. 1443] XXXIII, pp. 48–9, Qs. 1467–97.

[82] Of the suicides committed by pharmacists, photographers, and doctors, and their assistants, 86 per cent, 85 per cent, and 60 per cent respectively were by poison: Ogle, 'Suicides in England and Wales', p. 122, Table XII.

[83] In 1907 4 poisons—carbolic, oxalic, and hydrochloric acid and laudanum—accounted for 69 per cent of all female self-poisonings, and nearly 20 per cent of all female suicides. The same 4 poisons, plus prussic acid and cyanide of potassium, accounted for 53 per cent of all male self-poisonings: *Registrar-General's 70th AR*, pp. 438–9. In 1869–73 a wider range of poisons was used, and the four most popular poisons among women suicides accounted for only 39 per cent of female self-poisonings: *Registrar-General's 30th AR*, p. 192.

above the labouring classes; and from the 1870s onwards so successfully was the importance of disinfecting drains and sickrooms
rammed home by the public health movement,[84] that every respectable
urban household kept a supply of carbolic acid at hand,[85] in addition
to a number of other poisonous cleaning materials. The corollary of
this was that by 1899 an eighth of the women who took their own
lives did so by drinking carbolic acid.[86] The spread of the hobby of
photography among middle-class men also had its consequences, for
it made them familiar with cyanide of potassium and other poisonous
materials used in photographic developing, which was then usually
done at home. By the turn of the century, swallowing cyanide of
potassium had become quite a common male method of suicide,
although this was a poison almost never taken by women.[87] Again,
Edwardian families often made a point of keeping some laudanum in
the house, as most families keep aspirin today, for it was still regarded
as a good all-round item for the domestic medicine cupboard;[88] and

[84] In the 1890s the medical profession became divided over whether domestic use of
carbolic acid should now be discouraged. 'It would be a pity to ban such a cheap and
efficient disinfectant for drains', wrote J.R. Greenway, MD, in *The Lancet*, 1891, ii.
485, 29 Aug. In 1897, however, there was widespread criticism in Liverpool of its
continued ready sale: ibid., 1897, ii. 418, 688, 14 Aug. and 11 Sept. In Edinburgh the
Sanitary Department ceased to give out disinfectants after cases of infectious disease—
a step to which H. Littlejohn (who had been medical officer of health for Sheffield
before he became Professor of Forensic Medicine at Edinburgh) ascribed Edinburgh's
comparatively small number of suicides from disinfectant: Littlejohn, 'Medico-Legal
Notes: II. On Suicide', p. 228.

[85] As early as 1874 one daughter told Lankester at the inquest on her mother that 'we
had carbolic acid about always': GLC, Central Middlesex IR, Box 47, 18 July 1874,
inquest on Jane Lucy Martin.

[86] *Registrar-General's 62nd AR*, p. 258. In 1869–73 only 13 women were adjudged to
have committed suicide by swallowing carbolic acid, as against 16 men: *Registrar-
General's 32nd–33rd ARs*, pp. 184–5, *34th–35th ARs*, pp. 206–7, *36th AR*, pp. 208–9.
By 1887–91 these numbers had risen to as many as 138 women as against only 98 men:
PP 1893–4 (488) LXXI, p. 3.

[87] For an early example, when photography was the preserve of the well-to-do, see
the case of Samuel George Walton, ch. 4 n. 66. As time went on, reputable firms selling
photographic materials acknowledged this problem and adopted some precautions, such
as confining sales of cyanide of potassium and corrosive sublimate to professional
photographers: PP 1903 [Cd. 1443] XXXIII, p. 101, Qs. 3167a–3170a, p. 102, Q. 3201a.

[88] It was described as 'perhaps the most valuable remedy in the whole range of
medicine' in the first edition of *Black's Medical Dictionary* (1906), p. 550—a handbook
intended to be midway between a technical Dictionary of Medicine and one for the
domestic treatment of commoner ailments: see p. v. It was also still being recommended
as a domestic medicine, though with a caution, in the new edition of *Mrs Beeton's Book
of Household Management* published in the same year (see p. 1894); and according to
oral evidence collected by Berridge and Edwards 'everyone had laudanum at home', sc.
at the turn of the century: *Opium and the People*, p. 228.

in the 1900s laudanum was still a favourite suicide poison, even though it had lost its earlier dominating position.[89] Moreover, although vermin killers were less used in late-Victorian and Edwardian than in mid-Victorian urban households,[90] patent medicines and toilet preparations which contained poisons were much more widely bought;[91] while at the same time, in areas like north-east London where small workshops and artisanal occupations continued to predominate, corrosive acids were still very familiar—as familiar as the poisonous properties of sheep-dip in farming areas.[92] All these various facts of life were reflected in the use made of poisons for suicide.

Sex and generation, and still more class and occupation, inevitably affected the use of poison for suicide more than the restrictions imposed by the law,[93] for what mattered most was what familiar bottles and jars people had lying around in their drawers and cupboards and sheds at the critical moment, and this was settled by their daily habits of life

[89] In 1863–82 opiates were the most popular suicide poison among women and accounted for 17.4 per cent of female suicidal poisonings, while among men they were the second most popular suicide poison and accounted for 26 per cent of suicidal poisonings: Ogle, 'Suicides in England and Wales', p. 119, Table X. In 1907 they were the fourth most popular type of suicide poison among women, and accounted for 8.7 per cent of female suicidal poisonings; while they were the third most widely used suicide poison for men and accounted for 11.8 per cent of male suicidal poisonings: *Registrar-General's 70th AR*, pp. 438–9.

[90] In 1869–73 vermin killer was the poison most frequently used by women for suicide: *Registrar-General's 32nd–33rd ARs*, pp. 184–5, *34th–35th ARs*, 206–7, *36th AR*, pp. 208–9, and throughout the period 1863–82 it was used only slightly less often than laudanum, and accounted for 15.5 per cent of all female suicidal poisonings: Ogle, 'Suicides in England and Wales', p. 119, Table X. (Servants were very likely to have a packet of vermin killer to hand: see for an example GLC, Central Middlesex IR, Box 47, 14 Apr. 1874, inquest no. 23, Sarah Nicholls.) By the early 1900s, however, it was being used by only 1 or 2 women a year: see *Registrar-General's 70th AR*, p. 439.

[91] For an example of the use of a much-publicized patent medicine (namely, Anti-Kamnia) see ch. 5, p. 170.

[92] Westcott's lists of the poisons used for suicide in his District of North-East London in the late 1890s and early 1900s showed a preponderance of 'the violent and corrosive liquids used in the arts, and carbolic disinfectants': *On Suicide*, p. 9, and PP 1903 [Cd. 1443] XXXIII, p. 49, Qs. 1478, 1494. (These strong mineral acids were the very ones which came under sect. 5 of the 1908 Act, and were therefore subject only to labelling requirements.) For the use of sheep-dip, see ibid., p. 82, Q. 2754. Registered cases of suicide by sheep-dip were rare, however.

[93] Of the 4 favourite female suicide poisons in the 30 years from 1883 to 1913, oxalic acid had been in Part II of the Schedule since 1868; laudanum had been in Part II from 1868 and Part I from 1908; carbolic acid in Part II from 1900; and hydrochloric acid was not a scheduled poison, although under sect. 5 of the Act of 1908 it had to be labelled 'Poison', as did carbolic acid for agricultural and horticultural use and soluble salts of oxalic acid. The two favourite male suicide poisons, prussic acid and cyanide of potassium, had both been in Part I from 1868.

and work. After 1900 came a last indication that what counted was the integration of a poison into people's daily lives, with the simultaneously rapid spread of the gas cooker in Edwardian urban kitchens, and suicide by coal-gas poisoning, particularly among women. Not until the development of the pre-payment slot-meter in the 1890s did ordinary homes begin to have gas supply pipes, even for lighting; and the gas cooker—that painless, accessible, reassuringly familiar means of escape from this world—did not begin to oust the coal range until the turn of the century.[94] Thereafter, however, it never looked back; and neither did suicide by coal-gas poisoning. In 1903 this was still a rare and novel method, used by nine men and only one woman; but six years later, it accounted for 3.9 per cent of female and 3.5 per cent of male suicides, and by 1926 women were using this means of suicide more than any other. By 1928 so too were men; and it was impossible to restrict the sale of gas.[95]

What of that other means of suicide which became more popular in the generation before 1914 and might seem very easily controllable by law—firearms? In the 1860s only 6 per cent of male suicides shot themselves; but a generation later, in 1890–2, the proportion had doubled.[96] (The number of women who shot themselves was always negligible.) Moreover, although always less resorted to overall than hanging, drowning, poisoning, or the use of a knife or razor, shooting was the method most often used by young men in their late teens and early twenties, by soldiers, and by gentlemen,[97] so that the suicides accomplished by firearms could be claimed to deprive the community of human capital which it could especially ill spare. Restrictions on

---

[94] 'In 1900 the rule of the [coal] range was not seriously challenged': Ravetz, 'The Victorian Coal Kitchen', pp. 456, 458. Gas cookers spread most rapidly in London homes and most slowly in Lancashire and the West Riding: Daunton, *House and Home in the Victorian City*, p. 240, Table 10–1.

[95] *Registrar-General's Statistical Review, 1961*, Part III, p. 263, Table CXXXII. Isolated cases of suicide by coal-gas poisoning were recorded in the 1880s and 1890s (Westcott mentioned such a case as a bizarre curiosity in 1885: *Suicide*, p. 153), but 1904 was the first year in which there were more than 10. By 1909 the number had climbed to 130: *Registrar-General's 72nd AR*, pp. 470–1. The official comment offered in 1961 on the figures for suicide by domestic gases in the period 1912–60 was very much in Farr's vein: 'If suicide is the result of an impulse, as some contend, the high rates from gas poisoning may be partly due to its wide availability, and it is not possible to restrict this, as could be done in the case of solids or liquids, by restricting their sale': *Registrar-General's Statistical Review, 1961*, Part III, p. 264.

[96] *Registrar-General's 24th–31st ARs*, p. 124, *32nd–33rd ARs*, p. 122 and *53rd–55th ARs*, p. 200.

[97] Ogle, 'Suicides in England and Wales', pp. 121–2, Tables XI and XII.

the carrying of firearms, however, were peculiarly difficult to get on to the statute book. In Victorian England the universal right of Englishmen to bear arms was associated with deep-rooted feelings about the nature of English society and English liberty. Proposals to control the sale or carrying of firearms thus not only provoked cries from interested parties of 'interference with trade', just as happened with poisons, but also raised symbolic issues of class, constitutional rights, and national pride which cut deeply into the feelings of the sort of men who sat in Parliament. To some members of the legislature the control of firearms was objectionable as 'a game law bill in disguise', to others as 'a new agricultural tax', and to many more as against the national interest ('in the present disturbed state of Europe ... every ploughboy in the land should know how to pull a trigger').[98] It is thus not surprising that the restrictions imposed on the possession and sale of firearms in 1870 and 1903 were as loose and incomplete compared with those of 1920 and 1937, as were the restrictions imposed on the sale of poisons in 1868 and 1908 compared with those of 1920 and 1933.[99]

In securing the acceptance of these controls, moreover, the desire to reduce suicide played an even less significant part than it did in securing control of the sale of poisons. The avowed object of Gladstone's first Government in 1870 in requiring those who carried a gun to purchase an annual licence for 10s. from a post office was 'to check lawless habits'.[100] The proposal was unpopular with both sides of the House, and certain categories of people had to be exempted; but the issues which counted most in debate, apart from constitutional ones, were poaching, the protection of birds from schoolboys, and checking Irish violence in Britain; reducing accidents was little mentioned, and reducing suicide not at all. In 1893, when Asquith as Home Secretary in Gladstone's last Government brought in another and much more rigorous proposal for firearms control, things were different. This time the target was pistols and revolvers alone, and strict control was proposed over the sale and purchase as well as the carrying of these weapons;[101] and the bill was specifically presented as a safety measure

[98] *Hansard*, 3rd series, cci, cols. 1680–3, ccii, cols. 852–6, and cciii, cols. 763–70, debates of 30 May, 23 June, and 22 July 1870 on the Gun Licences Bill.

[99] The inter-war restrictions referred to are the Firearms Acts of 1920 and 1937, and the Dangerous Drugs Act, 1920, and Pharmacy and Poisons Act, 1933.

[100] *Hansard*, 3rd series, cciii, col. 768, 22 July 1870.

[101] Bill to Regulate the Sale and Use of Pistols, PP 1893–4 VI, Bill no. 425; cf. the bill as amended in Committee, ibid., Bill no. 458.

against suicide, as well as against accidental injuries and homicide. In July 1893 the Home Office furnished Returns which showed that suicidal deaths from revolver wounds had risen steeply from an annual total of 113 in 1890 to 183 in 1892, and that suicidal injuries caused by revolvers were usually fatal, although accidental injuries were not.[102] (Those who deliberately shot themselves with a revolver usually shot themselves in the head, and only about one in eight survived long enough to be taken to hospital—and even for these, death was more likely than recovery.)[103] That summer provided London with plenty of other reasons to favour controls on the sale of revolvers as an anti-suicide measure. These were the months when 'the new Wertherism' was at its height among the would-be Bohemian young, especially in the capital; and injuries and deaths from attempts at suicide with a revolver were far more common there (especially in well-to-do west London) than in the provinces.[104] (It was in August 1893, it may be remembered, that Ernest Clark used a revolver to play out the 'Ibsene' drama at Liverpool Street station which provoked so much press discussion).[105] Revolvers were always associated with crime, 'wanton mischief', and the follies of the young—unlike guns, which were the weapons of manly sport and patriotic rifle practice—and sober people had been deploring their spread since the 1870s;[106] but in 1893 feelings were particularly uneasy.[107]

Yet the truth is that the responsibility of revolvers for a rapidly rising number of suicidal deaths proved a very feeble argument for legislation to control their sale. As the chief critic of such 'grand-motherly' legislation said in the House, 'the notion that the Bill would have any effect in the repression of suicide was absurd, whilst so many

[102] PP 1893–4 (371) LXXIII, pp. 11, 26. Of the inquests held in 1890–2 on persons who died from revolver injuries, 83 per cent resulted in a verdict of suicide: ibid., p. 26.

[103] Of these cases 55 per cent died, as against only 19 per cent of those injured accidentally by revolver and taken to hospital: ibid., p. 11.

[104] In 1890–2 30 per cent of the revolver cases admitted by metropolitan hospitals were suicidal, as against only 18 per cent of those admitted by provincial hospitals, while at St George's, Knightsbridge, 75 per cent of the revolver cases admitted were suicidal, and all died: ibid., pp. 3–11.

[105] See ch. 7.

[106] For a typical comparison, see *Hansard*, 3rd series, ccii, col. 855 (Major Walker, 23 June 1870). Large numbers of cheap, single-action pocket revolvers, dubbed 'Suicide Specials', were manufactured in these years, and widely sold by mail order: Taylerson, *The Revolver, 1865–1888*, p. 39, and *The Revolver, 1889–1914*, p. 82.

[107] During the serious dock strike in Hull in 1893, there was talk of civil war if revolver sales were not controlled. Certainly sales of revolvers in Hull shot up: *Hansard*, 4th series, xii, col. 66 (Asquith, 4 May 1893).

other means of self-destruction were easily accessible.'[108] Judges and
police, as well as coroners and coroners' juries, constantly urged
that something should be done; but the only argument which could
overcome the resistance mounted by libertarians, traders, and manufacturers, and those who espied concealed class legislation, was that
controls would reduce accidents among children. It was this plea which
finally carried a very watered down private member's Pistols Bill on
to the statute book in 1903. If there was 'a great volume of public
opinion' behind this Bill, as its supporters claimed, it was a public
opinion anxious to prevent accidents, not suicide.[109] And what was
the result? After 1903 it became unlawful (with certain exceptions) to
sell or hire a pistol or revolver to anyone under the age of eighteen,
or to anyone else who lacked a gun or game licence.[110] A gun licence,
however, could be got at any post office for 10s.; and in any case the
act was imperfectly enforced.[111] Even so, by 1907 shooting accounted
for only about 8.5 per cent of all male suicides, as against 11.4 per
cent in 1902 and 13.5 per cent in the peak year of 1892; and in particular
the proportion of youths aged fifteen to nineteen who committed
suicide by shooting fell from 20 per cent in 1902 to 15 per cent in
1907.[112] Apparently, then, the Pistols Act did somewhat modify the
pattern of suicide.

Four conclusions seem justified about the environmentalist approach
to suicide prevention. First, when legislation was called for, this could
be secured only as a side result of other campaigns which had nothing
to do with suicide prevention. Secondly, although the success of efforts
to nip suicidal inclinations in the bud by creating a healthier environment necessarily remains an open question, Victorian and Edwardian
attempts to create an environment in which suicide was simply more
difficult certainly achieved something. Thirdly, however, the impact
of all these efforts was more than cancelled out by that of other aspects
of the Victorian and Edwardian environment which were the result
of general developments. Examples of this are furnished not only by
the industrial and domestic applications of poisons and poisonous

---

[108] C. P. Hopwood, MP for Middleton, South-East Lancs., used these words during
the debate on the second reading of the private member's Pistols Bill introduced in 1895:
Hansard, 4th series, xxx, cols. 1659–60 (27 Feb.). He had, however, used very similar
language against the Home Office bill of 1893: ibid., xvii, cols. 1256–7 (14 Sept. 1893).

[109] Ibid., cxx, cols. 1016–18, and cxxv, cols. 129–31 (2 Apr. and 9 July 1903).

[110] 3 Ed. 7, c. 18.

[111] *Hansard*, 5th series, cxxx, col. 657 (10 June 1920).

[112] *Registrar-General's 55th AR*, p. 200; *65th AR*, p. 262; *70th AR*, p. 438.

gases already noticed, but also by two methods of suicide so far ignored, one very personal, the other quite the opposite. About one in five of Victorian men who killed themselves, did so with their razors: not for nothing are open razors still known as 'cut-throats'. The frequency with which razors were used for suicide seemed a good argument for wearing a beard to William Farr (who wore one himself).[113] Between the mid-1850s and mid-1870s long, thick beards were much in fashion; but soon they were being trimmed, and by the 1890s younger men, at any rate, were likely to wear only moustaches and shaving boomed again.[114] Unfortunately until the 1920s the safety razor (which quickly captured the market in the United States) spread only very slowly in England, and on the eve of the First World War the intimately familiar cut-throat razor continued to lie conveniently in most men's drawers (and occasionally to be borrowed by their women when bent on suicide).[115] Long before this a major economic development had made an entirely new instrument of suicide almost as accessible: a country-wide railway network. In 1909 156 men and 27 women (a record number) threw themselves under a train.[116] A novel mode of suicide had thus been provided by 'modern life'—and one which could not be put out of reach.

The history of railway suicide, however, gives cogency to a fourth point: that the stress laid by mid-Victorian epidemiologists and reformers on the psychological environment, whether or not it had any practical effects, may not have been ill-judged as a piece of analysis. After all, what is striking about the use of railways trains as an instrument of suicide is not that it happened, but that it happened so slowly. The early Victorian years were the first railway age, but they were not the first age of railway suicide: railway trains were hardly ever used as a means of self-destruction until 1868. In that year a total of 20 men threw themselves under trains, as the newspapers reported

---

[113] Millar, 'Statistics of Deaths by Suicide among H.M.'s Troops', discussion, p. 192.

[114] Trends in men's hair fashions in this period are neatly summarized in Raverat, *Period Piece*, pp. 261–2.

[115] Cut-throat suicides did proportionately decline a little, but the fall was only from 21 per cent of male suicides in 1873–4, to 18 per cent in 1909: *Registrar-General's 36th and 37th ARs*, p. 208; *72nd AR*, p. 470. (After 1891 'Cut, throat' suicides were not separately recorded from 'Cut, stab' and 'Cut, other'. Before this, however, some 98 per cent were 'Cut, throat'—although some of these were certainly by knives and not by razors.)

[116] That is, 5.8 per cent of male suicides and, in this record year, 3 per cent of female: *Registrar-General's 72nd AR*, pp. 470–1.

in some detail;[117] and suddenly this became the fashionable method. When in 1875 Anthony Trollope, always immensely accurate in his topical details, needed to make a ruined financier destroy himself, he made him go to 'Tenway Junction' and walk into the path of the Euston to Inverness express.[118] Two years later that hard-headed commentator Edward Cox remarked that, 'Recently, suicide by falling before a railway train has exercised an extraordinary fascination for disordered minds';[119] and thereafter the proportion of total suicides accounted for by this method roughly doubled every decade until the 1900s. Even then, however, it was used by only about 5 per cent of men and little more than 2 per cent of women who took their own lives. Railways had thus covered the country for half a century before they became at all a significant mode of self-destruction; and this slow and limited use of railway trains for suicide provides a salutary reminder that changes in the physical environment by themselves do not necessarily affect the mode of suicide, let alone its scale.

In reality the existence of suicide facilities is relevant only when there is widespread awareness that that is what they are; and in Victorian and Edwardian England such awareness depended on family and local traditions, the songs and stories and images in current circulation, and (as contemporaries emphasized so tirelessly) the suicide reporting of the popular press. There are many examples of a particular method of suicide running in a family. Experienced coroners knew that one suicide was apt to breed another of the same type, and some made it a rule never to return the razor, cup or gun used for suicide to the relatives, even when they asked for them as a memento, since a suicide instrument had a dangerous fascination.[120] They tried, too, to stop local publicity being given to a suicide in the neighbourhood by an exotic method or in an unusual place.[121] Opinions differed over whether or not the act of suicide itself was likely to be the result of 'emotional contagion', but all agreed that the precise method or place chosen was

---

[117] *Registrar-General's 31st AR*, p. 186.

[118] 'He walked down before the flying engine—and in a moment had been knocked into bloody atoms': Trollope, *The Prime Minister*, ch. lx.

[119] Cox, *The Principles of Punishment*, p. 123. In 1886 Ogle remarked that this was a method of suicide 'only of late years come into use, but now on the increase': 'Suicides in England and Wales', p. 119.

[120] Westcott, *On Suicide*, pp. 10–11. Horsley remembered that an uncle who was a county coroner 'found suicide is like marriage in respect to one making many': 'Suicide', p. 510.

[121] For an example in Manchester, see n. 30.

often the result of imitation. Nor was the field of contagion necessarily limited to the local neighbourhood. The nation-wide publicity given by the press to outstanding sensations or 'human interest' stories wherever they took place was repeatedly shown to be baneful and regretted, and not only by epidemiologists concerned about moral contagion.[122]

It would surely be wrong, however, to suppose that it was only the influence of a spectacular or intimately known individual case which affected the consciousness of a family, a neighbourhood, or the public at large so far as methods of suicide were concerned, or even perhaps the onset of suicidal moods themselves. As the nineteenth century moved into the twentieth, increasingly specialized and detailed stereotypes of suicide seem to have established themselves in popular awareness, especially in the minds of the sort of people who read the popular press most avidly—'minds barren of ideas', as the moralists liked to put it. Even the most fundamental shift of all in modes of suicide, the move away from hanging—which began in the Victorian and Edwardian period but has gone so much further in the twentieth century—perhaps owed something to the country's changing suicide culture, as it certainly did to its changing social and occupational structure.[123] Hanging had always been the way taken by the humble unskilled worker and above all the agricultural labourer.[124] To the town dwellers and skilled and white-collar workers who made up an increasing proportion of the population, other methods were equally if not more convenient and accessible, and also more thinkable and emotionally acceptable. It was people like this, moreover, who were most likely to be conscious of what might almost be called an etiquette of suicide, a 'proper' way of committing suicide for a particular life situation, and even perhaps a 'proper' situation for suicidal behaviour.

---

[122] An outbreak of suicide by strychnia in 1857, for example, was attributed to widespread reporting of the Rugeley poisoning case: *Annual Register*, 1857, Chronicle, 21 Feb., p. 28. In 1844 a needlewoman who poisoned herself in central London had been 'heard to advert to the double suicide at Kilmarnock' then being reported, as a model to follow: ibid., 1844, Chronicle, 8 Nov., p. 134. In 1846 the press publicity given to extracts from Haydon's diary before his suicide and to Peel's generosity to his widow, encouraged imitation: Hayter, *A Sultry Month*, p. 107.

[123] Between 1861–70 and 1901–10 the proportion of suicides by hanging dropped from 44 per cent to 29 per cent of male suicides, and from 31 per cent to 18 per cent of female suicides: *Registrar-General's 24th–31st ARs*, pp. 124–5, *32nd–33rd ARs*, pp. 122–3, and *75th AR, Supplement*, Part III, p. xcv, Table XLV.

[124] Hanging was the method used by 55 per cent of agricultural labourers in 1878–83: Ogle, 'Suicides in England and Wales', p. 122, Table XII.

It could easily seem 'right' for a young woman of the working classes to drown herself for ill-usage in love; for a young man of the middle or upper classes with love or money troubles to shoot himself (especially with a revolver) or a woman in middle age who was depressed or sorrowful to poison herself with 'black draught' or, later, carbolic acid; for star-crossed lovers to make a narcotic suicide pact or an older business man in financial difficulties to throw himself under a train; and each of these juxtapositions may have become more likely in the 1900s than the 1860s not only because each was a convenient and accessible mode of suicide for the sort of people and situation concerned, but also, it may be surmised, because each had been made very easily thinkable for these people in these situations, as familiar and apparently appropriate stereotypes came to mind in moments of stress and excitement.[125]

Throughout the nineteenth and early twentieth centuries there were probably far more moralists who preached the need to correct the mental and moral environment if the growth of suicide was to be checked, than there were practical reformers who concentrated on the material environment and tried to raise parapets, install safety-nets, and so forth. Inevitably the moralists' style of argument was heavily based upon unspoken assumptions and fielded a restricted cast of villains, with 'the press' selected for a leading role markedly more often than clergymen, schoolteachers, and parents, or even novelists and poets. Nevertheless, if it would be a mistake to claim much for the practical importance of their efforts, it would surely be a still greater mistake to dismiss out of hand their analysis of the situation. Admittedly the impact of the cultural environment on the actual scale of suicide must have been far more complex and probably also far more limited than they believed; but its impact on the particular form of suicidal behaviour which was adopted by given sorts of people in given situations seems to have been real enough. In the last resort, however, it must be acknowledged that 'modern living', whether seen as a moral or a material phenomenon, and whether or not it bred desires and thoughts of suicide (that endlessly debated conundrum), did undeniably tend to make the actual accomplishment of suicide

---

[125] In 1886 Ogle concluded that the psychological differences between different ages must explain the marked preferences and aversions of particular age-groups for particular methods of suicide, where these methods seemed equally accessible to all: ibid., p. 120; but he did not consider how far these age related preferences and aversions might have been shaped by cultural factors.

quicker, surer, more convenient, and less painful. By and large, Victorian and Edwardian England was a place where suicide was becoming all the time easier, not harder to achieve; and that this was so makes it impossible to credit the environmental approach to the reduction of suicide with more than a very limited success. But was the contribution of clinical medicine, it must be asked, any more impressive?

II

The Role of Medical Men
in Preventing Suicide

Victorian and Edwardian medical men, like those of every other generation, could prevent death by suicide in two ways: by keeping alive those who had already tried to destroy themselves, and by preventing those who were potentially suicidal from becoming actively and successfully so. The first raised few professional problems. After all, when a medical man was summoned to attend someone who was semi-asphyxiated from immersion in water, or was vomiting or comatose after taking poison, or bleeding from cuts in the neck or arm, what was immediately required was plainly the routine treatment given in all such circumstances. True, there were other methods of suicide which tended to produce rather less commonplace injuries—such as hanging, shooting, or jumping from a height or in front of a train—but these were also less likely to make demands on medical skill, since they more often succeeded instantaneously. It was those who had resorted to drowning, and above all to poison or the use of a knife or razor, whose lives medical men were most often called upon to save.[1] Often indeed the survival of those who had tried to drown themselves chiefly depended on the first aid given on the spot by whoever chanced to rescue them; but a fair quota were taken to hospital (where they were treated with hot baths or, from the 1860s, with Marshall Hall's novel and at first controversial 'ready method' of artificial respiration),[2] and hospitals continually dealt with cut throats, slashed wrists, and

---

[1] As Maudsley pointed out, certain methods of suicide required a continued effort which some people could not sustain, so that (for example) cut-throats often failed, whereas those who used a gun usually succeeded: *The Pathology of Mind*, p. 181. (It should be noted that the terms used by Victorian and Edwardian medical men have been retained throughout this chapter. To translate them into modern medical terminology would be an undertaking entirely beyond my competence, as well as one fraught with risks of misleading anachronisms.)

[2] See ch 4 n. 69. The generalizations which follow are largely based upon the case histories studied.

various kinds of poisoning (apart from the exceptionally quick acting).[3] Fielding Blandford in 1871 referred to the 'hundreds of poor creatures ... brought to our general hospitals half poisoned, or with throats half-cut' in one of his lectures at St George's medical school,[4] and using the stomach-pump on would-be suicides and stitching up self-inflicted wounds from razors or knives was indeed part of the routine of hospital casualty work. The strictly medical treatment such patients required was very limited. John Marshall, that outstanding anatomist and surgeon, told his students at University College Hospital in 1870 that 'it consists mainly in stimulants', because

> though these patients may not necessarily have suffered a more or less prolonged period of exhausting mental stress previous to the attempts, or subsequently the loss of a large quantity of blood, they have almost always been governed at the moment by feelings of acute intensity, which are necessarily followed by a proportionate state of nervous depression.[5]

Certainly most of these non-fatal suicide cases were not at all serious, and many were discharged after only a few hours.

Why then, it may be asked, were they brought into the hospitals in such numbers? So far as the great hospitals of central London were concerned, part of the explanation lies in the long established habit among working people in their neighbourhood of taking there every kind of medical emergency. Thus when Francis Holden, a waiter living in the Smithfield area, stuck a penknife in his throat one morning in 1861, his wife 'pulled it out and got assistance and brought him to the Hospital', that is, St Bartholomew's;[6] and there can have been few people thereabouts who would not have done the same. Police practice also helped to funnel suicide cases into the hospitals, at least throughout the metropolitan area. It has already been noticed that in the second half of the nineteenth century it became increasingly common in London for working people confronted with a suicide attempt in their homes to send for a policeman, even when they also sent for a medical man; but a policeman equally often became involved because he encountered a suicide case on his beat, in the streets or a park, or

---

[3] For tables comparing the poisons used in unsuccessful and in successful suicide attempts, see East, 'On Attempted Suicide', p. 452, Tables XVI and XVII.

[4] Blandford, *Insanity and its Treatment*, pp. 165–6.

[5] *The Lancet*, 1870, ii. 634, 5 Nov. John Marshall (1818–91:*DNB*), himself the son of a coroner, was an exceptionally considerate man: Merrington, *University College Hospital*, p. 67.

[6] CLRO, CR, City, 15 Jan. 1861, inquest no. 13, Francis Holden

near a river or canal. Constables who found someone evidently in need
of medical attention in a public place had standing instructions to take
that person to the police station to be attended by the Divisional Police
Surgeon, or, if necessary, to summon the Divisional Surgeon to the
spot; only if he was not available or the case was critical was the
nearest available doctor to be summoned.[7] Whoever attended such
cases, however, seems usually to have given first aid, and then sent them
to the nearest hospital, whether or not there were serious injuries—
presumably in order to ensure a few hours' rest, attention, and observation. Indeed, a constable who considered the situation called for it
would himself take such a person straight to the nearest hospital in a
cab.[8] If he suspected poisoning, he might first hurry into a chemist's
shop for an emetic; but he might decide against this, for a chemist
might refuse to provide what was in effect a prescription, and hustle
such unwelcome customers out of his shop,[9] whereas in the metropolitan area no hospital would refuse admission even to the most
disturbed and violent case, since the police authorities had undertaken
to provide assistance with such patients on request.[10] In London, and
probably in other great cities as well, it was thus virtually routine for
those who unsuccessfully used certain methods of suicide to be taken
to the nearest hospital not only by their relatives and neighbours, but
also by the police.

Two sorts of people, however, rarely found themselves in a hospital
ward: those who had means, and those who lived in country districts.
Those who had means were much less likely to try to commit suicide
in a public place, and hence less likely to be encountered by a policeman
on his beat; and in their domestic emergencies, their relations and
servants were accustomed to summon private assistance to their

---

[7] In the metropolitan police district in 1918 about three-quarters of 7,201 such calls
for medical assistance were met by Divisional Surgeons: PP 1919 [Cmd. 336] XXVII,
p. vi, paras 8, 9.

[8] Apparently the Liverpool police were the first to have an ambulance service (a
horse-drawn one): *Graphic*, 27 Nov. 1886, p. 568, and Nott-Bower, *Fifty-Two Years a
Policeman*, p. 113. In London the 'Electro-Mobile Ambulance Service' came into operation in 1907: ibid., p. 313.

[9] See ch. 7 n. 73. First aid instruction was compulsory for the Edwardian City police:
Nott-Bower, *Fifty-Two Years a Policeman*, p. 314.

[10] The situation was different elsewhere. In 1907 the Chelmsford police refused the
local Infirmary's request for a constable to be left in charge of an insane carpenter who
had cut his throat in the street. Similar requests were reported to have been refused
since 1904, with the result that such patients were not allowed to remain in the Infirmary:
The Lancet, 1907, ii. 108, 13 July.

homes.[11] Where private patients were concerned, medical men always cultivated discretion. Thus when a general practitioner asked the editor of *The Lancet* in 1882 whether it was his legal duty to inform the police of a case of attempted suicide known only to himself and the patient's friends, the editor's reply was unhesitating: 'We believe he will be doing his duty to himself, his patient and the public by keeping a discreet silence.'[12] It is not surprising that W. W. Westcott's appeal through *The Lancet* in 1885 for information on attempted suicide brought few replies; nor that the general practitioners among those who responded believed that successful suicide attempts far outnumbered unsuccessful ones, whereas the hospital doctors were convinced of the opposite.[13] The family doctor, unlike those who worked in hospitals or held appointments as police surgeons, was likely to see a case of attempted suicide only rarely, and only when his services were indispensable; and since silence in such cases made sound professional sense, he would probably hear little from his rivals about such cases as came their way but escaped local publicity. Certainly it would never occur to him to send a patient with means to hospital, whatever his injuries: that would have been a radical departure from the customs of the day. 'Hospitals are for the poor who cannot be treated at home', *The Lancet* asserted categorically in 1907, and went on to give full editorial support to the Salford division of the British Medical Association in its condemnation of the Manchester police for removing to Ancoats hospital an elderly man bleeding from self-inflicted wounds in the throat, contrary to the advice of the family's doctor.[14]

In rural areas hospitals naturally hardly entered the picture, any more than police constables or Divisional Surgeons. There, private practitioners or on occasion poor law medical officers and panel doctors were called upon to try to save the lives of those who had attempted suicide. Rural medical men were probably confronted by this task more often than their city counterparts, for although the

---

[11] Norwood East took this for granted as an explanation of the fact that those remanded on a charge of attempted suicide included so few of the 'better-educated': 'On Attempted Suicide', p. 449. After Virginia Woolf's first suicide attempt in 1913 (a veronal overdose), her husband telephoned the neurologist whom she had recently seen for depression and her lodger Geoffrey Keynes dashed to his hospital (Bart's) to fetch a stomach-pump; naturally no one thought of rushing Virginia Woolf herself to Bart's: Keynes, *The Gates of Memory*, p. 116.

[12] *The Lancet*, 1882, ii. 930, 2 Dec.

[13] Westcott, *Suicide*, p. 157.

[14] *The Lancet*, 1907, i. 466, 607, 16 Feb., 2 Mar.

arrest rate for attempted suicide was far lower in country areas than in the great cities, this probably reflected a different policing situation,[15] and a lower recovery rate,[16] rather than a lower rate of attempts. Surviving inquest papers show local surgeons in the rural part of Sussex and Hertfordshire in the 1860s and 1870s giving standard emergency treatment to cases of suicidal poisoning, cutting, and stabbing, followed by assiduous home visiting. In December 1865, for example, Dr John Underwood, Surgeon to the Hastings Dispensary and one of the most highly qualified men then practising in the Rape of Hastings, was called out to the village of Fairlight and found a fifty-eight year old woman with her throat bound up with a wet towel. 'I never saw such an extensive injury to the windpipe', he told the coroner (and he had been practising for twenty years); 'I stitched up the wound, and saw her nearly every day, and sometimes twice a day.' For thirteen days, Underwood kept her alive by injections of port wine and beef tea, until she died 'of exhaustion'.[17] Here, plainly, was another difference between city and country: in the city, most cases of attempted suicide were funnelled to the police surgeons and the hospitals, while in the countryside rich and poor were treated by the nearest medical man— often something of a general handyman in his small locality. In neither city nor countryside, however, did the immediate treatment of these men and women raise any special problems: emetics, stomach pumps, the stitching and dressing of wounds, nourishment, rest and stimulants—such standard treatment was plainly what was called for in dealing with the half-poisoned, the bleeding or the semi-asphyxiated, whether their condition was self-inflicted or not.

Where suicidal tendencies and not suicidal injuries were concerned, the situation was altogether different. Here there was no standard routine to which medical practice could conform; and the medical men most often involved were not the hospital staff and police surgeons who bore the chief brunt of treating suicidal injuries (at least in the cities), but three quite different groups: general practitioners, prison medical staff, and asylum physicians. How alert were these men to recognize latent suicidal tendencies at an early stage? How often after

[15] See ch. 8, pp. 287–9.

[16] In country areas more certain methods were more commonly used, and the impulsive, moody young para-suicide whose attempt was little more than a gesture was rarer than in London: cf. ch. 5.

[17] 'Fairlight: Suicide', *Sussex Advertiser*, 30 Sept. 1865, p. 2, and ESRO, A 1684, 21 Sept. 1865, inquest no. 21, Mary Ann Andrews.

they had treated injuries from an abortive suicide attempt did they feel a duty to inquire into the circumstances or mental state of their patient, or appraise the chances of a further attempt? What treatment and care did they prescribe for those whom they knew or strongly suspected to be at risk? Professionally the three groups of medical men concerned were very dissimilar; and it is therefore not surprising to find among them three quite distinct clinical responses to the prevention of overt suicidal behaviour—so distinct, indeed, that they must be considered separately to be intelligible.

First, the general practitioners. These did not necessarily have a strong professional inclination towards the detection of suicidal tendencies. A family doctor who had been called in to treat a private patient for an injured windpipe, say, might well be chary of probing too far into what had happened, unless there were gross symptoms of mental disorder; while a 'club' doctor or poor law medical officer might be even less investigative, although for quite different reasons. In any case, it seems quite likely that most general practitioners were handicapped in detecting warning symptoms by sheer lack of appropriate knowledge and clinical experience. Certainly mental illness long remained something of a fringe subject, whose status was distinctly low. Only in 1885 did the General Medical Council give it any place in the medical curriculum,[18] at the close of twenty pioneering years which had seen the beginning in hospital medical schools of regular lectures in combination with clinical demonstrations at the nearest asylum;[19] and only in 1897 did the subject become a compulsory one.[20] Thus the proportion of registered practitioners who had received any formal instruction in mental illness must have remained very small

[18] O'Malley, ed., *The History of Medical Education*, pp. 244–5.
[19] The first appointment in England of a Lecturer in Mental Diseases was made at University College in 1865: Merrington, *University College Hospital*, p. 226; but in the same year the Senate of the University of London was compelled to refrain from requiring a clinical knowledge of insanity from candidates for degrees by the lack of clinical instruction: Maudsley, 'Memoir of the late John Conolly, M. D.', p. 165.
[20] 'The study of mental disease has now entered on a new era', was Clouston's comment in September 1898: *Clinical Lectures* (5th edn.), p. v. The Medical Directories of the period show that in 1861 no London teaching hospital included mental diseases in its curriculum, although in the next decade several for the first time appointed lecturers in this subject; and that while in 1907 every hospital offered lectures, not all had a Department for Mental Diseases, no scholarships were offered, and publishers advertised comparatively few manuals on this specialty. Some mention of the development of psychiatric teaching is included in Thomson, *The Story of the Middlesex Hospital Medical School*, pp. 62, 65, 102, 132, 161, and Lyle, *King's and Some King's Men*, pp. 208, 304, 408, and the histories of other teaching hospitals.

until well after the First World War, although no doubt those students who did attend such lectures in the days when they were voluntary were very committed.[21] Even at their best, however, lectures and asylum demonstrations could never provide the familiarity with the mild, early stages of mental illness which was what a general practitioner needed;[22] and as late as 1912 out-patient departments, which did offer students precisely such experience, were still rarities.[23]

On the other hand, the subject of insanity was very much in the forefront of educated consciousness throughout this period, and an ambitious general practitioner might well feel that he ought to seem knowledgeable upon it; while it was certainly in his own interests to be well-informed where suicidal probabilities were concerned. 'Ruin can follow the suicide of an influential patient', G. H. Savage of Bethlem and Guy's warned a crowded postgraduate audience in 1911, and he was indisputably right. 'Do what you will, suicides will happen', he went on; 'but it is your duty to recognise the danger and give warning.'[24] Not surprisingly there was a steady output of practical, explicit clinical manuals designed to meet the needs of practitioners as well as interested students. At first in the later nineteenth century this market was virtually monopolized by the magisterial *Manual of Psychological Medicine* produced by J. C. Bucknill and D. H. Tuke in 1858, which aimed to be 'sufficiently modern in its views and explicit in its teaching to satisfy the demands of the practitioner'.[25] Only in 1883 was this manual superseded by another heavyweight, T. S. Clouston's

[21] According to Ernest White, who held the Chair of Psychological Medicine at King's College Hospital between 1890 and 1910, when his course was voluntary 'the attendance was not large, although distinctly good'. His students had to travel to the City of London mental hospital 16 miles away for clinical instruction: Lyle, *King's and Some King's Men*, p. 304.

[22] This point was strongly made by Dr Bernard Hart in urging the establishment of an Out-Patient Department for Mental Cases at University College Hospital in 1912: Merrington, *University College Hospital*, p. 227.

[23] In 1912 Charing Cross, Guy's, St Thomas's, and St Mary's alone among London teaching hospitals possessed such departments: ibid., p. 227. The West Riding asylums seem to have pioneered out-patients clinics, beginning in 1890: Bullen, 'The Out-Patient System in Asylums', p. 491.

[24] Savage, 'Mental Disorders and Suicide', pp. 1334, 1336. 30 years earlier Clouston had similarly been impressing upon students that they should spare no pains to guard against a serious suicide attempt, 'so damaging to the reputation and foresight of the doctor in charge': *Clinical Lectures* (1st edn.), p. 112.

[25] Bucknill and Tuke, *Manual of Psychological Medicine* (1st edn.), p. iv. This work superseded earlier treatises, notably Prichard, *Treatise on Insanity* (1835), J. Conolly, *An Inquiry Concerning the Indications of Insanity* (1830), and Burrows, *Commentaries on the Causes, Forms, Symptoms and Treatment, Moral and Medical, of Insanity*

Clinical Lectures on Mental Diseases, which claimed to provide an even more clinical and practical treatment of the subject,[26] than that already available in a number of other (and briefer) published lectures.[27] To busy practitioners, however, all these may have been less acceptable than the handbook entitled *Insanity and Allied Neuroses: Practical and Clinical* which G. H. Savage contributed in 1884 to Cassell's series of 'Clinical Manuals for Practitioners and Students of Medicine'. Certainly there were many predecessors of Maurice Craig's successful manual of 1905, *Psychological Medicine*, which aimed to help the general practitioner in the early diagnosis and treatment of mental disorder;[28] and since general medical encyclopaedias had also long included a section on such topics,[29] it is clear that any general practitioner who wished could easily remedy the gaps of his student days and keep abreast of current thinking on mental illness.

What circumstances would have suggested a risk of suicide to a Victorian or Edwardian family doctor who had read a standard manual or attended a course of lectures on mental disease? First and foremost, he assuredly would have known that every patient suffering from mental depression (and hence incipient melancholia) was a potential suicide, but that suicide was comparatively rare in other forms of insanity. Secondly, he would have associated a risk of suicide with phobias, obsessions, and (from the 1880s) 'neuroses' of all sorts,[30] but

(1828). It 'had more influence, perhaps, than any other volume in disseminating the new outlook on lunacy and its treatment amongst the profession at large': *Munk's Roll*, iv. 102. On its distinguished authors, J. C. Bucknill (1817–97) and D. H. Tuke (1827–95), see *DNB* and *Monk's Roll*, iv. 102, 237.

[26] Clouston chose to discuss not interesting rarities, but 'good ordinary types and guides' from his long experience at the Royal Asylum, Morningside, Edinburgh: *Clinical Lectures*, p. vi. His work reached its sixth edition in 1904.

[27] By 1883 teachers with extensive asylum experience who had published their lectures included Sankey, *Lectures on Mental Diseases* (lectures delivered at University College London in 1865); Maudsley, *The Physiology and Pathology of Mind* (Maudsley was then Lecturer in Insanity at St Mary's Hospital Medical School); Blandford, *Insanity and its Treatment* (lectures delivered at St George's Hospital); Sheppard, *Lectures on Madness in its Medical, Legal and Social Aspects* (Sheppard was Professor of Psychological Medicine at King's College London).

[28] Craig, *Psychological Medicine*, p. v. This manual went into a fourth edition in 1926.

[29] E.g. the sections on 'Mental Diseases' in T. L. Stedman, ed., *Twentieth-Century Practice: An International Encyclopaedia of Modern Medical Science*, xii (1897), and T. C. Allbutt, ed., *A System of Medicine*, viii (1899) were latter-day descendants of the section on 'Insanity' in Forbes, Tweedie, and Conolly, *The Cyclopaedia of Practical Medicine*, ii (1833).

[30] The first of the standard textbooks to incorporate in its title this newly current and not then very narrowly defined term was Savage's *Insanity and Allied Neuroses*

particularly those connected with sexual potency or venereal disease, with hypochondrias of the throat, bowels, and reproductive system; with hysteria and any sudden shock to the feelings; with overwork and (again particularly from the early 1880s) with 'over-pressure'. Thirdly, he would have known that epileptics, puerperal women, and alcoholics (particularly those with delirium tremens)[31] were always at risk, and that certain acute diseases carried some risk of suicide either during delirium (as with erysipelas) or in the depression which was their sequel (as with gastric and bowel disorders, disorders of the reproductive functions, suppressed acute gout, and influenza—whose aftermath was much discussed in the epidemics after 1889).[32]

Yet how many family doctors did in practice seek guidance from these excellent manuals? How many kept in mind the three basic categories of patients to be regarded as suicide risks? Where such matters were concerned, general practitioners were apt to be hampered not only by lack of knowledge and experience, but by their conception of their professional province. In 1856 that founding father of British psychiatry, John Conolly, regretted that in the vital first few weeks and months of mental illness when the chances of recovery were best, patients (if cared for at all) were attended by general practitioners who were not only unfamiliar with these forms of disorder, but disconcerted and alarmed by them; and twenty years later it was being plainly said that the medical profession as a body ought to take more interest in the treatment of insanity.[33] From the mid-1880s, when the steep rise

(1884). Particular emphasis was placed upon watching neurotic patients, for in their case the most trivial causes might lead to a suicide attempt. The term was in common use among specialists giving evidence at inquests on deaths by suicide by the 1900s. In 1892 Savage was teaching that in cases of 'neurotic suicide' a family history of suicide was frequently found: 'Suicide and Insanity', p. 1231—not surprisingly, since neuroses had long been regarded as evidence of hereditary alienation or 'degeneration': Lewis, *The State of Psychiatry*, p. 90.

[31] When Bevan Lewis published a new textbook in 1899 which aimed to correct an alleged over-emphasis on the clinical aspects of insanity and stress its pathology, he emphasized that two-thirds of patients suffering from chronic alcoholic cerebral atrophy were determinedly suicidal: Lewis, *A Text-Book of Mental Diseases*, p. 292, and this view coincided with an increased emphasis in many quarters on the suicidal behaviour of alcoholics.

[32] These points summarize the common ground in successive editions of all the textbooks and lectures just mentioned and one or two others, notably D. H. Tuke, ed., *A Dictionary of Psychological Medicine* (1892) and Savage, 'Suicide as a Symptom of Mental Disorder'. (Savage's lectures drew particularly large audiences.)

[33] Conolly, *The Treatment of the Insane without Mechanical Restraints*, p. 279; Granville, *The Care and Cure of the Insane*, i. 328; and in similar vein, [Wynter], 'Non-restraint in the Treatment of the Insane', p. 447.

in the rates of both suicide and attempted suicide became a matter of concern to the mental hygiene lobby, *The Lancet* tried to persuade its readers that 'our duty it not limited to the feeling of pulses and the looking at tongues', and that 'the general practitioner should make himself seem available if help and counsel is needed'. He should be alert to signs of psychological as well as physical weakness, and encourage patients to have faith and courage: 'We ought to warn the man who is in a bad mental state that he is making trouble for himself in the future', just as a warning would be given to 'one living over a cess-pool'.[34] The tightly packed columns of *The Lancet*, however, were hardly likely to be closely studied by the average practitioner, who was more likely to glance through the less formidable pages of *The Practitioner*, that readable monthly which promised 'practical, every-day help to medical men in actual practice'; and it is significant that in 1915 this journal found space for a short piece entitled 'Suicide—From a General Practitioner's Point of View', which claimed to have been written because general practitioners so rarely encountered sui-cidal cases that they had difficulty in dealing with them, and offered a down-to-earth rehash of textbook orthodoxies.[35] Evidently the editor considered that most of his readers had not conned the clinical manuals very assiduously; and in all probability he was right.

It was not only his own ignorance, inexperience, or narrow-mind-edness, however, which might cause a general practitioner to fail to take appropriate action, but also that of his potential patients and their families. From the 1850s and 1860s supporters of the new psychological medicine who believed that those who committed suicide were nearly always suffering from mental disease continually reproached not only their colleagues, but also the public for their failure to take mental symptoms seriously.[36] In particular they urged that medical advice

[34] *The Lancet*, 1886, i. 407, 599, 27 Feb., 27 Mar. For further editorial views on suicide prevention, see ibid., 1891, ii. 361, 1405, 15 Aug., 19 Dec.; 1893, ii. 640, 9 Sept.; 1894, ii. 451, 25 Aug.; 1895, ii. 417, 17 Aug. From its earliest days *The Lancet* discussed editorially the latest serious books and papers on suicide, and provided in its columns a précis of their contents.

[35] Adams, 'Suicide—From a General Practitioner's Point of View', p. 470. Adams was a School Medical Officer in Bristol who held the certificate of the Medico-Psychological Association.

[36] This was the constant theme of Forbes Winslow and his *Journal of Psychological Medicine* throughout its existence (1848–63): see particularly 'Neglected Brain Disease—Suicide', x (1857), pp. 413–53. In 1879 W. F. Wade went so far as to argue that the Home Office should investigate the depositions where the verdict was one of 'suicide in a state of temporary insanity', 'with a view of determining whether the coroner had taken due

should be sought in cases of sleeplessness and unusual pains in the head, both of which were represented as harbingers of suicidal propensities.[37] Yet if most family doctors persisted in thinking that physical pain alone was their true province, so too did most of their potential patients.[38] Middle and upper middle-class reluctance to consult a doctor for intangible symptoms was no doubt much increased by the mid-Victorian development of the certification system. The stigma of legal confinement was something the better-off and respectable were anxious to avoid; and in matters of certification, medical judgement (to which the new lunacy laws gave a decisive role) was often regarded as lacking in common sense and disinterestedness.[39] Such prejudices, as well as ignorance, disbelief, and indifference, were continually blamed by mid-Victorian specialists for what they considered the lamentable failure to seek medical advice in the early stages of mental illness, or to follow it when given.[40] Someone's friends and relations would say that they 'only thought him a little low' and were sure they could deal with this passing trouble, or would plead that they were 'afraid to worry him' by bringing in a doctor. The poor, needless to say, were even less accustomed to seek medical advice when there was incipient mental disturbance, and for them the necessary staging-post to medical observation seems often to have been admission to the workhouse.

When a general practitioner did form the opinion that a patient ran some risk of suicide, his primary responsibility was not to prescribe treatment, but to advise family, friends, or the poor-law relieving officer where that treatment should be given. A recognized suicidal tendency was widely regarded as a strong indication that someone should be sent to an asylum.[41] For this there were two reasons. The

care to ascertain whether any one, and if so who, had been guilty of negligence in the matter': 'On the Prevention of Suicide', p. 533. See also H. Sutherland, 'The Prevention of Suicide in the Insane', *The Lancet*, 1892, ii. 1267, 3 Dec.

[37] Wakley was reported to hold that 6 out of 7 cases of suicide could be prevented if immediate medical advice was sought for sleeplessness or unusual head pains: 'Neglected Brain Disease—Suicide', *Jnl. of Psychological Medicine*, x (1857), p. 434.

[38] For example, evidence was given at inquests that an elderly weaver would not allow his wife to go for any medical man 'as he said it was in his mind', and that another man told his wife that 'a doctor could do him no good, as he had no pain': ibid., p. 429.

[39] For the agitation in 1858–9 and 1876–7 over wrongful confinement, see McCandless, 'Liberty and Lunacy: The Victorians and Wrongful Confinement'.

[40] Wade, 'On the Prevention of Suicide', p. 533.

[41] In Ireland too in this period 'an attempted suicide was taken to be irrefutable evidence of a person's insanity': Finnane, *Insanity and the Insane in Post-Famine Ireland*, p. 151.

most cogent was the fact that anybody with suicidal tendencies required constant watching, and this, so orthodox opinion held, was something the poor could never afford to give, and even well-to-do families who employed nurses could never guarantee; whereas from the 1860s surveillance was the overriding goal in the country's rapidly expanding county and municipal asylums, and in many private licensed houses or 'Homes' as well. Secondly, however, the standard treatment for those suffering from melancholia, overwork, emotional shock, and so on emphasized not only attention to diet, sleep, exercise, and the bowels but also change of scene, plenty of companionship, occupation, and amusement, so that it was often said that 'the essence of the treatment of melancholia is removal from relations and friends'.[42] In mild cases a doctor might advise a visit to relations, or (if it could be afforded) travelling with a companion or (from the end of the century) a stay at a hydropathic; but what of more serious cases? 'An asylum is not absolutely indispensable, if the patient's means will afford him what he requires elsewhere', that practical man, Fielding Blandford, told his audience of 'future family advisers' at St George's Medical School in 1871, for he well knew that any recommendation of legal restraint was quite likely to be met with every conceivable objection; 'but if the patient is a poor man, there is nothing for it but to send him to an asylum.'[43] For rich and poor alike, however, one thing usually settled the matter: an actual as opposed to a merely threatened attempt at suicide. One characteristic of the mid-Victorian faith in institutions embodied in bricks and mortar, was a growing popular belief (which seems slowly to have worked its way up the social scale) that the best place for the insane was an asylum,[44] or, in the case of the well-to-do, a 'Home'; and by the 1880s doctors were each year certifying as in need of confinement some 4,000 people with suicidal propensities.[45] True, progressives were by then calling for facilities for

---

[42] Thus Dr Bower at a meeting of the Medico-Psychological Association: *Jnl. of Mental Science*, xxxii (1886), p. 299. Here, however, Bower was only summarizing the advice long given in the standard handbooks.

[43] Blandford, *Insanity and its Treatment*, pp. 190, 362.

[44] Much has recently been made of the substitution among the working class of asylum for family care (cf. n. 126), but little detailed work on asylum admissions records has yet appeared, with the notable exception of Finnane, *Insanity and the Insane in Post-Famine Ireland*, pp. 129–74. Family circumstances as a whole were clearly crucial, and not only the amount of time and money available. For the solitary poor, for example, the only alternative to an asylum was the 'feeble ward' of a workhouse.

[45] *Lunacy Commissioners' 44th AR*, p. 59, Table XIX. Signing these certificates was

the voluntary early treatment of mental disorders along ordinary hospital and out-patient lines;[46] but these did not even begin to materialize until the 1890s,[47] and the usual assumption long continued to be that a suicide attempt was the surest proof that someone suspected of mental disturbance could not safely be left at liberty.[48] At common law the sole sufficient cause for depriving an insane person of liberty had traditionally been that he was a danger to himself or others; and although in 1845 Parliament had made the giving of care and treatment a sufficient ground for confinement, in this as in many other matters it was the age-old language of the common law which continued to shape the thoughts and speech of ordinary people.[49]

The upshot was that only three sorts of recognized suicidal patients were at all likely to remain long within a Victorian or Edwardian general practitioner's care: women suffering from post-natal mania or melancholia, fever patients attacked by delirious mania or post-febrile melancholia, and alcoholics. All these, but especially the last, bulked large in a typical practice throughout this period.[50] Their care was always regarded as part of general medicine, and they were therefore treated at home or in a general hospital, where apparently they usually recovered very quickly. Otherwise, however, the general practitioner's role in suicide prevention hardly went beyond treating the preliminary

'the most common of all the medico-legal duties thrown on medical men': Clouston, *Clinical Lectures* (5th edn.), p. 672; and medical handbooks and directories, as well as lectures to medical students on mental diseases, always offered much practical advice on certification.

[46] *The Lancet*, 1884, ii. 606, 4 Oct.; *The Times*, 16 Aug. 1888, p. 7, col. d. In 1841 W. A. F. Browne had urged a temporary asylum exclusively for those who had attempted suicide: *The Lancet*, 1840–1, ii. 370–1, 5 June 1841.

[47] See n. 23.

[48] 'A recognized suicidal tendency is often the principal reason, in the eyes of the public at least, for sending a patient to an asylum': Adams, 'Suicide—From a General Practitioner's Point of View', p. 470. Even Bucknill, in the midst of his criticisms of excessive use of asylums, acknowledged that 'it is right to place a lunatic with delusions leading to self-destruction in the greater security of an asylum', although 'it would be stupidly cruel to lock a man up in an asylum who had attempted his life under the depression caused by cholaemia or some other temporary influence': *The Care of the Insane*, p. 116.

[49] With some reinforcement from the statute law in this case, for when a pauper lunatic was discharged, his relatives or friends had to undertake in writing that he would be no longer chargeable to any Union, and would be properly taken care of and prevented from doing injury to himself or others: 16 & 17 Vict., c. 97, s. 81.

[50] The increasing rarity of such fevers as scarlet fever and smallpox was counterbalanced by the advent of major influenza epidemics after 1889.

symptoms of melancholia ('sleeplessness, depression, want of interest and irritability, with fears and suspicions of all sorts', said Clouston),[51] and ensuring, once he had recognized dangerous symptoms, that the patient was sent away—an onerous task in which fatal failures were probably commoner than medical men admitted publicly, even in their own gatherings,[52] given the scarcity of appropriate knowledge, experience, and interest. All things considered, the chief contribution of Victorian and Edwardian general practitioners to the prevention of suicide may have been the unconscious and fortuitous one implied in 1880 by that doyen of psychological medicine, J. C. Bucknill. 'The family doctor often treats and cures a case of lunacy almost without knowing it', wrote Bucknill of insanity as it occurred among the middle and upper classes, for 'without paying that attention to the mental condition which he ought to do, he treats the failure of bodily health upon which it depends, and the patient frequently recovers in mind and body';[53] and in so far as this was so, any practitioner who treated illness or debility at any social level may sometimes unwittingly have had a genuine share in averting certain sorts of suicidal behaviour.

A far more conscious and direct effort at suicide prevention was forthcoming from a very much smaller band of medical men: the medical officers (or 'surgeons') of the big city prisons which housed a large floating population of remand prisoners. Throughout the later nineteenth century and well into the twentieth, expert psychiatric attention was much more likely to be given to those whose attempts at suicide entangled them with the machinery of the law, than to those whose behaviour remained known only to themselves, their friends, and their family doctor. How did this rather surprising situation come about?

From the later 1860s, metropolitan magistrates made a practice of remanding those about whose mental state they felt some doubt to the

---

[51] Clouston drew students' particular attention to the few forms of insanity which were usually treated by the general practitioner. Those associated with a risk of suicide are discussed in his *Clinical Lectures* (5th edn.), pp. 482, 544, 692, 706. Much the same points were made, very briefly, in Adams, 'Suicide—From a General Practitioner's Point of View'.

[52] W. F. Wade told the Psychology Section at the annual meeting of the British Medical Association in 1879 that there was 'a class of cases in which we ourselves are to blame' for not preventing suicide, but that he believed it was a small one: 'On the Prevention of Suicide', p. 533.

[53] Bucknill, *The Care of the Insane*, p. 114.

House of Detention in Clerkenwell for observation by its new and energetic surgeon, Dr William Smiles; and they especially directed Smiles's attention to those remanded on a charge of attempted suicide.[54] In adopting this practice they were probably responding not to contemporary medical urgings that attempted suicide should always be regarded as a sign of insanity and equated with bodily disease, but to the campaign to secure asylum care for the insane poor after the much-discussed revelations in *The Lancet* in 1865–7 about the unsatisfactory state of sick and insane paupers in metropolitan workhouses.[55] However this may be, magistrates dealing with suicide charges in the metropolitan area anticipated by over twenty years the Home Office circular of 1889 which urged magistrates to obtain medical evidence as to the medical condition of prisoners in all doubtful cases, and to treat those considered insane as ordinary lunatics unless their offence was a grave one.[56] At the end of the century other developments reinforced this approach, for progressive penal reformers and administrators became increasingly convinced that most criminal behaviour had a physical basis in heredity and 'degeneracy', and above all in feeble-mindedness and inebriety.[57] Accordingly, not

[54] For example, in the 12 months before Oct. 1873, Smiles 'watched and certified to the state of mind of 113 prisoners supposed to be insane', and his attention was also 'directed to 64 males and 129 females committed for attempted suicide': House of Detention, Clerkenwell, Surgeon's Annual Report, GLRO, MJ/SP1873/Oct./16. Smiles (an Edinburgh graduate) replaced the elderly Henry Wakefield as surgeon to the Middlesex House of Correction and House of Detention in 1862. He long held an appointment as physician to the St Pancras Royal General Dispensary, and at various times was Vice-President and Secretary of the Medical Society of London, and a Corresponding Fellow of the Academy of Surgery of Madrid.

[55] This campaign stimulated the setting up of the Metropolitan Asylums Board in 1867: McCandless, ' "Build! Build!" ', p. 569. In 1867 2 people remanded on a charge of attempted suicide were for the first time recorded as having been sent directly from Clerkenwell to a lunatic asylum: Chaplain's Annual Report, GLRO, MA/RS/1/501.

[56] Walker and McCabe, *Crime and Insanity in England*, ii. 59. The numbers sent for trial for attempted suicide were always much too small for it to be likely that in developing this practice metropolitan magistrates were swayed by the concern for efficiency and economy which lay behind the Home Office circular of 1889.

[57] For an indication of general trends in criminology at this time see McDonald, *The Sociology of Law and Order*, pp. 81–2, and Walker and McCabe, *Crime and Insanity in England*, ii. 23–4; and for the popularity of a medical model of deviance, see Nye, *Crime, Madness and Politics in Modern France*, pp. 330–8. It is notable that in the late nineteenth century the chaplain's quarters inside prison were handed over to the medical officer 'whenever possible': Griffiths (1838–1908: *DNB*), *Fifty Years of Public Service*, p. 286; and that when Holloway was reorganized in 1902, the posts of Medical Officer and Governor were combined—a step as significant as the much more renowned combination of the posts of Chaplain and Governor at Millbank in 1837. For the diffusion among medical men in the 1870s of the belief that crime, alcoholism, epilepsy,

only was the prison medical service allotted a more central role, but knowledge of mental diseases came to be singled out as the one indispensable qualification in its members.[58] One sign of the times was that the new Medical Commissioner appointed in 1897 was interested in biometrics (whereas his predecessor had specialized in prison diet-aries);[59] another was that a leading specialist in mental defect, Sir H. Bryan Donkin, was appointed in 1898 Medical Adviser to the Prison Commission; and yet another was the entry into the prison medical service in the 1890s of a number of young registered practitioners with research interests and qualifications in psychological medicine—notably J. J. Pitcairn, G. B. Griffiths, W. C. Sullivan, and W. Norwood East. These young men were eager to use their unique opportunities to investigate one of the most discussed questions of the day, namely, the links between deviant behaviour, degeneracy, insanity, feeble-mindedness, and inebriety; and in this they were encouraged by the new style of prison administration developed at the Home Office after 1895.

With all five of these topical problems one action was held to be supremely associated: attempted suicide. Naturally, therefore, the cases of those remanded on such a charge were eagerly studied by prison medical officers of the new sort. Between 1885 and 1902 Holloway was probably 'the largest depot for untried prisoners in the world', and every year some 22,000 people drawn from an area of about 200 squares miles passed through the hands of its medical staff. Of these, about a thousand were kept under observation for indications of insanity, around half because the committing magistrate had specific-ally requested a mental report, and the rest on the strength of infor-mation from relatives or warders, or because of the special significance attached to their alleged offence.[60] Those charged with attempted suicide were invariably kept under this kind of observation, whether or not the committing magistrate had asked for a mental report. As a

and insanity were all the effects of a hereditarily diseased soma, see Jacyna, 'Somatic Theories of Mind and the Interests of Medicine', p. 255.

[58] The recommendation of the Gladstone Committee in 1895 that candidates for medical appointments in the prison service should be required to show that they had given special attention to lunacy amazed the old guard, who pointed out that the most important disease in prisons was tuberculosis: PP 1896 [C. 7995] XLIV, pp. 38–9.

[59] For the interests of the former (Herbert Smalley), see Sir E. Ruggles-Brise (1857–1935: *DNB*) in Goring, *The English Convict*, p. iii; and for those of the latter (R. M. Gover) see Griffiths, *Fifty Years of Public Service*, pp. 264, 286, 313.

[60] Pitcairn, 'The Detection of Insanity in Prisons', pp. 59, 62, and Tables I and II, p. 60.

result, each year throughout the 1890s well over 400 men and women who were alleged to have tried to commit suicide in the metropolis were psychiatrically examined.[61] The driving force behind this extensive psychiatric work at Holloway was not the senior Medical Officer there, who until 1897 was George Walker, a man with qualifications in public health and apparently no interest in psychological medicine, but his young assistant appointed in 1890, J. J. Pitcairn. After qualifying in 1887, Pitcairn had gone on to take the Certificate of the Medico-Psychological Association in 1889; and in 1897, he contributed a paper to the journal of that Association which drew attention to the procedures used at Holloway and claimed that virtually every latent case of insanity among those charged with attempted suicide was detected and 'filtered out' to a lunatic asylum.[62] In the same year Walker was replaced as senior Medical Officer there by James Scott, a progressive who was himself a member of the Medico-Psychological Association and had studied at Vienna as well as Edinburgh. In 1902 Holloway became exclusively a prison for women and the posts of Governor and Medical Officer were combined, thus creating an important new post of Deputy Governor and Medical Officer which went to another man with keen research interests, G. B. Griffiths of Parkhurst.[63] Facilities for observing suicidal and mental cases were at the same time much improved by converting the old male hospital to this use,[64] and in the twelve months from 1 April 1904 Griffiths placed 184 women charged with attempted suicide under mental observation in this special hospital accommodation.[65] Meanwhile, Brixton had become the prison

[61] For the figures for 1890–6 see Pitcairn, 'The Detection of Insanity in Prisons', Tables I–III, pp. 60–1, and for those for subsequent years, see the extracts from the reports of the Medical Officer of Holloway printed each year in the Appendix to the *Prison Commissioners' ARs*. It is striking that only 848 women were remanded to Holloway specially for observation and report in 1890–6, although 1,250 women charged with attempted suicide were kept under observation there in these years. Perhaps magistrates connected this offence so readily with the increased female drunkenness then so notorious that to them a mental report usually seemed unnecessary.

[62] Pitcairn, 'The Detection of Insanity in Prisons', p. 61. Successive editions of the *Medical Directory* give details of Pitcairn's career and publications (which included support for the treatment of inebriates in special reformatories instead of prisons).

[63] At Parkhurst Griffiths had initiated a now renowned piece of biometrical research designed to establish whether English convicts bore out the theories of Lombroso and the Italian criminal anthropologists: Goring, *The English Convict*, p. iii.

[64] *Prison Commissioners' AR*, 1902–03, p. 340.

[65] These 184 women accounted for a quarter of all the cases Griffiths placed under mental observation in that year, although they represented less than 7 per cent of the total number of Holloway's unconvicted prisoners: PP 1908 [Cd. 4215] XXXV, Table B, pp. 200–2. In 1890–6, however, attempted suicide cases had accounted for as much

to which men remanded on a charge of attempted suicide were sent; and since the Medical Officer chosen to inaugurate the new regime was James Scott, the procedures adopted there were naturally the same as those used in Holloway. Each year in the first decade after 1902 some 270 men charged with attempted suicide were placed in Brixton's hospital for mental report,[66] and again enterprising clinical research and experimental innovations were forthcoming from a young assistant, this time Norwood East, later one of Britain's most distinguished criminal psychologists. East had come under the influence of that leading specialist in suicide as a symptom of mental disorder, G. H. Savage, while a student at Guy's, and had spent a couple of years as resident medical officer in two mental hospitals before entering the prison medical service in 1899. At Brixton he undertook a systematic and wide-ranging study of one thousand consecutive attempted suicide cases remanded there between 1907 and 1910 (the results of which he reported to the Medico-Psychological Association in 1913), and embarked upon his first psycho-therapeutic interviews, choosing selected adolescent and adult men charged with attempted suicide for these experiments.[67]

Thus as early as the late 1860s nearly 200 men and women charged with attempted suicide in the metropolitan area each year underwent a week's psychiatric examination while on remand; and by the 1890s and 1900s this number had increased to about 450. In other words, the proportion placed under mental observation rose from just over half to almost four-fifths of all those taken into custody for attempted suicide by the Metropolitan Police.[68] What happened in other cities is uncertain, apart from the fact that at Walton prison in Liverpool about 100 prisoners charged with attempted suicide were being mentally examined each year in the later 1890s, when the deputy medical officer there was another keen young member of the Medico-Psychological Association who had entered the prison service after clinical experience

as 59 per cent of the female, although only 33 per cent of the male observation cases at Holloway: Pitcairn, 'The Detection of Insanity in Prisons', Tables I–III, pp. 60–1.

[66] East, 'On attempted suicide', Table I, p. 433.

[67] Home Office: East and Hubert, *Report on the Psychological Treatment of Crime*, p. 10, para. 33. For East's career (1872–1933), see *DNB*.

[68] The average annual number taken into custody for this offence in the metropolitan police district in 1867–75 was 353: *Miscellaneous Statistics of the U.K., 1867–75*, Crime &c: Metropolitan Police, no. 2. For the average annual number of apprehensions in 1893–7 and 1909–13, see Table 6.2.

in a lunatic asylum, W. C. Sullivan.[69] It is likely that the total extent of such work was considerable; and if the number of such investigations was high, their quality was probably not low, for posts at such prisons as Holloway and Walton were regarded as exceptionally demanding and accordingly were apt to be given to men who were particularly well thought of, and who were, moreover, better provided than usual with assistance.

Yet how substantial were the practical results of all this daily interviewing, note-taking, and observation? Did psychiatric investigation on remand make a notable contribution to the prevention of suicide? It is difficult to be convinced that it did. After all, its primary purpose was to assist not the person in question, but the courts. Before an examining magistrate discharged someone taken into custody, he needed to be assured that it was safe to do so, in the sense that the prisoner showed no indications of insanity and was sufficiently calm and rational for his promise not to do such a thing again to have some value; equally, before he committed him for trial (if that was what he contemplated), he needed to be assured that the accused was fully responsible for his actions, and not so mentally defective as to be incapable of benefiting from prison discipline. The primary object was thus simply to identify for the courts gross cases of certifiable insanity or serious mental deficiency among those alleged to have tried to destroy themselves. True, this must in its way be reckoned a contribution to the prevention of suicide. But how many cases of this kind were removed to the care of an appropriate institution through the work of the prison medical service? Clearly very few. Both inside and outside the service, the proportion of those who tried to commit suicide who were in some sense insane was endlessly debated. Informed estimates often ranged between a third and a seventh, with the proviso that insanity was more closely linked with completed suicide than with abortive attempts. No prison medical officer, however, would report as legally certifiable more than a very small proportion of those he considered to be suffering from some sort of mental illness or disturbance. Contrary to popular imaginings, medical men were notably

---

[69] Sullivan, 'Alcoholism and Suicidal Impulses', p. 259. Sullivan had studied in Paris as well as Cork and Dublin (where he held the Stewart Scholarship in Mental Diseases), and was a member of the Neurological Society as well as the Medico-Psychological Association. His first post was that of Clinical Assistant in Richmond Lunatic Asylum. After his initial appointment in the prison medical service at Walton, he was promoted to Pentonville and then to Holloway. In 1911 he went to Paris to look into intelligence testing: Walker and McCabe, *Crime and Insanity*, ii. 24.

cautious about certification, particularly after the libertarian outcries of the mid-Victorian years. Prison doctors were well aware that those on remand for attempted suicide were very unlikely to be their usual selves, even if the case was not complicated by the effects of alcohol. Confident young medical officers (unlike their elders) might think that a week usually sufficed to determine the presence of insanity; but even they acknowledged that seven days were not enough for a firm diagnosis of the particular form of insanity involved, and admitted that great difficulties arose from their patients' habit of keeping quiet about facts which they thought might prejudice them in court, and from the absence of case histories.[70] It was very often impossible to get sufficient evidence to certify them as insane, and in any event, many were genuinely hovering on the borderline between depression and melancholia, sanity and insanity.[71] The committing magistrate in his turn was likely to be reluctant to proceed with certification except in a very clear case, if only because every person sent to a local asylum placed a considerable burden on the rates;[72] and limited weight might be given to a mental report, at least by a lay magistrate. In 1910, for example, the principal Medical Officer at Brixton, S. R. Dyer (a very senior man who was shortly to become Medical Inspector of Prisons) reported that a certain remand prisoner was very depressed and nervous, that both he and his mother had previously been in an asylum, that two sisters and a brother had committed suicide, and that the prisoner himself admitted that he was quite unable to stop making suicide attempts. Dyer was clear that he would be better in an asylum: 'He is a skilled tailor and anxious to go back to his work, but one feels it would hardly be safe with these suicidal tendencies and histories.' Yet despite all this, the sitting alderman at the Guildhall merely gave this man some good advice, requested the City police to investigate the circumstances surrounding his purchase of laudanum, and discharged him.[73]

This magistrate's response may not have been typical; but certainly

---

[70] East, 'On Attempted Suicide', p. 473.

[71] See the remarks of James Scott in 1905 and Norwood East in 1922: *Transactions of the Medico-Legal Society*, ii (1904–5), p. 98, and xvii (1922–3), p. 38.

[72] Asylum care was reckoned to require 3 times more money from the rates than workhouse care. After 1877 prison care, including care in a criminal lunatic asylum, was paid for entirely by central government.

[73] It is true that the House Physician at Bart's had initially been of the opinion that this man was not definitely certifiable: CLRO, Guildhall Justice Room, Notes of Evidence, 1910, 15 and 23 Nov., ff. 70, 115, and 'Attempted Suicide', *City Press*, 26 Nov. 1910, p. 7.

the numbers sent direct from remand to an asylum were very small. Between 1867 and 1875, for example, only 13 of the 1,743 men and women remanded to Clerkenwell on a charge of attempted suicide were reported to have been sent thence to an asylum; and even in 1904, only seven of the 184 women remanded to Holloway on this charge were so dealt with.[74] In Liverpool too only 'a small proportion' of those remanded on this charge in 1896–7 were sent to an asylum on the prison medical officer's report.[75] It is true that Norwood East diagnosed insanity in as many as 12.3 per cent of the men remanded to Brixton on a charge of attempted suicide between 1907 and 1910;[76] but he is silent on how often certification was recommended for these men, as well as on how often the magistrates did proceed to certify them. Clearly not all those who were certifiable were filtered out at the remand stage, for some of those sent for trial for attempted suicide were subsequently found insane either before trial, or by a trial jury— proportionately far more, indeed, than in the case of those sent for trial for the ordinary run of offences;[77] and the mental report of the prison medical officer could be as crucial at this as at an earlier stage.[78] The absolute numbers involved, however, were again very small. In 1881–3, for example, only three men and two women (or 2 per cent) of all those sent for trial for attempted suicide in England and Wales were sent to a criminal lunatic asylum.[79] In short, a mere handful of people with active suicidal tendencies who were believed to be suffering from severe mental disorder were certified and sent to an asylum as a result of psychiatric observation of their case by prison medical officers either while they were on remand, or later, when they had been committed for trial. Once in an asylum, these people were indeed vigilantly protected from death by suicide, whatever their lot in other respects; but such people were few.

---

[74] House of Detention, Clerkenwell, Chaplain's Annual Reports to the Middlesex Justices, 1867–75, GLRO, MA/RS/1/501, 508, 514, 516, 521, 526, 531, 536, and MJ/OC/65; PP 1908 [Cd. 4215] XXXV, Table B, pp. 200–2.

[75] Sullivan, 'Alcoholism and Suicidal Impulses', p. 270.

[76] East, 'On Attempted Suicide', p. 472. Of these 123 men, 83 were diagnosed as cases of melancholia, 33 as alcoholic insanity, 3 as cases of stupor, and 4 as delusional: ibid., Table XX.

[77] In 1881–3, for example, such prisoners were almost 10 times more likely to be declared insane before trial than were the general run of offenders (those accused of murder excepted), and nearly twice as likely to be found insane by a trial jury: *Judicial Statistics, 1881–83*, Part I, p. 45.

[78] Pitcairn, 'The Detection of Insanity in Prisons', p. 61.

[79] *Judicial Statistics, 1881–83*, Part I, p. 45.

Was any other contribution to the prevention of suicide made by the large amount of time and public money expended from the later 1860s on providing close medical attention to those remanded on a charge of attempted suicide? In the first years of the twentieth century the socially concerned sometimes pressed for these medical observations to be used to filter out two other groups seen as both prone to suicidal behaviour and in need of specialized institutional care and control: inebriates and mental defectives. Since to attempt suicide was widely considered a sign of 'degeneracy' (that turn-of-the-century bogey), its relaxed treatment by the courts was inevitably deplored by those who were concerned for the welfare of the race. From the 1870s the lobby for inebriates' reformatories had claimed that enforced detention of habitual drunkards would reduce deaths from suicide,[80] and in the late 1890s this lobby acquired a valuable supporter inside the prison medical service in W. C. Sullivan, whose observations at Walton gaol convinced him that what lay behind over three-quarters of suicide attempts was alcoholism. Other medical men quickly pointed out that Liverpool was hardly a typical district.[81] Sullivan, however, zealously publicized his finding that statistically the incidence of attempted, as opposed to completed, suicide reflected very closely the incidence of alcoholism;[82] and many people were persuaded that there were links between the two. When such people also believed that alcoholism could be cured by two or three years in a reformatory, they naturally argued that the sure and certain way to reduce the number

---

[80] In 1870 the first private bill for such a reformatory defined a habitual drunkard as 'a person who, not being amenable to any jurisdiction of lunacy, is notwithstanding by reason of habitual drinking of intoxicating liquors, dangerous to himself or herself or to others, or incapable of managing himself or herself, or his or her affairs'; and this definition was ultimately embodied in the Habitual Drunkards Act of 1879: MacLeod, ' "The Edge of Hope" ', p. 219 n. 14.

[81] See the report of the discussion after Sullivan's paper: Sullivan, 'Alcoholism and Suicidal Impulses', p. 269.

[82] After the appearance of 'Alcoholism and Suicidal Impulses' in 1898 and 'Cases of Suicidal Impulse in Cerebral Automatism' in 1899, Sullivan published in 1900 'The Relation of Alcoholism to Suicide in England'. This much-discussed paper was summarized editorially in *The Lancet*, and its conclusions were debated by the Psychological Section of the British Medical Association at its annual meeting in 1900, and by John Macdonell, Master of the Supreme Court, in his introduction to the *Judicial Statistics* for 1899: *The Lancet*, 1900, i. 1081–2, 14 Apr., ii. 390, 11 Aug.; *Judicial Statistics, 1899*, pp. 38–41. In 1903 he published 'Inebriety and Suicide', and finally in 1906 his book, *Alcoholism: A Chapter in Social Pathology* (in which see especially pp. 54–5, 66–7, 74). The novelty of Sullivan's increasingly subtle argument lay in his association of alcoholism with attempted as opposed to completed suicide.

of suicide attempts was for magistrates to ensure that all those who came before them on a charge of attempted suicide committed under the influence of drink were sent thither. Their case was forcefully put by the Inebriates Acts Inspector, Dr R. W. Branthwaite. At present, he pointed out in his report for 1904, 96 per cent of those taken into custody for attempted suicide were allowed to go home, where with the best will in the world it would be practically impossible to keep drink out of their hands; while the few sent to prison received sentences which were too short to be curative, and lost any self-respect they might still possess. What was needed, therefore, was for magistrates to be given summary powers to send straight to an inebriates' reformatory all those charged with attempted suicide who were habitual drunkards. Meanwhile, they should make a point of sending them for trial on the two counts of habitual drunkenness and attempted suicide, so that if the court was satisfied that the attempt was made under the influence of drink, it could order detention in a reformatory for up to three years under Part I of the Inebriates Act of 1898. Branthwaite was confident that 'if freely done, this would materially reduce the yearly number of suicides';[83] and in 1908 a Home Office committee and forty-five expert witnesses agreed.[84] But was this ever freely done? Down to 1907 attempted suicide accounted for only 7 per cent of the offences which led to a reformatory sentence under Part I of the 1898 Inebriates Act; and in the whole period between 1903 and 1913, a mere 38, or just over 1 per cent of the 3,080 men and women sent for trial on a charge of attempted suicide were sentenced to detention in inebriates' reformatories.[85] These are figures of failure. In Brixton alone,

---

[83] PP 1905 [Cd. 2590] XI, pp. 14–15.

[84] PP 1908 [Cd. 4438] XII, pp. 16–17, para. 52; PP 1908 [Cd. 4439] XII, pp. 145–6. Only H. C. Bennett, with characteristic realism, insisted that already police magistrates in practice dealt summarily with cases of attempted suicide and had power to send such people to reformatories under the Inebriates Act of 1898, if they really were habitual drunkards: ibid., p. 41, Qs. 578–81. In 1905 a member of the Royal Commission on the Care and Control of the Feeble-Minded, the Revd. H. N. Burden (representing the National Institutions for Inebriates) elicited assent from Herbert Smalley, then Medical Inspector on the Prison Commission, to the proposition that 'more suicide cases might be sent by magistrates to Sessions and then dealt with at Sessions by being sent to inebriate reformatories or some similar institution': PP 1908 [Cd. 4215] XXXV, p. 192, Q. 3400.

[85] PP 1908 [Cd. 4342] XII, p. 5; *Judicial Statistics, 1909–13*, Part I, Table V and see ch. 8, n. 138. The greatest support for these reformatories came from the London authorities; and it will be remembered that in the metropolitan area magistrates did send those charged with attempted suicide for trial much more often in these years: see ch. 8, Table 7.1.

Norwood East recorded alcoholism as the cause of almost 40 per cent of his attempted suicide cases between 1907 and 1910; and in 1913 he considered that this figure should have been higher still, since some of those whom he had classified as having attempted suicide through weak-mindedness had been reduced to that state through alcoholism.[86] Clearly prison medical officers, however enthusiastic, were unable to channel towards reformatories more than a tiny proportion of the alcoholics with suicidal tendencies who came under their observation—and understandably, for these institutions cost too much to ratepayers and were too unpopular and draconian in their approach to become a central part of early twentieth-century penal practice.

What of the mental defectives whom they encountered? In these Edwardian years, mental deficiency seemed to many socially concerned people to be closely intertwined with all the problems which most disturbed them: poverty, illiteracy, petty crime, habitual drunkenness—and soaring numbers of suicide attempts. Prison medical officers informed committing magistrates when they considered that a prisoner on remand was feeble-minded, although not certifiably insane. In 1904 three of the 184 women remanded to Holloway on a charge of attempted suicide were reported in this way.[87] At Brixton between 1907 and 1910 East considered that as many as forty-six out of the thousand male prisoners charged with attempted suicide whom he studied were feeble-minded, although he did not regard their condition as the sole cause of their suicide attempt, nor did he record how many of them were officially so reported to the committing magistrate.[88] In any case, although such reports served to prevent a prison sentence (for feeble-mindedness both extenuated the offence and indicated incapacity to benefit from the discipline of prison life), they can hardly have done much to prevent another suicide attempt by the person in question. Before the Mental Deficiency Act of 1913,[89] the feeble-minded could not be compulsorily sent to a special institution for care and

---

[86] East, 'On Attempted Suicide', Table XX and p. 455. His 393 alcoholic cases included 141 cases of alcoholic impulse with amnesia, 171 of alcoholic impulse with memory retained, 31 of post-alcoholic depression, 33 of alcoholic insanity, and 1 alcoholic accident. It should be added that only in about a third of these cases was alcoholism recorded as the sole cause of the attempt, and that only in 61 cases did East diagnose alcoholism as a physical condition: ibid., p. 447.

[87] PP 1908 [Cd. 4215] XXXV, Table B, pp. 200–2.

[88] East, 'On Attempted Suicide', Table XX.

[89] This act is discussed in Simmons, 'Explaining Social Policy: the English Mental Deficiency Act of 1913'.

protection, unless they came under the Inebriates Act as habitual drunkards. A conscientious magistrate might take special care to entrust such a person to the care of his friends or a social worker or to bind him over for six months, or have him admitted to a 'feeble ward' of a workhouse; but he could hardly do anything else to safeguard him. In any case, most people remanded for attempted suicide seemed 'on the border-line', no more. They would have been helped by preventive psychiatric treatment as out-patients, Norwood East believed;[90] but even in 1913 such treatment was novel and in short supply, and since they were not clearly a danger to themselves or others, they were discharged by the magistrates in the way already described.

Yet it would be a mistake to suppose that the practice of placing those remanded on a charge of attempted suicide in a medical observation ward merely achieved specialist institutional care and custody for the very few who clearly needed this. It had a much more immediate and general usefulness. Most obviously, it ensured for all such people at least seven days of constant watchfulness against any further attempt. Very stringent precautions were taken by remand prisons after a Home Office investigation in 1879 had shown that their prisoners were among the most likely to commit suicide.[91] In the early 1900s 'very careful watching' was reported to have been required in Holloway, because many of the women remanded there for attempted suicide had been on reception 'acutely depressed'.[92] As a rule, however, those who had already tried to end their lives were not the prisoners most likely to try to commit suicide: remorse or lethargy often followed such an act, especially when it had been impulsive or more or less unconscious.[93] What they did nearly always need was favourable bodily conditions for recovering from shock, if not from tension and depression; and it was these which prison hospitals provided—and which would otherwise often have been unobtainable by the homeless, unemployed, hard-drinking, derelict men and women who largely

---

[90] East, 'On Attempted Suicide', p. 476, and see n. 23. In 1907 the new out-patients' department for mental diseases of Charing Cross Hospital offered to see cases referred by the Salvation Army's Anti-Suicide Bureau: 'Hospitals' Duty', *Daily Express*, 5 Jan. 1907, p. 8.

[91] *Prison Commissioners' AR, 1879–80*, pp. 18, 54–62. Clerkenwell (then the remand prison for Middlesex) was found to have had a far larger ratio of suicides than any other prison in 1874–9: *Prison Commissioners' AR, 1878–79*, Appendix 25, p. 84.

[92] *Prison Commissioner's AR, 1903–04*, p. 333.

[93] Cf. ibid., p. 40, and *Prison Commissioner's AR, 1904–05*, p. 37; East, 'On Attempted Suicide', p. 474.

made up the prison population for this offence. Ample plain food, quiet, warm clothing, a bed with sufficient bedding in a warmed and well-ventilated room, and knowledgeable and well-intentioned treatment—all these the hospitals of the metropolitan remand prisons claimed to give,[94] and probably with some justice. The hospitals of remand prisons were at least far more comfortable than either penal prisons or casual workhouse wards. Norwood East himself was firmly of the opinion that the medical, 'moral' (that is, psychological), and practical help given in Brixton did benefit the non-insane cases who made up the great majority of attempted suicides remanded there. Clearly he was far from an impartial judge. Yet whether or not the psycho-therapeutic interviews he conducted between 1907 and 1910 were as successful as he thought, and whatever the effectiveness of the various good samaritans bent on practical help who visited the hospital beds as they visited the cells, at least these days on remand were days of enforced rest and comparatively healthy routine. Cases of initial exhaustion and general debility were always quite common;[95] and for such people as well as for those who had already spent a week or two in a general hospital recovering from acute self-inflicted injuries, the observation ward of a remand prison provided a week's convalescent care which they would not usually have had otherwise. For one reason and another it is not too difficult to credit East's statement that when the Medical Officer suggested a second week on remand, 'not a few' agreed to become 'voluntary boarders', and that with a depressed but not certifiable patient the improvement during this second week was nearly always very marked.[96]

Nevertheless, however rosy a view is taken of the medical work done in remand prisons, by definition this work could help only a small minority of those with suicidal tendencies, and then only during a few short days. True, those days were often vital ones; and Norwood East at least found that only alcoholics and those who used a half-hearted suicide attempt as a means of getting access to shelter, work or 'charitable relief' were at all likely to return thereafter on the same charge.[97] The fact remains, however, that it was not in the country's remand prisons that long-term concentrations of men and women

[94] Ibid., p. 431.
[95] Of East's 1,000 Brixton cases, 291 were in bad or indifferent physical condition on reception: ibid., p. 447.
[96] Ibid., p. 431.
[97] Ibid.

believed to be in danger of suicide and specialists in their care and treatment were to be found, but in its lunatic asylums. Perhaps 600 people charged with attempted suicide were annually under observation in the large remand prisons in the 1890s; but on average 4,000 men and women with suicidal tendencies were admitted each year to institutions licensed for the care of the insane in the 1880s.[98] Figures like these make it clear that it was not prison doctors whose professional duties gave them the greatest opportunity to save lives believed to be at risk from suicide, but those employed in the care and treatment of the insane.

Among medical men, the heavy end of the task of suicide prevention thus fell to the asylum doctors. How well did they shoulder it? If this question is taken to mean simply, how successfully did they prevent asylum patients registered as having suicidal tendencies from taking their own lives, the answer is plain: very successfully indeed. From the first, the Commissioners in Lunacy as well as the public regarded the prevention of suicide as one of the most important duties of the officers of every asylum, and failure provoked not only critical comment in the local press, but searching official investigations and the apportioning of blame by name in the published annual reports of the Commissioners to the Lord Chancellor.[99] A series of suicides would ruin any asylum career. Everywhere, therefore, asylum staff gave priority to frustrating any suicidal propensities among their patients. The record of the

---

[98] The statutory 'Statement of Particulars' filled in on admission included the question, 'whether suicidal', from 1845 in the case of licensed houses and hospitals for lunatics (except Bethlem), and from 1853 in the case of county and borough asylums and Bethlem: 8 & 9 Vict., c. 100, Schedules B and D, and 16 & 17 Vict., c. 97, Schedule F. In 1879–88 about a fifth of the men admitted to licensed houses and over a quarter of those admitted to local authority asylums were registered as suicidal, while a quarter of the women admitted to private licensed houses and as many as a third of those admitted to local authority asylums were so registered, and altogether an annual average of 2,200 suicidal women and 1,750 suicidal men were admitted to these institutions: *Lunacy Commissioners' 44th AR*, p. 59, Table XIX. It is understandable that suicidal propensities were commoner among female admissions, since men were much less likely to survive suicide attempts; and also that they were commoner among local authority asylum admissions, since those who could afford to enter private licensed houses were much more likely to be able to arrange suitable care in such circumstances without having recourse to any custodial institution at all.

[99] The Commissioners in Lunacy directed legal proceedings to be taken against asylum staff whom they considered guilty of wilful neglect: see e.g. their *31st AR*, p. 109. All deaths in asylums were statutorily required to be reported within 2 days to the local coroner: see ch. 1 n. 30.

county and borough asylums was particularly good in this respect. Only a minute proportion of deaths in these institutions was ever caused by a suicidal act within them: 0.63 per cent in 1867, for example, and a miniscule 0.14 per cent in 1911.[100]

Asylum staff were understandably proud of such figures. How did they achieve them? 'Proper arrangements' and 'due vigilance' were the twin prescriptions of the Commissioners in Lunacy. Neither, however, was easily managed. First, there were problems of staffing. It was often hard for an asylum superintendent to squeeze enough money from either a local authority or a private proprietor to employ sufficient staff to ensure constant watching, day and night;[101] and at least until the end of the century it was quite as difficult for him to secure attendants who were of the right quality, and to discipline and supervise them adequately.[102] Secondly, there were problems of buildings, fittings, and equipment—problems whose solution could be delayed by professional disagreements as well as by financial constraints. In 1873, for example, the Commissioners in Lunacy published plans for a model 'Observation Dormitory' for new asylums, with single rooms opening directly off it, each with wide slits in the upper half of its doors, and they also recommended a series of other devices for ensuring efficient night watching; yet ten years later they had to report that only seventeen of the sixty-two county and borough asylums had made 'very good' provision for watching suicidal and epileptic patients at night, while six had made no provision at all.[103] Safety stops on all windows were elementary, as were such things as a strong dress with a special buckle, no hairpins, no tapes, no handkerchiefs, no sharp

---

[100] *Lunacy Commissioners' 22nd AR*, Appendix A, pp. 106–7 and *66th AR*, pp. 15, 43. At Colney Hatch, only 2 out of the 2,900 female patients treated there in 1851–63 committed suicide, and of the 243 patients who died in this vast county asylum in 1877, only 1 died by suicide: Hunter and Macalpine, *Psychiatry for the Poor*, pp. 188, 249.

[101] The Commissioners constantly reported that they had strongly urged stricter care upon a local Committee of Visitors but found that they 'did not concur in our views': for example, *Lunacy Commissioners' 22nd AR*, p. 81. On the other hand in the 1850s and 1860s the Visiting Justices 'willingly' sanctioned special attendants for suicidal patients at Colney Hatch: Hunter and Macalpine, *Psychiatry for the Poor*, pp. 86, 94.

[102] In 1890 certificates of proficiency and a register of qualified asylum attendants were introduced, and in 1895 the Asylum Workers' Association was founded to improve the status of mental nurses: Walk, 'The History of Mental Nursing', pp. 11, 16. By 1897 over 2,400 nurses held certificates from the Medico-Psychological Association: Wood, 'The Asylum Trained and Certificated Nurses of the Medico-Psychological Association', p. 530.

[103] *Lunacy Commissioners' 37th AR*, pp. 62–6. For their plans of a 'Ward for Epileptic or Suicidal Patients' see their *28th AR*, pp. 26–7 and Appendix C.

knives, thick cups and gutta-percha chamber pots.[104] Experience, however, continually revealed new hazards. Moreover, although a safe environment was literally vital, laymen and medical men alike outlawed the easiest way of achieving it: mechanical restraint. After the reforming crusades of the earlier part of the century, mechanical restraint was 'part of a condemned and exploded system'.[105] Its denunciation became a shibboleth, and in 1845 and 1853 Parliament required any instance of its use to be recorded in the weekly Medical Journal and Case Book which every asylum was required to keep.[106] As late as 1888 J. C. Bucknill, by then one of the old guard, vehemently denounced G. H. Savage (his junior by twenty-five years) in the columns of *The Times* when he discovered that he had used mechanical restraint within the Royal Hospital of Bethlem itself, a place which ought to be a model to the profession. The irrepressible Savage retorted that his rule was to do 'what is best for the individual' and not to worship a dogma of either restraint or non-restraint;[107] but less flamboyant men admitted to such practices only apologetically and with assurances that they had been sanctioned by the Commissioners in Lunacy. Even Sir James Lawrence, the President of the Royal Hospitals of Bridewell and Bethlem, thought it desirable to point out when he came to Savage's defence that the Commissioners themselves had said that restraint might be more humane by mechanical than manual means;[108] and Fielding Blandford, when he told his students at St George's Hospital in 1871 that he had used mechanical restraint at night with certain suicidal cases, hastened to add that this had been done at the suggestion of the Commissioners.[109] Mechanical restraint long remained something about which the profession felt deep inhibitions and against which the law raised safeguards; and even in 1890,

[104] For a long list of such precautions, see Craig, *Psychological Medicine*, pp. 428–9. Almost every report of the Commissioners in Lunacy in the 1860s and 1870s reveals how ingenious suicidal patients could be.

[105] By 1856 Conolly (who had abolished mechanical restraints at Hanwell in 1839) believed that non-restraint had been almost generally accepted, except in the smaller private asylums: Conolly, *The Treatment of the Insane without Mechanical Restraints*, pp. 314, 322.

[106] 8 & 9 Vict., c. 100, Schedule H, and 16 & 17 Vict., c. 97, s. 90.

[107] *The Times*, 22 Aug., p. 6, col. f, 23 Aug., p. 1, col. f, 28 Aug., p. 13, col. d, 1888. Savage denied that he had used strait waistcoats or handcuffs, and claimed that his 'soft gloves' were really a means of increasing the liberty which could be permitted to patients: *The Lancet*, 1888, ii. 738, 13 Oct.

[108] *The Times*, 26 Sept. 1888, p. 11, col. f.

[109] Blandford, *Insanity and its Treatment*, p. 211.

when Parliament allowed that such restraint might sometimes be necessary, it required a medical certificate to that effect to be given, and did not remove the obligation to keep a full record and furnish a report to the Commissioners whenever it was used.[110]

It was thus apparently no straightforward task to guard and control the many patients who had over their beds the pink 'caution cards' which the Commissioners insisted upon for those with suicidal tendencies. Still, it was accomplished; and although each year thousands of patients were admitted with 'suicidal' against their names, only a dozen or so successful suicide attempts were annually made within asylum walls.[111] Given figures like these, it seems impossible to deny that Victorian and Edwardian asylum staff made a very substantial contribution indeed to the prevention of death by suicide. Yet was their achievement really so impressive as these figures indicate? Two considerations suggest that their task may not have been so formidable as appears at first sight. The first is the fact that quite slight suicidal tendencies were often enough to get someone into an asylum. Bucknill and Savage, although so often at loggerheads, agreed that certification documents exaggerated the extent of suicidal propensities. Thus in 1880 Bucknill protested that since 1845 'the law providing that madmen, dangerous to themselves and others, shall be secluded in madhouses for absolutely needful care and protection' had been made to cover a motley crowd of persons of weak mind or low spirits and 'persons said to have suicidal tendencies if they are not always under supervision'. Four years later Savage reported that during his twelve years as resident physician at Bethlem only 5 per cent of the patients there had made serious attempts at suicide or seemed likely to repeat such attempts, although between 20 and 30 per cent were always registered as suicidal: 'there is much more cry than wolf.'[112] Perhaps

---

[110] 53 & 54 Vict., c. 5, s. 40.

[111] About a third of those patients who did commit suicide, did so when out of the asylum 'on trial'. Inside an asylum, suicide was far more likely to occur among those not registered as suicidal or reckoned to be convalescent, than among those regarded as actively suicidal and so kept under constant supervision: see, for example, the figures for 1911 given in *Lunacy Commissioners' 66th AR*, p. 43, and the cases of 'S.G.' and 'H.C.' at Colney Hatch in 1888 and 1886: Hunter and Macalpine, *Psychiatry for the Poor*, p. 189. For the insistence by the Commissioners on the proper use of 'caution cards', see ibid., pp. 189–90.

[112] Bucknill, *The Care of the Insane*, pp. 3–4; Savage, *Insanity and Allied Neuroses*, p. 169, and 'Constant Watching of Suicidal Cases', p. 17. Clouston's experience in Edinburgh was very similar. In 1883 he considered that only 1 in 20 of his melancholia cases at Morningside was really intensely suicidal, although four-fifths had spoken of or attempted suicide: *Clinical Lectures* (1st edn.), p. 122.

then, many of those pink caution cards were unnecessary, and only a quarter or less of those stated on admission to have suicidal tendencies were in reality actively and dangerously suicidal.

The preventive achievement of the asylums also seems less spectacular when the statistical profile of suicidal patients is taken into account, for the published admission records suggest not only that suicidal patients may have been rather easier than most to manage and control, but also—and this is far more significant—that they were much more likely to make a quick recovery. In 1884–8, for example, the typical suicidal patient was a married woman, aged between twenty-five and thirty-four or between forty-five and fifty-four, and among male patients, suicidal tendencies were commonest among the elderly and rarest among young single men;[113] while in both sexes suicidal propensities were associated with one form of mental disorder above all others: melancholia.[114] Between 1879 and 1888 half the asylum patients who were admitted with suicidal propensities were classified as suffering from melancholia, as against only 14 per cent of the other patients admitted; and as time went on the preponderance of melancholics among suicidal patients grew.[115] The practical implications of this must have been substantial, since melancholia, as one Victorian specialist after another pointed out, was the most transient and the most curable of all varieties of insanity.[116] Melancholia was also a form of insanity in which the greatest danger of suicide came at the beginning; and although half-hearted suicidal demonstrations were common when a hypochondriacal melancholic was among relatives and friends, this strategy was rarely used in asylum surroundings.[117] Admittedly the suicidal impulse was always liable to return suddenly, or to be called up by the sight of some means of self-destruction; but it was when the melancholic patient returned home to his old environment that the danger of relapse was greatest.[118] Moreover, as Sankey told his students in 1865, 'the true melancholic will openly

---

[113] *Lunacy Commissioners' 44th AR*, pp. 70–1, Table XXVI.

[114] The two were assumed to be virtually synonymous by laymen and early alienists: for an example of the latter, see Burrows, *Commentaries*, p. 413.

[115] *Lunacy Commissioners' 44th AR*, pp. 68–9, Table XXV, and *53rd AR*, Appendix A, pp. 142–3, Table XXX.

[116] Fielding Blandford taught that the prognosis was favourable even for melancholia with delusions and hallucinations, 'if the general health be not much broken': *Insanity and its Treatment*, p. 166.

[117] Clouston, *Clinical Lectures*, 5th edn., p. 107; Bevan Lewis, *Mental Diseases*, p. 147.

[118] Blandford, 'Insanity', pp. 112–13.

attempt suicide. There is no concealment about the act, and he will soon disclose the mode by which he will try to effect his purpose', and hence could easily be forestalled. The really important point, however, was that, as Sankey had found after much experience at Hanwell and in his own private asylum, 'with attention to the health, the propensity to suicide in the majority of cases of melancholia will not last for a very long period, perhaps a month or six weeks'.[119] Sampling of the records of Colney Hatch for 1853–82 suggests that those in charge of that other great Middlesex asylum would probably have agreed with him;[120] while in 1899 Dr Henry Rayner of Hanwell and St Thomas's also reported that 'over half' of those admitted to asylums with melancholia recovered.[121] Conversely, suicidal patients very rarely were recorded as suffering from the two forms of insanity listed in these statistics which were virtually incurable: senile dementia and congenital insanity.[122] True, a sizeable proportion were listed as suffering from mania: and for these patients the prognosis would have been much less good than for the melancholics, and the task of controlling them much more difficult, in view of their paroxysms of angry excitement and outbursts of violent destructiveness.[123] The proportion of such patients among suicidal asylum admissions between 1879 and 1888 was much smaller than the proportion among non-suicidal admissions, however; and as time went on it diminished further.[124] In short, the typical asylum patient 'with suicidal propensity' was increasingly a middle-aged married woman suffering from melancholia, and thus someone who was both relatively easy to manage and also had a comparatively good chance of recovery.[125]

[119] Sankey, *Lectures on Mental Diseases*, pp. 230, 45.

[120] Brief sampling of the asylum's Registers and Case Books suggests that perhaps more than half of the suicidal melancholics admitted may have been discharged 'relieved' or 'well' within 18 months, but that much depended on there being someone willing to take responsibility for these convalescent patients, who quite often had no kin, or at least none living in the area. Typical examples are Emma Crockford and Caroline Gotch, both admitted on 4 Dec. 1872 suffering from suicidal melancholia, and discharged on 13 and 14 May 1873 respectively: GLRO, Acc. 1038/193. A similar male case in 1854 is briefly described in Hunter and Macalpine, *Psychiatry for the Poor*, p. 189.

[121] Rayner, 'Melancholia and Hypochondriasis', p. 374. Similarly, Clouston reported that 54 per cent of his melancholic asylum patients recovered, half within 3 months and 87 per cent within a year: *Clinical Lectures*, 5th edn., pp. 124–5.

[122] In 1879–88 only 2.4 per cent of suicidal patients were classified as suffering from senile dementia and 1.4 per cent from congenital insanity: *Lunacy Commissioners' 44th AR*, pp. 68–9, Table XXV.

[123] Cf. Blandford, 'Insanity', p. 99.

[124] See n. 156.

[125] This conclusion, based upon the published statistics of age, sex, and form of

Altogether, the task of treating, controlling, and caring for these many thousands of suicidal patients must have been considerably less formidable than appears at first sight, and in some respects, indeed, less difficult than the task of treating, controlling, and caring for the general run of non-suicidal patients. Even so, the fact remains that it was carried out with some success, not only in the primary sense that their safety was almost completely ensured, but also in the sense that after a few months many were considered well enough to be discharged as recovered or relieved. What then were the methods of treatment used as part of this not unsuccessful story? The years after the Lunatic Asylum Act of 1845, when the number of patients received into asylums climbed steeply,[126] were also the years when purging and blood-letting were abandoned in the treatment of insanity, as they were in general medicine.[127] The drastic treatments common in the 1840s and 1850s—when insanity was still seen as usually the result of either a disorder of the stomach and viscera or congestion of the blood vessels of the brain and purging, emetics, setons, and blood-letting were the order of the day—were shunned by the men who entered the specialty after the 1860s.[128] Not for them, either, the wide-ranging speculations and

mental disorder, is not disturbed by consideration of the 'assigned causes of insanity', where they are available. Thus in 1888 nearly a third of suicidal as against less than a quarter of non-suicidal admissions were attributed to bereavement and domestic troubles, business and financial difficulties, anxiety, overwork, religious excitement, and love affairs; and rather more suicidal than non-suicidal female patients were believed to have become insane through physiological cataclasms such as pregnancy, childbirth, and the menopause, or through starvation or privation, and fewer through old age or congenital defect: *Lunacy Commissioners 44th AR*, pp. 60–1, 65, Tables XX, XXIII.

[126] The number of such patients increased by 44.6 per cent between 1859 and 1869. This was much the largest decennial increase recorded in the period 1859–1909: see *Lunacy Commissioners' 65th AR*, Part I, p. 9. Recently much has been written on the rise of the asylum , notably in Finnane, *Insanity and the Insane in Post-Famine Ireland*, and Donnelly, *Managing the Mind: A Study of Medical Psychology in Early Nineteeth-Century Britain*. For other recent work, see the references in Finnane, p. 174 n. 106; and for a more matter-of-fact treatment, see R. Hodgkinson, 'Provision for Pauper Lunatics, 1835–71', *Medical Hist.*, x (1966), pp. 138–54.

[127] Cf. Niebyl, 'The English Blood-Letting Revolution', p. 480. In 1871 Blandford in his lectures stated that 'nowadays general bleeding in insanity is entirely abolished' although to some extent local bleeding by leeches or cupping survived, and (unlike Sankey in 1866) he advised total abstention from blisters: Blandford, *Insanity and its Treatment*, p. 234; Sankey, *Lectures on Mental Diseases*, p. 216. Thereafter such publications ignore the subject of bleeding. (Setons in the neck were, however, being used in the case of suicidal melancholic patients at Colney Hatch in 1882: see e.g. GLRO, Acc. 1038/230, case 8430, 29 Nov. 1882.)

[128] For typical examples of such treatment see Bucknill and Tuke, *Manual of Psycho-*

zest for innovation characteristic of the generation which had grown to maturity amidst the reforming enthusiasms of the 1830s and 1840s, and had found crusading leaders in Prichard and Conolly.[129] Their forte was practical good sense, and their concern the clinical rather than the pathological aspects of mental disease. G. H. Savage may stand as their epitome. Born in 1842 and at the age of thirty appointed resident physician of Bethlem, Savage was as energetic in the wards and consulting room as at Hospital dances or in the Alps, but made no attempt to use his vast experience for the advancement of fundamental knowledge.[130] On clinical problems, however, he was a clear, racy lecturer and a prolific writer—talents which have bequeathed a plethora of detailed case histories which give a vivid if rosy picture of the best practice of the day and are far more accessible than the voluminous Case Books kept by the asylums, valuable though these plainly are.[131]

Where a patient suffering from melancholia was concerned, Savage's generation agreed on the paramount importance of attention to general health. Of Savage's own patients who were suicidal melancholics, the most famous today is surely Virginia Woolf;[132] and her treatment was altogether typical in its emphasis upon rest, short walks, and above all nourishment.[133] 'The first necessity in the treatment of a melancholic patient', wrote Charles Mercier of Westminster and Charing Cross

---

logical Medicine, Appendix of Cases, pp. 531, 537–9, 545, and Robinson, *On the Prevention and Treatment of Mental Disorders*, p. 197. On the rationale of these therapies, see Leigh, *Historical Development of British Psychiatry*, i. 53–4, 78, 152.

[129] Forbes Winslow (1810–74), Sankey (1814–89), and Bucknill (1817–97) were certainly members of this generation, and D. H. Tuke (1827–95), Blandford (1829–1911), and Maudsley (1835–1918: but Conolly's son-in-law) were born just in time to have some first-hand acquaintance with the reforming enthusiasts and pioneering ways; the men born after 1840—such as Savage, Clouston, Mercier, Craig, Bevan Lewis—grew up into an established specialty with established institutions and journals.

[130] See *Munk's Roll*, iv, 306–7 and some acute incidental comments by one of his successors at Bethlem, Sir Aubrey Lewis, in his *The State of Psychiatry*, pp. 88, 254. Sidelights on Savage appear in *'Under the Dome': The Quarterly Magazine of the Bethlem Royal Hospital*: e.g. new series, no. 4 (1882), p. 38. A bibliography of his writings will be found in Trombley, *'All That Summer She Was Mad'*, pp. 330–2.

[131] Patients' records remain confidential for 100 years. For a note on this valuable type of source, see Finnane, *Insanity and the Insane in Post-Famine Ireland*, pp. 237–8. These remarks are fully borne out by my own sampling of the voluminous Colney Hatch records now deposited at the GLRO.

[132] Virginia Woolf's treatment has recently been discussed at more length and with less knowledge of the historical context and care in the use of sources than might have been wished: see Trombley, *'All That Summer She Was Mad'*.

[133] At the end of her convalescence in 1915 Virginia Woolf found herself sitting in 'a mound of flesh': Nicolson, ed., *The Question of Things Happening: The Letters of Virginia Woolf*, ii. 70.

Hospitals in a standard reference book, *The Dictionary of Psychological Medicine*, in 1892, 'is to insist on the ingestion of abundance of aliment.' From W. H. O. Sankey to Maurice Craig (and there were fifty years between them) specialists agreed that the first essential for melancholic patients was to make sure that they had plenty of food, and after that to see that they slept, took abundant exercise, kept warm, and did not become constipated; stimulants and sedatives should be given only as the case required.[134] At Colney Hatch, so sampling of the records indicates, melancholics were given 'Extras' of tea, sugar, egg, and wine, and their weight carefully noted; only the very noisy ones were quietened with drugs.[135] On details of ways and means there was naturally debate and disagreement: for example, on when to feed forcibly, and whether to do so by a spoon, nasal tube, or stomach pump, on the easiest way to insert a feeding tube, and on the rival merits of bran bread, enemas, and various aperients to deal with constipation.[136] Naturally too the preferred stimulants and tonics varied, as did the recommended narcotics and sedatives, and indeed readiness to give drugs of any sort, whether for purposes of therapy or control. Opium, for example, which was still in routine use around 1870, had been replaced twenty years later in psychiatric as in general practice by what were regarded as more efficient sedatives, notably chloral and bromides.[137] In 1892 Charles Mercier reported that he found the most efficient sedative to be 'Easton's syrup' of the phosphates of quinine, iron, and strychnine, which had the advantage of stimulating the processes of digestion; but he insisted that copious feeding and exercise should be tried before any drugs were given.[138] In this, he was expressing the tendency, well established by that time, to

---

[134] Thus (in chronological order) Sankey, *Lectures on Mental Diseases*, p. 216; Maudsley, *The Physiology and Pathology of Mind*, p. 511; Blandford, *Insanity and its Treatment*, pp. 191–4; Clouston, *Clinical Lectures*, 1st edn., pp. 133–4; Mercier, 'Melancholia', pp. 787–96; Rayner, 'Melancholia', pp. 379–80; Craig, *Psychological Medicine*, pp. 120–1. (Craig, incidentally, was also consulted by Virginia Woolf.)

[135] For example, GLRO, Acc. 1038/230, case 8430, 29 Nov. 1882 and 1 July 1885.

[136] For different views on forcible feeding, for example, see Sankey, *Lectures on Mental Diseases*, p. 47, Blandford, *Insanity and its Treatment*, pp. 207–10, and Clouston, *Clinical Lectures*, 5th edn., pp. 108–9.

[137] In 1892, according to Mercier, opium treatment, which was 'for many years routine', was 'now seldom used': 'Melancholia', p. 794. In 1868, however, it was recommended by Maudsley 'in many cases': *The Physiology and Pathology of Mind*, p. 512; in 1871 by Blandford 'in sub-acute melancholia': *Insanity and its Treatment*, p. 191; and in 1874 by Bucknill in the third edition of his and Tuke's *Manual of Psychological Medicine*, pp. 714–27.

[138] Mercier, 'Melancholia', pp. 794–5.

disparage the drug therapy and 'chemical restraint' which had been practised by the generation which jettisoned mechanical restraint—a tendency which provoked a survivor of that generation, J. C. Bucknill, to belittle the asylums of his old age as places where 'a patient may get well if he will under good hygienic influences', but where the 'systematic attempts to aid nature by the resources of the medical art' common in his young days were rarely to be found.[139] Bucknill was too belligerently determined to grind his own axe to be fair to the new generation of asylum doctors, but his erstwhile collaborator, D. Hack Tuke, a younger, gentler, and more scholarly man, was more open-minded and appreciative. It is 'more rational therapeutics which we witness in 1881', was his approving verdict as he looked back to the 1840s and 1850s when croton oil, black draughts, and large doses of tartarized antimony had been in daily use in many asylums (not least Bucknill's own), and bleeding was freely employed—although he hoped for major advances from the growing interest which he discerned in the somatic aetiology of insanity and praised the experiments of Clouston, Savage, and a few others with certain drugs.[140] In the years which followed, some attempts were indeed made to use the rapidly developing scientific study of nutrition to throw new light on the aetiology of suicidal depression;[141] but only in some Scottish asylums (consistently the centres of innovation and experiment in this period) were meat and tea eliminated from the diet of suicidal patients in order to see whether lowering the level of uric acid in the blood would improve the circulation in the brain and hence relieve depression and cure suicidal tendencies.[142] In English asylums, faith in common sense and 'good hygienic influences' long ruled.

[139] 'Persistent efforts to relieve by medicine those bodily conditions upon which the morbid mental states depend have now gone out of vogue, and even the belief in them seems to be dead and gone': Bucknill, *The Care of the Insane*, p. 117. Bucknill's own favourite therapies when he was Medical Superintendent of the Devon County Lunatic Asylum in 1844–62 are abundantly illustrated in the Appendix of Cases which he contributed in 1858 to Bucknill and Tuke, *Manual of Psychological Medicine*, pp. 529–56.

[140] Presidential Address to the Medico-Psychological Association, reprinted in Tuke, *Chapters in the History of the Insane in the British Isles*, pp. 484, 487. Tuke made effective play in his address with the great variety of pharmaceutical remedies which had been tried in the treatment of insanity over the years: ibid., pp. 485–6.

[141] In 1911 Savage reported that he had found a rigid vegetarian diet sometimes useful in cases of gouty melancholia: 'Mental Disorders and Suicide', p. 1335; and in 1906 Lewis Bruce had much to say about the association of malnutrition and deficient excretion with melancholia, as well as about the role of metabolic, bacterial, alcoholic, and drug toxins in insanity: Bruce, *Studies in Clinical Psychiatry*, pp. 46–8.

[142] This was recommended by Alexander Haig (1853–1924: *Munk's Roll*, iv. 341–2),

Still, this did not mean that for English medical superintendents the treatment which they ought to prescribe for their suicidal patients was a foregone conclusion. 'Good hygienic influences' included what had long been rather misleadingly referred to as 'moral' treatment, that is, a cheerful and stimulating environment; and it was agreed that melancholic patients required amiable attendants, healthy occupation outdoors (in the shape of walks, caring for animals, gardening, and so forth), amusements and outings, new acquaintances, and such things as newspapers and games, all *mutatis mutandis*, and with visits and letters from and to home either banned or encouraged according to individual case history and medical judgement.[143] Every asylum made efforts of some sort in this direction, although few were in a position to rival Bethlem in Savage's day, with its band, smoking concerts, dances, charades, acrostics, trips to Kew and the Nore, and excursions to Westminster Abbey and the other sights of London.[144] Even in the vast country asylum at Colney Hatch, there were visits, weekly dances, and fortnightly comedy shows throughout the winter and outdoor equivalents in the summer such as 'the Haymaking Tea'; while weeding, reading, and 'accompanying another patient in instrumental music' might be a greater or lesser part of a patient's life all the year round.[145]

a pathologist who specialized in uricacidaemia. Haig read a paper on 'Suicide as a Result of Error of Diet' to the Psychology Section of the 66th Annual Meeting of the British Medical Association: *British Medical Jnl.*, 1898, ii. 680–2, 10 Sept.

[143] For outline advice on such 'moral' treatment, see e.g. Blandford, *Insanity and its Treatment*, pp. 367–8; Mercier, 'Melancholia', p. 794; Rayner, 'Melancholia', pp. 377–9.

[144] For some day-to-day details of these goings-on see *'Under the Dome'*, new series, nos. 3 and 4 (1892); and for more formal accounts see O'Donoghue, *The Story of Bethlehem Hospital*, pp. 358–9, and Savage, 'On some Modes of Treatment of Insanity', pp. 98–9. The Christmas party at St Luke's in 1851 was described in Charles Dickens's *Household Words*, 17 Jan. 1852 (reprinted in Stone, ed., *Charles Dickens's Uncollected Writings from 'Household Words', 1850–59*, pp. 382–91). Bethlem (like St Luke's) took only 'recent and uncomplicated cases' and sent patients away after a year, so that it had a far higher proportion of curable cases than did county and borough asylums. Moreover from W. C. Hood's time as Resident-Physician its patients were predominantly middle-class and not uneducated, and hence easier to treat in this way: cf. the review of Hood's *The Statistics of Insanity* in *Jnl. of Mental Science*, viii (1862), pp. 442–3.

[145] GLRO, Acc. 1038/56, Resolutions of the Committee of Visitors, 6 Apr., 28 Sept., and 5 Oct. 1888; ibid., Acc. 1038/76, fol. 510, case of Andrew Smith Flintoff, 1852. Before 1888 the Commissioners had often urged a better supply of comforts and amusements at Colney Hatch, for female as well as male patients: Hunter and Macalpine, *Psychiatry for the Poor*, pp. 138–40. (There was an inevitable tendency for female patients to be provided with less stimulus and exercise: see Showalter, 'Victorian Women and Insanity', pp. 167–8.) Details of similar activities in other county and borough asylums emerge in the Lunacy Commissioners' Annual Reports when a patient had

As a result, nowhere could a medical man in charge of suicidal melancholics escape a difficult decision: how far should suicidal tendencies be held to debar a patient from joining in such activities? Clearly any patient suffering from depression needed the stimulus of change and occupation, and a suicidal patient (so many held) particularly needed to be made to feel trusted; yet equally, a patient with suicidal tendencies needed not only to be kept safely out of reach of any opportunity to destroy himself, but to be closely and continuously watched. These needs could never be reconciled. Which then should be given priority?

Unremitting vigilance, day and night, was the prescription of the Commissioners in Lunacy; and this usually entailed putting all the suicidal cases together in special wards, and thus in an environment the very opposite of the one which was psychologically desirable. How many medical superintendents, however, obeyed this rigid policy of 'safety first'? Often a superintendent seems to have made a point of assessing for himself the real degree of risk with a new patient admitted with 'suicidal' after his name.[146] Yet even when he decided that it was not intense, the extent to which he departed from 'safety first' depended partly on circumstances (especially the ratio of attendants to patients in his institution), but chiefly on his own personality and therapeutic opinions. Not surprisingly, the ebullient, confident, extrovert Savage declared himself at a quarterly meeting of the Medico-Psychological Association held at Bethlem in February 1884 to be against constant watching, even in actively suicidal cases; and strongly against gathering such cases together in special wards. Preventing suicide, he told his fellow specialists, should be secondary to the cure of curable cases, and constant watching was not for the good of patients. Patients must be 'treated in a home-like way'. By encouraging self-reliance, the

---

seized the opportunity they provided to commit suicide: for example, *Lunacy Commissioners' 31st AR*, pp. 82, 89. It seems probable that too much has been made of the degeneration into mere custodialism in the later nineteenth century. According to two historians with intimate inside knowledge, 'custodial care was forced on asylums as a way of life only in the 1920s', and 'Victorian asylums were not prisons': Hunter and Macalpine, *Psychiatry for the Poor*, pp. 158, 41. Inevitably large asylums acquired the characteristics of all large residential institutions; but not until asylum records have been studied in a way which has barely yet begun will it be possible to get behind the polemics of our own day and of that time (expressed, for example, in Andrew Wynter's widely read article of 1870, 'Non-restraint in the Treatment of the Insane').

[146] Savage did this in the first few days after admission, and meanwhile put his patients at night in strong clothes and strong sheets in a single room: 'Constant Watching of Suicidal Cases', p. 19. Clouston listed carefully for his students the things which determined the real degree of risk: *Clinical Lectures*, 1st edn., p. 114.

patient 'very generally gets well'. 'No one can avoid suicide at all times unless he destroys all privacy, and makes the wards of asylums barracks with night-patrols', and this he would never countenance. Patients had repeatedly told him that when constantly watched 'they felt as if they were being dared to do a thing, and naturally set themselves to evade their tormentors.' In his usual bluff way Savage wound up: 'Some risk *must* be run if good is to result, and we must be considerate to each other when accidents do happen.'[147] It is a pity that the discussion which followed was not recorded, for Savage had been very provocative. Any suicide in an asylum caused an outcry; but he had said outright that he did not care what the public thought and had implied that he did not intend to be ruled by the Commissioners or professional shibboleths, and that medical superintendents should decide for themselves what was best. In subsequent years he seems to have practised more caution than he preached in 1884; yet he continued to condemn special dormitories for suicidal patients, and in 1911 wound up a lecture on mental disorders and suicide with a reference to this paper of 1884 and the warning that 'over-watching may be injurious'.[148]

Presumably the front rank of the profession could afford to be more venturesome than the rank and file working in county and municipal asylums; yet few even of Savage's peers seem to have been as bold as he. Charles Mercier in 1892, for example, preached constant watching as strongly as the Commissioners could have desired, and Maurice Craig in 1905 was prepared to concede only that when the patient seemed to be recovering 'certain risks must be taken', to encourage him.[149] At all levels differences in practice seem to have been considerable. For example, when the South-Western Division of the Medico-Psychological Association met to discuss suicide in asylums in April 1903, Benham of Fishponds, Bristol, who opened the discussion, explained that all his suicidal patients slept together in specially staffed observation wards, with caution cards, elaborate safeguards, and the most actively suicidal placed nearest to the watch; and that he rarely allowed a patient out on trial, since it so often had fatal results. Other asylum medical officers present, however, believed in smaller wards or changes of ward for their suicidal patients, and thought it important not to continue caution cards longer than necessary, or even claimed not to use them at all unless an actual attempt at suicide was made

---

[147] 'Constant Watching of Suicidal Cases', pp. 17–19.
[148] 'Suicide and Insanity', p. 1232; 'Mental Disorders and Suicide', p. 1336.
[149] Mercier, 'Melancholia', p. 795; Craig, *Psychological Medicine*, p. 429.

after the patient had been admitted.[150] On balance it seems likely that something of the 'stern vigilance' deplored in 1922 in a letter to the *British Medical Journal* was to be found in most asylums before the War,[151] and that there was a good deal of caution (especially probably in cities)[152] about allowing once suicidal patients out on trial or discharging them—and understandably so, since it was commonly the asylum medical officer who was blamed if former patients did commit suicide while they were out on trial or after they had been discharged.

It is obviously impossible to know how often a preference for caution and 'safety first' hindered recovery from suicidal melancholia. A considerable proportion of such patients were certainly considered fit to be discharged each year. Leading asylum superintendents and specialists said as much in their lectures and textbooks, as has already been remarked; and the asylum registers which have been sampled bear them out. Equally, magistrates' charge books and coroners' inquisition papers show suicidal patients moving quite frequently in and out of asylums and hospitals for the insane.[153] Statistics compiled after periodic re-certification had been made obligatory in 1890 showed that around a third of all those certified as insane and admitted into care in any one year had been discharged twelve months later, most of them as 'recovered'—and the proportion must certainly have been higher where melancholics were concerned, since theirs was the form of mental illness for which the prognosis was most favourable.[154]

How different, it may be asked, was the treatment of those asylum patients who suffered from some other form of mental illness than mel-

---

[150] Benham, 'Some Remarks on Suicide in Public Asylums', pp. 449–53.

[151] Letter from S. E. White, 'Suicide in Borderland Cases', *British Medical Jnl.*, 1922, i. 79, 14 Jan.

[152] In the discussion after Benham's paper in 1903, Dr Baskin, the young Assistant Medical Officer of Devon County Asylum (perhaps tactfully wishing to reconcile his differing elders) opined that patients from county asylums, 'not having to return to city life', could be discharged more freely than those from borough asylums: Benham, 'Some Remarks on Suicide in Public Asylums'. p. 453.

[153] In the matter of repeated admissions and discharges perhaps something of a record is held by Anne Hopwood, who was admitted to Witney Asylum 9 times between 1849 and 1856, having previously been admitted once to Gloucester County Asylum and once to the Warneford Asylum, Oxford—on each occasion after bouts of acute intoxication when she grew greatly excited and at times suicidal: Parry-Jones, *Trade in Lunacy*, Appendix D, p. 320. Discharge and readmission were also common in Ireland: Finnane, *Insanity and the Insane in Post-Famine Ireland*, p. 175.

[154] 34 per cent of all those admitted in 1909 had been discharged a year later, 28.2 per cent of them as 'recovered' and the rest as 'relieved' or 'not improved': *Lunacy Commissioners' 66th AR*, p. 14.

ancholia, but were regarded as at risk of suicide? Such patients were comparatively few—with one exception:[155] around a third of the suicidal patients in mental institutions suffered from some form of acute mania.[156] If such patients killed themselves, however, they were likely to do so merely accidentally, in the course of a paroxysm of excitement and destructiveness. In a sense, therefore, as the ever optimistic Savage argued, there was less danger with maniacs than with melancholics— although Fielding Blandford's gloomy comment was that in their wild fits, such patients 'will require all the appliances of a well-ordered asylum'.[157] By the 1890s it was being emphasized that the ideal goal for these patients as for melancholics was healthy exhaustion and natural sleep; but it was obvious that sedatives very different from these must still play a large part in their management and therapy. Strait jackets, handcuffs, and the like were outlawed; what then were the alternatives? Such drugs as opium, chloral, and hyoscine were successively in and out of favour. In 1858 Bucknill and Tuke in their *Manual of Psychological Medicine* lent their authority to opium treatment;[158] but by the 1890s a combination of bromide of potassium and tincture of cannabis indica was preferred by the leading textbook of the day. Whatever the therapy, however, in a really well-run asylum around the end of the century some 60 per cent of such patients would recover enough to be discharged.[159]

Altogether, perhaps almost half of each year's suicidal admissions recovered enough to be discharged, most of them never to be readmit-

---

[155] 'True suicidal monomania' was considered very rare and largely confined to the young: Blandford, 'Insanity', p. 100.

[156] In 1879–88 37.4 per cent of the total number of patients registered on admission as having suicidal tendencies suffered from mania, while in 1893–7 the corresponding proportion was 30.6 per cent: *Lunacy Commissioners' 44th AR*, pp. 68–9, Table XXV, and *53rd AR*, p. 143, Appendix A, Table XXX.

[157] Savage, *Insanity and Allied Neuroses*, pp. 193–4; Blandford, 'Insanity', p. 99.

[158] Bucknill described 3 cases of his own in which a maniacal patient had recovered after treatment with morphia in combination with warm baths, aperients, leeches, and cupping to the nape of the neck: *Manual of Psychological Medicine*, 1st edn., Appendix, pp. 537, 539, 545, cases 'G.N.', 'S.S.', 'A.W.'. For the third edition of 1874 (which introduced far more changes than either the second or fourth editions of 1862 and 1879), he provided a new chapter on treatment, but this still favoured the judicious use of morphia in the treatment of mania: see pp. 719–24.

[159] Clouston, *Clinical Lectures*, 5th edn., pp. 179, 174. In his presidential address to the Medico-Psychological Association in 1881, Tuke drew attention to Clouston's demonstration of the effect on mania of prolonged courses of certain narcotic medicines: Tuke, *Chapters in the History of the Insane*, p. 489.

ted.[160] No doubt very many of these people would have recovered anyway, given time. Time, however, was precisely what asylum vigilance ensured for them, since it virtually prohibited successful suicidal acts. Accordingly, unimpressive though such primarily custodial treatment of the mentally sick and self-destructive may seem today, in practical terms it cannot be reckoned a failure; and it would be ungenerous to deny that the contribution to suicide prevention made by asylum staff was more tangible and direct than that of either the prison medical officers or the country's general practitioners. True, it was limited to only one section of the suicidal—those certified as insane. Yet the contribution of general practitioners was also limited— in their case to those recognized by themselves or by relations or friends as at risk; while that of prison medical officers was not only restricted to those arrested for a suicide attempt and then remanded by magistrates, but also limited by brevity of contact and their own position as adjuncts of the judicial system. In reality, it is plain, no section of the Victorian and Edwardian medical profession ever encountered a true cross-section of the suicidal population. Each made its own distinctive contribution to suicide prevention; but in each case that contribution had its own in-built limitations and inadequacies.

[160] At Bethlem in 1856–60, 38 per cent of those admitted had 'meditated or attempted suicide' and 63 per cent of these patients were discharged 'cured' within a year: Hood, *Statistics of Insanity*, p. 93, Table XIVa. This, however, was certainly a better than average proportion: cf. n. 144. I have found no official figures for discharges and re-admissions which distinguish suicidal from non-suicidal patients. In 1900, however, the overall rate of recoveries at Colney Hatch was running at 30–60 per cent of admissions: Hunter and Macalpine, *Psychiatry for the Poor*, p. 232; and in 1911 the Lunacy Commissioners reported that nationally 'about 40 per cent of those admitted are discharged recovered', but that about 17 to 18 per cent of admissions in any given year were re-admissions: *Lunacy Commissioners' 65th AR*, p. 14. The proportion of suicidal patients discharged was probably somewhat above the global figure, because of the high proportion of melancholics among them.

CONCLUSION

What has emerged from this study? In the first place, an idea of the sorts of people most likely to commit suicide in Victorian and Edwardian England—with all its suggestive historical implications. For the official suicide statistics are not useless, despite their neglect; indeed, the peculiar English way of determining whether a death should be registered as suicide—so altogether lacking in uniformity and bureaucratic professionalism—arguably had its statistical compensations. The scale of suicide in Victorian and Edwardian England does indeed remain altogether uncertain (as it must in any society); but not the relative extent to which the likelihood of dying in this way was affected by living in a given place at a given time, or by age or sex, or by occupation. As always, however, it is only by looking behind averages and generalizations that historical understanding opens out. For example: in this period, men increasingly became more prone to suicide than women; but the reality behind this generalization was divergent trends between men and women in certain age-groups and in certain sorts of places. Among those under the age of twenty-five, suicide slowly increased among men but declined among women in big cities; while among those over the age of sixty-five, it increased steeply among men (especially those living in industrial towns), but fell steeply among women. Did urbanization, then, make life easier for both younger and older women? And was industrialization good for younger and middle-aged men, but not for their elders? This would probably be to draw too simple a conclusion. What is conjured up by the fullest statistics of all—those for London—is rather a complex network of changes in health, psychological environment, and material prospects whose general thrust was to aggravate the problems of old age for men but not for women, while making much easier the lot of young people in big towns and cities, and especially the lot of girls in their late teens.

As for the impact of place on the propensity to suicide, this turns out to have been less substantial than that of sex and age; but suicide was always comparatively high in the south-east and east midlands, and comparatively low in the south-west and north-east. Unexpectedly, the county suicide rates show that the steepest rise among men occurred in certain rural counties; and this does not seem to have been merely a reflection of variations in registration efficiency, or of demographic abnormalities. Were rising suicide rates, then, not especially associated with industrialization and urbanization after all—as has always been believed? District figures available for the 1860s suggest that only for men over the age of fifty-five did industrial towns and cities deserve their suicide prone reputation; indeed, in small and medium-sized new industrial towns and in small seaports, male suicide rates were substantially lower than in most rural areas. It was in historic county towns and new residential developments that urban suicide rates were high. This is surprising; but it becomes less so when the figures for occupational mortality from suicide are taken into account, for these show that suicide was most common in professional, artisanal, and service occupations, and least frequent among industrial and outdoor workers. Nevertheless, occupational geography cannot explain the spatial distribution of suicide among women—which indeed seems to be of little significance; or in Wales—where cultural deterrents and administrative laxity seem to have combined with occupational factors to keep suicide rates very low by English standards. As for change through time, given that the changes in the scale of suicide must remain an open question, the greatest alterations over these fifty years or so seem to have been in the age and sex of those most prone to suicide, and the least in their occupations.

The pattern of suicide among the dead has its historical significance, however, as well as that among the living. In this period the growth in the proportion of deaths caused by suicide was greatest of all among men who died in the prime of life. This—and the increasing rarity of every sort of premature death—must have increased the concern caused by the much-publicized rise in official suicide rates towards the end of the century, since only the most thorough-going Social Darwinists were prepared to welcome suicide as a means of eliminating the least fit from the nation's breeding stock. Suicide did not take much of its toll from the most productive sectors of the labour force or from women of child-bearing age, however, and its economic and demographic consequences cannot have been at all massive.

But what did this kind of death mean to those Victorian and Edwardian men and women who experienced it? Some exceptionally full coroners' papers have made it possible to tackle this second issue, and to recapture something of the experience of dying by suicide in certain parts of London and rural east Sussex. In London different paths to suicide prevailed in different districts, reflecting their widely varying socio-economic structures; and there were different paths too for women and for men. In 1861–2 London seems to have been a place where those who took their own lives were very often neither sober nor in good health; where both their living and their dying were improvised and rough; where the strains of close relationships had been very familiar but not those of loneliness; where the humblest and most destitute suicides of all were women, not men; and where in their last moments those who destroyed themselves rarely fully knew what they were doing. In rural east Sussex in the very same months, however, suicide seems to have been a less sordid and more sombre experience. There it could be a natural deliverance from failing powers, pain, or old age, or be tied up with loss of proper pride and neighbourly esteem or with brooding doubts of personal salvation. Evidently older pathways to suicide were still being trodden in the Sussex Weald. As for the deed itself, among these country people it was more often deliberate, direct, and resolute; more often a matter of hanging or drowning and seldom of poison (so particularly favoured by London women who took their own lives); and more often a door to death in solitude and without the intervention of others.

The experience of dying by suicide could vary with time, though, as much as with place. Some coroner's papers for Edwardian London demonstrate that by then alcoholism, loss of work, and brushes with destitution were less important than they had been fifty years earlier. In the early twentieth century people worried more about their own health and adequacy, and saw suicide as an escape from depression, disappointment, and self-reproach, in a way which a present-day psychiatrist might not find unfamiliar; while their approach to suicidal action was more brooding and long drawn out, and less casual and impulsive, than that of their mid-Victorian predecessors. Changes in family relationships, in work and business, and even more perhaps in health and everyday ideas about medication were matched by changes in the triggers of suicidal action and in the final nature of suicidal death. Dying by suicide was thus an experience deeply affected by its specific historical context. In mid-Victorian London it could be an experience which was predominantly squalid and rarely deliberate; in rural east Sussex in the same years it could be sombre and sturdy; or it could be essentially an introspective agony over private fears and feelings, as it tended to be in Edwardian London.

But what ideas and feelings about suicide had these people—and other Victorians and Edwardians—imperceptibly been absorbing since childhood? It is the suicide 'culture' of Victorian and Edwardian England which has been a third area of concern in this book. Most people's ideas and feelings about suicide naturally remained at the level of the clichés familiar from popular songs and stories, poems and visual images, melodramas and newspaper reporting. Among mid-Victorian Londoners, four traditional stereotypes of suicide—as sad, wicked, strange, and comic—were evidently well known; but the first and the last—the sad and the comic—had pride of place. From the 1840s there were two standard images of sad suicide: the deserted, fallen woman; and the defenceless victim of the harsh modern economy (most frequently, the ragged factory child or the starving seamstress). Yet suicide stories also provided some favourite parodies and much comic word-play and farce. Newspaper reporting, too, especially when it was aimed at a lower middle-class family readership, might treat an unsuccessful attempt at suicide humorously, although it usually adopted a tone of sentimental pity. Altogether mid-Victorian Londoners were conditioned to see suicide as a sad ending which deserved sympathy and forgiveness, but also as sometimes a bizarre and very occasionally a downright wicked deed; and they had plenty of encouragement to think that not every suicide attempt need be taken at its face value. This makes it the less surprising that when they were confronted with a real-life case of suicide they assumed that this had been a piece of abnormal behaviour which could probably be understood and condoned if the surrounding circumstances were fully known, although it could never be regarded as right. They expected suicide to be associated with unusual emotional or bodily states, such as depression, headaches, sleeplessness—and, in women, gynaecological disorders. They did not easily swallow the medical dogma then current that suicide was itself a sign of organic brain disease; but neither did they agree with the lawyers that anyone who knew his deed was wrong must be held fully responsible for his action. Humbler people, especially, were inclined to lay the blame on ill-treatment or 'fate', as well as illness or emotional upset. Evidence of calculation or secretiveness, though, meant that sympathy was forfeited; and suicide done deliberately in cold blood or as part of an evil design was reckoned a crime indeed.

Yet these ideas and feelings were not universal. In some rural areas folk attitudes seemingly survived, although probably as no more than half-beliefs and a manner of speaking. Rural responses to a particular suicidal death seem to have been harsher and more realistic than London ones; and provincial communities seem to have been readier to fasten responsibility on surviving near ones, and to mete out 'rough music' or withhold the exonerating verdict of 'temporary insanity' or 'mind unsound'. Some geographical variations can be detected; but whether these were linked with regional or local traditions, with types of settlement or predominant occupation, or even with local dynasties of coroners, remains problematic. Early twentieth-century Londoners were different again, although they had adapted rather than abandoned mid-Victorian attitudes. Ordinary people seem to have been uneasy about the *fin de siècle* romanticization of suicide, and to have continued to believe that suicide was something 'which the ordinary man did not do, and ought not to do', and hence to return verdicts of 'temporary insanity' or 'mind unsound'. By then, however, coroners' inquests, like death in general, were ceasing to be an everyday subject of interest and conversation; and for Londoners especially, the official process of investigating sudden death had become arcane and remote, with the replacement of out-houses and pubs by local authority mortuaries and coroners' court-houses, and the advent of full-time coroners' inquiry officers and highly professional coroners, appointed by the county council instead of elected at the hustings by all the county freeholders. Paradoxically, as suicide became statistically more common, it also began to seem a much more unfamiliar, untoward, and embarrassing affair.

Yet to those in positions of power and authority, as well as to those concerned to assist the suffering in mind, body, or soul, suicide and suicide attempts were problems which had to be tackled; and it is Victorian and Edwardian efforts to prevent suicide which have been a fourth and many-sided field of enquiry here. 'The sermons and sanctions of the law' were not entirely useless in maintaining the common feeling that suicide was both a sin and a crime, and better concealed for fear of trouble. True, the reluctance of coroners' juries to return a verdict of *felo de se* undermined the penal force not only of the criminal law (whose penalties for this crime were in any case abolished by 1882), but also of the civil and ecclesiastical law (although the desire of some Churchmen for greater strictness over the burial of suicides was also frustrated by the ending of the parson's monopoly over burials brought about by the needs of public health and parliamentary politics). On the other hand, the offence of attempted suicide began to be developed with the advent of the new police, whose goals of public welfare, public decency, and public order led to a crackdown on suicide attempts in public places. Urban magistrates, however (who dealt with the great majority of these arrests), unlike country justices, adopted a low-key approach and simply remanded most of them to prison for a week for reports from the prison chaplain and surgeon. Only around 2 per cent were sent for trial, and of these a decreasing proportion were given custodial sentences, and then short ones—except in Edwardian London, where progressive sentencing policies prescribed that prison sentences should be rare, but when given should be long enough to have some effect. Thus in the metropolitan area (where the bulk of arrests for attempted suicide were made), and probably in other big cities as well, the primary role of the law in suicide prevention proves to have been not to punish, but rather to promote public order, and then to identify suicide-prone individuals and channel towards them the attention of the social workers of the day.

Since suicide was seen as part of the problems of sin and poverty, each successive phase of Victorian and Edwardian evangelistic and philanthropic endeavour had as its by-product a characteristic phase of suicide prevention. At first evangelism alone seemed what was needed; but in the 1850s and 1860s a host of agencies for practical good works were developed, and these were widely used by the chaplains who worked with the many prisoners remanded on a charge of attempted suicide in London, whether they were low church Evangelicals, Home Missioners, Anglo-Catholic slum priests, or 'Sky Pilots'. From the 1890s, however, this welfare work was increasingly taken over by the new police court 'missionaries', who could provide long-term care, and who after 1907 often supervised as probation officers those put on probation for a suicide attempt. But the really radical innovation of 1907 was the Salvation Army's Anti-Suicide Bureau, which offered help to all and sundry who contacted it. These proved to be predominantly young, middle class and male, and to be suicidal often through financial difficulties, and not through the alcoholism, domestic troubles, or sheer feeble-mindedness which so often seemed to be behind the suicide attempts of which the police took notice. In many ways the Bureau foreshadows the advent of international samaritan agencies and a spreading awareness of suicide and attempted suicide as strategies used by people in certain situations.

Not all Victorians, however, regarded suicide as a by-product of sin and poverty. To a few influential people (notably William Farr), it was rather the product of a defective environment. These proponents of 'social science' believed suicide could be reduced first of all by fostering in the community healthy minds in healthy bodies, and secondly by creating an environment which made suicide difficult to accomplish on the spur of the moment. A few useful safety measures were accordingly introduced, and some restrictions were imposed on the sale of poisons after 1868 and of firearms after 1870—although these were mild and not strictly enforced, and were primarily designed to reduce accidents and homicide. In any case their impact was cancelled out by the general developments which were making suicide easier—developments such as the widespread use of poisons in the home for cleaning and disinfecting and in the new hobby of photography, or the advent of a railway network, or (after 1900) of domestic gas cookers. Yet the slowness with which trains came to be used as instruments of suicide, compared with the very rapid spread of suicide by coal-gas poisoning, is a reminder that it is not the existence of facilities for suicide which matters, but popular awareness of them as such; and this was something which the nineteenth and early twentieth-century environmentalists, for all their calls to the media of the day to cease reporting suggestive details, never succeeded in controlling.

Was the contribution of clinical medicine more substantial than that of social medicine? To keep alive those who had already tried to destroy themselves was simply a matter of applying standard emergency procedures; but to prevent incipient or threatened suicidal behaviour was no straightforward matter. General practitioners often lacked knowledge, interest, and experience where mental illness was concerned; and even when a family doctor decided that a patient was at risk of suicide, he himself treated only those whose suicidal tendencies were very mild, or associated with childbirth, feverish illness, or alcoholism. In other cases his chief task was to advise on certification and removal to a mental asylum. In contrast, the medical officers of large remand prisons increasingly possessed considerable relevant knowledge, interest, and experience. From the later 1860s metropolitan magistrates made a habit of asking for a 'mental report' on those whom they remanded to prison on a charge of attempted suicide; and from the 1890s a number of younger prison medical officers were specialists in 'psychological medicine' and eager to investigate the links between suicide, degeneracy, inebriety, and deviant behaviour generally. Yet their primary task was always simply to funnel out of the judicial process those few who were certifiably insane. For the rest, their efforts at most ensured a week's watching and rest, with warmth, ample food, and opportunities for talk and advice; and since those with comfortable homes were not the sort of people remanded in prison on this charge, these may have been genuinely helpful. Prison medical officers necessarily worked with their prisoner-patients for only a few days, however, and saw only those whom magistrates had chosen to remand.

Asylum doctors, in contrast, had to deal with large numbers of patients with suicidal tendencies—on average 4,000 such patients were admitted each year in the 1880s, whereas only 5–600 cases of attempted suicide were observed in remand prisons each year in the 1890s. Despite these large numbers, successful suicide attempts within an asylum were extremely rare, thanks to intense vigilance and continual efforts to eliminate all means of suicide. In any case a high proportion of the suicidal patients admitted were suffering from melancholia, and thus had a comparatively good prospect of recovery. From the 1860s they were increasingly treated by attention to their general health, instead of purging, vomiting, blood-letting, or drugs. Possibly as many as half of those admitted as suicidal recovered enough to be discharged, at least for a while. No doubt many of these would have recovered any way, given time; but time was what asylum vigilance ensured for them. In sheer numbers the greatest medical contribution to suicide prevention plainly came from the asylum doctors. Yet theirs was a contribution which was necessarily limited to those who had been certified as insane, just as the contribution of prison medical officers was limited to those who had been arrested by the police and remanded in prison by magistrates, and that of the general practitioners was limited to those acknowledged by themselves or by relations or friends to be at risk. In this, however, the exertions of medical men were no different from other Victorian and Edwardian efforts to reduce suicide: they were persistent and adaptable, yet each had its own in-built limitations.

Perhaps the same might be said of this book. Undeniably it burkes the fundamental issues and classic sociological questions, draws no parallels with current trends in suicide, and nowhere makes explicit the links between past and present controversies, attitudes, and pro-cedures. This, however, is no accident. After all, the first requirement on what is for historians a green field site is surely a structure in their own vernacular, and not one influenced by the structures of others, however impressive. It will be time to blend history and theory and compare past and present when much more work has been done on sources which have so far only been sampled. Here the focus has deliberately been upon particular people, in particular places, at particular times in the past; for this book represents an early staging post in what is likely to prove a long journey—the journey towards historical understanding of a uniquely resonant strand in human behaviour.

APPENDIX

I VICTORIAN AND EDWARDIAN OFFICIAL SUICIDE
STATISTICS

In 1858 a new official nosology was introduced which listed deaths from suicide separately from other deaths from violence; and thereafter deaths registered as caused by suicide appeared in the 'Annual Abstracts of Births, Deaths and Marriages' published in the Registrar-General's reports in precisely the same way as deaths registered as resulting from any other cause separately specified on the official form. Each year the Registrar-General related the death returns to a short list of causes of death (which simply specified 'suicide'), and also to a full list (which specified 'suicide by poison', 'suicide by asphyxia', and so on). Between 1858 and 1910 the units of tabulation were those created by the Civil Registration Act of 1836; and tables of causes of death were furnished not only for England and Wales as a whole, but for each of the forty-five registration counties, and for the registration division of London. (Between 1858 and 1880 tables were also furnished for the other ten registration divisions.) From 1911 the local unit of tabulation became the 1,885 administrative areas into which the country was divided, and the General Register Office accordingly began to provide voluminous annual tables giving mortality data for all the administrative counties, county boroughs, metropolitan boroughs, other urban districts, and rural districts, which made up these 1,885 areas. What contemporaries usually had in mind when they referred to 'the suicide figures', however, was either the brief figures always given by Farr in his annual 'Letter to the Registrar-General on the Causes of Death in England' included in every Registrar-General's report, or the table headed 'Deaths by Suicide in England and Wales' which formed one of the four regular tables on violent deaths provided annually in the Registrar-General's report after 1867.

In addition to these many annual tables, the Registrar-General's decennial supplements also included data on suicide in their special mortality tables. In the second and third decennial supplements, which related to 1861–70 and 1871–80 respectively, these gave age specific figures of the causes of death in each of the 625 registration districts into which England and Wales were then divided (and in 1861–70 these figures were sex specific also); while the fourth and fifth decennial supplements tabulated male occupational mortality in 1890–2 and 1900–2.

All these figures have been extensively used in this study; but so too have been the figures published by the Home Office. From 1856 the Judicial Statistics included among the police returns a 'Table of Coroners' Returns' which showed the returns made by each coroner of the number of inquests he had held in the course of the year (these numbers were age and sex specific), and gave the findings of the jury and the total amount of the costs incurred. From 1893 the finding 'Suicide' was subdivided into '*Felo de se*' and 'Other'. Coroners' jurisdictions, however, except in the case of a few borough coroners, did not correspond with the units of population used for census purposes, so that these returns (unlike the Registrar-General's figures) can as a rule only provide ratios, and not rates. By the end of the century the Judicial Statistics also provided figures for deaths caused by suicide among murderers, convicted prisoners, criminal lunatics, and those in inebriate reformatories, as well as statistics on the criminal offence of attempting to commit suicide.

Only two pieces of information sometimes given in the official suicide statistics of other countries are entirely lacking in the English statistics: an ascribed reason for the act of suicide, and—until 1911—the usual district of residence of the deceased. (Until 1911 deaths were allocated to the district in which the body happened to lie.)

II   CORONERS' CASE PAPERS

The coroners' papers which form the basis of Part II call for some description. Those which relate to the London area are to be found in three different archives. At the Corporation of London Records Office there are two series of coroners' records, since the coroner for the City of London was also coroner for the old Borough of Southwark. Each includes not only bound and indexed chronological registers of inquests held, ruled with five columns (giving the number and date of the inquest, name and age of the deceased, and verdict), but also (what is naturally far rarer) associated papers arranged chronologically in yearly bundles. These consist of the inquisitions themselves, endorsed with the inquest number and other brief details, and tucked inside them, first, the coroner's warrant commanding the beadles and constables of the parish to summon a jury to appear before him at a specified time and place 'to inquire on behalf of our Sovereign Lady the Queen touching the death of a certain person'; secondly, a list of those summoned, with ticks against the names of those who actually served, and a list of witnesses called; and thirdly—the heart of the matter—verbatim notes of the witnesses' depositions, rapidly written by the coroner himself, together with any pieces of paper handed in as evidence. After 1901 all these papers were bound; and heavy use was made by then of printed forms and clerical assistance, as described in Chapter 1. Among the muniments of the Dean and Chapter of Westminster Abbey are similar papers relating to the inquests taken by the coroner for the City and Liberty of Westminster, but no registers; while in the custody of the Greater

London Record Office are not only the registers of the coroner for Central Middlesex, but also forty-seven boxes of the case papers accumulated by Edwin Lankester while he held that office in 1862-74, with a few accumulated by his successor, William Hardwicke. (These papers were bought from Hardwicke's widow by his successor, G. P. D. Thomas: PP 1893–4 (373) XI, p. 34, Qs. 647, 652; and deposited at County Hall in 1930 by Thomas's own successor, Sir W. Schröder.) The Central Middlesex registers have eight columns (the three additional ones are headed 'Parish', 'Held At' and '£.s.d.'), and as usual provide a useful index to the case papers. These do not include the inquisitions, but consist of the forms and letters sent to Lankester by the police informing him of a death requiring an inquest, post-mortem reports, large specially printed blue sheets of notes of depositions, and occasionally other papers associated with the case. The sequences of inquest numbers begin and end at very short intervals. (In his first six months as coroner, for example, Lankester submitted his accounts three times to the Treasurer of the County of Middlesex, claiming reimbursement of expenses totalling £1,147. 17s. 6d. for 493 inquests.) Finally, the box of inquisitions taken by N. P. Kell and Charles Sheppard in 1859–66 as coroners for the Rape of Hastings now in the East Sussex Record Office normally contains for each case the inquisition itself, the coroner's warrant to summon a jury (and sometimes a jury list and other papers), and very lengthy verbatim notes of the witnesses' depositions. In each archive it is the date of the inquest which is essential to locate a particular set of papers.

BIBLIOGRAPHY OF WORKS CITED

(Place of publication is London unless otherwise indicated.)

I UNPUBLISHED SOURCES

BEDFORDSHIRE RECORD OFFICE, Returns of inquisitions taken before the coroner for Bedfordshire and the coroner of the Honour of Ampthill, 1841–1921 (C.O. 2).
— Returns of Deaths reported to the County Police, 1859–93 (C.O.3).
— Papers relating to coroners' pay and salaries, 1837–96 (C.O.4).
— Inquisitions taken before the coroner for Bedfordshire, 1831–1930 (C.O.11).
BERKSHIRE RECORD OFFICE, Coroners' Inquisitions, Liberty of the Borough and Manor of Hungerford, 1813–77 (H/JCi).
BRITISH LIBRARY, Peel Papers, Add. MSS 40,530 and 40,612.
CORPORATION OF LONDON RECORDS OFFICE, Coroners' Records, City of London and Borough of Southwark, 1861 and 1911: registers of inquests and inquest papers.
— Sessions Records, City of London: Guildhall Justice Room, Magistrates' Charge Books, 1861 and 1863, and Registers and Notes of Evidence, 1900 and 1910.
DEVON RECORD OFFICE (WEST DEVON AREA), Diaries of R. B. Johns, Coroner, Borough of Plymouth, 1892–7 (95/160–4).
EAST SUSSEX RECORD OFFICE, Coroners' papers, Rape of Hastings, 1838–66 (A 1684).
GREATER LONDON RECORD OFFICE, Coroners' registers, Western Middlesex, 1856–62.
— Coroners' registers and case papers, Central Middlesex, 1862–74.

GREATER LONDON RECORD OFFICE, Middlesex Sessions records: calendars of prisoners (MJ/CP/B), depositions (MJ/SPE), reports to quarter sessions (MA/RS/1), Minute Books (MJ/OC), Sessions papers (MJ/SP, 1873).

— Petty sessional records: Edmonton (PS.E/E) and Highgate (PS.H).

— Records of Colney Hatch lunatic asylum (Acc. 1038).

HERTFORDSHIRE RECORD OFFICE, Coroners' Records: Register of inquests, 1827–40; inquest papers (Hertford District), 1870–85.

LANCASHIRE RECORD OFFICE, Inquisitions, Manor of Prescot, 1847–59 (DDCs).

PUBLIC RECORD OFFICE, Home Office: Calendars of prisoners (H.O.140).

WESTMINSTER ABBEY MUNIMENTS, Coroners' Inquests and related papers, *c.* 1760–1880.

WESTMINSTER CITY LIBRARIES: ARCHIVES AND LOCAL HISTORY DEPARTMENT, MARYLEBONE LIBRARY, Registers of coroners' inquests, Paddington, 1840–64.

II NEWSPAPERS AND OTHER PERIODICAL PUBLICATIONS

Annales d'hygiène publique et de médicine légale (Paris)

Annual Register

Art-Journal

Assurance Magazine

Bayswater Chronicle

Bell's Weekly Messenger

Bentley's Miscellany

Birmingham Journal

British Medical Journal

City Press

Contemporary Review

Daily Chronicle

Daily Express

Daily Mail

Daily News

Daily Telegraph

English Churchman

Essex, Herts and Kent Mercury

Graphic

Guardian

Illustrated London News

Independent and Nonconformist

Journal of Mental Science

Journal of Psychological Medicine

Journal of Social Science

The Lancet

Law Times

Leicestershire Mercury

Life Saving Society, *Annual Reports*

Lloyd's Weekly Newspaper

London City Mission Magazine

London Epidemiological Society, *Transactions*

Marylebone Mercury

Medical Critic and Psychological Journal

Medico-Legal Society, *Transactions*

Monthly Review

Morning Advertiser

Morning Post

Morning Star

National Association for the Promotion of Social Science, *Transactions*

News of the World

Pall Mall Gazette

Quarterly Review

Ratepayers' Journal and Local Man-
agement Gazette [Marylebone]
Reformatory and Refuge Journal
Reynolds's Newspaper
Royal Humane Society, *Annual*
Reports
St Pancras News and Middlesex
Advertiser
Saturday Evening Post [Birmingham]
Saturday Review
Social Science Review
South London Chronicle
South London Press
Southwark and Bermondsey Recorder
and South London Gazette

Spectator
Standard
Star
Statistical Society of London [after
1870, Statistical Society; after 1886,
Royal Statistical Society], *Journal*
Sussex Advertiser
The Times
'*Under the Dome*': *The Quarterly*
Magazine of the Royal Bethlem
Hospital
War Cry
West Middlesex Advertiser
The World

III PARLIAMENTARY PAPERS

Censuses of England and Wales.
Judicial Statistics, England and Wales: Part I. Criminal Statistics.
Lunacy Commissioners, Annual Reports.
Metropolitan Police Commissioners, Annual Reports.
Miscellaneous Statistics of the United Kingdom.
Porter's Tables.
Prison Commissioners, Annual Reports.
Registrar-General of Births, Deaths and Marriages, Annual Reports and
Decennial Supplements.
[The above are cited by year or number only. For the appropriate volume of
the parliamentary papers, see the *General Index to House of Commons
Papers*.]

1834 (600) XIV, Report from the Select Committee on the Police of the
Metropolis.
1852–3 [1690] LXXXIX, Census of Great Britain, 1851: Religious Worship,
England and Wales.
1852–3 (908) LXXXI, Abstract of Returns, showing ... the Clergymen and
other Religious Instructors ... officiating in each Prison.
1854 [1772] XXVI, Reports and Minutes of Evidence, Commissioners
appointed to inquire into the state of the Corporation of London.
1857 (sess. 2) (294) XII, Report from the Select Committee of the House of
Lords on the Sale of Poisons &c Bill.
1859 (sess. 2) [2575] XIII.1, Report of the Commissioners appointed to inquire
into the Cost of Prosecutions.

1860 (193) XXII, Report from the Select Committee on the Office of Coroner; together with the proceedings of the Committee and Minutes of Evidence.

1860 (237, 237-I) LVII, Return of the Number of Coroners' Inquests held in England and Wales from 1849 to 1859 ... on which the Coroners' Fees were not allowed.

1860 (241) LVII, Return of all Orders and Regulations made ... since 1850, relating to the expenses of holding Coroners' Inquests; and of all Instructions ... to the County Constabulary, with reference to their Duty in giving Information of Deaths to Coroners.

1861 (180) IX, First Report from the Select Committee on Poor Relief (England).

1864 [3416] XXVIII, Sixth Report of the Medical Officer of the Privy Council.

1867-8 (89-I) LVII, Return relating to the Metropolitan and City Police.

1868-9 (22) XXXI, Report of the Inspectors of Constabulary for the year ending 29 Sept. 1868.

1870 (259) VIII, Report from the Select Committee on Prisons and Prison Ministers Acts.

1870 [C. 218] XIX, Fourth Report of the Commissioners appointed to inquire into the Rubrics, Orders, and Directions for regulating the course and conduct of Public Worship.

1873 (192) LIV, Return of Places having Stipendiary Magistrates.

1873 (388) LIV, Return of all Clerks in Holy Orders in the Commission of the Peace in any County in England and Wales.

1878-9 (245) LXI, Return showing each Workhouse and Prison in Great Britain ... with particulars as to Religious Ministration provided.

1880 (59) LIX, Return of Salaries paid and Allowances made to Chaplains in Gaols ... in 1878.

1882 (34) LII, Return of all Deaths from Drowning in the United Kingdom during 1880.

1882 (192) LII, Return of the number of Human Corpses found in the Thames River within the precincts of the City of London and Metropolitan Districts during the years 1877-81.

1882 (257) LIV, Return showing the number of Human Corpses found in the Regent's Canal and River Lea within the Metropolitan Police District area, during the years 1877-81.

1884-5 [C. 4402] XXX, First Report of the Royal Commission on the Housing of the Working Classes.

1892 (sess. 1) (265) LXVIII, Poor Law (In-door and Out-door Relief): Return.

1893-4 (371) LXXIII, Revolvers (Deaths and Injuries): Return.

1893-4 (373, 402) XI, First and Second Reports from the Select Committee on Death Certification; with the Proceedings of the Committee and Minutes of Evidence.

1893-4 (488) LXXI, Return of the Number of Deaths in England and Wales caused by the taking of Carbolic Acid, 1887-91.

1895 [C. 7684, 7684-I] XIV, Report of the Royal Commission on the Aged Poor; and Minutes of Evidence.

1895 [C. 7702] LVI, Report from the Departmental Committee on Prisons.

1896 [C. 7995] XLIV, Observations of the Prison Commissioners on the Recommendations of the Departmental Committee on Prisons.

1896 [C. 8154] XLIV, Report of the Departmental Committee on the Education and Moral Instruction of Prisoners.

1897 (312) XI, Select Committee on Burial Grounds: Minutes of Evidence.

1898 [C. 8790] XLVII, Statement by the Prison Commissioners of the action taken up to Jan. 1898 to carry out the Recommendations in the Report of the Departmental Committee on Prisons, 1895.

1903 [Cd. 1443] XXXIII, Report of the Departmental Committee on Poisons, Part II: Minutes of Evidence.

1905 [Cd. 2590] XI, Report of the Inspector under the Inebriates Acts, 1879 to 1900, for 1904.

1908 (150) IX, Minutes of Evidence taken before the Joint Select Committee on the Poisons and Pharmacy Bill.

1908 [Cd. 4215] XXXV, Royal Commission on the Care and Control of the Feeble-Minded: Minutes of Evidence, England and Wales, vol. I.

1908 [Cd. 4342] XII, Report of the Inspector under the Inebriates Acts, 1879 to 1900, for the year 1907.

1908 [Cd. 4438] XII, Report of the Departmental Committee appointed to inquire into the Operation of the Law relating to Inebriates.

1908 [Cd. 4439] XII, Minutes of Evidence taken before the Departmental Committee appointed to inquire into the Operation of the Law relating to Inebriates.

1909 [Cd. 4632] XLIV, Royal Commission on the Poor Laws and Relief of Distress, Appendix, vol. xx: Report . . . on Boy Labour.

1909 [Cd. 4782] XV, First Report of the Departmental Committee appointed to inquire into the Law relating to Coroners and Coroners' Inquests [Coroners' Committee]: Part II, Evidence and Appendices.

1910 [Cd. 5004, 5139] XXI, Second Report of the Coroners' Committee: Part I, Report; Part II, Evidence.

1911 [Cd. 5492] XIII, Second Report of the Coroners' Committee: Part III, Evidence and Appendices.

1913 [Cd. 6818] XXX, Report of the Departmental Committee appointed to inquire into Jury Law and Practice: II, Evidence and Appendices.

1919 [Cmd. 336] XXVII, Report of the Departmental Committee on the Metropolitan Police Medical Service.

IV OTHER OFFICIAL PUBLICATIONS

CONVOCATION OF CANTERBURY, *The Chronicle of Convocation: being a record of the Proceedings of the Convocation of Canterbury.*

CONVOCATION OF CANTERBURY, *Report on the Rubrics of the Book of Common Prayer presented to H.M. the Queen ... on July 31, 1879.*

DIOCESE OF LONDON, *Bishop of London's Fund for Providing for the Spiritual Wants of the Metropolis and its Suburbs; Annual Reports.*

Hansard's Parliamentary Debates, 3rd, 4th, and 5th series.

HOME OFFICE, W. Norwood East and H. de B. Hubert, *Report on the Psychological Treatment of Crime* (1939).

LONDON COUNTY COUNCIL, *Annual Reports of the Proceedings of the Council.*

— *London Statistics.*

— *An Account of the Bridges, Tunnels and Ferry belonging to the London County Council* (1898).

MIDDLESEX JUSTICES OF THE PEACE, *Report of the Special Committee appointed at the Michaelmas Session 1850, as to the Duties and Remuneration of Coroners, and Resolutions of the Court* (April Quarter Sessions, 1851).

OFFICE OF POPULATION, CENSUSES AND SURVEYS, Series DH1, no. 3, *Trends in Mortality 1951–1975* (1978).

— Series DH1, no. 4, *Mortality Statistics. Review of the Registrar-General on Deaths in England and Wales, 1976.*

— Series DH5, no. 3, *Mortality Statistics, Area, 1976* (1978).

REGISTRAR-GENERAL OF BIRTHS, DEATHS AND MARRIAGES, *Annual Statistical Review of England and Wales.*

Statutes of the Realm.

V   REFERENCE WORKS

Bacon's New Ordnance Atlas of London and the Suburbs, with Directory by G.W.B. (n.d.; *c.*1875).

BARTHOLOMEW, J. G., *The Survey Gazetteer of the British Isles: Topographical, Statistical, and Commercial, Compiled from the 1901 Census and the Latest Official Returns* (1904).

Black's Medical Dictionary (Edinburgh, 1906).

BOASE, F., *Modern English Biography*, 6 vols. (reprinted, 1965).

Catholic Encyclopaedia, 15 vols. (New York, 1910).

Clergy List.

COX, E. W. (ed.), *Reports of Cases in Criminal Law, Argued and Determined in all the Courts in England and Ireland, vol. vi, 1852–5* (1855).

Crockford's Clerical Directory.

Dictionary of American Biography.

Dictionary of National Biography.

Halsbury's Laws of England, 3rd edn. (1952–64).

HOUFE, S., *The Dictionary of British Book Illustrators and Caricaturists, 1800–1914* (Woodbridge, Suffolk, 1978).

International Encyclopaedia of the Social Sciences, ed. D. L. Sills, 17 vols. (USA, 1968).

Kelly's Post Office Directories.

Law List.

LEIGH, E. C. AND CAVE, L. W., *Crown Cases Reserved for Consideration and Decided by the Judges of England from Hilary Term 1861 to Trinity Term 1865* (1866).

London Manual, 1899–1900, ed. R. Donald.

Medical Directory.

MITCHELL, B. R. AND DEANE, P., *Abstract of British Historical Statistics* (Cambridge, 1962).

MITCHELL, C. & CO., *The Newspaper Press Directory and Advertiser's Guide.*

Munk's Roll, iv: *Lives of the Fellows of the Royal College of Physicians of London, 1826–1925*, compiled G. H. Brown (1955).

Official Year Book of the Church of England.

Oxford English Dictionary (reissue, 1933) and *Supplement*, ed. R. W. Burchfield (1972).

PARTRIDGE, E., *A Dictionary of Slang and Unconventional English*, 2 vols., (5th edn., 1961).

ROST, H., *Bibliographie des Selbstmords* (Augsburg, 1927).

Salvation Army Year Book.

Stevenson's Book of Proverbs, Maxims and Familiar Phrases (1947).

WATERS, G. M., *Dictionary of British Artists Working 1900–1950* (Eastbourne, 1975).

Who was Who.

VI   BOOKS AND PAMPHLETS FIRST PUBLISHED BEFORE 1914

ALDIS, C. J. B., *The Power of Individuals to Prevent Melancholy in Themselves* (1860).

ALLEN, GRANT, *Ivan Greet's Masterpiece Etc.* (1893).

— *The Woman Who Did* (1895).

ANSTEY, F., *Mr Punch's Pocket Ibsen* (1893).

ASHTON, J., *Modern Street Ballads* (1888).

ATKINSON, J. C., *Forty Years in a Moorland Parish: Reminiscences and Researches in Danby in Cleveland* (1891).

BAKER, W., *A Letter Addressed to H.M.'s Justices of the Peace for the County of Middlesex on the Subject of the Increase of Inquests* (1839).

— *A Practical Compendium of the Recent Statutes, Cases and Decisions Affecting the Office of Coroner* (1851).

BARHAM, R. H., *The Ingoldsby Legends: or, Mirth and Marvels by Thomas Ingoldsby, Esq.*, 88th edn., 3 vols. (1894).

BEETON, I., *Beeton's Book of Household Management* (1861).

— *Mrs Beeton's Book of Household Management*, new edn. (1906).

BENNETT, E. A., *Hilda Lessways* (1911).

BENTHAM, J., *Works*, ed. J. Bowring, vol. i (Edinburgh, 1843).

BIBER, G. E., *The Act of Suicide as Distinct from the Crime of Self-Murder* (1865).

BLACKSTONE, SIR W., *Commentaries on the Laws of England*, 8th edn. (Oxford, 1778).

BLANDFORD, G. FIELDING, *Insanity and Its Treatment: Lectures on the Treatment, Medical and Legal, of Insane Patients* (Edinburgh, 1871).

BLIGH, E. V., *Lord Ebury as a Church Reformer* (1891).

BLUNT, J. H., *The Annotated Book of Common Prayer*, 1st edn. (1866).

— *A Key to Christian Doctrine and Practice founded on the Church Catechism* (1871).

— *The Book of Church Law, being an Exposition of the Legal Rights and Duties of the Parochial Clergy and the Laity of the Church of England*, revised by W. G. F. Phillimore, 2nd edn. (1872) and 4th edn. (1885).

BONSER, T. O., '*The Right To Die*' (1885).

BOOTH, C., *The Aged Poor in England and Wales* (1894).

— *Life and Labour of the People in London*, 1st series, Poverty; 2nd series, Industry; 3rd series, Religious Influences; Final Volume; 4th edn., 17 vols (1902–3).

BOSANQUET, C. B. P., *London: Some Account of its Growth, Charitable Agencies, and Wants* (1868).

BOSANQUET, H., *Social Work in London 1869 to 1912: A History of the Charity Organisation Society* (1914).

'BOURNE, G.' [pseud. of G. Sturt], *Change in the Village* (1912).

BRUCE, L. C., *Studies in Clinical Psychiatry* (1906).

BUCHAN, W., *Domestic Medicine* (1830 edn.).

BUCKLE, H., *The History of Civilization in England* (1857).

BUCKNILL, J. C., *The Care of the Insane and their Legal Control* (1880).

— and TUKE, D. H., *A Manual of Psychological Medicine* (1st edn. 1858, 2nd edn. 1862, 3rd edn. 1874, 4th edn. 1879).

BULWER, E. L., *England and the English*, 2nd edn., 2 vols. (1883).

BUNYAN, J., *The Life and Death of Mr Badman*, World's Classics edn. (1929; first publ. 1680).

BUNYON, C. J., *A Treatise upon the Law of Life Assurance*, 1st edn. (1854); 3rd edn. with J. V. V. Fitzgerald (1891).

BURDETT, H. C., *The Necessity and Importance of Mortuaries for Towns and Villages* (1880).

BURN, R., *Ecclesiastical Law*, 1st edn., 2 vols. (1763); 2nd edn., 4 vols. (1767); 3rd edn. (1775); 4th edn. (1781); 6th edn., with additions by S. Fraser (1797); 8th edn., with additions by R. P. Tyrwhitt (1824); 9th edn., with additions by R. Phillimore (1842).

BURROWS, G. M., *Commentaries on the Causes, Forms, Symptoms, and Treatment, Moral and Medical, of Insanity* (1828).

BUTLER, A. M., *Suicide or Murder* (n.d. [1906]).

CARDWELL, J. H. et al., *Two Centuries of Soho: Its Institutions, Firms, and Amusements* (1898).

CHESTERTON, G. L., *Revelations of Prison Life,* 3rd edn. (1857).

CHRISTISON, R., *A Treatise on Poisons* (Edinburgh, 3rd edn. 1835; first publ. 1829).

CHURCH OF ENGLAND TEMPERANCE SOCIETY, *Missionary Efforts of the Church of England Temperance Society* (1894).

CLEGG, J. (ed.), *Autobiography of a Lancashire Lawyer, Being the Life and Recollections of John Taylor, Attorney-at-Law, and first Coroner of the Borough of Bolton* (Bolton, 1883).

CLOUSTON, T. S., *Clinical Lectures on Mental Diseases* (1st edn., 1883 and 5th edn., 1898).

CONOLLY, J., *The Treatment of the Insane without Mechanical Restraints* (1856).

COPLAND, J., *A Dictionary of Practical Medicine* (abridged edn., 1866; first publ. 1858).

CORNISH, F. W., *Extracts from the Letters and Journals of William Cory* (Oxford, 1897).

COX, E., *The Principles of Punishment, as Applied to the Administration of the Criminal Law, by Judges and Magistrates* (1877).

CRAIG, M., *Psychological Medicine: A Manual on Mental Diseases for Practitioners and Students* (1905).

CRIPPS, H. W., *A Practical Treatise on the Laws relating to the Church and the Clergy,* 1st edn. (1845); 3rd edn. (1857); 5th edn. (1869); 6th edn., by C. A. Cripps (1886); 7th edn., by A. T. Lawrence and R. S. Cripps (1921).

DEFOE, D., *A Review of the Affairs of France,* no. 60 (30 Sept. 1704).

DICKENS, C., *Sketches by 'Boz'* (1836).

— *Pickwick Papers* (1836).

— *Oliver Twist* (1837).

— *Nicholas Nickleby* (1838).

— *Martin Chuzzlewit* (1844).

— *The Chimes* (1844).

— *David Copperfield* (1849).

— *Bleak House* (1853).

— *Little Dorrit* (1857).

— *The Uncommercial Traveller and Reprinted Pieces Etc.,* introduced by L. C. Staples (The New Oxford Illustrated Dickens, 1958).

— *Charles Dickens' Uncollected Writings from 'Household Words' 1850–1859,* ed. H. Stone (Bloomington, USA, 1968).

DIPROSE, J., *Book about London and London Life* (n.d. [1872]).

DOWSON, E., *Dilemmas: Stories and Studies in Sentiment* (1895).

DURKHEIM, E., *Suicide*, trans. J. A. Spaulding and G. Simpson (1952; first publ. 1897).

EGERTON, J. C., *Sussex Folk and Sussex Ways: Stray Studies in the Wealden Formation of Human Nature* (Lewes, 1884).

'ELIOT, GEORGE', *Middlemarch: A Study of Provincial Life* (1871–2).

ELLMAN, E. B., *Recollections of a Sussex Parson* (1912).

ENGELS, F., *The Condition of the Working Class in England in 1844,* transl. and ed. W. O. Henderson and W. H. Chaloner (Oxford, 1958; first publ. Leipzig, 1845).

FARR, W., *Vital Statistics: A Memorial Volume of Selections from the Reports and Writings of William Farr,* ed. N. A. Humphreys (1885).

FORBES, J., TWEEDIE, A., AND CONOLLY, J., *The Cyclopaedia of Practical Medicine,* 4 vols. (1833–5).

FROUDE, J. A., *Shadows of the Clouds* (1847).

GALSWORTHY, J., *The Man of Property* (1906).

GAMON, H., *The London Police Court To-day and To-morrow* (1907).

GEERING, T., *Our Sussex Parish* (1925; first publ. 1884).

GORING, C., *The English Convict* (abridged edn., 1919; first publ. 1913).

[GRANT, J.], *Portraits of Public Characters,* 2 vols. (1841).

GRANVILLE, J. S., *The Care and Cure of the Insane; being the Reports of 'The Lancet' Commission on Lunatic Asylums for Middlesex, the City of London and Surrey, 1875, 1876, 1877* (1877).

GREENWOOD, J., *Unsentimental Journeys: Or, Byways of the Modern Babylon* (1867).

— *The Seven Curses of London* (n.d. [1869]).

GRIFFITHS, A., *Memorials of Millbank and Chapters in Prison History,* 2 vols. (1875).

— *Secrets of the Prison House, or Gaol Studies and Sketches,* 2 vols. (1894).

— *Fifty Years of Public Service* (1904).

GRINDON, J., *Compendium of the Law of Coroners* (1850).

GUERRY, A., *Statistique morale comparée de la France et de l'Angleterre* (Paris, 1864).

GURNHILL, J., *The Morals of Suicide,* 2 vols. (1900).

HAGGARD, H. RIDER, *Regeneration* (1910).

HAMILTON, W. (ed.), *Parodies of the Works of English and American Authors,* 2 vols. (1884).

HARDWICKE, W., *On the Office and Duties of Coroners* (1879).

HARDY, T., *Jude the Obscure* (1895).

HARFORD, G. AND STEVENSON, M. (eds.), *The Prayer Book Dictionary,* 1st edn. (1912); 2nd edn. (1925).

HAVILAND, A., *The Geographical Distribution of Disease in Great Britain,* 2nd. edn. (1892).

HAWKSLEY, T., *The Charities of London, and some Errors of their Administration* (1869).

HINDLEY, C., *The True History of Tom and Jerry, Together with a Vocabulary and Glossary of the Flash and Slang Terms, occurring in the Course of the Work* (1888).

HOLLINGSHEAD, J., *Ragged London in 1861* (1861).

HOLMES, T., *Pictures and Problems from London Police Courts* (1900).

— *Known to the Police* (1908).

— *London's Underworld* (1912).

HOOD, W. C., *Statistics of Insanity: Embracing a Report of Bethlem Hospital, from 1846 to 1860, inclusive* (1862).

HORSLEY, J. W., *Jottings from Jail*, 2nd edn. (1887).

— *Prisons and Prisoners* (1898).

— *'I remember'. Memories of a 'Sky Pilot' in the Prison and the Slum* (1911).

— with DAWES, N., *Practical Hints for Parochial Missions, Revised and Prefaced by the Rev. George Body* (1878).

JACKSON, H., *The Eighteen Nineties* (1913).

JAY, A. O., *Life in Darkest London: A Hint to General Booth* (1891).

JERVIS, SIR J., *On the Office and Duties of Coroners*, 1st edn. (1829); 2nd edn., ed. W. Welsby (1854); 3rd edn., ed. C. W. Lovesy (1866); 4th, 5th, and 6th edns., ed. R. E. Melsheimer (1880, 1888, 1898); 7th edn., ed. F. Danford Thomas (1927).

JUNIOR ETCHING CLUB, *Passages from the Poems of Thomas Hood* (1858).

KINGSLEY, C., *Yeast* (1851).

KIRWAN, D. J., *Palace and Hovel, or, Phases of London Life* (Hartford, Connecticut, 1871).

LANKESTER, E., *The Sixth Annual Report of the Coroner for the Central District of Middlesex* (1869).

— (ed.), *Haydn's Dictionary of Popular Medicine and Hygiene* (1874).

LECKY, W. H., *England in the Eighteenth Century*, cabinet edn., 7 vols. (1921).

LE GALLIENNE, R., *The Romance of Zion Chapel* (1898).

LEGOYT, A., *Le suicide ancien et moderne* (Paris, 1881).

LETHEBY, H., *Report to the Honourable Commissioners of Sewers of the City of London on Certain Imperfect Mortality Returns, Relating to the Verdicts of Coroners' Juries* (1856).

LEWIS, W. BEVAN, *A Text-Book of Mental Diseases, with special Reference to the Pathological Aspects of Insanity*, 2nd edn. (1899; first publ. 1889).

LEYLAND, J. (ed.), *Contemporary Medical Men*, 2 vols. (Leicester, 1888).

LITTLE, J. BROOKE, *The Law of Burial* (1888).

LOANE, M., *The Queen's Poor* (1905).

— *The Next Street But One* (1907).

— *An Englishman's Castle* (1909).

— *Neighbours and Friends* (1910).

LOW, S., *The Charities of London in 1861* (1862).

LOWER, M. A., *A Compendious History of Sussex*, 2 vols. (Lewes, 1870).

LOWNDES, M. BELLOC, *The Lodger* (1913).

MACKAY, C., *The Thames and its Tributaries, or, Rambles among the Rivers*, 2 vols. (1840).

MADDISON, A. J. S., *Hints on Rescue Work* (1898).

MAIGRON, L., *Le romantisme et les moeurs* (Paris, 1910).

MAUDSLEY, H., *The Physiology and Pathology of Mind*, 2nd edn. (1868).

— *The Pathology of Mind: A Study of its Distempers, Deformities and Disorders* (1895 edn.).

MAYHEW, H., *London Labour and the London Poor: A Cyclopaedia of the Condition and Earnings of Those that Will Work, Those that Cannot Work, and Those that Will Not Work*, 4 vols. (1861–2).

— *The 'Morning Chronicle' Survey of Labour and the Poor: The Metropolitan Districts*, intr. P. Razzell, 6 vols. (1980–2).

MINTO, W. (ed.), *Autobiographical Notes of the Life of William Bell Scott*, 2 vols. (1892).

'MONCRIEFF, W. T.', *The Scamps of London, or the Cross-Roads of Life*, Dicks' Standard Plays, no. 472 (n.d.) [Malcolm Morley Coll., London Univ. Library].

MOORE, C., *A Full Inquiry into the Subject of Suicide*, 2 vols. (1790).

MOORE, G., *The Power of the Soul over the Body*, 6th edn. (1868; first publ. 1845).

MORSELLI, H., *Suicide: An Essay on Comparative Moral Statistics*, English trans. (1881).

NEW COMIC AND SENTIMENTAL SONG BOOK, Davidson's Popular Song Books [1864], BL 11622.bb.33.

OKE, G. C., *The Magisterial Formulist*, 1st edn. (1850); 2nd edn. (1856); 3rd edn. (1862).

— *The Magisterial Synopsis*, 1st edn. (1848); 5th edn. (1857); 7th edn. (1860); 9th edn. (1866); 14th edn. (1893).

OLIPHANT, L., *Piccadilly: A Fragment of Contemporary Biography* (1870).

PATERSON, A., *Across the Bridges, or Life by the South London River-Side* (1911).

PEDDER, D. C., *Where Men Decay* (1908).

PERRY-COSTE, F. H., *The Ethics of Suicide* (1898).

PHILLIMORE, R., *The Ecclesiastical Law of the Church of England*, 2 vols., 1st edn. (1875); 2nd edn., by W. G. F. Phillimore (1895).

PHYTHIAN, J. E., *George Frederick Watts* (1906).

POLLOCK, F. AND MAITLAND, F. W., *The History of English Law before the Time of Edward I*, 2 vols., 2nd edn. (Cambridge, 1911).

PRESTON-THOMAS, H., *The Work and Play of a Government Inspector* (1909).

PRICHARD, J. C., *A Treatise on Insanity and other Disorders affecting the Mind* (1835).

'PRISON MATRON, A' [ROBINSON, F.], *Female Life in Prison*, 2 vols., 3rd edn. (1863).

RADCLIFFE, J. N., *Fiends, Ghosts and Sprites, including an Account of the Origin and Nature of Belief in the Supernatural* (1854).

READE, C., *It Is Never Too Late To Mend* (1856).

— *Put Yourself In His Place* (1870).

REFORMATORY AND REFUGE UNION, *The Metropolitan Reformatories, Refuges and Industrial Schools: Authentic Accounts of 54 Institutions*, 4th edn. (1859).

RICHARDSON, B. W., *Diseases of Modern Life* (1876).

RIVINGTON, W., *The Medical Profession* (Dublin, 1879).

ROBINSON, G., *On the Prevention and Treatment of Mental Disorders* (1859).

ROGERS, J., *Reminiscences of a Workhouse Medical Officer* (1889).

RUMSEY, H. W., *Essays and Papers on some Fallacies of Statistics* (1875).

SANKEY, W. O., *Lectures on Mental Diseases* (1866).

SAVAGE, G. H., *Insanity and Allied Neuroses: Practical and Clinical* (1884).

SELBY, C., *London by Night,* Dicks' Standard Plays, no. 721 (n.d.) [Malcolm Morley Coll., London Univ. Library].

SHEPPARD, E., *Lectures on Madness in its Medical, Legal and Social Aspects* (1873).

SMITH, J. TOULMIN, *The Right Holding of the Coroner's Court* (1859).

SPENCER, H., *Education: Intellectual, Moral and Physical* (1861).

SPRIGGE, S. S., *The Life and Times of Thomas Wakley* (1897).

STEPHENS, A. J., *A Practical Treatise of the Laws relating to the Clergy* (1848).

STEVENSON, R. L., *New Arabian Nights,* Skerryvore edn., 2 vols. (1924).

STEWART, A. P. AND JENKINS, E., *The Medical and Legal Aspects of Sanitary Reform* (1866; repr. Leicester, 1969).

STONE, S., *The Justices' Manual,* 21st edn. (1882).

STRAHAN, S. A. K., *Suicide and Insanity* (1893).

SULLIVAN, W. C., *Alcoholism: A Chapter in Social Pathology* (1906).

TAYLOR, A. S., *The Principles and Practice of Medical Jurisprudence* (1866 edn.).

THACKERAY, W. M., *Miscellanies: Prose and Verse,* vol. i (1855).

TODD, J. H., *A Letter to the Reverend George Deane, Rector of Bighton, Hants.* (1856).

TROLLOPE, A., *The Small House at Allington* (1864).

— *The Prime Minister* (1876).

TUKE, D. H., *Chapters in the History of the Insane in the British Isles* (1882).

WEBER, A. F., *The Growth of Cities in the Nineteenth Century* (New York, 1899).

WELCH, C., *History of the Monument, with a Brief Account of the Great Fire of London* (1893).

WELLINGTON, R. H., *The King's Coroner*, 2 vols. (1905).

WELLS, H. G., *Anticipations* (1902).

— *The History of Mr Polly* (1910).

WESTCOTT, W. W., *Suicide: Its History, Literature, Jurisprudence, Causation and Prevention* (1885).

— *On Suicide* (1905).

WESTERMARCK, E., *The Origins and Development of the Moral Ideas*, 2 vols. (1908).

WHARTON, J. J. S., *The Law Lexicon, or Dictionary of Jurisprudence*, 8th edn., ed. J. M. Lely (1889).

WHEATLY, C., *A Rational Illustration of the Book of Common Prayer*, 1st edn. (Oxford, 1710); 3rd enlarged edn. (1720); 8th edn. (1819), another edn. (1845), another edn., with additional notes by G. E. Corrie (Cambridge, 1858).

WHITE, A., *The Great Idea: Notes by an Eye-Witness on Some of the Social Work of the Salvation Army* (1909–10).

WIGRAM, W. K., *The Justices' Note-book* (1880).

WILLIAMS, M., *Leaves of a Life*, 2 vols. (1890).

— *Later Leaves: Being the Further Reminiscences of Montague Williams* (1891).

VII   ARTICLES FIRST PUBLISHED BEFORE 1914

BENHAM, H. A., 'Some Remarks on Suicide in Public Asylums', *Journal of Mental Science*, xlix (1903), 447–53.

BLANDFORD, G. FIELDING, 'Insanity', *Twentieth Century Practice: An International Encyclopaedia of Modern Medical Science*, ed. T. L. Stedman, xii (1897), 3–254.

BOWLEY, A. L., 'Rural Population in England and Wales: A Study of the Changes of Density, Occupations and Ages', *Journal of the Royal Statistical Society*, lxxvii (1913–14), 597–652.

BRAND, J., 'Is Suicide a Sign of Civilization?', *Pearson's Magazine*, ii (July–Dec. 1896), 666–7.

BREND, W. A., 'The Necessity for Amendment of the Law relating to Coroners and Inquests', *Transactions of the Medico-Legal Society*, x (1912–13), 143–97.

BROUC, M., 'Considérations sur les suicides de notre époque', *Annales d'hygiène publique et de médecine légale*, xvi (1836), 223–62.

BULLEN, F. ST. J., 'The Out-Patient System in Asylums', *Journal of Mental Science*, xxxix (1893), 491–7.

DAVEY, J. G., 'Life Insurance Offices and Suicide', *Journal of Mental Science*, vii (1861), 107–20.

— 'Life Insurance and Suicide', *British Medical Journal*, 16 Sept. 1865, 280–2.

— 'The Prevalence of Suicide', *Social Science Review and Journal of the Sciences,* iv (1865), 512–20.

— 'On Suicide, in its Social Relations', *Journal of Psychological Medicine,* iv (1878), 230–55.

DRUITT, R., 'Short Notes on Some of the Details of Sanitary Police', *Journal of Public Health and Sanitary Review,* i (1855), 15–22.

EAST, W. N., 'On Attempted Suicide, with an Analysis of 1,000 Consecutive Cases', *Journal of Mental Science,* lix (1913), 428–78.

GRIMSHAW, T. W., 'The State in its Relation to the Medical Profession', *British Medical Journal,* i (1887), 189–92.

HENSON, H. H., 'Suicide', *Oxford House Papers,* 3rd series (1897), 64–75.

HOPKINS, T., 'Suicides and Malingerers', *Law Times,* cxxiv (30 Nov. 1907), 110–11.

HORSLEY, J. W., 'Suicide', *The Fortnightly,* xxix, new series (1881), 504–12.

[JOHNS, B. G.], 'The Poetry of the Seven Dials', *Quarterly Review,* cxxii (1867), 382–406.

JOPLING, R. T., 'Statistics of Suicide', *Assurance Magazine,* iv (July 1851) and v (Oct. 1851), 32–54.

LITTLEJOHN, H., 'Medico-Legal Notes: II. On Suicide', *Edinburgh Medical Journal,* new series, VI (1899), 222–33.

MALLOCK, W. H., 'Is Life Worth Living?', *The Nineteenth Century,* ii (1877), 251–73, and iii (1878), 146–68.

MARTINEAU, H., 'Self-Murder', *Once a Week,* i (1859), 510–14.

MAUDSLEY, H., 'Memoir of the late John Conolly M.D.', *Journal of Mental Science,* xii (1866–7), 151–74.

MERCIER, C., 'Melancholia', *A Dictionary of Psychological Medicine,* ed. D. H. Tuke, ii (1892), 787–96.

MILLAR, W. H., 'Statistics of Death by Suicide among H.M.'s British Troops serving at Home and Abroad, 1862–71', *Journal of the [Royal] Statistical Society,* xxxvii (1874), 187–92.

MULHALL, M. G., 'Insanity, Suicide and Civilization', *Contemporary Review,* xliii (Jan.–June 1883), 901–8.

OGLE, W. H., 'Suicides in England and Wales in Relation to Age, Sex, Season and Occupation', *Journal of the [Royal] Statistical Society,* xlix (1886), 101–35.

PITCAIRN, J. J., 'The Detection of Insanity in Prisons', *Journal of Mental Science,* xliii (1897), 58–63.

[RADCLIFFE, J. N.], 'The Method and Statistics of Suicide', *Journal of Psychological Medicine,* xii (1859), 209–23.

— 'On the Distribution of Suicides in England and Wales', *Journal of Psychological Medicine,* xii (1859), 469–83.

— 'The Aesthetics of Suicide', *Journal of Psychological Medicine,* xii (1859), 582–602.

[RADCLIFFE, J. N.], 'The Classic Land of Suicide', *Medical Critic and Psychological Journal*, i (1861), 182–200.

— 'The Aesthetics of Suicide,' *Medical Critic and Psychological Journal*, i (1861), 563–86.

— 'On the Prevalence of Suicide in England', *Transactions of the National Association for the Promotion of Social Science* (1862), 461–73.

— 'English Suicide-Fields, and the Restraint of Suicide, *Medical Critic and Psychological Journal*, ii (1862), 701–10.

— 'On the Prevalence of Suicide in England', *Social Science Review*, i (1862), 172–3.

— 'On Suicide: Age, Sex and Method', *Social Science Review*, 8 (1862), 185–86.

— 'On the Distribution of Suicides in England', *Social Science Review*, i (1862), 201–3.

— 'Baits for Suicide: *Lady Audley's Secret* and *Aurora Floyd*', *Medical Critic and Psychological Journal*, iii (1863), 585–604.

RAYNER, H., 'Melancholia and Hypochondriasis', *A System of Medicine*, ed. T. C. Allbutt, viii (1899), 361–81.

[ROBERTSON, C. H. AND MAUDSLEY, H.], 'The Suicide of George Victor Townley', *Journal of Mental Science*, xi (1865), 66–83.

SAVAGE, G. H., 'Constant Watching of Suicidal Cases', *Journal of Mental Science*, xxx (1884), 17–19.

— 'On some Modes of Treatment of Insanity as a Functional Disorder', *Guy's Hospital Reports*, xliv (1887), 87–112.

— 'Suicide and Insanity', *Dictionary of Psychological Medicine*, ed. D. H. Tuke (1892), ii, 1230–2.

— 'Suicide as a Symptom of Mental Disorder', *Guy's Hospital Reports*, 3rd series, xxxv (1894), 7–41.

— 'Mental Disorders and Suicide', A lecture delivered at the Medical Graduates College and Polyclinic on 9 May 1911, *The Lancet*, 1911, i, 1334–6, 20 May.

SCOTT, B., 'Intemperance and Pauperism, Considered Particularly in Reference to the Severe Frost in London in the Winter 1860–61', *Transactions of the National Association for the Promotion of Social Science* (1861), 485–91.

SKELTON, R., 'Statistics of Suicide', *The Nineteenth Century*, xlviii (1900), 465–82.

STEELE, J. C., 'Numerical Analysis of the Patients Treated in Guy's Hospital, 1854–1861', *Journal of the [Royal] Statistical Society*, xxiv (1861), 374–401.

SULLIVAN, W. C., 'Alcoholism and Suicidal Impulses', *Journal of Mental Science*, xliv (1898), 259–71.

— 'Cases of Suicidal Impulse in Cerebral Automatism', *Journal of Mental Science*, xlv (1899), 338–40.

— 'The Relation of Alcoholism to Suicide in England, with Special Reference to Recent Statistics', *Journal of Mental Science*, xlvi (1900), 260–81.

— 'Inebriety and Suicide', *British Journal of Inebriety*, i (1903–4), 25–8.

TROUTBECK, J., 'Inquest Juries', *Transactions of the Medico-Legal Society*, i (1902–4), 49–58.

— 'Modes of Ascertaining the Fact and Cause of Death', *Transactions of the Medico-Legal Society*, iii (1905–6), 86–117.

WADE, W. F., 'On the Prevention of Suicide', *British Medical Journal*, 1897, ii, 533 (4 Oct.).

WALFORD, C., 'On the Number of Deaths from Accident, Negligence, Violence and Misadventure', *Journal of the [Royal] Statistical Society*, xliv (1881), 444–52.

WEIGHT, THE REVD G., 'Statistics of the Parish of St. George the Martyr, Southwark', *Journal of the [Royal] Statistical Society*, iii (1840), 50–71.

WELLINGTON, R. H., 'The Verdict of "Suicide whilst Temporarily Insane": A Legal Contradiction', *Transactions of the Medico-Legal Society*, i (1902–4), 78–91.

WESTCOTT, W. W., 'On Suicide', *Transactions of the Medico-Legal Society*, ii (1904–5), 85–98.

— 'Twelve Years' Experience of a London Coroner', *Transactions of the Medico-Legal Society*, iv (1906–7), 15–32.

— 'The Coroner and his Medical Neighbours', *Transactions of the Medico-Legal Society*, viii (1910–11), 15–26.

WESTERMARCK, E., 'Suicide: A Chapter in Comparative Ethics', *Sociological Review*, 1 (1908), 12–33.

WOOD, T. O., 'The Asylum Trained and Certificated Nurses of the Medico-Psychological Association', *Journal of Mental Science*, xliii (1897), 530–4.

[WYNTER, A.], 'Non-restraint in the Treatment of the Insane', *Edinburgh Review*, cxxxi (Apr. 1870), 418–49.

VIII   BOOKS AND PAMPHLETS PUBLISHED IN OR
AFTER 1914

ABRAMS, P., *The Origins of British Sociology* (Chicago and London, 1968).

ALVAREZ, A., *The Savage God. A Study of Suicide* (1971).

ANDERSON, M., *Family Structure in Nineteenth-Century Lancashire* (Cambridge, 1971).

— *Approaches to the History of the western Family 1500–1914* (1980).

ARIÈS, P., *Western Attitudes Towards Death: From the Middle Ages to the Present* (1974).

ARMSTRONG, A., *Stability and Change in an English County Town: A Social Study of York, 1801–1851* (Cambridge, 1974).

ARMSTRONG, J. A., *A History of Sussex, with Maps and Pictures* (Beaconsfield, 1961).

ARTS COUNCIL OF GREAT BRITAIN, *George Cruikshank* (catalogue of exhibition, 1974).

ATKINSON, J. M., *Discovering Suicide: Studies in the Social Organization of Sudden Death* (1978).

BAECHLER, J., *Suicides* (Oxford, 1979).

BAILEY, P., *Leisure and Class in Victorian England: Rational Recreation and the Contest for Control, 1830–1885* (1978).

BAYET, A., *Le suicide et la morale* (Paris, 1922).

BAYLEY, D. (ed.), *Police and Society* (1977).

BENNETT, A. *The Pretty Lady* (1918).

BERRIDGE, V. AND EDWARDS, G., *Opium and the People: Opiate Use in Nineteenth-Century England* (1981).

BLUNT, W. S., *My Diaries* (one-vol. edn., 1932; first publ., 1919–20).

BOCHEL, D., *Probation and After-Care: Its Development in England and Wales* (Edinburgh and London, 1976).

BOOTH, M., *English Melodrama* (1965).

BOWEN, D., *The Idea of the Victorian Church: A Study of the Church of England 1833–1889* (Montreal, 1968).

BOYCE, G., CURRAN, J., AND WINGATE, P. (eds.), *Newspaper History from the Seventeenth Century to the Present Day* (1978).

BRATTON, J., *The Victorian Popular Ballad* (1975).

BREND, W. A., *An Inquiry into the Statistics of Deaths from Violence and Unnatural Causes in the United Kingdom* (1915).

BRENT, C. (ed.), *Lewes in 1871: A Household and Political Directory* (Centre for Continuing Education, University of Sussex, Occasional Paper no. 9, 1978).

BRISTOW, E., *Vice and Vigilance: Purity Movements in Britain since 1700* (Dublin, 1977).

BURGESS, F., *English Churchyard Memorials* (1979 edn.).

CAPP, B., *Astrology and the Popular Press: English Almanacs 1500–1800* (1979).

CARTWRIGHT, F. F., *A Social History of Medicine* (1977).

CHADWICK, O., *The Victorian Church*, 2 vols. (1966, 1970).

CHAPMAN, C., *The Poor Man's Court of Justice: Twenty-Five Years as a Metropolitan Magistrate* (n.d. [1925]).

CHESTER, SIR N., *The English Administrative System 1780–1870* (Oxford, 1981).

CHURCH INFORMATION OFFICE, *Ought Suicide to be a Crime?* Report of a Committee convened by the Church Assembly Board for Social Responsibility (1959).

CLUBBE, J., *Victorian Forerunner: The Later Career of Thomas Hood* (Durham, North Carolina, 1968).

— (ed.), *Selected Poems of Thomas Hood* (Cambridge, Mass., 1970).

COBB, R., *Death in Paris: The Records of the Basse-Geôle de la Seine, October 1795–September 1801* (Oxford, 1978).

COCKERELL, H. A. L. AND GREEN, E., *The British Insurance Business 1547–1970: An Introduction and Guide to Historical Records in the United Kingdom* (1976).

COHEN, J. M. (sel.), *The Penguin Book of Comic and Curious Verse* (1952).

COOK, W. G. H., *Insanity and Mental Deficiency in Relation to Legal Responsibility: A Study in Psychological Jurisprudence* (1921).

CRITCHLEY, T. A., *A History of Police in England and Wales, 900–1966* (1967).

CROWTHER, M. A., *The Workhouse System, 1834–1929* (1981).

CULLEN, M. J., *The Statistical Movement in Early Victorian Britain* (Hassocks and New York, 1975).

CUNNINGHAM, H., *The Volunteer Force: A Social and Political History 1895–1908* (1975).

CURL, J. S., *The Victorian Celebration of Death* (Newton Abbot, 1972).

DAUNTON, M. J., *House and Home in the Victorian City: Working-Class Housing 1850–1914* (1983).

DAVIES, E. AND REES, A. D. (eds.), *Welsh Rural Communities* (Cardiff, 1960).

DAY, A. C., *Glimpses of Rural Life in Sussex during the last Hundred Years* (Idbury, 1928).

DENNEY, M., *London's Waterways* (1977).

DONNELLY, M., *Managing the Mind: A Study of Medical Psychology in early Nineteenth-Century Britain* (1983).

DOUGLAS, J. D., *The Social Meanings of Suicide* (Princeton, 1967).

ELLIS, P. B., *H. Rider Haggard: A Voice from the Infinite* (1978).

ELLMANN, R. (ed.), *Edwardians and Late Victorians* (New York, 1960).

ELLSWORTH, L. E., *Charles Lowder and the Ritualist Movement* (1982).

EVANS, H. AND EVANS, M., *The Man who Drew the Drunkard's Daughter: The Life and Art of George Cruickshank, 1792–1878* (1978).

EYLER, J. M., *Victorian Social Medicine: The Ideas and Methods of William Farr* (1979).

FEDDEN, H. R., *Suicide: A Social and Historical Study* (1938).

FINER, S., *The Life of Edwin Chadwick* (1952).

FINNANE, M., *Insanity and the Insane in Post-Famine Ireland* (1981).

FINNEGAN, F., *Poverty and Prostitution: A Study of Victorian Prostitutes in York* (Cambridge, 1979).

FRASER, W. H., *The Coming of the Mass Market, 1850–1914* (1981).

FREEMAN, H., LEVINE, S., and REEDER, L. (eds.), *Handbook of Medical Sociology* (Englewood Cliffs, NJ, 2nd edn., 1972).

GIBBS, J. P. (ed.), *Suicide* (New York, 1968).

GILLIS, J. R., *Youth and History: Tradition and Change in European Age Relations, 1770 to the Present* (1974).

GLASS, D. V., *Numbering the People: The Eighteenth-Century Population Controversy and the Development of Census and Vital Statistics in Britain* (1973).

HALBWACHS, M., *Les causes du suicide* (Paris, 1930).

HALEY, B., *The Healthy Body and Victorian Culture* (Cambridge, Mass., 1978).

HALL, P. G., *The Industries of London since 1861* (1962).

HARRISON, B., *Drink and the Victorians: The Temperance Question in England 1815–1872* (1971).

HARVEY, J. R., *Victorian Novelists and their Illustrators* (1970).

HARVARD, J. D. J., *The Detection of Secret Homicide: A Study of the Medico-Legal System of Investigation of Sudden and Unexplained Deaths* (Cambridge Studies in Criminology, vol. xi, 1960).

HAVIGHURST, A. F., *Radical Journalist: H. W. Massingham 1860–1924* (Cambridge, 1974).

HAYTER, A., *A Sultry Month: Scenes of London Literary Life in 1846* (1965).

HEASMAN, K., *Evangelicals in Action: An Appraisal of their Social Work in the Victorian Era* (1962).

HEENEY, B., *A Different Kind of Gentleman: Parish Clergy as Professional Men in early and mid-Victorian England* (Hamden, Connecticut, 1976).

HIGGINS, D. S., *Rider Haggard: The Great Story Teller* (1981).

HINDESS, B., *The Use of Official Statistics in Sociology* (1973).

HINGLEY, R. (trans. and ed.), *The Oxford Chekhov*, vol. ix, *Stories 1898–1904* (Oxford, 1975).

HOBHOUSE, H., *Lost London* (1971).

— *Thomas Cubitt, Master Builder* (1971).

HOBHOUSE, S. AND BROCKWAY, A. F. (eds.), *English Prisons To-day: Being the Report of the Prison System Enquiry Committee* established by the Labour Research Department (1922).

HOBSBAWM, E. J. AND RUDÉ, G., *Captain Swing*, Penguin edn. (1973).

HOWE, G. M., *National Atlas of Disease Mortality in the United Kingdom* (1st edn., 1963).

HOWELL, D., *Land and People in Nineteenth-Century Wales* (1978).

HOWGEGO, J. L., *The Victorian and Edwardian City of London from Old Photographs* (1977).

HUNTER, R. AND MACALPINE, I., *Psychiatry for the Poor. 1851 Colney Hatch Asylum—Friern Hospital 1973: A medical and social history* (1974).

IGNATIEFF, M., *A Just Measure of Pain: The Penitentiary in the Industrial Revolution, 1750–1850* (1978).

ILLICH, I., *Medical Nemesis: The Expropriation of Health* (1975).

INGLIS, K. S., *Churches and the Working Classes in Victorian England* (1963).

JACKSON, R. M., *The Machinery of Justice in England*, 5th edn. (1967).

JASPER, R. C. D., *Prayer Book Revision in England 1800–1900* (1954).

JERVIS, E., *Twenty-Five Years in Six Prisons* (1925).

JOHNSON, D., *Southwark and the City* (Oxford, 1969).

JONES, G. STEDMAN, *Outcast London: A Study in the Relationship between Classes in Victorian Society* (Oxford, 1971).

JONES, P. d'A., *The Christian-Socialist Revival, 1877–1914: Religion, Class and Social Conscience in late Victorian England* (Princeton, 1967).

KELLETT, J. R., *The Impact of Railways on Victorian Cities* (1969).

KENT, J., *Holding the Fort: Studies in Victorian Revivalism* (1978).

KEYNES, SIR G., *The Gates of Memory* (Oxford, 1981).

LASLETT, P., OOSTERVEEN, K., AND SMITH, R. M. (eds.), *Bastardy and its Comparative History* (1980).

LATHAM, R. AND MATTHEWS, W. (eds.), *The Diary of Samuel Pepys*, ix, 1668–9 (1976).

LEE, A., *The Origins of the Popular Press in England 1855–1914 (1976).*

LEESON, C., *The Probation System* (1914).

LEIGH, D., *The Historical Development of British Psychiatry*, i (1961).

LEWIS, SIR A., *The State of Psychiatry: Essays and Addresses* (1967).

LIECK, A., *Bow Street World* (1938).

LYLE, H. W., *King's and Some King's Men* (1935).

MCBRIDE, T., *The Domestic Revolution: The Modernisation of Household Service in England and France 1820–1920* (1976).

MCCONVILLE, S., *A History of English Prison Administration*, i, 1750–1877 (1981).

MCDONALD, L., *The Sociology of Law and Order* (1976).

MCFARLANE, J. W. (ed.), *The Oxford Ibsen*, vii (Oxford, 1966).

MCCINTOSH, P., *Physical Education in England since 1800* (1952).

MCLEOD, H., *Class and Religion in the Late Victorian City* (1974).

MACKENZIE, COMPTON, *Our Street* (1931).

MACKENZIE, G., *Marylebone* (1972).

MALCHOW, H., *Population Pressures: Emigration and Government in late Nineteenth-Century Britain* (Palo Alto, Calif., 1979).

MANCHESTER, A. H., *A Modern Legal History of England and Wales 1750–1950* (1980).

MARSH, P., *The Victorian Church in Decline: Archbishop Tait and the Church of England, 1868–82* (1969).

MARTIN, J. P. AND WILSON, G., *The Police: A Study in Manpower. The Evolution of the Service in England and Wales 1829–1965* (1969).

MEACHAM, S., *A Life Apart: The English Working Class 1890–1914* (1977).

MEISEL, M., *Realizations: Narrative, Pictorial and Theatrical Arts in Nineteenth-Century England* (Princeton, 1983).

MELLER, H., *Leisure and the Changing City, 1870–1914* (1976).

MERRINGTON, W. R., *University College Hospital and its Medical School: A History* (1976).

MILLER, W. C., *Cops and Bobbies: Police Authority in New York and London, 1830–1870* (Chicago, 1977).

MILLS, D. R., *Lord and Peasant in Nineteenth-Century Britain* (1980).

MINGAY, G. (ed.), *The Victorian Countryside*, 2 vols. (1981).

MORRIS, T. P., *The Criminal Area: A Study in Social Ecology* (1958).

NEALE, R. S., *Bath 1680–1850, A Social History: or A Valley of Pleasure, Yet a Sink of Iniquity* (1981).

NEATE, A., *The St. Marylebone Workhouse and Institution 1730–1965* (St. Marylebone Society Publications no. 9, 1967).

NEWSHOLME, SIR A., *Fifty Years in Public Health* (1935).

NEWTON, J. L., RYAN, M. P., AND WALKOWITZ, J. R., *Sex and Class in Women's History* (1983).

NICOLSON, N. (ed.), *The Flight of the Mind: The Letters of Virginia Woolf,* i, 1888–1912 (1975).

— *The Question of Things Happening: The Letters of Virginia Woolf,* ii, 1912–22 (1976).

NORMAN, E. R., *Church and Society in England, 1770–1970* (1976).

NOTT-BOWER, SIR W., *Fifty-Two Years a Policeman* (1926).

NYE, R., *Crime, Madness and Politics in Modern France: The Medical Concept of National Decline* (Princeton, 1984).

OBELKEVICH, J., *Religion and Rural Society: South Lindsey 1825–75* (Oxford, 1976).

OBERSCHALL, A. (ed.), *The Establishment of Empirical Sociology* (New York and London, 1972).

O'DONOGHUE, E. G., *The Story of Bethlehem Hospital from its Foundation in 1297* (1914).

O'MALLEY, C. D. (ed.), *The History of Medical Education,* UCLA, Forum in Medical Sciences, 12 (Los Angeles, 1970).

OSSOWSKA, M., *Social Determinants of Moral Ideas* (1971).

OWEN, D., *The Government of Victorian London 1855–1889*, ed. R. MacLeod (1982).

OXFORD BOOK OF MODERN VERSE, 1892–1935, THE, chosen by W. B. Yeats (Oxford, 1936).

PARRY-JONES, W. LL., *The Trade in Lunacy: A Study of Private Madhouses in England in the Eighteenth and Nineteenth Centuries* (1972).

PARSSINEN, T. M., *Secret Passions, Secret Remedies: Narcotic Drugs in British Society 1820–1930* (Manchester, 1983).

PEARL, C., *The Girl with the Swansdown Seat* (1955).

PEASTON, A. E., *The Prayer Book Revisions of the Victorian Evangelicals* (Dublin, 1963).

PELLEW, J., *The Home Office 1848–1914* (1982).

PELLING, M., *Cholera, Fever and English Medicine, 1825–65* (Oxford, 1978).

PETERSON, M. J., *The Medical Profession in Mid-Victorian London* (1978).

PHILIPS, D., *Crime and Authority in Victorian England: The Black Country 1835–1860* (1977).

PLOMER, W. (ed.), *Kilvert's Diary*, 3 vols. (1960 edn.).

PRINGLE, J. C., *Social Work of the London Churches: Being Some Account of the Metropolitan Visiting and Relief Association 1843–1937* (1937).

PUCKLE, B. S., *Funeral Customs: Their Origin and Development* (1926).

RAVERAT, G., *Period Piece: A Cambridge Childhood* (1952).

READ, G. AND JEBSON, D., *A Voice in the City: 150 Years History of the Liverpool City Mission* (n.d. [1979]).

REED, J. R., *Victorian Conventions* (Ohio, 1975).

RICHARDSON, D. M., *Pilgrimage: Backwater* (1938 edn., first edn. 1916).

RICHARDSON, SIR J. (ed.), *The British Encyclopaedia of Medical Practice: Medical Progress 1972–73* (1973).

RIDLER, A. (ed.), *Poems and Some Letters of James Thomson 1834–82* (1963).

ROBERTS, R., *The Classic Slum: Salford Life in the First Quarter of the Century*, Pelican edn. (1973).

ROSE, G., *The Struggle for Penal Reform: The Howard League and its Predecessors* (1961).

ROSEN, G., *A History of Public Health* (New York, 1958).

— *Madness in Society: Chapters in the Historical Sociology of Mental Illness* (1968).

ROWELL, GEOFFREY, *The Liturgy of Christian Burial: An Introductory Survey of the Historical Development of Christian Burial Rites* (1977).

ROWELL, GEORGE (ed.), *Plays by W. S. Gilbert* (Cambridge, 1982).

RUCK, S. K. (ed.), *Paterson on Prisons, being the Collected Papers of Sir Alexander Paterson* (1951).

RUMBELOW, D., *I Spy Blue: The Police and Crime in the City of London from Elizabeth I to Victoria* (1971).

RUSSELL, JOHN, 2nd EARL, *My Life and Adventures* (1923).

SADLEIR, M., *Forlorn Sunset* (1947).

SAINSBURY, P., *Suicide in London: An Ecological Study* (1955).

SAMUEL, R., *East End Underworld*, ii, *Chapters in the Life of Arthur Harding* (1981).

SANDALL, R., *The History of the Salvation Army*, iii, *1883–1953. Social Reform and Welfare Work* (1955).

SHEPPARD, F., *London 1808–1870: The Great Wen* (1971).

SHORTER, E., *The Making of the Modern Family* (1976).

SIMEY, M. B., *Charitable Effort in Liverpool in the Nineteenth Century* (Liverpool, 1951).

SKULTANS, V., *Madness and Morals: Ideas on Insanity in the Nineteenth Century* (1975).

SLATER, M. (ed.), *Dickens 1970* (1970).

SMITH, F. B., *The People's Health 1830–1910* (1979).

SMITH, R., *Trial by Medicine: Insanity and Responsibility in Victorian Trials* (Edinburgh, 1981).

SMITH, S., *The Other Nation: The Poor in English Novels of the 1840s and 1850s* (Oxford, 1980).

SMITH, W. D., *Stretching Their Bodies: The History of Physical Education* (Newton Abbot, 1974).

SMITH, W. S., *The London Heretics 1870–1914* (1967).

SPILLER, G., *The Ethical Movement in Great Britain* (1934).

SPROTT, S. E., *The English Debate on Suicide from Donne to Hume* (La Salle, Illinois, 1961).

STEEDMAN, C., *Policing the Victorian Community: The Formation of English Provincial Police Forces, 1856–80* (1984).

STERN, W. M., *The Porters of London* (1960).

STONE, L., *The Family, Sex and Marriage in England* (1977).

SUTHERLAND, G., *Policy-Making in Elementary Education, 1870–1895* (Oxford, 1973).

SWAN, A. S., *My Life: An Autobiography* (1934).

TAYLERSON, A. W. F., *The Revolver, 1865–1888* (1966).

— *The Revolver, 1889–1914* (1970).

TAYLOR, S., *Durkheim and the Study of Suicide* (1982).

THOMAS, J. E., *The English Prison Officer since 1850* (1972).

THOMAS, K., *Religion and the Decline of Magic* (1971).

THOMPSON, F., *Lark Rise to Candleford*, World's Classics edn. (1954).

THOMPSON, P., *The Edwardians* (1975).

THOMSON, H. C., *The Story of the Middlesex Hospital Medical School* (1935).

THURSTON, G., *Coroner's Practice* (1958).

TILLOTSON, K. (ed.), *The Letters of Charles Dickens,* Pilgrim edn., M. House and G. Storey, gen. eds., iv, 1844–6 (Oxford, 1977).

TILLY, L. A. AND SCOTT, J. W., *Women, Work and Family* (New York, 1978).

TROMBLEY, S., *'All that Summer she was Mad': Virginia Woolf and her Doctors* (1981).

TRUDGILL, E., *Madonnas and Magdalens: The Origins and Development of Victorian Sexual Attitudes* (New York, 1976).

VICINUS, M. (ed.), *A Widening Sphere: Changing Roles of Victorian Women* (Bloomington, Indiana, 1977).

VINCENT, D., *Bread, Knowledge and Freedom: A Study of Nineteenth-Century Working-Class Autobiography* (1981).

WALKER, N., *Crime and Insanity in England: i. The Historical Perspective* (Edinburgh, 1968).

— and MCCABE, S., *Crime and Insanity in England: ii. New Solutions and New Problems* (Edinburgh, 1973).

WALKOWITZ, J., *Prostitution and Victorian Society: Women, Class and the State* (Cambridge, 1980).

WARD, W. R., *Victorian Oxford* (1965).

WEST, D. J. AND WALK, A. (eds.), *Daniel McNaughton: His Trial and the Aftermath* (Ashford, Kent, 1977).

WHITTINGTON-EGAN, R. AND SMERDON, G., *The Quest of the Golden Boy: The Life and Letters of Richard Le Gallienne* (1960).

WILLIAMS, G., *The Sanctity of Life and the Criminal Law* (1958).

WILLIS, F., *101 Jubilee Road: A Book of London Yesterdays* (1948).

WOHL, A. S., *The Eternal Slum: Housing and Social Policy in Victorian London* (1977).

WOOD, C., *Victorian Panorama: Paintings of Victorian Life* (1976).

IX ARTICLES PUBLISHED IN OR AFTER 1914

ADAMS, J. B., 'Suicide—From a General Practitioner's Point of View', *The Practitioner*, xciv (1915), 470–8.

ADELSTEIN, A. AND MARDON, C., 'Suicides 1961–74', *Population Trends*, ii (1975), 13–18.

ANDERSON, O., 'The Incidence of Civil Marriage in Victorian England and Wales', *Past & Present*, 69 (1975), 50–87.

— 'Did Suicide Increase with Industrialization in Victorian England?', *Past & Present*, 86 (1980), 151–73.

— 'Suicide in Victorian London: an Urban View', *Bulletin of the Society for the Social History of Medicine*, 26 (1980), 18–21.

ATKINS, P. J., 'The Retail Milk Trade in London, *c.*1790–1914', *Economic History Review*, 2nd series, xxxiii (1980), 522–37.

BARTEL, R., 'Suicide in Eighteenth-Century England: The Myth of a Reputation', *Huntington Library Quarterly*, xxiii (1959–60), 145–58.

BÉDARIDA, F., 'Londres au milieu du xixe siècle: une analyse de structure sociale', *Annales*, xxiii (1968), 268–95.

BERRIDGE, V. AND RAWSON, N., 'Opiate Use and Legislative Control', *Social Science and Medicine*, xiii, A (1979), 351–63.

BESNARD, P., 'Anti- ou anté-durkheimisme? Contribution au débat sur les statistiques officielles du suicide', *Revue française de sociologie*, xvii (1977), 313–39.

BLAUNER, R., 'Death and Social Structure', *Psychiatry*, xxix (1966), 378–94.

BRIGHTFIELD, M. E., 'The Medical Profession in Early Victorian England, as depicted in the Novels of the Period (1840–1870)', *Bulletin of the History of Medicine*, xxxv (1961), 238–56.

CHAMBERLIN, J. E., 'An Anatomy of Cultural Melancholy', *Journal of the History of Ideas*, xlii (1981), 691–705.

COLEMAN, B. I., 'Southern England in the Census of Religious Worship, 1851', *Southern History*, v (1983), 154–88.

COOTER, R. J., 'Phrenology and British Alienists, *c.*1825–45', *Medical History*, xx (1976), 1–21 and 135–51.

DAVIDOFF, L., 'Mastered for Life: Servant and Wife in Victorian and Edwardian England', *Journal of Social History*, vii (1973–4), 406–19.

DINGLE, A. E., 'Drink and Working-Class Living Standards in Britain, 1870–1914', *Economic History Review*, 2nd Series, xxv (1972), 608–22.

DOUGLAS, J. D., 'Suicide: Social Aspects', *International Encyclopaedia of the Social Sciences*, xv (1968), 375–84.

DUNNING, SIR L., 'Discretion in Prosecution', *The Police Journal*, i (1928), 39–47.

DYOS, H. J., 'The Slums of Victorian London', *Victorian Studies*, xi (1967–8), 5–40.

ENGELHARDT, H. T. Jun., 'The Disease of Masturbation: Values and the Concept of Disease', *Bulletin of the History of Medicine*, xlviii (1974), 234–48.

FLETCHER, I., 'The 1890s: A Lost Decade', *Victorian Studies*, iv (1960–1), 345–54.

FORBES, T. R., 'Coroners' Inquests in the County of Middlesex, England 1819–42', *Journal of the History of Medicine and Allied Sciences*, xxxii (1977), 375–94.

—— 'Crowner's Quest', *Transactions of the American Philosophical Society*, lxviii (1978), part 1, 3–50.

GATRELL, V. A. C., 'The Decline of Theft and Violence in Victorian and Edwardian England' in V. Gatrell, B. Lenman, and G. Parker (eds.), *Crime and the Law: The Social History of Crime in Western Europe since 1500* (1980), 238–370.

GATES, B., 'Suicide, *Bentley's Miscellany* and Dickens's *Chimes*', *Dickens Studies Newsletter*, viii (1977), 98–100.

GIDDENS, A., 'The Suicide Problem in French Sociology', *British Journal of Sociology*, xvi (1965).

GILBERT, E. W., 'Pioneer Maps of Health and Disease in England', *Geographical Journal*, 124 (1958), 172–83.

GORHAM, D., 'The "Maiden Tribute of Modern Babylon" Re-examined: Child Prostitution and the Idea of Childhood in late-Victorian England', *Victorian Studies*, xxi (1978), 353–79.

GRAY, D., 'The Uses of Victorian Laughter', *Victorian Studies*, x (1966–7), 145–76.

GREENWOOD, M., MARTIN, W. J., AND RUSSELL, W. T., 'Deaths by Violence 1837–1937', *Journal of the Royal Statistical Society*, new series, civ (1941), 146–63.

HAIR, P., 'Deaths from Violence in Britain: A Tentative Secular Survey', *Population Studies*, xxv (1971), 5–24.

HARE, E. H., 'Masturbatory Insanity: The History of an Idea', *Journal of Mental Science*, cviii (1962), 1–25.

HENRIQUES, U. R. Q., 'The Rise and Decline of the Separate System of Prison Discipline', *Past & Present*, 54 (Feb. 1972), 61–93.

HOCHSTADT, S., 'Social History and Politics: A Materialist View', *Social History*, vii (1982), 75–83.

HOLLOWAY, S. W. F., 'Medical Education in England, 1830–1858', *History*, xlix (1964), 299–324.

HOWKINS, A., 'The Voice of the People', *Oral History*, iii (1975), 50–75.

HUNNISETT, R. F., 'The Importance of Eighteenth-Century Coroners' Bills' in *Law, Litigants and the Legal Profession*, ed. E. W. Ives and A. H. Manchester (1983), 126–39.

JACYNA, L., 'Somatic Theories of Mind and the Interests of Medicine in Britain, 1850–79', *Medical History*, 26 (1982), 233–58.

JAMES, L., 'Cruikshank and Early Victorian Caricature', *History Workshop*, 6 (1978), 107–20.

JONES, D., 'Women and Chartism', *History*, lxviii (1983), 1–21.

JONES, D. J. V., 'Crime, Protest and Community in Nineteenth-Century Wales', *Llafur*, i, 3 (1974), 5–15.

JONES, G. STEDMAN, 'Working-Class Culture and Working-Class Politics in London, 1870–1900: Notes on the Remaking of a Working Class', *Journal of Social History*, vii (1973–4), 460–508.

JONES, I. G., 'Dr. Thomas Price and the Election of 1868 in Merthyr Tydfil: A Study in Nonconformist Politics', *Welsh Historical Review*, ii (1964–5), 147–72, 251–70.

LILIENFELD, D., ' "The Greening of Epidemiology": Sanitary Physicians and the London Epidemiological Society (1830–1870)', *Bulletin of the History of Medicine*, lii (1978), 503–28.

LOGAN, W. P. D., 'Mortality in England and Wales from 1848 to 1947', *Population Studies*, iv (1950–1), 132–78.

LOMAX, E., 'The Uses and Abuses of Opiates in Nineteenth-Century England', *Bulletin of the History of Medicine*, xlvii (1973), 167–76.

LONG, O. W., 'English Translations of Goethe's *Werther*', *Journal of English and Germanic Philology*, xiv (1915), 169–203.

LOW, A. A., FARMER, R. D. T., JONES, D. R., AND ROHDE, J. R., 'Suicide in England and Wales: An Analysis of 100 Years, 1876–1975', *Psychological Medicine*, xi (1981), 359–68.

MCCANDLESS, P., 'Liberty and Lunacy: The Victorians and Wrongful Confinement', *Journal of Social History*, xi (1977–8), 366–86.

—— ' "Build! Build!" The Controversy over the Care of the Chronically Insane in England, 1855–1870', *Bulletin of the History of Medicine*, liii (1979), 553–74.

MCCLURE, G. M. G., 'Trends in Suicide Rate for England and Wales 1975–80', *British Journal of Psychiatry*, 144 (1984), 119–26.

MACDONALD, M., 'The Inner Side of Wisdom: Suicide in Early Modern England', *Psychological Medicine*, vii (1977), 565–82.

MACDONALD, R., 'The Frightful Consequences of Onanism: Notes on the History of a Delusion', *Journal of the History of Ideas.* xxviii (1967), 423–41.

MACLEOD, R., ' "The Edge of Hope": Social Policy and Chronic Alcoholism, 1870–1900', *Journal of the History of Medicine,* xxii (1967), 215–45.

MALCOLMSON, P., 'Getting a Living in the Slums of Victorian Kensington', *London Journal,* i (1975), 28–51.

MARRINER, S., 'English Bankruptcy Records and Statistics before 1850', *Economic History Review,* 2nd series, xxxiii (1980), 351–66.

MITCHELL, S., 'Sentiment and Suffering: Women's Recreational Reading in the 1860s', *Victorian Studies,* xxi (1977–8), 29–45.

NIEBYL, P., 'The English Blood-Letting Revolution, or Modern Medicine before 1850', *Bulletin of Historical Medicine,* li (1977), 464–83.

PETERSEN, A., 'Brain Fever in Nineteenth-Century Literature: Fact and Fiction', *Victorian Studies,* xix (1975–6), 445–64.

QUEN, J., 'An Historical View of the M'Naghten Trial', *Bulletin of the History of Medicine,* 42 (1968), 43–51.

RAVETZ, A., 'The Victorian Coal Kitchen and its Reformers', *Victorian Studies,* xi (1967–8), 435–60.

REDDAWAY, T. F., 'London in the Nineteenth Century: IV. The Freeing of the Bridges, 1800–1880', *The Twentieth Century,* cli (1952), 163–77.

ROBERTSON, A. B., 'Children, Teachers and Society: The Over-Pressure Controversy, 1880–1886', *British Journal of Educational Studies,* xx (1972), 315–23.

ROEBUCK, J., 'When does Old Age Begin?: The Evolution of the English Definition', *Journal of Social History,* xii (1978–9), 416–28.

ROSEN, G., 'The Fate of the Concept of Medical Police, 1780–1890', *Centaurus,* v (1957), 97–113.

— 'History in the Study of Suicide', *Psychological Medicine,* i (1971), 267–85.

RULE, J. G., 'Social Crime in the Rural South in the Eighteenth and Early Nineteenth Centuries', *Southern History,* i (1979), 133–53.

RUSSELL, JOHN, 2ND EARL, 'The Ethics of Suicide', *Transactions of the Medico-Legal Society,* xvii (1922), 24–56.

SAINSBURY, P., 'Suicide: Opinions and Facts', *Proceedings of the Royal Society of Medicine,* lxvi (1973), 579–87.

SELLIN, T., 'The Significance of Records of Crime', *Law Quarterly Review,* lxvii (1951), 489–504.

SHOWALTER, E., 'Victorian Women and Insanity', *Victorian Studies,* xxiii (1979–80), 157–81.

SHYROCK, R. H., 'Nineteenth-Century Medicine: Scientific Aspects', *Journal of World History,* iii (1957), 881–908.

SIMMONS, H. G., 'Explaining Social Policy: the English Mental Deficiency Act of 1913', *Journal of Social History,* xi (1977–8), 387–403.

SLUIS, I. VAN DER, 'The Movement for Euthanasia, 1875–1975', *Janus*, lxvi (1979), 131–72.

SPEER, J. B. Jun., Essay Review of T. R. Forbes, *Crowner's Quest*, *Annals of Science*, 37 (1980), 353–6.

STEARNS, P. N., 'Old Women: Some Historical Observations', *Journal of Family History*, v (1980), 44–57.

STORCH, R. D., 'The Plague of the Blue Locusts: Police Reform and Popular Resistance in Northern England, 1840–1857', *International Review of Social History*, xx (1975), 61–90.

—— 'The Policeman as Domestic Missionary: Urban Discipline and Popular Culture in Northern England, 1850–1880', *Journal of Social History*, ix (1976), 481–509.

SUMMERSON, J., 'The Victorian Rebuilding of the City of London', *London Journal*, iii (1977), 163–85.

SWINSCOW, D., 'Some Suicide Statistics', *British Medical Journal*, 1951, i. 1417–23, 23 June.

THANE, P., 'Women and the Poor Law in Victorian and Edwardian England', *History Workshop*, vi (1978), 29–51.

THOMAS, P. H., 'Medical Men of Glamorgan: William Thomas Edwards (1821–1915): part 2', *The Glamorgan Historian*, viii (n.d. [1972]), 121–45.

WALK, A., 'The History of Mental Nursing', *Journal of Mental Science*, cvii (1961), 1–17.

WELLS, R. A. E., 'Social Conflict and Protest in the English Countryside in the early Nineteenth Century: A Rejoinder', *Journal of Peasant Studies*, 8 (1980–1), 514–30.

WILLIAMS, A. B., 'Customs and Traditions Connected with Sickness, Death and Burial in Montgomeryshire in the late Nineteenth Century', *The Montgomeryshire Collections*, lii (1951–2), 51–61.

WILLIAMSON, J. G., 'Urban Disamenities, Dark Satanic Mills, and the British Standard of Living Debate', *Journal of Economic History*, xli (1981), 75–83.

ZILBOORG, G., 'Suicide among Civilised and Primitive Races', *American Journal of Psychiatry*, 92 (1935–6), 1347–69.

X   UNPUBLISHED THESIS

SHERRINGTON, E., 'Thomas Wakley and Reform, 1823–62' (Oxford D.Phil. 1974).

INDEX